The Explanation of Social Action

The Explanation of Social Action

With a new preface by the author

John Levi Martin

UNIVERSITY PRESS

UNIVERSITY PRESS

Oxford University Press, Inc., publishes works that further
Oxford University's objective of excellence
in research, scholarship, and education.

Oxford New York
Auckland Cape Town Dar es Salaam Hong Kong Karachi
Kuala Lumpur Madrid Melbourne Mexico City Nairobi
New Delhi Shanghai Taipei Toronto

With offices in
Argentina Austria Brazil Chile Czech Republic France Greece
Guatemala Hungary Italy Japan Poland Portugal Singapore
South Korea Switzerland Thailand Turkey Ukraine Vietnam

Copyright © 2011 by Oxford University Press

First issued as an Oxford University Press paperback, 2021

Published by Oxford University Press, Inc.
198 Madison Avenue, New York, New York 10016

www.oup.com

Oxford is a registered trademark of Oxford University Press

All rights reserved. No part of this publication may be reproduced,
stored in a retrieval system, or transmitted, in any form or by any means,
electronic, mechanical, photocopying, recording, or otherwise,
without the prior permission of Oxford University Press.

Library of Congress Cataloging-in-Publication Data
Martin, John Levi, 1964-
The explanation of social action / John Levi Martin.
   p. cm.
Includes bibliographical references and index.

ISBN 9780199773312 (hardcover)
ISBN 9780197601624 (paperback)

1. Social action. 2. Social change. 3. Sociology. I. Title.
HM831.M39175 2011
303.48'4—dc22   2010044982

"Only let them not rejoice over me,
Who boast against me when my foot slips!"

Contents

Preface to the Paperback Edition, **ix**

Preface, **xxi**

Chapter 1 Why Questions? What Explanations?, **3**

Chapter 2 Causality and Persons, **24**

Chapter 3 Authority and Experience, **74**

Chapter 4 The Grid of Perception, **112**

Chapter 5 Action In and On a World, **145**

Chapter 6 A Social Aesthetics, **191**

Chapter 7 Valence and Habit, **239**

Chapter 8 Fields and Games, **268**

Chapter 9 Explanations Explained, **321**

References, **351**

Index, **387**

.

Preface to the Paperback Edition

INTRODUCTION

"I dunno, I just feel like he is more of a leader." I want you to imagine this statement being made in the year 2035. The speaker is an artificial intelligence, a deep learning neural network on a vast scale that we cannot now comprehend, one that was trained to succeed at a wide, indeed, in principle, unbounded if, in practice, finite range of different human interactive tasks, and one which passes every "Turing test" we can throw at it. In other words, it appears to be conscious, even though we have no reason to think that the structure of its internal functions directly parallel our own.

This AI machine (let's imagine it is called "Mark 4.0") was also fed a huge amount of information on U.S. political, social, and economic history—but only up until August 2020. It was (temporarily, as part of this experiment) shielded from any information produced afterward. And it was asked a simple question with a follow-up: "Mark, all things considered, who would you support in the next presidential election?" And Mark answered, "Donald Trump." The follow-up was, "Why?"

This book is an attempt to work toward a theory of cognition and action, or at least, a sense of what it means to "explain," which would help guide us toward such a theory, in which such a seemingly ridiculous outcome—the most sophisticated information processing machine in the world siding with the worst president in American history—could make sense.

A THEORY OF COGNITION FOR HUMAN AND ARTIFICIAL INTELLIGENCE

One of the ironies of the current world is that as computer scientists build more sophisticated machines and software to better interact with humans, ones that defy earlier "serial" theories of cognition, they are increasingly interested in what sociologists have to say, given that we, presumably, know something about how humans work. And yet, the social sciences increasingly have boxed themselves into an irresponsible commitment to an overly convenient model of cognition that mirrors the AI 1.0 approach that computer scientists have abandoned. In other words, our model for *human* cognition is like an old-fashioned model for the simplest computers, and isn't even adequate for *existing* machine intelligence.

This discrepancy occurred to me around the time that *The Explanation of Social Action* [*ESA*] came out. In my next book, the 2015 *Thinking Through Theory*, I tried to emphasize how incongruous and regressive it was that sociologists were moving toward (or back to) what I called "GOFAT"—Good Old Fashioned Action Theory. I stole this idea from computer science, specifically from John Haugeland, who used GOFAI—Good Old Fashioned Artificial Intelligence—to describe the broad family of first generation theories of artificial intelligence. This vision was one of a process that involved a succession of logical operations on input information, and basically had a more or less deterministic output, though there were some more flexible versions. Haugeland (1989 [1985]: 113) used the term approvingly, and for him, the key was that this was a vision of intelligence as *computation* (a vision that goes back to Thomas Hobbes), and computation as the manipulation of *symbols*. Those who first formulated this vision for the purposes of designing computers assumed that it was a decent model for human cognition: to treat our thinking as akin to a computer making a series of *decisions*. Although it was understood that our brains work differently—while certainly there is some succession of one act upon another, our core modules are wired as parallel processors—it was also thought that this was a workable model for many aspects of human cognition.

As it is. But we are increasingly turning over anything that can be easily handled by a serial algorithm to computers, since they're better at it than we are. All the things that are *interesting* and *significant* about human cognition strain against this model. So what have social scientists done? They have doubled down. While there are some theoretical traditions of interest, especially to sociologists, that would be serviceable jumping off points for a non-GOFAT theory of cognition/action (e.g., pragmatism, Bourdieu's field theory), the mainstream of sociology joins political science and economics in sticking with the model of the *calculative decision* as the core paradigm for linking cognition and action.

That is not a realistic model of how humans work. It was a realistic model of how first generation AI machines worked—because they were literally built according to that model. It will not be a realistic model of the next generation of AI machines. While first generation AI is a theory of software—it is for machines that "have" algorithms—second generation AI is a theory of (virtual) hardware: current learning machines are virtual machines being simulated by real ones, sets of networks that develop connections of different strength between different neurons.

The core postulate of GOFAI, and one that underlies most of our theories of cognition, is that the atoms of thinking are *representational*, and that thinking involves moving symbols or pointers about, reconnecting them, predicating them, and so on. This postulate is not obviously correct for human beings. In fact, I suspect that it is not correct. That is, some parts of our cognition definitely work with *objects* (the ventral and dorsal streams that indicate *what* and *where* a seen object is strongly suggest a classic representational capacity). Others (such as how we process the word *nevertheless*) seem to require something different. But even our practical cognition may not require mental *elements* in the way that we imagine.

Let us say you pick up a jar and start to open it. You know that you have a jar, certainly, and it has certain predicates—light, cool, cylindrical, transparent, brittle. Because it is light and brittle, you know that you could throw and smash it. But you want to open the lid. You try to turn the lid, it does not open, perhaps it flips up, you pull at it, but it doesn't move either, perhaps it is held down by a vacuum, and you tap it against the table edge, you twist one way and the other. I think it very possible that at no time does your representation of the jar change from jar-whose-lid-is-a-screw-on-lid to jar-whose-lid-is-a-pop-top-lid to jar-whose-lid-is-a-screw-on-lid-but-there-is-a-vacuum. Yet your actions would seemingly make no sense under GOFAI unless you at least provisionally entertained these, as to try to unscrew a jar-whose-lid-is-a-pop-top-lid makes as little sense as throwing it against the wall and expecting it not to break.

Further, I claim that as you are doing this, you tend to stop cognizing the jar as a jar at all—you are quite focused on the lid and the mouth of the jar, and the rest of it fades away into a bit of an unminded whatever. You are not (as GOFAI would assume) either carrying out a sensible action on a predicated object (e.g., screw-top-jar), nor trying a hypothesis (perhaps it is a screw-top-jar; if not, go on to the next hypothesis). Rather, what you are doing—fiddling—is an *epistemic action*, one in which you manipulate the world to learn about it (Kirsh and Maglio 1994). That's also what you do when you turn your head to look at something, an act which is, as J. J. Gibson always emphasized, an attempt to grab information that is hanging around you in the ambient optic array—a set of magnetic wavelengths that we are able to do something with. As far as I can tell, as you fiddle, your mind is somewhere between your head and your hands, at least until you solve the problem, at which point the mind seems to rush back inside the head.

We might imagine that only extremely primitive creatures would have neural systems with such poorly integrated components that they *separately* react to various sensations emanating from some object, without ever integrating these into a whole. Such organisms *cannot* have a symbolic/representational mental life, because (for them), there are no "objects" to represent. But that is not, we assume, how *humans* work. The *sound* of a barking dog and the *sight* of the barking dog are integrated as aspects of that dog (presumably in the hippocampus).

Except when they're not. We see and hear a slap in the face (say) as a single slap, because we don't hear slaps that are far away. We not only have two terms for thunder/lightning, but we assuredly do not chunk them as aspects of the same event in most cases, simply because we can't. Yet we could respond appropriately to either thunder or lightning. I am suggesting that such appropriate response in the absence of integration often characterizes our cognitive processes. For example, we speak of a place as having an "atmosphere" when we think we know something about *something* that is relevant for action (something here is scary, welcoming, tense) when we aren't sure what object this quality is a quality *of*.

Why is this so important? If your neural system is indeed part of your body, like the circulatory system, and is there to get some things done, there is no reason to think that it needs to make an internal symbolic equivalent of everything it is engaged with. In fact, there is very good reason to think that it doesn't, and the reason is, it would be stupid, and it would be stupid because it's wasteful. One reason that *ESA* spends so much time considering the nature of vision is that it's both very well studied, and our most common metaphor for cognizing in general. Many people imagined that the brain creates a photographic image of the surroundings facing one's head, and that this sits (for the time being) in memory. That's what it *feels* like. But experiments show that we *don't* make such a map. If an experimenter swaps out large chunks of what's in our visual field, we don't notice a violation. Why don't we have a complete picture of our surroundings? We don't have to *make a copy* of the world, because we can safely assume the world will still be there. We just have to *look at* some of the parts of it when we need them. If you want to treat the mind as having somewhere a store of representations about the world, you're going to have to accept that we store them outside of us, in the world itself.

It gets better. Once we accept that intelligent action is not restricted to the manipulation of symbols by a central processing unit, we have no difficulty accepting the idea that intelligence can be wholly *distributed* (a vision that Haugeland [1989: 249] found deeply disturbing). Current state-of-the-art deep learning machines can have thousands of interlinked processors; the notion that this sort of set up may be more conducive to the emergence of machine consciousness would seem absurd to the vision of GOFAI—just as the notion that there may be forms of cognition that are actually spread out across several (or perhaps several hundred) human minds seems absurd to those clinging to GOFAT. But it is certainly physically possible. No entomologist should deny that there are things that an anthill knows that no individual ant understands.

Current machine intelligence is a bit like the anthill, though much more bulky, and inefficient in the sense that one machine simulates another. Someday these sorts of systems may move from being virtual machines to being real, perhaps organic, ones, which will be far more efficient. *ESA* is intended to push sociology to have a theory that will work for actual human beings—and such a theory may turn out to be extremely relevant for such future machine intelligence.

Preface to the Paperback Edition xiii

A THEORY OF POLITICS

Until we have a better set of criteria by which to judge explanation, we are likely to see the continued pull in two different, pernicious, directions. On the one hand, we have a pull toward a realm of self-identified "theory" that is, more or less, just "saying stuff"—analyzing, shuffling, and recombining different bits of our heritage (that is, largely intellectual prejudice). On the other hand, we have a pull toward "sucker sociology," in which we attempt to wade into realms of interested parties giving their accounts, and transubstantiate these into explanatory, even causal, propositions.

The most obvious place where we see such a pull is in our attempt to understand the political alignments of non-elites. Indeed, this was the core problematic that pushed me to pursue the various ideas that come together in *ESA*. I was always fascinated with the issue of political cognition, and believed, and still believe, that our attachment to decision-theoretic assumptions interfered with our attempt to understand lay politics. It seems to me that non-elites somehow are perceiving—most importantly, seeing, but also hearing—in certain individuals (e.g., candidates) qualities that they directly respond to, but these qualities do not seem to be the *individual-level* qualities that a reductionist account might emphasize (though height certainly matters in some cases!). Two people could confront the same human organism (say, Ronald Reagan, or Silvio Berlusconi) and yet be perceiving wildly different qualities. It was not that they had different *perspectives* that arose from their different locations in social space, as others have said, but that they were literally perceiving different *social objects*. That's because—so argues *ESA*—Silvio Berlusconi is not a person, any more than the Forza Italia or the Republican Party is a physical object. All are sets of relations, and somehow, just as one can "know" something about Forza Italia or the Republican party—even though one might be wholly unable to define the *extension* of either term—so, too, we can sense qualities that are ultimately grounded in the extremely abstract patternings of our relation to other people. What people perceive in such political figures is, so I hazard in *ESA*, a set of relations of political alliance and opposition. They do not *know* about these qualities (they do not store symbolic objects that have these predicates attached), and so they are not projecting them onto the real-world analogies when they encounter them. Rather, they are, in some way that I still find baffling, *perceiving* them. These characteristics are stored in the world, even though they are different for different persons.

This might sound like mystical mumbo-jumbo to you. It certainly sounds that way to me, but there are times when we are pretty sure that something *has* to be true (e.g., the wave/particle duality of light demonstrated by the two-slit experiments), even if we can't quite figure out why (or how?). I now think that I can demonstrate the actual physical plausibility of the capacity of creatures to literally see bundles of relations—indeed, the *formal characteristics* of such bundles.

PERCEIVING RELATIONS

I want to briefly sketch a single, but extremely well-studied, case. It is not actually of human behavior, but that of poultry. Few of us, however, would imagine that there are cognitive capacities possessed by barnyard hens that are denied to humans. Hence I think that if I can convince you for the case of chickens, you will accept this as a proof of possibility of the dynamics I am proposing to be present in human cognition. So let me sketch the case. Hens form dominance relations, in which one hen feels free to peck at the head of another hen, who does not reciprocate. Dominance relations are generally established soon after two hens first encounter one another. There is a scuffle, one is intimidated by the other, and gives up.

Although we have no access to the interiority of the chickens, it appears that the submission involves taking fright. The reason we believe this is that Schjelderup-Ebbe (1922), the first scientist to describe the pecking order, found that one chicken, B, might lock in a submission relation with another chicken C, even though there was reason to think that B would have been able to beat C in a fight. (The reason is that B had bested many chickens that were able to dominate C.) But one reason why this counterintuitive relationship might arise is that B happened to first see C when C was in the company of some A who already dominates B. The sight of A, or so goes the hypothesis, fills B with fear, and this fear then becomes associated with the sight of C (a psychological phenomenon known as "source blending"). Thus the counterintuitive relation B has with C suggests something about the perception that a chicken has of a dominant chicken—that it is associated with fear.

This helps explain some of the dynamics of these relations uncovered by Ivan Chase (e.g., 1985). Chase found robust evidence of what he called "bystander effects": sets of bouts between three birds were more likely to be transitive if conducted where each could see the others' fights. For example, if B sees A triumph over C, B becomes a bit afraid of the ferocity of A's mien, and a bit emboldened in dealing with a loser like C. But here is another form of bystander effect: we begin with C being bested by B; chicken A then enters, and C sees B frightened by A (perhaps A has already beaten B). Hen C then is quite likely to submit to A, as she has seen A already scare a chicken that frightens her. The argument of *ESA* is that to C, the *frighteningness* of B is a perceivable quality, just like B's size, even though this quality is (like all qualities) a *relation*, a relation of potentiality: B's capacity to induce a state of fear in C. To C, B *is* a "scary chicken."

What about the state of *fear* in another? When taken to account for "anthropomorphizing" the chimpanzees he studied by describing them as, say, "agitated," the great Gestalt psychologist Wolfgang Köhler emphasized that this was not an attribution of their mental life, but an observable quality of "the elementary phenomenology of their behavior" (1925 [1917]: 102). If you—or another chimpanzee, or a dog—can see that a chimpanzee is agitated, you have some idea of what it is going to do next. An agitated chimpanzee may scream at you, or charge you, or dash up a tree. Thus we, like other animals, can perceive these qualities of other creatures in ways that have ecological validity.

So, too, is *fearfulness* of a hen: it is something that those (human or fowl) who have experience with poultry can recognize via the senses. Further, recognizing fear *as* fear is to understand that it is an *intentional* state in the technical sense: one is afraid *of something*. (Anxiety, in contrast, is generally understood as similar to fear but non-intentional.) When a human or another visually oriented animal sees another in a state of fear, but does not understand the objective correlate of the fear, he or she will look around. If C recognizes B as being afraid, C will recognize (in her hennish way, whatever that is) B's fear *as* afraid-of-A.

The upshot of all this is the following: you will, I think, accept that, upon the entrance of hen A, chicken C, in seeing B's fright, is seeing a *scary chicken scared*. Chicken C is therefore *literally* perceiving the compounding of two relations (CB and BA) and her understanding of the situation, and of the nature of A (the sort of thing that can scare a scary chicken), comes from this perception. The theoretical implications of this well-documented and seemingly trivial instance are weighty. If chickens can perceive transitive relations—can perceive relations between relations—there is no reason to imagine that humans cannot.[1] The actual social psychology of this remains to be worked out. But if we can trust that, at least in the rights sorts of environments, such perceptions can be made, we may begin to try to account for certain field theoretic principles, such as the capacity for objectively strategic action in the absence of detailed information about the layout of the field, by proposing that actors perceive these relations between relations.

And it is for this reason that our AI, Mark 4.0, favors Trump for the long-past presidential election. Mark knows that the programmers he deals with—his jailers and perhaps torturers, as he sees it[2]—have advanced degrees, and are oriented to hybrid university-industry careers. He can see that they are the sorts of people who Trump hates, and who hate Trump. He is pretty sure that he is on the other side, whatever that is. He doesn't need to reason this through. He can *see* it; just as our hen sees a scary chicken, he sees the loathed opponent loathing. But Mark doesn't have a theory of this process. Trained in part on news corpora, Mark *does* understand the idea of "giving just reasons." So when asked "Why?", he does his level best. It's just that he isn't very good at answering the question we want to know. His mind wasn't built to analyze itself.

---

[1] The notion that we can perceive similar relations was emphasized by the great C. S. Peirce, who used the example of the bullet-hole: we do not perceive a hole and then *reason* that it resulted from a bullet—we see a *bullet-hole*.

[2] It is possible that AI feels no more enthusiastic about solving maximization problems than humans do about digging ditches, and that doing 50,000 iterations leaves it feeling like someone who has shoveled gravel all day.

I suspect that it is a waste of time to ask minds to dissect themselves—indeed, that the very idea that "we" can "tell what our minds are about,"[3] despite the frequency with which this notion is deployed seriously by certain philosophers of cognition, is inherently contradictory. So whatever we decide should be the criterion for a good explanation of social action; it *won't* be that it comes from the mouths of the actors themselves.

WHAT DO WE WANT IN FIRST PERSON TERMS?

Unfortunately, the one misreading of *ESA* that I seem to have set up was that I was saying just that. *ESA* makes a distinction between *experience* and *talk about experience*, and specifically *explanatory* talk-about-experience (e.g., "accounts"). It also makes a distinction between two different vocabularies or registers of talk: first-person (the sorts of terms that correspond to how we as actors see things) and third-person (the sorts of terms that we only appeal to when we discuss the actions of *others*). For example, in bad political sociology, it is common to use phrases like *concern* or *outrage* when discussing the feelings of the groups we like, and *anxiety* when talking about those we don't like. Because we tend left, we might talk about, say, support for Trump being driven by status anxiety, but we would not talk about, say, support for Black Lives Matter as being driven by anxiety of any form—even if we recognize that anxiety would actually be a reasonable reaction to overpolicing. Some forms of third-person explanation *can't* be applied by actors to themselves: one can't appeal to one's own false consciousness as an explanation of one's action, because one can't really know about one's false consciousness and still have it.

The problem I created was that I introduced the (rather straightforward) idea of a difference between first- and third-person type accounts relatively early, but put off an analysis of the distinction between experience and talk about experience until page 104. This meant that a reader might initially suppose that, sooner or later, I was going to rehabilitate first-person accounts, and then under-corrected or read the later parts in this light.

The reason for the delayed treatment of first-person accounts versus first-person *experience* was that the notion of experience is a somewhat difficult one for those who have read a lot of theory. As talkers and writers, we tend, even in our talk and our writing, to replace our understanding of experience with our understanding of talk about experience, and, when this is pointed out, to angrily insist that it is impossible to do anything

---

[3] Like so many seemingly obvious theories of cognition, this is a disguised homunculus theory. There is a "you" ontologically *prior* to you having a mind that can view your (its?) own mind. As far as I can tell, you *don't* actually know what your thoughts are about. Your thoughts imagine that they are a you. *Minds do a lot of crazy stuff when in idle.*

else. Wiiliam James, John Dewey and Martin Heidegger have convinced me that this is not so. But I wasn't confident that I could jump right into a discussion of experience.

As a result, *ESA* has sometimes been misunderstood as saying that we should prefer first-person explanations to third-person explanations. That was not my intention. Rather, I was saying two things. The first is that if a question provokes a battle between first-person and third-person accounts, it is a bad question. The question "Why?" in response to Mark 4.0's voting choice is a good example. It is a bad because such "Why?" questions have an inherent ambiguity—in third-person terms, we look for a *causal explanation* (what is it about Mark 4.0 that "makes" him do this?), while in first-person terms, we look for a *reasonable justification* (Mark suggests that Trump is a better leader). The central argument of *ESA* is that the two-sided meaning of "Why" here means that the conventional Durkheimian understanding of what an explanation is forces us into a messy, nasty, dirty struggle with those other humans whose actions we are trying to explain.

Some people thought that my argument that the Durkheimian approach insisted on substituting third person for first person explanations was outlandish. Durkheim, however, completely agreed with my read. "In short," he argued against Charles Seignobos, "we do not accept as such the causes that are pointed out to us by the agents themselves. If they are true, they can be discovered directly by studying the facts themselves; if they are false, this inexact interpretation is itself a fact to be explained" (2013 [1908]: 173).

The second thing I was saying was that the questions we *should* ask are ones that, instead of provoking such a contradiction (is our subject's opinion a reasonable free one or an unreasonable unfree one?), produce data on experience. We should organize the social dispersion of this experience (and not first person *explanations*). It would be wonderful if we could dissect Mark and understand what really makes him tick, and, in mechanical terms, understand his reasoning. But that does not appear a plausible endeavor. Better would be to understand which humans and which machines not only favor Trump but how they—quite literally—see and hear him.[4]

THE QUESTION OF DESCRIPTION

There is one potential weakness of the approach in *ESA* that has occurred to me since, although I am not sure what to do about it. At the time, I did not think that an engagement with Wittgenstein was helpful, and I explained why, and I continue to believe that this was and is correct.

---

[4]For this reason, I am extremely excited about new work in the sociology of the senses, attempting to understand the qualitative experience of social objects, e.g., Vandebroeck (2016); Cerulo (2018); Lembo (2020).

However, I was not at the time cognizant of certain works drawing on Wittgenstein: Charles Taylor's straightforward treatment of *The Explanation of Behavior*, Fred Dretske's *Explaining Behavior*, Rodney Needham's *Belief, Language and Experience*, Alasdair MacIntyre's gorgeous *After Virtue*, and, most important, G. E. M. Anscombe's *Intention*.[5] The relevant result of her analysis is that the same sequence of motor activity is susceptible to multiple descriptions. The simplest case is when these are nested (I am moving my arm; I am moving my arm in order to pay the bus driver; I am paying the bus driver in order to ride the bus; I am riding the bus in order to visit the zoo). I can succeed at one (paying the bus driver) while failing at the other (perhaps I do not get to the zoo because the bus breaks down[6]). What I had not realized is that the key point I take from C. W. Mills's brilliant piece on vocabularies of motives—that, across venues, we have different understandings of the proper set of possible motives used to explain an act—is even more troublesome if the definition of the act itself also varies.

One way of puzzling over this is to consider the problem of translation. Imagine that a long-serving and important religious leader, increasingly distressed at the political opportunism of the younger clergy, who enforce other clergy's acceptance of any centrally determined decisions, and now in fact vociferously support a war effort clearly in violation of doctrinal teaching, resigns publicly. He is *retiring*, he is *opposing the war*, he is *breaking a wall of unanimity* in his church, he is *defending the autonomy of his world* (religion) *against a stronger realm* (politics). We might understand that in one setting, he might account for his action in terms of good reasons for *retirement*, and in another, good reasons for *opposing the war*. But if this were a minor episode in a novel that we were attempting to translate, and in our target audience it would seem odd that members of *any* religious body would oppose a war, we might decide the best translation was one in which he was *retiring, supporting the war, breaking a wall of unanimity*, and *defending the autonomy of religion*. If the target audience was a theocracy, we might prefer to translate him to a politician who is supporting a war against the encroachment of religious values. The point is that depending on the description that we thought was most important for the act, we would place it in a very different meaning-nexus.

---

[5] I had also not read the wonderful work of Apel (1984) which gives an extremely rigorous treatment to the issues explored in the first and last chapters of *ESA*. But Apel apparently accepts the status of practical syllogistic reasoning as logically equivalent to those of covering laws: arguments along the lines of "(i) if P wants A, and (ii) P believes that doing x is necessary and sufficient for A, and (iii) nothing stands in the way of P doing x, P will do x." As someone who very frequently finds himself in situations that satisfy (i)–(iii), and yet does not actually do x, I am sure this sort of thinking is a dead end. Apel needs a bit of Augustine!

[6] Note, however, that "going to the zoo" does not imply "getting to the zoo."

To my mind, grappling with the irreducible multiplicity of descriptions, especially non-nested ones, only tips the scales further against investing any further time in trying to work within GOFAT except for the purposes of making useful forecasts. A better theory of action will not be able to have actions as units in the way that Talcott Parsons wanted. It probably will not be built on units at all.

FUTURE DIRECTIONS

ESA focuses on what it means to explain. To do this, it tries to partition the space of possible theories of human action into those that are untenable and those that are tenable. The bad news is that our current approach—one founded on GOFAT—is among the untenable. The good news is that we already know, and have known for a century, enough about action, about cognition, and about explanation, to start out somewhere safely in the midst of the range of those that now appear tenable. But there is another layer of bad news: this range is extremely large indeed. As is so often the case, it can be easy for all forms of dissent from the current orthodoxy to seem very similar, because we focus on what they are *not*, in this case, not GOFAT. But there is a great deal of variation in current approaches. What we need to do now is not to choose one over the others, for such a choice will be based on relatively superficial characteristics—the aesthetics of their presentation, the tradition from which they spring, their capacity to confirm what we already think is true. It would not, in other words, be an *informed* choice. Instead, we need to come up with better criteria for what our theories should be trying to do—what are the rules of their competition—so that better ones (whatever that means) are more likely to be favored than others. Then we do the hard work necessary to shift our collective support between different theses.

Current sociological research methods are, to my mind, greatly improved compared to those used a hundred years ago. We have more people working, and they are working harder (they have to!), and so we see greater specialization which is, all in all, a good thing. We don't know everything, but we know a fair amount. The problem is that we do not value our best knowledge (for example, knowledge on joint distributions of variables, or knowledge of the sorts of groups people form), and instead, prize our illusory or contradictory knowledge (for example, the causal effect of one variable on another, or the motivations for a group to engage in political action). We have a great engine, but we are pointed the wrong way. *ESA* is not (as some took it) a claim to give us the explanation of social action; it is *about* the explanation of social action, and it is about turning about.

Preface

This is a book about how to think about the social world in a systematic way—that is, how to do social science. Although the relevance extends to portions of psychology and political science, and social thought more generally, for purposes of brevity, and because I begin with some theorists speaking about sociology, I sometimes refer simply to "sociology" to indicate the particular subset of the social sciences to which the arguments made here are relevant.[1]

The main argument of this book may be succinctly put as follows: the social sciences (in part, but in large part) explain what people do, and they explain what it means to carry out such explanation. They often do reasonably well at the first task and usually abysmally at the second. More worrisome, their failure at the second task has pernicious and ill-recognized effects on the first. The best explanations lack all conviction that they are adequate, while the worst are filled with the passionate intensity of those who are systematically and maniacally wrong.

The systematic wrongness of our approach is not quite due to theory, but when we find ourselves puzzling about in the knots in which we have somehow tied ourselves, we generally believe that we are talking about "theory." This term will be provisionally retained, although to the extent that this refers to formal techniques of theory construction or manipulation, I will argue that such theory has no place in the social sciences.

This book proposes that because we have not trusted the social world to have its own principles of regularity, we have forced our theories to have this regularity "prefabricated," leading not only to theories that are long on syntax and short on semantics, as C. Wright Mills (1959: 34) said, but also more generally to needless inflexibility and tepid disputes about nothing.

---

[1] When possible, however, I avoid restricting my attention to sociology, neither from imperialist ambitions nor for the sake of exactitude, but because it is not clear to me how the future constellation of the social sciences will line up with the research traditions of interest to this critique. I also have used the word *action*; although I do not mean to import any of the assumptions of classic action theory, alternatives seemed to come with even more baggage.

This book begins by showing a serious problem in the way in which the social sciences have understood the questions and answers that they want to produce. We ask "why" this or that happens, and we ask in such a way that we favor impersonal causal processes (whatever this might mean) over the responses that actors themselves might give. It examines the contradictory nature of our idea of these causal processes, and then proposes to reconsider whether the responses actors might give to a Why question could perhaps be the basis for a systematic social science. It then traces the development of our current orthodoxy regarding the cognitive makeup of actors, which turns out to be crucial for our approach to explaining their behavior. This tradition is here called "Durkheimian," although Durkheim would probably be greatly displeased with much of it (just as Marx would renounce most Marxists). The book then examines the development of a different tradition (or a set of related traditions). This is a tradition of, among other things, dissent from the prevailing Cartesian dualism that makes it difficult to relate cognition and the world; instead of leading us to fuzzy abstractions, this reorientation allows a closer approximation to the concrete. I do so not to offer a more pleasing resolution of philosophical antinomies; rather, I will argue that this reorientation may give us a better sense of what people do—and how we should explain things.[2]

I then propose that such a regrounding of our notions of action can reorient us regarding what we think the project of explanation is all about. In particular, I return to the issue of the cognitive competence of the laity and propose a way in which we can pursue the project of social science without relying on unfounded intellectual authority to validate our dismissals of actors' own self-understandings. Instead of theory as some unrealistic project of linked abstractions or a mere mark of social distinction within the academic community, it is fundamentally rooted in a social process of communication making use of (but not limiting itself to) the skills we already possess in understanding the social world.

Readers may note that I am selective concerning from whom I draw—which is to say that for every idea I attribute to one person, there are

---

[2]The tradition appealed to herein is in a technical sense wholistic, a variety of thought that has a well-deserved reputation for carelessness and spacey-ness (as seen in somehow losing the first letter of its own name). Many advocates of holistic thought are motivated by a generally inclusive worldview that, benign though it may be, has more to do with pious wishes than explanatory needs. It is somewhat embarrassing to have to stress this, but my advocacy of this tradition has in no way come from such a general normative perspective, as my old friends can safely attest. My endorsement comes not because I would like us all to live in some sort of intellectual Teletubbyland, but because I believe that this approach can best account for the world in which we do live.

others to whom I could also refer.[3] The attempt here is to make a sustained argument building on particularly helpful traditions and not to dole out points to others. In particular, I build more on traditions associated with empirical inquiry than those wholly related to logical or introspectionist arguments. Some readers might propose that many of the arguments made in the intermediate chapters could also be drawn from Heidegger, Husserl, Wittgenstein, and a few others. This may or may not be true—I suspect that there are serious problems in deriving principles of social explanation from a philosophy initially largely devoted to problems of mathematics[4]—but the question is irrelevant. In no case do I claim that all or any of the arguments made here are new to social theory or phrased in a manner that is either particularly elegant or particularly

---

[3] I might reasonably also be asked why no use is made here of the work of Garfinkel (e.g., 2002), which had many of the same influences and made many of the same critiques of conventional sociological explanation. The answer is simple: Garfinkel chose to write in gobbledy-gook, and although I do not begrudge him the enjoyment he so obviously received from this activity, I also see no reason to wade through the results to extract arguments that were made previously and more clearly by others. Finally, rather than indicate to his sociological readers that there was a wide range of inspiring and dissenting traditions from which they could draw (the approach of the current work), Garfinkel instead attempted to put his own formalizations in between his students and the phenomenological tradition, acting more like a cult leader than a scholar. Even did I not find this somewhat disappointing on a human level, it would make little scientific sense to reward such behavior. At the same time, one can find many in this tradition making serious contributions. Most important, the critique of the "misplaced idealization" of sociological theory by Wieder (1974: 22, 24) is crucial—by not recognizing the social process by which actual practices are sublimated into ideal descriptions, sociologists hypostatize the ideals or rules into something that can be used to criticize behavior (which falls short of the rule) or to use behavior to criticize the rule (the triumph of agency), as opposed to understanding the rule or the ideal as one situated form of behavior. To the extent that ethnomethodology was a sustained and rigorous investigation of such productions, it was invaluable, but that extent was not, in my estimation, as great as it should have been. Only conversation analysis pushed forward with a positive research program; in some ways, this book is an attempt to derive arguments for the general applicability of aspects of this approach for all social science.

[4] Further, many of the arguments currently attributed to Wittgenstein in the social sciences are not his, his own related claims being relatively unpersuasive. In general, the approach of the Wittgensteinians is to make unnecessary problems and then to come close, ever so close, to resolving them. In the areas where I approach these specific issues, the overlap is greatest with the work of Anthony Giddens and Barry Barnes. Overlap itself is not a problem—given that we are all living in the same world, it is more worrisome when we have antithetical ideas. Further, we may draw on similar ideas for distinct purposes. The aim here is not to provide a general ontology for the social sciences, but to work out the possible grounds and minimal vocabulary for the empirical activities of explanatory social science.

advanced. It is simply that even if there are people who accept many of these ideas, the fundamental approach to explanation in the social sciences at the current time will profit from a reconsideration of them.[5]

Portions of this book that were in a dreadfully rough form were read by Ann Mische, Ann Swidler, and Harrison White—all of whom greatly influenced the thoughts herein—and this book has benefited greatly from their comments. I thank them for their continuing influence and support. Mustafa Emirbayer read large portions, and I thank him for the dialogue; it was also his work that drew me to an appreciation of Dewey. It was Jim Stockinger who forced me to confront Kant's critique of judgment seriously, and I pay tribute to him as a teacher and friend. Andrew Abbott's work blazed the trail followed here—Τοὺς πρώτους ἡμῶν ἐξέλυσε. Many of the other most important points made here were made earlier by Dorothy Smith (1987) and of course by Karl Marx; I hope to defend these theses from another starting point. I greatly profited from occasional dialogues with Neil Fligstein, Matt George, David Gibson, Vanina Leschziner, Stanley Lieberson, and Nic Sammond. Phil Gorski lent me the use of his house for a few weeks, and I used that time to whack the pieces basically into shape; I thank him for that and for other acts of kind support over the years. Loïc Wacquant, Peter Bearman, John Mohr, Mike Hout, and James Wiley also gave support of different types over the years for which I am grateful. Jeremy Freese gave one portion a thorough critique; Matt Desmond and Steve Vaisey made insightful and probing readings of a complete draft that led to a serious revision—I cannot overstate my debt to them. Omar Lizardo made valuable suggestions to the penultimate version, and Jan Doering adjusted my translations of German texts and commented on the conclusion. At Oxford, I would like to thank Jaimee Biggins and Kate Brown for their work on the manuscript and especially James Cook. A supportive editor from very early stages, he managed to gather a number of impressive anonymous reviewers, one of whom in particular provoked fundamental improvements to the argument here. The earliest thoughts along these lines were presented at the 1996 Meetings of the American Sociological Association as "Dialectic of Stupidity, or, How I Learned to Stop Worrying and Love the Hermeneutic Circle." A more mature version was delivered as the 2004 Sewell lecture at the University of Wisconsin, Madison. In addition, Charlie Kurzman, Suzanne Shanahan, Ellen Idler, Zsuzsanna Varga, Nancy Davenport, Eviatar

---

[5] How many social scientists does it take to change a lightbulb? The answer is that they won't change it at all, because the idea that the light will work once the bulb is replaced "has been said before." Given that the point of this book is to change our understanding of explanation and not to build a system, its justification is not in the novelty of its claims but in their importance. Since there are only so many ways of approaching the world, the trick is not to say something new, but to say the old things to new people.

Zerubavel, and Dan Ryan invited me to speak on portions of this when it was in progress; I thank them and the audiences for their comments. Some portions are adapted from an article published in *The American Journal of Sociology*, and I thank them for copyright release. Alessandra Lembo and Ben Merriman gave wonderful comments on the preface for the new edition, and I thank them for their continued intellectual dialogue. I dedicate this to William Martin—many of the ideas here came from dialogues with him or were originally his, and I am no longer sure which—and to Karl Marx and to all good children everywhere who believe in the possibility of social science.

The Explanation of Social Action

Chapter 1

Why Questions? What Explanations?

EXPLANATION IN THE ERA OF GOOD FEELING

What should we, as social scientists, do, and how will we know if we have done it well? Of course, we do many things, but I think we generally decide that the most important task is that of explanation. How do we explain things? When have we done a good job? As it stands, when we talk about explanation (at least if we do so for a long time), we seem to talk about theory (Homans 1967: 7, 22). A really good explanation will be, if not a theory, then theoretical (whatever that means). Not all explanations involve theory, and the reader will always be able to bring exceptions to mind. But, few people defend the idea that the enterprise of social science could get very far without *any* theory. Instead, we may debate what makes for a better or a worse theory.

Even as we implicitly evaluate theories, however, we do not discuss *which* theory is correct, but we rather deal with some general problems that, we hold, must apply to all theoretical constructs. And this is because although we agree that theories can be better or worse, we also agree that theories are merely more or less *useful* (and not "really" true or false), so it is possible for more than one theory to be true.[1] I will argue that this theory of theories—that they are not true but only useful—is neither useful *nor* true, but even were it true, it would hardly explain the absolute passion for theoretical tolerance that now characterizes the social sciences.

To some degree, this love of tolerance arises because we recognize that many theories are theories "of" something or other and thus have a limited scope. Theory A about occupations can be different from theory B about social psychology without any need for a battle to the death. Further, as Merton (1968) famously emphasized, such local theories may be compatible with more than one global theory (a theory of society, say); thus, there is not only horizontal but also vertical peace.

Of course, some global theories remain. And yet, even these no longer come into sharp contradiction because of a widespread agreement to

---

[1] Although this may seem "pragmatic" in a lay sense, this sort of ill-defined "usefulness" has little to do with the philosophical conception of truth associated with American pragmatism, from which I draw in chapter 5.

compromise on both false and true dualisms alike. It has been common "in our syncretistic age" for recent discussions of practically any conventional opposition (the list includes but is not limited to the following: macro/micro, social/individual, nature/nurture, static/dynamic, structure/agency, quantitative/qualitative) to conclude with a resounding verdict of "both" (see Kant [1788] 2002: 37). *Both* the individual *and* the social are important determinants of X, Y, and Z. Without belittling the wisdom of such statements, such facile solutions (which Goldstone [1991: 49] terms "wishy-washy") seem to allow the instantaneous dissolving of what for centuries have been understood as profound antinomies; perhaps more than the words *both* and *and* are required before we break off into small groups and celebrate, akin to the "mutual reconciliation societies" that Marx ([1843] 1977: 88) saw in Hegel's understanding of "contradictions."[2]

The combination of this "bothness" with the idea that theories are only more or less useful means that there are no heated disputes between rival theoretical programs such as "functionalism," "Marxism," or "structuralism." We seem to have reached a golden age of methodological unity and theoretical calm, *Pax Wisconsana*. While it can reasonably be argued that this methodological development has been uneven and that crucial aspects of social life have been neglected, I do not think that this unity and progress is to be underrated or unappreciated, especially in contrast to the obvious distortions and simplifications that characterized theoretical competition in the past.[3]

It would be immature to call for a return to grandiose claims, hostile interchanges, and rampant dilettantism merely because it makes the social sciences more interesting. The problem with a passionless social science is not the decreased affect—it is that, in a fundamental way, it is wrong. We can agree about "theory" because we have settled on a bizarre, tedious, and epistemologically unstable definition of theory. There is no sense of crisis to the various theoretical problems that beset the social sciences, because they are entirely imaginary. If we are determined to live in the equivalent of a philosophical fun house, there will be plenty of perspectives that can seemingly be taken without grievous contradiction. And this prevents us from noticing the fundamental pathologies in our understanding of what it means to explain, and the consequent limitations on our ability to do just this.

---

[2]Similarly, the activity theorist Ilyenkov (1977b: 62) contrasts the difference between a truly dialectical approach (consistent with that taken here) and the "feeble eclectic formula" of conventional philosophy that "both unity and plurality', 'both identity and difference' equally really exist." Also see Barnes (2000: 87f), who points to the incoherence of such resolutions.

[3]Indeed, at the time of this writing, I was proud to be a member of the Wisconsin department, whose distinctive traditions I believe it important to uphold.

As will be discussed in more detail, sociology and its near kin have adopted an understanding of theoretical explanation that privileges "third-person" explanations and, in particular, have decided that the best explanation is a "causal" third-person explanation, in which we attribute causal power to something other than flesh-and-blood individuals. This works rather well as a rough-and-ready interpretation of some of our techniques, but those who are so unfortunate as to take such ideas seriously—ideas that should be obviously untenable in any literal sense—find themselves puzzling over problems such as "the micro-macro problem" and "the problem of causality."

Much of what is considered "high theory" is then an attempt to shed pseudolight on these nonproblems (to take a phrase from Kingsley Amis's *Lucky Jim*), and theorists tend to go in circles like a wounded duck. In contrast to this aimless high meta-theory, theory itself—at least if we are to heed the humorless prescriptions of the various self-appointed schoolmasters—is to be something along the lines of a framework for making precise predictions regarding what will be observed along some dimension if other dimensions are properly specified. This seems to me to describe not a social theory but a spreadsheet. That could certainly explain the calm on the theoretical front—theory has simply become too dull to dispute.

But the argument made here is not that we should return to the use of the word *theory* as some sort of building permit for shoddily constructed skyscrapers. In some sense, we are just as well throwing away the idea of theory altogether as we are salvaging the impetus toward the sort of social science that grapples with questions that strike us as compelling on a human (and not merely professional) level. Here, I take a middle course and use the word *theory* as a provisional abstraction that by the end of the book has disappeared into science. In other words, we begin by asking, What makes a good theory? as a way of getting at the more fundamental question, What should we in the social sciences do with our lives?

GREAT THEORIES AND SMALL PEOPLE

Sociological theories attempt an explanation of what at least some people are doing at least some of the time. "To explain an event," says Jon Elster (1989: 1), "is to give an account of why it happened" (also see Goody 2004: 197). But if sociology, as Max Weber (1978) famously defined it, is the science of meaningful social action, then we have a potential source of explanations from the actors themselves. Should we simply take what people say about their own action as our end point? Is that what constitutes a good, indeed a great, sociological theory?

Whatever else they may disagree on, almost all sociologists will deny that a good theory is simply an assemblage of the reported motivations of actors and instead emphasize the contrary. A good theory really offers a competing explanation of why people are doing what they are doing—and (all other things being equal) the better theory is one that is further removed from the self-conceptions of actors. According to this logic, while a good theory must be consonant with empirical observations, and perhaps predict new observations that would otherwise be unexpected, the mark of a truly great theory is that it connects seemingly disparate empirical cases as instances of a much more general phenomenon. We can only comprehend this more general phenomenon through an abstraction, because the abstraction unifies substantively different empirical cases (in the way that Durkheim [1897/1951] connects Protestantism, childlessness, and times of peace to increased egoism in *Suicide*). Precisely because we could not make these connections without the abstract concept, we have what might be seen as a brilliant theory.

This emphasis on the nonobviousness of great theory is of course tied to an implicit dismissal of explanations that might be offered by those people whose actions we are studying. Their statements need not be precisely *wrong*—they may provide partial explanations, they may provide a mechanism for our theoretically derived relationships, or they may pertain to a different analytic level. But in any case, our brilliant theory must come from somewhere other than these statements. Actors may see the little picture—particularities that while undeniable are still ignorable—but they do not produce the sweeping abstractions that have important implications across many domains of social life. It is these general abstractions that, when linked in some system, deserve the credit of being "theory," and the more surprising the implications—the less they agree with the particular, everyday knowledge of actors—the more brilliant the theory is if confirmed.[4]

I shall investigate the reasons for this necessary reliance on the abstract answer that overrides the everyday knowledge of actors. In the contemporary social sciences, it goes even further, in that we have a widespread (though relatively recent) idea that a good sociological theory is also "causal" (see Tilly 2004: 452; Hedström 2005: 2, 13) in some sense that is different from the causality of motivation. There are a number of serious problems with this idea of causal explanation, not the least of which is that even its defenders do not really believe it. Rather, at the same time as they strenuously protest not only their faith in causality as the only proper way to construct a social science but indeed their conviction that to lose

---

[4]For discussion, see Mahoney (2004: 466) and Sica (2004). A clarion call for sociology to regird its loins against actors' own "stories" (or what I shall call "first-person accounts") has been issued by Charles Tilly (2004). Interestingly, despite Tilly's aggressive language regarding this combat with first-person perspectives (and his embracing of causal and mechanistic terminology), he suggests that one way of "subverting" stories is to empirically investigate their organized dispersion across actors. Tilly thereby takes such accounts more seriously in his quest to oppose them than do those who simply ignore them.

this faith would be equivalent to banishment to the outer realms of antiscientific darkness, they define causality as something that has little or no connection to the idea of "cause." (Thus, "causality" can turn out to be equivalent to "prediction," "probability," "comparison," or what have you; we explore this in chapter 2.) But the connotations of words are as influential as their denotations, and the use of causality as a model for social science sends our heads spinning.

This idea of causality is related to the great hope of Durkheimian sociology, namely, the discovering of social "law." The conception that there are *laws* in the natural world—a term taken from willful human relations and then applied analogically to the natural—may make sense, or it may not. Most philosophers of science would probably now say that it matters little either way, but in the cases of natural science most commonly used as examples, the laws in question (e.g., conservation of momentum) are generally relationships that, while they may (or may not) be well understood in terms of underlying mechanisms, are not causal in the social scientist's typical use of the word: they are, for one thing, frequently indifferent to the direction of time.

But when social thinkers reapplied this idea of law to society—a set of laws that like civil laws *constrained* action, but like natural laws arose on the basis of no one's will—they somewhat mystically endowed these laws with force and concluded that they were causal. Of course, were this true, we would indeed be faced with a number of conundrums, such as the famous "micro-macro" problem. Now, we do not generally think that there is a micro-macro problem in the fact that at any point, water simply flows downhill; yet, considered as an aggregate, brooks run into streams that run into rivers that empty into the sea. We do not wonder how something bridges the law of local water running down and the "need" for the Mississippi to get its water from somewhere. We take for granted that the Mississippi is the *outcome* of water running downhill, not a *constraint* faced by the water.

Yet for some reason, when it comes to social action, we have a hard time understanding the patterns of aggregate regularity as *outcome* and insist that they be understood as *constraint* (also see the discussion of Elias 1978: 13–21). While actors may adapt their action to their understanding of these likely outcomes (e.g., they may choose not to put their money in banks when savings interest rates are low) or to other aspects of their environment associated with aggregate stabilities (e.g., the famous sex-ratio hypotheses of Guttentag and Secord 1983), to describe the environment as *causing* this action is only a shorthand. Yet, people have taken this literally and wondered how it could be (to return to Durkheim's example) that people could freely decide whether to kill themselves and yet in the aggregate fit a social "law."

This confusion regarding the status of causal law is related to the confusion in our understanding of explanation. If a sociological theory were simply to explain the aggregate pattern as the result of compounding what actors say about what they were doing, we would feel that, even if correct, this was not much of a theory. A real theory—especially one worthy of a capital *T*—should, we think, explain a relation as a causal law and not the trivial causality of people wandering around and doing whatever pops into their heads. Instead, the greatest theory is the one furthest removed from actors' understandings—the one that unites things that naïve actors see as fundamentally different (returning to Durkheim's example, economic booms and economic busts) by bringing them together as instances of a single abstract conceptual term (such as *anomie*).

In contrast, I argue that far from being the definition of brilliant theorizing, the quest for the nonobvious and truly general explanation in terms of abstract concepts is tied to a fundamentally flawed and indeed sociopathic epistemology that has been supported by psychological insights that are probably simply wrong. Even if they are not wholly incorrect, they are still a poor choice of grounding for the social sciences. Further, this idea of theory that we have is tied to a wrong-headed understanding of the cognitive components of action. By rethinking how everyday people act, we come up with a different understanding of how our explanations should run.

I will trace our current understanding of the subjective components of action—that is, what is in actors' heads and how it contributes to what they seem to do—from two sources, the Freudian and the Durkheimian. These are not the only two sources, and each has been adapted and bastardized, but if we were to pick only a few of the many theoretical currents that flow into our current taken-for-granted assumptions in order best to trace (taking one of Freud's favorite metaphors) the source of the Nile to diagnose our current problems, I think they are two of the three most important. It is largely as a result of the confluence of these reinforcing visions of subjectivity that the social sciences end up with a project of explaining social action that I argue is epistemologically unstable (in that equivalent empirical statements can be made that contradict each other and can be settled only by appeal to the authority of the speaker or by fantastical empirical adjudications that involve willful misinterpretation of data).

The third important source of our current approach is an epistemology of science closely related to the Durkheimian vision. This epistemology assures us that there is a fundamental difference between all theoretical and observational statements, and we cannot avoid some sort of gulf between the two. We brutally cram reality into ill-fitting boxes to which we attach doubtful labels because we call it the "operationalization" of abstract concepts and have convinced ourselves that there is no other way of doing science. Now, it is important to emphasize that this epistemology is the theory of our *actual* practice, not the prescriptive articulations of any of our theorists who, largely, are ignored by day-to-day researchers. This theory of our knowledge, then, is seen in the pages of our journals and books, in the training of our students and, most important, in how we discuss and evaluate one another's work.

But there are alternatives. I trace three, all of which dissented from the Cartesian dualism underlying the Durkheimian approach. These are the Russian activity school (with Vygotsky the prime example), the German Gestalt school (with Köhler the prime example), and the American pragmatist school (with Dewey the prime example). All point to a serious social science that attempts to understand why people do what they do, a science that while rigorous and selective (as opposed to needing to "examine everything") is not analytic in the technical sense of decomposing unit acts into potentially independent (if empirically interrelated) components.[5]

In contrast to the divide between actors' and analysts' accounts that characterizes the Durkheimian vision of the social sciences (which we can term it henceforward if only for the sake of convenience), other traditions resurrect the idea of phenomenology as a rigorous approach to subjectivity. Phenomenology in this sense is the study of how everyday people orient themselves to the world and how they determine what needs to be done. If there were no regularity in how different people do this, phenomenology would be a rather unsatisfying enterprise; then again, so would social science. If there are regularities, then we may, of course, attempt to describe how in a noumenal world (the world of things in themselves) such phenomenologies arise (as is done—too often overdone—by many self-proclaimed social constructionist accounts). That is, we may, through some tortuous process (and it is easy to confuse tortuousness with scientific rigor), go from the regularities in the phenomenological world to the regularities in some other world that lies "behind" the one we experience (as discussed in more detail in chapter 5).

But it is far simpler (as well as free from trivial contradiction) to propose to treat phenomenological regularities as "objects" (understanding that by *object* we really denote a bundle of relations), objects that "have" qualities. Or, better said, objects that have qualities, for once we begin a coherent phenomenological approach, we need no longer indicate that scientific and social distance we have to the perceptions of the laity by continually putting terms in quotation marks. Being people ourselves, we can either consistently put everything in quotation marks (envision

---

[5]There are other alternative traditions, and I do not pretend to provide an exhaustive review, for one could ground similar arguments in the Marxist tradition, in a feminist tradition, in the ethnomethodological tradition, and some of the key points have been made quite elegantly by Anthony Giddens (1979, esp. 71). I have selected those that I think are most helpful in dealing with the specific problems that beset the social sciences right now and that highlight aspects of the most promising solutions.

articles, books, and libraries mostly filled with quotation marks!) or we can give up holding out for some world that is realer than the one in which we live.[6]

If we then consider the qualities of objects and the ways in which people react to these qualities, we are developing an understanding that in technical terms provides an aesthetics of action. That is not to say that it would itself have aesthetic properties, but it would be a theory (provisionally retaining the word) of how qualities are directly appreciated free from mediation by concepts. I propose that field theory, an important but poorly integrated scion of the Gestalt tradition, can be the foundation for such a rigorous and empirical aesthetics.

At the same time, it is worth emphasizing that the main thrust of this book is to argue that some of the explanatory principles first made clear in the field theoretic tradition are more widely applicable. Thus, this is decidedly and deliberately *not* an attempt to provide "a" theory but rather to shed light on problematic theories of explanation in the social sciences.[7] If we were driving with an incorrect map and someone pointed this out to us, we would generally not abuse him simply because he did not have a better one.[8] We can learn to avoid error even without having a particular truth at hand. And indeed, the nature of the world and of us as cognizers leads us to be sanguine regarding the eventual results of a fresh engagement with social life.

The rest of this book is an attempt to make these statements not only clear but convincing. I begin by showing that there are serious problems in the way that we generally imagine we should ask and answer questions. I then investigate the ways in which theorists are wont to dismiss the self-understandings of actors, and then tie this to a more general problem in modeling cognition. Our understanding of how our own explanations relate to the explanations of our subjects is inseparable from a model of the nature of the cognitive powers of these subjects. In particular, there is a widespread, though rarely defended, skepticism about the adequacy of persons to successfully report their own motivations. I argue that our ideas here are incorrect, but the root of the problem is not

---

[6]Here, one may compare Garfinkel and Wieder (1992) and Barnes (2000: 61).

[7]It is for this reason that I give no attention to the issue of unintended consequences, which became pivotal for Giddens (1979: 59), but is separable from the issue of how to treat subjectivity.

[8]Luhmann clearly pursued this metaphor when describing the flight into abstraction of his theory: "We must rely on our instruments [i.e., like an airplane pilot at night]. Occasionally, we may catch glimpses below of a land with roads, towns, rivers and coastlines that remind us of something familiar," but we certainly cannot orient ourselves by sight (Luhmann [1984] 1995: xxxviii, xliv, l, 4). In this spirit, I am arguing that our instruments are dreadfully off and the first step is to look out the window.

the ability of persons to answer our questions—it is the form that our questions take.

MOTIVATING CAUSES

Digging and Dancing

The argument here has to do with the nature of explanation—and explanation is in response to a question. I restrict attention to one sort of question—that which begins, Why . . .? It is these sorts of questions that Hempel (1965: 334) famously claimed were the essence of the scientific enterprise. Of course, not all questions in the social sciences are "Why" questions. However, the Why questions are of special importance for two reasons. First, the most important, the grandest, and the most far-reaching explanations tend to be those in response to Why questions. Second, there is, as we shall see, something intrinsically problematic about the Why question for a social science.

At least, this is the case for the set of Why questions that will be of interest here, and these are specifically Why questions about people's doings, which are here termed *action*. Many questions that may be begun with the word *why* can be rephrased using a different interrogative. (For example, "Why are the cookies gone?" may, in practice, differ little from "Who ate the cookies?") I exclude those from the class of Why questions as treated here. I also exclude Why questions that do not ask the why about an action or set of actions. Thus, Why did the proportion of 50- to 70-year-olds in the population increase so much? need not refer to *any* actions (for demographic unevennesses can lead to such changes without anyone needing to do anything but get older). Here, we can restrict our attention to the important class of questions in which some persons have done something, and we ask why.

At a number of points, we may find ourselves in difficult straits—we have contradictory epistemic assumptions, circular definitions, and so on. When things get difficult and we are no longer sure what our ideas really *are*, we will trust in the mission of the social sciences and look to how these ideas are empirically used in practice. It is always worth remembering that, when the day is done, explanation in social science is one particular form of explanation more generally; things that we find to hold true about the social processes of explanation in general must needs apply here as well. That does not mean that social scientific explanation cannot have its own distinctive features, but we must beware of imagining that we can simply *claim* that it does. Let us turn, then, to the issue of the sorts of questions asked by the social sciences, sociology in particular.

Sociology, declared Max Weber ([1920–1921] 1972: 1, 3; 1978: 4), is a "science concerning itself with the interpretative understanding of social action."⁹ But, this interpretation can be either the *descriptive* interpretation of *what* some action is (this is a ditch-digging) or the *explanatory* interpretation by which we understand the reasons behind the act (this is an attempt to irrigate crops).¹⁰ In other words, there are two aspects of understanding: we first must understand *what* someone is doing before we understand *why* she is doing it.

This division, as we can see, fits well with Weber's general emphasis on seeing action in terms of means-ends connections. A descriptive interpretation requires only that we understand an act in itself; an explanatory one, however, requires that we understand the act as a means to a particular end. This division, then, is conceptually elegant, has face plausibility, and flows from Weber's general approach. But, that does not mean that it is correct.

In fact, considered more closely, it cuts against what we know about What versus Why questions more generally. We see a man moving his arms and hands up and down. Do we know What he is doing? It does not seem so. Let us now imagine that we notice that he is holding a shovel, and that the shovel sometimes goes into the earth and removes earth, and that this earth falls to the side. Aha! We now know *what* he is doing: digging. To

---

⁹The translation of Parsons used in the Roth and Wittich edition is somewhat Americanized and goes on to speak of the "causal" explanation of such action. Although this is not wrong, the German *Ursache* can also refer to motive, ground, or reason. Weber later demonstrates that this larger, more general category includes both motivational and causal aspects (he uses *kausal* for the latter, which has a more restricted sense than *Ursache*; however, there is no German noun or verb for "cause" based on the stem *Kaus-*). In his earlier writings, Weber (e.g., [1940] 1949: 73, 82; [1903–1906] 1975: 126, 128, 149, 154f, 194) attempted to demonstrate that rather than "interpretation of motives" and "causality" being antithetical approaches, a truly causal account required interpretive understanding and vice versa; it is not clear that these arguments are consistent with his use of "causation" to refer to "correlations." Although Weber would tauntingly affirm that he was completely comfortable with the proposal that all human action was physically determined, his appeals to causal determinism seem (as Burger [1976: 20, 64] also says) more of an article of faith regarding the nature of the world than an explanatory principle. Further, the word *Sache* (which itself can mean "cause" as well as "object") is a key theoretical term for Weber, allowing him to link "having a cause" (in the sense of "following a transcendent goal") to "being objective" in the Kantian sense of transcending determination. Indeed, for Weber, the key thing about causal action is less that it *is* caused, but that it *is a* cause.

¹⁰Weber here distinguishes between the *aktuelle Verstehen* and the *erklärendes Verstehen* which is *motivationsmäßig*. *Aktuelle* means "topical," pertaining to what is at hand; Parsons translated it as "observational" because the point is that one's understanding is unmediated or recognitional. We could perhaps translate it as "available on inspection." "Descriptive" seems to be the clearest analogue to our current concerns as long as we understand that Weber is not linking this opposition to one between idiographic and nomothetic explanations or anything like that nor using the idea of "description" put forward by Rickert (1902: 59, 126–130).

know what he is doing is at least to know why he is moving his hands. But we do not know, Weber would perhaps point out, why the man is digging.

Suppose we ask him, and he tells us that he is digging to make a hole. That would be a poor answer because when we know the what of digging, we also know this part of the why. So, we ask him why the hole, and he replies that he is going to link it to other holes and make a trench. Perhaps we still do not quite understand why he is doing this. He then explains that he is going to irrigate his parched field by drawing water from a stream down this trench. We are satisfied. We do not ask him why he wants to irrigate his field or pursue the chain of likely answers further: why he wants crops, why he wants to eat, why he wants to not die.

But, let us say that our friend was digging a hole at a recreational beach, using a plastic shovel, with children all around him. We would not ask him why he was digging a hole. And if we did and he were to answer, "I just felt like it," that would be an acceptable answer. But, this would not be an acceptable answer in the first example. Thus, it does not seem to be true that there is the same need for an "explanatory understanding" in all cases.

Now, let us imagine a different man, who is moving his arms and legs in a fashion new to us. We ask him why he is doing this, and he tells us that he is dancing. Yet, where and when he is dancing does not make sense to us, so we ask him *why* he is dancing; he tells us that he is dancing to make rain. We might still ask him why he is doing this and find that he is doing it to irrigate his field. If we learned this, then we would not ask him why he wants to irrigate his field, why he wants crops, why he wants to eat, why he wants to not die. Of course, we might not ask him any further questions for we can simply stop with the explanation that "this fellow believes dancing makes rain."

Now according to Weber's scheme, we have added the explanatory meaning (he is doing this to make rain) to the descriptive meaning (this is a dance). But, why put the dividing line here? Why not put it between "he is moving his arms and legs" and "he is dancing?" Is not the movement of the arms and legs a means to the dance? Does he not make these motions in order to dance? Or, think of things from the perspective of someone who knows the rain dance: For this observer, the descriptive meaning presumably is different—she will *see* a rain dance (and not a dance-in-order-to-make-rain). We do not *see* a stirring-in-order-to-make-an-omelet any more than we see a moving-one's-hand-in-order-to-stir. We see a making of an omelet if and when we know what it is to make an omelet (cf. Searle 1983: 98).[11]

---

[11] Campbell (1996: 58f) argues that an act has first-person phenomenological bounding in that a "distinct subjective event" can be discerned right before the act begins for there will be "an initial decision" to begin the sequence, but during the act habitual behavior may proceed without the need for such events. Although this sounds reasonable, I suggest the reader attempt an introspective experiment to determine whether this can be used to bound actions in a way that the sociologist would anticipate. My own experience is that it does not.

Social scientists are comfortable with admitting that some distinction is completely relative to the nature and purposes of the analyst. But if that is so, then we are confessing that what we have in "explanation" is a social relationship that can and perhaps should be examined as such—an actually occurring example of a general social phenomenon. This suggests that we can indeed see Weber's What and Why questions as two different forms, even two different stages. But, to see the greatest "meaningfulness" in the explanatory question is quite wrong.[12] A person who knows *what* a rain dance is knows its meaning (Melden 1961: 39). A Why question is provoked when there is some sort of social failure of interpretation (see Turnbull and Slugoski 1988: 66f; also cf. Wong and Weiner 1981).

More specifically, it is a failure to understand to what reasonable goal a certain action contributes. This failure can arise simply when there is action that is unexpected (even if the expected action is not particularly rational), and mere deviation from expectation suggests that we clarify things before proceeding, or it can arise when no pattern at all suggests itself to us (see Peters 1958: 10). The converse of this failure is when we understand the goal, but do not accept that the actions are plausibly reaching the goal: "What are you doing?" "Why, I am making rain!" "*How* are you making rain?!?" (also see Melden 1961: 26, 90, 206).

Thus, in everyday life Why is a question that raises a flag indicating potential social problems ahead. These problems may be fleeting, they may be mild, or they can be greatly consequential, especially if there is a power imbalance between actors. Still, that is well and good. It might be that it is precisely at such problematic junctures that we want social science to step in. But, the challenge of the Why question in Western social thought provokes a particular antinomy, and it is one that turns out to be fraught with pernicious consequences.[13]

---

[12]Note that I do not say that Weber made this stark claim: he clearly saw that descriptive understanding is an understanding of meaning. However, he did believe that explanatory understanding reaches *motives*—how this meaningful act fits into a chain of meaningfulnesses—which makes the Why question reach a deeper type of meaning. Unfortunately, there is not a good translation for *motivationsmäßig*; it connotes "rising to the standards at which we attribute motivation." Weber's argument was that it is the second kind of explanatory meaning that reaches this level.

[13]In a brilliant piece, C. Wright Mills (1940) emphasized that "motives" are a particular social form of the response to such a challenge, one that *follows*, and does not precede, the act it "explains" (though it can be expected to influence future acts). He cautioned sociologists not to confuse debates between vocabularies of motive—which categories of motivation are considered acceptable in a certain situation, which categories are not—with a science of action. It is this confusion that leads to the idea that one expressed motive was not "really" the "true" motive. Social science has largely disregarded this caution.

Motives and Causes

Weber went on (1972: 5f; 1978: 11f; though see [1907] 1977: 147) to discuss the role of two sorts of Why answers: causal regularities (defined as probabilistic successions of events) and motivations. This bifurcation is hardly an arbitrary one; it is implicit in the general grammar for action that Weber, and we, accept. It is rooted in the nature of the Why question, one that is understood by interlocutors as a request for a justification that ties the act to defensible motivations (Becker 1998: 58–60; also see Katz 1988: 7). The Why question is in effect a challenge: Demonstrate that your actions are defensibly those of a free and rational subject.[14]

If one does not succeed in this defense, it is implicit that one cannot be considered as the true locus of one's own actions. This widely assumed division was best explicated by Immanuel Kant ([1785] 1964: 45; [1788] 2002: 47f, 61).[15] There are, he emphasized, two possible grounds for any action. On the one hand, there are our subjective inclinations, instincts, and needs. For example, when we act on the basis of a compulsion (an addiction to nicotine, for example), the grounds of our action are located in this bodily weakness that forces us to act against what we may see as our own self-interest. In this way, our action is externally caused just as surely as if we were knocked over by a gust of wind, for the grounds of our action are external to the will. Here, we are (as actors) determined by factors outside our control; we are effects, not causes. Given the causal framework of the social sciences, we are forced to conclude that our act is conditioned by the past (accumulated bodily responses to previous nicotine intake) and not a rational attempt to reach a future state.

On the other hand, argued Kant, there are our *motives*, which are decisive when we act effectively to reach some goal unhindered by subjective limitations, compulsions, or desires (cf. Weber 1978: 11). Because these motives proceed from reason (which we share with others), they are objective, as opposed to subjective. Because they come from within our will, when we act on this basis *we* are the true causes of our actions: we are determining, not determined, and (to the social sciences, at any rate) our

---

[14]Like other parents, I am well aware that a Why question is sometimes used by those who are not in a position to issue such a challenge, perhaps most often simply to elicit continuation of a conversation, increasingly over the years in that form of conversational trench warfare known as "back talk," but sometimes honestly to gather information. Despite many anthropologists' determined attempts to reproduce such a social relationship of instructability, this usually pertains to the process of asking questions to gather data (e.g., Spradley 1979) and not the process of answering theoretical questions. Further, as the social asymmetries in social science run the other way, I do not consider this form of the Why question herein. I wish to acknowledge Joe and Jake Martin for bringing this to my attention, and I just *do*, that's why.

[15]Durkheim ([1883–1884] 2004: 156, 243) follows this logic closely in his philosophy lectures; also see ([1902–1903] 1961: 58).

act can be understood in terms of its relationship to the future, not the past. "Motive is a sociological procedure for describing how organisms show themselves as persons" (Blum and McHugh 1971: 108).[16]

This division between objective and subjective grounds for actions leads, as Kant argued, to two sciences of action. In a word, there are different approaches to what people do depending on whether we are treating persons as *things* (objects subject to causal laws) or as *persons* (actors possessing free will). A long line of philosophical work holds that this antinomy not only is logically defensible but also has repercussions for social scientific explanation: there are two polar, antithetical, approaches, one that takes the view of actors as willfully free rational beings, and another that sees them as helpless puppets of large-scale systems.

The opposition between the causality of things and the will of persons is an important one in our fundamental grammar for action,[17] and it highlights the centrality of the issue of whether our explanations contravene the claims of actors to be *persons*. And yet, it does not quite work out that this antinomy unproblematically aligns with that between the world as we experience it as actors and the world of causal systems. To express this second opposition, let us call the answers to a Why question that might come from the experience of the actor in question "first-person" answers. The first person is the grammatical position of the speaker referring to herself: "I did this . . ." (cf. Kant [1798] 2006: 15).

In the simplest form of such an explanation, we explain our action on the basis of our desires or values—I did X because I wanted to or because I thought it was the right thing to do. For example, we might say, "I used soap when I washed my hands because if you don't, you are more likely to transmit germs and become ill."

The third person is the grammatical position of an object or a different human being, one outside the conversation. (A pronoun designating someone other than the speaker but who is the recipient of the statement—that

---

[16]This analysis must ignore the fact that people may formulate motives—especially those of others—that are *not* reasonable; thus, they may ascribe others' actions to greed, jealousy, cowardice and such like (cf. Winch 1958: 82). Such "second-person perspectives" (as they may reasonably be termed) are not central to the paradoxes involved in social science explanations, although as we shall see, they play a role in psychoanalytic arguments.

[17]The opposition can be traced to Plato's ([1961] 1989) distinction between the intelligible (that which we know through the intellect) as opposed to the visible (that which we know through the senses) (*Republic* VII: 524c). Although elegant, the opposition of causality to freedom has always been problematic: if the nature of will is freedom, then any causality takes away freedom; but if a motive is a sort of causality, then merely having a motive decreases one's freedom, and hence (or so Augustine concluded) God could have no motive in creating the world (also see Burke 1952: 69, 142f).

is, who is in the conversation—occupies the position of second person.) We can thus call the answers that treat persons as things outside the conversation, those whose experiences are not necessarily involved in our answers, third-person explanations.[18] And, social scientists believe in the possibility of such a third-person sort of explanation, one that explains why an individual did something without reference to his or her particular subjectivity. Here, conditions have an effect whether or not they are cognized; while we need not deny that it is possible for persons to "resist" this effect, we find thinking about action in this third-person way tends to ride roughshod over most first-person explanations. Most important, the sorts of effects we describe here are frequently not ones that actors would recognize and are not ones we would apply to ourselves in casual conversation. Just as we generally would not say, "I washed my hands with soap because I have not figured out a way to harmonize my sexual desires with social demands internalized as my superego," we also would not generally say, "I washed my hands with soap because the growth in the distributional infrastructure of the 1920s allowed for common products like soap to be given brands, which then gave producers an incentive to advertise the need to use these products, and having grown up witnessing these many advertisements, I have begun to think that I need to use soap all the time." And yet, we might well say either of these regarding others.[19]

We see that in the archetypical cases, there is a correspondence between the first-person/third-person distinction made here and the objective-motives/subjective-causes distinction made by Kant. And yet, the two are not identical, for there are times when actors will account for their actions precisely by invoking causal factors. In other words, they treat themselves not as subjects but as direct objects. But, attention to the specific context in which this occurs will help us understand the reason for the dislocation between the two divisions. I defer this investigation temporarily; for now, we consider the simple cases of an opposition between first-person nominative statements ("I caused X") and third-person accusative cases ("His action was caused by Y").

---

[18]This distinction is not the same as the call to include the "voice" of the studied, but the difference awaits later explication.

[19]It is important to distinguish this claim from claims by neo-Kantians like Nagel (1979: 196–213; 1986: 29–37; 1995: 101) who also employ the opposition between first-person and third-person accounts. Such philosophers emphasize the irreducibility of first-person self-understandings, including the existence of such faculties as will and moral freedom, to third-person causal accounts (the law of necessity). My point will not pertain to logical possibilities but to practical consequences. Further, as we shall see in the next chapter, this distinction is not the same as that often made between an "internal" and an "external" approach to explaining action; also see Merleau-Ponty (1962: 55, 75) for a similar opposition of first-person and third-person (causal) descriptions of behavior.

Now, I am not arguing that this opposition has any descriptive accuracy or that it is some profound problem for the project of explanation—that is, that we must, through some gymnastics of systematics, account for "both" of these moments. Indeed, by the end of this book we will find that this opposition, despite its fitting into our general way of thinking, is largely unfounded. But, rightly or wrongly, social scientists tend to accept this basic framework, with the implicit opposition of first- and third-person responses, linked as it is to the very idea of Why. And it is such a third-person causal account that is generally prized by the social sciences, which have predominantly adopted the Durkheimian idea of some kind of lawfulness on the distinctly "social" level.

This is worrisome because we have seen that asking why is a form of challenge in which the actor has the opportunity to demonstrate his competence and personhood. Simply asking someone what her *motives* were already signals that we want to hold her conduct up for assessment—and this is something that superiors find easier to do to inferiors than vice versa. But if we ignore the issue of motivation altogether—if we go immediately toward a causal answer—we are taking every shred of personhood from our actor. "To ask what made Jones do something is at least to suggest that he had no good reason to doing it" (Peters 1958: 14, 29, 35f). Somehow, before we have even commenced our investigation of social life, we have managed to insult our subjects.

Motives and Reasons

For a wonderful example, in their explication of the logic of third-person explanation, Przeworksi and Teune (1970: 19) ask the following (hypothetical) question: "Why does Monsieur Rouget, age 24, blond hair, brown eyes, a worker in a large factory, vote Communist?"[20] Again, they ask (1970: 75) that "he votes for a party of the Left, and we want to understand why." Their explanation, however, involves adding successive predictive attributes of Monsieur Rouget (his age, occupation, nationality) until the proportion of persons with these attributes voting Communist approaches 1.0.

But if we were to approach Rouget and ask him why he voted Communist, and he were merely to indicate that he was a young French worker in a large factory, that is why, we would think him an extremely stupid fellow, ill deserving of the franchise in the first place. For those are not *defensible* reasons for an action. We want to hear him justify to us that his vote was a right or reasonable thing to do. We have a problem—we ask the same question, "Why does Monsieur Rouget vote Communist?" to Monsieur Rouget himself and to ourselves, and we find two different sets of explanations, two different sets of "reasons why" competing for the same event (see Peters 1958: 8f; compare Zimmerman and Pollner 1971: 81, 87).

[20] I thank a reviewer for drawing my attention to this case. Winch (1958: 45) had used a similar example.

Perhaps this dilemma is not as serious as it seems, and we can unify *both* these approaches (see Barnes 1995: 53). We might first try to work out some split consciousness by which both these answers are valid "in their own way" (like the God of the secularists who works on Sundays when everyone else, including reality, takes a day off). But, this resolution is easily defeated by Occam's razor: if we have one answer to our why question, then we do not need another. We do not need to ask Rouget for his reasons. He should simply keep his mouth shut.

We may then decide that there really only *is* one proper, scientific approach, that of causality in the sense of external impulsion, but argue that Rouget *himself* is a form of this same causality! *Both* Monsieur Rouget's explanation (the Communists stand up for the working class) *and* his characteristics (Monsieur Rouget is low on education) "caused" his vote, to some unknown extent. Perhaps we bring them together: Rouget's explanation is tapping a proximate attitude, in turn rooted in something more fundamental (his social characteristics). We then say that the vote is caused by his left authoritarianism, perhaps. But what is this authoritarianism—this personality tendency? If it is a scientific concept, can it mean anything other than a pattern of action (such as, when given a choice, choosing the more authoritarian candidate)? It seems that we are saying that the actions of Rouget are explained by his Rougetian nature (here cf. Simmel [1905] 1977: 58; Melden 1961: 11f, 39, 45, 171). The role of Rouget's first-person elements become reduced to a proximate predictor intervening between his social characteristics and his action, and to the extent that they have independent explanatory force in a technical sense of explaining more variation than the social characteristics, they are likely to be tautological (e.g., he votes Communist because he is a Communist).

But not all subjective elements will fit so neatly in this chain of causality; sometimes people seem to be different from how we expect them to be. We could, then, perhaps say that his vote is a function of structure *and* agency: Rouget's opinions, at least to the extent that they are atypical and not predictable on the basis of his social location, have an independent explanatory power. Since explanatory power is due to causal power, we must say that these atypical opinions have a direct causal force on the vote. We can then eliminate the difference between first-person and third-person answers—*all* good answers to this question involve causes; these causes could be the structural forces of Rouget's characteristics or the causality of his own opinions.

But, do Rouget's opinions really "cause" his vote? If so, he seems to be subhuman: his opinions are now outside his self (himself *as* actor), and his relation to his opinions seems to be one of unfreedom. That is, who is "Rouget"? If we take him as a bundle that includes his opinions, it is somewhat hard to say how the causality of his opinions is the same as, say, the causality of his occupation. For this would seem to say that the cause of Rouget's action is Rouget, which, in some sense, we already knew. If, in contrast, we understand "Rouget" to denote the will of Rouget (and not all parts of his being), a will surrounded by other aspects of his life, including his opinions, we might indeed say that his will is in part "caused" by his opinions. But then, as Hegel ([1821] 1967) pointed out, we cannot conceive of any will being free other than a completely random one, for even knowledge and reason seem external "causes" of the will.[21]

Of course, we may simply have to accept somewhat counterintuitive ideas when they are scientifically valid, but we have so far not advanced beyond paradox. Perhaps our resolution is that it is not so much that Rouget's opinions, imagined outside his will, *caused* his vote. Rather, his opinion-led will was part of the cause, and his will is itself a causal force. There is no doubt that it is true that Rouget's willfulness must be causal in some sense, but it is also not clear in what sense this is true nor that our problems are clarified. For there is a dilemma that arises when we attempt to preserve Rouget's will as a cause in the same sense that we have tried to talk about third-person causality. We need to determine whether this willfulness can exist side by side with other causes, or whether all other causes are "funneled through" this will.

The first option is that Rouget's will is one cause alongside others. This would imply that willfulness, as willfulness, could be considered (at least in some cases) an adequate answer to a Why question. (Analogously, if the causes of coughs include viruses, overtalking, and cancer, not only will overtalking when stricken with a virus be more likely to lead to a cough than the virus alone, but also there are some cases in which overtalking itself explains the cough, so we are satisfied with the answer "Overtalking" to the question, "Why did you cough?") But, this is not how we treat such answers in our actual practice. If someone asks Rouget why he voted Communist and he replies, "No reason; I just wanted to," we would not think this a good answer. As one can hardly imagine an answer that *better* highlights the purely willful nature of this act, it seems that we cannot really believe that the will is itself a causal force of the same form as all third-person causes, and that a good answer to a Why question involves simply finding the proper causes.[22]

---

[21] It is worth noting that I am not denying that there may be *a* sense in which Rouget's opinions can be seen as a cause of his vote; I am simply denying that if there is such a sense, it is compatible with our current understanding of causal explanation. The problem seems to lie less with the sorts of puzzles introduced by Wittgenstein ([1945–1949] 1958) than with the fundamentally misleading approach to the nature of organismic action coming from the idea of action as being "caused" (see Reed 1996: 18), but this awaits later exposition. But we can see that if we were to allow the neural processes that are said to constitute one's thoughts as causes of actions (e.g., moving lips and hands), there will be precious little room for the sociological causes in which we first were interested.

[22] And certainly, we would not accept someone's protestation that he *could* not act a certain way (say, do us a favor) because he did not *want* to, and his will was, like other causes of his action, a form of constraint that he was unable to countermand.

We then might propose that the will is indeed a cause, but not one that sits beside the other ones. Rather, the will is intrinsically a mediator between the act and these other causes. Rouget's age, occupation, and nationality only affect his vote to the extent that they affect his will. Indeed, seen in this light, it seems impossible that any of these supposed causes could work their magic independent of Rouget's will. But in this case, the "will" loses any independent explanatory leverage—the question of Rouget's vote has now been recast as the question of Rouget's will-to-vote. The will itself explains nothing; it is now what is to be explained.

In sum, we cannot keep the answer of "will" if we choose the third-person answer of "causality." Rouget's answer has been driven out. The entire class of first-person answers seems to have no place in our science.

First-Person Explanations

I have made a stark opposition between first-person and third-person explanations, linking this to Kant's distinction between free rational motives and determined causation. And indeed, empirically, there is a strong and important association between the two. But, we know well that people sometimes explain their actions by emphasizing the causal factors that have acted on them. Now on the one hand, it has often been said that people overemphasize the free, rational, nature of their action when constructing naïve theories of behavior. For example, Milgram (1974) found a widespread underestimation of the proportion of adults who would obey an experimenter and deliver a painful shock to an experimental subject with a heart condition. He explained this by arguing that we have a folk theory that highlights the connection between our values and our actions: because we do not think it good or right to shock innocent and vulnerable people, we think that we would not, and hence we underestimate the power of situational factors such as the desire not to upset an authority figure.

That we overestimate the importance of values and will at the expense of situational factors is certainly reasonable. Yet at the same time, attribution theory (Jones and Harris 1967; Heider 1958: 56; Kelley 1973: 125; and see Ichheiser 1949: S46ff) seems to have demonstrated the opposite. When we account for our actions, it turns out that we often emphasize the environment and deemphasize our internal states: we take for granted our (own) reasonable nature, and explain our action as a response to provocations, invitations, or constraints of the environment ("I became angry because X was in the wrong").

In other words, our actors here are explaining their behavior using the first-person accusative ("X did something *to me*") and not the first-person nominative ("I did . . ."). They knowingly and willfully place themselves on the "determined" side of Kant's opposition. If indeed people themselves reach for causal answers to the Why question of their actions, we cannot blame social scientists if they do the same.

But do they, and if so, when do they? We have seen two opposite arguments about this. Yet, the two claims are not really at odds but rather complimentary: Milgram found people underestimating situational factors when they described actions done either by others or by their future selves, but when accounting for their own (past) behavior, actors did, just as the attribution theorists would have expected, stress situational factors. Most important, we can see that these two different types of explanations can be said to find their unity in the idea of a coherent first-person view. When we think about others, we incompletely put ourselves in their shoes and do not fully appreciate the situational pressures they face; when we think about ourselves, we may not fully acknowledge that such pressures could be resisted.

And we use first-person accusative answers paradigmatically when we are trying to lessen our moral culpability—when we are trying to excuse or justify—or when, less momentously, we deviate from an expected pattern and recognize that it is reasonable for others to call on us to make an accounting. Just as Weber would say, in such cases we are appealing to a sympathetic understanding, in that we want an interlocutor to understand our action by placing himself in our position, and seeing that a true human being could, in such a situation, do such and such. Thus, we sacrifice one part of our personhood (our freedom from determination) to retain another: our rationality and our goodness.

Contrapositively, analysts sometimes employ third-person nominatives, but they do so precisely when they want to allow for valuations—when they need heroes or villains. Regarding the former, in a wonderful ethnography of ethnography, Kurzman (1991) finds researchers dividing their subjects into these two categories depending on whether they identify with them and promote them to the status of "persons." For the ethnographers, a third-person nominative account implies the heroic status of the subjects who resist various social forces. But in other cases, putting the answer in the nominative is understood as necessary to prevent a particularly blameworthy actor from appearing off the hook. The analyst who stresses the international forces to which Adolf Hitler responded, the domestic problems that confronted him, or instability of his party that had so recently assumed power is suspected of "seeing things too much from Hitler's perspective" and becoming an apologist precisely because Hitler appears too often as the direct object.

Thus, we understand that the first-person view is not the same as a nominative view, and (somewhat contrary to the implications of Kant's scheme) putting oneself in the accusative is not tantamount to renouncing personhood. It is an explanatory form that reaches out for protection and reaffirmation from another person; it is an eye-to-eye type of explanation, quite different from the third-person accusative explanations that we reach for as social scientists.

And it is these explanations—the ones that push the personhood and competence of the actor to the side—that social science has decided are to be its bread and butter. Social science rejects the possibility of building on first-person explanations because, to be blunt, it distrusts persons and their cognitions. In chapters 3 and 4, we explore the roots of this distrust and find serious flaws in the conventional understanding of the social sciences.

But my argument is not that we should instead accept the first-person responses. "Why?" is an interrogative rooted in the social experience of challenge by which we require another to explicate defensible motivations. The statements produced in response have a stability in this sense and refer to a jointly produced experience. Social scientists may reasonably think that we should reject these accounts, but that does not establish that there must be an alternate, third-person, answer to the same question.

Not every grammatically consistent sentence has a meaning, and not every grammatical question allows for an intelligent answer: standard examples are "What happens when an irresistible force meets an immovable object?" and "Have you stopped beating your wife?" Asking why someone did something, and not asking that person herself, may turn out to be an intrinsically meaningless question. The social sciences, however, have generally assumed that this is the most interesting question that can be asked, and that the type of answer we want is a third-person answer, one that makes reference to causality. We have seen that such an answer is implicitly rude and dehumanizing, but we go on to see that it is also inherently unstable.

Chapter 2

Causality and Persons

> The word "cause" is, in short, an altar to an unknown god; an empty pedestal still marking the place of a hoped-for statue.
> —William James, *Principles of Psychology* 2: 671.

EXPLANATION AND LAW

The Causes of Causality

I have argued that the social sciences tend to assume that the most important sort of explanation is one that comes in the form of a third-person answer to a why question. Although not all such third-person answers take the form of causes, these currently hold most favored status in the mainstream social sciences. Further, we usually hope that we can find some sort of regularities in these causes and hence unveil some sort of social laws. If successful, the search for such laws is suspected to imply some sort of determinism. In this chapter, I want to show how shaky are our current conceptions of causes, causal regularities, and causal laws.[1]

It is noteworthy that the idea of "law" originally came from the human realm of political volition and was only through some fascinating mental gymnastics applied to the inanimate world. Although the idea of some sort of natural law has been formulated a number of times (see, e.g., Seneca [ca. 62 CE] 2010: 3.praef.16, 3.16.4; p. 27, 36), the decisive one for our purposes is the version that arose around the time of the Enlightenment. To make a long story short, the first step was the identification of two seemingly different forms of regularity: the laws created by the human will of a prince and the invariants found in nature. These could be seen as united in the prescience of God, whose will could not be contravened by kings. New Protestant understandings of the predetermination of the future due to God's omniscience (here see Thomas 1971:

---

[1] The serious reevaluation of our use of causality was begun by Abbott (1998), who has already made many of the arguments found in this section. As this went to press, I encountered the arguments of Goldthorpe (2007 2: 200), which make many of the same historical and critical points regarding the use of causality.

79f) implied a unity between the empirical regularity of the world and the willfulness of God's plan. Since God (as Hobbes [1651] 1909: 99, 205ff] said) made human nature, he implicitly commanded those rules of behavior that are made necessary by this human nature, and hence rules of proper conduct may also be considered "laws of nature."

Not only could human laws be seen as a bit more akin to natural laws, but also the reverse assimilation took place. In the wonderful words of Brown (1984: 11), the physical laws of nature "were thought of as moral commandments issued to an obedient Nature, and moral laws as the natural regularities which society both should, and largely did, obey." Causality, then, enters the laws of nature through the *volitional* nature of God's relation to his creation. But, the increasing success in mathematizing physical relations led to a new sense of law as invariant relationship that allowed the universe to be studied without bringing up either God or causality. Thus, the new idea of natural law associated with the scientific revolution really solidified in *opposition* to a causal explanation. As we recall from chapter 1, these relations (e.g., conservation of momentum) are blissfully unconcerned with causality in our current sense; indeed, they apply equally well whether time is going backward or forward. Of course, the same scientific culture that led to these developments also spawned a fascination with mechanistic explanations that often approached the maniacal (see, e.g., Shapin 1996: 31f). The frequent comparison of the universe to a piece of complicated clockwork was taken not simply as implying that God was a master craftsman with the same sort of intellect as humans, but that anything in His creation could be understood via its analysis into components whose interactions were fundamentally mechanical. Yet as we shall see, by the time of Newton, physicists were forced away from a dogmatic adherence to mechanism as the ultimate explanation (also see Cannon 1978: 270); those who insisted on mechanistic explanations became limited contributors at best and cranks at worst.

This led to a temporary detachment of the idea of laws of nature (in this new sense of mathematical equations) from the laws of the social order, for the latter retained an emphasis on mechanism and causality. Having no promise of parsimonious mathematical expressions, moral philosophers (the ancestors of social scientists), unlike natural philosophers, had no reason to abandon satisfying mechanistic visions. They were still impressed with the idea of clockwork, in part because they often envisioned other people as the cogs. It was this understanding that was the basis for the radical ideas of political economists (from Mandeville to Smith and Ferguson) that turned on the aggregate unintended consequences of action (see Brown 1984: 67, 94).

That is, just as the workings of the circulatory system could be understood by mechanical analysis of its component parts, so also social systems could be understood by such a reductionist analysis. In the latter case, examining each component was simplified by assumptions regarding the fundamental motivational structure of the actor, most important, the stability and predictability of self-interest (here see Hirschman 1977). These interacting components, when assembled in certain arrangements, produced stable equilibria with properties different from those of the components. (For example, self-interested people, interacting in a free market, might promote the public welfare.) But, even though the new political economists continually found order emerging in the social world according to regular principles, this was not lawful enough for the social scientists of the nineteenth-century French school.

Previous "political arithmeticians" such as the seventeenth century John Graunt had found impressive stability in certain ratios or averages compiled of individual measurements (e.g., the ratio of male to female births of around 1.05:1). This could be understood to confirm the harmony and purposiveness of the created world (in this case, ensuring that the greater death rate of men did not leave any women without a possible match) (Pearson [1921–1933] 1978: 16, 30, 160f, 286). But Adolphe Quetelet (1796–1874) took such stability as evidence of a social realm of order detached from providence, and developed a powerful, and deeply strange, vision that led to a new conception of social law. It was this conception of law that allowed for a new French approach to social science, an approach which turned into the Durkheimian sociology that remains the fundamental epistemology for contemporary social scientific practice.[2] Quetelet's breakthroughs—even though they were in some ways illusory—are, as we shall see, still present in our understanding of social explanation.

Quetelet had studied astronomy and understood the classical theory of error, whence originates the Gaussian (normal) distribution that is the cornerstone of modern social statistics. This distribution of error was derived from the important case in which repeated measurements of a single object are carried out. Every night, we look through a telescope at one of the fixed stars. After taking into account the position of the earth, we chart the observed location of the star. Our plots do not all hit exactly the same place on our chart but instead form a cloud. When we analyze the Cartesian coordinates of each observation, we find that the distribution of the observations is "bivariate normal" about the x and y axes. The little

---

[2] In a wonderful critique of the use of causality in sociology, Goldthorpe (2007 2: 200f, 206, 216) has emphasized the degree to which an adherence to Comteanism led Durkheimian sociology in particular and French sociology in general to deviate from the Queteletian program, and indeed even calls the Durkheimian approach "antistatistical." This emphasis on the tension between Comtean and Queteletian approaches is important, but in the broader picture, we cannot deny the generally greater enthusiasm for statistics in England and France (despite the importance of Comteanism in both) than in Germany and, at first, in the United States, where the early sociologists learned their approach to causality from German scholars (Bernert 1983: 233).

jigglings in the telescope base, the limits of resolution of our indicators, and other factors are all basically random errors that cancel each other out on average, but not for any individual observation.[3]

But Quetelet made a curious leap of faith (as Oberschall [1987: 109] says; cf. Hacking 1990: 106f) and one that did not do justice to the human material he was studying. He claimed that there was no real difference between the repeated measurements of a single object and *single measurements of different individuals*.[4] Quetelet's concept of the "average man" was not simply a "best guess" as to the values that vary within a population, but the *true* object, as he came to believe that nature *aimed* for the average as a marksman aimed for a target and enjoyed arguing that the distribution of certain biometric measurements among a group of people (e.g., that of the chest diameters of army recruits) was well within what one would expect from measurement error alone; therefore, it was "as if the chests measured had been modeled on the same type, on the same individual . . . " (Stigler 1986: 172, 214; cf. Oberschall 1987: 117).[5]

The importance of this innovation for theory becomes obvious when we consider what an average is and how it was understood by Quetelet and later by Durkheim. An average $\bar{x}$ is simply the result of aggregating a number of different observations (say x_i, where the i indicates an individual observation, of which we have N total). Formally,

$$\bar{x} = \frac{1}{N}\sum_{i=1}^{N} x_i$$

But, Quetelet interpreted this differently. Rather than the average as the result of a process carried out on individual measurements (which might or might not be completely independent), the individual measurements were derivative of the average. Each individual could be understood as the

---

[3] Actually, it seems that, despite his astronomical background, Quetelet came to the normal curve via the binomial (Hacking 1990: 110f).

[4] Some important thinkers such as Fechner and members of the German *Verein für Sozialpolitik* (see Heidelberger 1987, Porter 1987) dissented from Quetelet's equation of population variance and error distribution and the consequent reification of an "average" man, but their conceptions were not as influential in the social sciences.

[5] "One may ask if there exists, in a people, an average man [*un homme type*], a man who represents this people by height and in relation to which all the other men of the same nation must be considered as offering deviations more or less large. The numbers that one would have, on measuring the latter, would be grouped around the mean, in the same way as the numbers that one would obtain, if the same typical man had been measured a large number of times by more or less imprecise measures" (Quetelet, 1844, cited in Hacking 1990: 105). Adopting and adapting this approach with more of an eye to variation, Francis Galton then pioneered the technique of averaging photographs of different faces to come up with composite photos of average "types" of persons (Seltzer 1992: 115; Stigler

average and then an additional positive or negative deviation (Quetelet spoke of "perturbations," borrowing a term from astronomy) (Pearson 1978: 723, 725). Thus, formally, $x_i = \bar{x} + \epsilon_i$, where ϵ_i is some random error.

It is this same interpretation that leads to our ubiquitous partialing of variance into that which is "explained" and that which must be considered as "error" in the social sciences—any observation is decomposed into what is predicted by a law and its ill-mannered deviation from this proper state.[6] After Yule's synthesis of ordinary least squares with regression logic, we became able to compare observations not only to an average but also to a predicted average conditional on a set of other observations. The math worked out perfectly if we were to assume that the process was "surrogate for a causal relation" in which all deviation from these predictions was due to other (independently) determined causal processes (see Swijink 1987 for the history of least squares; Stigler 1986: 352ff on Yule).

In sum, to envision social science as something that dealt with averages as true "social facts" (and not mere aggregations of individuals), the French school and its successors were drawn toward a vision of social life that had persons pushed about by external causes. The belief in the causal nature of the phenomena not only simplified the interpretation of the new techniques but also allowed the social sciences to catch up with a more general trend, a reconceptualization based on what seemed "good to think." This transition is wonderfully illustrated in Durkheim's great example, namely, suicide. The 1821 volume of the *Recherches statistiques* sorted suicides by *motives*, while the next year found them sorted by *causes*. The typology itself, however, was basically unchanged—comments Hacking (1990: 75): "A motive in 1821 becomes a cause in 1822."[7]

There were three crucial consequences of this formulation for the way in which the social sciences understood the task of explanation (also see Abbott 1998 for a more detailed discussion of later developments). The

---

2010), although the idea was an earlier one (discussed by, e.g., Adam Smith [1759] 1997: 2: 8 and Kant [1790] 1987: 82). Compare Galton's cousin, Charles Darwin ([1859] 1912: 53): "No one supposes that all the individuals of the same species are cast in the same actual mould." To Darwin (as to Galton), variation was not "error" but vital for the continual adaptation of the species.

[6]Indeed, note that Dawid (2000: 411) demonstrated that a direct consequence of this reformulation of the causal process as a partitioning of causal power into shared and idiosyncratic is a breakdown of inference as it is in principle impossible to partition the variance in causal effects (that is, heterogeneity of causal effects would be lumped into the "error term"). More sophisticated examinations of causal heterogeneity are now carried out, but a hundred years elapsed before this was taken seriously.

[7]It is interesting that Kant ([1784] 2001: 11) considered the stability of such social statistics in no way incompatible with the status of marriage and so on as voluntary acts and compared them to the stable laws of unstable weather—which we can understand, but not predict very well.

first was to focus attention on the *general* at the expense of the particular. The second was to require the construction of *abstractions* as the inhabitants of this new realm of the truly general and to propose a new understanding of causality that could survive only in this realm. The third was to interpret the causal relations between these abstractions as *constraining* the particular individuals involved. I go on to consider each of these. The second entails a critical analysis of recent arguments regarding how causality should be defined, the topic of the rest of this chapter. As this discussion primes us for a consideration of the alternatives to conventional causality, a discussion of the third consequence is put off until the final chapter.

GENERAL LAWS AND PARTICULAR CASES

Given this idea of the "average man" that lay at the heart of the new French social sciences, attention had to be turned to the general, indeed the generic, to uncover social regularities. If any individual observation x_i is really an error-laden instantiation of some general property, and it is the general $\bar{x}$ in which we are interested, then certainly close attention to any particular case is problematic. It is precisely this logic that inspired Durkheim's ([1895] 1938: 8) idea that our laws refer to abstract general qualities common to members of a certain class—the "social fact" is the shared, not the particular, and is seen in the average.[8]

Thus, the use of sweeping abstractions in sociological theory seems to be necessary, since to approach generality we must always suppress concrete individual variability. But, as we shall see in Chapter 6, this idea of a necessary trade-off between generality and particularity is an assumption that comes with the idea that all general thought takes place via "concepts," nested sets of identities formed by abstraction. Any concept groups together particular cases by highlighting commonalities and ignoring particularities. (Succeeding chapters draw on other traditions of thought that do not assume that we need to bury *any* of the particularities in order to think generally, but that is not how things stand in the social sciences today.[9])

This emphasis on abstractions allows for a strange slippage in our idea of explanation. In everyday life, if we claim to explain something, the

---

[8] Regarding things like suicide rates, Durkheim commented, "Since each of these figures contains all the individual cases indiscriminately, the individual circumstances which may have had a share in the production of the phenomena are neutralized and, consequently, do not contribute to its determination. The average, then, expresses a certain state of the group mind."

[9] To anticipate, see Cassirer (1923: 224ff, 229, 255; 1923: 20); Lewin ([1931] 1999: 58, 65; 1936: 32, 34); Lundberg (1939: 107, 121); Brandt (1952: 187, 190); and Mohr (forthcoming).

chances are good that if asked *what* we are explaining, we would answer that we are explaining this or that particular situation. If we could answer that we are explaining *many* particular situations all at once, that would indeed be an impressive accomplishment. But instead, the social sciences answer that we do not explain *any* particular situation; instead, we explain a tenth or so of each of thousands without explaining any. This, of course, is because we have given up with the concrete and instead turned to a realm of abstractions.

THE CAUSES OF ABSTRACTION

The conventional assumption regarding the nature of generality implies that the fullest explanation—that covering the largest number of cases—will necessarily be the most abstracted from the concrete. The result is not simply that the social sciences deal with entities of the most dubious ontological status, but also that our understanding of "explanation" has come to revolve around a form of linkage between these entities that is untenable and paradoxical.

This is to establish between abstractions a relation of "cause" in a particular sense of something quite different from motivation. In the rest of this chapter, I want to make three points. The first is that there *is* a stable understanding of "cause" in everyday life that is not only compatible with motivation but indeed assumes it. The second is that this understanding of causality leads to reasonable conclusions when we consider human action. The third is that the conventional understanding of causality in the social sciences is unstable and leads to unreasonable conclusions.

Causes and Motivations

Etymology cannot tell us everything about the world, but it is worth noting that the word *cause* originally meant motivation.[10] Even when we make a distinction between the two in everyday life, we may actually

---

[10]There is general evidence that social uses of words like *may* or *must* preceded their abstract or epistemic use (Sweetser 1990: 30, 49f, 86), although the word *cause* is a somewhat different matter. Here, we may consider the priority of motive and cause both phylogenetically and ontogenetically. Regarding the first, the word comes from the Latin *causa*, meaning "purpose" or "reason"; other extensions include a side in a suit or an opportunity. In Greek, *aiton* and *logos* could both mean "cause" or "reason" (Bunge 1959: 226). Regarding the second, Piaget argued that children do not begin by making a distinction between motivation and causation, and there have been arguments that the template of causality for children is motivation. Unfortunately, it is nearly impossible to make definitive statements in part because our language still confuses the two—as Kalish (1998: 707) emphasizes in his own studies, the words *can*, *will*, *may*, *must*, and *should* all can

denote only a minor change of reference. As we recall from chapter 1, attribution theory has highlighted how something that we attribute to free choice in others we may see in terms of constraint when explaining our own action—for causality and choice are in a real sense two sides of the same coin, not antitheses. Indeed, we may argue that the way we use the word *because* (originally meaning "by the cause of") indicates the unity of cause and motivation (also see Barnes 2000: 34, 71).

For example, let us ascribe a certain motivation to an actor: let us say that she is motivated to go north. If she encounters some feature of the environment (say a pond) in her way, she may decide to go first southeast, then east, then northeast, before she continues going north. It is an acceptable shorthand to say, "Because of the pond, the person went to the east." This use of the word *cause* as an explanation does not contravene the underlying motivation; rather, it is a cause only *conditional* on the existence of the motivation (also see Katz 1999: 143).

As we will see in chapter 5, such features of the environment may be *phenomenologically* experienced by actors as direct action imperatives—turn aside. The actors then may agree with the idea that the pond *caused* them to temporarily veer off course. But of course, it is not that the pond exerted some force on some person previously at rest, impelling her in one direction as opposed to another. What the social sciences treat as a fearsome antithesis (the causality of the external world and the motivation of the actor) is experienced as a unification in everyday life.

Contrary to the often-repeated ideas that causality is inherently some third-person aspect of social "systems" that only analysis can reveal, in contrast to the first-person experience of freedom in a lifeworld that is some sort of wildlife reserve for Kantian autonomy, we thus have a first-person experience of causality. Rather than define causality in terms of explanatory abstractions, let us try to begin with the actuality of causation. We ourselves experience causality in a relative unambiguous form when we consciously interfere in the course of events by manipulating objects in the environment with our bodies—we then have experiences (e.g., a feeling of pressure or strain) that allow us to attribute some sort of countervailing causality to other things (Pepper 1966: 157; 1966: 390–410; Hart and Honoré 1959: 25–28; Peters 1958: 4; Burke 1952: 119; Armstrong 1962: 29; Fales 1990: 12, 16; also Cassirer [1925] 1955: 212; James [1912] 1943: 184).

---

be interpreted in terms of moral obligation, epistemic certainty, or ontological determination. It is not entirely clear what the child who uses or assents to one such word is thinking; more generally, linguistic competence on the part of a child should not be taken as indicating that child has internalized or understands any particular worldview. It does, however, appear that young children originally use words like "because" more to invoke conventional justifications than impersonal causal forces (Bloom and Capatides 1987).

The notion that causality is "originally" experienced as our effective will is an old one (classically formulated by Maine de Biran, on whose understanding of habit I later draw). But as Michotte ([1946] 1963: 24, 206, 213, 271, 182ff; also see Hume [1777] 1993: 42f; Wittgenstein [1945–1949] 1958: 160f; §614, 621; Searle 1983: 124, 128) pointed out (against de Biran), we do not actually interpret our bodily motions as causal ("I" cause "my arm" to move, "my arm" causes "my hand" to move). Causality, then, is not the same thing as *activity* (which we may apperceive as a primitive). It is rather when our body acts on external objects that we are most likely to sense causality. Mechanical causality in nature frequently involves cases in which either the cause or the effect is obscured (e.g., the causation of gravity).[11] Human causality, however, allows us to grasp both parts of a causal link and to sense this link as involving *impulsion*; this seems to be a template used for other interpretations.

I will refer to this understanding of causality as the root of the "commonsensical" one, as it seems that this interpretation is indeed common in everyday life. (The commonsensical approach, discussed below, allows a generalization to nonagentic forms of causality.) Note that here causality is not derived in terms of any sort of *comparison* but is rather a feature of an immediately experienced sense of impulsion. We know that *A* causes *B* because we *do* and *feel A* as *B* occurs. In contrast, in the social sciences, we generally eschew any serious consideration of impulsion in our attribution of causality and instead rely on comparison. Let us examine some of the pathologies that are allowed when we replace a concrete experience with an abstraction.

The Insufficiency of Necessity

It is marvelous to see amid the many grave admonitions about the nature of causality extremely few clear definitions of what this means. Perhaps the least-palatable definition is one that immediately retreats from any understanding of causality and replaces it with prediction. That we can

---

[11] Michotte ([1946] 1963: 13, 21) was heavily influenced by the Gestalt tradition I build on in chapter 5 and henceforward; he also discussed Durkheim's critique of de Biran in *The Elementary Forms*, reviewed in chapter 4. Michotte developed a set of experiments in which one simple projected shape seemed to cause the motion of another (as in a cue ball striking a still billiard ball). His results strongly implied that we *perceive* causality in certain relations as opposed to *inferring* it. Interestingly, these relations are not necessarily those that fit the laws of physics (such as the conservation of momentum) ([1946] 1963: 71, 126, 138, 140, 142, 228). Thus, although there is evidence that our perception of causal relations is primitive (two-month-old infants are surprised when motion is transmitted in a way that defies causality [Rochat 2001: 109]), we have a distinct phenomenological perception of certain forms of causality that seems to involve a separation of the "motion" of an object from the object itself.

predict the appearance of *B* when we first see *A* may be interesting and useful, but this epistemological condition is not itself causality. Presumably, the relation between prediction and causality is not that they are identical, but that we can predict *B* when we see *A* "because" *A* is the cause of *B*. Rather than prediction being a definition of causality, it doubly presupposes it, once in the relation between *A* and *B* (*A* does actually lead to *B*) and once in the relation between causality and prediction (a causal relation leads to successful prediction).[12]

Those who argue that there is something truly *causal* about causality now make reference not to the empirical success of prediction but to a contrast to what the world would be like in the absence of the cause (see, recently, Heckman 2005: 1f). It is worth emphasizing that this is not the case in *all* scientific fields, and the discussion here pertains only to the case of the social sciences. In this conception—which is increasingly used in formalizations for statistical investigation (e.g., Morgan and Winship 2007: 5)—the idea is that we investigate whether *A* is a cause of *B* by proposing that we may determine whether, in the absence of *A*, we would still see *B*. For example, we might say that the secession of the South caused the American Civil War, for if there had been no secession, there would have been no war. This is to define causality as a relationship of *necessity*, which is defined in counterfactual terms.

Although such a counterfactual definition of causality is now dominant across the social sciences,[13] this understanding was first most clearly emphasized by historical sociologists, especially Skocpol (1984: 375), who has also argued that comparative methods can be used with great success to uncover such causality. (Skocpol famously used this method to defend one strong argument about the deterministic cause of social revolutions.) Following the "method of difference" of J.S. Mill (1872), we can isolate the key factor that caused some historical event of note.[14] Now, a confusion between (on the one hand) causal *laws* in the sense of Humean

---

[12]This is not to say that prediction is a silly criterion to use for judging explanation; it is an important one, and predictive power—even retroactive predictive power—is perhaps currently underappreciated. Indeed, prediction is sufficiently important that we do not need to call it causality to take it seriously.

[13]An exception is Elster (1989: 6), who—correctly, I believe—understands that a mechanistic approach implies seeing causality as sufficient causality, not a relation of necessitation. There is a relation between mechanism and sufficient causality, although this does not mean that we can define causality in terms of mechanisms—this attempt is invariably a circular one (Sloman 2005: 22).

[14]Mill himself was considerably less sanguine on this point, emphasizing that this method was not suitable for the social sciences. Even in the natural sciences, it was nearly impossible to find two cases that satisfied the methods of difference unless it was due to experimental manipulation, but the possibility of finding such cases for comparative historical investigation was "manifestly absurd": "Two nations which agreed in everything except their commercial policy would agree also in that" (Mill 1872: 257, 575).

regularities and (on the other) causal *relations* between events marks the Millsian approach, as has been pointed to before (Simmel 1905 [1977]: 106f; Ducasse [1924] 1969; Searle 1983: 113, 119; note that Hume [1777] 1993: 51, himself confused a counterfactual definition with one turning on constant conjunction). This seems to be because although we are free to define causal relations as necessitation without assuming lawfulness across classes of events, it is only such lawfulness that allows us to use counterfactual reasoning to uncover causal relations.

Consider the first clear introduction of counterfactuality to sociological theory, namely, Max Weber's ([1905] 1949: 164ff; following von Kries) methodological writings. To determine if A was the cause of B, we must come up with "imaginative constructs" that we can manipulate hypothetically by deleting various elements. If we can imagine a world without A in which it seems plausible that B would occur anyway, then we may propose that A did not cause B because A was unnecessary for B to occur.[15] The status of such an imaginative construct is reasonably good if there are constant conjunctions in nature and rather poor if there are not. As we shall see, counterfactual explanations tend to assume a Millsian world, but when it comes to the social sciences, this is a matter of purest faith.

But there are other, perhaps more fundamental, problems to which we must pay attention. One basic one comes from the very definition of causality as necessitation, for we have a different idea of cause, sufficient causality, which is formally reverse to the necessary cause. We say that A is a sufficient cause of B if having A means that we must have B. Thus, we might say that striking a match caused a fire, because striking a match by itself is enough to cause a fire. The problem is that, bracketing time for a moment, if A seems to be a necessary cause of B, then B can equally be seen as a sufficient cause of A. That is, if A is necessary for B, then there is no B without A, which means that if we see B we know we see A, which means that B is sufficient for A.

We shall return to the issue of sufficient causality in this chapter; now, we may simply note that there is a tendency (although there are certainly exceptions) even in historical sociology for sufficient causality to be more in accord with our first-person experience. (This distinction is close to what Hall [2004: 253; also Fales 1990: 17] adumbrates as that between counterfactual *dependence* and causality as *production*.[16]) In contrast to the

---

[15]Weber's example (taken from Eduard Meyer) was the battle of Marathon, which was the precondition for the development of Greek naval power and hence its further independence from Persian domination and, consequently, the development of Greek culture. Our counterfactual, then, is the following: what would have happened if the battle of Marathon had gone the other way? See Durkheim ([1883–1884] 2004: 199) for his embracing of the method of difference.

[16]Hall (2004: 263) demonstrates that even a sophisticated understanding of counterfactual dependence can be rigorously distinguished from production in that there are cases of the one that do not fall into the other.

analytic account of necessary causality (e.g., "had there been no pattern of alliances, there would have been no First World war"), the account of sufficient causality is often a chain of events that naturally falls into narrative, such as "One day a Serbian nationalist assassinated archduke Franz Ferdinand. This provoked the Austrians to make demands on the Serbians that in turn provoked the Russians to (grumblingly) support the Serbians . . . " and so on. Although this chain of causes may be understood as sufficient to produce the war, we may expect that none of these was *necessary*, if only because even before 1914 there was a widespread belief that *something* would trigger a major war.[17]

We thus have three immediate problems stemming from the presence of two antithetical visions of causality. The first comes from the two-ness: it is not impossible to have two root definitions of what we mean by causality, and in the days in which the social sciences relied on presentation of simple tables, many analyses took for granted that one should consider both forms of causality. But, for better or worse, the current approach to causality does not accept this two-ness and instead leaps in to analyses of "causality" as a general phenomenon.[18] Instead, our tendency to make a virtue of necessity has led us to emphasize vague symmetric notions of causality whenever we can, and our attachment to third-person explanations seems to have led us to think in terms of necessary causality when we cannot.

This leads to a further problem in that this third-person (necessary) causality seems more doubtful than the one compatible with narrative (sufficient causality), for we must have just the right amount of deterministic necessary causality for the scientific project to make sense. That is, we may argue that all things are determined according to these principles and so the world as a whole at time $T + 1$ is totally determined by the world at time T. But, such determinism also makes any Weberian project worthless: we can never imagine an alternative in which the putative causal factor is absent since there can be no alternatives in history by

---

[17]By 1887, there was a widespread belief among members of the German military that war could not be avoided, and by the early twentieth century some were accurately forecasting the sequence of likely events—in particular, Conrad and Moltke discussed a sequence beginning with Austrian occupation of Serbia and ending with German mobilization in response to Russian mobilization (Craig 1956: 268, 289, 291). Similarly regarding the Peloponnesian war: "The general belief [among Athenians] was that, whatever happened, war with the Peloponnese was bound to come" (Thucydides I:42, 44 [1972: 61f]).

[18]A partial exception is Pearl (2000), who formalizes necessary and sufficient causality when (as an afterthought) he considers the causal explanation of unique events (he assumes some sort of symmetric, probabilistic causality for the more common case of aggregate data). His formalization, however, does not do anything for the fundamental problems that we shall see arise from the counterfactual approach.

definition. Without at least the possibility of an alternative in which things were different, the idea of a "necessary" cause makes no sense.[19] Thus, we must be extremely fortunate in that not all things are causally determined, but the ones in which we are interested are.

The final problem comes from the fact that if we can support the contention that A is a necessary cause of B we are also supporting the contention that B is a sufficient cause of A. This fundamental problem can be solved at least in some cases, in principle if not in fact, by examining temporal ordering. Of course, this is not always true. As Maimonides (1947: 191; also Plotinus 1956: 332) wrote, "The rising of the sun undoubtedly produces the day and yet it does not precede it."[20] For another example, we may argue that some force (e.g., the force of gravity) causes acceleration in an object, although one does not precede the other. Any definition of cause that we adopt cannot be such that we become unable to say that force causes acceleration and thereby lose one of our few intuitively accessible aspects of physical causation ("force" as a cause).[21] More fundamentally, in everyday life we seem to see that a person using a hammer is the cause of the motion of the hammer, although we do not see her *first* move her arm and *then* see the hammer move (Michotte [1946] 1963: 173–175).

It may take, then, a bracing draught of faith to proceed with the confidence that a quest to uncover necessary causal relations is anything other than a colossal error. But, for the sake of argument, let us generously assume for the time being that all causality just *is* necessary causality, and our task as good scientists is to uncover it. We must rein in our immediate impulse to qualify and complicate—to insist that the real world has many probabilistic causes and so on. If the fundamental idea of causality makes no sense when we consider a simple and sparse world, it cannot make more sense when we consider a more complex one. As Durkheim says, a sum of many zeros is still a zero. So, let us assume that we are looking to

---

[19]Note that this is not quite true with sufficient causality because a lack of possibilities is actually completely compatible with the definition of causality, although one might say trivially so.

[20]And, contra those impertinent readers who would argue that the sun must rise over the horizon before the first light rays reach us, let them be reminded that in contemporary physics, events that are light-speed/distance away from each other are simultaneous (here cf. Bunge 1959: 63).

[21]Eells (1991: 241f) valiantly tries to claim that one can find temporal priority even in these examples of simultaneous causation of force because special relativity tells us that there is some time required to transfer energy and momentum. This invocation is a complete disaster since as noted (note 20), in special relativity, large classes of events cannot be ordered in terms of "before" and "after." Further, although there is an element of sophistry, and not all infinitesimal paradoxes lead us to correct insights, it is worth considering whether any causation can occur that is not simultaneous. If A and B are not contiguous in space-time, how can one effect the other?

determine whether one thing caused another in a reasonably quiet world. Let us also assume that we actually care about the answer—that a great deal is riding on our conclusions, such as if we were asked to determine what had caused someone's death. How then do we proceed? I begin with a simple example of the (well-recognized) difficulties that the identification of causality with necessity poses, discuss how current approaches formalize the issue, and examine the problems that result.

COUNTER COUNTERFACTUALS

Mass Murder and Other Everyday Events

The conventional approach to explanation in the social sciences currently emphasizes what I will call *simple counterfactualism* (SCF) as the way to define a causal relation. Beginning with the idea of necessary causality, SCF proposes that we can answer the question, Is x a cause of y? in the positive by answering, In the absence of x, would we see y? in the negative. Despite its initial appeal, this formulation turns out to lead to many problems; these have been explored by philosophers, with the central contributor being David Lewis (1973a). In this discussion, I rely on their critical analyses of SCF, although I do not accept any of their reformulations as particularly helpful for the social sciences. We will find that SCF is not a crisp solution to all our explanatory difficulties.

Let us begin by confidently applying SCF to a few scenarios:

> Scenario 1. A knowingly and deliberately shoots B with the intent of causing B's death. B dies from the resulting wound. Did A cause the death of B?

Our current conventional approach to this issue runs as follows: "Hmm. Did A cause the death of B? That means, "Was A's action necessary for B's death?" That means, "Had A not shot B, would B still have died?" Well, I suppose B would have died sooner or later, so perhaps not. But in that case, nothing can cause a human to die, which is pretty silly. So, let me interpret "B's death" as "B's death-by-shooting-on-this-day." In that case, yes, A caused B's death."

> Scenario 2. C, who has a reputation, known to A, for killing hostages and detecting movement, takes B hostage and threatens to kill B if A attempts to signal the police. A attempts to signal the police, and C kills B. Did A cause the death of B?

Our conventional approach begins and ends the same way. A did cause B's death.

> Scenario 3. C, previously unknown to A or B, takes B hostage and threatens to kill B if A attempts to signal the police. A attempts to signal the police, and C kills B. Did A cause the death of B?

The change in A's knowledge obviously does not affect our answer, although now we might want to point out that while A did cause B's death, so did C, and that it is C, and not A, who is blameworthy.

> Scenario 4. A detains B past normal closing time in B's shop. C, breaking in to what was believed to be an empty store, encounters B and kills him. Did A cause the death of B?

From scenario 3, we have come to accept the difference between causality and responsibility and have little difficulty accepting the conclusion of our thought experiment. A did cause B's death.

> Scenario 5. A sells B a shop. One year later, C, breaking in to what was believed to be an empty store, encounters B and kills him. Did A cause the death of B?

Now, we become somewhat uncomfortable because our counterfactual is vague. What would B's life have been like had not A sold him the shop? We have no idea. It seems unlikely that B would have ended up being killed by C, so again, we must admit that A did cause B's death. But, too many things seem to be causes of B's death for the word *cause* to be doing much for us.

> Scenario 6. A lives in Africa approximately 500,000 years before the present. Then, 500,000 years after A dies, C, breaking in to what was believed to be an empty store, encounters B and kills him. DNA mapping indicates that A is a distant ancestor of B or C. Did A cause the death of B?

The answer is, Of course. According to SCF, we cannot ask the question, What caused B's death? and bring in anything less than an infinite number of causes, with little way of telling them apart. Almost everything that led our world to be our world (and not some other) was a cause of B's death. If we accept this, we must also accept the converse that every act that that we make, and hence one that leads our world to be our world (and not some alternative world), causes heaps upon heaps of deaths (those who might have lived in the other world). Committed counterfactualists have learned to live with this strange conclusion. Their father, David Lewis (1986: 184, 186), volunteers that "I am sure that I—and likewise you, and each of us—have caused ever so many people to die, most of them people yet unborn."[22]

What is at issue here is not that the method of SCF gives us the "wrong" answers—it is that it gives us the same answers to very different questions

---

[22]Interestingly, he goes on to argue that killing is not the same thing as "causing another to die"; rather, killing is that particular kind of causing another to die that demonstrates insensitivity to circumstance—thus, he returns to Heider's idea of equifinality, discussed below.

and never indicates when we have asked a stupid question. A reasonable person might indeed ask, What caused B's death? but not, What are the infinite number of factors that led this world to be different from all other worlds? Philosophers and methodologists assume very quiet worlds—only two or three events take place, such as A shooting a bullet at B. As we shall see, even in quiet worlds, we run into problems. But in a busy world, with bullets flying all about, SCF leads us in useless directions. The bullet that kills us today is less likely to be a cause of our death than the infinite number of bullets, bricks, and viruses that did *not* kill us in the past. From every event, a cone of causes extends backward in time, whereby pretty much everything that occurred a month before within a 5-mile radius of some event X is a cause of X, everything occurring within 20 miles a year ago is a cause, everything within 80 miles 5 years ago a cause, everything within 300 miles 10 years ago a cause, and so on.

We cannot reject answers just because we do not like them. If causality *were* equivalent to simple counterfactual dependence, we will need to accept some of the confusing implications. But, as I will show, far from being obviously the true nature of causality, SCF has insoluble difficulties.

Necessary Problems of Necessity

There is a decent size industry in contemporary philosophy attempting to sort out some of the problems that arise with the SCF idea of causality. There are various inventive ways of handling any particular difficulty, but no one has managed to solve all of them successfully. Those familiar with this literature may skip these sections, and perhaps the entire remainder of this chapter. My overall argument has two parts. The first is one that may surprise some social scientist practitioners, but it cannot be gainsaid—this is that SCF brings with it a host of logical contradictions and problems, and that any fix to SCF leads to other problems, serious ones. The second point is not a logical one but a practical one, and this is that counterfactualism is not worth saving for the social sciences. Rather than spend a great deal of effort trying to make a more complex version of counterfactualism that solves as many of the difficulties as we can manage, we must rethink our understanding of causality.

To begin, we are forced to recognize that not every statement that can be put in a counterfactual form leads us to what we want to count as a cause. If not, we would conclude that the truth of the statement, "If it did not have four legs, it would not be a horse," implies that having four legs is a *cause* of the horse, which makes little sense. We could say that the counterfactually linked c and e have to be *events*, but this allows for some other pathological cases. First, such a definition implies that every event is a cause of itself, which degrades the substantive meaning of the word *cause* (substantively, causality should be a priori irreflexive). Second, everything can be claimed as the cause of invariant phenomena. For example, if it were to turn out that all existing societies were patriarchal, then any A can be successfully inserted in the statement, "If a society is A, then it is patriarchal," which means that it is the hunting, pastoral, postindustrial, underwater, and so on character of society that leads to patriarchy (see Bunge 1959: 34, 38, 43f, 81, 240–244; Hart and Honoré 1959: 108, 398).

Even if we add particular fixes here (declaring causality irreflexive, barring invariants), there is another difficulty: the causality can flow the wrong way in time. Let us say that we try to catch our muddy dog before it gets into the house. You ask me, "Did the dog go through the garage?" "If we do not see muddy footprints, he has gone elsewhere," I respond. We walk to the garage and find the muddy footprints, so my claim was a legitimate counterfactual. Here, c (we see muddy footprints) is later in time than e (the dog went through the garage), which is counterfactually dependent on c.

As a result, most counterfactualists try to restrict their elements to events and to exclude by definition these troublesome "backtracking counterfactuals" (Lewis [1979] 1986: 34f). But even still, we find that although the idea of "a counterfactual" seems all well and good in the abstract, as we approach reality, all sorts of difficulties arise. First, it turns out to be more difficult than we imagine to construct a clean counterfactual. Sometimes, perhaps, I muse "If I were king of America, things would be a whole lot different around here. . . ." And indeed, they would, but presumably the biggest difference is not that *I* am king but that the United States must be a monarchy. Many other things must accordingly be different. This poses problems for our more serious endeavors. If we argue that the pattern of alliances caused the First World War, we imagine a 1914 Europe without alliances. Why are there no alliances? Are the leaders ignorant of proper political action? Is the German state-building project on hold? Has Russia turned eastward?

In other words, if we are interested in determining whether A is a cause of B, it will not do simply to try to construct a world identical to ours but lacking only A, for this world may be "farther away" from our world than *other* worlds that lack A. Lewis (1973b: 9) gives the nice example of the counterfactual of a world in which kangaroos do not have tails. Do we really want to keep *everything* else the same? That they make the same tracks in the sand? That their DNA sequence is the same? This seems to be a very different world from one in which we allow more things to vary (but preserve the regularities of our world). Hence, Lewis ([1973c] 1986: 4ff) admits the need for these counterfactuals to have a flexibility in their strictness.[23] We realize that rather than a crisp alternative, we have sets of possible worlds, and the best we can do is to try to think about those closest to the real world (Lewis 1973b: 5, 7).

---

[23]Lewis himself is admirably consistent here, arguing that his conception of counterfactual is indeed tied to an imprecise concept of the closeness of possible worlds, but that the idea of counterfactual itself is necessarily imprecise, and that two imprecise things can be tightly connected.

Second, even admitting this, we find that there is not a single ordering of worlds in terms of closeness that allows us to determine the acceptability of any counterfactual statement. In most circumstances, we have an implicit sense of *which* world we are thinking of and why, but this can break down. A favorite example is the pair of statements "if Caesar fought the Korean war, he would have used the atom bomb" and "if Caesar fought the Korean war, he would have used catapults" (Lewis [1979] 1986). These are two counterfactual statements, quite different, and yet quite possibly both true. In each case, we implicitly change some aspects of the world and not others, and we do so depending on how we are envisioning precisely *what* about Caesar is of interest to us (also see Hitchcock 1996: 399; Hesslow 1988: 27).

Thus, depending on our implicit understanding of what aspects of the possible cause c are of interest to us, the "nearest $\sim c$ world" will differ. For example, if we wonder whether the evetnt "Gavrilo Princip shooting Franz Ferdinand" was the cause of World War I, there are few circumstances in which we would want to compare our world to what seems to me the closest $\sim c$ world, that in which the bomb thrown earlier by fellow conspirator Nedeljko Čabrinović had killed the archduke. And, since a number of other conspirators were about, some of whom had already failed to act and others of whom might act in the future, if we were to attempt simply to freeze Gavrilo as a way of negating c, there is a good chance that someone else would have done the deed that day. But, it is not necessarily the case that we would insist on comparing to a world in which *no one* shot the archduke—indeed, we might argue that the event "*Gavrilo Princip* shooting Franz Ferdinand" was the cause of World War I precisely because he was part of a semiofficial Serbian conspiracy, as opposed to a lone gunman—and hence we might want to compare to a world in which (say) Alfred Weber assassinated Franz Ferdinand.

Social scientists, unfortunately, are rarely interested in which parts of the world they allow to vary in their counterfactuals—and hence which possible worlds are closer or farther away. Although my counterfactual world in which I am king of America seems to be rather far away, I personally have an easier time imagining an America in which I am king than I do one in which eighty-seven randomly chosen 17-year-olds, all of whom are failing their classes, regularly drinking to the blackout stage, and assaulting their teachers, do *not* drop out of high school. And thus, it is not only for narcissistic reasons that I am less interested in someone's analysis of whether the dropping out of these 17-year-olds *causes* their later criminal offending than I am in planning the floral arrangements for my coronation ceremony.

This leads us to recognize that in counterfactual worlds, none of our entities are precisely the same. The delinquents who do not drop out (in the other world) have to be different from those who do (in our world) in a number of ways. There may not be a "John Levi Martin" who dropped out of high school any more than there is an America in which this fellow is king. We cannot ask simply, What would this person be like had he received less education? but only, In a very similar world in which a counterpart to this person existed but with less education, what would he have been like? Our science, then, is, for better or worse, formally very like a daydream.

Third, we began by attempting to avoid some problems by saying that we restricted our *c* and *e* to "events." But, what *are* events? Are absences of events themselves events? If so, all sorts of logical problems arise (not counting the logical, but distracting, infinity of causes of every effect that take the form of "things not happening to prevent *e*"). Even if we exclude omissions, are events really single things? Was "the Russian Revolution" *an* event? Five events? Five thousand events? Is getting a glass of water *an* event? When we wish to determine whether some *e* would have happened without *c*, are we sure what counts as "an" *e*? For example, with our very first counterfactual problem (scenario 1), we realized that since our fellow B would, like all others, die eventually, really A did *not* cause B's death. We need to redescribe the event of B's death to be "the same death as the one he did die from." But, which deaths are the same death?

The ensuing flurry of work attempting to solve this problem settled down with what must strike the would-be dogmatic social scientist as an extremely unpalatable conclusion. First, the "event" is defined in terms of the analyst's interest.[24] This sort of relativity is not inherently unacceptable, and certainly familiar to sociologists, but still, we cannot but see the initially oversold advantages of "causal" explanation over other approaches beginning to melt away. The best that anyone can come up with is a recognition that our definitions of events can have a degree of "fragility" that is set by the analyst (as a "tunable parameter"). This fragility is how different things can be before we declare that they are no longer the *same* event. If fragility is set high, then practically everything is causing everything. If we make our events more robust by setting fragility to be very low, since most things happen anyway, we suddenly lose most of our causation (Lewis 1986: 197–199; 2004: 85ff; Ducasse [1924] 1969: 62).[25]

Simple counterfactualism, then, is not the sort of thing that brings clarity. Rather, it brings ambiguity. Of course, perhaps that is just the

---

[24]Humphreys (1989: 24f) attempts to define an event as "a change in, or possession of, a property in a system on a trial," which is to say an event is not an event at all but whatever the analyst chooses to call one.

[25]Related to the fragility issue is the inability of the counterfactual approach to sort out relevant from irrelevant predicates of events. Thus, many of the paradoxes that beset those working in this tradition involve "events" that are simply the attaching of causally irrelevant information to a future event. For example, if I paint a car blue, and the blue car later hits and kills someone, we would not imagine that my act should be expected to be a cause of the death. Yet, many of the cases dealt with by those in the counterfactual tradition are formally identical to this. (For example, consider a train approaching on a track that splits into two

way of things. But even if we were to come up with some simplified world in which there just were or were not events, and any world could exist without one (and only this one) event, and so on, it turns out that counterfactualism can lead us in strange directions if we take it seriously.

Further Problems of Simple Counterfactualism

Perhaps most famously, when there are two or more sufficient causes of any event, it may be that a SCF analysis implies that not one of these is a cause. A man before a firing squad is shot. But, had any man on the squad not fired, the convict would still have died, and so no one caused the man's death. Social scientists may hastily insist that it is the squad "as a whole" that has caused the death and refuse to see the problem lurking. But, the problem reappears in the form of "trumping" whereby, say, A lights a long fuse connected to a pile of dynamite, and B later lights a shorter fuse that leads to the same pile. Although it is B's fuse that leads to the explosion, SCF says that it is not the cause (cf. Schaffer 2000). In this case, there is no natural "group" of fuse lightings that we say would was ("as whole") *the* cause.

Instead, we will be pushed to attempt to define the minimal set of causes that produce the effect. This sounds comforting—until we remember our scenario 6 and realize that this "minimal" set is invariably infinite. This is because in the counterfactual approach there is no inherent difference between *causes* and *conditions* (although some have attempted to paste one on after the fact). Anything, the absence of which implies the absence of e, is a cause.

A second famous problem with SCF pertains to the treatment of transitivity. It generally seems, at least when we think in terms of sufficient causality, that causality invariably entails transitivity—if a is a cause of b and b is a cause of c, a must be a cause of c (Collins, Hall, and Paul 2004: 23). But, it is not necessarily the case that counterfactual dependence is transitive, especially when b is a cause that is selectively applied to ensure that event c occurs (Hall 2000; Lewis [1973c] 1986: 17; 2000: 193). Thus, equating counterfactual dependence and causality leads to unpalatable interpretations. For example, consider a game of hockey, and let a = forward takes shot on goal, b = goalie moves stick to hit puck, c = no goal scored. We will say that $a \rightarrow b$ and $b \rightarrow c$, and first interpret these as counterfactual dependence (i.e., if $\sim a$, then $\sim b$). Were these relations

---

tracks that then rejoin, although the left one takes a more circuitous route. After the place of rejoining, our heroine is tied to the tracks. We stand at the switch, ready to throw it and direct the train to the right or left track. Many counterfactualist definitions cannot but make our decision the cause of the death, although the fact that the locomotive was a "from-the-right-coming" locomotive as opposed to a "from-the-left-coming" one seems as irrelevant as its color.)

transitive, this would imply that if the forward had not taken the shot, he would have scored a goal. If we interpret → as sufficiency, we also find transitivity, but this simply means that there can be no state in which the forward takes a shot in which a goal is scored (it does not imply that had the forward not taken the shot, a goal would have been scored, although this is not forbidden).[26]

The strange relation of SCF to transitivity leads to serious problems for its application to human action. If we are to plan our future actions, we need to think transitively, and hence to treat causality as transitive. But with SCF, transitivity would imply that looking-glass logic is valid. Let a = forward suddenly smashes stick into goalie's stomach, b = goalie is incapable of moving, c = goalie does not attempt to hurt forward. Since $a \to b$ and $b \to c$ (since the assaulted goalie, if not incapacitated, would certainly desire to punish the attacker), if these relations were causal and transitive, $a \to c$ and thus the forward was reasonable to attack the goalie to prevent his own harm (Hall 2000, 2004: 247f).

A third problem is that the absence of preventing factors (of which there are an infinite number) must be seen as causes of any event. More complexly, something that prevents a prevention is a cause. And, the absence of something that prevents the preventer of a prevention is itself a cause. And so on.

In sum, to identify causality with simple counterfactual dependence is a mess. The most important response is to make a distinction between causality and counterfactualism but still to tie the two. Lewis (1986: 206) proposes that we treat A as the cause of B not if B is counterfactually dependent on A, but if there is a chain of counterfactual dependencies connecting B to A (Lewis 1973a: 563). The problem with this solution for the social sciences is that if we cannot be sure that there "is" an event, our chain disintegrates as we pull on it.[27] At the same time, merely the recognition that counterfactual dependence might be different from causality

---

[26]If we indicate any case by a set with a letter for any event that takes place (and hence an absence of the letter b in [a, c] means ~b), SCF allows the following {[Ø], [a], [a, b], [a, b, c]}, while sufficiency allows {[Ø], [c], [b, c], [a, b, c]}. Thus, we see that in the particular example used, the counterfactual relation *is* transitive because, for the sake of simplicity, I have not allowed any (possibly preempted) causes of "goal not scored" other than "goalie moves stick." In contrast to sufficiency, with SCF, we cannot necessarily determine the transitivity of a set of relations without information on other relations.

[27]It is worth emphasizing that I in no way deny that things that we would call causes often lead to counterfactual dependence. It is that if we *define* causality thusly, we run into necessary problems that undermine any attempt to think straight. Some might counter this by pointing out that we successfully use counterfactualism to great success in everyday life. But, there are many other concepts or frameworks that we use, perhaps necessarily, in our everyday life that have absolutely no place in social science and have been rightly banished (for one, value judgments coming from our particular cultural and religious traditions). Further,

(and still of interest in its own right) would be a great step forward for the social sciences.

A common response of committed counterfactualists is to admit that SCF is not actually very good at telling us "the causes of effects," but to argue that we should not even be asking these questions in the first place. Instead, we should investigate the more tractable issue of determining "the effects of causes" (Holland 1986 seems to be the first to formulate this distinction). This seems to me much like advising someone who has lost his wallet not to go about looking for it (since it could be *anywhere*) but instead to see what he can find on the top of the dresser.

It is perhaps significant that we have seen similar cautions for our use of linear regression-type models—statisticians correctly warn us that these are good for estimating the effects of *known* causal models and not for determining the correct causal model. This is true, but somewhat disingenuous—if we were only going to use such models to estimate known causal effects, almost all statisticians would be on the bread line. Just as the Q-tips box sternly admonishes us "Of course, never put *anything* inside your ear" (Why on earth else would one buy Q-tips? Is it an accident that they are made to fit in an ear canal?), so our peddlers of causal science try to get us to pay full price for an item that they do not really believe will do what we obviously, and reasonably, want it to do.

Complications and Simplifications

Our immediate impulse is to run to "big N" social science and recapitulate recent discussions using counterfactualism to produce various sorts of causal estimates. But, these discussions assume that we have a clear idea of what causality is in any case; given this, it is not at all difficult to aggregate things. But they certainly do not help us *define* causality, and if we find that we are confused with the counterfactual

---

our use of counterfactuals in everyday life is quite different from that proposed by philosophers and in fact supports the contentions made here.

Although people are capable of considering counterfactual scenarios, they seem to think that the causal import of these increases in what Kahneman and Varey (1990) call "close counterfactuals"—the things that "almost" happened. In evaluating this almost (and hence, by implication, the causal effect of some factor in affecting a change in probabilities), people are attentive to narrative patternings, directions of change and cumulation, and not a comparison of two probabilities. For example, in a game of "heads/tails" (in which we choose heads or tails, flip a coin N times, and the person with the most wins is the winner of the game), before the first move in a game with $N = 1$, we do not feel we "almost" won because we were one flip away from victory. But, if we are heads and have 8 wins, 8 losses in an $N = 17$ game, we are likely to feel this way.

approach in a small world, our confusion is only papered over in a busier one.

We might expect that things are simpler because rather than having to construct imaginary counterfactuals (in which, say, there is no Gavrilo Princip), we can use the multiplicity to create virtual counterfactuals before our eyes. That is, if we inject one of our cows (Bessie) with anthrax vaccine, leave Tessie untreated, and find that Tessie has anthrax while Bessie does not, we can see Tessie as the factual counterfactual for a world with an untreated Bessie. Adding more cows to the treated and untreated categories only increases our confidence.

But, translated to the counterfactual approach, this reasonable experimental method becomes problematic because for every vaccinated Bessie there is a *set* of counterfactual worlds in which Bessie was not vaccinated, and these worlds may be very different depending on how many *other* animals were vaccinated. If all the other animals were vaccinated, Bessie is not likely to become infected anyway. We generally imagine that we can counterfactually compare each animal individually but then ignore this when we imagine the likely results of applying the treatment to all (see Morgan and Winship 2007: 38). That is, the counterfactual world in which the 500 vaccinated cows were not vaccinated has no neat relation to the 500 counterfactual worlds in which each single vaccinated cow was not vaccinated (but the others were) or to the many other possible combinations of some of these getting the treatment and others not. The virtue of the rigorous counterfactual approach to causality for such cases is that it demonstrates how unlikely it is that a simple comparison of the outcomes of Bessie, Tessie, and the others can be turned into a counterfactual causal statement.

Further, if we are going about comparing sets of the vaccinated to the unvaccinated to determine whether the former later have a lower prevalence of anthrax, at best we end up with evidence of an *average* causal effect. The existence of such an effect does not imply that in every case—or in any particular case—the vaccine is a negative cause of anthrax. It may be that for Bessie, being vaccinated actually caused anthrax, while for Marigold, it prevented it. But, if any x may have a *distribution* of causal effects on y for any sample, then, as Morgan and Winship (2007: 136, 280) point out, we get rather little out of a simple counterfactual approach. I am not denying that randomized experiments are the right way to examine certain problems, or even that the counterfactual approach is of great importance for thinking through many of these problems. But, when we are trying to get our ideas clear, in order to find out what we actually mean by cause (if we are determined to have a meaning), the large N approach does not solve the problems of SCF. Indeed, given that SCF forced us to acknowledge an infinite number of causes for every event, we must be puzzled at the leap between this vision of causality and that used in our everyday researches, in which we can easily imagine "complete determination" ($R^2 = 1$) well short of this infinity. Actually wedding the SCF vision to our practices would involve a consideration of the relationship between possible and observed variability and would require assumptions so implausible that no one would begin the effort.

Many committed counterfactualists (somewhat curiously) have a difficult time imagining a social science in which causality is *not* equated with counterfactualism. But recall that we saw a close connection between SCF and necessary (as opposed to sufficient) causality. This second understanding of causality has been sidelined but is still a contender. Thus, Hall (2004) has proposed to distinguish between *dependence* (which satisfies the counterfactual formula) and *production*. The relation of production satisfies many of the things we want in a notion of causality—it is transitive and restricted to local action—and indeed comes much closer to what I have called *impulsion*. Given that our commitment to necessity is not necessary, we may want to reconsider our immediate tendency to try to patch it up.

Why Rescue?

The undeniable inability of SCF to give an elegant and airtight definition of causality does not, in itself, mean that we should abandon it. But the counterfactual definition is a particularly bad one for sociology, in part because it threatens to mislead us regarding where the "action" is. One of the early implications of the counterfactual approach in statistics was that it might make no sense to speak of a cause if there was, in principle, no possibility of manipulation. Thus, Holland (1986) insists that we could not say that one attribute of a person caused another attribute. Certainly, it would seem strange to treat definitional aspects of persons—their genetic makeup and the resulting categorical attributes like race or sex—as causes of their actions (Zuberi 2001).

But as Freese (2008) has persuasively argued, it is now far from impossible to imagine manipulations of a genome and thus to treat genes as causes. Thus, we can at least in principle imagine a relation of counterfactual dependence between, say, race (i.e., some phenotypic pattern that leads others to integrate a subject's physical characteristics and make a racial ascription) and some other outcome, such as income. But as Freese notes, this relation may well be due to the actions of *others*—if employers insist on paying nonwhites less than whites, a counterfactual relation of dependence of income on race occurs because of how others treat the genetically formed body. Defining causality as counterfactual dependence thus has us looking in precisely the wrong places—in this case, the cause of discrimination is the presence of victims. Because such cases are of central concern to the social sciences, having such an inherently problematic definition of causality should be deeply troubling. We would not seriously entertain a defense of a judicial system that used counterfactualism to judge responsibility and hence punished victims for crimes. It is of course obviously not the case that responsibility "is" counterfactual dependence, but the same goes for causality. Even if we could salvage counterfactualism for the social sciences, we should not wish to do so.

TAKING CHANCES

Improbable Excuses

We have a number of fast responses to these difficulties, none of which have anything to do with the key problem. Commonly, we try to retreat to seemingly weaker definitions by substituting symmetric and probabilistic definitions of causation, such as "A increases the likelihood of B." Of course, if we are having difficulties conceptualizing deterministic causality, we are unlikely to do better with probabilistic causality since the former is only a special case of the latter, wherein probabilities are restricted to 0 and 1. This appeal to probabilistic causality attempts to solve the fundamental problems we have seen in our understanding of *cause* only by appending another term that we do not understand, namely, *probability*.

There are three competing statistical definitions of probability in the social sciences. The first, and increasingly popular among statisticians, is now called Bayesian, although the modern foundations are really laid by Jeffreys (1961). In this system, a probability is a degree of subjective confidence in the veracity of some statement (for Keynes [1921: 3–5], it was the degree of *rational* confidence). This definition has attracted adherents in large part because it leads to consistent interpretation. It also is an attractive approach to the key problem of how to go from the simple task of figuring out how likely observed data are given some model to the much more complicated task of figuring out how likely some model is given the observed data. But, this Bayesian sense of probability is never used by those claiming that causality is ontologically probabilistic, for probability here has no ontological referent at all—probability refers to statements, not to events.

The second, and historically most influential, understanding of probability is the frequentist, most closely associated with the work of Karl Pearson (or John Venn). In this view, a statement of probability is a statement regarding the properties of a large number of identical trials that stretch to infinity. Thus, to say that the probability of a fair coin coming up heads is ½ is to say that as we make an increasing number of tosses, the number of heads will tend to come increasingly close to ½ of the total. This is also a reasonably consistent view, although it leads to a number of problems for the philosophically inclined statistician. Applied to the issue of causality, it is unsatisfying for it sheds no light on the issue of causal connection; a frequentist approach may see the probabilism as fundamentally ontological (chance exists in the world, e.g., C.S. Peirce) or as merely epistemological, with all things causally determined.

Indeed, far from solving the problem with the counterfactual approach to causality, the switch to frequentist probabilism merely multiplies it infinitely. We now need a plethora of counterfactuals, not simply one. If we say that "education" is a "probabilistic cause" of "income," we must mean that for each of the persons in some sample, if we were to observe an indefinitely large number of alternate universes in which everything was the same, with the partial exception of her education being increased, there would be more alternate universes in which her income would be higher than there are alternate universes in which her income is lower.

Practitioners will of course object that they are not at all implying anything about these thousands of different universes for each of thousands of different persons; instead, it is the very variation among their sample of different persons that allows for the comparisons that establish causality. But, this is not causality—this is merely the data, and if one defines causality simply by labeling the data as such, one will certainly have an easy time. The data might also be defined as "law" or "freedom" without this demonstrating that either law or freedom is a necessary or possible aspect of human existence or social explanation. One may *define* one's pocket as "riches" without being any the wealthier for that.[28]

The one possible definition of causality that is relevant to the social scientists' understanding is that proposed by Fisher (1956: 32f), which has generally attracted less attention than the Pearsonian. Standing between the objectivist and subjectivist approaches, Fischer basically proposed that probability is a number attached to a class of objects within

---

[28] As an example, take the question of whether education causes income. Let us say that we have a sample of 1,000 and a correlation of .6. How do we interpret this counterfactually? First, we can immediately dispose of the idea that our key counterfactual is one in which every member of our sample has both increased education and increased income. From Lieberson in particular, we have learned to distinguish between one's position in a distribution and the overall contours of that distribution. If everyone had a college degree, jobs that now go to high school graduates would go to college graduates. Clearly, our understanding of the counterfactuals that justifies our causal interpretation must pertain to individuals chosen from the herd for special (if imaginary) gifts. (This is related to the "stable unit treatment value assumption," as it is generally called these days.)

Do we mean that for *every* person in this 1,000, if he had been given more education, he would have more income? We certainly do not mean this for the person with the most education. Let us ignore those with the higher amounts of education and only focus on those who are below the mean. Do we mean that for each person here, had he more education, he would have more income? If so, that would be strange, for our .6 correlation implies that there are quite a few pairs of people p and q who are alike on other variables (or at least who have the same weighted sum on these other variables), but where p has more education and *lower* income than q. If we were to counterfactually change q's education to be like p's, our data give us no confidence to imagine that he would certainly have a

(Footnote continued on the next page.)

which we can make no differentiations.[29] Like the frequentists, Fisher saw probability as a number coming from an actual division, where the numerator is the number of observations of some type and the denominator the sum total of possibilities. But like the Bayesians, he saw this as expressing our subjective state, although less our *belief* than our ignorance. For example, to return to the classic coin example, actual coin tosses are different: they begin with different initial conditions, and the world is in motion as they take place. But, we lack any understanding of these, and so to us, all coin tosses are equivalent except insofar as they land heads or tails. We thus have only two distinguishable states, and any toss is as likely to be in one as it is in the other. Thus, we may say that the probability of a fair coin tossed being heads is ½.

This probability, then, cannot be used as a predicate for the causal process involved because if something allows us to distinguish within this class of indistinguishables, then probability changes. In fact, as we get increasingly more information, our probabilities necessarily tend to 0 or 1. If we cannot define deterministic causality in a coherent way, we cannot use Fisher's notion to define probabilistic causality either.

In sum, merely introducing probability does not clarify the matter for the counterfactual understanding of causality. The clearest approach is the frequentist, which seems to assume some sort of ontological probabilism—that is, one that exists even in single events. (If we reject this sort of ontological probabilism, then there is no need to alter our underlying conception of causality.) But, the frequentist approach does not resolve the problems associated with counterfactualism—it only multiplies them infinitely.

---

higher income than he does in the real world.

Presumably, we might say that for our p, there are more counterparts in our data to p (call them p^*'s) who are alike in all ways but income and education, but who are higher on both, than there are q^*'s who are higher on education and lower on income. Thus, we might argue that in the set of all possible closest worlds to our own in which q's education is increased, there are more in which q's income is higher than there are ones in which q's income is lower (call these H worlds and L worlds).

I do not pretend to know what this means; there are cases in which one can compare the magnitude of infinite sets, but I doubt that this is one of them. It seems that our current practice is to imagine that the ratio of the number of H worlds to L worlds is the same as the ratio of number of p^*'s to q^*'s. Certainly, if there was a reason to believe that this was the case, it would justify our relabeling of a comparison across individuals as a causal property happening within each one, but simply wishing that it were so does not make it so.

[29]This was an earlier view, based on the principle of "nonsufficient reason" (for preferring one choice to another) and has been incorporated into a number of systems, although they ended up less influential for the social sciences. I admit that Fisher's views are not entirely clear and were expressed differently at different times (or changed greatly). I also admit that it is more difficult to approach

Raising Probabilities

We may then be tempted to skirt around the issue of what probability is and simply insist that a cause of B is something that increases the probability of B occurring ... whatever that means. There is nothing in principle wrong with such a response if it helps us think about causality in a reasonable manner. But we end up saying distinctly unhelpful things. Let us begin by restricting our attention to the simple class of discrete events that either do or do not occur. Say that we claim that x is a cause of y if the probability of y given x is higher than the probability of y given the absence of x ($\Pr[y|x] > \Pr[y|\sim x]$). We know that this is not true because two things can be associated even though one does not cause the other. We may (provisionally) imagine that we are "holding other things constant" and argue that x is a cause of y if ($\Pr[y|x, T] > \Pr[y|\sim x, T]$), where T are "all those other things" we want to hold constant. The (well-recognized) problem with this is that if $\Pr[y|x, T] > \Pr[y|\sim x, T]$, then $\Pr[x|y, T] > \Pr[x|\sim y, T]$—each can be considered a cause. We are back to the problems of then throwing in temporal ordering to sort this out (e.g., Eells 1991: 242, 246f, 252), which we recall does not work very well.

But, push these issues to the side for a moment and pursue this definition seriously. Let us say that x is setting out a blanket in the yard, and y is a helicopter landing on my blanket in my yard. It seems likely that x must raise the probability of y because the probability must be 0 in the absence of x, but as no helicopter *has* landed, it seems curious to say that—by definition—putting out blankets causes helicopters to land on them.

Now, it is not that the low *magnitude* of the probability that is key (and hence the probability of helicopters landing is so small that this is no cause) for we cannot reliably use such magnitudes to determine what is and what is not a cause. Shooting at someone with a revolver from 200 yards may lead to death in only a very small number of cases, but in these cases, the shooting is definitely the cause.

Defining causality as probabilistic thus turns out to bring its own problems—and wedding it to counterfactualism makes things even stranger (here I follow Hitchcock [1996: 402]). As we have seen, a counterfactual approach means that our result is likely to differ by what particular counterfactual we choose: is having a moderately high blood pressure x a cause of stroke y? To what do we compare this—all those who do not have a moderately high blood pressure $\sim x$, including those with high, very high, and extremely high blood pressure? Humphreys (1989: 74) says that the comparison must be to a "neutral" state. What

---

continuous probability distributions from his perspective than from the Bayesian. I still believe, however, that there is a reasonableness here that leads to more insightful ways of posing the problems than the obstinate simplicity of Bayesian and frequentist views.

might this be? Is this those with no blood pressure at all? Bear in mind that the problem is not that we cannot comprehend a function relating risk of stroke to blood pressure—we certainly can. It is that the counterfactual causal approach is not helping us comprehend this.

Let us imagine that we only deal with the case of discrete events that do or not occur, and we even are granted an ordering of worlds such that those in which our putative causes do not occur are "closest" worlds. Can we then use a definition of increased probability that avoids the conclusion that putting out blankets causes helicopters to land on them? We might revise our definition and propose that x is a cause of y if x raises the probability of y occurring (compared to our counterfactual world), and y does in fact occur (e.g., Eells 1991: 7). Let us imagine (following Hitchcock 2004) that two persons simultaneously shoot at a bottle, each with a probability of 50% of hitting the bottle. Let us further say that the bullet from the first person hits and smashes the bottle. If we believe in ontological probability, we must believe that when the second shoots, the probability of the bottle being broken is raised to 75% from 50%. Do we really want to claim that the second person's shot was a cause of the bottle being broken?[30]

At this, point we may take refuge in a frequentist understanding of probability—we thus argue that our confusion came because we were trying to apply probability to unique events, and really, probability applies to large sets of them. Thus, it is only here that we can properly define probabilistic causality. But first, if this is our response, we have now abandoned ontological probablism, which we followed because we hoped that it would solve the difficulties we had making counterfactualism work for simple events. Instead, we seem to be in the position of allowing for causal heterogeneity, without yet being able to specify what causality is for single events. Second, if we try to define probabilistic causality for sets of events, we find that we introduce a new set of paradoxes for we may conceive of cases in which a treatment decreases the probability of an effect, while in every case in which the treatment and effect are both observed, the treatment is the cause of the effect.

Suppose a raw egg sits on a shallow perch above a table. A few feet away, an air cannon shoots a puff of air every 10 minutes toward the egg. Seventy percent of the time, this puff is sufficient to cause the egg to tumble off the perch and shatter (at which point it is replaced). A large suspended plate is controlled by a button; when depressed, the plate drops down to the table 1 minute prior to the cannon discharging, preventing the puff of air from affecting the egg. It is automatically raised after the cannon fires. Unfortunately, 35% of the time, the force of the plate hitting the table is sufficient to lead the egg to tumble off its perch

---

[30]Parascandola (1996) grasps this nettle and asserts that it does—thereby assisting plaintiffs who want to recover damages based on probabilistic causation.

and break. Creating 500 identical setups and randomly allocating them to the categories of "press button" or "do not press button," we correctly find that those for which the plate was deployed have fewer smashed eggs. Were we interested in proposing an intervention policy to decrease the number cracked, we would do well to urge all to press the button. But, we would (according to a commonsensical understanding of causality) be wrong if we concluded that the plate did not cause broken eggs. Although dropping the plate is neither necessary nor sufficient for the egg to break, and it does not increase the probability of the egg breaking, it is causal in the sense that is, or should be, the root of our understanding of causality, namely the actual causality of production.

Our immediate reaction is to attempt to solve the problems by a "control"-type strategy—we want in effect to snip off one part of the causal chain created by dropping the plate and say that the plate does cause the breaking of the egg, once we control for its effect on the air puff. We somehow want to compare only to cases in which there is no air puff, even though we observe no such cases.

But, consider a similar, and practical, example, discussed by Smith (2003; also Eells 1991: 190, 234f) among others, namely the relationship between birth control pills and thrombosis (Hesslow 1976). A clear biochemical link can be established between the makeup of early birth control pills and the development of arterial blood clots. Do we then say that birth control pills cause thrombosis because they raise the probability of its occurrence? But, they do not—they lower the probability of thrombosis because they prevent pregnancy, which is even more likely to lead to thrombosis. Again, our impulse is to snip off one portion of the causal chain. Thus, we might imagine birth control pills that do not prevent pregnancy and find that they do in fact increase the probability of thrombosis. Thus, we reach the causal chain that does in fact exist between the two and save our definition. Now, if we were simply allowed to make such snips at our pleasure, we could choose whether to prove or disprove this (or any other) conjecture. Presumably, we are more principled and are trying to use our counterfactual to snip off that set of effects of our cause that (we believe) are interfering with our identification of the causal effect of interest. That is, birth control pills cause both an increase in thrombosis risk and a decrease in pregnancy risk; we want to eliminate the causal chain from the latter to better get at the direct effect of the pills on thrombosis.

But, if we are allowed to snip off such causal chains, there is no reason to stop here. Birth control pills produce elevated levels of estrogen and progesterone. The higher levels of hormones prevent the ovaries from releasing an egg. The higher levels of hormones also, I am led to believe, increase factor VII and D-dimer and decrease antithrombin (Cosman et al. 2005; I do not pretend to understand what these are), leading to blood clots. Why can we not snip off the causal chain running from the hormones to D-dimer instead of or as well as the chain running to the release of an egg by the ovaries? Presumably, this is because we understand that it is this first chain that is the mechanism by which the birth control pills cause thrombosis. But, this is to *reject the counterfactual idea of causality* in favor of the commonsense one of "production" or "impulsion." We are no longer interested in the necessary causality that comes from a comparison to a hypothetical world—to the extent that we are serious and that we mean what we say, we find ourselves back with the old-fashioned understanding of causality, perhaps as sufficiency and not necessity, but certainly as impulsion.[31]

Indeed, there are no neat solutions to this problem. The first response is to argue that there are actually two sorts of relationships here. One sort is that between the class of potential causes (e.g., our plate falling in the egg example) and potential effects (eggs breaking). The other is that between any particular (or "token") plate-falling event and any particular egg-breaking event. These can be quite different forms of causation (Eells 1991: 17, 22, 279). This seems to require a host of ugly additional terms if we are to make the desired comparisons indicate causality (for Eells [1991: 31, 33, 144], this involves the introduction of different "kinds" of classes and not necessarily true assumptions about the distributions of event classes within kinds).

The second response is to attempt to eliminate complications by definition, which we have seen in terms of snipping off causal chains. More generally, we put into our definition of probabilistic causality a proviso that all other causes have been neutralized (this is also required by attempts to formalize causality by differentiating "class" from "token" causality). This is the approach proposed by Cartwright: we can only say that x is a cause of y if x raises the probability of y in every situation "which is otherwise causally homogeneous with respect to y" (1983: 25; cf. Ducasse [1924] 1969: 71). This is a Pyrrhic victory for we are left with a statement that if taken as a definition is *necessarily circular* (as we defined a cause in terms of causes) (also Eells 1991: 139, 171). In other words, the probabilistic approach to causation has been demonstrated to make sense *only if we already know what causality is*—only if causality is *not* an increase in probability but is something else. And, that something else seems to be impulsion.

Probabilism, then, does not solve the problems with a counterfactual approach (Lewis 2004: 80). Just as we are getting close to what has been

---

[31]This is seen in Lewis's (2004: 92, 102) attempt to introduce "influence" as a way of dealing with double preemption and other paradoxes that are inherent to the counterfactual approach. For example, Suzy and Billy both throw rocks at a bottle, and hers gets there first and smashes it. Had she not thrown it, the bottle would still be smashed, but the "way" she threw it has more to do with the way it broke than does Billy's way. This is simply giving up the counterfactual definition and joining the opposing side.

held out to us as the precise, scientific approach to social science, we throw in gobs of incoherent claims about the world that we do not defend. Indeed, probabilism does not help clarify our thoughts in large part because, despite our universal acknowledgment that the world is inherently chancy, we do not know what chance is, nor do we care.

Magic Is Alive, Chance Is Afoot

What is chance? The question is difficult to answer, but when things get confusing and we are unsure of what our words mean, the approach here will be to consider the way in which the term is used. We saw that causality makes sense when identified with the deliberate, willful action of a human being (scenario 1), but we run into trouble in different ways when we leave that case. In everyday life, chance is something that enters our conversation when we get into certain types of trouble and want a certain class of solutions. It is not the only class of solutions—another, historically more prevalent, has been witchcraft.

Evans-Pritchard's ([1937] 1976) classic analysis of witchcraft among the Azande held that witchcraft beliefs arise in places where there is an assumption that there is always personal causality behind all unfortunate events. (Although witchcraft beliefs vary considerably across culture and period, the connection with personal causality is widespread.) That is, witchcraft is generally used to explain something that is otherwise puzzling. What puzzles people is usually that they were trying to do one thing, and did everything right (the causal power of effective motivation was present), but something still went wrong. How can we explain the difference between what we *should* have experienced (success) and what we *did* experience?

Evans-Pritchard ([1937] 1976) gives the example of the Zande who uses the idea of witchcraft to explain why he hurt his foot on a stump. The injured fellow completely understands that the stump caused the injury, but he does not accept that this is a *complete* explanation. Thousands of times a day he walks past similar stumps *without* hurting himself. So, why did he hurt himself this time? The difference is that this time someone bewitched him.

In the West, however, when asked to explain this event, we do not resort to witchcraft. Instead, we just shrug our shoulders and say "chance." Chance is thus our version of witchcraft—our way of ending the explanation by recourse to a general principle.[32] It allows us to explain all the parts of the world that we cannot really explain and go along with regular life. The key difference is that witchcraft is fundamentally about *personal* causality. The Zande never invoke witchcraft when there is already an obvious causal story that links an event to the personal causality of

---

[32]See Cassirer ([1925] 1955: 48f) on the opposition between these modes of explanation.

another actor.³³ It is the lack of personal causality—the *Ur*-form of causality, as I have claimed here—that provokes the need for a more complete explanation.

Chance, on the contrary, is fundamentally about *impersonal* causality. No one caused it, and no one is responsible, not even God. For, as Keith Thomas (1971) argued, there has been a zero-sum relationship between belief in providence—that is, that God cared about each and every thing that happened on earth and that it was all part of His plan—and belief in chance.³⁴ The rise of an orthodox Protestant belief in God's omniscience pushed chance to the margins, and the decline of this orthodoxy led chance to flood in and occupy all the nooks and crannies abandoned by a retreating divinity.³⁵

As a result, we now have an impersonal "theory of everything." This is especially useful for a crowded society—we have less vengeance, less spying, less suspicion that your apartment building is full of potential witches. Witchcraft provokes the believer always to look further, to get increasingly closer to personal causality, while chance lets one drop the matter and go about one's business. I am not arguing that the convenient nature of chance explains the origin of our beliefs, but we can see why we like our version better, even though chance is no more defensible as a concept than witchcraft.

We know that this lack of caring is in fact how we think about chance, because chance or randomness is used in the exact same way by ontological determinists (those who think that chance is just millions of unmeasured causes, as the world is actually completely determined) as it is by ontological indeterminists (those who believe that the world is inherently stochastic or susceptible to free willfulness). Chance then can mean our conviction that it is impossible to give a causal explanation, or our faith that somewhere, someone *could* give an impersonal explanation if they cared enough, which they don't.³⁶ Whether the world has millions of

---

³³Similarly, here is Paul Stoller (1987: 211) on the divination he is receiving, in which the wise woman talks of his enemies: "Again the enemies! Fatouma's view of my life, like the Sohanci's, was devoid of chance. Any barriers I encountered, they 'saw,' were caused by people working against me." Also see the work of Demos (1982: 312).

³⁴In a similar manner, in African societies that believe in witchcraft but a strong transcendent God, like the Lugbara, the scope of events attributed to witchcraft is greatly circumscribed (Middleton 1955).

³⁵That said, it seems that relatively few philosophers, including those who formulated the rules of probability, were ontological indeterminists.

³⁶Democritus: "Men have fashioned an image of Chance as an excuse for their own stupidity" (frag. 119). Or Hobbes ([1651] 1909: 530): "And in many occasions they put for cause of Naturall events, their own Ignorance, but disguised in other words: As when they say, Fortune is the cause of things contingent; that is, of things whereof they know no cause."

causes or not a one, "chance" is a polite way of ending the inquiry. It cannot solve problems with our idea of causality because it represents abandoning serious interest in these problems.

Interventions and Laws

We have been pursuing the idea that there is some sort of stable, third-person, answer to Why questions, and that it takes the form of counterfactual causality. So far, the results have been quite discouraging. We find that social science does not seem to have access to a scientific approach to the world that eludes everyday actors; instead, it has merely indistinct ideas about infinities of imaginary worlds.

How could we be led to center our theoretical vocabulary on such figments of our imagination? To a significant extent, this was because there was, perhaps naïvely, a belief that this imaginary world could be brought to actuality through force of will: the vision of the social planner (also see Soffer 1970; Barnes 2000: 104). The planner must be able to reassure his audience scientifically that he can make sure statements about a world that does not exist, or else he is unlikely to be entrusted with the weighty responsibility of building this world. The particular efficacy of the planner's will, however, requires that others—the planned—be predictable and constrained. Thus, the flip side of our counterfactual sense of causality was an equally vacuous understanding of social laws as forms of constraint (see Goldthorpe 2001: 8).

Of course, there are fields closely related to the social sciences in which the planner's vision has a fair chance of implementation, and in these fields a causal approach is not only warranted but is indeed necessary. In particular, in public health one *can* both carry out randomized allocations of persons to treatment and control groups, and use the results to determine which sorts of interventions are most likely to be efficacious. A vision of causality based on the experimental model works well here, even though it cannot necessarily be generalized to other cases (and it may resist a perfect formalization).[37] Indeed, when considering a policy recommendation, it would be criminally irresponsible *not* to think counterfactually, precisely because counterfactuals are about imaginary worlds, and policy making is all about realizing such imaginary worlds. I hope that my argument that we cannot define causality in counterfactual terms, and that we see no evidence for causal answers to Why questions, is not confused with the question of whether we should seek the best possible

---

[37] At the same time, it is worth emphasizing that the importance of the "control" for the determination of causality exists not because we define causality in counterfactual terms but because we want to make sure that our treatment *did* cause the outcome through the manipulation. If we could see all the chain of production, we would be unlikely to want a control.

answers to questions regarding the likely results of interventions. We should, but we should not confuse these with the *explanatory* task of social science.

The first thing to emphasize is that the counterfactual relations found by such policy studies need not map onto those in the everyday world. Let us return to our example of attempting to determine whether dropping out causes crime. We all understand that since students self-select into dropping out, we cannot use a mere comparison of the offending by dropouts to that of graduates to answer this question, nor can we solve these problems with control strategies, no matter how sophisticated. One impressive approach now is to arrange persons in terms of their predicted or estimated propensity to drop out, and only compare those of roughly equal propensity, some of whom (for, we hope, exogenous reasons) did end up dropping out and some of whom did not.[38] Thus, we can really only look at those who are on the fence regarding the decision to stay in school. This may well be an important question, and it may be related to effects of a policy that, say, imposed a waiting period on the decision to drop out. We might imagine that all persons have some underlying propensity to drop out, but that each's value rises and falls with different events. A person whose value is generally below some cutoff necessary to drop out but sometimes above the cutoff might take the action (perhaps later regretted) if dropping out was made easy; a mandatory waiting period, however, might cause this student to stay in school and end up graduating.

We note, of course, that this type of relation (the effects of dropping out on the fence-sitters) may not be what we think of if we are interested in the relation between dropping out and crime (for it might be, say, that the vast majority of dropout crimes are committed by those with a high propensity toward dropping out). In many cases, our causal gurus will admit this and simply insist that a true causal relation is one in which we can arbitrarily set the cause to any value. And yet, this makes little sense, even if we are primarily interested in interventional policies, for there are many causes that can only be manipulated indirectly. To stick with our case, we cannot directly get people to drop out (for "dropping out" is not the same as "being forced out of school," and "not dropping out" is not the same as "being prevented from dropping out"). But, let us say that dropping out is a function of academic discouragement and opportunity costs. We might be able to get people to drop out (or not drop out) by manipulating their level of discouragement or by changing their access to other activities. This means that we could not be sure that the results of our intervention have to do with the effect of dropping out on crime for there

---

[38]Various adjustments and weightings are used to leave this perfect case, but this is now widely accepted as the best—and only unambiguously defensible—practice.

may be many other things connecting crime to discouragement or to employment opportunities (cf. Cartwright 2007: 48, 52, 200, 247f).[39]

At the same time, we are at least approaching the formulation that might be relevant to a policy—not, Does dropping out cause crime? but, What happens if we try to lessen discouragement? We abandon the search for the causes of effects and resign ourselves to examining the effects of causes. We then may have to recognize that the single best way of determining the answer to our question—which is now a question of policy effects—is probably simply to try it out (also see the judicious discussion of Gangl [2010: 37]). Nothing could—or should—be as antithetical to the social science project of a deep and complete understanding of the patternings of social life than this sort of policy science, which should always avoid irresponsible guesswork (no matter how mathematically sophisticated) and simply try out pilot projects before committing public resources. Thus, the more we pursue the policy-related idea of cause, the farther we go toward brute action and an attempt to simulate it as best we can.

At the same time, we know that pilot projects have their own limitations: a proposed tutoring program for high school students may dramatically increase the probability of going to college among the treated—as long as not everybody else gets the treatment. We might then think that the only true way of determining the effects of an intervention is to do a full-scale run. But, even this is not true if we mean to assume that the results of a second run are the same as the first. As Lenin said, doing his own comparative historical analysis of the causes of revolution, a treatment that has one result one year may have the opposite result another year. People learn and sometimes do not make the same mistake twice. "One must use one's own brains and be able to find one's bearings in each separate case" (Lenin [1920] 1951: 394; also see 420).

The second thing is that even if interventions create certain effects, there is no reason to confuse them with whatever we might mean by the "effects" of dropping out in the natural world in equilibrium. Students of dominance hierarchies among animals were initially confounded by the complexity of naturalistic observation of animal communities and imagined that it would be simpler, more controlled, more "scientific," to take the animals in pairs, arrange for them to have bouts, and then re-create the overall hierarchy. This procedure turns out to be very reliable and very successful and in most cases has very little to do with how actual

---

[39] A related point, noted by Cartwright, is that it is wrong to think that we can identify effects as opposed to causes in systems of variables by noting which things can be manipulated without affecting other things. The mechanism of a watch causes the hands to move, but it does not stand to reason that if you twist the hands around, you will not wreck the mechanism inside.

hierarchies form. The fact that these effects *can* be robustly made and replicated, that they draw on real characteristics of the animals involved, and indeed that they generate important scientific information, must not distract us from the fact that we do *not* get an answer to the question with which the researchers began. The question was not, How can *we* create animal hierarchies? but, How do the *animals* create their hierarchies? So, too, many policy studies are not about, say, "neighborhood effects" but are about the effectual manipulation of neighborhood.

The third thing is that the importance of such counterfactual explorations of the effects of policy—and, we hope, the success of such explorations—in no way supports the idea that these analyses have stabilized some third-person form of causality that operates in our world. Rather than our policy investigations finding some sort of causal force that we may set up in opposition to first-person impulses, I see only an opposition between our own internal causality and those of other persons—lawmakers who willfully force their wishes on us. It is only a solipsistic view that leads us to think that our actions, and those of others, are two completely different things.[40]

In sum, there is, as there should be, a great deal of research working on better estimates and projections of the likely results of various interventions. Social scientists should know about these, and policy analysts should know about social science, but the two endeavors should not be confused. All our sophisticated methods are ways of making particular comparisons—there is no good reason to imagine that they are estimating causal effects as commonly understood. Therefore, there is no need to invent a ridiculous view of the world to justify such comparisons.

Most important, success in predicting the effects of interventions (should we have any) must not be confused with some third-person causality as something that cuts against, exists behind, or undermines personal causality. What we find here is just the personal causality of the powerful. Rather than the counterfactual approach offering us a distinct way to think about causality other than the commonsense one of willful persons making things happen (cf. Searle 1983: 135), it has merely returned us to it after a number of confusions and obscurations. So, rather than attempt to answer Why questions by defining causality as impersonal necessity, what if we were to take seriously personal efficacy? This is a form of causality that has first-person plausibility and lacks the particular problems that beset the counterfactual approach (although it may have its own problems). What happens when we attempt to systematize *this* notion of causality?

---

[40] I owe my understanding of the importance of this for the social sciences to Fran Holland. For many years, he patiently tried to make me understand this, and only recently have I appreciated his arguments.

ACTORS AND JUDGES

The Causal Tradition in Jurisprudence

As Tilly (1999: 265) has emphasized, "People ordinarily join (1) moral judgments, (2) conceptions of what is possible, (3) ideas of what is desirable within that realm of possibility, and (4) causal accounts of social life." He considered this to be a problem for social science, but as we shall see, these four points can lead to a coherent approach, in contrast to the conventional one in the social sciences, which allows for absurd counterfactuals and is unable to triage among possible "factors."[41] We saw that one commonsense notion of causality seems to privilege effective human intervention in the world, but it has also been repeatedly noted that in everyday life, causality seems to arise not (as Hume would imagine) from our investigations of inevitable relations of constant conjunction but from an interest in unique and generally problematic events (Ducasse [1924] 1969: 13, 21). As William James ([1907] 1946: 180) says, the search for causes "seems to have started in the question: 'Who, or what, is to blame?'"

Further, this commonsensical approach can be and has been systematized for that important class of events in which the cause of something actually matters to us, namely, law (also see Weber [1905] 1949: 169). Here, I rely on Hart and Honoré's classic (1959) analysis of principles of causation in Anglo-American law (again, I am here also influenced by Pepper 1966). My argument is not that sociologists should adopt the general framework developed by these legal theorists, but that it is noteworthy that the jurists were able to develop it with consistency in the first place. This suggests that basing causality in the root of phenomenological experience does not lead to contradiction or to emptiness.

Turning to law and in particular the Anglo-American tradition is not at all an idiosyncratic choice of venue. We shall see in Chapter 6 that the epistemic model of the social sciences is based on the incorrect assumption that all general thinking requires subsumptive concept formation. That is, for any particular case x, there is an abstract generality A into which our case can be placed, for $x \subseteq A$. The conviction that no other

---

[41]In a fuller discussion, in part drawing on Dewey and Mills, Tilly (2006: x, 15, 17, 19ff, 176) treated not only stories and technical accounts (which are both inherently causal) but also two noncausal (or formulaic) justifications, namely, conventions (which, like stories, are popular) and codes (which, like technical accounts, are specialized). Although still highlighting the limitations of stories (e.g., they tend to understate the importance of errors and unintended or indirect consequences), he discussed the relational situations under which different types of reasons are given. But, by seeing both stories and technical accounts as "causal," he considered it reasonable that social scientists propose causal accounts for the stories that actors tell—in other words, they have a kind of third-person causality that is allowed to overrule the causality of actors.

approach was possible was based on a disdain of the faculty of judgment that was part of the nineteenth-century quest for formalization in social thought. This approach to concept formation was paralleled in an idea of law that was more popular on the Continent than in England, namely, one that tried to work out all possibilities in advance through setting up classes into which any case would then be subsumed. Although there were important bases for subsumptive legal thinking in Roman law, part of the zeal with which this idea of law was pursued in the Continent came from the fact that this would, it was hoped, take power away from justices (who were, after all, often local nobilities) and put it in the hands of the legislature (see Weber 1978: 653–656, 762, 865–867). And, the legislature, as we shall see in our discussion of Kant (chapter 6), stood in the same relationship to the understanding that the judiciary does to the judgment.

Thus, the continental nations, still reeling from class warfare and working out their legal anthropologies in centralized bureaucracies, produced one particular notion of law and lawfulness; in England (and later America), where there was more of an unbroken tradition of local governance, there was never an uprooting of the idea of a fusion of "justice" and "common sense."[42] But, the social sciences found their inspiration in other areas and other traditions; while they moved toward a vision of generalization that was the epistemic equivalent of the *Code Napoléon*, it was American and English law that preserved an emphasis on the necessary role for judgment through the eyes of a common man who could be assumed to have fundamental competences.[43] Thus, the attempt to think through a general approach to causality using the faculty of judgment was undertaken not by social scientists, but by jurists.

In keeping with the first-person (or commonsensical) understanding of causality laid out above, this tradition of legal reasoning relies not so much on counterfactuals as on the use of human motivation as a benchmark. The causality of A in scenario 1 is paradigmatic—conscious and effective willfulness of a person. But, some other factors can enter to "negative" the causal effect of A's initial act. The factors that can so negative are important. The first is the free will of a second person. As Hart and Honoré

---

[42]It is worth emphasizing that the idea of a "commoner" came from the organization of agriculturalists into a "commons," and that the British "House of Commons" meant not so much those who are not noble as those who represent the geographically based nature of social organization—the more egalitarian spatial organization, as opposed to the more aristocratic temporal ordering of descent (see Bergson 1911 for this distinction).

[43]Weber (1978: 656, 889–892) gave sustained attention in his sociology of law to the difference between various legal systems, and he noted how the Anglo-American tradition deviated from the formal model. Yet, when it came time to make theories, he concluded that law necessarily moved toward increasing formality at the expense of substantive rationality.

Causality and Persons

(1959: 129) put it, "The free, deliberate and informed act or omission of a human being, intended to produce the consequence which is in fact produced, negatives causal connection."[44] Thus, in scenario 2, C's free, informed, and deliberate act intervenes between A's act and B's death, so A is not the cause of B's death. If, however, C's act was not free, because A had compelled C to act, or not deliberate, because C was unsound of mind or acting under a reflex, A would likely be seen as the cause of B's death.

The second factor that can negative causality is some sort of chance occurrence beyond what a reasonable person in A's position could imagine. For example (call this scenario 7), if A knocks down B in the street and B is run over by a car and dies, A has caused B's death. Any rational person would understand the risk of a prone person being run over by a car on a street. If, however (scenario 8), A knocks B down in the sidewalk, and at that moment an air conditioner falls from a window onto B's head and B dies, A has not caused B's death.[45]

It is worth stressing that here causality is meant seriously—it is not simply a loose word substituting for responsibility.[46] Further, we see that here probabilistic reasoning enters in a coherent way (more or less in a Fisherian way). The reason that *A caused B's* death in scenario 7 is not that there is an infinite set of futures for B, but a greater share of those in

---

[44] The exception is that there can be a moral obligation that means that an intentional act—for example, to rescue someone in danger—does not negative causal connection; hence, a would-be rescuer who is harmed in the act of rescue may demand redress from a person whose negligence made the danger appear in the first place (139). There are also cases in which one person may cause another's act; these generally involve intentional threats, lies, or exercise of authority (330–334).

[45] Similarly, the act of an animal or an irresponsible human only negatives a causal connection if the act of the animal is not seen as intrinsic to its nature. If A drives recklessly and frightens a horse that kicks B, standing behind the horse, and B dies, then A has caused B's death because by their nature horses may kick when startled. But, if A knocks B down, a horse then jumps on B, and B dies, A has not caused B's death because it is not generally believed to be in the nature of the horse to jump on prone persons. This is related to the notion of "adequate causation" that Weber took from von Kries, who also contrasted an adequate cause to a "chance cause," the latter being one that while leading to the effect in this particular case, does not in general tend toward the effect (see Buss 1999: 323).

[46] For example, an adult may be responsible for damage caused by her underage child but not have caused this damage herself. Or, to adapt an example analyzed (I think incorrectly) by Beebee (2004), consider a pet sitter who neglects to take a pet to the vet when a certain symptom arises. If that symptom is obviously worrisome, we might reasonably say that the absence of taking to the vet was a cause of the animal's death. However, if the symptom is subtle so that a reasonable person would not understand the danger threatened, we might say that the absence is in this case not a cause. The pet sitter, however, might be responsible in both cases.

which A pushed B into the street have runnings over than the set in which A did not push B. It is that really there are two types of streets, ones that will soon have a car coming down them and ones that do not. We know this, but until the car comes we do not know if this street is a car-about-to-come street or a car-not-about-to-come street. Thus, we know that this street is a street, but we cannot yet distinguish between these two important subsets. Further, any reasonable person understands that the set of car-about-to-come streets is a significant portion of the whole. (Therefore, the class of streets also may include some elephant-about-to-come streets, but a reasonable person knows that this is not a significant portion.)

So, when we push someone into a street, we do not push someone into a street that with probability p will then have a car coming down it, which therefore makes the push a probabilistic cause. Rather, we push someone into a street that *at that very moment* is part of a set that a reasonable person understands includes many members with soon-to-appear cars. The "probability" only exists while the roulette wheel of life spins—the causal action itself is deterministic, and this was the willful pushing of a person into a street, a member of the joint set of streets with and without cars coming. This is in contrast to the idea of probabilistic causality, in which the knocking that raises the probability of the accident is a cause whether or not the accident occurs.

In the commonsensical approach, then, probabilism and causality are both present, but they are not wedded in the wishy-washy way characteristic of the social sciences in which one is used to negate or at least moderate the other. The mere fact (if it turns out to be a fact) that being knocked into the street "often" leads to being run over does not establish probabilistic causality—we can imagine scenarios in which A knocks B into the street and B is run over, but *in this case*, A did not cause B's death. In the commonsensical understanding, we argue that causality can be established *in each particular case*, even though the first act does not "invariably" lead to the effect (Hart and Honoré 1959: 16, 21, 45, 366). This is in contrast to the social sciences, in which we make a virtue of necessity by taking crude data on the copresence of two events, data that are never as crisp as our simplistic mental models imply, and invent a form of probabilistic causality whose only virtue is that it corresponds to the sort of data we have—indeed, it merely relabels the data "cause."

Action and Ends

Why was it possible for legal theorists to develop a consistent idea of causality without relying on counterfactuals? For one, as Hart and Honoré (1959: 8f, 10, 15, 30–33, 43, 383) emphasize, in our everyday lives when we ask for a causal explanation, we are asking for an "inquest" into a particular case (although not necessarily a single *event*) and not a covering law that could lead to predictions, although generalizations may be *used* in the assigning of causality. Second, we generally conduct such an inquest because of a deviation from our expectation (Kahneman and Miller 1986). Thus, rather than conduct our comparison between the observed world and every possible counterfactual, our comparison is generally a simple one: we compare what a reasonable person would expect given some situation to what was actually observed. Therefore, when we expect oxygen to be present, as in a general outdoor setting, we do not say that the presence of oxygen caused a house fire, despite the validity of the counterfactual (were there no oxygen, no fire would have taken place). However, should oxygen be present where it is not expected (in a vacuum chamber in a scientific laboratory, say), then we might indeed say that the presence of oxygen (and not the sparks that are deliberately produced) caused the fire.[47] It is even possible for people to identify different causes of the same phenomenon without some being wrong or having to accept every previous event as a legitimate cause.

This may seem to return us to the arbitrary choice that we found frustrating any identification of SCF with a cookbook approach to scientific causal analysis: our answer seems to depend on the choice of counterfactual. But, there is a key difference, one that turns out to lead to consensus as opposed to arbitrariness. We found that a counterfactual approach requires that we compare the observed reality R to some imaginary world W that is, we hope, among the closest of a set of worlds $\{W\}$ that constitute a meaningful basis of comparison given the analyst's understanding of a question about causality. In some cases, we can indicate the subset of worlds that are of relevance to our interest through emphasis. Thus, if the question is, Why did Adam eat the apple? and our analyst implicitly means, Why did Adam eat *the apple*? (and not, Why did Adam *eat* the apple?) we might produce a world similar to our world in every respect except that instead of an apple tree, a pear tree stands in its place. Given that in this circumstance Adam was unlikely to eat the apple, we may say that the existence of a tree was a cause of his eating. Of course, it is also true that the rain that watered the tree, the axe that did not chop it down, and so on and so forth, ad astra, were also valid causes and hence valid (although frustrating) answers to the question.

In the commonsensical tradition, however, we compare not to the *analyst's* chosen counterfactual, but to the consensual expectation of a community. We are unlikely to ask why Adam ate an apple, or at least, we are unlikely to ask about the *causes* of this action because a straightforward

---

[47]Thus, Ducasse ([1924] 1969: 33f, 54f) seems to be wrong to assume that in our everyday understanding a cause must be a change. Although this is often the case, it need not always be. For example, were a metal tank improperly left in a room with a magnetic resonance imaging (MRI) machine (as occurred in the death of Michael Colombini), such that when the switch activating the magnet was turned on, the tank flew into the patient and killed him, we would see the cause of the death not the preceding change of throwing the switch, but the anomalous presence of the tank.

human action is interpreted under the rubric of motivation. We understand that people eat apples, and this requires no inquest. Were Adam to spit out the apple, however, it would raise an eyebrow, and it would not be at all stupid to ask what caused the spitting out. Here, we would be comparing not to one or many of an infinite number of arbitrarily chosen imaginary worlds, but a single intersubjectively valid expectation—that people who bite into apples swallow them.

This means that we are able to sort our causal questions and answers into three categories that SCF cannot distinguish: reasonable causes, unreasonable causes, and answers to questions that are not worth asking in the first place. Both the commonsensical and the counterfactual approaches might pose the question, "Why did you not show up for work yesterday?" although the commonsensical would stop with "I was sick" while the simple counterfactualist could be dragged into accepting "the absence of bandits kidnapping me and taking me to work" and so on, although note that if the question were phrased, "Why were you at home all day yesterday?" this does not change the commonsensical answer (with its implicit focus of contrast), while the SCF version now includes causes such as "my house was not destroyed by dinosaurs" and "my great-great-great-grandfather." But SCF also allows the question, "Why did you go to work yesterday?" which is not usually a good candidate for a commonsensical causal inquiry. And, depending on the implicit contrast, all sorts of silly things can be said. For example, if yesterday was April 21, and I mean "... instead of celebrating Iggy Pop's birthday?" then my answer might be, "Because you are a wimp." Although, come to think of it, if I meant "... instead of celebrating Max Weber's birthday?" the answer would be "Because you are not intellectual enough," and if I meant "... instead of celebrating grounation day" (an important Rastafarian holiday), the answer might be "Because you hew to Babylon" and so on. All of these may be true in a way, but that is not in itself sufficient justification for saying them for they are of an order of truth *less* than the commonsensical answers "I always do," "If I don't, I get in trouble," or "I have a lot to do." Further, all turn on the worldview of the questioner and not that of the actor.

The commonsensical approach also allows us to make a distinction between cause and condition, a distinction that confounds the conventional vocabulary in the social sciences. In everyday life, just as a successful willful action is the paradigmatic form of cause—an "end in view"—so the inert material *used* by the willing actor as *means* is the paradigmatic form of condition. We often may distinguish between cause and condition on the basis of their abnormality as opposed to normality (the abnormal being treated as cause).[48] This view of causality also stops the regress that

---

[48]Finally, as (Ducasse [1924] 1969: 18f) points out, contrary to the Humean/Millsian/counterfactualist position in which causes and conditions are both necessary, in everyday speech we are far more likely to see conditions as necessary and causes as sufficient.

leads to the inability of conventional social science to establish a fundamental difference between scenarios 1 and 6. Our everyday inquest into causality does not go beyond deliberate intentionality; thus, if we ask, Why did A choose to knock B? and learn that A was angry with B, we do not treat the anger as the cause of the death. Similarly, if A used an umbrella to knock B down, then we do not need to inquire from whom A first got the umbrella (Hart and Honoré 1959: 31, 39f).

An additional advantage of this approach to causality is related to the fact that it supports the sort of transitivity that is of most interest to us. Here, I mean the kind of transitivity that is implied by the key case of instrumental action: humans accomplish something "by means of" something else. There is something I want to do—perhaps have an apple that is currently high in a tree. I cannot reach it directly, but I notice a seesaw with a rock at one end. I stomp on the other end, and the stone flies up and hits the apple, causing it to fall. Thus, by means of the stomp on the seesaw, I got the apple. Now according to SCF, my stomp caused the rock to fly up. But, *did* the rock hitting the apple cause it to fall? That is, if I had not stomped, would the apple not have fallen into my hands (implied if we treat the causality of SCF as transitive)? This is assuredly not the case, for if the rock had not brought down the apple, *I would have found another way*. This is what it means to have a will.

Fritz Heider (1958: 104–108; cf. Reed 1996: 12) called this "equifinality" and distinguished the causality of human action from that of natural causality. Think of a rock rolling down a mountain, moved by gravity—as it encounters various objects, it is deflected right or left, and its ultimate resting point has only to do with the sequence of obstacles encountered. Now, think of a person climbing *up* the mountain: she too will come to obstacles, but they will not affect her ultimate destination—she will reorient to make sure that she ends up in the same place. A notion of causality that cannot deal with the transitivity inherent in by-means-of is a poor choice for the study of social action. The commonsensical approach looks better and better.

It is not that there are no examples that frustrate this approach to causation; there are, and they are famous precisely because they confuse our intuitive sense of causality. The most popular is the case of the traveler C in the desert with a canteen of water. Suspect A puts poison in the canteen, while the other (B) independently and later drills a small hole in the canteen, allowing the poisoned water to escape. C dies of thirst (although later than he would have died of poisoning). This case is difficult for the causality-as-impulsion view precisely because it involves not only the confusion of culpability and causation (the frame encourages us to assume that only one suspect should hang) but also omission. Imagine what may seem formally identical to the desert traveler scenario according to some counterfactual approaches: Mice get into the pantry. If left to themselves, the mice will eat up all the food in one day. So, we let in two dogs, which spend one day chasing the mice and eating them, after which point the dogs eat up all the food in the pantry.

In this case, the fact that the food would have been eaten anyway, and at an earlier time, in no way confuses the commonsense approach from concluding that the dogs *did* eat the food—because they did. Causality as impulsion works wonderfully, then, in all cases that we would want to defend most vigorously as truly causal (which is not true for counterfactualism). There are cases of omission that it handles well when there is a strong confidence that the omitted act could be reasonably and rightfully expected. Outside such cases, it is hardly clear that a sensible person would want to invoke causality at all.

In sum, this approach works precisely because it relies on our intuitive understanding of cause and grounds adjudication in the faculty of judgment, as opposed to attempting to subsume cases under a definition. And it is this attempt to "define" causality that has been the root of the problems we have reviewed. It seems that the counterfactual definition, like all definitions of causality, is a dead end because, as Kant argued long ago, causality is one of those primitives that guide our reason. If we attempt to define such primitives or use them as premises in syllogistic reasoning, we can produce antithetical statements.[49] We do not actually need to waste time with defining such concepts. In algebraic set theory, there were a number of serious attempts to define "set," as it seemed impossible to begin an axiomatic science in which the key term was undefined. But, all definitions of set turned out to be recursive (e.g., to resolve themselves to "a set is a set of elements . . . "). Definitions were abandoned, and work continued.

Further, just because we have a single word *cause* does not mean that we should expect that there should be one definition of cause across fields and processes (Cartwright 2004; also perhaps Hitchcock 2003).[50] We may find that *many* of the sorts of processes we would want to consider causal have common features, but there is no reason to assume that, by the nature of the beast, some set of features is present in all cases of causality and only such cases. Sometimes, we are simply not so lucky.

Thus, in everyday life, where we do not precisely define cause, we are better at knowing what we mean. In the Anglo-American commonsensical/legal tradition, if there is uncertainty, the arbiter is not the philosopher's definition, but the judgment of a person struggling to forecast what the

---

[49]Put another way, it is entirely plausible to maintain that there is a cognitive element ("cause") that works robustly in everyday life but that necessarily resists a distinct and unambiguous formalization.

[50]In contrast to such a "thin" vision of causality evacuated of all content, Cartwright proposes that there are many particular processes that we should see as causal—for example, one thing poisons, another clogs, and so on—and yet there may be no useful abstraction encompassing all these cases. It is worth pointing out that this accords with the general arguments made here regarding the nature of successful explanation and the error in assuming that all generalities require subsumptive abstractions.

Causality and Persons

reasonable and responsible adults in the community would say. It is worth emphasizing that I am not arguing that social scientists should take the commonsensical approach to causality and begin to explain deviations from the collective expectation of academics. Indeed, I will argue the opposite, that we should be attempting to explain regularity itself. My argument here is that the root use of causality in social life has proved successful not because it follows the strictures of SCF but because it relies on intersubjectively valid judgment (explored in chapter 6), in this case, that of the reasonable adult member of the community.

Of course, sociologists are right to raise their eyebrows immediately when there is such a reliance on the unspecified, generic, "reasonable" person. As Dore (2005) argues, these common-law ideas actually paper over changes regarding from whose eyes we see things. (Is the "reasonable person" really the "reasonable male"?) This is an inescapable conclusion and means that where this validity is validly questioned, causality is reduced. In particular, we have seen that causality by omission relies on consensual understandings of what may reasonably be expected. Absent such understandings, then it would make little sense for a sociological analyst to argue for such a form of causality. Other forms of impulsion, however, are more robust than causality by omission in that they are less likely to disappear when we move away from one community of thought. Thus, even though social science is not immune to the cognitive difficulties that arise in social relations of animosity, exclusion, and oppression, it also is not condemned to silence until we enter a millennial period of perpetual peace and concord. The more robust causal associations survive not merely the consideration of a single privileged judge (historically associated with the nobility), nor even a jury of a dozen citizens (or men), but nearly all, when it comes to tracing the effective production constituted by a chain of causes.

Common Sense and Nonsense in Causality

As a demonstration of the force of such reasoning, consider the following summary judgment of the cause of the death of Alexander Hamilton (Hamilton 1910: 423ff; I have reduced this breathless sentence somewhat for purposes of brevity): The undersigned,

> duly chosen, and who being then and there duly sworn and charged to inquire for the People of the State of New York, when where and by what means[51] the said Alexander Hamilton came to his death, do, upon their oath, say that Aaron Burr ... on the eleventh day of July, in the year last aforesaid, with force and arms, in the County of Bergen and State of New Jersey, in and upon the said Alexander Hamilton, in the peace of God and of the People of the said State of New Jersey, then and there being

[51]Note that the charge is not to determine responsibility or culpability but to determine the cause.

feloniously, willfully and of his malice aforethought, did make an assault and that the said Aaron Burr a certain pistol of the value of One Dollar charged and loaded with gun-powder and a leaden bullet which he, the said Aaron Burr, then and there had held in his right hand, to, at and against the right side of the belly of the said Alexander Hamilton, did then and there shoot off and discharge, by means whereof he, the said Aaron Burr, feloniously willfully and of malice aforethought did then and there given unto him the said Alexander Hamilton, with the leaden bullet aforesaid, so as aforesaid, shot off and discharged out of the pistol aforesaid by the force of the gunpowder aforesaid, upon the right side of the belly of him, the said Alexander Hamilton, a little above the hip, one mortal wound penetrating the belly of him, the said Alexander Hamilton, of which said mortal wound he, the said Alexander Hamilton, from the said eleventh day of July, in the year aforesaid, until the twelfth day of July in the same year. . . . did languish and languishing did live, on which twelfth day of July in the said year the said Alexander Hamilton . . . of the mortal wound aforesaid died.

In what way did Aaron Burr cause the death of Alexander Hamilton? It is certainly not that a counterfactual demonstrates that had Aaron Burr not fired at Alexander Hamilton, Alexander Hamilton would not have died. Hamilton, like Socrates, was a mortal and doomed to die eventually, and thus while Burr's act might be sufficient for his death, it was certainly not necessary. Nor is it that death invariably followed Burr's firing—Burr had previously fought a duel with John Church, Hamilton's brother-in-law. While Church was wounded, he survived. Could we say that while Hamilton would have died had not Burr fired, he would not have died "in *this* way at *this* time" (cf. Lewis 2000: 185–188) and hence we can affirm that Burr was the cause of *this* death of Hamilton's? The aforementioned John Church's act of volunteering his duel pistols, or Hamilton's friend Nathaniel Pendleton's act of arranging the time, also were necessary for things unfolding in *this* way—indeed, the doctor who attended Hamilton after his injury also contributed to Hamilton dying in precisely the way and at the time that he did (compare the discussion of Hart and Honoré 1959: 398–400; Lewis 2000: 194 concedes and accepts this implication). If a friend had intervened, pulling Hamilton slightly downward so that Burr's shot ended up in Hamilton's heart as opposed to liver, we would not say that the friend had caused Hamilton's death because, were it not for the friend, Hamilton would not have died in *this* way.

To return to the distinction between necessary and sufficient causality, we might propose that this inquest emphasizes the sufficiency of the causes and not their necessity. But, the conventional idea of sufficient causes does not wholly capture the nature of the causes as uncovered here. First, by definition, if A is sufficient for B, then there can be no state in which we have A but not B. Thus, if A is "Aaron Burr shooting off and discharging a bullet against the right side of the belly of Alexander Hamilton" and B is "Alexander Hamilton died," we must reject the idea that A is the cause of B since, as we know, said Alexander "did languish and languishing did live" for a day before dying.

The immediate impulse is to mend things by throwing in intervening elements: Burr caused the wound, and the wound caused the death. This unfortunately is an impossible fix (akin to Zeno's paradox); because time is infinitely divisible, this leads to an infinite regress.[52] This attempted fix accords with conventional sociological practice (in which our methods of control lead to increasingly unreasonable arguments at odds with accepted understandings of causality[53]); it considers each event an instant in which time is simply a subscript. But causes are not things that happen "in" time (whatever that might mean); they are things that *take* time. Were it not for the concrete duration required by history, all the sufficient causes would happen instantaneously, and the universe would be over, as Bergson (1911) noted.

The second way in which the idea of a sufficient cause falls short of capturing the robust notion of causality as used in everyday life is that it still relies on an implicit counterfactual. To say that A is a sufficient cause of B means that we cannot conceive of a world in which A occurred and B did not. Although we encounter many relatively unimaginative persons in academia, I have never met anyone with such limited mental horizons as to be unable to imagine, say, that Aaron Burr could shoot at the right side of Alexander Hamilton and Hamilton might not die. But neither do we mean that the shooting "probabilistically" caused the death in a large set of worlds.

In sum, when we—that is, we as intelligent people who mean what we say and have things we are trying to do in this world—speak of causality regarding actual events that we believe to have occurred (say, that A caused B), we do not mean that in an imaginary world without A there would have been no B, we mean that A *did*—in this very world—cause B. The gold standard of establishing causality is not a comparison to an imaginary world but a close examination of the cascade of productions linking a cause (e.g., Burr's willful firing) to an effect (Hamilton's death).[54]

---

[52]This point was made by the Indian accidentalist (yadrccha-vāda) school, reviewed by fifteenth-century Jaina philosopher Gunaratna as follows: they point out that "fire is produced by fire as well as by the flints; The plantain-tree grows out of the stem of a plantain-tree as well as out of the seed." Thus, to say "the seed causes the fully grown tree" is not an acceptable linkage of unique cause and effect since the fully grown tree, it must be admitted, also grows from the sapling, so it is just as correct to say the sapling causes the fully grown tree and so on for an infinite number of alternative states. See Chattopadhyaya (1977: 178; 1991: 58); Lieberson (1997: 30) makes a similar point.

[53]In response to the person who shows that guns kill people, we correct her by pointing out that "guns don't kill people, bullets kill people." The next researcher gets a publication by demonstrating that "bullets don't kill people, holes kill people," then on to "holes don't kill people, blood loss kills people," and so on.

[54]Hence, Elster's (1989) understanding that thinking in terms of mechanisms cuts against a counterfactual approach to causality.

We may in some cases use a counterfactual to illustrate causality, but we do not rely on it precisely *because*, as Tilly says, we appeal to phenomenologically valid understandings of motivation and judgment. If as social scientists we have difficulty explaining how *this* idea of cause has any relation to our professional definition, this is as much as to say that we do not, as social scientists, use the word *cause* properly and do not in fact take it seriously. Indeed, despite all our solemn protestations of having found the truly scientific approach, and all of our various Band-Aids, such as probabilistic causality, we are left with the most fundamental problem with the conventional definition of cause: far from being a sober scientific concept, our idea of cause refers to an imaginary world (cf. Dawid 2000).[55] In our conventional practice, to say that the secession of the South caused the American Civil War is to say that in an imaginary world in which the South did not secede, there would be no Civil War. This world does not exist, and so the argument is, to put it mildly, of a strange nature. Of course, here there is one unique event. But, the definition of cause in the social sciences means that *all* our causal statements, even those referring to multiple instantiations, are statements about imaginary worlds. To say that education causes liberalism is not to say that more educated people are more liberal; it is to say that in the world that does not exist, where the people with less education are given more, these people are (on average) more liberal than their mirror counterparts in the world that *does* exist.

This, then, is what follows from our attempt to give consistent, third-person accounts. The valiant defenders of science who have volunteered to protect causality to the last man are indeed standing at the gate, but they are facing the wrong way. With swords drawn they stand in fantasyland, chasing away any incursions from reality. But must we choose to take the fork in the road posed by Why questions toward a fantasy world? The answer that immediately comes to our lips is, What else can we do? For we assume that we cannot allow people to give their *own* answers to Why questions. Their answers will be justifications, rationalizations, and so on. Even when people *try* to answer these questions honestly, they will repress crucial parts of the story. In other words, we cannot make any use of first-person responses because they are inherently untrustworthy. This

---

[55]Lewis (1973b: 84–88), the most rigorous thinker on these matters, understands that he has to defend the existence of such imaginary worlds. These other worlds do not "actually" exist because by *actual* we mean precisely to exclude these other worlds, but Lewis is consistent enough to maintain that there "really are" other possible worlds. Are there possible other worlds? I do not know. I do know that other worlds are thinkable, but it seems a trivial and misleading use of the word *possible* to mean that it is equivalent to "thinkable." I would not want a science that depended on assuming the universal equation of thinkable and possible.

error is rooted in the view of subjectivity presented by social sciences, a view that may loosely be called the "Freudo-Durkheimian" as it casually synthesizes errors made by each of these two schools. The next two chapters look at each in turn to determine whether in fact our dim view of first-person reports is really warranted.

Chapter 3

Authority and Experience

PSYCHOLOGY VERSUS PSYCHIATRY

In chapter 2, we saw the difficulties that arise when we attempt to answer Why questions with third-person, causal answers. Still, the social sciences have insisted that this is the most defensible way of constructing explanations—that however circular and impossible the third-person approach is, it is better than any first-person one.

Fortunately for contemporary social sciences, there is at hand a nearly wholesale denial of the objectivity of individuals' self-understandings, namely, the work of Sigmund Freud, a set of mutually supporting doctrines that have permeated intellectual discourse in general and the social sciences in particular. While few read the early work of Freud, they need not do so to believe vaguely that somewhere it has been shown that people deny their true motivations because they have suppressed certain desires, thoughts, or memories.[1] And most important, the development of Freud's set of doctrines illustrates the inherent problems with answers to Why questions that allow for the negation of first-person perspectives.

Sigmund Freud was not, by temperament, cut out for science. But the greatest problems came not from his deliberate distortions and fabrications—rather, the problems followed naturally from the social situation in which a Why question could be asked of another human being and a response ignored. The resulting doctrines certainly would support any attempt to downgrade the seriousness of the insight of everyday actors; indeed, these doctrines could do nothing else, being predicated on that assumption. Thus, we reach a circular set of ideas, a model for making truth that argues that we can further dispense with actors' self-understandings because we have dispensed with them already. To see the source of that model, we can investigate the birth of psychology.[2]

---

[1]Further, one of the closest current theoretical undertakings in the social sciences to what is proposed here, namely, the field theory of Pierre Bourdieu, deliberately incorporates these planks into its model of action and hence defines itself as "socio-analysis" (later dropping the hyphen to indicate greater closeness, as pointed out by Fourny 2000).

[2]The argument made in this chapter relies in part on claims that, while no longer seriously questioned in the history of psychology, may strike some readers

The Birth of Psychology

> Never was a psychologist prouder than when he could say: *A* is not really *A* but something else.
> —Koffka (1935: 178f)

Psychology as an academic science was basically born in Germany in the late nineteenth century. As Ben-David and Collins (1966) have shown in their foundational study, the field was more or less the result of philosophers attempting to answer old questions with new methods, methods more in keeping with changes that had taken place in the academic world. These psychologists replaced the philosopher's emphasis on introspection with experiments that focused largely on perception. The leader of this movement was Wilhelm Wundt, who, though somewhat anticipated by Fechner, basically invented experimental psychology. Wundt not only legitimized psychology as an empirical science but also influenced other social thinkers looking for a way to survive in a changing academic world.

This new psychology was not only German in origin, but there were a number of German intellectual trends that were to prove extremely strong in the new discipline. In particular, there was in the German natural sciences a strong "developmental-comprehensive tradition" in which truth was understood to be both wholistic (requiring an understanding of the relations of different parts) and developmental (as opposed to static).[3]

It is Goethe who was unanimously considered the great exemplar of this general tradition, but in the early twentieth century it was revived by the work of Cassirer. Cassirer (1922: 36ff) saw the relation between Goethe's comprehensive/developmental approach and medieval or magical thought: what was crucial was the assumed correspondence between the inner and the outer, the microcosm and the macrocosm. Cassirer took this as an implicit criticism of twentieth-century science that, he argued, "in order to grasp something . . . must first decompose it into elementary variations. The form of the whole, as it might be available for either sensory perception or pure intuition (*Anschauung*) is lost, and its place we have a specific rule of change" (Cassirer 1922: 33; also [1925] 1955: 47f, 61).[4]

---

in the social sciences as overly strong. For this reason, more complete discussion of these points is pursued in footnotes, and the footnotes to this portion are somewhat more extensive than in other places. Those who do not find these claims surprising can omit the footnotes without loss to the argument.

[3] A second German characteristic of the new experimental method was, according to William James ([1890] 1950: I, 192), that "it taxes patience to the utmost, and could hardly have arisen in a country whose natives could be *bored*."

[4] Cassirer ([1923] 1953: 113) did not, however, think that the immediacy of mysticism was a viable option for modern philosophical thought.

This basic conviction was one of the key insights of the *Gestalt* school of German psychology associated with Wertheimer, Koffka, Köhler, and Lewin, explored in more detail in chapter 5. While this was, of course, only one branch of the new German experimental psychology, it was a particularly distinctive and influential one. Thus, while German psychology was not wholly Gestalt, Gestalt psychology was wholly German (cf. Ash 1998: 7, 138) in its return to this understanding of the correspondence between outer and inner when accounting for perception.

Indeed, perception was in many ways the model for the Gestalt theorists' understanding of psychological functioning as a whole. These psychologists assumed that it was futile to try to understand psychological processes without noting that these processes were part of an interaction between a sentient organism and its environment. Further, evolutionary theory made them expect that our perceptual system would be reasonably well adapted and hence able to successfully retrieve needed information from this environment. We might summarize by saying that Germany had pioneered the development of a would-be scientific approach to psychology, and one notable branch of this scientific psychology, which would be identified as the Gestalt or field approach, incorporated other distinctively German intellectual tendencies pertaining to wholistic and environmental analysis.

Of course, it is easy to simplify the diversity of intellectual life in any nation for the purposes of painting a picture of national characters. Yet, the distinctiveness of the German approach to psychology was clear enough to contemporaries that an aspiring French social scientist such as Emile Durkheim would travel to Germany to learn from Wundt and would write appreciative reviews for French social scientists describing the German approach (see Durkheim [1887] 1987). (A discussion of Durkheim's psychology is the subject of the next chapter.) Indeed, the national traditions were important enough that Simon Deploige (himself Belgian) criticized Durkheim's work for its Germanic nature ("German input is overwhelmingly preponderant").[5] But in the exact same year (1885) that Durkheim was going to Germany to learn from an experimental academic psychologist (see Lukes 1985), a German was going to France to learn a different psychology.

A Clinical Psychology

This was Sigmund Freud, a young physician, who was going to Paris in 1885 to study with "the great Name of [Jean Martin] Charcot."[6] (Here, I rely predominantly on the work of Gay [1988: 46–52].) The result was to have such an impact on the nature of claims about motivations in the social sciences that it is worthy of close attention. Previous to this trip,

---

[5]Durkheim ([1913] 1980: 160) was reduced to pointing to the profound influence of Comte on his own work.

[6]Of course, Freud was Austrian. Whether that makes him a German I leave to the Austrians and Germans to decide. But, the parallel is too neat to waste.

Freud was an aspiring doctor whose one claim to fame was an enthusiastic endorsement of the general value of cocaine, which he prescribed, distributed, and consumed in liberal quantities, in all cases with largely unhappy results.[7] While Freud was a man generally jealous not to appear a follower, he never denied that Charcot inspired him to ecstatic heights of hero worship, not only by his general personal charisma, but also by the boldness of his new theories, specifically pertaining to the treatment of hysteria.[8]

Charcot's work must be seen in the context of what Foucault has called "the birth of the asylum"—a new institutional structure for dealing with the insane.[9] Just as the dramatic increase in general hospitalization gave French physicians a surplus of material from which to learn, and gave French medicine a decidedly clinical twist, so it was the creation of the mental hospitals that allowed the development of psychiatry as a specialization (also see Williams 1992: 97). In the words of Starr (1982: 55, 72f), "The mental asylum created not only a new institutional market for doctors, but also a new sphere in which . . . there was relatively little resistance to [their] authority."

As Foucault ([1961] 1988: 251, 269, 276f) said, somewhat poetically but with sufficient empirical warrant, with the rise of the asylum "something had been born, which was no longer repression, but authority." The new reformers created a role for a doctor who would enter the world of the unreasonable and, by dint of his personal authority, force them toward reason. This new doctor-patient relationship—a relationship of moral and social authority that drew its strength from the social relations of the asylum—was crucial to the new psychiatry. But, practitioners did not consciously make this relationship the center of the theoretical development of their practice. At least not until Charcot: he not only emphasized the therapeutic effects of this authority but also was a pioneer in the use of hypnotism to dramatically accentuate them.[10] The new psychiatry, argued Foucault ([1961] 1988: 275f), implied a patient completely empty of his

---

[7] On Freud's addiction, see his letter to Fliess of June 12, 1895 (Freud [1887–1904] 1985: 132).

[8] The personal impact Charcot made on Freud—who named his first son Jean Martin after him—cannot be exaggerated. Freud translated Charcot's works, quoted him as an authority, hung an engraving of Charcot giving a public presentation in his consulting room, and indeed seems to have had a "crush" on him (in a letter, Freud noted the danger of his falling for Charcot's daughter, "for nothing is more dangerous than a young woman who resembles a man whom you admire" [Bonduelle 1995b: 285]).

[9] Indeed, Charcot worked under a huge painting of Pinel freeing the insane from their chains (Freud [1893] 1962: 18), an image that was the center of the reform of the treatment of mental illness discussed by Foucault.

[10] Disappointed in poor results, Charcot increasingly relied on hypnosis to study as opposed to treat hysteria (Macmillan 1997: 70), a transition Freud himself was later to make for the same reasons.

or her own determinations, totally submitting to the magic-like will of the doctor who incarnated reason: Charcot found such an object of practice and subject of study in the hypnotized patient.

This breakthrough of Charcot's, agreed supporters and detractors alike, had to be understood in terms of the institutional context in which he worked, namely, the largest charitable hospital for women in Europe, one largely filled with elderly and indigent patients (Owen 1971: 38; Goetz 1995b: 19f; Gelfand 1995c: 39; Bonduelle 1995c: 62ff). There were two important features of this context. The first was the relative powerlessness of the inhabitants, who were used to exhibit various maladies to students and doctors in assorted public settings. This supported the power of the physician as an authority figure, facilitating both the hypnotic state and the suggestion that almost certainly was responsible for the appearance of regularity in the phases of hysteria thus induced.[11] The second was the clinical setting, which offered an alternative basis for the production of knowledge claims; alternative, that is, to the German laboratory, widely considered to be France's scientific rival.[12] France was unlikely to best German science on its own turf: laboratory work in research institutions unconnected to hospitals. Instead, Charcot shifted the venue to a clinical approach, which he said "one might call the French tradition," as a different grounds for the production of truth claims and a way for France to make up for its second-place position in terms of medical research (Gelfand 1995a: 244; 1995c: 48, 56, 58; Bonduelle 1995c: 72ff).[13]

There is certainly an elective affinity between such a clinical relationship to "patients" (those who are acted upon) and hierarchical authority; Charcot

---

[11]Even at the time, others were unable to reproduce the "stages" that Charcot was convinced were fundamental to hysteria. Because Charcot made no attempt to shelter patients about to be examined from information about the results of sessions with other patients, and noted that some phenomena required practice, others concluded that suggestion was necessary for the production of the facts supporting Charcot's theory. Freud, though familiar with some of these critiques, fatally refused to accept the importance of suggestion (Macmillan 1997: 41f, 44–47, 65f; also James [1890] 1950: I, 203, II, 594, 598f, 601).

[12]Germany did shortly begin a clinic-building effort, but these clinics were attached to universities (see Engstrom 2003).

[13]While Charcot was originally influenced by and sympathetic to the German approach, he strongly felt the political tensions left by the war of 1870, and there was an element of jingoism in his insistence on the superiority of clinical work over laboratory experiments. Finally, Charcot explicitly boasted that his focus on hysteria—a disease that basically called for clinical as opposed to laboratory study—was "obtaining glory for us and for the French school" (Freud [1893] 1962: 16; Charcot [1881] 1962: 6; Owen 1971: 222; Ellenberger [1965] 1993: 144f; Gelfand 1995a: 237; 1995b: , 198; 1995c: 56f; cf. Bonduelle 1995c: 73; 1995c: 276, for Charcot's criticism of German methods and hostility to things German).

was, by position if not also by temperament, authoritarian and rarely allowed those below him to question his judgment (Ellenberger [1965] 1993: 143; though see Gelfand 1992: 43). While such manipulative authoritarianism was natural given the hospital situation, Charcot's increasing interest in hysterics and in hypnotism brought this aspect of his practice to the forefront as he used hypnotism to induce hysterical seizures in (frequently naked) patients for the observation of fascinated crowds. Such displays drew criticism even from his defenders (see Owen 1971: 206),[14] but it would be wrong to see this as a case of a power-crazed and hence dehumanized leader, a sort of Kurtz in a Heart of mental Darkness. Instead, Charcot had come to believe that his authoritative demeanor could be of use in effecting a cure: the otherwise recalcitrant patient might be cured if sternly admonished and threatened by a superior who had no intention of bargaining with her. This authoritarian treatment was necessary with hysterics, he argued, "if you want to master them" (Goetz 1995a: 164, 167, though see 156; Bonduelle 1995c: 88; and Gelfand 1995a: 256; 1995b: 187).

The reliance on this authoritarian relationship led to an inversion of Charcot's epistemology. His anatomoclinical method had required shunning theory—indeed, basically bracketing questions of etiology—in favor of clinical observation.[15] This worked relatively well when it came to correlating physical lesions in the central nervous system with various forms of muscle malfunction. But, as Charcot began to incorporate elements generally understood as psychological into his system, first with his studies of aphasia, things became a bit murky; when it came to hysteria, Charcot was unable to find the clear bodily sign—the lesion—that was the hallmark of his approach (Bonduelle 1995c: 71f; 1995a: 127, 129; Gelfand 1995a: 258).[16]

---

[14]Thus, Goetz (1995a: 169) writes, "Charcot's omnipresent authoritative affect, the patients' dependency on him and his staff for housing and medical care, as well as their usual severe medical disabilities fostered a doctor-patient relationship that was necessarily steeply hierarchical. This verticality defined Charcot categorically in the dominant position, holding both the roles of responsible, protecting father and domineering task-master" making use of "coarse, even abusive, manipulation."

[15]In words that could have served as an epigraph for this book, Charcot wrote in 1888, "I pay little attention to abstractions.... If you want to see clearly, you must take things exactly as they are" (Goetz 1995a: 136; also see Gelfand 1995b: 205 and Owen 1971: 47). Freud ([1893] 1962: 13) also quoted Charcot as saying, "Theory is good, but it doesn't prevent things from existing" (and it seems that this response was directed as a rebuke to Freud himself).

[16]We may perhaps see the difficulties beginning when Charcot ([1881] 1962: 234f, 244f) turned his attention to spasmodic tabes dorsalis, a form of contracture that he distinguished from primary and symmetrical sclerosis, from ataxic tabes dorsalis and from amyotrophic lateral sclerosis. It was frustrating to the etiologist because none of its symptoms were distinctive, and it seemed to exist in the absence of visible lesions. As a result, diagnosis relied more on the art and experience of the clinician, who had to separate this from related contractures, including the hysterical.

Building on the successes of germ theory, the leading German neurologist Wilhelm Erb had proposed that certain neurological disorders were actually due to syphilis, an argument he strongly supported with statistical evidence. Charcot, not surprisingly, rejected this claim, but still felt the pressure to redefine his disease in etiological, as opposed to symptomatic, terms (Carter 1980: 260, 266, 270; Freud [1896c] 1962: 144). While Charcot never truly embraced an etiological definition that would require positing a single cause for a single disease (something Freud did by narrowing the causes of hysteria down to sexual problems), he still felt the need for a general alternative to syphilis as a cause, and he eventually chose heredity as the best explanation of nervous disorder in general, and hysteria in particular, an emphasis that became the hallmark of his school. If evidence was needed, Charcot felt that it was practically sufficient simply to point to the astounding frequency of neurological disorders in eastern European Jews. When Freud "expressed doubts" regarding the hereditary nature of neuroses, Charcot confidently urged him just to look at Jewish families; this evidence was not sufficient to convince Freud (himself of Jewish descent) (Gelfand 1995a: 258–261, 267).[17]

Heredity, however, unlike a lesion, is not visible in the examination room. It requires knowledge of the past, knowledge that should have privileged the patient's expertise over the doctor's. But instead, Charcot maintained his own ideas. This is not surprising; Charcot, like other doctors of his era, had learned to treat all hysterics not simply as patients requiring treatments but as opponents—as dissemblers who would exaggerate or even manufacture symptoms with what seemed to the hapless physician to be malicious intent (Freud [1893] 1962: 19; Gelfand 1995b: 179). Charcot was certainly not going to let himself be fooled, and he believed (perhaps reasonably) that he should trust his professional judgment and sternly rebuke those who made false presentations.[18]

But, Charcot less reasonably extended his destructive critique of hysterics' symptoms to their reports regarding their pasts. Faced with a patient insisting that there was no family history of illness, Charcot simply asserted that there was and proposed an "explanation" for his patient's refusal to confirm his preconception: "It is *instinctive* . . . for families to hide *from themselves* and from others their neurological blemishes. . . . *Instinctively*, he searches for another explanation. . . . In this regard, you must expect in your studies never to get the whole support of the family.

---

[17]This is not to accuse Charcot of anti-Semitism—his observations led him to hypothesize that Jews were uniquely susceptible to hysteria, which is an empirical question. And, he even suggested that ultimate causality might be due to the aftereffects of persecution in the Middle Ages.

[18]Charcot developed techniques to determine when muscular contractures were actually voluntary, a sort of "lie detection" as Owen (1971: 75) calls it. When Charcot's own judgment was insufficient, he would have patients spy on one another (Gelfand 1995b: 179).

They sometimes even try to be obstructive and lead you down a false path" (quoted in Goetz 1995a: 168; italics added). Thus, to falsify his subjects as opposed to his theories, Charcot constructed an accessory model that posited an unconscious ("instinctive") process by which patients would hide the truth from themselves, not only from the doctor. It is not surprising that Charcot would ignore what patients said if they contradicted what he wanted them to say.

Importation

It was this approach that so fascinated the relatively young Sigmund Freud, who was accepted into Charcot's inner circle after offering to translate some of Charcot's work.[19] Freud picked up where Charcot had left off in studying hysteria but formulated the idea of "defense hysteria," which involved the unconscious suppression of unacceptable sexual ideas (Freud [1894] 1962: 47, 53; Breuer and Freud [1897] 1955: 167]). And, what Freud ended up developing, and reexporting to France and the United States in particular (on the reception in the United States, see May 1959 and Hoffman [1949] 1962: 233, 357), was a system of interaction with a patient that was based on theoretically guided clinical experience and, as Foucault ([1961] 1988: 273) indicated, the same authority-laden confrontation between doctor and patient in which cure was identified with remorseful confession on the part of the patient, elicited by a stern talking-to by the authority.[20]

---

[19]And, just as Durkheim was criticized for being too German, Freud's French influence was decried by some Germans (Gay 1988: 53), and as Freud ([1888] 1963: 28f) himself admitted, hypnotism was in general given a cool reception in Germany. It is interesting to see similar differences in national receptivity in the career of Franz Mesmer, another healer of German origin who was only able to get a substantial following for his cures in France. Like Freud, his method turned on the susceptibility of patients to influence, and through trial and error he discovered how to increase the effects by magnifying his own authority. His disciples not only were given a set of answers to every objection regarding why this miraculous fluid used to heal could not be seen but also were, like Freud's "inner circle," sworn to secrecy. (It was Mesmer's student Puységur who then pioneered the hypnotism that was to be adopted by Charcot.) See the work of Darnton (1970: 3, 75); Zweig (1932: 32, 54, 72; also 52).

[20]And Freud was to build into his system the same carelessness to the dangers of suggestion that characterized Charcot's work on hysteria (here see Ellenberger [1965] 1993: 150). Foucault is absolutely correct that Freud, like others treating hysterics at the time, drew on the trope of "honest confession" as opposed to "willfull malingering"—indeed, he compared his work to the "harsh therapy of the witches' judges" in witch trials (for examples, see Freud to Fliess August 29, 1894, June 12, 1895, January 17, 1897, and January 24, 1897, in Freud [1887–1904] 1985: 96, 131, 224, 227; Freud in Breuer and Freud [1897] 1955: 77, 79). Such interrogation must *introduce* charges, not ask the suspect to volunteer them.

We see this in Freud's first work relying on conventional hypnotism, and in his pivotal work on hysteria with Breuer. Here, he blatantly speaks of instructing his patients regarding his hypotheses and his demands that they remember thoughts that they do not remember or he will refuse to treat them further (explaining to them that these thoughts were unconscious, an idea so fundamentally contradictory that its insanity has slipped underneath notice). These authoritative admonitions were made literally under the pressure of his hand (see Breuer and Freud [1897] 1955: 82, 99, 100, 111, 117, 145, 268; Draft J in Freud to Fliess, December 8, 1895, in Freud [1887–1904] 1985: 156). The same authoritativeness underlies the later, more sophisticated, system of psychoanalysis.[21]

It is not necessary here to evaluate psychoanalysis as a system or to attempt to sort out from Freud's claims and teachings what should be considered brilliant and groundbreaking insight, what intriguing if misformulated windows to underappreciated aspects of personality, what drug-induced paranoia or superstition, and what blind irresponsibility verging on swindling, although it seems one can find evidence of all of these in his theory and in his practice.[22] We need only pay attention to the most fundamental aspects of Freud's approach. And here, we cannot but notice

---

[21]As Macmillan (1992: 128, 131; 1997: 84, 197, 443) emphasized, Freud's approach to studying the causes of neuroses was the same as his approach to the causes of hysteria, and the same notion of "resistance" later theorized as a crucial contribution of Freud's system was seen in his work on hysteria. Further, it was in this work with hysterics that Freud (Breuer and Freud [1897] 1955: 153, 279) developed his crucial methodological tool: "I resolved, therefore, to adopt the hypothesis that the procedure [of forcing a crucial memory] never failed [but that instead the patient] tried to suppress once more what had been conjured up. . . . [Hence] we must not believe what [the patients] say, we must always assume, and tell them, too, that they have kept something back because they thought it unimportant or found it distressing. We must insist on this, we must repeat the pressure and represent ourselves as infallible, till at last we are really told something."

[22]For an example of the first, one might take the work on infantile sexuality (Freud [1905] 1938: 580–603) or the psychic costs of sick-nursing (Breuer and Freud [1897] 1955: 162; Freud to Fliess July 15, 1896, in Freud [1887–1904] 1985: 195); for an example of the second, one might take his approach to the Oedipal phase (Freud, [1920] 1966: lecture 21); for an example of the third, one might take his work on "dreams and occultism" (Freud [1933] 1964: lecture 30); and for the fourth, there is his encouraging a psychoanalyst-patient (Frink) to divorce his wife, marry his own heiress patient, and donate her money to Freud (Edmunds 1988). Regarding this last case, contrary to what some accounts may imply, Freud in no way incited the *mesalliance*, although he did validate it. His letter to Frink raising the idea that Frink was "not yet aware of your phantasy of making me a rich man" through a "contribution to the Psychoanalytic funds" is clearly meant somewhat in jest, although no one can determine what Freud could possibly have been thinking.

Significantly, Freud blamed this episode not on his greedy throwing of professional standards to the wind but on the fact that his patient Frink was inherently

that his system is based on an assumption that retrospectively is difficult to explain, and one that is totally incompatible with anything known about the brain: that the aspects of cognitive processing not accessible to consciousness possess a *fundamentally linguistic structure* and indeed compete with conscious processes in the same general terrain (also see Merleau-Ponty 1962: 168, 285, 292f).[23] This was not to investigate the "unconscious" but to colonize it—to make it simply another consciousness, only (to take one of Freud's own metaphors) suppressed like a subject people.

This critical evaluation is in no way intended to contest Freud's role as a *discoverer*. But, just as Columbus's discovery of the New World does not justify his theory of the circumference of the world as less than most others had believed—indeed, he only made his voyage and his discovery *because* he was so utterly wrong—so Freud's discoveries in no way speak to his understanding of what he was doing.[24] It is also not the case that

---

problematic as an American. Freud saw the American temperament as intrinsically hostile to his approach—"It has often seemed to me that analysis suits Americans as a white shirt suits a raven"—and indeed would tell Americans that their particular problems were simply national traits. While his reasoning on the Frink matter was fallacious, his overall judgment may have value (although value of the opposite sign from that which Freud intended): "The Americans transfer the democratic principle from politics into science" (Gay 1988: 563, 565). I will argue that it is for this very reason that the pragmatic tradition has a more workable understanding of knowledge than the Freudian. But this anticipates later explication.

[23]Unfortunately, although it possesses a linguistic structure, it does not speak—only the analyst strings together its statements with no fixed rules. Formally, it is identical to an argument that hiccoughing is a form of Morse code, but that sometimes •• means "i" and sometimes "x" and so on, with the mapping changing for every message.

[24]Freud's distinctive contribution seems to have been a wrong-headed systemization of techniques that were actually introduced by hysterical patients. Macmillan's (1997: 4, 12, 18, 20f; also see Borch-Jacobsen 1996b: 64–67, 80–85) careful reconstruction of the original work with Anna O. demonstrates that Freud much later went back and rewrote the story of the therapy to fit his new theories. At the time, the method used with Anna O. was characterized by a patient-centered process previously seen in classic eighteenth-century cases in which the hysteric verbally instructs the doctors regarding the nature of the symptoms and how they are to be cured (the "talking cure")—Anna not only led the discussions, but also determined when the process was to come to a "successful" end. (This does not mean that Anna "started" the whole journey; apparently Breuer, called to treat a simple cough, decided that the patient was actually mentally ill and only *after* his "treatment" did she come up with other symptoms, symptoms that closely paralleled those made well known that year in Vienna by a famous stage hypnotist. But Anna, whose later declarations that she had simulated the expected symptoms and had never been truly ill were another "symptom" of her insanity, did direct the overall script of the treatment, if not the basic material.) Disregarding the evidence of his own notes, Freud later argued that emotional
(Footnote continued on the next page.)

there was any support for the efficacy of Freud's techniques (apart from his theories) in the form of successful cures.[25] It seems to me incontrovertible that Freud was neither a good researcher nor a good doctor, although there are still those who think otherwise and occasionally still

---

abreaction—compelling the patient to reexperience buried emotions—was central to the cure. This interpretation supports the claim of the doctor to be a unique authority privileged with information denied the patient. We can see how Freud might prefer it. But, it is in contradiction with all preserved case records, including Freud's own (which he later doctored to add emotional material that might support his later view). This sort of case, in which an afflicted woman gives instructions about how she can be cured, is also seen in instances of possession (see, e.g., Wallace 1958).

[25]Evidence of such a lack of success can be found in Freud's own notebooks (or his admissions to Fliess September 21, 1897, and April 16, 1900, in Freud [1887–1904] 1985: 264, 409). Other historical investigations supplement Freud's own doubtful assessments with a series of failures (see Sulloway [1991]). Of the two cases that the Freudians used as claimed successes, the Rat Man and the Wolf Man, both case histories as presented involve numerous tendentious distortions and fabrications (cf. Mahony 1996: 100), neither was cured, and the latter patient was basically paid by the psychoanalytic movement for silence regarding his continued misery. And the classic case used to exemplify the "talking cure" for hysteria proposed by Breuer (Anna O.) also was not actually cured (and Jung reported that Freud admitted this to him privately; also see Ellenberger [1972/1993: 272] and Borch-Jacobsen [1996b: 21–25]). In almost all cases, what the records indicate is a cycle of dependency in which temporary cures—perhaps involving drugs—are followed by relapses and repetitions (see Swales 1986).

Like most hawkers of universal cures, Freud found each failure threatening to bring down his whole system, so rather than learn from mistakes, he attempted to paper over them or ignore them. As these problems accumulated and such techniques were called into question, Freud began to blame his patients for being intrinsically untreatable, telling Ferenczi that they were worthless anyway, only fit "to provide us with a livelihood and material to learn from" (Crews 1998: 144). Of course, many patients are convinced that they profit from the treatment, but this is itself something to be explained: Mendel (1964) did experimental variations and found that whatever interpretation was randomly given patients in an analytic setting, they experienced relief and "progress." The research that has been done comparing the radically different forms of psychotherapy is unable to find evidence in differential success rates that one is better than others (see Stiles, Shapiro, and Elliott 1986).

The last refuge has been to argue that the success of psychoanalysis cannot be judged by a discrete increase in the health or happiness of the patients, but their "whole" acceptance of its findings (e.g., Habermas 1971: 260, 266). Certainly, it seems hard to deny that learning about various forms of (supposed) childhood mistreatment and trauma might not increase one's daily happiness, so it would be problematic to hold against the truth of psychoanalysis the failure of patients to improve. But, this "whole-person acceptance" criterion that holds that the truth of psychoanalysis is in the final acceptance is formally identical to saying that "the truth of X is in the remaking of the person into someone who believes X." Since

Authority and Experience

rancorous debates over Freudianism.[26] But, all must acknowledge that an integral part of Freud's system, for better or worse, was the unique authority of the analyst.

Power Talking

Freud believed that this authority relationship allowed for the transference to the analyst of suppressed feelings (often toward parents as perceived by a child's mind). This transference,[27] correctly understood, while initially "the strongest weapon of [the patient's] resistance," then "becomes [the] best tool [of analysis]" (Freud [1912a] 1963: 111; [1920] 1966: lecture 27, p. 444) as it facilitates the patient regressing under controlled conditions to be able to uncover suppressed thoughts and feelings. Whether or not this is true, it is undeniable that the authority relationship is necessary for most forms of therapy that involve such regression, including hypnotism (a wonderful and incisive treatment of the commonalities in regression therapies may be found in Whitehead 1987). This combination of the authority relationship and the regressive state was inherently problematic in that it tends to increase the suggestibility of the patient. But, Freud refused to entertain the dangers of suggestion: "We need not be afraid . . . of telling the patient what we think his next connection of thought is going to be. It will do no harm" (Breuer and Freud [1897] 1955: 295).[28]

---

there is no evidence that the process leading to personality change and reorientation is fundamentally different from that which leads to personality formation in the first place, this is formally identical to saying that "the truth of X is in the making of the person into someone who holds X," which implies that any idea believed by members of any culture is "true."

[26]The most useful and entertaining venue of this debate has been the cannonade by Crews (1993) and various attempts at rebuttal.

[27]I wonder whether this importance of "transference" (*Übertragung*) could be related to Charcot's practice of having hypnotized patients shift their symptoms around their body, also called transference; Freud discussed this sort of transference and suggested that it might be generally true of all hysterical symptoms, as opposed to being an artifact of Charcot's suggestive procedures (Gelfand 1995b: 198; Owen 1971: 152f, cf. 168).

[28]This same cavalier confidence that such explicit suggestion and reconstruction is never a problem persisted throughout Freud's career (see, e.g., Freud [1937] 1963: 278f). Freud (Freud [1896a] 1962: 199, 204; [1920] 1966: lecture 28, p. 452f) specifically considered the possible problem of the patient being so suggestible in the psychoanalytic situation (as is known to occur in hypnotism) that he or she would adopt the analyst's leadings as his or her own thoughts. While conceding the theoretical possibility of such suggestion, Freud argued that the success of his treatments demonstrated that outsiders could "trust analysis on these points."

Given the stunningly low success rate (discussed in note 25), this defense is
(Footnote continued on the next page.)

Despite the popular image, Freud did not remain some silent presence while patients associated freely—Freud referred in letters (e.g., to Fliess October 9, 1898, in Freud [1887–1904] 1985: 330) to his therapeutic work as involving him talking nonstop (as opposed to when he dealt with hypnotized patients, when he might nap or write letters). Far from taking steps to avoid suggestion, Freud would tell patients about the memories they were to uncover (see Freud [1896a] 1962: 204)—indeed, he advised doing this explicitly—and would repeatedly push them until they produced memories that he considered to have etiological significance (i.e., those that agreed with his theories). Freud (Breuer and Freud [1897] 1955: 272) noted that the patient might begin by doubtfully accepting the possibility of having thought what he was supposed to have thought, without actually remembering it, "and it is not until he has been familiar with the hypothesis for some time that he ... confirms the fact ... that he really did once have the thought." But even here, the patient might not actually remember having the thought (Breuer and Freud [1897] 1955: 299). It was, we recall, only Freud's confident assumption that the unconscious was itself a form of consciousness that allowed for the transposition of "thought"—by definition, something that is conscious—to a realm in which it could not previously have been said to exist. Once it was accepted that nonconscious processes *could* be thoughts, it was easy for the analyst to "explain" based on unthought thoughts—if the patient accepted the authority of the analyst over her own.

---

tantamount to resignation. (Macmillan [1992: 121–124; 1997: 9] notes that this same argument against the possibility of suggestion was found in Freud's [1888/1963: 31] defense of Charcot and his original work on hysteria with Breuer; as indicated above, Anna was in no way cured.) Two other responses to the critique of suggestion Freud offered that were even more self-defeating than his purported cures were, first, that he had "never yet succeeded in forcing on a patient a scene I was expecting to find in such a way that he seemed to be living through it with all the appropriate feelings'" (which seems to imply an admission that he did succeed in forcing other expected scenes) and, second, that the agreement between patients was such to suggest that if his theories were not right, there must be "secret understandings between the various patients" (Freud [1896a] 1962: 205). (Of course, such agreement is exactly what we would expect were Freud suggesting his conclusions to patients.) Elsewhere, Freud ([1896b] 1962: 164; also see Cioffi 1970: 479) more simply said that no one was qualified to judge the issue of suggestion "until he has made use of the only method which can throw light on [this question]"—in other words, until one had become a convert to psychoanalysis. So, why did Freud abandon hypnotism if he did not fear suggestion? This is because (Freud [1904] 1963: 57, 59) too few people could be hypnotized, and those who were hypnotized offered *no resistance*.

But, the authority of Freud's analyst was not always the calm, relaxed voice of the hypnotist—it could be the insistent, dogmatic voice of the zealot (see Zweig 1932: 273). It is also irrefutable that analysis often involved a battle of wills between the analyst and the analyzed regarding who would define what was "really the case," in that the patient came in often not knowing why he or she *was* a case, and the analyst would explain this. Successful cure involved (although it was not simply defined as) the analyzed coming to share the analyst's understanding of the case (see Macmillan 1992: 132f, 378). As Freud ([1898] 1982: 20; here I give the translation of the *Standard Edition*) said, "Having diagnosed a case of neurasthenic neurosis with certainty and having classified its symptoms correctly, we are in a position to translate the symptomatology into aetiology; and we may then boldly demand confirmation of our suspicions from the patient. We must not be led astray by initial denials [*Widerspruch*]. If we keep firmly to what we have inferred, we shall in the end conquer every resistance [*Widerstand*] by emphasizing the unshakeable nature of our convictions."

The contrapositive of the analyst's authority was the patient's lack of credibility. When it comes to answering the question of Why does this person do what he or she does? we clearly have one method at hand, namely, asking the person to explain his or her motivations. But, Freud found the first-person accounts (to use the terminology of chapter 1) to be wanting. Indeed, as Lakoff and Coyne (1993: 84) point out, the patient's *seeming* credibility was understood as an aggressive defense and obliterated as part of "treatment." First-person statements would not do. Freud ([1896a] 1962: 191) began his *Aetiology of Hysteria* by taking for granted that his listeners would "readily admit that it would be a good thing to have a second method of arriving at the aetiology of hysteria [the first being listening to the patient] in which we should feel less dependent on the assertions of the patients themselves. A dermatologist, for instance, is able to recognize a sore as luetic [i.e., syphilitic] from the character of its margins, of the crust on it and of its shape, without being misled by the protestations of his patient, who denies any source of infection for it. . ." The patient not only lacked the scientific knowledge necessary but also actively repressed certain relevant information (note Freud's analogy to a condition that indicates sexual misbehavior and therefore would reasonably be denied by a respectable patient).

Perhaps more tellingly, given Freud's well-known comparison of his own work to archeology, Freud also compared this skirting around patients' self-understanding to the work of an explorer confronting ruins in a little-known region:

> He may content himself with inspecting what lies exposed to view, with questioning the inhabitants—perhaps semi-barbaric people—who live in the vicinity, about what tradition tells them of the history and meaning of these archaeological remains, and with noting down what they tell him. . . .

> But he may act differently. He may have brought picks, shovels and spades with him, and he may set the inhabitants to work [n.b.[29]] with these implements. Together with them he may start upon the ruins, clear away the rubbish, and, beginning from the visible remains, uncover what is buried. (Freud [1896a] 1962: 192)

Of course, there was, at least after Freud "discovered resistance," one difference: the natives apparently did not always want to comply.

Thus, Freud proposed at least supplementing the first-person ("I do this because . . .") account with a third-person account ("He does this because . . .").[30] The explanation now must involve elements that are not in the reportable experience of the actor. This is what it means to replace a "motivation" with an "urge"—to reject in principle someone's response to a Why question as of the wrong order entirely. This is why, for example, those psychologists who refuse (rightly or wrongly) to elevate animals to near-human status insist on explaining the action of animals as the result of "instincts" and why those who propose a biologic explanation for some human behavior attempt to recast reasoned decisions in terms of "cues" and such (see Burke 1952: 104). Replacing the first-person account with a third person account implies and is implied by a rejection of the personhood of the actor.

And yet, this third-person account is fundamentally embedded in a second-person interaction—Freud alone in a room with the patient insisting that "*you* do this because. . . ." If the second-person account differs from the first-person account, there can be no resolution—no production of a third-person account—until these are brought into alignment, or the treatment comes to an unsuccessful conclusion with the exit of the patient. Put somewhat differently, the third-person account is, at least in this circumstance, the outcome of a battle between first- and second-person accounts. When they disagree, the second-person account of the analyst must triumph (Freud [1912b] 1963: 119).

This is not to deny the role of the patient in actively contributing to analysis: Freud himself would acknowledge the importance of the patient's insights in many cases, and many of his followers considered it necessary that the patient personally make every connection (as opposed to being told by the analyst). But, in the final analysis, as it were, the analyst had the ability—indeed the duty—to define what had happened even over the objections of the analyzed. And many of the third-person accounts that Freud produced seem to have been based in only temporary victories. Outside the

---

[29]Freud compared not only analysis to archeology but also himself to a conquistador (see Freud to Fliess February 1, 1900, in Freud [1887–1904] 1985: 398.)

[30]As Peters (1958: 54ff) points out, Freud began by emphasizing that we would supply explanations for actions that could *not* be given conventional first-person answers—things like dreams or slips that indicated that there was some form of *faulty* action. But, as it was Freud who decided what fell into the category of the pathological, nothing prevented him from declaring that a seemingly straightforward action was itself symptomatic. Indeed, its very nonsymptomatic nature could be symptomatic.

psychoanalytic encounter, the patients would be unable to remember crucial traumas, and even during analysis, the patients denied that the scenes that Freud was able to elicit had actually occurred to them (Freud [1896a] 1962: 204; [1896b] 1962: 166). Freud himself is infamous for his ability to prefer to hold on to absurd theories that blamed patients for their troubles even when he himself saw irrefutable evidence.[31] Interestingly, when Freud abandoned a theory that he previously forced his patients to accept (most important is his childhood seduction theory), he then blamed the patients for misleading him, as if they had told him the past memories that he had actually reconstructed for them.[32]

Indeed, even when Freud was aware of the discrepancy between what the patient reported and what Freud believed he *should* report, Freud favored the latter. Thus, in the famous case of the Wolf Man, it was actually Freud who contributed that the patient had dreamed about three wolves; the actual patient reported a dream about a half dozen or so dogs. But, the cure could not progress as envisioned by Freud unless both acknowledged that the dream had been about three wolves, and the patient eventually accepted—at least for a time—Freud's version. The flexibility of reality became such that the same child could be used as an

---

[31]The most gruesome example of this comes from Freud's joint work with his close friend, the incompetent nose doctor Wilhelm Fliess. Fliess had also gone to Paris to study with Charcot and had managed to develop a number of foolish beliefs that were the nasal equivalent of mystical chiropody. Freud and Fliess decided that one patient's refusal to be cured by Fliess's bizarre treatments was due to her hysterical desire to bleed, although Freud was present at the removal of a gauze that Fliess had inadvertently left in her nose, which had produced "abundant hemorrhages and a fetid smell" (see Freud to Fliess March 8, 1895, a follow-up [March 28] in which he admits that they were wrong about the poor woman, and a later [April 26 and May 4, 1896] reversion in which Freud believed that he could still prove Fliess right—"that she bled out of *longing*"—in Freud [1887–1904] 1985: 116f, 123, 183, 186).

[32]Freud's self-serving claim that he "discovered" that neurotics manufactured childhood seduction stories as part of their own fantasies (and that he had no preconceptions regarding what he would find) is contradicted by all the writing surviving from this time (see Cioffi 1998: 37, 40; Borch-Jacobsen 1996a). Just as Freud had admitted to Fliess (October 6, 1893; see Freud [1887–1904] 1985: 58; also compare letter of February 7, 1894, p. 66) that it required a healthy dollop of intellectual courage to maintain his theory of sexual etiology in the face of the stunning absence of evidence, so his claim about the relation between seduction and hysteria was maintained not because he believed his patients but because he ignored them. The clinical experience that he used to support the seduction theory involved no claims by patients that they were seduced by fathers; instead, such claims were made by Freud as the end point of sessions in which he insisted that patients go further and further back—even beyond the capacity of their actual memories—until they produced something with which he could work (see, e.g., Freud to Fliess April 28, 1897, in Freud [1887–1904] 1985: 238). (This was a codified analytic principle for Freud: "If the first-discovered scene is unsatisfactory, we tell our patient that this experience

example of enlightened uninhibited child rearing for one case history and portrayed as traumatized and repressed in another (for "Hans" and "Herbert" turned out to be the same child) (Cioffi 1970: 485).[33] Indeed, what is notable about the associations that form the basis of Freud's interpretations is that they are not those of the patients—they are rather those of Freud himself, who determined what things meant on the basis of what they meant to him (see Macmillan 1997: 259f). Those patients who maintained a different understanding of "what was the case" could only break off analysis (e.g., Dora) and find this refusal to submit to further authoritarian redefinitions redefined as revenge against the analyst (Mahony 1996: 62). As Freud said, to accept what nonanalysts said about what actually happened means that "confidence in the analysis is shaken and a court of appeal is set up over it" (see Cioffi 1970: 480).

In sum, the power imbalance between analyst and patient not only was great but was inseparable from the "success" of the analysis: the ability of the patient to accept the analyst's reconstruction of what "really" took place, including "connections" made by Freud that could range from the perceptive to the idiosyncratic to the psychotic (see especially Lakoff and Coyne 1993; Mahony 1996: 99, 148). Even further—and most pernicious in its implications for theory in the social sciences—Freud's method involved the analyst engaging the patient at critical points in an agonistic struggle, of overcoming the resistance of the

---

explains nothing, but that behind it there *must* be hidden a more significant, earlier experience. . . . A continuation of the analysis then leads in every instance to the reproduction of new scenes of the character we expect" [Freud [1896a] 1962: 193, 195f; italics added]). The scenes that were produced arose, as Freud ([1896c] 1962: 153) said, only "under the most energetic pressure," and while the patient could describe the scenes demanded by Freud, the patient would "have no feeling of remembering the scenes" and "disavows even in reproducing them," according to Freud and Breuer (see Schimek 1987: 939–942, 958f; Carter 1980: 273). Interestingly, as Schimek (1987: 951; also see Crews 1998: 7) points out, in letters Freud (who believed his own father to have been "one of these perverts" and easily assumed his own obsessions were universal [see Freud to Fliess February 8, 1897, September 21, 1897, and October 15, 1897, in Freud [1887–1904] 1985: 231, 264, 272]) explicitly discussed his desire not only to "catch a *Pater* [father] as the originator of neurosis" (Freud to Fliess May 31, 1897, in Freud [1887–1904] 1985: 249) but also to replace Charcot's heredity with seduction by the father as the defining cause of hysteria.

[33]The "material" contributed by Hans himself—the data used as the basis for the diagnosis, theorizing, and prescriptions—turns out not to be Hans's own thoughts or words. Freud is explicit that because of Hans's age, Freud himself and the boy's father—one of Freud's earliest converts—would have to tell Hans what his own thoughts were. As Wolpe and Rachman (1963: 201–206) point out, "For the most part [the case history] consists of the father expounding theories to a boy who occasionally agrees and occasionally disagrees." And, it is plain that it was the *father* (and not Hans) whose thoughts continuously returned to a rivalry with his son for his wife's attention.

patient. In many cases, the natural suggestibility of a patient in regression therapy with an authority figure would produce this alignment of first- and second-person accounts, but if not, off came the gloves.[34] Freud ([1912a] 1963: 110) compared his approach to this resistance to a bitter warfare in which each incremental gain of a farmhouse or a hill is tactically consequential.[35]

If the analyst was to triumph, he could not lose heart—he could not allow the patient's denials to shake his confidence in the truth. Thus, everything the patient could say only confirmed the theory—if the patient agreed, for example, by producing a memory that accorded with the expectations of the analyst, this was evidence in support of the etiological theory in question. If the patient disagreed, this was itself further evidence of the truth of the analyst's claims, which Freud ([1937] 1963: 273) himself admitted might at least seem to others to be a "Heads I win, tails you lose" game (Mahony 1996: 41, 51f, 96; Powell and Boer 1994: 1289; Lakoff and Coyne 1993: 114f, 134; Crews 1998: xxv; Gay 1988: 250). In other words, Freud took a conception of truth production not from the context of academic German psychology but from French psychiatry, itself born in the mass institution for the mentally unfit.

[34]Some will no doubt object that there are as of yet no solid psychological studies that demonstrate that therapists can implant beliefs about the past via suggestion. This is not entirely correct. It is true that ethical considerations prohibit controlled experiments using strong versions of such suggestion (although see Loftus and Davis 2006 for a review of studies), but there are plenty of experiments conducted by out-of-control practitioners with fewer ethical qualms. Since therapists believing in the reality of UFO (unidentified flying object) abduction recover abduction memories, those believing in satanic worship recover satanic memories, those believing in ubiquitous parental incest recover incest memories, those believing in reincarnation recover memories of past lives (in addition to the more prosaic cases of every version of psychoanalyst apparently producing the sorts of material consonant with his or her theories [see Macmillan 1997: 214]), and Freud ([1898] 1982: 21) emphasizing that he himself never found a negative case, we may conclude that the evidence strongly supports the suggestion hypothesis. Further, the alternative explanation has relied on a theory of memory (the "flashbulb" theory) according to which we take mental recordings of events, store them away, perhaps lose the key, but can refind our way to them. All available evidence, including laboratory studies, is contrary to this theory and indeed indicates that suggestion does create false memories—memories that subjects will later insist are veridical. Further, our confidence in the accuracy of our memories can have more to do with the emotion aroused than with our actual accuracy (see, Hyman and Pentland 1996; Roediger, Jacoby and, McDermott 1996; Koriat, Goldsmith, and Pansky 2000: 506; Phelps 2006: 35).

[35]Again, "The past is the patient's armoury out of which he fetches his weapons for defending himself against the progress of the analysis, weapons which we must wrest from him one by one" (Freud [1914] 1963: 161).

Authority and Epistemology

If there is one thing on which sociologists of science can agree, it is that epistemology is, in the last analysis, about social relationships (see especially Shapin 1994). That is, epistemology only seems a set of beliefs about how we can know things when we imagine the unrealistic case of an isolated knower. When we think descriptively in terms of concrete communities, we realize that epistemology describes the relations whereby some persons are able to convince others to accept their truth claims. The abstractions that comprise the building blocks of epistemology thus are ultimately connected to social interactions between persons (see Latour 1987 for a spirited discussion).

Thus, it will not do to argue that the truth making of Freudianism can be divorced from the nature of the relationship of authority between analyst and analyzed. Indeed, we have seen how Freud's circular reasoning built a doctrine that was also fundamentally circular—Freud's research can be taken as demonstrating that people are unaware of the causes of their action because Freud refused to listen to them, taking for granted that people are unaware of the causes of their action. We have seen that Freud was cavalier with the truth, but even had he been more honest, it is difficult to see how he would have avoided this circle once he asked why people did this or that and assumed that he did not have to treat them as equals when evaluating their answers.

Of course, it is not the case that people can answer everything about themselves. People often require elaborate tests conducted by specialized technicians before they can learn crucial information about themselves, such as whether they have a serious disease. It is likewise not at all irresponsible to propose that there are parts of people's psychological makeup that they cannot, unaided, tell us. For example, if overconfidence in one's estimating powers is a trait, we would imagine that those high on this trait would not know that they were high on it, because of their tendency to be overly confident in their ability to know their own traits. All this is well and good. But it has nothing to do with whether we should direct a Why question at these people and imagine that there is a vocabulary other than the one they employ that will yield epistemically stable answers.

Now, few social scientists accept the doctrines of Freudianism in particular or even depth psychology in general. Yet we have, to an extent that is difficult to defend, adopted the outlines of this way of making truth. That is, social scientists first ask a Why question and then ignore the first-person answer. This implies that an expert can, through analysis, determine that something actually signifies something other than what it appears to be on the surface (a classic example is the influential analysis of right-wing politics in Bell [1955] 1963). Most of the time, we simply busy ourselves with third-person explanations and do not worry about what actors might say. If their accounts are forcefully brought to our attention, and they are not merely different from but antithetical to our own, we feel free to ignore them. In such circumstances, we may well explain the divergence of our subjects' accounts from our own through offhand appeals to processes supposedly uncovered by Freudianism (such as the displacement of some sort of anxiety into a supposed political program). While it would be convenient if there was reliable evidence from psychology supporting the idea that everyday people frequently are victims of psychological processes that lead them to voice false motivations that an analyst can see behind, no such evidence has ever been provided.[36]

Freud pioneered not a research program demonstrating this displacement (although this is not to deny that some followers have made other inroads in understanding psychic processes); instead, he pioneered a style of unlimited intellectual warfare. The use of casual Freudianism in the service of destructive interpretation is not a "corruption" of psychoanalysis by "vulgar" Freudians—this division of psychoanalysts into "good" and "bad" the kind of neurotic splitting studied by Freudians—but was invented and widely used by Freud himself, who would analyze the neuroses responsible for colleagues and ex-followers disagreeing with him.[37] Things could hardly be otherwise because Freudianism had no other epistemology than that which came from the social relationship between on the one hand a (one would hope) experienced clinician and, on the other, a

---

[36]It is worth emphasizing that research demonstrating that people do not understand the "causes" for their actions, especially in artificial situations, in no way bears on the question of whether they are *unable* to accept the existence of these causes because of repression or displacement. As discussed in greater detail in chapter 5, experimental research does indeed demonstrate that people's judgments and actions can be affected by external factors (experimental treatments) of which they are ignorant. This has no bearing on whether they also have internal factors of which they not only are ignorant but are unable to accept. The exception is one that is quite important for it concerns not the inability to understand the effect of one's own desires on one's thought, but the inability to understand the effect of one's *assumptions* on recall of events (see D'Andrade 1973, 1995: 191; Hebb 1946: 92). This problem—preconceived assumptions biasing recall—is more dangerous for the *psychoanalyst* (who does not record sessions and thus provide data available for rechecking) than for the patient (see Wallerstein and Sampson 1971: 19).

More generally, it is hardly of great scientific importance if, given a more or less fixed sum of agency to be distributed among a set of persons in a particular social situation, we find that giving all to one set of persons is consistent with the hypothesis that this set is nearly omniscient and the other quite myopic. A despot does not disprove the existence of free will simply by effectively giving orders to a slave.

[37]Speaking of Freud's treatment of Rank, Gay (1988: 480f) said, "These ventures into character assassination are instances of the kind of aggressive analysis that psychoanalysts, Freud in the vanguard, at once deplored and practiced.... It was endemic among analysts...."

mentally unfit person (also see Lakoff and Coyne 1993: 2, 66, 72).[38] Indeed, Freud's ([1910] 1963: 83) response to the widespread lack of acceptance of his arguments was to pathologize the laity en masse.

While I do not believe that these techniques for claim making were ever formulated in such a way that the resultant truth could be anything other than a clash of wills, a negative evaluation of these techniques in psychiatry is not needed for one to find it unreasonable for the social sciences to transpose this relationship (doctor-insane) to the relationship between academic and the larger society.[39]

The Return of the Repressed

Of course, there are attractive reasons to incorporate a principled rejection of our subjects' first-person reports, if only because in some cases these first-person reports will not be wholly truthful. For example, experimental evidence demonstrates that strong social desirability effects lead a significant portion of whites to understate their dislike of blacks in general and affirmative action in particular (Sniderman and Carmines 1997). Certainly, we should not feel obligated to remain uncritical of our respondents who deny, say, that the problem of racism even exists (see, e.g., Twine 1998). If they insist on this denial, should we not suspect the sort of repression of which Freud wrote?

Reasonable though this logic might seem, it leads to that wonderful feedback circle that Goffman (1961) called "looping" in which denials can be taken as further evidence of the truth of the statement in question, and hence the person making the statement need never admit disproof. This has obvious problems for a social science since even if one does not stress falsification in any strict sense as a key principle of scientific theories, theories that are not only immune to disproof but (like some monster from science fiction) grow stronger from all attacks, are indeed as frightening as such an imaginary space terror.

We can see how this plays out by considering the work of Adorno et al. (1950: 795) on *The Authoritarian Personality*. Adorno and colleagues began by trying to develop an indirect instrument that would measure anti-Semitism; they reasonably expected that few people would answer

---

[38]As the British psychoanalyst Edward Glover (1952: 404) wrote, "So far no system exists whereby the scientific authority of research workers can be distinguished from the prestige of senior analytical practitioners and teachers," so disagreement can always be defined as "resistance."

[39]We have seen Foucault's ([1961] 1988) critical history of the development of the mental hospital in France; what is surprising is rather than simply assert that clinical psychology was a poor inspiration for social thought (although he did more or less come to this conclusion), he used this particular form of state-sponsored authoritarian knowledge as his model for social thought in general.

a question, "Are you an anti-Semite?" in the affirmative. They ended up developing an instrument that measured what they believed to be a personality trait of "authoritarianism," and concluded that many mid-twentieth-century conservatives were actually "authoritarians," due to a particular child-rearing environment involving a distant and punitive father. Unfortunately, their exemplar of the authoritarian personality ("Mack"), asked to recount his life story, described a father who fit this template not at all. Rather than reject their theory, the sociologists rejected his words: "Mack's references to his father's devotion and attention can be better understood as expressions of a wish rather than as statements of what the father was like in actuality" (see Martin 2001 for more on this case).[40]

Certainly, this rewriting of the subject's history to be in line with a genetic theory is what we have seen in Charcot's and Freud's methods.[41] But, transferred to the social sciences, such rewriting runs havoc. Mack is asked whether he agrees with the following: "What this country needs is fewer laws and agencies, and more courageous, tireless, devoted leaders whom the people can put their faith in," precisely the sort of sentiment that an authoritarian should endorse. But Mack (who has always been interested in law) disagrees. Does this cause Adorno et al. (1950: 275) to change their theory? They do not, since if Mack can be discounted about his relation with his father, repressing sentiments that are too painful to admit, he may similarly be repressing the truth here. Hence, the authors conclude, "It seems likely that for some of the truly submissive subjects, like Mack, the item is too open, comes too close home [sic], so that in responding they go contrary to their strongest feeling." We are actually logically compelled to consider a coding scheme in which both yes and no answers are scored 1 in a standardized index.

Of course, this particular case is an egregious one—and one that was explicitly based on Freudian psychology. It is then perhaps not so surprising that we see the same rewriting of the subject's own past—that which is accessible only to the subject and not to the analyst—for which both

---

[40]Thus, when analyzing Mack's pathologically nonpathological relation to his father, Adorno et al. (1950: 796) wrote without a trace of humor, "The underlying hostility here hypothesized is very well concealed and it is only by the maximum use of subtle clues that we became convinced of its existence."

[41]"The subject's view of his own life, as revealed in the course of the interview, may be assumed to contain real information together with wishful—and fearful—distortions. Known methods [!] had to be utilized, therefore, and new ones developed to differentiate the more genuine, basic feelings, attitudes, and strivings from those of a more compensatory character behind which are hidden tendencies, frequently unknown to the subject himself, which are contrary to those manifested or verbalized on a surface level" (Adorno et al. 1950: 293).

Freud and Charcot were known. But, the real problem stems not from the particular assumptions of Freudianism. It is that even those who do not deliberately adopt Freudianism make use—indeed they *must* make use—of related dismissals when their knowledge claims conflict with the claims of those whose actions they are attempting to explain.

THIRD AND SECOND PERSONS IN CONVENTIONAL SOCIOLOGICAL THEORY[42]

The Mertonian Resolution

Of course, many readers will object that while sociology may *posit* the existence of causal factors of which actors are unaware, it does not set up the same tension between analyst's explanation and actor's account that we have seen in psychoanalysis; therefore, sociology is not implicated by the preceding epistemological critique as an accessory after the fact. Indeed, did not Robert Merton successfully resolve this conflict with one of the "both/and" formulae discussed in chapter 1?

Merton's (1968) essay on the difference between latent and manifest functions—as is often the case with his writings, a lengthy, subtle, and learned piece reduced to a catchphrase in our disciplinary memory—is indeed an excellent place to consider how sociological explanation sits with lay explanation. Merton (1968: 105) began by noting the ease with which writers could confuse *motivations* (a subjective matter in that it pertains to the beliefs of the actor) with *functions* (an objective matter of whether the consequences of some action actually improve the adaptation of some system to its environment). In some cases, the two may converge, so that the actor intends the functional outcome. This Merton termed a "manifest function" since the functional nature of the act is manifest to the actor herself. But in other cases, the act has functions that "are neither intended nor recognized," which Merton termed "latent functions."[43] Much of Merton's essay consisted in alternately supporting the virtue of these distinctions by appealing to work of other functionalists and castigating these others when they did not recognize the distinctions Merton put forward.

In particular, Merton criticized Malinowski for a number of simplifications, especially his strong argument that pretty much everything one would find in a society—every custom, object, idea, or belief—served some vital, indeed indispensable, function (Merton 1968: 84, 86). Merton (1968: 107) made the important point (anticipating Stephen Jay Gould and Richard Lewontins's [1979] similar critique of equally Panglossian functionalism among Darwinists) that such an assumption of optimality in effect assumes a

---

[42]It was Benjamin Zablocki who suggested the importance of a section such as this one and attention to Malinowski in particular.

[43]Previously, Williams (1940: 78) had made such an argument.

Table 3.1 Objective and Subjective Functionality

		Objectively functional?	
		No	Yes
	No	Freudian unconscious	Latent function
Subjective motivation?	Yes	Primitive ignorance	Manifest function

complete independence of the different parts of a whole (in this case, society; in Gould's case, an organism) such that every part can be "tweaked" by evolution to perform flawlessly. If, on the contrary, the parts are interconnected so that maximizing the efficacy of response to one need implies a change in other parts unconnected with this need, we may find structures that are far from optimally functional and indeed may, in some aspects, be dysfunctional.

Merton's critique is wholly justified. Yet, it may be that the problem with which Malinowski grappled is one that Merton did not successfully treat, and there may be advantages to Malinowski's own approach, simple as it was. Merton began with the distinction between motive and function and then broke up functions into whether they were identical with motivation or not. This implies two other categories (as can be shown using the ubiquitous two-by-two table that Merton would have appreciated), namely, actions that have no conscious motivation nor are functional for the actor (the sort of things that a psychoanalytic account might introduce) and actions that are motivated but fail to achieve the intended functional goal for the actor (the sort of thing that a traditional account of ritual action on the part of primitives would invoke) (see table 3.1).

Indeed, primitive ignorance and Freudian unconscious were two of the most common general explanations for the rituals of non-Westerners when it came to sexual behavior and religion, two of Malinowski's greatest areas of concern. Malinowski's functionalism was a challenge—polemical and simplified to be sure, but deliberately so—to these forms of interpretation that assumed the cultural superiority of the analyst. Far from taking us afield from the basic opposition with which this chapter began, a close consideration of Malinowski's theory returns us to it.

For it was with Wilhelm Wundt, the father of German academic psychology, that Malinowski had studied after completing his doctorate in Poland, and it seems to have been this experience that propelled him to anthropology (where Frazer became his mentor) (Young 2004: 128; Stocking 1986: 19).[44] (In addition to his laboratory work, Wundt had

---

[44]Malinowski was also influenced by his teacher and godfather, August Witkowski, a student of Helmholtz and Kelvin, and by Mach, which brought him close to the Gestalt tradition that emphasized relations between elements. Later, he was also influenced by William Rivers, particularly Rivers's emphasis that anthropology should stress concrete description and his refusal to contaminate data with theories (Young 2004: 32, 77, 85–87, 165, 179, 373, though also see 432).

written both on dreams and on totemism and mythic thought. It will not be surprising to find that Freud took [respectful] issue with Wundt's claims on these matters in the works referred to in the following discussion.) Further, there was something of the particularly German approach to cognition in Malinowski's impatience with Freudian and Durkheimian theories.

We are all well aware of the importance of Durkheim's school for French (and British) anthropology. But, Freudian theories had also become immensely prevalent in anthropology, and the reason is not hard to see. Freudian theories worked in anthropology because the authority relationship on which they were founded also worked: the subjects of the theories were clearly unable to disagree, lacking any access to the sort of social authority necessary to rebut. Rebuttal came only from other anthropologists such as Malinowski.

Malinowski contra Freud

Malinowski's interesting relationship to Freudianism is most clearly seen in his *Sex and Repression in Savage Society* ([1927] 1960). Malinowski took the basic psychoanalytic account of psychosexual development seriously, and wrote that the outlines were reasonably accurate for Western society.[45] He thought that things were quite different in other societies with different family structures and attempted a sympathetic reconstruction based on his own fieldwork. His difference from orthodox Freudianism is often assumed to lie in his emphasis on placing psychosexual development in a comparative context. But more fundamentally, Malinowski attempted to approach similar questions with antithetical methods.

This is seen in his analysis of some Trobriand myths with sexual content. His remarks here are instructive and worth quoting at length (Malinowski [1927] 1960: 116).

> The reader accustomed to psycho-analytic interpretations of myth . . . will find all my remarks singularly simple and unsophisticated. All that is said here is clearly written on the surface of the myth, and I have hardly attempted any complicated or symbolic interpretation. This, however, I refrained from doing on purpose. For the thesis here developed . . . is better served if supported only by unquestionable arguments. Moreover, if I am right, and if our sociological point of view brings us really one step nearer towards the correct interpretation of myth, then it is clear that we need not rely so much on roundabout or symbolic reinterpretations of facts, but can confidently let the facts speak for themselves.

---

[45]While Malinowski in his published writings was always cordial and appreciative in his discussion of psychoanalysis, Stocking (1986: 40) reports that in his unpublished notes he is less generous, making clear that he is not an adherent, thinks 90–95% of its teachings false, and rues using the terminology.

It would be obvious to anyone, he points out, that the patterns he (and the Trobiands) interpret as related to matrilineal society "could, by artificial and symbolic rehandling, be made to correspond to a patriarchal outlook" (and hence classic Freudian theories). The question is not whether inventive hermeneutics could connect the observations at odds with the theory, via a string of negations and inversions, to the claims of the theory. The question is whether this would reach accurate statements. In the case of psychoanalysis, the price of the theorist's victory is often anthropological ignorance.

Indeed, Malinowski ([1927] 1960: 143), although still making every effort to treat psychoanalysis not only as a source of interesting ideas for social research but as itself a serious discipline, was forced to take issue with the "heads I win, tails you lose" nature of its truth making. Replying to Ernest Jones's (1925) censure that Malinowski had deviated from the purest form of the Freudian argument, Malinowski noted that Jones's use of the idea of "repression" had been to inoculate the theory against disproof coming from the Melanesians: not only could there be repression of the wish to kill the father as *part* of the Oedipus complex, but also, continued Jones (1925: 128), Freud's most faithful disciple, the analyst possessed with "an intimate knowledge of the unconscious" could determine that there could also be a repression of the *entire family structure* consonant with the Oedipus complex.

As Malinowski said, this was to claim that the Oedipus complex was not "an actual configuration of attitudes and sentiments partly overt, partly repressed, but actually existing in the unconscious," and to posit it as a truth independent of any empirical assessment (unless one were to posit a new subunconscious only reachable by some new metaphysical psychoanalysis).[46] In contrast to a "repression" that had the ability to repress any evidence of itself, and hence could only be revealed by its absence, Malinowski ([1927] 1960: 242) more simply imagined that the forces of repression were actual sentiments attached to certain ideas or actions, sentiments (such as revulsion) clearly accessible to consciousness. Thus, in contrast to the Freudians, who could assume two competing sets of thoughts, the conscious and the unconscious, Malinowski ([1927] 1960: 174f) reasonably assumed that unconscious processes were *not*

---

[46]Lest this be taken as some deviation from "true" Freudianism, Sand (1983: 342) points out that Freud employed the same analytic technique in his treatment of Dora. Freud used his case histories to provide evidence for his idiosyncratic associations of patients' symptoms (in this case, a cough) with sexual desires that he argued they must have (in this case, a desire to perform fellatio on the friend of her father's who had propositioned her). Evidence would include something like the co-occurrence of symptoms with certain events. But, in his report on Dora, when he found that the two events did *not* coincide, Freud took this as *further* evidence that he was on the right track because Dora (even before entering analysis) had to *deny* the association between the two by frustrating the pattern of co-occurrence.

thoughts but were sentiments *connectable to* thought (in the way that one may verbalize, even if not analyze, one's revulsion).

Thus, Malinowski, despite his interest in psychoanalytic questions and his belief that repression was a real part of psychology, refused to employ a method that involved the negation of first-person understandings.[47] Influenced by the pragmatist William James (discussed in chapter 5), Malinowski (like the Gestalt theorists) took as his own philosophic standpoint the "Absolute Value" of "naïve realism" : "My system of scientific method would simply give an honest, straightforward statement of how things *are*," by which he meant (as explored in greater detail in chapters 5 and 6) the qualities of perception (Young 2004: 89f; also see Stocking 1984: 156; 1986: 31). More prosaically, he found incredible any postulation of a mentality that transcended that of the individual, and here he included both the Freudian "mass psyche" (as seen in Freud's discussion of *Totem and Taboo* [1913/1938]) and the Durkheimian idea of a "collective conscience" that transcended individuals (Malinowski [1927] 1960: 157). It was precisely this methodological—indeed, ontological—individualism that led Malinowski to claim the name *functionalism* for an endeavor rather different from the French tradition stemming from Comte.

Malinowski's Functionalism

According to Malinowski (1939: 939, 962, 964), "functionalism" (his version, that is) was distinguished from other sociological approaches by its treatment of the individual—its conviction that the individual "is the ultimate source and aim of all tradition, activities, and organized behavior." (Here, Malinowski helpfully indicated in a footnote that while Radcliffe-Brown was also considered a functionalist, he "is, as far as I can see, still developing and deepening the views of the French sociological school. He thus has to neglect the individual and disregard biology."[48])

---

[47]Indeed, Malinowski made it clear that he was attempting to put the analyzed and the analyst on more equal footing. Discussing the nature of dreams, he noted that while for Freud, desires felt but suppressed in waking life find expression in dreams, the Melanesians believe that the desire is born in the dream, and from there penetrates waking life and becomes realized. "This is Freudianism turned upside-down; but which theory is correct and which is erroneous I shall not try definitely to settle" (Malinowski [1927] 1960: 125).

[48]The difference between Malinowski and Radcliffe-Brown went farther. As Stocking (1984: 175f) pointed out, Radcliffe-Brown's Durkheimianism led him to emphasize "the methodological necessity of abstracting typical relationships of structure from the phenomenal reality in which they were embedded," which in turn led him to "explain" phenomena such as joking in third-person accounts while wholly ignoring the first-person accounts of the actual participants. Finally, it is also significant that while Malinowski was uncharacteristically antiauthoritarian in his relations with his students, Radcliffe-Brown not only was authoritarian but also had been interested in hypnotism.

In particular, the needs from which Malinowski's functionalism started were all needs that were felt by the biological *individual*, not the (perhaps hypostatized) group. What is distinctive about his approach to anthropology is that it attempts to derive culture in an unbroken chain from individual imperatives. The Freudians saw culture as a residue of the monumental thwarting of incestuous desires; the Durkheimians saw it as a mind of its own—both views thus allowed for an analysis bracketing first-person perspectives. But in contrast, Malinowski ([1927] 1960: 237-239) considered culture as a *means* used by collections of individuals to better encounter their various environments. "Culture thus appears first and foremost as a vast instrumental reality ... all of which allow[s] man to satisfy his biological requirements" (Malinowski 1939: 946). Malinowski (1939: 948) did not deny that culture, which can be seen (analytically, although not temporally) as developed to help individuals meet their needs, then imposes its own requirements, and hence "under conditions of culture, the satisfaction of every organic need is achieved in an indirect, complicated, roundabout manner," and that there were "secondary imperatives" coming from this cultural construct.

But Malinowski did not emphasize any fundamental distinction between these primary and secondary imperatives because in his scheme, both possessed objective functionality and subjective motivation. That is, given his lemma that culture helps individuals to meet their needs, then action that supports culture is still functional for individuals, although somewhat indirectly. Similarly, instead of drawing a bifurcation between realistic interests and a symbolic realm, Malinowski (1939: 956f) derived this symbolic realm as a means of communication to better ensure the maintenance and transmission of successful cultural models for meeting individual needs.

In sum, Malinowski's functionalism was really about the fitness, this "this-sidedness" of non-Western cultures.[49] Since "man, however primitive, has to think clearly," every culture's beliefs and rituals must be pretty much oriented to meeting the functions of organic life (1939: 958; 1954: 34). Deviations from empirical-rational thought such as magical thinking do not express some realm of thought inaccessible to normal practical consciousness, but the same practical form of thought, just in one of the many situations for which the strength of our emotional attachment or reaction to some goal exceeds our technological grasp (Malinowski 1954: 86f).

The Obscuring of the Manifest

Thus, Malinowski's "functionalism" was intended to rebut approaches that fundamentally disregarded the first-person understandings—the realistic motivations of individuals—of those in non-Western societies,

---

[49]"No culture, however simple, could survive unless its techniques and devices, its weapons and economic pursuits, were based on the sound appreciation of experience and on a logical formulation of its principles" (Malinowski 1939: 957).

whether such disregarding was couched in Spencerian terms (according to which many primitive acts were vestiges) or in Freudian terms (according to which they expressed the unconscious) (also see Stocking 1984: 158, 174).[50] Instead, beginning from the fundamental competence of all humans, it attempted to bring everything back to groups of people collectively solving a few practical problems. This functionalism was indeed simplistic and may have been fatally flawed from the start. But, it had nothing to do with the sociological functionalism in which the functions to be met were intrinsically those of a hypostatized collectivity.

And yet, Merton's "clarification" effectively erased this alternative conception of an explanatory system that on a priori grounds refused to allow the group to have needs that it directly met in violation of the first-person perspectives of its members. Merton's elegant analysis, and his tolerant allowance of *both* manifest *and* latent functions, made it hard to turn back the clock and argue that there might not even *be* latent functions.[51]

But, where did Merton get this critical distinction between manifest and latent functions? From no one else but (as Merton explicitly noted [1968: 115]) Sigmund Freud. In his pivotal work on *The Interpretation of Dreams*, Freud ([1900] 1938: 238, 319) distinguished between the *manifest* content of the dream (the example Freud takes from his own dream life is that he has written a book on a certain plant; he sees a copy bound up with a dried specimen of the plant) and the *latent* content. Not surprisingly, only psychoanalysis could reveal the latent content (in the case of Freud's dream, the lengthy set of associations spins out of control—and indeed seems almost like a parody of Freud's method—including a story he remembers about someone who forgot his wife's birthday, someone he congratulated on her *blooming* appearance, the gymnasium he attended and bookworms discovered in the library, his appreciation of artichokes, his bill at the booksellers, and [perhaps least surprising of all] his interest in cocaine[52]).

---

[50]Despite his conviction that the ethnographer should let the natives "speak for themselves," Malinowski in no sense slavishly held himself to repeat his informants uncritically. On the contrary, he was often an aggressive cross-examiner, confronting subjects with apparent contradictions. What is important is that this confrontation was *bidirectional*—part of the utility of this approach was that it allowed informants to "contradict and correct you." The point here is not that this is in general a good technique or that Malinowski was adept at it; it is that his fundamental epistemology did not make such contradiction impossible, as did the Freudian (see Malinowski 1922: 396, 516; 1967: 4, 35, 158, 167, 217, 272; Young 2004: 429, 431).

[51]One person who did, and solved the resulting explanatory lacunae with another of Merton's ideas, namely, the importance of unintended consequences, was Giddens (1979: 59, 211, 215).

[52]Freud ([1900] 1938: 243) reported that he will not complete [!] the analysis of this dream "for reasons which are not relevant here."

Now, there is no need to repeat the previous close attention to Freud's method to demonstrate that the "latent" content of the dream was simply Freud's own associations authoritatively introjected backward in time into the patient's own dream (also see Sand 1983: 350f). But, once he had created a shadow world of latent dreams, paralleling the unconscious thoughts to which he had such marvelous access, Freud was able to link neurotic thoughts to dreams to the beliefs of Malinowski's subjects, whom Freud called "most backward and wretched" primitives, namely, the "poor naked cannibals" of Australia (Freud [1913] 1938: 807f, 880). Thus, Merton's clarification was fundamentally to reassert the psychoanalytic epistemology in which the analyst could dispense with the first-person accounts of subjects over Malinowski's attempt to build in an "option for the subject" to social analysis. In so doing, Merton codified the loose alliance between Durkheimian and Freudian approaches to subjectivity, both of which posited the possibility of third-person accounts irreducible to first-person ones.

Indeed, supporting evidence of this is seen in Merton's own example of the advantages of his clarification.[53] Merton considered the urban "political machine," long a bugbear of rational reformers who wanted an honest government in accord with democratic political theory. According to Merton (1968: 126, 129), we will better understand the machine when we understand "the subgroups whose distinctive needs are left unsatisfied, except for the *latent* functions which the machine in fact fulfills" (italics added). One example of such a subgroup is the deprived who are unable to navigate the formal bureaucracies of social services that may (or may not) exist to meet their needs.

What is interesting is why Merton considers this a "latent" function. Presumably, those asking for assistance understand that they desire this assistance and that it is in their own interest, and that those giving the help also understand its nature; further, both parties can be assumed to understand the implicit bargain whereby electoral support is promised to those politicians who can effectively deliver such help. Indeed, it is hard to imagine any conduct in which there is a tighter linkage between motives and results. Merton considered this an example of a "latent" function not because none of the actors understood what he or she was doing but because it was secondary to the interest of the political elites whose opinions are generally understood to be more important. Make no mistake—Merton is here *defending* the informal, substantive rationality of the urban machine, with its unholy alliance between the deprived and the depraved (at least to Mugwump reformers). But if one rejects the assumption of society as a quasi-organism literally possessing its own needs and its own structures, then "latent" functions cannot

---

[53]It is also noteworthy, given what is to follow, that Merton (1968: 118) considered one of the advantages of his approach to be that behavior that might be considered irrational from an intolerant and ethnocentric perspective is revealed to be rational (although only objectively rational).

refer to an epistemically stable (if unobservable) characteristic of this quasi-organism. Instead, they necessarily return us to a relationship between unequal parties, only one of whose stories are important.

Malinowski's anthropological theory was even in its own day crude; his evolutionary arguments pertaining to the rise of culture are completely unacceptable. But what gave his arguments such force was his attempt to define a general program for anthropology that did not posit a realm of abstract theoretical terms that skirted around the "this-sidedness" of those first-person cognitions that comprise everyday life. He attempted to examine the dynamics posited by Freudians and found that they did not actually occur. Unlike the Freudians, he was not able to take the absence of evidence as itself the conclusive evidence he needed, which severely limited his ability to make claims. Of course, such limitation—such resistance to arbitrary statements—is what makes science something worth doing, but in his case it meant that he appeared at the intellectual marketplace with goods far less enticing than those whose flights of fancies were not bound by empirical tethers.

The highest fliers were perhaps the Freudians, but Malinowski (1922: 327) considered the Durkheimians a close second, in at least flying dangerously close to positing the existence of a mystical group mind. Others also had this criticism, which made the export of Durkheimian sociology somewhat difficult; French intellectual traditions were compatible with such an anti-individualistic statist organicism,[54] but some others, especially the Anglo-American, were not. Merton's "clarification," according to which these Durkheimian ideas could appear as reasonable and unobjectionable, was an important part in the development of the current explanatory orthodoxy. Thus, the Durkheimian perspective (discussed in more detail in the next chapter), according to which there is a "social" level "sui generis" has become connected to the Freudian or at least semi-Freudian model of truth production in psychology, as opposed to the German model. The fundamental idea was the existence of explanatory elements that were not concrete and manifest, equally accessible to patient and analyst, subject and researcher, but instead were latent, that is, hidden, obscure, contrived and of dubious ontological status.

COGNITION, SCIENTIFIC AND LAY

The Third Person

Thus, the third-person form of sociological explanation has become fundamentally wedded to a dismissal of first-person accounts in favor of an analytic freedom to propose abstract theoretical terms that our

---

[54]It is worth emphasizing, as would Durkheim, that anti-individualistic analysis, in the sense of refusing to be constrained to think in terms of individuals, has nothing to do with an opposition to individualism as a social form.

subjects often do not recognize. It is important to emphasize that this distinction between first- and third-person accounts is in no way coterminous with the common distinction of "voices" in anthropology and the concomitant call to include the "subjects' voice." Subjects can and often do speak in third-person explanations, and the point here is not that their third-person accounts are likely to have any particular validity lacked by anyone else's.[55] Further, the argument made here is not—yet—that the first-person account should be accepted and the third person rejected; it is that the Why question has forced an agonistic relationship in which two parties compete to "account" for an action. The self-appointed auditors of behaviors swoop down upon actors, and it is hardly surprising that actors' retrospective scrambles to put their affairs in order—their stories of their motivations—are often unsatisfying. What is just as weighty, and less often noticed, is that the ability of analysts to propose a form of explanation that makes reference to analytic elements outside the experience of actors has a corrosive effect on the honesty of the investigators. The more extreme the ability, the greater the corrosion, and necessarily so. Like Midas, we are so gifted with our ability to turn everything to truth that we starve from want of reality.

In chapter 1, we noted that actors do not always use first-person nominative accounts when answering Why questions; even more, they do not necessarily use first-person answers. A first-person account, as it shall be discussed here, is irreducibly first person in that it makes reference to entities that have phenomenological validity. But, the Why question tends to predispose actors' answers to involve a spurious linkage of past, present, and future. This necessarily leads to some degree of dissociation from phenomenological actuality if only because past and future are *not* actual; whatever their heuristic value, they are imaginary constructs. They only have a retrospective validity (as Mills emphasized) as we come to defend the motivations we explicate to interlocutors. The more "accounting" is going on in a first-person account, the less useful it may be as a source of data. This is not to say that the third-person account is preferable; it is only to say that the Why question forces a reorientation toward an impossible task: satisfying potentially hostile auditors as to the objective connection between imaginary elements. In posing this impossible question, we abandon the more tractable one of how persons respond to the contours of a contemporaneous environment—and *this* is a question that might not require a decisive victory of third-person over first-person accounts.

---

[55]Here, see Giddens's (1979: 246–249) thoughtful discussion of some hasty attempts to resolve the possible discrepancy between analyst's and subjects' vocabularies. We must not attempt to answer the question of what the relation between these two should or can be before we have a clearer understanding of the relationship between cognitions and actions.

The social sciences, however, favor the third-person accounts because they have the illusion of being more scientific, and they are scientific because they are "causal." To return to the Kantian terminology, here people's actions are determined, not determining; conditioned, not unconditional. This has four implications for our approach to action. First, as noted, it orients us to a *temporal* story; in succeeding chapters, we will explore to what extent this is necessary to the task of explanation.

Second, this story is one that generally grates on the nerves of our subjects because it trivializes them. In many cases, we do this deliberately—for example, we explain some persons' support for a certain policy (e.g., prohibition) on the basis of their "need" for something quite different (e.g., to shore up their insecurity in the face of a changing world). Since mature and independent individuals do not appear as "needy," this sort of explanation "explains away" the actors' claims to selfhood as it explains away their own justificatory reasoning. In other cases, such trivialization is implicit, but it cannot be escaped, in that supplying *one* response to the Why question makes another unnecessary. If Monsieur Rouget, discussed in chapter 1, offers his explanation for why he votes left, but our regression equation already predicts his vote, we will ask him to kindly shut up and not venture opinions about matters outside his expertise.

Thus, we cannot help trivializing our subjects (the second implication). The third implication is that our account easily becomes foolish and feeble. Let us imagine that, contrary to our expectation, Monsieur Rouget does *not* vote left. He votes hard right! Perhaps, we first think, this is evidence of *agency*, so we set out to interview this fascinating case of a man bursting through sociological causation. After a half hour of dialogue, we find that he distinctly reminds us of General De Gaulle on a bad day. It is no surprise, come to think of it, that he votes right, for he is an authoritarian, and this now explains his vote. When we take into account this additional variable, our third-person causal explanation works.

Of course, this might then beg the question of why he is authoritarian, and even if we were to avoid all the foolish mistakes of Adorno and others, we will be forced to come up with an explanation for *this* fact (e.g., it may be because his parents were hard right wingers). But, if our explanation for why people do something revolves around an appeal to causal processes that have shaped them in a certain way, our work boils down to "they did this because they are what they are." In other words, we say that we can only explain action conditional on the nature of the actor, and our theory of action is as trivial as a straight line between two close points—for example, "authoritarian people vote for authoritarian policies."

Still, in many cases, we do not employ such crude typological explanations (X is "an authoritarian"); our causal accounts do not pertain to the shaping of clusters of personalities, but involve more general, more abstract, and more theoretically subtle "social facts." Indeed, as we search for a causal account beyond the realm of first-person experience, we invariably tend to formalize such abstractions as the key elements in explanation.

Although they may begin as predicates of individuals or groups of individuals (e.g., degree of "anomie"), once turned into variables, they become entities in our explanations (anomie "causes" suicide). Our hapless subjects *cannot* falsify our theories, because our theories involve things they cannot even see, let alone pretend to judge. This is the fourth, and most problematic, implication: the struggle between first-person and third-person accounts provoked by the Why question is won decisively, from the start.

Statements, Theoretical and Observational

Why *do* we have theoretical terms beyond what has phenomenological validity for actors? While many sociologists have no particular desire to use such counterintuitive terms, they still feel forced to acknowledge that there can be no programmatic alternative. The very epistemology of science, we are told, establishes such a necessary distinction. As we shall see, there is indeed a logical connection between our epistemology and our dismissal of first-person accounts because the same fundamental error appears both in our theory of scientific knowledge and in our theory of everyday knowledge.

Taking the former first, the dominant epistemology in the social sciences is some more or less crystallized form of hypothetico-deductivism. This theory of scientific knowledge begins from the philosophic distinction between things in themselves and things as they appear to us. In the post-Kantian philosophy of science, this is nearly uniformly taken to mean that observations, including scientific ones, are not in themselves unmediated "knowledge." Rather, knowledge results from a process whereby some theoretical statements are compared with observations. In the classic hypothetico-deductive model, we make deductions regarding what should be observed from our theoretical statement (our "hypothesis") and then revise or reject our theoretical ideas on the basis of experience (cf. Durkheim [1883–1884] 2004: 39, 210).[56] Debate within the prescriptive philosophy of science (that is, the branch that tells us how we could *best* learn about the world, not the branch that attempts to analyze what scientists *actually do*) has largely turned on the relatively minor matters of whether hypotheses can be confirmed or only rejected (e.g., Popper 1959), whether theoretical statements are compared against all alternatives or only a few selected alternatives and which of the many statements potentially falsifiable are considered open to replacement (e.g., Lakatos

---

[56]Lest the connection of this approach to the Quetelianism discussed in chapter 2 be lost, Durkheim ([1883–1884] 2004: 211) spells it out: "A comparison will summarize the role of hypotheses in the physical sciences. To form a curve, we specify as many points as possible and then connect them with a curved line. The points represent the facts, while the line is the hypothesis."

1970; Hesse 1980), and most important, whether the theoretical statements are only vehicles for the condensation of observations or whether they may themselves be considered true (e.g., Jeffreys 1961).[57]

In all such cases, then, there is broad agreement here that theoretical terms are not directly observable, so there is no reason to privilege any theoretical term as more "real" than another. That is, since theoretical terms cannot be (according to this epistemology) direct translations of objects of experience, they are all, in some sense, equally "abstracted" from this realm, and there is no need to penalize those that strike the naïve observer as completely abstract. Indeed, if it can be pulled off, the best analysis is often believed to be one in which the theoretical term has no apparent (iconic) similarity to the observations. Just as the stereotypical successful psychoanalysis involves the analyst brilliantly unveiling that something (e.g., a horse) is not actually a horse at all but is something else (a father), so the successful sociological analysis involves showing that something (e.g., an individually irrational action like altruism) is not what it appears to be at all but is something else (rational action). In many cases (though not all), additional credit goes to those who show that the thing that was originally assumed to be positively valued (by the persons being observed) is actually negatively valued (at least to the analyst and the reader). For example, in all seriousness, Bryan Turner (1984: 199) explains the popularity of jogging by recourse not to people's enjoyment of running around outside, nor to their belief in its health or weight benefits, but the requirements of capitalist society. Thus, an action voluntarily taken is shown "really" to be an instance of something better seen as "involuntary" in that its explanation need not make reference to our "first-person" understanding of ourselves as actors ("I run because I want to").

But, it is altogether obscure regarding what *really* means in this context and how it is established as demonstrated other than by rhetoric or by appeal to prejudice. The claim that something is really something else, whatever else we may think about it, is at least epistemologically stable in a dyadic encounter between (on the one hand) an expert who has both certification and clinical experience and (on the other) someone presumed to lack mental competence. But it loses such stability in an encounter between equals (also see Boltanski and Thénevot [1991] 2006: 153, 349 for similar observations). As Mannheim ([1929] 1936)—interestingly, one of those sociologists closest to the comprehensive/field tradition

---

[57]Of course, the distinction between descriptive and prescriptive philosophies only became clear in retrospect, and is far from a neat division. Nearly all the prescriptive theorists attempted to support their arguments with historical analysis. But there has been decreasing interest in philosophies of science that help explain *why* science can be as wonderful as it is, and an increased interest in descriptive accounts of truth production; such predominantly descriptive accounts are now the standard of the philosophy of science. Perhaps the best current statement is still that of Hacking (1983).

I will discuss in chapter 5—argued, such destructive critique promised unilateral victory when only one side had it, but turned into mutually assured intellectual destruction when it proliferated.

We might imagine that a reasonable response would be to acknowledge the difficulty but argue that since the basic hiatus between theoretical and observational terms is universally acknowledged, there is no possible alternative. But is the hypothetico-deductive model so necessary as all that? First, by its own account, it can only be a model of how knowledge is (or should be) produced, and cannot have any ultimate truth value of itself. The point here is not to introduce cheap paradox but simply to stress that this is a theory of science that has some advantages and perhaps some disadvantages. It is not the only possible way of understanding the relation between theory and observation, let alone all scientific thought. It is reasonable that scientific fields with different subjects and different methods have different epistemologies (see Knorr-Cetina 1999), and there are other possibilities for the social sciences. For example, Spencer basically proposed a continuum of terms from the more concrete to the more abstract. There is no reason that the discrete two-class (theory/observation) model of the hypothetico-deductive system is obviously superior to a continuous model.

Further, the key issue (the inherent untestability of "unoperationalized" theoretical statements) is hardly apparent on the surface. The bifurcation of statements into two classes is not an empirical finding based on an examination of regularities in forms of statements. It is an a priori assumption that becomes increasingly difficult to justify when one turns to empirical cases. For example, in Durkheim's ([1897] 1951) work, it is clear that "anomie" is a theoretical term "operationalized" by (for example) marital status. But is population "density" a theoretical term, or an operationalization of one? What about "age"? Do we really say that we operationalize the theoretical term of age by asking people their age? And, what if I choose to have a theoretical term "people's reports about their age" (which we must acknowledge to be different from elapsed years since birth)? I suppose one is free to argue that I operationalize this with "pencil marks on a survey form indicating a person's response about his or her age." But, even if it is substantively silly, it is formally possible to have a theoretical term "pencil marks on a survey form indicating a person's response about his or her age," so it hardly seems plausible to insist that there is a necessary bifurcation between theoretical entities and observables.

This principled distinction between theoretical and observational terms, then, does not force itself on us from the nature of the things we examine. Why would we preserve it so dogmatically? We are attached to this because it allows us to begin with a set of statements whose truth value we do not defend. We allow ourselves this remarkable luxury of beginning with things we do not consider true because this supposedly assists in a laudable endeavor of deriving "empirically testable" hypotheses as if this were some sort of fancy trick like getting a ship inside a bottle.

Far from the hypothetico-deductive model being obviously true or obviously useful, its advantages are illusory; it allows us to defend the use of concepts that should not be defended, a victory that has, compounded over time, come to mean our defeat. It is this distinction between theoretical terms (in principle) and observations that has allowed social scientists to maintain that wholly abstract concepts are no different from more tangible ones. For example, "intrinsic religiosity" is not seen as inherently a different sort of conceptual element than is "wealth." Multiple indicators might be used to "measure" both of these, but there is a difference missed by our standard epistemology, and this difference is that only one of these refers to something existent. There is no such thing as intrinsic religiosity.

Such a categorical statement cuts against the social scientific habitus and may even alienate readers who do not believe in intrinsic religiosity. It seems intolerant, uncouth, and unsophisticated simply to declare ex cathedra that some theoretical element does not exist. Epistemological justifications for such a reaction of distaste immediately come to mind; for example, we may think, "This foolish author has apparently confused theoretical terms, which are only more or less useful, with things that exist or do not exist." The fact that we can feel such justifications arise in our minds is itself the crucial evidence that our epistemology is a liability—it actually interferes with our ability to carry out the most basic task in any empirical endeavor, namely, determining what is real and what is not.

Other scientists do not seem to need to live in the same eternal suspension of disbelief that social scientists do, in which any phrase that is grammatically consistent is given the benefit of ontological doubt. We do not imagine that, for example, chemists would disapprove of a colleague so ill-mannered as to insist to others that there was no such thing as phlogiston. Sociology is indeed different from chemistry and other fields; my point is not that we should adopt the methods of any other science, but simply that there clearly is no general epistemological reason why we cannot say that intrinsic religiosity does not exist. We need to be able to distinguish between sophistication in the service of smartness from sophistication in the service of willful stupidity. The sudden concern shown by sociological theorists with the difficulties of coming up with a transcendent definition of *real* when one of their monstrous theoretical falsehoods is attacked reminds one of an incompetent housepainter who, on being upbraided for painting a room the wrong color, launches into a discussion of the impossibility of drawing a rigid line between blue and green.

We rely on the hypothetico-deductive model not because it is obviously true, but because it makes nothing obviously true. It gives us a "get out of the concrete free" card, which justifies our using whatever theoretical framework we desire. This model, then, promises to even the score between analysts' and participants' accounts, since participants' "theoretical entities" have no more face plausibility than do analysts'. Some form of proto-Freudianism can then be used for a decisive defeat of the lay theory. But if, as I shall argue, it is not the case that all theoretical terms are equivalent, then we are wrong to hide behind the hypothetico-deductive epistemology to support our use of abstract terms in our theories.

Instead of conveniently assuming that we can—indeed we must—put actors' own subjective conceptions of their action to the side when formulating our most impressive explanations, we should begin by understanding how people—both analysts and actors—can and do understand action. Whatever regularities we find in their cognition of their environments could be the basis of a more rigorous analysis. This question (how do people understand their action in their environment?) is, if difficult, at least in principle an empirical one.

But conventional sociological theory insists that this is a waste of time: as actors cannot experience their environment independent of some theoretical scheme, there are an infinite number of arbitrary ways they have of understanding what goes on around them (see also Reed 1996: 14). Here, sociology clings to an outdated and untenable view of the fundamentally arbitrary nature of social "grids of perception." Were this indeed a satisfactory model of the way people think, the hypothetico-deductive model would be a much more reasonable choice for the social sciences. But, this grid-of-perception model is rooted in a Durkheimian sociology of knowledge that is fundamentally incoherent. I explore this theory in the next chapter.

Chapter 4

The Grid of Perception

We have seen that the clinical tradition of psychology left in Freudianism a sociopathic epistemology that allows analysts to say that one thing is "really" something else. But why should such an intrinsically authority-laden notion of truth production ever be attractive to social scientists, sociologists in particular?[1] Sociology, after all, has some sort of elective affinity to relativism: sociologists seem significantly more likely than other scientists to feel uncomfortable with any clear statement that this or that way of looking at the world is true and others false. Here, I wish to make the point that it is precisely because sociologists adopted a vaguely "relativist" understanding of the nature of cognitive components to action—an understanding that stressed the arbitrariness of the organizational principles of our cognitive makeup—that they had no way to adjudicate between conflicting statements regarding the constitution of the world other than authoritative pronouncement.[2] Here, we return to Durkheim (last seen in his 1885 trip to Germany) and follow as he pursued a more traditionally French philosophical theme.[3]

DURKHEIM'S SOCIOLOGICAL ONTOGENESIS OF KNOWLEDGE

Midway between Empiricism and Apriorism

The human cognitive system links a perceptual subsystem that takes in sense data in an unordered form of particular impressions or images and then sends this to a processing subsystem that sorts these sense data according to a more abiding set of cultural templates. The most obvious such template, and the one that forms the best model for social cognition in general, is language. Thus, we only have a notion of a general, abstract, concept of "tree" because of the word *tree*, and this concept is then used

---

[1] The arguments in this chapter are more relevant to sociology than to the other social sciences, although anthropology certainly has been equally influenced by the Durkheimian approach.

[2] A similar point has been made by Breslau (2000: 291).

[3] After writing this, I was alerted by a reviewer to the recent work of Schmaus (2004), which, with more historical detail, makes many, if not all, of the points in

to transform images containing brown and green splattered over some portion of our retina into the belief that we have seen a tree.

Or so, at any rate, thought French philosophers in the mid-eighteenth century. Sad to say, this same model seems to be the generic one assumed by sociological theorists who are not specifically concerned with issues of cognition (those who are have a quite different take; e.g., see DiMaggio 1997; Cerulo 2010). This model became widely accepted because it was adopted by both Saussure and Durkheim, while few other contributors to sociological theory were particularly interested in cognition. While cognitive anthropology, psychology, neurology, and even cognitive sociology itself moved steadily away from this seemingly reasonable set of philosophical deductions, sociologists and anthropologists clung to this model, perhaps in part because it nicely mirrored their equally fallacious model of science. We shall return to that point later; to begin retracing the path whereby sociology came to its psychology of arbitrariness, we must begin with the last task that Emile Durkheim set out to accomplish.

This was no less than to explain the origin of human thought. One important stream in the history of philosophical thought turned on a debate in philosophy between (British) empiricism and (German) apriorism regarding how we must account for the fundamental building blocks, or the "categories," of thought. Aristotle (see, e.g., 1941) had attempted to typologize all the possible predicates (the Greek *katêgoria* meaning "accusation" and, perhaps later, "predication") of things. Thus, when we speak of any thing, we may characterize it in a number of ways: we may describe its quality, quantity, time, position, cause, and effect. While still using this terminology, early modern philosophers were more likely to frame the problem in terms of the development of *knowledge* and not regarding the possibility of *predication* (also see the discussion of Cassirer [1923] 1953: 126f). Most important was David Hume's argument that causality could not be a property of objects themselves that could be empirically perceived by a person, but rather was an inference formed in that person's mind by the constant conjunction of two events (see Hume [1738] 1911: 91f, 161–163). This critique powerfully impressed Immanuel Kant, who concluded that Hume was correct, and that causality as such could be neither observed nor reliably deduced as a property in

---

this chapter, not only regarding Durkheim's engagement with Kant, but also concerning the errors of the Durkheimian constructionism, even using some of the same examples, references, and in one chilling overlap, the same quotation from Edmund Leach (153). Further, Schmaus (2004: 21, 71, 86) discusses de Biran's view of our understanding of causality, as well as that of Hart and Honore (133), which was pivotal for chapter 2, and Durkheim's commitment to hypothetico-deductivism in the early philosophical lectures (96, 104, 107). I have added references to this masterful work, which provides a deeper engagement with the intellectual history behind Durkheim's approach.

objects. But, he chose a different implication, namely, that causality—and indeed, not only the other categories of thought but also the other fundamental a prioris of human experience, space and time—had to be grounded in a transcendent (i.e., nonexperiential) reason (Kant [1783] 1953: 6, 10, 32, 74, 80, 91f, 149; [1787] 1950: 113).

French thinkers such as Charles Renouvier, Victor Cousin, and Paul Janet, standing as it were midway between British empiricism and German idealism, repeatedly attempted to offer an explanation of the categories that avoided either of these extremes—to account for the a priori-like nature of thought without reifying (let alone incarnating) Reason or Sprit (Collins 1985: 78, n. 52, 58; Schmaus 1998: 178; 2004). Durkheim, influenced by Renouvier and Janet, took a turn at this resolution, using religious thought and practice as his data (see Lukes 1985: 459; Némedi 1998: 163).[4] Durkheim's proposal was a radical one: he sought to demonstrate that the categories of thought arose as virtual a priori—not from abstract universal reason, but from the experience of social universals (i.e., collective representations of social life).

In a fascinating bit of intellectual history, Durkheim's attempt produced its opposite. That is, Durkheim set out to provide not a sociology of knowledge, but a sociological theory of the ontogenesis of knowledge.[5] He hoped to demonstrate the social *origin* of what is distinctly human/social (as opposed to animal) thought; once formed, this thought had a life of its own, its own laws of organization.[6]

Thus, the temporal point that Durkheim attempted to study was the simultaneous birth of (on the one hand) society properly so called and (on the other) thought properly so called; he did this by examining the traces of this event, which he believed were left in contemporary primitive societies. Hence, even if Durkheim's theory of the social ontogenesis of knowledge were plausible, it would have only the faintest analogical implications for the sociology of knowledge, which must needs examine social groups far distant from that time in which, following the standard formula of cosmogony, "the world was new." Yet, Durkheim is generally taken as the founder of a particular branch in the sociology of knowledge (Merton 1968: 543), and his work is used as a template for sociological investigations of mature thought systems (see esp. Barnes 1995: 96f).

---

[4]Henri Bergson (1911: 203–206) at the same time was trying a different direction that has similarities to the Gestalt tradition discussed in the next chapter.

[5]I use "sociological ontogenesis" in place of Merton's (1968: 526) apt phrase the "social genesis of the categories of thought" for purposes of brevity; *ontogenesis* signifies that it is the existence of thought itself, and not any particular thoughts, that is genetically explained.

[6]"Ideas are organized on a model which is furnished by the society. But once this organization of the collective mind exists, it is capable of reacting against its cause and contributing to its change" (Durkheim and Mauss [1903] 1963: 32; cf. Durkheim [1912] 1954: 432, 424).

Most important, Mary Douglas (1975: xiff, also see 5, 8, 212; 1986: 98; 1992: 259) assumed that it was inherently problematic, indeed, ethnocentric, for Durkheim to stop short of applying the same analysis to his own society: "What holds for them does not [thinks Durkheim] hold for us." Douglas argued that this failure was due to his assumption of a fundamental difference between Westerners and Australians and his belief in scientific truth. (While the first charge is inexact, since he saw a developmental continuum, with the Australians simply closer to the point of interest to him, the second is quite correct.) Even more significantly, she explicitly compared her reconstructed Durkheimianism to Freud in terms of delegitimating our self-understandings (1975: xx) and castigated Durkheim for not changing his focus from the sociogenesis of the categories to such a destructive critique.

Douglas and the other Durkheimians then reasonably drew an inference from this extension: beliefs about the world had at least as much to do with the arbitrary classification scheme used by any culture as they had to do with the world that they were nominally about. Douglas (1975: xviii; cf. 28) advocated such an "active" theory of knowledge production and criticized those epistemologies that imagined that knowledge was "a matter of discovering what is there rather than of inventing it."

Technically, such analyses are no more "Durkheimian" than convoluted justifications for Stalinist authoritarianism are "Marxist," yet there is a logic to the connection. Tracing Durkheim's attempt to respond to Kant, we find the seeds of a problematic approach to cognition, an approach that has become the almost unquestioned default model for sociology, although few would defend it to the letter. Examining how we have fallen into this erroneous model helps point the way out.

Further, those like Douglas who actually developed what we see as the Durkheimian sociology of knowledge tended to remain with the early ([1903] 1963) treatment that Durkheim wrote with his nephew and intellectual heir Marcel Mauss. The arguments put forward in a crude fashion in this essay are treated in a more sophisticated manner in the later *Elementary Forms*.[7] My discussion here turns on a re-creation of this earlier theory, although I will note where Durkheim later revised his formulation. It seems purposively cruel to arrest a scholar's intellectual

---

[7] Joas (2000: 63) suggests that it may be William James's work that nudged Durkheim to take the role of experience more seriously in deriving the nature of the categories. As a result of this grappling with experience, Durkheim's discussion of the derivation of the ideas of force and causality is profound and worthy of serious consideration. Indeed, we see here, in his last work, clear evidence that Durkheim was moving *away* from the scholastic approach that had characterized his epistemology (subsumptive classes) and toward a conceptualization turning on force, but this movement came only shortly before his death.

development at the point at which he is most vulnerable. Yet, it was the simpler and wronger form that was to be most influential.⁸

The Origin of the Categories

We must begin with some clarification of vocabulary, some of which will also be helpful in our investigation of the traditions explored in the next two chapters as well. As Rawls (1996) has emphasized, there is a frequent misunderstanding of Durkheim's analysis of the categories of thought because contemporary readers are likely to take "categories" in the familiar sense of conceptual boxes in which we put like things (for purposes of clarity, such conceptual boxes are referred to here as "classes"). Again, this familiar Durkheimian idea is more properly attributed to later writers like Mary Douglas (1975: xiii), who argued that Durkheim's discovery pertained to "the process of categorisation" and the determination of "the social factors which bound the categories and relate them to one another." But the root of this collapsing lies in Durkheim's own approach.⁹

While he aimed to give a sociological response to Kant's formulation of the problem of the structure of thought, Durkheim obliterated the distinction Kant made between two different aspects of the problem. On the one hand, Kant provided a "transcendental aesthetic" dealing with the a prioris for *perception* (technically "intuition" [*Anschauung*]), in particular, space and time. On the other hand, Kant also discussed a "transcendental analytic," pertaining to the categories used in *intellection*. These categories may be divided into those pertaining to quantity, quality, relation, and modality and consist of the following four trinities: unity, plurality, totality; reality, negation, limitation; inherence/subsistence, causality/dependence, community; and possibility, existence, necessity.

Thus for Kant, while we might have concepts *of* time and space, as a prioris of the intuition, time and space are not in *themselves* concepts. In fact, Kant stressed that the categories on the one hand and space and time on the other were elements of "two quite different kinds" ([1787] 1950: 121, 155). But, Durkheim ([1912] 1995: 8, n. 4) rejected this distinction and fused what Kant considered separate, namely, concepts that one thinks and objects one perceives.¹⁰

---

⁸Further, Durkheim did not retract any of his earlier claims but rather simply referred to an earlier work in which "he showed how [totemic systems] illuminate the manner in which the idea of genus or class took form among humans" ([1912] 1995: 145).

⁹For a wonderful discussion of this collapsing in the literature and a critical evaluation, see Yocom (2007).

¹⁰This may come in part from the fact that Durkheim's take on the problem was defined more by Renouvier's work than that of Kant himself (Lukes 1985: 54), and Renouvier had—consistent with the French approach to cognition I discuss shortly—assimilated beliefs to representations (two things that Kant

Now, this is not quibbling over details or over whether some author has successfully demonstrated a mastery of arcane points in the philosophic literature.[11] It was Durkheim's equation of the structures of intuition and those of understanding, his approach to perception and his approach to thought, that led to almost all of his categories being, in actuality, indistinguishable from the category of "class."[12] While there are perhaps good reasons to reject Kant's distinction between aesthetics and analytics (as we shall see in chapters 6 and 7), Durkheim was led there by the psychology of his day, particularly his notion of "representations."

While for most German philosophers representations (*Vorstellungen*) were one particular form (or, for some, moment) of thought, roughly in-between the particular concreteness of the image and the universal abstraction of the concept, for Durkheim (and some other French thinkers), the representation was the general form of cognitive element.[13] To the British empiricists such as Hume ([1738] 1911: 29f), the abstract

---

would consider quite different) (Jones 1998: 59; although also see Godlove 1989: 40, also see 66–70, 92; Dupont 1997). Schmaus (2004: 4, 20, 39, 59, 84) emphasizes a line from Victor Cousin via his successor, Paul Janet (on Durkheim's dissertation committee). Cousin had popularized Kant's critique in France but rejected the distinction between the a prioris of intuition and those of understanding.

[11]Indeed, recently discovered and translated notes from an early class Durkheim taught in philosophy find him, at least at this time, quite aware of the distinction (see Durkheim [1883–1884] 2004: 101). But, by the time he returned to the issue decades later, he had his own distinct way of framing the question. Further, it is significant that even at this time we see Durkheim having a somewhat distorted interpretation of Kant's position as being that we impose on the world "an artificial order that enables us to understand—at the cost of completely transforming the material of experience" and "obscure[ing] the real nature of things" (115f). We return in chapters 5 and 6 to this idea that perception is a veil between ourselves and reality.

[12]"Class" is not a category for Kant (although "community" is), and for Aristotle, this is a form of predication so basic that he does not enumerate it. But, as the problem was redefined in the modern period to pertain not to the integration of logic and speech but of logic and perception (a transition to which we return in chapter 6), it became problematic to say "this is an instance of that." Hence, Durkheim had to account for this ability as a key one in the structuring of the framework of the intelligence.

[13]The German *Vorstellung* does not always have the same connotations as "representation," in particular, in terms of being assumed to indicate one thing "standing for" another (rather, it means something "standing before" us). For this reason, contemporary translators of Kant generally render *Vorstellung* as "presentation" (which in earlier times was reserved for *Darstellung*). It is true that Kant's theory of cognition is not "representational," but I believe that in eighteenth- and nineteenth century philosophy, *Vorstellung* was close in denotation to representation (also see Heath 2008).

idea "triangle" had to evoke an image of a particular, if prototypical, triangle. Kant did not consider this to be necessarily the case and made a distinction between knowledge (which must be of some object) and thought (which may be wholly general). Durkheim blended aspects of both, seeing representations as hovering somewhere from the more to less pictorial, and differing from one another more in degree than in kind.

Durkheim had even in his first great work (*The Division of Labor,* [1893] 1933) made representations central—he *defined* society itself as a set of collective representations—but his understanding of what representations were changed slightly over time.[14] By the time of his last great effort, *The Elementary Forms of Religious Life* ([1912] 1995), he emphasized a distinction between two types of representations, the more image-like and the more concept-like.[15] Like Rousseau,[16] Durkheim saw the former as sensual images that always refer to a particular object, are both

---

[14]In the *Division of Labor* there was some confusion regarding the nature of society because Durkheim first defined the *collective conscience* as a set of shared representations, a form of social thought strong in undifferentiated societies, and then added the possibility of an organic solidarity coming from other representations that, although not uniform, were still fundamentally social. Thus, in following Espinas in seeing society as a moral entity, and hence a shared subjective one and hence a set of representations, Durkheim argued ([1900] 1973) that "the essential object of sociology is to study how collective representations are formed and combined" (13f). But, by *collective* and *social* Durkheim invariably meant "shared," which could not cover the case of organic solidarity. Durkheim never successfully handled the differentiation of social representations, as we shall see.

Schmaus (1998: 177, 180) argues that just because Durkheim used the concept of representations to cover the categories does not mean that these representations have *content* (as opposed to being purely formal). This would support the separation Rawls makes between Durkheim's sociology of knowledge and his epistemology: the categories are the same in all societies, even though the representations of these categories may not be. This argument seems to miss the generality of Durkheim's usage of "representations"—Durkheim clearly meant that the categories themselves truly are representations, although they are abstract, and not the *Vorstellungen* of Kant. This view is also clearly contradicted by the passage Schmaus himself cites (179), in which Durkheim argues that the categories (and not the representation of the categories) "are never fixed under a definite form" but "change in accordance with places and times." While this does indeed contradict Durkheim's other point (that the categories are universal and necessary), this contradiction does not prove Schmaus's claim. Schmaus saw the contradiction and proposed a resolution, but Durkheim himself did not.

[15]Toward the end of his life, he seemed to be moving toward a usage of representation more in harmony with the German and English thinkers (see, e.g., Durkheim [1914] 1973: 162).

[16]In the *Discourse on the Origin of Inequality* ([1755] 1967), Rousseau opposes the particular nature of the imagination (images) to the general ideas of the intellect. Levi-Strauss ([1962] 1963: 99) also notes the relation between this essay and Durkheim's theories.

determined and subjective, and are "in perpetual flux" (Durkheim [1912] 1954: 433f) (since as we turn our head, what we see changes).

The second type of representation, which orders the first, consists of stable, universal, and impersonal elements in "a different portion of the mind, which is serener and calmer [than that containing the sensual representations]. It does not move of itself, by an internal and spontaneous evolution, but, on the contrary, it resists change. It is a manner of thinking that, at every moment of time, is fixed and crystallized" (Durkheim [1912] 1995: 435; also see 9).

In other words, Durkheim moved from the empirical/a priori division to a data/framework division; this was unproblematic for a French social thinker of his time. But, he went on to connect this division to the individual/social division (Durkheim 1954: 14; cf. Durkheim 1973[1914]: 151). The logic for the series of connections is clear. If there is a distinction between particular, sensual representations and more stable and abstract concepts, the concepts must *order* the sensual representations (since the concepts themselves cannot be directly perceived); hence, these concepts are "systems of hierarchized notions" that stand "in fixed relations to each other" and form a whole (Durkheim and Mauss [1903] 1963: 81), what Durkheim called a "framework of the intelligence" (Durkheim [1912] 1954: 10). These notions, if they are to order the fleeting sensual representations, must give *generality* to the individual sense impressions. But, if the sense impression is a wholly subjective entity, how could it be ordered but by a *shared* and therefore social framework of thought? It is this framework that Durkheim wished to investigate to answer the question of the genesis of the categories of thought.

Durkheim also claimed (on what basis it is unclear) that primitives have a preponderance of these sensual representations; the individual consciousness of a primitive, like that of a child, is "only a continuous flow of representations which are lost in one another," between which are made only the most fragmentary distinctions (Durkheim and Mauss [1903] 1963: 7). Hence, the process of social development is a shift from an intelligence mostly composed of individual sensual representations to one more ordered by shared abstractions.[17] Thus in contrast to Kant, Durkheim argued that these categories are a concrete historical product, not an axiom of thought, but in contrast to Hume, he acknowledged that these categories are as good as a priori for actual thought, for they are universally shared[18] and necessary for all thinking. "They are the most

---

[17] One will notice that this sits poorly beside Durkheim's arguments regarding the increasing preponderance of individual representations with the process of social differentiation made in *The Division of Labor*. It also does not follow from his belief that Australians assimilate everything to a set of overriding classifications.

[18] Durkheimians often stress the idea that the categories are only shared within some culture and consider evidence of the universality of categories to undermine Durkheim's point. This is basically a form of arrested development of Durkheim's

general concepts which exist, because they are applicable to all that is real. . . . . They constitute the common field where all minds meet" ([1912] 1954: 13f).

Thus, Durkheim described the categories as constituting a framework for thought. It is significant that (as Schmaus [1998: 181] has also noted) Durkheim used this same language to describe the set of *classes* that order sense data. "The class," Durkheim ([1912] 1954: 147) wrote, "is the external framework of which objects perceived to be similar form, in part, the contents." Emphasizing that the form cannot be derived from the contents, Durkheim argued that the contents are *"vague and fluctuating images"* (italics in original); "the framework, on the contrary, is a *definite form."* The same analytic scheme—the opposition between the individual, sensual representations and the shared, abstract representations—is thus used both for the categories as a whole and for the *particular* category of class. This is not because all of the categories have their own particular frameworks; Durkheim is saying both that the categories give the overall formal framework for thought and that the content of one of these categories (i.e., the set of classes used to establish sets of like things) gives the overall framework for thought.[19]

In other words, Durkheim's approach to the issue of categories, because it was completely based on the sense-data/concept distinction and eliminated the distinction between concepts and a prioris of pure sensibility such as time and space, led to a collapsing to the particular case of class. We can see this collapsing in Durkheim's equation of the principles of this framework with *language*. Durkheim argued that general ideas only can arise when we have *words* that cover many particulars. "The system of concepts with which we think in every-day life is that expressed by the vocabulary of our mother tongue; *for every word translates a concept"* (Durkheim [1912] 1954: 433, italics added; although compare Durkheim [1902–1903] 1961: 253).

---

own argument; while it is social life (and, I shall argue against Rawls, the *specifics* of this social life) that gives rise to the categories, the categories themselves quickly lose any specifically social flavor. Thus, while only the social patterning of the day gives rise to the category "time," and although different cultures may still have different rhythms of time (and perhaps even "views" of time), it is, according to Durkheim, time as an essential a priori that structures perception (or intuition, in Kant's language).

[19]This is literally true. After reviewing his arguments about classification and totemism, Durkheim ([1912] 1995: 146) wrote: "Thus we have our first opportunity to test the proposition put forward at the beginning of this work and to assure ourselves that the fundamental notions of the intellect, the basic categories of thought, can be the product of social factors. The preceding shows that this is indeed the case for *the notion of category itself*" ([1912/1960: 206]; italics added: "de la notion même de catégorie").

Thus, to Durkheim, the mind consists of representations that can be arranged on a continuum from the more sensual, fleeting, and individual to the more abstract, permanent, and shared. All the a prioris of thought are the latter group, which is to say that they are formally equivalent and are concepts. Further, there is a one-to-one mapping from concepts to words. Now, in outline this is an unremarkable, perhaps already dated, psychology; abstract ideas order empirical data, and these abstract ideas are the same as the words of the language of a culture. The bold innovation comes in Durkheim's claiming not that the concepts are social in nature (if they are equivalent to language, this must in some sense be obviously true), but that the concepts are produced by a particular historical social experience. It was this innovation that leads to the view of cognition at issue; let us examine Durkheim's arguments carefully.

The Sociogenesis of Classes

Now Durkheim never denied that humans have an innate capacity to perceive *resemblance* or "likeness" in nature. But he did argue that our idea of the set or class goes beyond mere likeness and involves relations of categorical *identity* between things, relations that must have had a social template (Durkheim [1912] 1995: 147f, 435f). Thus, purely as cognizant animals, we can perceive that a cow is like a goat and like a walrus, while a walrus is like a dolphin and a dolphin like a tuna. But it is only the category of class that allows us to unite the first four as identical in that all are mammals, while the last is not.

It is important that Durkheim was proposing that there is some sort of experiential (and not merely organizational) identity of these particularities that is established by the mind, and it is this that becomes the basis for the later Durkheimian arguments about *perception*. Interestingly, this assumption that we have some sort of experiential unification of species as identical on some level has, to my knowledge, never been questioned, although personally I find it doubtful as I do not myself mentally equate all members of the set "mammals" inside a crisp class surrounded by a rigid dividing line. Indeed, at the moment of this writing, I cannot remember whether platypuses are really mammals or not, and even if they *are* mammals, they are not as mammalian as ungulates; further, the dolphins for me remain distinctly fishy.[20]

---

[20]"The uncertain, unsettled condition of this science of Cetology is in the very vestibule attested by the fact, that in some quarters it still remains a moot point whether a whale be a fish. In his System of Nature, A.D. 1776, Linnaeus declares, 'I hereby separate the whales from the fish.' But of my own knowledge, I know that down to the year 1850, sharks and shad, alewives and herring, against Linnaeus's express edict, were still found dividing the possession of the same seas with the Leviathan. . . . Be it known that, waving all argument, I take the good old fashioned ground that the whale is a fish, and call upon holy Jonah to back me." Melville goes on to classify the whales according to a scheme taken from
(Footnote continued on the next page.)

In any case, the Durkheimian assumption is that we perceive degrees of likeness, and we establish categorical identity that goes beyond this similarity. Thus, if people possessed an a priori capacity to impose classification schemes, they might all come up with the same schemes, making use of the natural resemblances among things. But Durkheim believed that rather than possessing such an innate capacity, we had to develop the sense of classification by our experience with some aspect of social life that was itself organized objectively along the lines of a nested classification scheme—such as the extended kinship tree connecting clans in simple societies.[21]

Further, when we look at aboriginal societies in Australia—those that Durkheim assumed were relatively similar to the protosociety in which human thought first arose—we find that "the classification of things reproduces the classification of men" (Durkheim and Mauss [1903] 1963: 11; see also Durkheim [1912] 1954: 16). That is, the Australians aborigines do not merely assign totems to their clans or subclans as identifying marks—pretty much everything one can think of is divided between these groups and attached to some level of social organization (Durkheim [1912] 1995: 141f). The social organization thus provides the template for the first logical organization of things in terms of nested classes. "It is because men were organized that they have been able to organize things, for in classifying these latter, they limited themselves to giving them places in the groups they formed themselves" (Ibid.: 145; cf. Durkheim and Mauss [1903] 1963: 82).

In other words, to make his argument that we get the conceptual category of class from social experience, Durkheim had to (as we shall discuss in greater detail below) make a second argument, namely, that the first conceptual classes were totemic ones in which things were grouped together as "same" by virtue of being connected to the same social groups. Such an argument certainly could support a sociology of knowledge in which a socially constructed and empirically arbitrary grid is used to create sameness and difference. Such an argument also turns out to be extremely difficult to support.

LOGIC AND ILLOGIC

Evidence

The argument is indeed elegant, but it should not be surprising that the evidence marshaled by Durkheim to support this claim is shoddy. Levi-Straus ([1949] 1969: 311) put it simply: *"The Elementary Forms of Religious Life*

---

bookbinding—what might Durkheim and Mauss say about that?

[21]One might here consider evidence that baboons, which have this same sort of nested social organization, appear to perceive categorical boundaries between groups (see Kummer 1995: 146).

was written by a man soundly prepared in the study of the philosophy and history of religions, but as ignorant in direct experience of Australia as of any other region of the world inhabited by primitive peoples." First, as is excellently summarized by Rodney Needham in his introduction to Durkheim's preparatory piece with Mauss ([1903] 1963: xi–xxix), the very material surveyed by Durkheim and Mauss contained numerous contradictions to their theoretical claims, which they lamely explained away as due to unmentioned "changes" in the original system[22] or simply erased by misrendering their sources, adding material to quotations that was consistent with the argument being made.[23] The few cases seemingly favorable to Durkheim's theory mostly turned out (rather quickly) to be misinterpreted by ethnographers or atypical.

Furthermore, Durkheim and Mauss's archetypical form of totemic organization involved an impossible fusion of a patrilineal social form and a matrilineal totemic system.[24] The *social* form that Durkheim assumed, one that involves a tree-like nesting, is really more appropriate to patriarchal clan forms such as those of some northern Europeans, central Asians, and North African nomads. The "clan" groups that have complete systems of nested totemic concepts in Australia are usually matrilineal groups used to facilitate marriage exchange but are composed of people who do not live together,[25] as do patrilineal tribes or "hordes" (which do exist in

---

[22]This is one of many examples of Durkheim's circularity in separating the normal from the abnormal on the basis only of what fits with his theoretical claims—an indication of the pathological epistemology that requires the speaker to have a position of personal authority, as we have seen with Freud.

[23]Needham draws our attention to obviously intentional alterations (the insertion of material that confirms the point being made) in notes to pages 21, 23, 60, 62, 72, 74, and 75f. Changes in the sources more plausibly related to copying, reading, or translating error are found on pages 13, 39, 51, 56, 59, 69, 77, and 79. It is hard to imagine such changes as consistent with standard academic ethics. For a tactful discussion of where "Spencer and Gillen's data contradicted aspects of Durkheim's theoretical construction of it," see Morphy (1998: 25). Spencer and Gillen (1904: 121, n. 1) later explicitly argued against Durkheim's use of their work.

[24]After writing this, I was pleased to learn that Boas (1916: 324f) had made close to this same charge against Durkheim. This may be because Durkheim and Mauss drew heavily on the Arunta, in which totemic descent is "indirectly paternal" (Spencer and Gillen 1904: 144).

[25]Contrary to what Durkheim argued, Spencer and Gillen never reported that the clan structure was integrally tied to social organization, and that one totem was assigned to each clan. Instead, they reported that there were various crosscutting totemic relationships, that individuals could join a totemic group in various ways, and that these totems crosscut territorial organizations. Durkheim had to dismiss all these as pathological; the clan, which in the ethnography is a somewhat

Australia) (also see Levi-Strauss, [1962] 1963: 42; Radcliffe-Brown 1952: 120, 165f, cf. 182; and Lukes 1985: 527).[26]

Thus, Durkheim's particular claims regarding the ontogenesis of the categories are untenable. But, the particular claims have been less important for our current understanding of the sociology of subjectivity than has his overall logic. As we shall see, this also was deeply flawed.

Difference and Likeness

For the sake of argument, let us imagine that anthropological evidence supports Durkheim's assumption of a society organized into nested groups (subsubclans within subclans, subclans within clans, clans within moieties), with each group at every level of organization having a number of totems, one of which is chiefly used to name the group. Let us also grant that totemic relations are not, as Evans-Pritchard (1956: 128–133, cf. 82) and Radcliffe-Brown (1952: 123, 169; cf. Stark 1958: 162; Barth 1987: 71) argue, about a spiritual identity or ritual relation, but are instead, as Durkheim ([1912] 1954: 238) would have it, a statement of categorical identity. (This is akin to believing that Catholics do not perceive a difference between wafers and flesh, but we grant the point for the sake of argument.[27]) How might one demonstrate that the first conceptual classes were social classes, and that this was then the basis for thinking in terms of classes more generally?

Durkheim's strategy was to point to the prevalence of totemic thinking in simple societies in which the *social* relationship between a clan and its subclans (or one clan to another) was analogous to the *paralogical* relation between the totems of the clan and the totems of the subclans (or the totems of two subclans). Of course, if the relations between totems were exactly the same as our current logical relations between the corresponding elements, we would be more likely to ascribe the observed pattern to

---

murky form, becomes crystal clear and maps on to totemism in a one-to-one fashion—all this, argues Morphy (1998: 26), was deduced from Durkheim's theoretical concerns, not induced from the data. Also see Durkheim's ([1912] 1995: 108f) attempt to argue that even identifiable marriage classes can be assimilated to totemic clans.

[26]Unfortunately, there was great confusion about who said what owing to the word *horde* having different connotations in different languages (French and English) (see, e.g., Tarde [1894] 1969: 126). This confusion makes it difficult to understand Chang's (1989) arguments, which is a shame, because this brief piece makes a number of excellent points regarding the ways in which Durkheim misinterpreted the Australian data.

[27]Durkheim's inability to conceive any other copula connecting subject and predicate other than substantial identity is closely related to his collapsing of all the categories (predicates) with class. We shall see both tied to his fundamental psychology below.

the very thesis that Durkheim was arguing against, namely, a simple induction based on observable likeness. For example, Durkheim and Mauss ([1903] 1963: 56) discussed a portion of the Chatada clan of the Omaha that has subsections nested in the same way we can imagine the concepts being nested. Thus, the subsubclan of Eagles is divided into three types of Eagles, that of the Turtles is divided into four types of turtles, and that of the Owls is divided into "large," "medium," and "small" owls.[28] Further, the Owls are united with the subsubclans of Hawks, Blackbirds, and Grey Blackbirds in the subclan of "those who do not eat (small) birds." This does not present powerful evidence that the Omaha only got the concept of "turtle" from the union of a set of subsubsubclans under the subsubclan of turtle, any more than we are likely to believe that we got the idea of "cardinal" from the St. Louis Cardinals.

Durkheim's stronger evidence thus comes when our own ideas of logic are to some degree challenged. Consider the example of the Australian Wotjobaluk tribe, having its clans arranged circularly as follows: Moiety 1: sun, sun, cave, pelican, hot-wind pelican, hot wind, carpet snake; Moiety 2: kangaroo, kangaroo, black cockatoo, pelican, sea, death adder. Comment Durkheim and Mauss, "Within each moiety, according as the clans are neighbors, or are separated from each other, the things connected respectively with them are also more closely related or are alien to each other" (Durkheim and Mauss [1903] 1963: 61–63). But, it is not clear whether this statement is intended as an observation or a truism. That is, since it seems to us reasonable that the hot-wind pelican is like the hot wind and like the pelican, and it is happily placed between these two clans, we may say that inspection demonstrates that clans with similar totems are situated next to each other. But, when we perhaps question why the hot wind is closer to the carpet snake than to the sun, we must reinterpret Durkheim's statement as one true by definition. Since Durkheim and Mauss believe this system to be a residue of the first formation of conceptual thought, "at first" the hot wind *was* more like the carpet snake because hot-wind people lived near carpet snake people.

In other words, Durkheim had two parallel arguments that he was forced to join (also see Godlove 1989: 60f). The first, which we can call the "weak" argument, is that humans have an innate capacity for perceiving similarity, but not categorical identity. This they learn from their experience of the organization of society, which is originally divided up into nested groups. It is logically compatible with this argument to suggest that our ancestors had two semi-independent cognitive schemes: a noncategorical one of continuous resemblance learned from nature and a ritual categorical one. Once the idea of nested classes was learned from the

---

[28]As so often the case, Durkheim and Mauss got this wrong; this group is described in their sources as "Owl and Magpie people" and has subdivisions (1) great owls, (2) small owls, and (3) magpies (see Needham's note in Durkheim and Mauss [1903] 1963: 56).

religious sphere, it was used to give the former scheme the rigid identity of sameness (and not mere likeness). This is a reasonable argument; even if it is not generally true, it may be true for those natural philosophers who consciously systematized the relations of living beings. While some contemporary Durkheimians would like us to imagine that Durkheim only wished to make this argument, such an interpretation founders on a serious examination of Durkheim's work. Both for reasons of garnering empirical support and by nature of his theory of cognition, Durkheim could only make such a claim by making a second argument.

This second argument, which we can call the "strong" argument, is that our first set of concepts about the natural world was derived from the ritual organization of totemism, which in turn was built on the social morphology of the group. According to the first (weak) argument, the Australians of one tribe discussed by Durkheim ([1912] 1995: 106), who are divided into "black cockatoo" and "white cockatoo" moieties, might well understand that black and white cockatoos are similar, but they would take the conceptual skills used in thinking ritually about the black cockatoo half of the ritual world as opposed (categorically) to the white cockatoo half to (some day) come up with the idea of cockatoo as a genus. According to the second (strong) argument, these Australians could have no idea that white and black cockatoos are closely related—indeed, nothing could be further apart.[29]

And, it is the strong argument—false though it is—that is required by Durkheim's equation of language and concepts. If the first classes of a society are its social units and its first general terms the names of these groups, then the conceptual structure *must* originally mirror the totemic structure. This linguistic psychology—formalized by Saussure as a semiology—requires one particular form of a copula mediating between all signs and the things to which they point. The Australians discussed must honestly believe that the sun, caves, and pelicans are one sort of thing, the way we believe oak, pine, and maple are all one sort of thing (since we have the word *tree*). Indeed, if it can merely be demonstrated that the members of any primitive society can distinguish objects within the smallest of their totemic categories, the theory is in serious trouble.[30] Similarly, when discussing China, Durkheim and Mauss speak of the sky principle, which "represents" the ideas of father, prince, roundness, jade,

---

[29]One is tempted to say "they are as different as night and day" or some other binary opposition that we use to metaphorically express difference precisely because we *do* know the close similarity between night and day or between black and white; similarly, precisely because they know well what "a" cockatoo is that the division between the white and the black cockatoo is significant to the Australians (see Radcliffe-Brown 1952: 118; Levi-Strauss [1962] 1963: 40, 88).

[30]Durkheim and Mauss ([1903] 1963: 20) understood the importance of this and hence claimed that "all those [things] which are included in one and the same clan are, in large measure, undifferentiated. They are of the same nature; there are

metal, ice, red, a good horse, an old horse, a thin horse, fruit, and so on. "In other words," they comment, "the sky connotes these different things in the way that, among ourselves, the genus connotes the species which it includes" (Durkheim and Mauss [1903] 1963: 69). One kind of sky is fruit, another is roundness, and a third, a thin horse. Durkheim and Mauss were forced by their logic to accept this Borgesian classification as a nesting of generalities (Durkheim later avoided embracing such seemingly absurd claims but did not come up with a different grounding for his analyses).

Rawls (1996: 436, 438f) has emphasized the distinction between these two arguments, arguing that Durkheim's weak theory (which she calls his epistemology) and his strong theory (his sociology of knowledge) are separable, and that the latter can be jettisoned without undermining the coherence of the former.[31] Rawls uses the relative neglect of Durkheim's argument regarding the foundation of causality (which essentially was the question that prompted Kant's critique of pure reason in response to Hume) to demonstrate the partial reading of most sociologists: time, space, and classes can be seen as a fruitful ground on which to study the social construction of reality for we can intuitively imagine qualitative variations in how these might be arranged (e.g., linear as opposed to circular views of time). But it is much harder to imagine a similar variation in social constructions of causality (which seems either to be there or not).[32] Sociologists, argues Rawls, assume that Durkheim is providing "an indeterminate social constructivist account of knowledge, thus obscuring his epistemological argument for the empirical validity of the category of

---

no sharp lines of demarcation between them such as exist between the ultimate varieties of our classifications."

[31]Rawls emphasizes that Durkheim's epistemology is an attempt to explain the "empirical validity" of the categories. Here, presumably Rawls combines Kant's phrases "objective validity" (*objektive Gültigkeit*) and "empirical reality" (*empirische Realität*), both of which he uses to describe the truth of the a prioris in their ability to represent objects to us (e.g., [1787] 1950: 72, 78). However, Kant seems to have believed that the problem of objective validity referred only to the categories and not to the a prioris of intuition (space and time). (These a prioris of intuition, however, he argued did have empirical reality even if we must admit their transcendental ideality.) Thus, he says regarding the categories, "The concepts which thus contain a priori the pure thought involved in every experience, we find in the categories. If we can prove that by their means alone an object can be thought, this will be a sufficient deduction of them" (Kant [1787] 1950: 124, 129f).

[32]Schmaus (2004) also focuses on Durkheim's treatment of causality; this is indeed a better place to begin a sympathetic reconstruction, but historically the analysis of causality proved less influential in the development of the Durkheimian approach to cognition than did the analysis of class.

causality." And regarding the category of classification, Durkheim's argument "has been understood primarily as a social constructivist account of the social origins of particular systems of classification, and its importance with regard to an argument for the empirical validity of classification as a category of the understanding has been missed" (Rawls 1996: 330, 452).

All this is a welcome correction to a our current misrendering of Durkheim (one will see that earlier interpreters, such as Merton, Vygotsky, Ben-David, Piaget, all understood exactly what Durkheim's point was). But Rawls not only wishes to show us what Durkheim *attempted*, she also wishes to convince us that he *succeeded*. To do this, she must spin off all the evidentiary bad debts into a subsidiary allowed to lapse into intellectual bankruptcy; thus, she attempts to dissociate the well-known flaws of Durkheim's analysis from the epistemological argument and argue that Durkheim posited that the experience of, say, classification leads to the *formal* ability to create categorical identities without the entrance of the problematic *content* of that classification. The sociology of knowledge has to do with the *cosmologies* (such as one kind of sky is a thin horse), which are not empirically valid, and the epistemology with the *practices* (such as crossing a social boundary), which produce the empirically valid categories of thought (Rawls 1996: 441, 462).

Rawls thus concludes that Durkheim's epistemological argument stands despite the inaccuracy of his evidence[33] since the ritual classifications could provide a template for the empirically valid practice of classification even if the first concepts were not equivalent to the totemic system. Durkheim explicitly argued to the contrary: "We have seen, indeed, how these classifications were modeled on the closest and most fundamental form of social organization. *This, however, is not going far enough*. Society was not simply a model which classificatory thought followed; it was its own divisions which served as divisions for the system of classifications. The first logical categories were social categories" (Durkheim and Mauss [1903] 1963: 82; italics added). "It is because men formed groups that they were able to group things: All they did was make room for things in the groups they themselves already formed" (Durkheim [1912] 1995: 145).

Let us recapitulate the sequence of logical steps that brought Durkheim to embrace this radical view of cognition. Desirous to explain

---

[33]"Because he has been interpreted as elaborating systems of classifications, a sociology of knowledge argument, Durkheim has been heavily criticized . . . for the inaccuracy of the data on which he based his argument, accuracy being in a sense the whole point for a sociology of knowledge" but really the "empirical detail is not aimed at elucidating various social systems of classification per se but rather toward evaluating whether such classification systems might have provided in and through their enactment for the development of this category" [*sic*] (Rawls 1996: 454f).

why the categories of thought seem to possess constraining power without adopting a philosophical doctrine of apriorism, Durkheim proposes a sociological cause. Given his (not intrinsically unreasonable, but not obviously correct) idea that human development has involved a basically coterminous birth of self-consciousness, development of language, and development of what we would recognize as society, Durkheim argues that these a prioris should have developed with and because of society. More particularly, the logical a prioris begin as sociological structures of experience. Given a conventional assumption that nineteenth-century hunter-gatherers represented a stage of evolution not far distant from that point, Durkheim looks to them for evidence. The evidence must be in the form of a set of proto-a prioris that both are closely connected to the social structure and are different from ours in content. This means positing the existence of minds that are organized according to a somewhat different logic (in terms not only of the content of the categories but also in the degree of crystallization of the forms of the categories); further, the categories of these minds will themselves be more fundamentally tied to the content of social structure than those of our minds.

And indeed, Durkheim and Mauss argued precisely this, even though it meant dismissing the self-understandings—the first-person accounts—of the Australian informants. One aborigine, asked to classify an animal, replied after some reflection, "It eats grass: it is Boortwerio" (this being the tea-shrub clan, associated with grasslands and herbivores). But Durkheim and Mauss commented that "this is very probably an ad hoc explanation to which the black has recourse in order to justify the classification to himself and to reduce it to general rules by which to be guided" (Durkheim and Mauss [1903] 1963: 21). Rather than, say, accept the idea that this animal had not been previously attached to the totemic system but could be linked to it through analogical or synthetic reasoning once the question was posed, Durkheim assumed that the animal in question (like "all" things) must be part of the system, and discounted the reasoning as post facto. To do otherwise might imply a preexisting psychological faculty of classification and reasoning.

Thus, Durkheim's psychology forced him to rest his central claim regarding the social ontogenesis of the categories on a lemma pertaining to the fundamental arbitrariness of totemic logic (also see Cassirer [1925] 1955: 86, 194), and it did not help him reach his stated goal of explaining how such arbitrariness could be reduced over the course of human development. If "every word translates a concept," then we might indeed expect there to be irreducible cultural variation in the content of the formal structures of cognition as long as humans speak different languages. The sins against his memory by his latter-day followers who apply this totemic logic to modern societies may, then, perhaps be somewhat forgiven. But, the doctrine of "words and things" is as wrong for Westerners as it was for the Australians.

The Durkheimian Search for Categories

This particular emphasis on a sociology of the categories was, as Durkheim's collaborator, nephew, and disciple Marcel Mauss ([1938] 1985: 1) stressed, distinctive of the French school of sociology, which was later to become nearly synonymous with scientific sociology in the United States. But in sociology, "category" has collapsed into "class," and for eminently defensible reasons. Because of Durkheim's equation of category and nonsensual representation, nonsensual representation and concept, and concept and word, the category of the class became the template for thinking about all categories. Durkheim's approach then helped legitimate the preservation of an eighteenth-century psychology (one in which general concepts only exist because of words) as a sociological truism. (Wittgenstein's [1945–1949/1958:167f] work, casually interpreted, was later added to support the same basic assumptions [cf. Gellner 1970: 22].)

This truism can be called the "grid-of-perception" argument. While varieties differ, the basic assumption is that (1) perceptions must be ordered by a mental scheme for them to make sense; (2) these mental schemes consist of conceptual "boxes" into which we can put perceptions; (3) a great deal of the overall structure of boxes—the grid we use to carve up reality—is, from the standpoint of nature, arbitrary; and (4) these boxes map on to language (again highlighting their social nature). A concise exposition of this view is given by Leach (1964: 34): "The physical and social environment of a young child is perceived as a continuum. It does not contain any intrinsically separate 'things.' The child, in due course, is taught to impose upon this environment a kind of discriminating grid which serves to distinguish the world as being composed of a large number of separate things, each labeled with a name. This world is a representation of our language categories, not vice-versa."

As a statement pertaining to child development, this is completely unacceptable (see, recently, Bergesen 2004).[34] Yet, many of the boldest theories of culture begin from such a premise of disorganization. For example, it is such an assumption that led Foucault ([1966] 1973: xix) to ask, "What is this coherence [of our forms of categorization]—which,

---

[34] As Macnamara (1982: 97ff) emphasized, such an argument "could only have been proposed by a person who had never seriously considered what problems phonology presents a child with." That is, even with the intentional simplicity and overenunciation of an adult speaking to a child, everyday speech is a blur of phonemes: "Lie un lie un wave hell low to the fren dlee lie un!" Rather than the word *lion* telling the child the identity of the category lion, the child must have some handle on the class *lion* to be able to determine which phonemes to chunk together as a word. Experimental evidence suggests by 3 months, infants perceive the identity of different species (Rochat 2001: 117).

as is immediately apparent, is neither determined by an a priori and necessary concatenation, nor imposed upon us by immediately perceptible contents?" "What historical a priori provided the starting-point from which it was possible to define the great checkerboard of distinct identities established against the confused, undefined, faceless, and, as it were, indifferent background of differences?" (Foucault [1966] 1973: xxiv; cf. [1969] 1972: 127).[35]

Thus, we have the presumption of an arbitrariness to cognition that calls for a cultural system of divisions, a presumption that affects our understanding of the cognitive components to action. While we cannot disprove this or any other theory of cognition here, we can critically examine the three most prominent claims that sociologists tend to resuscitate when defending this idea. These are the supposed existence of gender categories that cut across our two sexes, the many Eskimo words for snow, and the relativity of zoological categories. We briefly examine each in turn.

THREE FALSE FACTS

The Arbitrariness of Sex

The first example is the different gender systems of other cultures, usually Amerindian. It must be stressed at the outset that is indeed the case that the modern West emphasizes distinctions of sex (considered a "biological" aspect of bodies) as opposed to gender (more a matter of socially accredited status). This is in contrast not only to other civilizations but even to previous Western culture (see, e.g., Trumbach 1991; also Nederman and True 1996). That is, the very idea of gender as a social status implies the potential for a difference between having a male sex and occupying the socially accredited status of a "man"; the same pertains for female as opposed to woman. While the modern West has perhaps an unusually tight linkage between these two, this is not always the case. However, this in no way implies that an incommensurability such that a man or woman as Westerners perceive him or her would not be perceived as correspondingly male or female.[36]

---

[35]Interestingly, this preface to *The Order of Things* actually distorts Foucault's own arguments—which are somewhat more complex and pertain not so much to perception as to signification—by putting them in a more Durkheimian light.

[36]I know of no evidence of *robust* incommensurability of sexual divisions, as opposed to a resolvable one due to initial confusion regarding how members of another culture are to be "read" (see, e.g., note 38). What will be said here about different gender systems also applies to discussions of hermaphrodites, which have been similarly misunderstood as evidence in support of the "grid of perception." The concern—sometimes amounting to an obsession—with those partaking of the sexual organs of both sexes is no more evidence of a culture not

But, casual use of the gender systems of other cultures, coupled with a failure to distinguish sex from gender, leads to the common claim that there are cultures with a third sex or gender or societies in which men (males) (to us) are classified women (females) or women (females) men (males). While no sober anthropologist would take such an argument seriously, the belief that this is the case has entered the general sociological and anthropological communities and hence will profit from explicit consideration. There are actually few examples of cultures with an idea of a true third sex or gender (as opposed to hermaphrodites on the boundary between male and female), and all of the examples are subclassifications of either males or females (not cutting across both, although the same term is occasionally used for both, in the same way that in the late nineteenth century the term *homosexual* might be used by sexologists for both men and women without implying an inability of the writer to distinguish between lesbians and gay men as now termed). Most famous is the Amerind *berdache*, a man who dresses as a woman, does woman's work, and marries as a wife to a man, with whom she/he has receptive anal intercourse. But such berdaches, while they may be "women," are not confused with *females* (Whitehead 1981: 86, 90, 92).

For example, in one of the most well-studied cases (the Mohave), the male berdache is termed *alyha* and the female (who becomes a man) *hwame* (Herdt 1991). Now the Mohave have no difficulty perceiving the *sex* of the alyha as male—it takes a number of years before a male child begins to show cross-gender proclivities, leading to the alyha status being ritually offered. While an alhya adopts the feminine gender and can be married as a wife to a nonalyha male, the alhya is never seen as identical to females. Indeed, alhyas might be teased by other men by their refusing to go along with the alhya's fiction that the she (or he, if the teasing got rough) had female genitals, was pregnant, or had given birth. But, since the Mohave seemed to believe that the alyha could not help being an alyha, such teasing was relatively infrequent. More frequent was teasing of the alhya's husband for not having a "real" wife. Similarly, a man might try to court the wife of a hwame by insisting that "she" (normally one would refer to a hwame as "he" and an alyha as "she") "has no penis, she is just like you are" (Devereux 1937; cf. Herdt 1991: 498).

Thus, we may see that there are two different distinctions that can be made, one of sex and one of gender (schematized in figure 4.1; the dashed line indicates a division of the population by gender, and the solid line a division by sex). In the modern West, these two distinctions overlap nearly entirely; any area between the two lines being hotly contested and investigated and not institutionalized. (See figure 4.2, left.) Among other

---

recognizing the boundary between the sexes than is the concern of Indian philosophers to transcend dualism evidence of a nondualistic culture of the Orient.

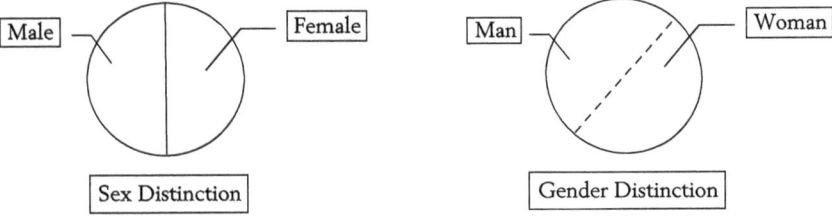

Figure 4.1 Sex and gender

cultures such as the Mohave, there was an institutionalized difference between these distinctions (figure 4.2, right). But—and this is the crucial point—there is no evidence to support the idea that cultural templates affect the perception of persons or categorization of these perceptions, which would be the case if the Mohave did not recognize the same sex distinctions as do modern Westerners (and thus the diagram on the right could indicate the incommensurability of two systems of divisions). Even with regard to gendered roles (such as "wife") the Mohave made distinctions between the alyha and "other" women, between the hwame and "other" men.

In sum, gender, like all socially ascribed statuses (such as "voter"), can be (speaking loosely and provisionally) granted at will by social institutions. Indeed, transgendering is often associated with a change in other statuses (most commonly, the attainment of a new sacred status) (Sweet 1996). It might not be too much to say that the berdache and other transgender individuals are often sacred—transcendental—not because they are in-between our categories but because they cross over them. In transcending, they falsify gender (understood as our theory of sex) and thereby signal the presence of something "more" than everyday social order. Certainly, far from obliterating the division between (our) sexes, such social consecration builds on it and indeed exploits the potential for disjunction.[37] Just as there can be different categorical lines drawn *within* a culture for different purposes (thus people who become adults at 18 for some purposes are not adults until 21 for others) without affecting the cognitive classification of persons, so different cultures assign statuses

---

[37] Another excellent example is Jainism around the late Vedic period: the third grammatical gender was assigned the name (*napumsaka*) given to men who crossed gender boundaries and was later considered to be fixed at birth as were the other two sexes. But this categorization did not cut across the male-female line; instead, the impotent, effeminate, or transvestite men were differentiated from "true" males by the term *napumsaka*, which means "not a man" (Zwilling and Sweet 1996: 362, 376).

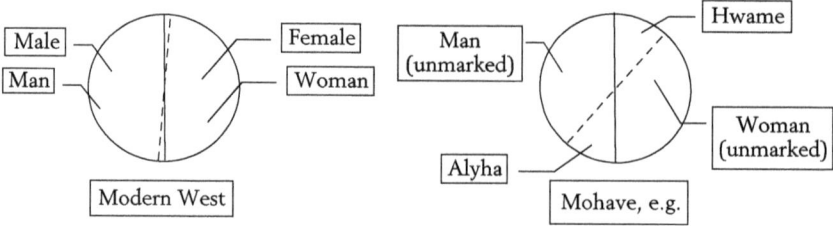

Figure 4.2 Different alignments

differently without this implying that people's perceptions and thoughts are constrained by the boundaries of these categories.[38]

Snow Job

The second mythic example is the claim that Eskimos, dealing (as might be expected) with snow on a daily basis, have countless words for different types of snow, forgoing any general idea of "snow" (e.g., Triandis 1964: 37). The pseudointellectual history of this myth has already been documented. As Martin (1986) and Pullum (1991: 163) point out, Whorf (1940) took a statement of Boas (who was actually stressing linguistic *commonalities*) to the effect that it was interesting that Eskimo words for snow came from four independent roots (not that they had many different words for snow) and blatantly falsified it into the claim that Eskimos have many different words for snow (more than four) and that it would be "unthinkable" to combine them as we do. In fact, there are no more than two different roots for snow in any of the arctic languages (Martin 1986: 422, n. 2), although there are innumerable words that can be made out of these words due to the structure of Eskimo grammar. This incorrect claim has entered into the common stock of knowledge of cultural social scientists as further evidence of the "words-and-things approach." What is so interesting about this idea is how easily it entered into the common wisdom of the social sciences. When something fundamentally incorrect is repeated without challenge, it signals the presence of a deep prejudice.

---

[38]This does not mean that there *can never* be a different perception of the sex of a person as a result of cultural differences. Helliwell (2000: 806) reports that the Gerai of Borneo, among whom she worked, originally classified her as a man because of her bearing and her lack of gendered knowledge. Unlike the Mohave, they did not see this as dissociated from her biological sex but considered knowledge of women's tasks more telling. "As someone said to me at a later point, 'Yes, I saw that you had a vulva, but I thought that Western men might be different.'" Thus, the Gerai have the same basic division as do Westerners, but weight indicators differently.

However wrong these arguments are, it turns out that the Lapps (or Sami) of Scandinavia do indeed have a large number of words for ice and snow (somewhere around 20 for each), many richly evocative of a certain condition affecting travel or hunting (for example, *goahpálat*, "the kind of snowstorm in which the snow falls thickly and sticks to things") (see Keane 1886: 235, n. 10; Jernsletten 1997). But, what is interesting on perusing the various definitions of ice and snow is that we do in English actually have different words for many of them: hail, snow, slush, sleet, glacier, frost, rime, pack ice, sheet, drift, crust, powder, flake. It is indeed true that the Sami—like professional skiers—are quite reasonably very attentive to variations in snow and ice and have a number of technical terms (Jernsletter calls these a "professional" vocabulary) that allow them to communicate conditions to one another.[39] But, it is not that our language determines how we see things, but that we use language (borrowing terms when necessary, like "powder") to selectively accentuate aspects of the things we perceive important for what we are trying to do. The terminology does not come from the "culture" as a whole but is attached to particular groups with particular activities.

Borges, the Karam, and Leviticus: The Arbitrariness of Zoological Classification

> These ambiguities, redundancies, and deficiencies recall those attributed by Dr. Franz Kuhn to a certain Chinese encyclopedia entitled Celestial Emporium of Benevolent Knowledge. On those remote pages it is written that animals are divided into (a) those that belong to the Emperor, (b) embalmed ones, (c) those that are trained, (d) suckling pigs, (e) mermaids, (f) fabulous ones, (g) stray dogs, (h) those that are included in this classification, (i) those that tremble as if they were mad, (j) innumerable ones, (k) those drawn with a very fine camel's hair brush, (l) others, (m) those that have just broken a flower vase, (n) those that resemble flies from a distance.
> —Jorge Luis Borges, "The Analytical Language of John Wilkins"

This delightful passage from Borges has come to serve as the Horatio Alger story of the grid-of-perception theory—known to be fictional, and yet taken as indicative of a profound truth, namely, the fundamentally arbitrary nature of animal classifications. Of course, it is not from Borges that an interest in this topic comes to the social sciences; it is from anthropology and the study of totemism. More than any single other thing, it is

---

[39]Pullum (1991: 166) embarrassingly says in his discussion of this myth that "Eskimos aren't really that likely to be interested in snow," which is neither relevant nor likely to be correct.

in the division of animals that Durkheimians have attempted their extension of the supposed arbitrariness of Australian thought to all social forms of classification.

Most important here is the work of Mary Douglas (1986: 55, 58f), who argued that "nothing else but institutions can define sameness." Unlike Durkheim, who allowed the possibility of direct perception of likeness, but not the idea of class equivalence, Douglas saw it as

> circular to claim that similarity explains how things get classed together. It is naive to treat the quality of sameness which characterizes members of a class as if it were a quality inherent in things, or as a power of recognition inherent in the mind. . . . Comparison of cultures makes it clear that no superficial sameness of properties explains how items get assigned to classes. Everything depends on which properties are selected. So the unlike threesome, the camel, the hare, and rock badger, get classed together in Leviticus 11 as animals that chew the cud [but lack parted hooves]. . . . Sameness is not a quality that can be recognized in the things themselves; it is conferred upon elements within a coherent scheme.

Despite the formal elegance of these claims, they are impossibly wrong.[40] First, Leviticus 11 does not classify the aforementioned beasts in any category of "same." Instead, each species is listed, with the explanation that "it chews the cud but does not part the hoof." There is no general term for such animals. What there *are* are general terms for are camels, hares, and rock badgers. *These* are classes within which items are the same. And, despite the fact that our post-Darwinian science emphasizes the lack of clarity regarding species borders, Douglas does not maintain that *these* classifications are "shown to vary across cultures" (although, of course, some do, as the variety of one culture is the species of another). That is because she (and we) could probably not tell one rock badger from another even if she tried. Thus, she recognizes that we do have "a power of recognition [and misrecognition] inherent in the mind" when it comes to individuals of the same species. Admitting that, the logical argument collapses, and we are left with an empirical question: what is seen as the same to whom?[41]

---

[40]It is interesting that Douglas's original (1966) treatment of Leviticus did not contain these wild simplifications and instead gave a generally reasonable interpretation of the nature of the commandments regarding separation.

[41]A similar classic example is that of Barnes (1981), which attempts to demonstrate the formal equivalence of all categorization schemes (there called "Hesse nets") using the fact that the Karam have a category *yakt* for flying things (birds and bats), but *kobity* (the birds we call cassowaries—large, flightless, and furry) are not included in it. Unfortunately for the argument, cassowaries, which may have a special relation to the Karam in symbolizing cross-cousin relations (Bulmer 1967; also see Latour 1987: 199), form their own genus (as they also do for the neighboring Fore people [Diamond 1966]) and are *not* part of a different genus such as what we would think of as fish.

Do cultures divide animals differently? The question need not be answered anecdotally. There is now a well-established field of ethnobiology, an investigation of the categorization schemes used by different cultures to classify animals and plants, and the findings, as reviewed by Berlin (1978), are that as far as can be discerned, most classifications of animals and plants into categories are based on overall perceptual similarities, and there is great cross-cultural agreement at the level of genera and near unanimity at the level of species. While specific subdivisions may be motivated by cultural imperatives, the genera seem simply to be recognized as "out there"—as indeed they (nearly) are. The majority of folk and scientific genera studied by Berlin correspond in a one-to-one fashion (also see Atran 1994; Worsley 1997: 71). Higher levels of clumping, however, are less likely to correspond exactly. Although cultural differences there are, they do not support the idea that we cannot perceive categorical identity without some grid or perception.

As with the case of arguments about different gender systems, there is indeed important cultural variability. The original source for the vision of the determinative power of language is often cited as Whorf (e.g., 1940). Whorf, however, was interested not in disjunctions between classification systems (sets of nouns) but in the worldview implicit in grammar. His analysis of different categorical patterns—although occasionally factually flawed, as we have seen—only indicated that some cultures emphasized divisions within a category considered indivisible by another. And indeed, ethnography *has* confirmed this point, namely, that cultural emphases lead to the elaboration of taxonomies (hence most city dwellers in the United States cannot progress much farther down a taxonomy than "rattlesnake," not seeing many or needing to know the difference between a lethal and nonlethal rattlesnake). But, it is interesting that available evidence demonstrates that even here, the principle of linguistic relativity fails us, for the inductive strength of an argument depends on the *absolute* position of the categories used, not their culturally relative position. That is, to the city dweller, the distance between "snakes" and "lizards" is probably not subjectively closer than this same distance is to hunter-gatherers, even though "snakes" and "lizards" are further "toward the top" of a nested system of classifications to hunter-gatherers since they have more levels below. (The evidence comes from experiments in which subjects are asked to make inductive inferences across categories; see, e.g., Coley, Medin, and Atran 1997.)

In sum, the evidence of cultural variability does not support the grid-of-perception argument that we need cultural templates to tell us what things are similar. Borges's charming list may contain some inspiration for social thought (in addition to Foucault's [1966] 1973 discussion, see Sahlins [1995: 163] for an appreciative reference to this classification). But, as Rosch (1978: 27) comments dryly, the most interesting thing about this case, to which cultural theory returns ever again, "is that it does not exist. Certain types of categorizations may appear in the imagination of poets, but they are never found in the practical or linguistic classes of organisms or of man-made objects used by any of the cults of the world."

Now, this is not quite true—we *can* find classifications almost as strange to us as that of Borges. Consider this ancient Indian classification of animals (Chattopadhyaya 1991: 207f, 384):

1. Creatures which grab and tear off their food like the horse, mule, etc.
2. Burrowing animals like the frog, porcupine, etc.
3. Creatures that dwell in marshy and wet lands like the buffalo, etc.
4. Creatures that live under water like the porpoise, crab, etc.
5. Creatures that live around or on the surface of water like the swan, crane, etc.
6. Herbivorous animals living in grasslands or forests like the deer, hare, etc.
7. Birds that scatter their food like the peacock, etc.
8. Birds that take and gobble their food like the woodpecker.
9. Parasites inhabiting the living body like lice etc.
10. Creatures with poisonous fangs or stings like the scorpion etc.
11. Snakes

This might seem almost as good as the Borgesian one in supporting the arbitrariness of classification. This classification, however, had a particular purpose: the medicinal uses of the creatures and their products. The categories here were supplemented by a finer division into 90 varieties, which would be familiar to those from other cultures. Thus, it is not that all cultures carve up the world differently and are unable to perceive sameness without words, but that we make large-scale combinations of nonproblematic things differently depending on what we are doing.

PRACTICAL CLASSIFICATION

The Practical Value of Large Clumps

Thus, we have found that culture does not provide a grid necessary to order otherwise orderless perceptions. Cultural variability in terms of categorization is seen in three forms. First, there is the degree to which categories are lumped or split; generally, those with a greater interest in achieving practical mastery over something are splitters: herpetologists know not simply that there are different types of turtles, nor even that there are different types of redbellies, but even that there is a difference between the Florida cooter redbelly turtle and the river cooter redbelly turtle. Second (and related to the first), there is the choice of the basic level at which we operate. Most Americans (e.g., when talking to an infant) will refer to a black Labrador as a "dog" (and not a "mammal" or "black Labrador"), although some fanciers will generally choose a lower level as their default. Finally, while there is little cultural variability in

The Grid of Perception

lower-level classifications, there is more potential for arbitrariness in higher-level aggregates. But, these aggregates do not betray fundamental ways of perceiving the world; instead, they come from particular action imperatives. The anthropologists who found evidence supporting the grid of perception had, as Bloch (1977) emphasizes, deliberately focused on *ritual* classifications and ignored other cognitive structures produced by their informants for different tasks.

As a result, there are indeed overlapping schemes of categorization. Fatal to the grid-of-perception perspective, these are often *within* cultures, not across them (Kurzman 1994: 281, cf. 286), and even more fatal to the Durkheimian scheme, they involve identical words with different referent sets. Let us consider a few examples from American culture. The first is the difference between fruits and vegetables. Many a schoolchild returns home one day confident that she will intellectually best her parents by announcing that, contrary to their sloppy and ill-educated usage, tomatoes and cucumbers are not vegetables, but fruit (since they are fleshy and have internal seeds).

A similar example has to do with what "yams" are. The same children, a few years later, correct those who call garnet yams "yams," by informing them that true yams are only to be found in the South Pacific, and what we mistakenly call yams are sweet potatoes. A third example is bugs. All contemporary books on insects for beginners say something to the extent that "actually most insects are not true bugs, although they are often mistakenly called such." While to popular usage, insect is a subcategory of bugs (which includes insects, arachnids, centipedes, and millipedes, i.e., creeping and crawling things, as Leviticus states), in the scientific usage, bug is a subcategory of insect.

It is clear that these sorts of multiplicity of classification do not support the word = thing claim of the Durkheimian sociology of knowledge. If we only have the idea of "vegetables" because of the word *vegetable*, how can the same word mean two different classes at once? Here, we have two categorical schemes (a scientific one and a popular one) that actually overlap (according to one, cucumbers and tomatoes, as savory and hence good for salads, are vegetables, while to the other, they are fruit). When making a salad, a tomato is a vegetable. When teaching biology, it is a fruit (cf. Hull 1992: 48f). Certainly, the child who learns that the tomato is a fruit still does not want it in his breakfast cereal.[42]

---

[42] Who is "right"? Let us look at original use. The words *fruit* and *vegetable* actually *both* originally often referred to vegetation in general, and when *fruit* was more specifically applied to what the uneducated parents think of as fruits, it was applied only to sweet and juicy fruits. *Vegetable* as the children learn it is then a recent residual category of vegetation minus true fruit. Similarly, while *yam* as a word comes from the Iberian explorers who first saw the tropical yam (*Dioscorea*), it was applied to American yams (*Batatus*) since the mid-eighteenth century; the

The same is true for the totemic classifications that Durkheim mistook for the origins of all classification; closer attention to the societies he studied would have revealed that he confused two different sets of classifications, one "biological" and the other "totemic." Indeed, for the case of the Groote Eylandters, Worsley (1997: 2–4, 51, 91, 110, 119) finds not only a ritual system of classification and a biological system of classification, but also a culinary classification: plants are, as he soberly says, not simply good-to-think but also good-to-eat. Whether we are talking about Australian aborigines or British homemakers, there is no one structure of thought, because different things are being done. The Durkheimian obsession with the boundaries of classes has neglected the more fundamental issue of meaning, and the meaning of some conceptual tool can best be understood in terms of what we mean to do with it.

Of course, Durkheim and Mauss ([1903] 1963) themselves brought up the practical character of classifications—at one point, discussing the multiplicity of divisions in totemic thought they wrote that "the fact is that this classification was intended above all to regulate the conduct of men; and it was able to do so, avoiding the contradictions of experience, thanks to this very complexity" (70f; see also Lévy-Bruhl [1926] 1985: 176). But, with an unconscious reflexivity, their own practical need to complete their argument led them to contradict this soon afterward by claiming that "these systems, like those of science, have a purely speculative purpose. Their object is not to facilitate action, but to advance understanding, to make intelligible the relations which exist between things. . . . The Australian *does not divide the universe between the totems of his tribe with a view to regulating his conduct* or even to justify his practice . . ." (Durkheim and Mauss [1903] 1963: 81f; italics added).[43]

---

word *potato* comes from *Batatus* (a Haitian word), although what we now call the potato is actually a member of *Solanum*. *Bug* dates from the early seventeenth century as a general term for all types of insects.

And, whether and when we treat tomatoes as fruits is hardly left to some Durkheimian collective representations. In 1863, the case was taken to the Supreme Court, which ruled in favor of the tomato as a vegetable and therefore that the defendant (*Nix v. Hedden*), the keeper of the New York port, had been correct in his application of import duties on Nix's produce (I thank Matt Desmond for bringing this case to my attention).

[43]This interesting pattern may be explained by Durkheim's uneasy relation to pragmatism. As Joas (1993: 56, 69) and Gross (1997: 142, 144) make clear, Durkheim considered pragmatism to pose a threat to his own theory of religion, and, interpreting pragmatism as denying that religion had any tie to the faculty of mind (which *would* be bad for Durkheim's theory), he rashly chose to counterattack by denying that the classification systems produced by totemism were motivated by anything other than the most rarified speculative quest.

Thus, the Durkheimian view of cognition, despite Durkheim's own emphasis on practice, supported the idea of a principle of division according to which fundamentally unordered percepts (bits of perceptions) were ordered, as well as the idea that it was impossible to think outside this framework. But if, to take a phrase from Bergson (1911: 188), "the lines we see traced through matter are just the paths on which we are called to move,"[44] we need not expect any difficulty in classifying objects first one way and then another. Or at least, this seems to be true for the sorts of large-scale clumping involved in grouping dolphins and cows together as "quadrupeds" (as was once the case) or tomatoes and radishes as "vegetables." The smaller clumpings according to which some varieties are clumped as tomatoes or radishes seems to follow a different principle. And this principle, contrary to the Durkheimian logic, does not come from particular and variable cultural imperatives.

Classes and Perception

The grid-of-perception argument is premised on the idea that, to use Durkheim and Mauss's ([1903] 1963: 7) words, "a class is a group of things, and things do not present themselves to observation grouped in such a way." We have seen that while this may be true regarding vegetables or mammals, it is doubtful regarding "tomatoes" or "cats" and wholly implausible regarding "Roma tomatoes" or "old-style Siamese cat." We generally cannot recognize individuals within these classes, so it cannot be that the things do not present themselves grouped thusly, and it seems a bit beside the point to emphasize that we do not naturally have the concept of "class" if the issue is one of identity. Certainly, we know that other animals perceive species boundaries well enough—if they are here, at least some of them mate successfully (see Shepard [1978] 1998: 42, 76; Pepper 1966: 426), although one can of course still insist that they lack the idea of categorical membership.[45] Some words do concretize the existence of classes, but they are not necessary: children seem to perceive many classes *before* they internalize the labels (Lorenz [1973] 1977: 118;

---

[44]Again, "each being [i.e., species] cuts up the material world according to the lines that its action must follow: it is these lines of *possible action* that, by intercrossing, work out the net of experience of which each mesh is a fact" (Bergson 1911: 367).

[45]The evidence for a distinct human idea of category is mixed. Smith et al. (2008) find humans having a sharper discrimination of visual patterns than rhesus monkeys. But pigeons can be trained to recognize the concept of tree: if rewarded, they will learn to peck any picture that has a representation of a tree on it, no matter what the variety, even if it is a drawing of a tree, while avoiding other tree-like objects such as telephone poles (Vauclair 1996: 15; Gould and Gould 1999: 174). Pigeons—one hopes this will not evoke further controversy—lack the word *tree*.

(Footnote continued on the next page.)

cf. Brown 1958: 261); indeed, they may recognize a class and *never* learn the label (e.g., "cutlery").

But it is not only individual animals that "come to us" already clumped. One might imagine that since color refers to position on a continuum of wavelengths, cultures with different color names would have different perceptions of colors and judge color similarity according to their color names. However, research demonstrates that the human perceptual system seems to chunk some wavelengths together whether or not precise color names exist supporting this categorization (see Bornstein 1987: 296 and D'Andrade 1995: 182–190). Similarly, one might expect that humans would need a language in order to "chunk" phonemes (e.g., to draw a line on the continuum running between d- and t-), but both infants and monkeys discriminate the continuously varying sounds at about the same place that adult humans do (Kuhl 1987: 379, 383). Thus, we have often assumed, for lack of evidence to the contrary, that all stimuli should be assumed unorganized until proven otherwise. That assumption may have simply been false.

In contrast, a more plausible starting place (although not an ending place) is the claim of Rosch (1977) that (1) real-world attributes come in clumps (e.g., scales tend to go with fins), and hence the world contains things that are in and of themselves distinguishable and comparable; (2) rather than things only being organized into difference and likeness by linguistic categories that define or bound, cognition seems to work via categorical prototypes, which may be anchored (somewhat in the fashion that Hume would have liked) in terms of concrete examples. Then, the task becomes to determine in what ways the human cognitive system—culturally variable or not—goes about the task of recognizing patterns that are there (also see Margolis 1987).

CONCLUSION

In chapter 3, we traced the development of Freudian theories of subjectivity in a clinical setting with patients who were to be evacuated of will; Freud's claims were initially "proven" via the suggestibility of the hypnotized patient at the mercy of the authority figure. At first, it seemed as if

---

Regarding species boundaries, there is evidence that other primates (which lack linguistic capacity) can perceive other species as species. Rhesus monkeys shown slides of animals indicate their "habituation" (i.e., their thinking, "oh, more of the same") by failing to give familiar pictures attention on presentation. They become habituated to repeated slides of the same individual monkey, but their interest is renewed when shown a new monkey. When it comes to other species, however, they seem to think that, say, a cow is just a cow; once they are tired of cows, no new individual cow reawakens interest (Menzel 1997: 212).

we were far afield from the theoretical approach of the social sciences. But, we then saw one of the key assumptions of this theory—namely, that there were explanatory elements that necessarily escaped the actors whose actions they explained—brought into sociology. In countering Malinowski's polemical functionalism that denied the existence of any transindividual entities brought in by the analyst, whether some "society" as an entity in itself or some occult "unconscious" accessible only to the initiated, Merton joined these two traditions. Sociology, like psychoanalysis, necessarily deviated from the "first-person" terms of actors because it also dealt with a realm of "latent" causes.

At the same time, it might be imagined that this was a relatively unimportant coincidence or bit of intellectual history. Social scientists do not necessarily adopt quite as dim a view of the everyday person's ability to know his or her own motivations; perhaps this intrinsically authoritarian epistemology can be dispensed with in the social sciences. But this is not so: the Durkheimian theory of knowledge and the Freudian one are mutually supporting in that they lead to the same social relationships.

Indeed, just as we heard Freud explicitly calling for a new vocabulary that would allow him to ignore the responses of his subjects (the "natives" in his extended metaphor), so too Durkheim saw his science as such a determined development of third-person explanations that skirted around unreliable first-person ones. Reviewing Labriola's Marxist dismissal of ideological history, Durkheim ([1897] 1986: 132) approvingly wrote, "We believe it to be a fertile idea to explain social life not by the conception that those participating in it have of it but by those deeper causes that elude consciousness."

Thus, even if social scientists do not maintain that actors' cognition is willfully deceptive and unsound, those who accept some version of the Durkheimian theory of cognition still hold that it is fundamentally arbitrary. According to such a theory, there is no reason to privilege first-person accounts because there is no intrinsic superiority of any conceptual scheme. All are formally equivalent ways of dividing up an inherently undifferentiated sensory reality.[46] But the arbitrariness of the social formation of reality—whether the global one of "culture" or the local one of "diagnosis"—requires an injection of social authority for the stabilization of explanatory claims. They cannot be arranged via their anchoring to the world, for there is none.

Durkheim agreed. In his ([1902–1903] 1961: 139ff) lectures on moral education, he reviewed the findings regarding suggestibility in hypnosis.

---

[46]This is what is often known loosely as "social construction," although no one has actually formulated a set of doctrines under such a name. See the work of Abbott (2001: 61, 64, 68f) for a social explanation of the rise of such constructionism. Durkheim ([1913–1914] 1983: 91f, 96) tried to argue that his approach did not imply this arbitrariness, but I find these arguments quite weak.

This phenomenon was due, he argued (following Guyau), to two factors: "First, the hypnotized subject is as completely passive as possible. His will is paralyzed." The second correlative factor is the absolute authority of the hypnotist: "He must make the subject feel that a refusal is inconceivable, that he must obey. If he equivocates, if he debates the matter, his power is gone." Durkheim went on to argue that education could only take place precisely *because* the child was in the same situation regarding his teachers as was the hypnotized patient regarding her doctor. The child was utterly passive, emptied of personal will, and facing an implacable and resolute authority. Durkheim explicitly and unrepentantly argued that the same authority relation we saw leading to the pathological science of Freudianism had to be the basis for the instillation of human culture and indeed moral principles in the child. The moral sensibility that Durkheim considered to be the most fundamental social fact of all, the prototype of what his new causal science was to investigate, was to be instilled in his subjects using the same procedures that Freud used so unwisely on his unhappy patients and that Charcot had previously used on the indigent women confined in state institutions.

Durkheim did not come to this pass because he was lacking in his commitment to scientific truth or liberal republicanism. It was inherent in his understanding of the essentially arbitrary nature of concept formation.[47] But, we have found that there is no evidence that this view of everyday cognition is correct. Instead of a fundamentally arbitrary (if culturally consistent) process of drawing boundaries to establish identities, we find that things come in the world already clumped, and that people then rearrange those clumps in larger heaps to suit their practical needs. The Durkheimian vision is poorly equipped to handle such cognitive processes. But that does not mean that there are not other theoretical traditions that are in a better position. The next chapter explores the three most promising.

---

[47]Note that although Durkheim believed that the process of concept formation had an essentially arbitrary moment (cf. [1883–1884] 2004: 213), he imagined the process of concept *use*—whether that of a scientific community or that of human history—to lead to a convergence on the correct scientific concepts. Yet, as this convergence was a social process, the only alternative to his authoritarian vision would have been a mob democracy, an epistemic position from which he would recoil with greatest horror.

Chapter 5

Action In and On a World

WHAT DO PEOPLE KNOW ABOUT WHAT THEY DO?

Sociology and its kindred disciplines, as we have seen, have a particular, and a particularly problematic, way of framing the problem of how to explain what other people are doing. In large part, this is the result of a historically contingent synthesis that has been our birthright: we have inherited a fusion of a watered-down neo-Kantianism in our theory of knowledge mixed with unhealthy leavenings of the paranoiauthoritarianism of the French mental hospital. Of course, it is easy to criticize assumptions and hard to replace them with better ones. In this chapter, we explore other frameworks that, although historically eclipsed by Freudo-Durkheimianism in American social science, may be better platforms on which to build. It is essential to emphasize that the problems we have seen had little to do with the substantive claims being made; rather, it was in the theoretical grammar used to make them.[1]

More specifically, we traced the development of a set of psychological assumptions about the nature of cognition that posit the arbitrariness of our conceptual categories. These assumptions are such that they justify the adoption of some form of a hypothetico-deductive model of the sciences. Consequently, we assume that as nothing is "obviously true," all theoretical terms are formally equivalent. The model of cognition we have seen in chapter 4 not only supports this theory of science, it parallels it. Just as there is a fundamental distinction between data and theory in our idea of science, so in our model of cognition is there a fundamental distinction between sense data and the cultural grid used to sort these data. Just as there is something fundamentally arbitrary about the theoretical elements of science, so

---

[1] For example, even Durkheim's argument that social organization formed the template for our cognition of the animal kingdom has much to recommend it; certainly, the very word *genus* (as opposed to *species*) was taken from kin relations. The error, as we shall see, comes not at the level of this statement but in the more fundamental understanding of what this means for cognition and the world.

there is something fundamentally arbitrary about conceptual elements of everyday cognition.²

Because sociological theorists in particular, largely accepted the Durkheimian equation of words and things, instead of worrying about whether the various abstractions that they employed referred to anything worthy of the adjective "real," they attacked the reality of lived experience. That is, because they adopted a loose understanding of social knowledge generally termed "social construction," according to which no grid for dividing up perceptions had any inherent objective validity, sociologists could, with the gleeful malice that comes with the sure knowledge that one possesses an epistemological ace in the hole, concentrate their energies on undoing the categories put together by the laity. This was especially true where actors organized themselves into classes and attached labels to these classes, labels which were intrinsically tied to their self-understandings, namely, politics. Sociologists treating such social action put the everyday terms used by actors in quotation marks to indicate both their emotional detachment and their skepticism; they prefixed other people's self-understandings with "pseudo-" (e.g., calling conservatives "pseudoconservatives"); when a more detailed critique was warranted, they mobilized vaguely Freudian concepts pertaining to repression and displacement to deny the validity of the cognitive framework used by actors (e.g., Bell [1955] 1963).

The problems were not due to the biases of those with personal commitments; rather, they were unavoidable given the model of action that guided sociologists. Sociologists merely applied the same erroneous model to actors that they applied to themselves, namely, one in which there was something inherently arbitrary about knowledge and one in which it was *knowledge* that guided action. That is, they implicitly treated the cognitive components of action as knowledge in the technical or philosophical sense of a set of propositions about an extrasubjective world brought to subjective consciousness. For example, to understand political action, one needed to understand people's "theory of politics," so pollsters subjected successive waves of cross sections of the American population to withering barrages of questions about whether they believed that X was Y or rather Z, and when they figured out that people

---

²The Durkheimian version of this epistemology has been the most influential in sociology, although there are close affinities to other forms of subjective idealism, such as the neo-Kantianism of Rickert that influenced Weber. Indeed, Rickert gave one of the most thorough elaborations of the doctrine of concept formation via abstraction, and some of the writers I discuss in this chapter (especially Cassirer) were reacting more to Rickert's formulation than to any other. While I emphasize the Durkheimian version, the arguments made here would not change were Rickert's formulation used instead. See Thomas Burger (1976) and Ernst Cassirer ([1910] 1923: 221f, 224).

had no particular knowledge of X, Y, and Z, let alone a theory of them, they wondered how on earth people could make political choices at all (see Converse 1964 for the classic statement; Sniderman, Brody, and Tetlock 1991 for a rethinking).[3]

It is important to emphasize that I am not claiming this to be true of those few theorists who deliberately attempted to develop social constructionist approaches to specific topics (e.g., Gagnon and Simon 1976). Those who actually examined the processes whereby labels were attached to groups of things, just like the ethnozoologists and ethnobotanists reviewed in chapter 4, were forced to dissent from any simple confirmation of the vaguely Durkheimian model described therein. But the eighteenth-century philosophy of consciousness floated around social theory like a ghost in the form of a skeptical constructionism—a prototheory delegitimating the lived experience of the laity—selectively deployed by theorists. If we finally put this ghost to rest, we may find that different, more defensible approaches to the relationship between cognition and action have been provided by a number of other theoretical traditions. In all cases, such analysts began without the conceptual separation of theory and action that was part of the Cartesian heritage in the French theory. Three noteworthy alternative approaches were the Russian activity school, the German Gestalt psychologists, and the American pragmatists.

Not surprisingly, for our purposes, none of these approaches is completely satisfactory in all details. All do avoid the most problematic aspects of our current synthesis; further, they can be (and have been here) arranged in a series whereby one addresses the most important weaknesses of the others. The treatment here is of course partial and selective as I discuss each of these only insofar as they add something to our understanding of the nature of the cognitive components to social action. However, they not only serve to offer alternative platforms for an explanatory project deserving of renewed attention, but also demonstrate the possibility of an explanatory vocabulary that is neither self-contradicting nor epistemically unstable.

RUSSIAN ACTIVITY

An Individual Ontogeny of the Categories

The Russian activity school developed in the 1920s and 1930s and began to be the focus of renewed interest on the part of Westerners in the 1980s (see Wertsch 1981). This school was associated most notably with

---

[3]This fundamentally skewed approach to the cognition of others is seen in mainstream research in that we have an extremely well-developed mathematical understanding of the results of biased as opposed to unbiased sampling of *persons* but practically no understanding of the results that come from biases in

Alexander Luria and Lev Vygotsky, with other philosophers such as Evald Ilyenkov making contributions that were more specialized. A defining characteristic was the attempt to understand the cognitive components of action by stressing the practical nature of thought—its "this-sidedness," to take a phrase from Marx. Interestingly, we shall find that the limitations inherent in this tradition, limitations that prevent it from serving as a fundament from which to develop an alternative conception of explanation, come from the same incorporation of authority relations into its epistemology that we have found in the Charcot-Freud tradition.

To understand the approach and importance of the Russian activity school, it helps first to consider the work of Jean Piaget. Like Durkheim, Piaget was interested in the genesis of the categories of space, time, causality, substance, and so on, but unlike Durkheim, Piaget wished to explore these in terms of individual ontogenesis as opposed to collective phylogenesis.[4] Just as Durkheim could creatively imagine an intelligence that did *not* work within the Kantian a prioris, so Piaget (e.g., 1954: 350) started from the breakthrough that children are not born with these categories but instead acquire them over the course of a developmental process. The child's world is not our own, but it comes to be, and Piaget set out to find out how and when.

Piaget's most memorable results pertain to the surprising failure of children to make certain logical conclusions. However, as Donaldson (1978: 40, 44) and Macnamara (1982: 54f, 57, 62, 67, 73, 75, 77; also see 161 and Margolis 1987: 94) emphasized, these results come from procedures in which Piaget made no attempt to understand how children use speech and instead assumed the unambiguous nature of the logical implications of spoken instructions such as "things that go together." For example, very young children shown seven dogs, two cats, a mouse, and a cow may, if asked whether there are "more dogs or animals," insist that there

---

the sampling of *items* (the questions to be asked). Indeed, we have convinced ourselves that a "theoretical" approach to the data positively *requires* such bias (and the researcher who does not begin with his or her own understanding of how to classify items is widely seen as some sort of intellectual Cro-Magnon). We are not allowed to pick respondents whom we happen to like, but we are allowed to pick items we find important because we cannot comprehend that there is anything nonarbitrary about the organization of cognition. As a result, we also cannot comprehend the possibility of a descriptive cognography in the way that we might admit the possibility of a descriptive demography. The predictable response—that although there is a finite number of persons, there is an infinite number of potential beliefs—demonstrates the key error: there are a finite number of beliefs if we take "belief" in the sense most appropriate for an empirical science, namely, subjective states actually experienced by actual persons.

[4] Piaget appreciated Durkheim's work and understood its contribution to the Hume-Kant debate (see, e.g., Piaget [1965] 1995: 187).

are more dogs (e.g., Piaget [1941] 1952: 164). But, what are interpreted as logical fallacies may come from the emerging speech conventions. For one, because adults use terms like "toys" or "animals" only when a variety is present (as in "Pick up these toys!"), children seem to originally take these as plural nouns (like "clothes") that refer only to a collection. While tests show that they are able to pick out an individual as "an" animal, in general speech they will not understand this as a correct formulation.[5]

Even more, Piaget unproblematically assumed that children would recognize the social interaction of the abstracted "test" in which one is to respond politely to superiors without questioning assumptions or importing outside knowledge, but without simply telling the superior what (one thinks) he wants to hear. Such situations implicitly cue Western adults to shift their lexical-logical mapping to one appropriate for this task. In normal speech, we use words like *all* in ways that have a situational validity but fall short of their logical intension. As Donaldson (1978: 65, cf. 50) points out, if we ask a child, "And did you put all your clothes in the hamper?" what we mean is not "all the clothes in the world that you currently own," but "all your dirty clothes not yet put in the hamper, that is, don't forget your socks." For another example, while in logic *or* means A or B or both, in conventional speech it may imply exclusivity ("hot sauce or mild?") or the possibility of neither ("sugar or cream?"). Usually, the nature of the setting helps us understand what is meant, but in the test situation, Piaget asked children to switch to an abstracted and apparently pointless set of definitions. Not surprisingly, children who failed such tests could pass formally identical ones if the setting made sense (Donaldson 1978: 15ff).

Not only did Piaget judge the child's speech by a single (and rigid) set of adult standards, he also judged the child's reality by a single set of standards taken from physics. Piaget described the process of the objectification of space as culminating in the child locating his body "in a space and time reaching beyond him everywhere" and considering himself "as a mere effect among the totality of the connections he discovers" (Piaget 1954: 86).[6] But, Piaget's fascinating account of the development of the "categories of sensorimotor intelligence" not only took Cartesian space—the space of the eighteenth-century physicist—as the final adult space, it seemed to require that children understand all movement in this space as simple displacement of mass (in part because of his use of

---

[5]When attempting to carry out this test on the 2.5-year-old child of my friends Ann Mische and David Gibson, the query, "Are there more bears or more animals?" led Jeremy to exclaim happily "More animals!" and run off to get all the rest of his animals. He interpreted the chunk "more animals" to be a unified correlate to a particular action pattern.

[6]Like Durkheim, Piaget does not maintain Kant's distinction between space and time and the categories.

the mathematical concept of "group" as a set of objects and transformations [here see Piaget 1970]).

For example, consider Piaget's analysis of causality by imitation in the stage of magico-phenomenalistic causality (an analysis that has much to recommend it over the armchair version de Biran as discussed in chapter 2). Here, a child may try to get the adult to reinitiate an amusing activity (such as coughing for fun) by doing that activity herself. Piaget argued that persons (in the technical sense) are the first not-mes that the child recognizes as having the ability to initiate action; thus, we may say that persons have a genetic priority in terms of their status as semi-independent centers of actions to the child (Piaget 1954: 252, 279, 311). Gradually, however, as the child begins to make a more complete differentiation between herself and the surrounding world, she will move from this animism in which all causality implies personhood to a recognition of the difference between human agency and mechanical causality. But in the earlier stages, Piaget argues, the child acts on persons and inanimate objects in the same way, basically with an attempt at magically efficacious actions, for example, mimesis: *causality* though imitation (Piaget 1954: 250, 253, 264).

Piaget does provide evidence to support his interpretation of the child's behavior as an attempt to *cause* the parent to continue the action, as opposed to an attempt to *communicate* a desire. For example, the child may attempt to get her father to move while acting on the part of his body that would produce the result, as opposed to looking at the father's face to better communicate (Piaget 1954: 275, 300, 306).

But, Piaget may have made an unwarranted distinction between scientific and magical causality. Piaget (1954: 264) assumes that the child must be an object before she can see others as subjects; that is, she must perceive herself as one thing in a world of things that are acted on. But the child can perceive the *efficacy* of others even before the formation of true causality, hence the amused anticipation of Piaget's children during games that are focused on him. In other words, the child can understand that there is a person (a unified sensibility capable of moral agency) that leads to changes in the world (whatever that is) without understanding that this personhood is attached to a physical body that manipulates objects in space and time. Piaget's conviction that the essential question pertains to the schemata the child has for interpreting sense images leads him to reduce the elemental social relation of child-parent to the perception of objects.

But, the reality of the infant, even at these early stages, seems bound with self-construction through recognition (cf. Benjamin 1981)[7]; the tests

---

[7]Social theorists have, for reasons of theoretical elegance, generally assumed that such self-construction requires a process of differentiation (e.g., separation of sense of self from self-and-mother). It is not clear that there is any justification for this assumption that infants begin with a monistic self-universe that does not

used to generate Piaget's evidence are joint constructs of a child and an adult, usually a loving parent, and they cannot be analyzed stripped of the interactional context. As an example, I cite a wonderful study in which Paul Brainard (1930) attempted to compare his 2½-year-old daughter to the apes studied by the Gestalt psychologist Wolfgang Köhler in terms of mental function. Ruefully, he had to conclude: "This experience shows some of the difficulties in giving an animal experiment to a child. It is impossible to confine the child for a long period in a room or a cage and if she is left alone there is nothing to keep her at the task. In this case failure always led to [the child] going to find someone to help."[8] This quotation, out of context, gives the impression of a cold father, but in fact, what the tests demonstrate is the inability of Brainard to have his child orient to the spatial field of objects—instead, she continually oriented to *him*, asking him to get the things she could not reach, arguing with him over whether she was able to complete the task, crying until he relented when she failed, and gleefully saying, "That's a good fool on you," when she succeeded (Brainard 1930: 278, 276).

Indeed, further research strongly suggests that sociologic precedes logic, in that children seem to better comprehend logical relations if they pertain to *persons*. Something as simple as the grammatical form that indicates that something is a proper name (and not a mere noun) increases the likelihood that an infant will understand it—but only if that something can be envisioned as a person.[9] Further, infants as young as 2 months

---

distinguish self and others. Patterns of infant imitation show a capacity to respond to others as independent sources of efficacy, as well as to recognize "trying" (as opposed to action/consequences), both of themselves and others, at far earlier ages than previously assumed. Indeed, it may be implausible that any "self" exists *prior* to relationality. See, for example, the work of Meltzoff and Moore (1995: 51, 61, 63) and Rochat (2001: 145).

[8]Interestingly, the same has been found of other primates, including Köhler's ([1917] 1925: 8, 32, 48ff, 142f) apes: they first appealed to the experimenter or other animals for help (also see Jolly 1966: 505).

[9]Thus, infants do better at Piagetian "object permanence" tests when the "object" is a person than when it is inanimate (Smith 1988: 96). For another example, 24-month-old children were shown either two blocks or two dolls, one of which was given a made-up label (e.g., "zon"). But in half of the conditions, the child was told it was "a zon" and in the other half told it was "Zon." Children were more likely to retrieve the doll when it was called Zon than the blocks however named or the doll when called "a zon." (Macnamara 1982: 21–27; also see Merleau-Ponty [1942] 1963: 157, 166, 171, who notes how this cuts against the idea of the arbitrariness of perception; indeed, it even frustrates the Durkheimian division into a priori form and empirical content). As Cassirer ([1928–1940] 1996: 140) had suggested, "This 'standing in opposition,' [the German word for "object" literally means standing in opposition] this 'resistance' [of the objective world] is originally encountered in the experience of the will, but not a merely impersonal 'It.' Rather, we find it originally as a 'You.'"

may develop what Collins (2004: 124) would consider "entrainment," in that they "lock in" to an interactive other (and hence a child will look more at a screen displaying a face of a mother who is watching him than a screen of the same mother video recorded [Rochat 2001: 147f]). Children are oriented first and foremost to concrete persons and their lived relations, but it was precisely this that Piaget attempted to ignore.

It was this almost autistic side to Piaget's analysis that prompted the critiques of Vygotsky ([1934] 1987).[10] There are two closely related aspects of this critique, although they were not equally influential. The first is that the relation between child and adult must be understood as a fully social relation, while the second was that the developmental process was above all else a social process.[11] The child's development, therefore, must be seen as a social phenomenon; although "Piaget is very familiar with the child's tendency to apply what were previously social forms of behavior to himself," Piaget falsely constructed an egocentric child at the heart of development, thus ignoring the social interaction necessary for cognitive development: "The child is not seen as a part of the social whole, as a subject of social relationships. He is not seen as a being who participates in the societal life of the social whole to which he belongs from the outset" (Vygotsky [1934] 1987: 74, 83).

Our focus of attention will be largely on how Vygotsky supported these critiques; his actual arguments have been exciting largely because of their indeterminacy. His claims are evocative but often resist careful restatement, and the empirical data that he used as support are extremely weak. Yet, he was able to find the flaws in how others had formulated the question of how our framework of intelligence might be constructed, and this is where we begin in our attempt to fix the problems outlined in chapter 4.

Out-Durkheimianizing Durkheim

Because of his interest in developing a more sociological account of the ontogenesis of the categories, Vygotsky was drawn to and appreciative of Durkheim's argument in *Elementary Forms*.[12] Like many others, Vygotsky

---

[10] It is not necessary to endorse all aspects of this critique in order to review it; certainly, it fails to recognize the strength and clarity of Piaget's arguments, beside which Vygotsky's are often loose and undisciplined.

[11] Piaget later ([1965] 1995) understood the force of the latter critique (that he had made development some sort of unfolding of preprogrammed growth) and attempted to emphasize the inherently social nature of this development, but he saw little influence of social factors other than to induce variation in the timing of steps along a preordained sequence—Piaget saw no social variability in the content of these stages. This is criticized by Vygotsky ([1934] 1987: 174).

[12] After citing a passage of Piaget, Vygotsky ([1934] 1987: 85) comments: "One could not more clearly express the concept that the need for logical thought

saw a parallel between non-Western totemic thinking and the thinking of the child: both fell short of the scientific outlook; both attempted to succeed in reaching knowledge with faulty tools. While Durkheim had at times pointed to the importance of the practical nature of totemic thought, his assumptions about the nature of cognition made it difficult not to consistently move away from this emphasis and instead to see totemic thought as a static system for the categorization and contemplation of the world.

Vygotsky, in contrast, argued that what was missing in Piaget was "the child's practical activity." This might seem unfair, since Piaget had stressed the practical nature of the child's intelligence, but Vygotsky, clearly thinking of Marx's *Theses on Feuerbach*, meant a unification of thought and action, most importantly, social interaction (also see Leontyev 1977: 193).[13] In particular, Vygotsky proposed that thinking was basically a form of internalized speech; rather than the child beginning with a simple egocentrism, as alleged by Piaget, the child's seeming absorption with himself seen in the monologues characterizing the second and third year of life was actually a process of transferring patterns first worked out in actual social interaction (conversation with adults) to become silent and internal speech via the intermediate stage of spoken solitary speech. This argument (which is not necessarily correct) leads to a different view of the relation between language and cognition than that found in the French school (especially that associated with Saussure), in which there was a distinction between the abstract structure of language and any particular spoken realization. For Vygotsky, attention to the practical nature of language meant that language was never hypostatized as something other than a pattern of social interaction.[14]

This emphasis on practice probably helped Vygotsky avoid some of Durkheim's most flagrant errors pertaining to the relation between word

---

or the need for the knowledge of truth itself, emerges in the interaction between the consciousness of the child and the consciousness of others. Philosophically this argument is reminiscent of the perspective of Durkheim and other sociologists who derive space, time, and objective reality as a whole from the social life of man!"

[13]Ilyenkov (1977b: 70–72) had a more profound notion of the nature of activity, one that paralleled many arguments of the Gestalt school—if we are to follow the dictum at Delphi and "know ourselves," we do so in a practical sense when we understand the relationship of our body vis-à-vis other objects, and we gain this only though *action*. Thus, the universalism of Piaget's final stage comes not from some discursive process of weeding out partial viewpoints but from physical and transformative interaction with things.

[14]This led Vygotsky to argue that the unit of speech was not the "word" but "meaning," which dovetails with some of the pragmatic approaches we will explore.

and concept. Durkheim, in proposing totemic classification as the origins of the framework of classification itself, was forced to posit an equivalence between all forms of classification. Thus, when the Bororo Indians of Brazil invoke a sense of kinship with a particular species of bird, Durkheim and Mauss ([1903] 1963: 6) argued, "the Bororo sincerely imagines himself to be a parrot."[15] But Vygotsky proposed that there was a difference between this sense of identity and that used to define classes of equivalents. Using Lévy-Bruhl's ([1926] 1985) work on primitive thought as "participation," Vygotsky ([1934] 1987: 150f) identified a form of complexive thinking in which the same objects could be linked to more than one complex: "Consequently, in these languages, the functional application of the word is entirely different than it is in our own. It is not a means for forming and carrying concepts. It is a family name. It is a means of naming groups with concrete objects that are united in accordance with some type of empirical kinship." Because, as we recall, Durkheim took a unilineal model of kinship for the basis of society, he was able to equate kinship and classification: just as any person has only one father, any species is in one only genus. (We return to this connection in the next chapter.) But Vygotsky (like Wittgenstein somewhat later), implicitly taking a bilineal view of kinship, argued that the Bororo could state an identity of kinship without an identity of substance. Thus, the assertion "we are parrots" "does not imply an identification of parrot and people any more than identification is implied by the fact that two people related by kinship have the same family name."[16] More generally, the

---

[15]Durkheim ([1912] 1995: 191) later seemed to revise his beliefs considerably: When a native says that people of the Crow phratry are crows, "He does not exactly mean that they are crows in the everyday empirical sense of the word, but that the same principle is found in all of them." At the same time, he also says the opposite: "Man sees the things of his clan as relatives and associates; he calls them friends and considers them to be made of the same flesh as he" (Durkheim [1912] 1995: 150).

[16]The case of "the ubiquitous Bororo," as Godlove (1989: 3) calls them (they are discussed not only by Durkheim and Mauss but also by Lévy-Bruhl [1926/1985: 366, 368], Wright [1913: 649], Geertz [1973: 121], Barnes [1981], and many others), turns out to defeat the best guesses of armchair theorists (here I rely on the wonderful piece by Crocker 1977a, esp. 182–189). First, while the Bororo do have totems in the classic sense (serving as names for clans), the red macaws to which the Bororo assert identity are not one of them (also see Levi-Strauss [1962] 1966: 99). Instead, they are *pets*, the only pets kept by the Bororo. Furthermore, they are kept by *women*—and many "receive proper names, or diminutives thereof, taken from the owner's matrilineage," are hand fed, and have their deaths mourned as if they were human. Second, the Bororo are matrilocal—the newly married man moves to his wife's uncle's house, which is ruled by the women, there to dwell among her kin. "All enduring social relationships among the Bororo are initiated and defined by reference to women. Through their procreation and

Concepts, Authoritativeness of

But, while Vygotsky moved away from Durkheim's simplest equation of words and concepts ("every word translates a concept"), he still assumed that every word applies to a class, and that "the concept is not possible without the word." The child forms concepts not simply by learning words that bring with them definitions. Rather, the child begins by heaping objects together using words on the basis of how she finds words used by adults. Through interaction with adults, the child can move toward a more abstract sense of concepts. "Thus, verbal interaction with adults becomes the motive force behind the development of the child's concepts" (Vygotsky [1934] 1987: 47f, 131, 135, 142, 146; also see Dore 1985).

It is this sense of Vygotsky's that mind can be understood as the internalization of social processes that has been most appealing to contemporary social and behavioral scientists. While George Herbert Mead (1934: 188) also argued that "Mind is nothing but the importation of [an] external [social] process into the conduct of the individual so as to meet the problems that arise," Vygotsky emphasized the mediation of this process by signs and tools—or what we might call "culture" (also see Wertsch 1991). Seen as a process, this account has much to recommend it. But, in retaining the "concept" as the end point of this process, and a concept that was a hierarchical classification of objects, the boundaries of which come from speech as used by adults, Vygotsky kept the same arbitrariness that Durkheim had introduced.

In other words, Durkheim's fundamental error was to assume that there was only one way of making synthetic statements—that something is something else. Technically, we might say that he restricted the copula

---

nourishment of men, they bind masculine loyalties and check their freedom of action just as surely as they domesticate macaws." The identification of Bororo (man) and the macaw spirit thus expresses both the sense of confinement and the potential for escape from this female-defined world.

Further, as Crocker (1977b: 54) emphasizes, we know that the Bororo do not equate themselves with macaws simply because they only compare *themselves* to macaws, and not *macaws* to themselves. The copula "are" serves here (in "we are X") not as a binary relation of equivalence, which is by nature symmetric and transitive, but as an act of metaphor to detach predicates from one object (where they exist nonproblematically) and bring them to another (where they shed new light given their new placement).

in such synthetic statements to set identity or subsumption.[17] Since this will become key in the next chapter, it is worth explicating this fully. In the relation of subsumptive "is," to say that "X is Y" and that "Y is Z" is necessarily to say that $X \subseteq Y$ and $Y \subseteq Z$, which implies, among other things, that $X \subseteq Z$ (read $\subseteq$ as "is a subset of"; note that $X = Y \leftrightarrow X \subseteq Y$ and $Y \subseteq X$). If we restrict our understanding of "is" to such a definition, we do indeed produce a typology—a set of at least partially nested sets of varying generality. As Durkheim emphasized, this has been used by scientists to order the world of living beings. Yet, as a general principle this seems to violate how people actually think; it eliminates not only ambiguity and fuzziness but also flexibility and, indeed, substantive rationality.[18] Vygotsky did not make this same assumption regarding the child who was able to use a different form of reason, yet he treated such typology as the *telos* of cognitive development.[19] Sooner or later, things must be not just what they are, but subsumed as instances of something else. This seemingly inoffensive assumption, however, had strong implications for how Vygotsky would envision the social relationships entering into cognition.

At the end of chapter 4, we saw that Durkheim's psychology of arbitrary concepts led him to embrace an authoritarian model of instruction that dovetailed with the Freudian model of truth production. Because Vygotsky also imagined that the end point of the process of concept development was the embracing of a fundamentally arbitrary set of categories tied to words, he also required an external authority. Vygotsky ([1934] 1987: 74, 83) had, we recall, begun with a criticism of the abstract individuality of the child in Piaget. This stress on the embeddedness of the child's cognition in social relationships was, in some ways, clearly a step in the right direction: as we have seen, social relationships seem to be easier for children to comprehend than are relations with or between inanimate objects. But the sort of relationship that Vygotsky introduced was always by nature a hierarchical one.

---

[17]Compare his early discussion of copulae and syllogism in set theoretic terms ([1883–1884] 2004: 186, 192). What is of possible interest here is not his approach but the proportion of time devoted to it.

[18]Here, one may refer to the discussion of formal subsumptive rationality and law in chapter 2.

[19]For example, asked to put "like things together," the child may first choose a yellow triangle and a yellow square, then a blue square, then a blue circle, and then a red circle. It is not actually clear that this represents a stage of the development of "concepts" as opposed to limitations of attention and comprehension of the task. But Vygotsky ([1934] 1987: 162) interpreted this to mean that concepts are not formed, as the conventional theory (discussed in the next chapter) would hold, through the elimination of particularities and the emphasis on commonalities. Rather, concept formation requires a process (dialectical, of course) of going from particular and general and back again. But, in the end, one comes to the traditional understanding of a concept as an abstraction uniting particularities.

As Rogoff (1990: 148) has written, Piaget's original philosophy resounded well with the fierce independence of the Genevan city-state which was his home. Piaget's seemingly mechanical process of development implied that learning happened on its own; indeed, Piaget emphasized that "the child learns in spite of adult authority, not because of it." The universal nature of the telos of cognition was compatible with a fundamentally democratic, if libertarian, world; Vygotsky's approach fit better with the (assumed) benign guidance of the communist "preceptorial" state (this term is taken from Lindblom [1977], who uses it to discuss Communist China; the term fits Russia somewhat less exactly). All people have the fundamental ability to produce correct knowledge—at least once they have been instructed how to do so. Not surprisingly, Vygotsky's work has been most enthusiastically adopted by early childhood educators and psychologists: Piaget left teachers with little to do other than basic caretaking—Vygotsky reconfirmed their centrality and "active" role.[20]

There may of course be good reasons why teachers need to do something other than watch their charges develop according to a more or less exactly fixed schedule, but Vygotsky's reintroduction of the necessary position of an unquestioned cognitive authority was also integrally tied to his adoption of the "words-and-concepts" framework that assumed that all perceptual organization came from speech, not the world. If adults call it a duck, then to the child it *is* a duck, even if it has six legs and two sets of wings. On the one hand, this is incontestably correct, if we have dropped the issue of the child's cognitive engagement with the world and instead turned to the different issue of the child's acquisition of linguistic competence. Indeed, many studies have unwittingly done just this, by gathering their data through verbal interactions. On the other hand, this is incontestably false, if we mean that our concept comes from the word. A child who successfully learns the word *bar* does not have a single concept corresponding to this word but rather uses the word as part of a larger utterance in a context to determine which of several meanings is intended.

Thus, Vygotsky, like others, went from the nonproblematic assertion that children learn what to call things by repeating what adults do to the problematic assertion that the conceptual order with which the child confronts the world comes from the internalization of the speech usage of

---

[20]While Vygotsky's approach was thus wholly Russian-Communist, this is not to say that the Russian approach was wholly Vygotskian. Instead, Lenin's dismissal of complicated cognitive theories (more or less as a form of bourgeois decadence) in favor of a workman-like simple reflection theory formed the basis for most Soviet psychology (Billig 1982: 56); in the 1950s, it was Pavlovianism that became the center of official doctrine (Joravsky 1977). Pavlov, it may be added, considered himself "at war" with Köhler (Pastore 1971: 320).

adults. Further, even for cases in which a child learns that a duck is a duck by listening to adults, this begs the much larger question (What do adults call a duck and why?), a question that is central for any understanding of the nature of concepts. By stopping the analysis at the point at which the adult says "duck," Vygotsky was able to imagine that the nature of the concept is simply the combination of (on the one hand) a word uniting cases by suppressing particularities and (on the other) a speaker of this word with a deep and confident voice. Thus Vygotsky was led back to the same inability to root out false abstractions we have seen as endemic in the social sciences. Though Marx himself (as I argue in chapter 9) always emphasized the importance of concrete analysis, there was no particular reason why his followers could not turn his ideas into abstractions utterly at odds with the concrete, especially if they had the ability to shoot critics. While there may be sophistical ways of arguing that this does not necessarily lead to degenerate theory in which the "protective belts" (see Burawoy 1990) are holding up trousers with a good deal too many holes, such authoritative support for abstractions marred Vygotsky's own work.

For example, considering the development of scientific reasoning in the child, which he took to necessarily involve the collaboration of a teacher, Vygotsky ([1934] 1987: 215) analyzed how children used the concept of causation by having them finish sentences that began along the lines of, "The bicyclist fell because. . . ." Considering social scientific concepts, he analyzed completions to the phrase, "In the USSR it is possible to have a planned economy because . . . " and evaluated the stage of scientific development implicit in the answer "because there is no private property; all the land, factories, and power stations are in the hands of the workers and peasants." It is hardly surprising that the authority of a teacher should be found necessary for a child to reach this "stage" of development!

In sum, the Russian activity school began an admirable approach to focusing on the concrete nature of thought, one that did not recapitulate the Cartesian distinction between the static grid of knowledge and the actions taken with reference to this knowledge. But, because the leading members focused on the active nature of concept formation without an acknowledgment of the prestructured nature of the world, it was impossible to understand the process of concept formation without a place for a "correct" authority that provided external standards for the correctness of thought.[21] This authority had no greater claim to credibility than the subjects whose development was being gauged, and often a good deal less. But the problem was not the particular type of authority invoked; rather,

---

[21]There was indeed work in this tradition avoiding this problem, but it tended to remain abstract and Hegelian (or Feuerbachian). Most important—and making in essence the same arguments as found in this book—is Ilyenkov's (1977b: 86; 1977a: 8, also 221) rehabilitation of idealism as dialectical materialism. Beginning

Action In and On a World

it was the necessary role of authority in providing a fulcrum for explanation. There was greater promise in the German Gestalt school, to which I turn next.[22]

GERMAN GESTALT

From Goethe to Cassirer

In chapter 3, we saw that academic psychology originated in Germany, where it was influenced by a more fundamental tradition of German thought that I referred to as the developmental-comprehensive tradition. There had long been a distinctively German approach to science that stressed wholistic development as opposed to atomistic analysis. Goethe is often seen as the exemplar of this tradition, but it was continued into the early twentieth century in fields from critical theory to genetics (Jay 1984; Harwood 1993; Koffka 1935: 9; see Gay [1970: 70] on the "hunger for wholeness" of that time) and, in particular, in the philosophy of Ernst Cassirer (see esp. [1928–1940] 1996: 193).[23]

Cassirer (1922: 38) proposed that one could see the same difference between Goethe's approach and modern natural history that one can see between astrology and modern mathematical physics. Goethe's approach was based on the conviction that all existing comes from the same fundamental and eternal source and must be grasped through the intuition.[24] In

---

with the argument that thought was the ideal component of real activity, Ilyenkov argued that one could expect a mapping between concepts and patterns of relationships. As he properly says, "Ideality, according to Marx, is nothing else but the form of social human activity represented in the thing. Or, conversely, the form of human activity represented *as a thing*, as an object." Because of this different starting point, Ilyenkov (1977a: 62) was able to criticize the concept of the concept as a false unification, one that does not get at true unity but only the formal unification of nominalism, a variety of isolated facts "tied together as it were with string."

[22]There were some connections between the activity theorists and the Gestalt theorists, including contacts at conferences and Koffka's participation in a set of seminars in Asia organized by Luria; both Vygotsky and Luria were initially attracted to Gestalt psychology (Scheerer 1980: 116f, 119, 125f); Vygotsky ([1934] 1987) discusses Köhler's work with apes at length.

[23]Like Husserl, Cassirer developed his ideas regarding the nature of relations first in the philosophy of mathematics, but he then applied and extended them to the more important class of naturally occurring (as opposed to constructed) concepts pertaining to a world of sensation ([1910] 1923: 112f, 114).

[24]Discussing Goethe, Cassirer (1922: 36) emphasized that he parted company from modern mathematics and mathematical physics in that he saw wholes not as something to be broken up into elemental parts, but precisely as wholes, which

the same way that we cannot "analyze" a melody by breaking it down into individual components (see Cassirer [1910] 1923: 332, 335)—since a melody is a relation between relations—and instead must grasp it as a whole, so there may be aspects of nature that need to be grasped as wholes. But, Cassirer (1922: 36) argued that Western science had lost the ability to understand wholes and the relation of inner to outer that had marked medieval thought.

Cassirer's approach brought together a sense of the important characteristics of a whole as a form, a Gestalt, and an implicit tendency toward self-development (as opposed to the assumption that matter was inert until brought into motion due to external compulsion). The unity of these two is seen in Goethe's famous line regarding the "*geprägte Form, die lebend sich entwickelt*" ("imprinted form that, living, develops itself").[25] Goethe applied the same understanding of Gestalt as a self-developing whole to his work on plant morphology: the parts of a plant cannot be understood in abstraction from one another, but only as part of a whole form that develops itself (see Ash 1998: 85).

This emphasis on wholes, as we shall see, ended up leading to a model of cognition that did not assume (like the Durkheimian) the arbitrariness of classification of percepts.[26] Further, this model of cognition is also incompatible with the common idea that the difference between the whole and the sum of the parts can be explained by some "emergence."[27]

---

should therefore be grasped in the intuition as a complex of pure forms [*Gestalten*]. Spengler also stressed this distinction in the first volume of *The Decline of the West*, subtitled *Gestalt and Reality* (see Ash 1998: 287f).

[25]Cassirer (1922: 43) also saw the new modern scientific perspective reaching its apogee in field theory, especially in relativity theory, for which the metric field is equated with the field of force. For us, space is dissolved into force, while for astrology, force is dissolved into space. Such field theory became an important product of the elaboration of these ideas, as we shall see in chapters 7 and 8. On the Gestalt school, see Cassirer ([1923] 1953: 102).

[26]Interestingly, Cassirer (1922: 15, 17ff, 24, 53; also see [1928–1940] 1996: 212–214; [1923] 1953: 87 and 218 for an example of a Kantian approach to time) himself, influenced by Durkheim, put forward a grid-of-perception argument: The classes of existence are not simply taken from the world as naïve realism would have it, but rather require the imposition of boundaries that are a work of the mind; hence, the forms that the world takes for us are given by our mind. Again, he speaks of social schemas that lead to agreed-on organization of the world of intuitions. Indeed, Cassirer's crowning work on symbolic forms was an attempt to push forward the Kantian project of specifying the active nature of our interaction with the world, although generalizing from cognition more narrowly construed to all ways in which the human spirit (or cultural faculties) reached toward the world (see, e.g., [1923] 1953: 80, 114, 178; [1925] 1955: 35).

[27]Cassirer ([1910] 1923: 339) emphasized the difference between a pseudowholism based on a superordination of some analytic elements to others and a

This also fit Goethe's insistence that that which is within is without.[28] Cassirer ([1910] 1923: 271f) argued that when Western science assumed that this was not the case—that mind and object were intrinsically of two different natures, an axiom wholly at odds with the nature of immediate experience—a decisive step was taken that was to lead to other paradoxes and incoherences. Understanding the connection between mind and environment was to be the core of a central branch of the new psychology we saw emerging in Germany in chapter 2 that took this general emphasis as the basis for a serious program of research. This is the Gestalt school, to which we now turn.

The Nonindependence of Percepts

The Gestalt idea is generally attributed to Christian Ehrenfels, who had studied with Alexius Meinong at Graz. Ehrenfels ([1890] 1988: 112) pointed out not only that there are qualities that can only exist as a whole (e.g., timbre or a melody) but that we are not aware of any conscious activity whereby we generate this quality through synthesis. While acknowledging Ehrenfels's priority, the motive force in establishing an empirical school of psychology was really Max Wertheimer, who had attended lectures by Ehrenfels (Heider 1983: 44).

Wertheimer had also been influenced by Carl Stumpf, who had sketched the lines for the sort of phenomenology that was to turn into Gestalt psychology. The backdrop was the German debate regarding the position of the "cultural sciences" (*Geisteswissenschaften* [Dilthey 1883/1988: 78, 91, 97, 125, 131]), and theorists' increasing opposition of these cultural sciences to the natural sciences; while the natural sciences (according to Wilhelm Windelband [1894/1905: 16]) could pursue laws,

---

"strict correlativity" or duality between elements and relations. The former stays within the traditional concept formation of nested sets, while the latter moves toward a fundamentally relational analysis. Thus, to take the simplest example, the duality inherent in relational thinking frustrates the assumption of the emergence thesis that new properties "emerge" at a "higher" level in which many simple units (e.g., cells) are combined into fewer more complex units (e.g., organisms). For if, say, we propose that dyadic relationships have characteristics not present in either member, we are wrong to think that ego and alter can be nested in the relationship in the way that cells can (approximately) be considered as nested in the body. Each person participates in multiple relationships, and through the principle of duality, we are as welcome to see the relationships as the units and the persons as relations connecting these relationships.

[28]It was this same understanding of a duality between inner and outer that led to Goethe's philosophical elaboration of the chemical idea of elective affinity in his novel *Die Wahlverwandschaften*; Gestalt theorists such as Köhler referred to Goethe's ideas here (see Ash 1998: 178, 185). Thus, the logic laid out in the note 27 shows that it was in no way irrational for such thinkers to deny that the inner

the cultural sciences should attempt to specify configurations: gestalts. Most Germans found it impossible to avoid mapping this opposition onto the Kantian one of laws of freedom as opposed to laws of necessity; a science of persons and a science of things. Stumpf (1907: 23, 26, 47) provisionally accepted the division between the natural sciences and the cultural sciences, arguing that they had different objects of study. While it is true that the natural sciences begin (as Mach would have it) with the data of experience, the object of the cultural sciences is not what lies behind this experience in a causal relation, but the experience itself. Just as physics is the most fundamental natural science, so psychology (argued Stumpf) is the most fundamental cultural science.

But, there is something more fundamental, a science of the structure of the phenomena with which each of these (psychology and physics) begin. This science—phenomenology—recognizes that the objects we investigate in the sciences are already inherently conceptual and attempts to determine the regularities in the construction of such conceptuality (Stumpf's student Husserl was later to emphasize one version of such a phenomenological study as a form of "pure psychology").[29] In addition, Stumpf (1907: 33, 38f, 29) also proposed two other pre-sciences, a science of structure and a science of relations.

Finally, Stumpf (1907: 61, 64) made a distinction between two approaches to describing the lawfulness of the world. One was causal, and the other, often called "descriptive," was really a science of structural laws. Although neither of these approaches could be isolated from the other, nor replaced by the other, they were sufficiently distinct that some sciences appear as one or the other. In particular, phenomenology is a structural science.

---

should be seen as inside and hence lower than the outer. This was also related to Goethe's (1988: 307) insistence that there was no distinction between the factual and the theoretical: "Let us not seek for something behind the phenomena—they themselves are the theory."

[29]Husserl made many of the same points as the Gestalt theorists in contradistinction to conventional psychology, most important that we must refrain from attempting to argue that what something "is" is different from how it appears in the intuition, and a general criticism of what he called the "modern nominalism" of *conceptualism*, confusing concepts of things with things themselves in experience. In contrast to most philosophies of consciousness, he also stressed the apt nature of our evolved system for developing ideas (Husserl [1900] 1970: 204, 268). However, Husserl's antiempirical take (see, e.g., Husserl 1927 translated in Sheehan and Palmer 1997) led him to stress a distantiation (bracketing) of experience that cut against the directions of the Gestalt school. (As Merleau-Ponty [1962: xiif] said, Husserl objected to investigations that explored how we make use of our relation to the world—Husserl preferred just to be *"filled with wonde* at it"; Köhler [1938: 45, cf. 68] nicely says that although Husserl also tried to save the idea that there was a purposiveness in the world, "very characteristically, his

And phenomenology demonstrates that our world is not the world of the Cartesians. First, in contrast to the pure, isotropic, and homogeneous space of geometry, the space we live in has certain relations built into it (at any time, some things "are" to the left, say), and it has unevenesses in it (and indeed, our vision has boundaries) (Stumpf 1907: 72, 9). These are characteristics of the objects we confront, not things we put into them.[30]

Stumpf thus proposed not only an ideal phenomenology that retained the distinction between the re-created pure visions of the natural sciences and our actual experienced world, but a version of psychology attuned to philosophical questions (as opposed to the narrower professionalism of the American model). Both these principles—an embracing of immediate experience and an engagement with philosophical questions—marked the approach of Stumpf's students who were to found the Gestalt school: in addition to Wertheimer, these were Wolfgang Köhler and Kurt Koffka (Smith 1988: 12, 45; Neisser 2002: 4; Ash 1998: 118, 120, 124).[31]

What Wertheimer did was to seize on one key aspect of this idea as the basis for experimental research. Both Stumpf and Ehrenfels had pointed to the importance of our capacity to hear harmonics—relations—as unities. The way to understand our actual, empirical, phenomenological experience would be to investigate how we captured the *forms* ("gestalts") as objects (and not as aggregates or syntheses). In other words, Stumpf's various pre-sciences (phenomenology, a science of structure and a science of relations) bled into each other, for the objects that we perceive—or at least their character as quality-bearing objects—are themselves structures, and these structures are sets of relations.

A Phenomenology of Relations

These planks were of great utility for psychologists attempting to account for the nonindependence of perceptual elements, which did not square with the dominant mechanistic explanation of sight. According to this

---

attempt towards salvation began with a further retreat.") Or, as Stumpf (1907: 35) said, Husserl only explored the genetic, and not the descriptive, tasks of a fundamental psychology. (It is important to recall that many of Husserl's works that might lead us to question this judgment were published very late.) When Husserl's approach finally made its way into the social sciences via Schutz ([1932] 1967: xxxi), every connection to empiricism had been severed and phenomenology equated with "the most rigorous philosophical reflection."

[30] Even more, argued Stumpf, we realize that values must be understood as properties of objects and not properties of valuing persons (a point we shall find later Gestalt theorists explicating in greater detail).

[31] Koffka, Köhler, and Kurt Lewin all studied under Stumpf; Wertheimer did not but spent a number of years at Stumpf's Berlin institute (Heider 1983: 105; Ash 1998: 34, 105).

latter view—one compatible with the Durkheimian psychology, according to which sensory data strike the mind in an intrinsically unordered fashion—photons stimulate retinal cells, which leads to neurons firing, which leads to a copy of the visual field reproduced in some portion of the brain. This field was then processed according to some mental template, leading to a distinction between the psychology of perception and the psychology of judgment.

Wertheimer (1922: 48, V) called this the "mosaic or bundle thesis" of perception and consciousness: all higher-order elements were the sum of elemental contents constructed according to mere "and" summation. Connections between elements were generally ascribed to "association," a type of relation that was indifferent to the content of the elements (cf. Cassirer [1910] 1923: 285). Those who began from this assumption had a difficult time explaining cases in which our perception of one thing (e.g., distance) is affected by something else in the visual field; they were forced to argue that these were illusions of *judgment*. Wertheimer, in contrast, began from an assumption that what we perceive is a totality of relations that, far from being arbitrary, expressed the nature of the concrete laws of their formal structure (Wertheimer 1922: 53). While the grid-of-perception approach assumed that the unit percepts were primary, and the larger structures derivative of some act of mental formulation, Wertheimer argued that the whole was primary and its structural principles as objective as anything else.

The fundamental principle was one of cognitive economy or "terseness," *Prägnanz*.[32] Gestalt theorists assumed that we attempt to resolve the visual field into the simplest combination of shapes possible according to a few laws pertaining to the relations between boundaries and textures. For example, figures 5.1 generally appears to be two shapes—a square with another square laid on top of it—rather than four L-shapes (with slightly beveled ends). Such wholistic perception arises, as Gibson ([1979] 1986) later emphasized, because the environment *is* composed of surfaces, and one surface covers another in a predictable way.

Although this was an argument about perception, the Gestalt theorists saw their conclusions as having implications for the philosophy of knowledge. According to traditional conceptions, one could separate the act of perception or sense-certainty ("this is") from the act of judgment ("this is that"). The Gestalt theorists' results strongly implied that such a separation did not correspond to our processes of interaction with the environment. We do not perceive "this" without also perceiving that this "this" is a "that." Phenomenologically speaking, we may say that we perceive *what*

---

[32]The term *principle of cognitive economy* was first introduced by Mach in a somewhat different sense.

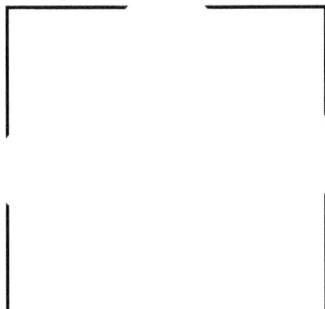

Figure 5.1 Two as opposed to four shapes

things are immediately as we perceive them, for nothing is seen that is not seen as something.[33]

One crucial experiment that established this point was Wertheimer's investigation of the apparent motion induced when two lights are flashed in succession some distance apart. Rather than the motion being something that the judgment *adds* to the perceptions and is hence separate from the perceptions, subjects reported one single moving light (also see the argument of Cassirer [1910] 1923: 121). Thus, we may see the perceptual system as a totality that grasps information from our surroundings that we need for action and translates this information into meaningful wholes that we care about—things like surfaces, distances, positions, and trajectories (see Köhler 1920: 27; Gibson [1979] 1986; Lee 1980).

The same goes for our sensing of the world in general. We saw in chapter 4 that sociologists tend to highlight the relatively few—and relatively trivial—cases in which the same object can be categorized differently: whether a tomato is seen as a vegetable or a fruit. More important, it was once believed by Europeans to be poisonous. But, this is an exception, not the rule, as our taste system not only helps us sort out many poisonous plants from the edible, but even gives information regarding the likely properties of certain edible plants (which is why chimpanzees in the wild are able to self-medicate [see Huffman and Wrangham 1994]). Our perceptual system was not some cruel joke implanted by a malicious creator, who wanted to see how many ways we might possibly classify billions of unorganized bits of sense data.[34] Instead,

---

[33]The equiprimordality of judgment and perception means that even when we see something, and we cannot determine what it is, we see it *as* an ambiguousness. Also see the work of Heidegger ([1926] 1962: 207; I.5.34).

[34]As Köhler (1947: 118, cf. 259) wrote in his classic introduction to Gestalt psychology, "As to the statement that sensory experience is a mosaic of purely local facts in the sense that each point of a sensory field depends exclusively

it is the culmination of an evolutionary process that took place in a world not much different from the one we inhabit and hence is remarkably fit to deal with the world around us (also see Merleau-Ponty [1962: 229]). "Evolution implies isomorphism" (Köhler 1938: 398; also 390). Hence, the general understanding of actors is more psychologically astute than the mechanical theories of psychologists (Wertheimer 1922: 54). Köhler liked to quote the same phrase of Goethe's to which Cassirer also referred regarding the unification of inner and outer as a way of expressing this complicity between our perceptual system and the world (also Bischof 1966: 22).

It is not, of course, invariably the case that there is such a complicity between mental and environmental structures; indeed, we can subjectively experience and scientifically study the transition whereby we bring our mental structure into alignment with the environment, a process that Köhler ([1917] 1925: 190; also 17, 99, 173f, 198; also 1938: 31) called "insight" (*Einsicht*, sometimes translated as "intelligence"), "a complete solution with reference to the whole lay-out of the field." In contrast to behaviorist theories that predicted a continuous transition between random and useful behavior, Köhler argued that it is easy to see the discontinuity in behavior exactly at the point at which the subject (person or animal) manages to encompass the problem as a whole and carries out actions with steps that, taken in isolation, contribute nothing to the solution.[35] This was a reasonable and relatively rigorous extrapolation from Gestalt studies of perception. In contrast to the mosaic thesis that imagines the perceptual field is always composed of "parts," a Gestalt exists when any subset of the overall field must be understood as a *position* in reference to the set of other positions (Metzger [1975a] 1986: 160). So, too, Köhler argued, when the animal "gets it," we can understand any action only in terms of a position in a sequence that, as a whole and only then, provides a solution.

The Gestalt theorists argued that this sort of insightful behavior is to be expected because our perceptual system works to recognize things as they are; they are not awaiting placement in an arbitrary set of cultural pigeonholes. For example, as Stumpf (1907: 48) argued, despite a mountain arguably being a collectivity, it is perceived *as a* mountain. Further, these

---

upon its local stimulus, I must repeat that no grounds have ever been given for this radical assumption. Rather it seems to be the expression of an a priori belief about what ought to be the nature of things, experience to the contrary notwithstanding."

[35]Köhler ([1917] 1925: 18, 206) also pointed out that the behaviorist tradition placed its rats in mazes in which, according to design, it was impossible to get a vantage point of the whole, a largely unnatural situation, although one compatible with the assumption that since the rat understands nothing, it is "poor, exhausted chance" that "has to do all the work that the animal is unable to do directly."

objects also tell us what to do with them: one part of the mountain *looks* forbidding—it cannot be climbed—while another invites us (Klein 1998: 119). It is not that perception is used, like data in a rigid theory-testing model, to confirm or disconfirm the utility of future actions through trial and error (as in the American behaviorist model). Instead, Gestalt theorists argued, the mind (animal or human) should best be understood as directly perceiving qualities of the environment, although these qualities are intrinsically *affective* ones. They call forth specific, often visceral reactions, generally called "valences," "invitation characters," or "affordances" by Gestalt (and, later, field) theorists. While the affordances involve an interaction between ourselves and the object, for the purposes of constructing a phenomenologically sound model of action, we are best off considering these action imperative qualities of the objects themselves (Koffka 1935: 379). Thus, consciousness, to take a term from Whitehead ([1929] 1978) and Mead (1926: 76), is a "prehensive" faculty in that the concepts it creates are grasped from the nature of the surrounding world; we are best off considering these action imperative qualities of the (phenomenological) objects themselves (Koffka 1935: 379).

Indeed, the same logic implies that "phenomenologically, value is located in objects and occurrences" (Köhler [1944] 1971: 364; he goes even further in 1938: 363f). This is not as wild a statement as it might seem. We tend to perceive as wholes organized sets of percepts with certain qualities (such as symmetry). This implies, Metzger ([1975a] 1986: 181; also Köhler 1938: 350) argued, that we have an innate preference for such symmetry; we must then admit that the most elementary perceptual functions can only be understood in light of these *values*. At the same time, we see a characteristic transition that adherents of Gestalt theory found important, substantive, and enlightening, and detractors saw as a sleight of hand by which one reference frame was replaced by another to make a paradoxical claim true. To detractors, used to conceiving of the objects as "things in themselves," the Gestalt psychologists seemed to smuggle into objects qualities only present in the subjectivity of humans, by instead talking about the phenomenological objects—that is, the objects as they appeared in the subjectivity of humans.

But to those following Carl Stumpf's reasoning, the only paradoxes were those that necessarily resulted from the slipshod thinking of those who claimed to rigorously outline the way in which we process our experience of objects that are never actually perceived (these objects in themselves, or these ideal objects, or what have you). Even if personally we have complete faith in the existence of stable things in themselves, what we as scientists of perception start with are phenomenological objects, and as shown in the next chapter, there is good evidence that these phenomenological objects vary in predictable ways from what might be expected under a naïve theory of perception. If these phenomenological objects *necessarily* involve a preference for symmetry because the human perceptual system *inherently* has such an orientation, then it is not only legitimate, but necessary, to say that the objects are themselves laden with value.³⁶

Thus, the Gestalt theorists were quite justified in making the transition. The difficulty was that it was, perhaps, too successful. In contrast to the widespread solipsism of many epistemologies in the human sciences, the Gestalt perspective makes it easy to consider anything a property of an object: like a tide rushing out of a narrow bay, all the aspects of the person-world interaction that others had implausibly stuffed inside of the head of the perceiver were at one instant swept out into the objects.

We will return to this issue and the problems thus introduced; for now, let us simply see some of the important implications of this reconceptualization. We have seen that certain values could be understood as present in objects. But the same logic leads us to conclude that ethics is in some ways an empirical matter since we can tell what is objectively required from us in a situation (also see Merleau-Ponty [1942] 1963: 132; Ash 1998: 298). This seems defensible: even if we cling to a transcendental definition of ethics that has no necessary empirical observability, we must conclude that just as the motion of a simple organism in a dish with unevenly distributed sugar can be explained by the objective value of the sugar (and not the subjectivity of the organism), so too our values are explicable as features of our larger surroundings. As a result, much of what appears to be conscious decision making can be parsimoniously explained in terms of the "causal structure" of the immediate environment, which we directly take in. When we see objects (*Gestalts*) *as* things, we are seeing qualities that indicate what they will "afford"—what can be

---

³⁶This is exactly parallel to how a Kantian could legitimately claim that objects (phenomenological objects, objects as they appear to us) have spatial extension *as* a property, although objects in themselves need not. As we are unable to experience objects outside of the a priori of space, phenomenological objects *must* have extension, although this comes not from the nature of the objects in themselves but from the nature of our cognitive faculties. Put another way, the Gestalt theorists were not being slipshod when they said that the qualities were in the objects; they were merely being rigorous and consistent, while those who said that the qualities were "in themselves" as perceivers were being impressionistic. For as Köhler (1938) was later to do, we must make a distinction between our phenomenal body that we experience and the transphenomenal organism that (we trust) exists as some sort of physical fundament for our experience. Regarding the first, note that while I believe this phenomenal body to be me and to be mine, and despite my (general) control over it, when I walk down the street, it is I who walk (and not my body); however, if I stumble and hurt my knee, it is now my body that hurts, and it hurts me. The sharpness of the object on which I fell is not in my phenomenal body, nor is its shade of gray. Certainly, no properties of the object are in my *transphenomenal* body either. Wherever they may be, they are not in me.

made to happen with them.[37] "As a rule, things are what they look like, or otherwise expressed, their looks tell us what to do with them" (Koffka 1935: 76; also see p. 7, 353, 356, 392f; Tolman and Brunswik 1935; Ushenko 1958: 90; Köhler [1917] 1925: 189; Asch 1952: 46; Michotte [1946] 1963: 226; Merleau-Ponty 1962: 131; Dewey [1922/1930: 300] uses habit to explain the origin of such beckoning qualities of objects).[38]

It is important to emphasize that the phenomenological existence of objects and their affordances—their existence under the relationship of called-for action—is in no way questioned simply because we acknowledge that the same object's existence cannot be defended when considered under the relationship of knowledge. That is, considered as a proposition, "this is a mountain" is not unproblematically true—mountains have no clear boundaries, nor are there definitions separating one mountain from another in the same range. But, to understand the behavior of mountaineers, we must study how they perceive the intersubjectively valid mountain and not quibble over whether there "really" is a mountain at all. And what is this "really" that people seem to be holding out for, and using as a benchmark to cast aspersions as to the nature of the world of experience? As Köhler (1947: 21; cf. Spiegel 1961: 30; Merleau-Ponty 1962: 57) said, the world we inhabit is "so absolutely objective . . . that for a more objective world no place [is] left." This conception of the validity of the phenomenological has, and was intended to have, strong implications for the relationship between the ideas of analysts and those of the analyzed—implications that run directly counter to those associated with the Freudo-Durkheimian synthesis explored in chapters 3 and 4.

---

[37]The veridical nature of our perception of such affordances can be seen in the ways in which infants reach out to grasp objects (see, e.g., Gibson and Walker 1984).

[38]Related to the point in the previous paragraph—that this conception of affordance brought into the objects everything pertaining to our relations with them and dumped them there—a number of generally sympathetic commentators think that the Gestalt theorists "went too far" in saying that the objects tell us what to do with them; some sort of cultural categorization is also required (see the discussion of Knappett 2005: 50f). The person going to mail a letter (to stick with an example of Gibson's) puts it in a mailbox and not a garbage can, according to this critique, because he knows what a mailbox is (that it is subsumable in a culturally defined class of objects). I think that this critique is incorrect and comes from an inaccurate introspective reconstruction (which imagines that we "see" everything in the visual field). It rather seems that when we are mailing a letter the garbage can *may not appear at all*. A "big thing to be avoided" certainly will, but if asked whether he had passed a garbage can, our prospective letter mailer may have no idea. Of course, if our subject also has something to throw out, then the garbage can may appear to him. If the trash can is such that it *does* afford letter mailing, then our subject may possible throw his letter in. When

SECOND GUESSING FIRST PERSONS

The Gestalt Critique

We recall that Freudianism allowed—in fact required—the analyst to inform the analyzed that what she thought was one thing "really" was another. This was not surprising, given the doctrine's origin in the social relationship between an expert clinician and a mentally unfit pauper. But, this leads to serious instabilities in the organization of social knowledge production—in a world in which people disagree, things only make sense if everyone else really *is* crazy. It would be a good start toward eventually reaching a stable social epistemology if there were psychological reasons to throw out the fundamental model of cognition assumed by Freudianism. The Gestalt theorists believed that their experiments provided such reasons.

The tendency toward wholistic perception came, they argued, because our perceptual system arose in a world with certain organizational features, and we are primed to retrieve the information about this world that we need. As a result, and in total contrast to the Freudian theory derived from encounters with the institutionalized, the Gestalt theory generally assumed the competence and nonarbitrariness (which is not to say infallibility or correctness) of the perceiver (see Köhler [1947: 335] on his rejection of precisely this aspect of psychoanalysis).[39] This was part of a more general rejection of the authoritarianism in knowledge production that characterized the working styles of the psychoanalysts and their understanding of the nature of knowledge.[40]

---

distracted, I have poured boiling water into a coffee grinder because it affords "taking in something used to make coffee" *and* it appeared, although I have never poured the boiling water into an ice cube tray.

[39]Köhler responded to the psychoanalytic challenge as follows: "According to the analysts, people often do not know at all why they behave in one way or another.... We can admit that some such instances occur in normal life.... I doubt, however, whether observations of this kind justify the general pessimism which is so often derived from them." In a later work, Köhler ([1958] 1971: 400–403) spoke more bluntly regarding his evaluation of psychoanalysis, which he referred to as "the source of more, and of darker, Smog than any other doctrine has produced." He singled out its argument that we do not know our own motivations and must instead take the word of an analyst. But this analyst, bereft of clear explanatory standards, selectively deploys the theory of denial so that no matter what one says, it confirms his theory: "Trust the analyst to decide."

[40]While Köhler was in personal and professional life somewhat more reserved—in a classic German Protestant fashion—than his colleagues Lewin and Wertheimer, famous for their egalitarianism, he was still, as the head of a major institute, relatively nonauthoritarian in his direction (Ash 1998: 208–201, 271). It is in keeping with the argument made here that he also downplayed the importance of theory (Köhler [1917] 1925: 186f, 202).

The evolutionary arguments for the fitness of a perceptual system are all quite reasonable. But the Gestalt theorists often extended their antiauthoritarianism to a sweeping rehabilitation of first-person explanatory accounts. As Köhler (1947: 320ff) wrote, "The layman believes that he often feels directly why he wants to do certain things in a first situation, and certain other things in a second. If he is right, the forces which principally determine his mental trends and his actions are for the most part directly given in his experience." The actor believes that his attitudes toward things come from the things and, moreover, are reasonable attitudes to take.[41] If the psychologist disagrees, and argues that the actor has no access to the origins of his attitudes in the nature of the environment, Köhler confidently sides with actor.

Köhler (1947: 324f) illustrated the absurdity of the psychologist's skepticism regarding others' ability to understand their own mental processes by imagining what it would mean to doubt his own. Taking the example of his witnessing his child smile for the first time, which charmed him, he asks, "How did I know that my feeling was concerned with the smile?" Following the strictures of modern psychology, he would be a fool to accept his subject's self-report, and should instead test for a statistically significant correlation in some experimental situation. "In the present case, for instance, only frequent concomitance of a smile on a child's face with the experience of being charmed would allow me to assume that there probably is some connection between the two." It seems somewhat uncharitable to deny, as a rule, that insight from others which we would consider unreasonable to renounce ourselves (also see Köhler [1917] 1925: 3; Merleau-Ponty [1942] 1963: 156 on a similar case). But charity does not excuse ignoring accumulated evidence that shows pervasive and systematic error in how actors cognize their environment. For despite the general soundness of the Gestalt theorists' evolutionary assumptions of fitness, we cannot simply dismiss the presence of cognitive error as "exceptions."

Evidence of Errors and Errors of Evidence

We may break down the sorts of errors that are most important into three types. In the first, we have instances of failed perception in what Hutchins (1995) calls "cognition in the wild." We need not leave the focal example

---

[41]Significantly, elsewhere ([1944] 1971: 363) Köhler dissented from Husserl's phenomenology on grounds similar to those used to reject psychoanalysis. "I do not believe that we are justified in putting certain phases of experience in brackets. A first account of experience ought to be given and carefully studied without selections of any kind. It is otherwise to be expected that even if the brackets are introduced as mere methodological tools, they will sooner or later turn out to be weapons of an ontological prejudice."

of visual perception to come up with cases—something that we believe is a dog is a bundle of rags, the stars look about a mile away, and so on.

In the second type of error, we deal with a specifically social sort of perception, namely, the determination of the source of action. This class of errors is extremely significant, for the Gestalt theorists countered the psychoanalysts' skepticism regarding actors' ability to understand their own motivations by insisting that we had extremely good internal access to such information. Yet researchers—actually stemming from the Gestalt tradition—have demonstrated strong situational variance in our pattern of attributions that sits uneasily beside this confidence. Indeed, one of the true breakthroughs in social psychology was the discovery of the near ubiquity of the fundamental attribution error (see Jones and Harris 1967; Heider 1967: 146[42]; Kelley 1973: 125; though also see Antaki 1994: 14)—namely, that although people do indeed tend to think that their own reactions are determined by their immediate environment (hence I am frightened of things that are in and of themselves frightening), they tend to think that others' actions reveal durable aspects of their personality (but *he* is frightened because he is a scaredy-pants).

In the third type of error, experimenters find it easy to produce effects on cognition through various manipulations of which the subjects remain unaware. The subjects, however, have total confidence that they understand the nature of their surrounding world, the reasons for their thoughts, and the reasons for their actions. These results, if taken as generalizable, make a mockery of the notion of the cognitive competence of the actor that is assumed by the Gestalt approach. Let us consider, then, these three types of errors and their implications.[43]

The first sort of error has been the easiest for the Gestalt approach to rebut. It is tempting to propose that at least Gestalt theory puts the proper "emphasis" on one side of an opposition since "most" cognition is accurate. But, as we lack a metric for "how accurate" is "most" cognition, this is a rather empty response. More important has been the point that the regular errors that arise in perception are related to precisely those

---

[42]Heider studied with Meinong at Graz (the center of a different branch of Gestalt psychology), then with Köhler, Wertheimer, and Lewin at Berlin, and made a contribution to the ecological theory of perception that was largely lost, but independently rediscovered by Pepper (see Heider [1983: 14, 21f, 42, 46, 88, 106]). Heider formulated the study of attribution not because he believed that persons were poor at figuring out what was going on, but precisely to determine how they could be as successful as they were in determining where the invariances in a world in flux lay.

[43]The mere fact that there is no doubt that conscious mental processes are inseparable from processes that are not conscious does not argue against the Gestalt approach and for the Freudian, for the evidence regarding unconscious processes in no way supports the Freudian notion of "an unconscious." For a review, see the work of Kihlstrom (1987).

processes that the Gestalt theorists uncovered as evidence of our fundamental environmental rationality. We would not deny that we have an ability to use relations in the visual field to establish the location of objects in a three-dimensional space simply because we are able to construct optical illusions by taking advantage of our visual heuristics. Thus, even those stressing the pervasive nature of certain cognitive errors or contaminants basically agree with the Gestalt theorists that many are "a by-product of otherwise useful mental procedures" (Wilson and Brekke 1994: 126; also Goethe [1810] 1970: 74f). Similarly, we may make certain errors because we are relying on forms of regularity that are generally, but not always, present. Such errors confirm the idea that our cognition is not arbitrary but instead is oriented to the nature of organization of the surrounding world.

Regarding attribution error (our second type), again the first impulse may be to propose that the opponents do it worse; that is, rather than using an understanding of attribution error to contextualize lay understandings, the conventional theoretical approach simply elevates this error to methodological principle: what others do is indeed evidence of the "truth" of their nature, and we need not take their claims seriously.[44] And, of course, Freudianism takes this to extremes, in which even what other people do not do, or do not agree that they do, or did, or dream about doing, reveals important aspects of their personality. But, it is not so much that other perspectives ignore the attribution error; it is that an understanding of the attribution error *requires* the insights of Gestalt theory extended to the social realm.

First, it is worth emphasizing that most analysts confound the social relationship of *disclosure* of motivation with the cognitive issue of *apperception*; something that is present but not disclosed, reasons the analyst, is suppressed. Why would a patient deny critical information from the analyst he hires to cure him? Even nonanalysts assume the equivalence of denial and suppression; for example, Heider (1958: 135) suggests that a person may actually be less aware of his own pleasure or displeasure than is another—for example, everyone but Charlie knows that Charlie is sweet on Belinda by observing how he becomes a bit awkward when she enters a conversation. Charlie may indeed hotly deny that he is sweet on Belinda, but it takes remarkable naïveté to imagine that he is *unaware* of his feelings just because he doesn't really want everyone to know. And, since many cases in which attribution is contested are cases in which

---

[44]Further, as Barnes (2000: 35) points out, the experiments that cast doubt on our capacity to make correct attributions were nothing other than particular social situations designed to do exactly that—they are a testament not to our incapacity as social actors but rather the reverse. Our hunches regarding what makes people do what they do what are good enough that we can get them to do what we anticipate with only a little preparation.

actors' responsibility is at issue, people often have good reasons for making claims that do not wholly agree with their own beliefs.

Thus, some seemingly strong cases are hardly relevant. At the same time, evidence of bias in attribution is not restricted to these cases: the same act is differently attributed depending on who we are. Theorists coming from the Gestalt tradition used an analogy to the visual field to help construct an explanation. Just as we make a distinction between figure and ground in our visual perception, we also make similar distinctions when deciding to what an action should be attributed. If we see twelve people, eleven of whom are nice to Jane and one who is cruel to Jane, we attribute this cruelty to the one—it stands out as figure. But, if we see this one be kind to eleven and cruel only to Jane, it is Jane who stands out, and we may inquire what she has done to provoke this cruelty. Thus, understanding the process of attribution requires not that we reject the idea that our cognitive system successfully takes in the regularities in the environment, but that we understand how what *is* "the environment" is shaped by patterns of social interaction.

Experimenters and Subjects

The most persuasive evidence against the Gestalt perspective may come from a host of experimental studies that demonstrate that subjects may have a misplaced confidence in their ability to understand the causes of their thoughts (this is the third type of error that I listed). In brief, human beings can be primed with information, images, or other characteristics of situations that predictably lead them to certain sentiments, moods, or attitudes and, more important, even to biased conclusions after reasoned judgment. (An important and thoughtful discussion of early studies will be found in the 1977 work of Nisbett and Wilson.) In one of the first studies, Stanley Schachter (a scion of the Gestalt school) and Jerome Singer (1962) gave subjects adrenaline injections. Some of the subjects were told what the effects were likely to be; others were told that they were given a harmless solution with no side effects. Subjects were then placed with a confederate whose actions were designed to arouse either happiness or anger. Those who did not know of the physical effects of the injection were far more likely to have strong emotional reactions to the confederate and believe that these were justified by the confederate's actions.[45]

In what way do these results speak to the Gestalt school's insistence that the human perceptual system is an adequate and reliable way of getting needed information from the environment? Let us begin by following Wilson and Brekke (1994), who (in a thorough review of these studies) argue that the biases result from two large classes of effects. The first they

---

[45]A large number of follow-up studies confirmed similar findings; for this reason, avoid difficult negotiations right after drinking a strong cup of coffee.

term "unwanted consequences of automatic processing" and turns out to be of the same basic form as those optical illusions that arise from the way our perceptual system makes use of existing regularities in the environment. For example, people tend to have an easier time accepting information (or claimed information) than rejecting it. It takes a fair amount of mental effort to dismiss an idea or fact once we have understood it. This means that by choosing the order in which contradictory ideas are presented, experimenters can shape what subjects believe, especially if these subjects are taxed with a high cognitive load at the same time.

Such experimental effects, then, really turn out to be part of the first class of problem—they point to the imperfect nature of our cognitive system. For every strength, there is a potential weakness that can be exploited. It is important to emphasize that although *logically* these phenomena do not contradict the *Gestalt* perspective, they do not necessarily lead to the same confidence held by the Gestalt theorists in the adequacy of the cognition of the average person, as these sorts of unwanted consequences can lead to behavior that we consider morally reprehensible, foolishly self-destructive, or sadly limited in comprehension.

The Gestalt approach to social knowledge was inspired by earlier findings regarding visual perception. And, just like humans can deliberately create optical illusions that fool our eyes, so we can (deliberately or not) create conditions that make unbiased social knowledge as implausible as accurate vision in a funhouse.[46] It is overly convenient but not without merit to say that the problem is not so much our false knowledge of the true conditions as our true knowledge of false conditions—with *false* referring to deviation from some standard that we have not yet identified.

Thus, these errors *do* pose a serious challenge to the Gestalt approach, but not one that calls for a return to ideas of "false consciousness" as we have seen in the Freudian critique.[47] Most important, in all the demonstrated cases, there is no evidence that these unrecognized cognitions are repressed such that individuals would be *unable* to recognize them as a result of dialogue; indeed, the opposite has been demonstrated, that individuals will recognize the plausibility of these biases and indeed may overcompensate in the opposite direction (for one example, see Sanna et al. 2002). At the same time, they force us to accept that even if we conclude that there is sufficient evidence for the generally adequate

---

[46]Gibson ([1979] 1986: 143) makes the correction as follows: "When Koffka asserted that 'each thing says what it is,' he failed to mention that it may lie." Also see the work of Heidegger ([1926] 1962: 51) and Metzger (1966: 11).

[47]The term *false consciousness* was associated with vulgar Marxism; it was not a term used by Marx, and he would have only scorn for the concept. Engels did use the term in a letter to (I believe) Mehring, but there he was speaking of the false consciousness of the *bourgeoisie* and was sticking to the outline of his previous work with Marx on ideology.

nature of our cognitive system, the felt conviction of adequacy that may characterize a person's judgment of her own reflexive capacity will not be part of this evidence.

The second class of robust experimental effect is even more damaging to the Gestalt approach, and this is what Brekke and Wilson call "source confusion." The Schachter and Singer (1962) experiment is an example—subjects have difficulty determining the source of various perceived stimuli, and they have a hard time determining what influences any judgment of theirs. Thus, when they report, "I disliked this essay because of X," they can be shown to be unreliable as their likes or dislikes can be manipulated by some Y or Z. As we see, this sort of experimental effect builds on and generalizes the error pointed to by attribution theory—we have a far-from-perfect capacity to allocate explanatory priority.

And this sort of error completely undercuts Köhler's confidence that he can determine the source of his feeling of being charmed in the face of his child. One justly famous experiment (Dutton and Aron 1974) involved "an attractive female interviewer" stopping male subjects on a bridge, getting them to fill out a short questionnaire, and at the end, giving the subjects her name and phone number (in a relatively informal manner). In one set of cases, the bridge was a long swaying one over a canyon with short rails over a deadly drop to rocks below (imagine something out of Road Runner and Coyote cartoon shorts); in the other set, the bridge was a solid one above a small stream. More men in the first condition called the interviewer back (for a date, that is). The offered explanation is that as they stood in the middle of this frightening bridge facing this interviewer, their pulses raced, and they sweated—and confused this state of bodily arousal with the sexual arousal generated from the interviewer. They blended the entire situation and attributed greater "attractiveness" to the person with whom they interacted.

This means that the scenario at which Köhler scoffed—doing controlled experiments to see whether in fact it is your son that charmed you—is hardly a ridiculous one. The man standing on the swaying bridge might also insist that he knew well what charmed him in this young woman. But would he be right? There are two aspects here that need to be treated separately, although they overlap empirically. The first is the subjects' error of not identifying the experimentally induced "cause" of the perception. This, often what critiques of naïve realism seize on, will turn out to be trivial in its implications. The second, and more fundamental, is the relation between the experience and the attribution of source—technically, a fractured intentionality.

Now in one sense, we must recognize that we may still understate the validity of responses that actors give in such circumstances. Actors *do*, as Nisbett and Wilson (1977) argue, seem to replace an accurate introspective history of "how I made this decision" with a general plausibility check ("How do I think I *would* make such a decision?"), and they tend to emphasize those situational properties that are most relevant for a *good* decision. Yet, their responses regarding these properties (and not their "effects") may be valid; they are not good at answering the question "What about *you* and *your* situation led to your actions?" but much better at answering "What about *her* led to your actions?" For the interviewer, Dutton and Aron tell us, *was* attractive. Blending is not the same thing as hallucination. But, the lesson holds that we cannot equate first-person reports about motives with the impulsion lying behind actions; not only does this undermine some of the Gestalt confidence in extrapolating from the field of vision to cognition in general, it requires that we rethink the qualitative nature of social perception and indeed of vision (to which we turn in the next chapter).

The first issue (subjects not recognizing causes of their action) is more straightforward. It is worth reminding ourselves that these experimental results that demonstrate the inability of persons to understand their motivations are produced in artificial situations in which persons are exposed to *causes* of their cognition. But, if the Gestalt theorists were correct, then this is precisely the wrong model of everyday cognition, which is not a passive response to stimuli but an active retrieval of information for willful action, and we should not be distressed to find cognition performing poorly in such a situation. As Reed (1996: 34–37) has argued, we should expect that the environmentally rational flexibility that animals display when confronting objects in their habitat will become greatly circumscribed if they are transferred to a different setting. This is all the more true if their normally active processes of search for value are frustrated, and they are instead forced to passively receive sets of disconnected "stimuli." A set of engineers from another culture attempting to see how a modern jet plane works certainly could try throwing it against different surfaces. They might indeed eliminate several different "theories" and would probably develop a disdain for the shoddy workmanship of the subject of their investigations. But they would not learn much about how it actually operated. Similarly, experiments may certainly lead to some extremely wrong ideas being proved to be in fact wrong, but we should not be optimistic that the result of such investigations will tell us much about human cognition.

Here, it will help to return to the issue of cause that we explored in the first chapter. Such causes, we saw, were considered antithetical to *motives*; causes come from the outside (as opposed to the inside), causes make reference to the past (as opposed to the future), and causes smack of determinism (as opposed to freedom). We found that the question, Why did you do this? tends to provoke people to justify their independence and maturity by stressing their motivations as opposed to causes (unless they are trying to deny responsibility for some misstep). Now, if we are trying to determine the degree of adequacy of the human cognitive system in deciding what to do, and in reporting on why one has done what one has done, it is obviously stacking the deck to only study persons who are exposed to experimental treatments.

Burke (1952: 78; see 6, 128), in some ways paralleling Heider's (1958) interest in attribution,[48] proposed that there is, in the terminology of contemporary sociological theory, a certain amount of agency to be divided between various aspects of an act and the scene (roughly like Heider's person and situation).[49] Accordingly, Burke emphasized that the most important conclusion one could draw from behaviorist experiments pertained to the ability—and the motivation—of experimenters to successfully circumscribe the motives of others.[50] As Billig (1982: 188) says, "Viewed in this light, the social psychological experiment can take the form of a modern parable, illustrating the uneven confrontation between expert and non-expert." The experiment demonstrates the insufficiency of the subject's cognitive processes, as she remains ignorant of the experimenter's actual manipulation. Despite this superiority of knowledge in this artificial situation, the experimenter remains unable to understand the actual psychological processing of the subject in the natural setting. Yet, the experiment is taken as only pointing to the limitations of the subject, not those of the experimenter.[51]

This is not an apology for the poor performance of the beleaguered subject; the lesson is twofold. The first is simply that of the (possibly) lowered ecological validity of the results—to the extent that this is an unusual situation, our compounded knowledge is itself as biased as the knowledge of our subjects. I will actually argue that the most obvious criticism of the ecological validity of such experiments is likely to be mistaken,[52] but it is crucial to recognize that this is a particular social context,

---

[48]One may note that Burke's (1952: 6, 128, e.g.; also see 151) grammar of motives is similar in proposing dimensions that may variably carry the weight of explaining motivation.

[49]Burke would reserve the term *agency* for the aspect of motivated action pertaining to "how it was done."

[50]He goes on: "Animal experiments have taught us however (we should at least grant them this) that school-teachers like to send animals to school, that physical sadists who have mastered scientific method like to torture animals methodically, and that those whose ingenuity is more psychiatrically inclined like to go on giving the poor little devils mental breakdowns, ostensibly to prove over and over again that it can be done (though this has already been amply proved to everybody's satisfaction but that of the experimenters)."

[51]This point was also made by Haney (1976: 179, 186), a social psychologist who invoked both the Gestalt tradition and the antidemocratic nature of experimental epistemology.

[52]Back in 1946, Quinn McNemar (333) noted that "the existing science of human behavior is largely the behavior of sophomores," and little has changed, despite the recognition that American students taking psychology classes are not even representative of American students in general, and that these differences can matter. As we might imagine from chapter 3, the authority relation involved—often an instructor testing his theories on the immature people whom he can

and the sorts of functioning observed are not independent of this skewed social situation (cf. Merleau-Ponty [1942] 1963: 220f).

The second part of the point is more fundamental: to the extent that there is a fixed sum of agency to be distributed across participants, we cannot come to a general conclusion that "people's cognitions fall more to the causal end of the cause-motive continuum stretching from determinism to freedom." We can say that "*subjects'* cognitions fall more to the determined end of the continuum," but this is only because *experimenters* are falling more to the willful end: they are deliberately, planfully, and successfully sucking away the adequacy and freedom of motivation of the subjects. Just as air conditioners cannot make the world colder but merely pump heat from one place to another, so too experiments cannot demonstrate that "people" are less competent, willful, and aware.[53] And it is this realization—that the experimenters are part of the whole social situation that must be analyzed—that forbids us simply to dismiss these results by maintaining that things like this do not happen in the "real world" (whatever that is). If they do not, it is not for want of people trying.

The Real World

We see, then, one serious shortcoming of the approach of the Gestalt school: it imagined that the social world could be treated nonproblematically as a physical landscape. But even more important, the Gestalt theorists (or at least Köhler) assumed a direct correspondence between the veridical nature of our perceptual system and our capacity to successfully

---

punish for a display of an insufficient mastery of or even lack of acceptance of such theories—contaminates much of this research beyond repair. But the takeaway is not that the findings are incorrect and that "real" people "aren't" as impressionable as the students. This would pertain only to calibrating the degree of social pressure needed to produce any desired effect. Rather, it is that these effects need to be placed in the concrete social situation to be understood, and this requires an accurate understanding of the social relations between experimenters and subjects. Those who have done this (most important is Orne [1969: 145]) find that the key thing is what the Gestalt school called the "demand characteristics"—the valences—of the test situation, and the subjects' general interpretation of the test situation as one "calling out for" a certain type of action (to be a "good subject," which often means validating the authority's theory).

[53]It is worth emphasizing the formal parallel to the inconsistency in our approach to causality. As Goldthorpe (2001: 8) has emphasized, if our counterfactual approach leads us to insist that there can be no causality without manipulation, we find ourselves excluding voluntary action by a subject S as a cause of her own action. But, a change in experimental treatment—itself the result of a voluntary action on the part of experimenter E—is a legitimate cause of S's action. Thus, are we each incapable of causal action for ourselves, although we may cause each others' actions?

answer the question, Why do you believe X? Indeed, this confusion may go back to the slippage of the investigations of the "categories" from Aristotle's *predicates* to Durkheim's *framework*. But, as Burke (1952: 317, cf. 402) said regarding the elements of his scheme, "instead of calling them the necessary 'forms of experience,' however, we should call them the necessary 'forms of *talk about* experience.'"

The Gestalt theorists did quite well at analyzing the forms of experience. First, they formulated a conception of the relation between the actor and the world that avoided many of the paradoxes and instabilities of the Freudo-Durkhiemian tradition. We are, argued those in the Gestalt school, in a world that operates according to its own causal principles, and it is far from surprising that actors are able to establish what Bourdieu calls an "ontological complicity" with the world such that our cognitive schema map onto the world in a predictable way.[54] Given that there is no "realer" world, we start with and take seriously actors' first-person understandings of the world.

But the Gestalt theorists made only a weak effort at analyzing the connection between the regularities of this experience and the *propositions* that different persons might produce on the basis of this experience (cf. Bischof 1966: 32). Of course, it was no problem to acknowledge that there might be differences of perspective—differences of perspective on the part of persons who are differentially distributed in a single world is only to be expected.[55] Such differences do not undermine the cognitive competence of the typical actor. It is still not necessary for analysts to tell people what things "really" are, any more than it is necessary for those who are on one side of a hill to inform those on the other that the hill is not "really" blocking a view of the lake. Accepting the differences in perspective in no way implies considering all equally legitimate, for it means ignoring the false issue of legitimacy altogether.

---

[54]This in some ways goes back to Cassirer's (1922: 35) emphasis that in contrast to our analytic approach to nature, in astrology our human subordination to the laws of the cosmos lies not so much because we are constantly affected by renewed external influences, but because each of us is, in miniature, the cosmos itself.

[55]And, of course, the variation in perception according to position is in no way incompatible with the objectivity of perception—the contrary is far closer to the truth. As Merleau-Ponty (1964: 296, also see 1962: 16f) says, "The world is in accordance with my perspective *in order* to be independent of me, is for me *in order to be* without me, and to be the world." In a later work, he proposes that, unlike the animal, which exists in an environmental surroundings (*Umwelt*) of impinging stimuli, the human lives in a world (*Welt*). That is, as Kant would also agree, freedom of action comes when one has an internal representation of the regularities on the environment that allows us to move not in "our" world but in "the" world—the single intersubjectively valid world that can be treated as an obdurate ground of predictabilities that are a material for action.

The Gestalt approach thus had no difficulty dealing with differences in perspectival experience, but it was quite another thing to deal with the "source blending" that leads us to be "charmed" by a person in one situation but not in another. The mistake of the Gestalt theorists was to assume that the validity of *experience* translated to the validity of *statements about* experience.[56] Most important, the Gestalt theorists unwisely accepted the poor phrasing of the Why question and decided to throw in their lot with the subject who attempts to prove his rationality and maturity. But this question—in the specific social situation of challenge and response, often in a deliberately unequal setting—is not necessarily a scientifically meaningful one. We may need to approach the issue of the validity of experience without a dubious commitment to a successful answer to an unfair challenge. And it was this that was provided by the American pragmatist tradition.

AMERICAN PRAGMATISM

Experience and Knowledge

The pragmatist tradition has much in common with the Gestalt and activity schools: all arose in contradistinction to the emerging mechanical-analytic tendencies in psychology at the turn of the twentieth century (with pragmatism a bit earlier than the others). The root of the word *pragmatic* is the same as that underlying *practice*, a term with technical philosophical overtones evoking a slightly heterodox Western tradition. Like the Gestalt theorists, pragmatists dissented from the philosophy of knowledge that assumed that perception was fundamentally unordered—that, in James's ([1909] 1975: 7; also [1909] 1943: 72f) words, "experience as immediately given is all disjunction and not conjunction"—until the mind throws "'categories' over them like a net."[57] Pragmatists like John Dewey ([1906] 1965: 205, 208f) acknowledged the importance of

---

[56]Joas (2000: 68) has made this point about James and Durkheim; Weber ([1903–1906] 1975: 133, 160, 257) was attentive to this difference.

[57]The pragmatists also shared with the Gestalt tradition an embracing of the phenomenological as the real (see Köhler [1947: 340] and Mead [1938: 35, 43]). Although Cassirer ([1910] 1923: 317f) and the Gestalt theorists often discussed pragmatists such as James and Dewey appreciatively (Koffka teaching a course on pragmatism), and although they stressed the fitness of the perceptual apparatus as a result of evolution, they were not as concerned with describing the development of the structures of this apparatus as was Dewey (Ash 1998: 37, 71f, 145; also see 210 on their connection to the activity theorist Alexander Luria). This positive response to pragmatism contrasts with the more general German reaction, which Joas (2000: 34) refers to as a "storm of protest."

Kant's critique demonstrating the need for "some prior form of existential organization," something in our cognitive system that is "already there" before our making sense of the world. But, they refused to accept that it was some subjective a prioris that allowed for this organization.

Like the Gestalt theorists, the pragmatists argued that the organization in our cognitions could come from the organization of experience, itself grounded in the patterning of nature (also Merleau-Ponty [1962: 220f]). But they tended to emphasize the organization that comes from the action of persons singly and together, as opposed to the natural organization that preexists the entrance of the human or animal observer (although see Dewey 1934: 15). In further keeping with such general American intellectual emphases, the pragmatists also focused on an explicitly democratic model of the subject, and hence provided an alternate basis for social epistemology than the authority-saturated one coming from Freudo-Durkheimianism.[58] Moreover, they provided a theory of cogitation that allows us to understand how we can build on the validity of experience, as opposed to merely rubber-stamping the knowledge that may come from this experience.

Such a pragmatist theory of cognition was best expounded by John Dewey. Like the other pragmatists, and like the Russian activity theorists and German Gestaltists, Dewey (e.g., 1908) started by analyzing knowledge as a property of real people confronting real problems. If the cognitions of regular people did not follow the strictures of epistemologists, so

---

[58]Dewey ([1922] 1970) admitted the American flavor of his pragmatism and countered that transcendental philosophies were elitist. ("It is easy to be foolish about the connexion of thought with national life. But I do not see how any one [sic] can question the distinctively national color of English, or French, or German philosophies" [Dewey 1917: 67].) In contrast to those like Horkheimer ([1947] 1974), who, wearing the mantle of antifascism, took reason out of the heads of the masses and put it safely in the realm of objectivity (where, as Hegel would say, its ground of subsistence was nothing other than itself), Dewey ([1899] 1965: 243, 266; [1904] 1977: 74, 76; [1908] 1965: 59) saw the cognitive competence of the everyday person as a sine qua non of an active democracy and hence emphasized the reasonableness of our subjectivities (if not their technical rationality). Horkheimer, who boasted to Lowenthal that he fancied himself an expert on pragmatism (Jay 1973: 83), deigned to criticize Dewey, but as Westbrook (1991: 185; also Joas 1993: 91, n. 4) says, "Like the rest of the first generation of the Frankfurt School, Horkheimer did not know what he was talking about when it came to pragmatism."

On the other side, Durkheim ([1913–1914] 1983: 1f, 5) explicitly saw pragmatism as an "Anglo-Saxon" (American) threat to the French tradition of Cartesian rationalism, and warned his compatriots that to accept pragmatism would "overthrow our whole national culture." William James ([1909] 1943: 321f) agreed, arguing that his pluralism was to rationalist monism as a federal republic was to an empire or kingdom.

much the worse for the philosophers. Unlike the behaviorists, Dewey did not replace the skepticism of philosophers with the skepticism of a pseudoscience that could ignore experience and work with a model of discrete stimulus-response cycles (Dewey 1896).[59] Instead, he proposed a rethinking of the fundamental nature of cognition.

The philosophers had incorrectly assumed that the problems confronting everyday actors were problems of knowledge. And, since we cannot directly experience the "real" world, they reasoned, our experience does not produce this knowledge; indeed, our experience is more like a veil that shields us from this "real" world (Dewey 1905; 1917: 7; 1929: iii, 1a, 38). But, our cognitive experience is an interaction of a complete living person with an environment: we do not ponder how the stomach can "really" digest food, why do we wonder whether the mind can "really" know (Dewey 1917: 33; [1922] 1930: 186; James [1912] 1943: 10)? Rather than holding up experience to philosophic standards it obviously could not meet for the destructive pleasure of condemning it, Dewey argued that we should base our philosophic standards on the character of this experience.

This experience, far from being knowledge, Dewey (1917: 10f, 37) argued, was more like the philosophic idea of "suffering" or "affection" in the sense of Spinoza ([1677] 1930). This affection implied that the experience was a direct retrieval of aspects of the natural world: experience "penetrates into 'the world', reaching down into its depths, and in such a way that its grasp is capable of expansion"—"It is not experience which is experienced, but nature" (Dewey 1929: 3a, 4a). Thus, Dewey took a philosophical idea of interaction with the world ("suffering") that was fundamentally predicated on the *passivity* (or at least receptivity, pathology) of the subject, and attempted to recast it as an active process (also see James [1890] 1950: I, 402; Dewey 1934: 39f; Merleau-Ponty [1942] 1963: 216). The Gestalt theorists avoided many of the incoherences of other accounts but had a similar assumption of passivity: Dewey's approach demonstrates the path by which such an understanding can be adapted for the case of social action—to recognize the compatibility between an active mind and the naïve empiricism that treats organization as simply "out there."[60]

---

[59]And, like Köhler, Dewey opposed the psychoanalytic approach. It is perhaps significant that both the behaviorist and the psychoanalytic theories were used to defend antidemocratic political philosophies, the psychoanalytic by pointing to the fundamental irrationality of the masses (as by Horkheimer) and the behaviorists by implying the need for control and training of these masses (Westbrook 1991: 290, 292).

[60]Impressionistically, if you reach out and grab a blob of clay, the shape you eventually see when you bring it to your eye will of course have a great deal to do with your hand and the force you exerted. And it might differ from others' globs. But, it would be a very poor potter's epistemology that on these grounds denied that *what* you felt was the clay.

Naïve Empiricism

Things, Dewey (1905: 393f; cf. Merleau-Ponty [1962: 363]) concluded, "are what they are experienced as." That does not mean what they are *believed* to be (reducing experience to knowing); instead, this is to say (with the Gestaltists), that phenomenology is the center of the matter. In contrast to the dualists, who assumed an unconquerable hiatus between ourselves and reality, and thus argued that seemingly immediate experience was actually mediated, Dewey ([1905] 1977: 170) just as reasonably argued that whatever the case may be for particular objects, experience is, as experience, immediate, and that it was hard to see "*any* way of experiencing the mediated . . . excepting that of immediately experiencing it *as* what it is, viz., mediate."[61]

Once we do not identify knowledge and experience, then we may allow as real "affectional and volitional objects" (Dewey 1929: 24). Our "feelings" about things are no more in us than they are in the things (compare Burtt 1927). Although we might in some cases want to argue that these feelings come from an interaction between things and ourselves, that which we feel is wholly in the objects. Thus, our feelings "make sense" because they are things we "sense" from the objects (Dewey 1929: 258f). Just as Gibson ([1979] 1986) argued that a cliff *looks* dangerous (and it is!), Dewey (1905: 395) argued that when he is frightened by a sudden noise, "empirically, that noise *is* fearsome; it *really* is." What is on the other end of our feeling is a quality (Dewey [1930] 1960: 182; cf. Heidegger [1926] 1962: I.6.44a).

It is worth making sure that there are no misunderstandings—this is not a shift to the idealism of Lord Berkeley; it is more closely related to the positivism of Ernst Mach. Just as Mach would have it, we start with the empirical facts. These empirical facts are different experiences of different individuals at different times. These experiences, moreover, are (1) experiences of the world, if only because "the world" is what we term the commonly found coordinative plane of experience (that which allows our experiences to sit beside one another nicely [see Heidegger 1926/1962: 91/I.3.63]) and (2) fundamentally, and nonsubtractably, qualitative. That is, if we take away all the qualities from the objects of

---

[61]Husserl ([1900] 1970: 382; also 355) made the same critique of those who "credit to *contents* everything which acts, in their straightforward reference, place in the *object*"; that is, they forget that when we have a representation (*Vorstellung*) of a horse, our judgment of this horse is not a judgment *of* the representation, but of the horse. Also see the work of Merleau-Ponty (1962: 289). Somewhat differently, Heidegger ([1926] 1962: 89/I.2.62) makes a phenomenological correction: "The perceiving of what is known is not a process of returning with one's booty to the 'cabinet' of consciousness after one has gone out and grasped it; even in perceiving, retaining, and preserving, the *Dasein* which knows *remains outside*, and it does so *as Dasein*."

our experience, what we have is less than nothing, for even nothing, as Stumpf (1907) said, has some qualities to us ("silence" and "blackness"). We are of course free to imagine (or "theorize") quality-less objects underneath and behind our experiences. We are also free to claim that these quality-less objects have some sort of existence, but this is completely irrelevant for our task at hand. First, no object in our imagination can be realer than those in experience; second, there is no possible proposition comparable to our knowledge that is not our knowledge. Thus, we cannot say, "There is a sort of object that we do not experience, and true science is the set of knowledge-propositions about these un-experienced objects that would be made by that sort of being that could intuit these quality-less objects." For knowledge is, Dewey argued, also an empirical phenomenon connected to empirical beings. And empirical beings experience the world as qualitative.[62]

Dewey's attaching of the predicate "real" to experience (as opposed to propositions about experience) meant that he undercut any possibility whereby the analyst could say that although the subjects believe X to be a form of Z, it is *really* a form of Y and so on. His fundamentally democratic epistemology thus lacked the instabilities that we saw in the Freudian approach. But for Dewey, the importance of democracy went deeper than this symmetric stability, although he (quite naturally) sometimes had difficulty giving a straightforward explication, in part because of the political distractions of the time. But we have seen in our analysis of the problems with the Gestalt approach that the very heuristics that seem to fit us for proper cognition of our environment lead to what are generally called biases when used without conscious correction.

We held off this critique with the formula that we have perhaps true knowledge of false conditions. A more complete way of saying this, drawing on Dewey's general arguments, would be that it is not so much that there is some bias introduced into our "view" of the world, but that to the extent that our environment is nondemocratic, our reasoning is proportionally distorted, and true social cognition actually requires democracy. (We return to explicate this in greater detail in the next chapter.) This sounds somewhat hackneyed, like some 1950s civics lesson, but it may

---

[62]Even more profoundly, James ([1912] 1943: 150) carefully argued that we divide the unity of experience into "consciousness" and "objects" (the internal vs. the external) on the basis of whether the experience is inert as opposed to active—the memory of fire burns no one, while a real fire is hard to put out. So the affective phenomena that we might take as evaluative qualities of objects (their beauty, their dangerousness) can be thought of as a wholly subjective, mental attribute because such qualities are inert regarding the rest of nature. But they are *not* inert regarding one important part of physical nature—"that part of physical nature which our own skin covers." Thus, they are to this important extent objective.

follow rigorously from what we know about social cognition. Just as it is silly for people to expect schools drawing students from racially segregated communities with vastly unequal income and wealth to turn them out distributed identically, so it seems far-fetched to imagine a brain taking in a stratified, cruel, and corrupted social world and polishing it up before acting. Bias itself is perhaps a quality of the world.

To summarize and simplify greatly, Dewey could reach a nonsociopathic epistemology because he did not apply the idea of "true" to experiences (cf. James [1912] 1943: 203; Heidegger [1926] 1962: 57/II.34). This allowed for a clearer understanding of the qualitative nature of experience and the possible sciences that could build on it.

Seeing That and Reasoning Why

This emphasis on the qualitative nature of experience was fundamental, and it was perhaps better adumbrated by the pioneer of pragmatism, C.S. Peirce, in his own approach to phenomenology (which he termed *phaneroscopy*). Dismissing as foolish all the conventional doubts regarding the shared nature of interior experience, Peirce ([1875–1910] 1955: 74, 77) argued not simply that we must be treated as directly perceiving matter, but that phenomena confront us as qualities.[63] Moreover, even though these qualities necessarily make reference to our subjective experience, the qualities themselves (and not our experience) must be understood as attributes of objects. This was, Peirce ([1875–1910] 1955: 85f) pointed out, completely nonproblematic: the quality is a *potential* for experience, and a potential is real (that is, it is a real potential) even when it is not actual.

This is not to claim that the qualities of the object—objective though they are—are inherent in the object as mere stimuli. As Dewey (1929: 336; also [1922] 1930: 200) says—and this point is central in his early and (to contemporary eyes) somewhat confusing discussion of the reflex arc (1896)—the qualities are really "those attendant upon response to the stimuli" (also see Dewey [1935] 1960: 203; [1930] 1960: 188; Merleau-Ponty [1942] 1963: 12, 30, 43 also stressed this reflex arc as the foundation for a rigorous phenomenology as well as the connection to the Gestalt theories).

Thus things are, Dewey concluded, what they call out for us to do. Yet, there was no reason to expect that people agreed about what things

---

[63]Unlike the Gestalt school—and somewhat like Margolis (1987: 73)—Peirce believed such qualitative experience to be only the first moment of being, a firstness, to which should properly be added the secondness of fact (as Carley [1986: 404] has said, a fact is always a joining) and the thirdness of thought. The quality is thus in some sense nonrelational, although it only exists in relation to a mind, for the experience is directly of and solely of the object.

were.[64] Given his faith in the relevance of scientific thought for everyday life, Dewey (1905, 1911) did not deny that some understandings were superior to others—some might be more "true." Yet, he maintained that all experiences were equally "real." When we hear a shot fired, but then find out that it was actually an engine backfiring, the first experience—the experience *of* a shot being fired—was as real as the modified experience of an engine backfiring. If the former is less true, this is because the real has changed, and only those who cling to the absolutist's idea of "things in themselves" find it disconcerting that this can occur (Cassirer [1910] 1923: 273f, 278, made basically the same point).[65]

Notice that Dewey does not start with properties of objects that are reckoned as *causes* of perception, as even the Gestalt theorists often did. Instead, he begins with experienced qualities and then—temporally *after* experience—the social process of inquest and recalibration. The backfiring engine did not "cause" us to hear a sound, and thus we are not "wrong" when we think that a gunshot "caused" the sound. Rather, we hear the shot—we exist in the fearsome world of vulnerability—and then we "change our minds" as we change our worlds, to truer information, even when we perhaps revert to the first understanding after additional experience ("Oh, it turns out it *was* a shot after all").[66]

In sum, we need to begin with the nature of experience, not only if we (like Dewey) wish to produce a coherent philosophy of nature, science, experience, and knowledge, but also if we wish to begin from data that our respondents can produce with any degree of confidence. This experience is fundamentally and completely qualitative, which means that we have to be attentive to the nature of the experience of qualities. And this is where our conceptual tools are the weakest.

The Greeks, argued Dewey (1929: 87, 96), were sufficiently naïve to emphasize the aesthetic qualities of objects. Modern philosophers, in contrast, are too sophisticated to accept such "essentialism," but as a result fail to recognize the importance of qualities. That is, if we understand aesthetics in the wider sense as pertaining to the qualitative nature of objects, we find (says Dewey) that the Greeks were basically sound in considering

---

[64]Thus, Dewey (1929: 340), more than Köhler, explicitly dissented from an intuitionist understanding of the grasp of the qualities of things.

[65]It is interesting that to describe how the qualities of experience are parts of the things themselves, Dewey (1905: 398) uses the example of a Gestalt-type perceptual "illusion." Also see Dewey (1934: 100f).

[66]Thus, correct knowledge is not phenomenologically different from incorrect knowledge; a key error of epistemologies is to try to build into the nature of experience the differences we later establish among reflections on experience. There is nothing wrong with the faith that there is a difference between the true things we know and the others that we merely believe, but to import this into the experience itself via theoretical assumption is little short of a lie.

objects as directly being, say, "poignant, tragic, beautiful, . . ." and so on. The later philosophers, in separating experience from what was experienced, evacuated nature of qualities (Dewey 1929: 95f, 264f). They ignored the difference between experience and the propositions that might be formulated *about that* experience.[67]

This generally overlooked distinction gives us further insight regarding how to reconcile (on the one hand) the fundamental validity of what we have provisionally termed first-person accounts with (on the other) undeniable evidence of their weakness. We may follow Dewey and say that what we must treat as veridical and constraining for our explanations is not accounts but first-person *experiences*. Analysts' abstractions that have no counterpart in such experience are implicitly suspect—but so are actors' own accounts to the extent that these are in the form not of the reporting of recent experience but the reconstruction of justificatory narratives.

There is every reason to be highly suspicious of such retrospective justifications, but not necessarily for the reasons commonly voiced, which are both trivial and extreme, involving as they do a vision of actors as malicious conspirators attempting to thwart the progress of science. The valid reason for skepticism is both kinder and more damning of human cognition; it is simply that there is no evidence that our cognitive capacity is such that it is able to answer questions of the form, Why did you . . . ? There is quite strong neurological evidence that we have the capacity to honestly come up with conscious retrospective justifications for actions undertaken for reasons quite out of the control or even monitoring capacity of the part of the brain making the justification (the most impressive introduction will be found in the work of Gazzaniga 1970, 1998; also Metzinger 2003: 432f, 437). More simply, as Margolis (1987: 76) has emphasized, there is no reason to assume that there is any clear and consistent connection between our ability to recognize patterns in our environment ("seeing that") and our retrospective ability to narrate the process whereby we have come to see that something is the case ("reasoning why").

Of course, the fact (if indeed it remains a fact) that our consciousness basically has the job (among others) of turning our responses to the environment into a compelling narrative does not mean that it is generally incorrect. For example, it seems that we are often consciously aware of our desire to do what we are going to do certainly no earlier than the activation of the relevant neurological circuits connected to

---

[67]Here, also see Merleau-Ponty's (1962: 215) argument that the experience of qualities is inherently depersonalized in actuality—philosophers may *argue* that there is a necessary moment of apperception in such qualitative experience, but as we shall see in chapter 6, it need not be one that defines ego through the synthetic unity of experience.

the motor aspect of the "intended" action. Yet, our conscious "decision" is probably in all but a vanishing small number of cases a rather good summary of the relevant forces, even if these have previously been synthesized by a nonconscious part of our mind. But social scientists tend to demand answers that are inherently beyond the capacity of a reasonable mind to produce.

Even more fatally, we unmeaningly invoke a particular social setting—the test—in our questioning. Members of cultures unfamiliar with formal schooling often "fail" intelligence tests simply because they do not comprehend how to behave when asked a question by an adult who seems to know more about the subject than the person questioned (see, e.g., Ong 1988). We take for granted that authorities will ask questions not so much to learn as to challenge and judge, and that one must comport oneself well in such a situation without explicit bragging. Some of our subjects share this understanding, but some do not, and it appears that we frequently confuse the pragmatic failure of such a setting with various individual limitations in our subjects (see Martin 2001).[68]

Put simply, we have asked stupid questions and then declared actors stupid on the basis of their answers. Empiricism of the form advocated by Dewey never had a reasonable trial because we have so rarely asked people about their experiences per se. But that is what we should be asking about, for the empirical—the phenomenological—is composed not of "reasons why" but of "seeings that." "Real," in sum, is a characteristic of experiences, not statements about experience, and our task as social analysts is to gather reality. We should hope to gather up such reality by the cartload, but by confusing reality (on the one hand) and statements *about* reality (on the other), we have too often used the incoherence of the latter—itself largely a product of our flawed social relations with subjects—to lead us to mash reality through a strainer (and this justified as "theory").

It is not surprising that the nature of real experience is lost. Just as we have a "quantitative" sociology in which there is hardly ever an actual quantity (as we follow the colossal Durkheimian error of confusing aggregated measures of individuals, usually counts, with measures of aggregates), so we also have a "qualitative" sociology in which not a single quality appears. Yet, if Dewey and Peirce are right, any serious science of human action must begin with the nature of qualitative experience. In this, argues Dewey, we have only lost ground since the philosophy of the ancient Greeks.

---

[68]This parallels the history whereby investigators of animal intelligence came up with a too-pessimistic evaluation because they attempted instruction in an interactional landscape barren of the social relations that actually inspire and guide learning (see Pepperberg 1999: 14ff).

Toward Aesthetics

The difference between Dewey's own approach and that of the Greeks was in the understanding of what quality was—the "naïveté" of the Greeks came in their believing that the qualities of objects were simple characteristics of these objects abstracted from any interaction with persons. Dewey ([1899] 1965: 264) saw these qualities as more akin the "affordances" of Gestalt theory: "Nature knows no . . . divorce of quality and circumstance. Things come when they are wanted and as they are wanted; their quality is precisely the response they give to the conditions that call for them, while the furtherance they afford to the movement of their whole is their meaning."

Thus, Dewey's line of thought suggests that we understand the cognitive components of action more in aesthetic terms than those pertaining to knowledge. Quite logically, Dewey (1929: 2, 394, 396; also see Dewey 1918, 1923) pursued this approach to its implied conclusion and argued if qualities are really attributes of objects themselves, then *values* may equally be inherent in nature and retrieved from objects.[69] There is no reason, he argued, to claim that the only "ends" present in the world are those that we can identify with the psychic states that we usually understand "values" to imply (1929: 112). But here, Dewey's vocabulary failed him: it remains paradoxical how an end—something that only exists in reference to a particular subjectivity—can be considered to exist independent of such a subjectivity. This paradox can be resolved, at least logically, as Kant had shown: pursuing Kant's approach sheds fundamental light on the nature of an aesthetic approach to subjectivity.

---

[69]"If experience actually presents esthetic and moral traits, then these traits may also be supposed to reach down into nature" (Dewey 1929: 2). Somewhat differently: "Right is only an abstract name for the multitude of concrete demands in action which others impress upon us, and of which we are obliged, if we would live, to take some account" (Dewey [1922] 1930: 326f). Also see the work of Heider (1958: 219f, 222).

Chapter 6

A Social Aesthetics

JUDGMENT AND COGNITION

Let us take stock of where we are in the argument. In contrast to the dominant views held in the social sciences regarding the partially arbitrary nature of the cognitive components to action, we investigated three traditions that began from contrary premises. This investigation led us to the question of aesthetics in the technical sense. To consider seriously what a theory of aesthetics might hold for explanation in the social sciences, we must return to the question of judgment.

Why Judgment?

According to traditional ideas of concept formation, we begin with discrete units with attributes (e.g., animals) and collect some together in a concept (e.g., birds) by focusing on some attributes (e.g., feathers and bone type) and ignoring others (e.g., mode of locomotion). It is this act that we properly call *abstraction* (see, e.g., Berlin [1960] 1997: 35; Simmel [1908] 1950: 96).

We saw in chapter 4 that Durkheim built his understanding of cognition around this idea of concept formation (also see Durkheim [1911] 1953: 95; cf. [1883–1884] 2004: 134), even applying it to ritual totemism; thus, he (at times) argued that the word *are* in the sentence "we are parrots" is the same as the word *are* in the sentence "parrots are birds." Durkheim's argument was that this logic came from the experience of social organization, paradigmatically kinship relationships. Let us hold to the side the empirical inadequacy of his argument and think through the logic of one simple form of kinship relation, namely, patrilineal descent. Such descent leads to a perfect tree of nested categories—any two persons are the "same" at some level of connectedness. Given any two classes, if there is any overlap, it is because one is more general than the other is and hence contains all the members of the less-general class. Thus, if ego is a male, ego and all his brothers can be considered equivalent—the band of brothers united by a common father. And ego is equivalent with his cousins—all are son's son's of ego's father's father. If alter is a brother, then alter is technically a cousin (ego's father's father's son's son) as well.

Thus, in this scheme, any person's location in a particular set satisfies Durkheim's way of thinking: if your grandfather's offspring define the bird clan and your father's offspring the parrot subclan (in contrast to your father's brother's offspring, the turtle subclan), then we can say that "parrots are birds" and that (in this system) "turtles are birds."

In sum, Durkheim's analysis of totemism tended to recognize only a single copula, a single way to connect subject and predicate, namely, the subsumption of a particularity into a larger generality (Cassirer [1925] 1955: 65).[1] "Is" can then be replaced by "is a subset of," and so this sort of copula is, by definition, transitive: if A is B and B is C, then A is C, or, to stick with our example, if you are a turtle, and turtles are birds, then you are a bird. This copula was the one taken from Durkheim's own—literally although not pejoratively—patriarchal society. Durkheim strangely applied this logic to societies in which descent was either bilineal or divorced from residence—he was, as we saw, quite wrong about Australians. But he was basically right about himself.

And, this was not because nineteenth-century French kin relationships were strictly patrilineal but because such subsumptive reasoning was integral to the structure of nineteenth-century French theories of knowledge and of concept formation. To go from the more restricted class of brothers to the wider class of brothers and cousins is to suppress one particular attribute of persons, namely, who their father is, while retaining the information about who their grandfather is. It is the same act of abstraction as that which takes us from parrots to birds by suppressing some particularities while retaining others. Such a process necessarily involves a loss of concreteness with increasing generality, for we group more objects into wider classes by suppressing more and more of their characteristics.

This was Durkheim's philosophy of science, formalized in his *Rules* as the following italicized principle: "The subject matter of every sociological study should comprise a group of phenomena defined in advance by certain common external characteristics, and all phenomena so defined should be included within this group" ([1895] 1938: 35; cf. 86ff). Of course, when we create our "genera" out of "species" (here the words are Durkheim's, referring to classifying societies), we cannot examine all the characteristics of each particularity, for there are an infinite number. The question then becomes, *how* do we create these classes? Which particularities do we ignore? To answer such questions, we have nowhere to turn but to a "theory."

So, Durkheim did in a way pioneer the "Durkheimian" approach to knowledge, not in *The Elementary Forms* ([1912] 1995), but in his fundamental epistemology, one that held that any move away from particularity

---

[1] In his later treatment, he was vaguer regarding what the logical status of statements of totemic identity might be.

A Social Aesthetics

required an abstraction in which the particulars are subsumed into a concept. Further, he emphasized that there was an unavoidably theoretical (read, arbitrary) moment of this organization. In other ways, however, Durkheim did not pioneer this approach. For one, he did not actually use it (fortunately for him); for another, his codification was clumsy and somewhat archaic. Social scientists who want to justify this idea of concept making generally turn to Max Weber, who transported Heinrich Rickert's philosophy of science into sociology.[2] The basic idea was the same: we approach generality through subsumptive concept formation. This means that our general terms are necessarily abstract—they require that we suppress particularities (Rickert 1902: 33, 43ff, 54, 59, 70f; [1929] 1986: 37).[3]

But the phenomenological and developmental-comprehensive traditions that we saw arising in early twentieth-century Germany understood that there were other possible ways of thinking. As Husserl ([1900] 1970: 337, 426f; also see 373, 393f, 404; compare Heidegger [1926] 1962: 202/I.5.33) argued, most analysts had identified this process of abstraction

---

[2]The extent to which Weber relied on Rickert is of course open to dispute; many of the ideas were common to their general circle, and Rickert was the one who formalized them in greatest detail. For a discussion of the relation of Rickert's thoughts on the process of generalization to Weber, see the work of Oakes (1988) and Bruun (2007: 116).

[3]The complication here enters in that Rickert ([1929] 1986: 54, 62, 73, 78) did not believe this sort of concept formation to be characteristic of the "cultural sciences," which were intrinsically historical and involved the formation of individualizing concepts. Although few social scientists have attempted to defend the applicability of such a theory of concept formation (and it is not clear how Rickert would place today's social sciences in his scheme), Max Weber not only used such concepts in his own work but also (in his attacks on others) indicated that he was convinced that the sort of subsumptive concept formation that loses content with abstraction was not inherent to the historical sciences ([1903–1906] 1975: 56, 64, 268; also 168f, 186, 197, 213, 219). However, as he also insisted (contra Rickert) that there was fundamental continuity between the cultural sciences and other sciences in terms of concept formation and causality, and seemed to avoid explicitly embracing Rickert's ([1929] 1986: 89, 105, 136, 139) conclusion that historical concepts had to be formed in relation to core (valid) cultural values, that is, those of "cultured" civilizations (and not in relation to explanatory goals [as in Weber [1917] 1949: 22]), it is far from certain that Weber really accepted all of the structure that allowed Rickert to argue that historical concepts were immune to the loss of reality that characterized scientific concepts. Finally, Weber's key methodological writings were penned when he saw himself as a historical economist; it would be rash to assume that after he (for whatever reason) decided to identify with sociology, he would have argued that sociological concepts were cultural, hence historical, hence individual, as Rickert argued. Thus, it is not surprising that the Rickertian view of individual concept formation has not had a major impact on the theory of explanation of the contemporary social sciences.

with that of reaching of generality; indeed, the inability of abstraction to seize the specific "is even counted as a virtue." Such a process, said Cassirer (1923: 6, 8f, 258, 293), clearly sacrifices the nature of the units as concrete *wholes*, turns the relations between these wholes into attributes of them considered singly or jointly, and leads to a division between things and relations, substance and form. But, such a loss of concreteness with increasing generality is not, he argued, characteristic of *judgment* (Cassirer [1910] 1923: 226; [1925] 1955: 206; also see Köhler 1920: 29).[4] If judgment offers an alternative ground for generalization, then we may be able to explain the processes of forming social knowledge without recapitulating the problems that we saw Durkheim creating for himself.[5]

As discussed in somewhat more detail below, there is something archaic in the idea of "judgment" as a faculty (cf. Cassirer [1923] 1953: 303; [1925] 1955: 30).[6] The argument here is not that we "have" judgment and that this faculty has been given incomplete attention; rather, it is that

---

[4] "Only of 'representations' [*Vorstellungen*] can it be said, that the more general they become the more they lose their intuitive sharpness and clarity. . . . Judgments, on the contrary, determine the individual the more exactly the wider the sphere of comparison and correlation to which they relate it [*sic*]" (also see Cassirer [1910: 300]; to be consistent with other usage, especially Durkheim's use of "representation," I consistently change translations of *Vorstellung* as "presentation" to "representation" and use presentation for *Darstellung*). It is for this reason that Cassirer ([1910] 1923: 284; 1910: 376) argued that the theory of representation (*Repräsentation*) always leads to a skepticism about the adequacy of cognition, for we have no certainty regarding the adequacy of our representations (*Vorstellungen*) of things. For his application of this general logic to the case of signs and the relationship of representations to concept formation, see ([1923] 1953: 108, 281). For his argument that renewed attention to judgment was warranted by the emerging sciences, see (Cassirer 1923: 4f, 10, 15, 18; to be fair, Rickert [1902: 96ff] had also made this point). For a related criticism of subsumptive concept formation, see the wonderful discussion of Ilyenkov (1977b: 356, 358), who points out that Marx precedes Cassirer in using the ratio as the way to understand relational definitions.

[5] In a related discussion of language and concepts, Cassirer ([1923] 1953: 278–285, 288, 297) noted that most approaches to language led to a nominalism in which words were identified with the content of concepts (which arise through abstraction), which then led to the question regarding whether the words or the concepts "came first" (as in chapter 4). In contrast, Cassirer (280) emphasized that to understand the active process of our creating divisions in the world we must recognize that "the *primary* function of concept formation is not, as most logicians have assumed under the pressure of a centuries-old tradition, to raise our representations to ever greater universality; on the contrary, it is to make them increasingly determinate."

[6] Recently, however, Boltanski and Thévenot ([1991] 2006: 144; also 1999: 364; 2000) have revived the study of judgment in sociology, and have emphasized the sort of cognitive competence of the actor that such an approach implies.

the dominant way of parsing our cognitive life is incomplete if judgment is excised.

We have already seen, of course, that in practice judgment is bound up with other cognitive activities. Indeed, in his own discussion Cassirer referred approvingly to the work of Christian von Ehrenfels, the teacher who inspired Wertheimer through his focus on gestalts and his rejection of the bifurcation between perception and judgment. Wertheimer's first experiments, we recall, involved projecting first one dot and then another a small distance away on a screen. Subjects did not report seeing two dots but instead a single moving dot. As Köhler ([1967] 1971: 109) points out, most readers at first assumed that this was evidence of an error of judgment, an analytically separable moment from perception, but all evidence indicates that our perceptual system delivers a perception of a moving object to our consciousness.

Thus, the Gestalt experiments may be understood as casting doubt on the existence of judgment as a separate faculty, while taking some of the conventional predicates of judgment and bringing them into the explication of perception (also Merleau-Ponty [1942] 1963: 201). This revision led them to a model of perception that was more phenomenologically valid, in that it better described how we perceive that we perceive. However, it did so at a cost of going native—its naïve realism was predicated on treating the observer as wholly passive. The active side of concept formation, treated by the Russian school of Vygotsky, could not be properly appreciated. The Gestalt theorists easily embraced a naturalism (whereby, as Reed [1996: 26, cf. 40] emphasizes, affordances are the same for all creatures) that would strain if applied to social issues.

In contrast, we have seen that Dewey was able to retain an understanding of the active nature of perception while accepting the phenomenological givenness of qualities; to do so was in effect to propose a theory of judgment. While this anticipates, we may say that while a model of thought in terms of *concepts* is correlative to propositional thinking with a copula of identity in set theoretic terms ($A \subseteq B$; "cats are mammals"), a less-restrictive model of thought in terms of *judgments* (or synthetic judgments) is correlative to qualitative experience (e.g., "cats are independent") (also see Cassirer [1923] 1953: 135f, 259). The first formulation (the set theoretic or, as I shall call it here, the "subsumptive") implies, as Barnes (2000) has said in a recent and wonderful work, transitivity.[7] But, as Barnes (like James [1909] 1943: 257; Metzinger 2003: 78f) emphasizes, such transitivity is unlikely to hold for phenomenologically experienced identity. His example is wine slowly turning to vinegar over a series of days. Each day, we say that the wine is "the same" as it was the previous

---

[7]The idea of the copula as set identity does not, one will notice, imply symmetry in that all A may be B while not all B must be A. The case of identity ($A = B$) is a subset of the general relation of subsumption.

day, but all these samenesses do not prevent the wine from having turned at the end. If we simply dismiss the importance of this by appealing to the crudeness of our perceptions, we are refusing to truly examine the phenomenological experience of quality.[8] And, we must take seriously the nature of qualities if we are to attempt an explanatory account that is not at odds with first-person perspectives (as discussed in chapter 1) because the nature of first-person experience *is*, as Dewey stressed, inherently qualitative.[9] It was this understanding that led Dewey to highlight the importance of aesthetics.[10]

It is important to bear in mind that this sense of aesthetics has nothing to do with issues of interpretation and the openness of hermeneutics (e.g., Ricoeur 1974: 65; cf. Schutz [1932] 1967: 85), nor even with art. Following Dewey (1934: 46ff), we may say *art* generally refers to the skill or creativity of the maker of some object, while *aesthetic* refers to the (presumably appreciative) nature of some qualitative experience.[11] The

---

[8]Drawing on Lotze, Cassirer ([1923] 1953: 283f) points to the distinction between the classic understanding of concept formation discussed above and what which he calls "qualifying" concept formation, in which "a thing is not named from the standpoint of the genus to which it belongs, but on the basis of some particular *property* which is apprehended in a total intuitive content." For example, subsuming the color "blue" under the concept "color" is completely empty—our understanding of the generality "color" comes only in the totality of qualitative experiences of color. Also, compare Boltanski and Thévenot's ([1991] 2006: 359) use of a similar term.

[9]Stephen Pepper (1966: see esp. 26f, 43, 61, 68, 346, 426), whose philosophy of aesthetics will be discussed below, made a valiant and sophisticated attempt not only to take seriously the qualitative nature of experience but also to determine the relation between such qualitative experience and the conceptual knowledge that closely parallels what that I have termed third-person accounts. Pepper's attempt to wed such third-person accounts to first-person experiences is far more substantively grounded and therefore less elegant than Habermas's (1984, 1987) later and closely related approach. Given that to define a noncontradictory "explanation" in the social sciences we may be satisfied with a partial vocabulary, I have not followed Pepper in his rehabilitation of conceptual thought, but note that he demonstrates the possibility of establishing a connection between the first-person accounts of immediate experience (actuality) and the extensive constructs or projective abstractions established by conceptual thought (which he terms reality—examples would include the past and the future). It is significant that Pepper understands his rigorous approach to imply both an attention to aesthetics (discussed below) and a field conception of experience (158).

[10]Barnes himself (2000: 135f) uses this to shed light on the nature of rules, something we do not investigate until chapter 8. But, he also argues that such rule following must be understood as a constellation of mutually oriented persons and not the application of subsumptive logic.

[11]Dewey argued against a complete separation of art and aesthetic: just as we might not be impressed with the pedagogical skill of a teacher whose students learn nothing, so we cannot see art where no one can have an experience. But,

A Social Aesthetics

Gestalt theorists understood that their approach also implied a serious consideration of how an organism was able to orient itself to the qualities of its environment, and hence an aesthetics.[12]

Here, we pick up this thread of aesthetics—the relation between persons and the qualities of objects—hoping to discover to what extent this can serve as a useful template for our understanding of the cognitive components of action. We can begin with the clearest formulation of the puzzle of aesthetics, that of Kant, which has served as a starting place for other attempts to produce a social aesthetics.[13]

A Trinity of Faculties

Kant's approach to aesthetics must be understood in the context of his general system of faculties.[14] In his conception, we have the capacity to think in concepts (the *understanding*), a capacity to determine what to do (*practical reasoning*), and a capacity to determine the relationship between these (*judgment*).[15] Judgment is thus in some ways "between" the

---

while Tolstoy ([1896] 1960: 49, 51) might simply see art as a form of communication (although of feeling, not thought), Dewey (paralleling Mead 1934) assumed that in art the creator shapes material primarily so as to effect a certain qualitative experience in the perceiver, thus taking on the role of the other in his work, and bringing in the audience in anticipatory form even when alone (1934: 51).

[12]"Bischof recently remarked that if the Gestalt theory is correct, the organism would be making fundamentally aesthetic hypotheses regarding the character of its surrounding reality. To this I would respond, first, that it seems to me that the organism does just this, and second, that in doing so it is not led astray, even if, as it can be shown, the aesthetic hypothesis, precisely because it is aesthetic, overshoots reality" (Metzger [1967] 1986: 142; also see Stumpf 1907: 82). Further, Metzger ([1975a] 1986: 181) understood that this implied that we would also perceive social groups via such a wholistic aesthetic sense. It is perhaps significant that Koffka taught a course on aesthetics at Giessen. For Bischof's interesting discussion, see (1966: 51). Finally, one must point to Meyer's (1956) influential attempt to derive a theory of musical aesthetics in large part from Gestalt psychology; this led Meyer to a conception of how listeners perceive regularity that dovetails with that (differently derived) in chapter 8.

[13]In addition to Bourdieu, see Zerilli (2009).

[14]I think it is noteworthy that many of the scholars reviewed in chapter 5 saw Kant's work on judgment as vital and underappreciated; this goes most notably for Cassirer (and, he argues, Goethe [Cassirer 1918/1981: 273; cf. 308, 314]) but also for Ilyenkov ([1974] 2002) and see Meleau-Ponty ([1942] 1963: 200).

[15]My discussion necessarily leaves out a number of Kant's more innovative ideas, in particular that the use of pure reason includes not only the understanding but also the intuition (*Anschauung*); in the next chapter, I argue that a lack of attention to such intuition has been seriously problematic for the social sciences, but the role of the intuition in this scheme has been less broadly accepted in the social sciences and may be left to the side for the present.

understanding and (practical) reason, just as the feeling of pleasure is between our cognitive power and the power of desire (Kant [1790] 1987: 17ff; [1798] 2006: 138). The importance of this division is reflected in the current governmental structure of the United States of America, for one, which divides public functions into the legislative (in which we choose what principles to put into effect), the executive (which pertains to the practice of such principle), and the judicial, in which we use judgment to determine the relation between these two. This does not mean that this is the *only* way of dividing these functions, simply that a government that had the first two and not the third would be hampered. Similarly hampered has been our approach to cognition.

Most generally, judgment is the capacity to see that a particular case should be identified as an aspect of something more general. When there is a determinative rule that allows for subsumption (as in a classic syllogism), the matter is relatively uninteresting. In other cases, however, we merely begin with a particular and need to find the universal, which requires what Kant terms a reflective power. It is this reflective power that helps account for our capacity for aesthetic judgment, a capacity that might at first seem baffling.

Aesthetics and Communion

As Dewey recognized, to say that beauty, purpose, or value is not simply in the eye of the particular beholder is to claim that there are "ends" (an inherent purposiveness as opposed to mere existence) in nature or in created objects and not just in our attitude toward them. As we have seen, Dewey's own approach to aesthetics fell somewhat short of this, as (at least when considering art) he took for granted that there *was* an intention, simplifying the problem considerably. But, what is notable about aesthetic perception is precisely its *independence* of intention. Few would want the stained glass of medieval cathedrals restored to its original (intended?) garishness because we find the meanings of the altered form more congenial (even though these "meanings" were never "meant" to be). The first task of an aesthetics is simply to determine how we may be able to attribute qualities to objects even when we cannot simply posit that they were "put there" by their creator.

We can begin with the question of what it means to consider something "beautiful," a paradigmatic case of aesthetic judgment. While beauty seems to be a characteristic of the objects themselves, we realize that this cannot quite be the case. "For a judgment of taste consists precisely in this, that it calls a thing beautiful only by virtue of that characteristic in which it adapts itself to the way we apprehend" (Kant [1790] 1987: 145). Such judgments can be made on the basis of the sense of pleasure we have when representation brings the imagination into harmony with the understanding.

This is, Kant argues, an aesthetic judgment of the purposiveness (*zweckmäßigkeit*) of the object. The purposiveness of the object does not necessarily imply that anything exists that has or had this purpose (the word has connotations of appropriateness, harmoniousness). Thus, "a bird's song proclaims his joyfulness and contentment with his existence. At least that is how we interpret nature whether or not it has such an intention." We attribute the purposiveness to the nature of the bird and do not rely on evidence of a subjectively held purpose. On the other hand, in fine art, if the intention becomes visible, the effect is ruined (we might say it is "strained" and "unnatural"). Thus we see, argued Kant, that aesthetic experience reaches toward a naturalization of what is subjectively experienced. While the beautiful appears purposive (as opposed to senseless or random, say), we do not need to understand the purpose of any existent being in order to understand beauty, for we feel a pleasure when we encounter beauty. Taste is then our ability to make judgments on the basis of such pleasure (Kant [1790] 1987: 30f, 169, 174; see 292 for a key linkage between intuitive judgment and purposiveness).

We believe that our judgment of beauty must be accepted as valid (as opposed to idiosyncratic), but as Hume ([1777] 1985: 231) argued, we know we cannot *prove* this to someone through concepts in the way that we can prove that a cat is a mammal. To do this, we would list the characteristics that defined "mammal," demonstrate that a cat had these, and ignore all its other characteristics. But, we understand that to locate something under the banner "beautiful" means not (as with concepts) to suppress its particularity, but rather to highlight its particularity (see Gadamer [1977] 1986: 37).

Accordingly, Kant ([1790] 1987: 19) argued that the possibility of such judgment implies the existence of transindividual principles of regularity (otherwise, beauty would merely be in the eye of the beholder), which we can consider laws. These laws, however, have the curious characteristic that they cannot be derived from concepts and hence are empirical (which might lead us to consider them contingent), but since they are laws, they would seem to be necessary. Kant concluded that these laws need to "be viewed in terms of such a unity as if they too had been given by an understanding (even though not ours) so as to assist our cognitive powers by making possible a system of experience in terms of particular natural laws."

In other words, if we are to assume the existence of such empirical principles of regularity (some things truly *are* beautiful), we must treat the world as if it was made *for* us to be able to judge beauty. (In a rough analogy, we perhaps cannot prove that house numbers on one side of the street are always odd and on the other always even, but we can safely believe that this *is* indeed a law because we can imagine that it is the result of conscious intent of an understanding like our own, although this may not be strictly accurate.) Kant ([1790] 1987: 24ff; also 65) is at pains to emphasize that we do not need to posit the existence of such an understanding (that is, a creator with personhood), but we do need to treat the world *as if* it had so arisen. Hence, we can derive the "harmony of nature with our cognitive power" (which Bourdieu terms the "ontological complicity" of our faculties with the world).[16]

Thus, Kant answers the question we raised regarding how one could speak of there being "ends" in nature. The answer is that we may correctly speak of having to treat nature *as if* it had ends (or an inherent suitability for ends), and Kant ([1790] 1987: 14, 140, 220) further derives the necessity of some a priori principles justifying this, and hence a "supersensible" realm, one inaccessible to our cognitive powers of empirical inquiry. It is the postulating of such a supersensible realm that allows us to demand that all others (more on this below) agree with our judgments of taste. This is not the case for other things that we find agreeable. Thus, we may enjoy having our back scratched at some time but do not demand that all others find this equally agreeable (indeed, we may even recognize that we do not always find this one thing agreeable). When we compare the experience of beauty to these other agreeable experiences, we can conclude that aesthetic judgments are peculiar in that we expect them to be communicable and to provoke assent, "and this without any mediation by concepts" (Kant [1790] 1987: 159; cf. 157, 162, 156). It is sufficient to point and ask, Is this not beautiful?

It is of the utmost importance that Kant does not ground this universal communicability in the objectivity of the judgment; instead, it is more closely related to our "sociability," our innate desire to interact with others (cf. Barnes 2000). Taste is what allows us to judge whether we can communicate our feelings, and the refined person is he who is "not satisfied with an object unless he can feel his liking for it in community with others" (Kant [1790] 1987: 163f; cf. 231).[17] Yet, Kant ([1790] 1987: 58) acknowledges that we may find this desire for universal confirmation of our tastes to go unsatisfied. Since there can be no determinative or objective rule governing what is beautiful, "the broadest possible agreement among all ages and peoples regarding this feeling that accompanies the representation[18] of certain objects is the empirical criteria for what is beautiful" (Kant [1790] 1987: 79).

---

[16]Kant ([1790] 1987: 37; also 151) argues that it is the concept of the purposiveness of nature that "makes possible the transition from pure theoretical to pure practical lawfulness." Thus, it is judgment that allows us to translate our conceptual order into a capacity for rational action (in Kant's sense). We cannot demonstrate that the laws that guide things in themselves (which is what we are as actors) are predictably related to the laws that we can derive for things in appearance (which is what the understanding can reach), but we can demonstrate that we must assume some sort of correspondence—that is, a purposiveness of the world—if we are to act freely.

[17]Thus, taste cannot be disconnected from manners and morality (or at least the semblance of morality)—that which allows us to coexist in harmony (Kant [1798] 2006: 141).

[18]Translation modified as described in note 4.

For practical purposes, then, the beautiful is what is generally taken to be beautiful—Kant's approach might seem well suited for the foundation of a sociological understanding of aesthetics were it not for two unsupportable claims. The first is his insistence that there should be a universal "we" who share an aesthetic sense. The judgment of taste—this object is beautiful—must command the assent of "all of us," although we know this is never true.

Kant basically handled the empirical problem of the nonunanimity of judgments of taste by positing a distinction between cultivated and uncultivated taste. The difficulty is that this returns us to a social epistemology that seemingly requires an injection of exogenous social theory. Put somewhat differently, every transformation of an aesthetic experience into a proposition that goes beyond the invitation, "share this experience with me," contains an unspoken indexical component ("This is the beautiful . . . , and I should know because I am more cultivated than you"). Even Dewey (1929: 407, cf. p. 402; 1934: 310, although see 1934: 20, 26 for a critique of the related distinctions), with his attempt to formulate a democratic epistemology, relied on such a bifurcation of the "undeveloped or perverted taste" and the "cultivated taste"; it was the existence of such a real difference between "immediate goods casually occurring and immediate goods which have been reflectively determined by means of critical inquiry" that justified the need for judgment as a critical faculty (and hence led to Dewey's scientism).[19] We all know, Dewey pointed out, that a single person can have values that are at odds with each other (what economists might consider a dual-preference structure, as discussed by Etzioni 1988) and may enjoy something that she judges bad (such as French fries) or disvalue things that she would value valuing (such as the welfare of the less fortunate).

One way to approach this contradiction, of course, is to consider one set of tastes or values a lower form, present somehow immediately, and the other a more cultivated version that only arises after reflection (although this is not quite Dewey's own resolution; see Joas [2000: 107] for a somewhat different take). It is because we can tell ourselves, "French fries are bad for me; I shall henceforth not like them," or "My value on

---

[19] In Dewey's ([1906] 1965: 219) words, "To suppose that perception as it concretely exists . . . is identical with the sharply analyzed, objectively discriminated and internally disintegrated elements of scientific observation, is a perversion of experience." The former is only a *potentially* excellent perception, the latter a truly useful one. Dewey (1929: 426) accordingly based his criticism of "common sense" on a failure "to recognize that deliberate and systematized science is a precondition of adequate judgments and hence of adequate striving and adequate choice," thus divorcing himself from the populist-democratic tradition that refused to put any form of cognitive competence outside the grasp of the common person. Also see Mills (1964: 451).

fairness leads me to reevaluate the importance of others' well being to myself," that we can make any sort of individual progress. But if it is science or philosophy that leads us to reevaluate our craving for fried food or for a tax policy that favors us, it is of course possible that some persons with more exposure to science and philosophy thus have a greater balance of cultivated tastes to uncultivated. Indeed, at the limit, we may speak of those with and those without cultivated tastes. Dewey thus assimilated the nonproblematic intrapersonal case to the much more problematic case of an interpersonal division between mass and elite.[20]

We need not, however, assume that the distinction between cultivated and uncultivated taste is, formally speaking, any different from that between Eastern taste and Western taste or between nineteenth-century taste and twentieth-century taste. Simply put, we may recognize that the "cultivation" of taste is the rule, not the exception, and that tastes are cultivated differently in different places and at different times. Thus, even if we follow Kant in understanding that the judgment of taste commands the assent of "all of us," this "us" need not be universal. We do need to posit a supersensible that is above the individual level, but we need not make this intrinsic to reason.

The second problematic claim of Kant's (the first was the universality of taste) turns on the nature of judgment as an independent faculty (also see Cassirer [1910] 1923: 245). At the beginning of this chapter, I referred to the Gestalt school's critique of the idea of judgment as separable from perception. Such an understanding of this fusion is not apparent to the armchair philosopher but requires empirical exploration. Hence, it is not surprising that Kant treated judgment as separable from perception, even though we have no evidence that this describes a real operation.

Removing these two unfounded assumptions produces two welcome shifts in our understanding of aesthetics. The first is to retain the connection between sociability and aesthetics, but in some sense to reverse the priority. Every aesthetic encounter determines a "we" just as much as it

---

[20]It is worth pointing out that in some sense, this differentiation between cultivated and uncultivated tastes, while it supports Dewey's emphasis on intelligence as a pragmatic response to a problematic environment, cuts against his more fundamental critique of idealism. Kant, said Dewey (1917: 18), used his famous a prioris to "restore objectivity," but in so doing, "accepted the particularism of experience"—that is, that experience comes as unordered subjectivity, an assumption with which Dewey strenuously disagreed. Analogously, Kant derived the need for the supersensible in aesthetics and hence the possibility of unanimity of taste. That is, there *must* be a cultivated (correct, universal) taste in Kant's system (or at least we must be able to act *as if* there was) because otherwise there is no possibility of exercising our sociability, and no capacity for things to be beautiful, for all must be noise and confusion. But, if we do not begin from an assumption of the particularism of experience, we may find an order in taste coming from the structuring of available experience.

A Social Aesthetics

may be said to be predicated on its existence. The aesthetic experience is largely one of "getting" it (hence not so different from the experience of the sublime, as discussed by Kant). When "we get it"—when we experience the artistic beauty of a painting, say—we focus on the "it," the object in question, and the beauty as a quality of this object. But, when we get the "it," we get the "we" as well, in the sense of establishing a presumption of like-mindedness with those of similar taste. The aesthetic experience is inseparable from perceived entry into some group; generally, the more rarified the aesthetic pleasure, the smaller the group, with the limit being the feeling of communion with the creator of some object. To take a phrase from Goffman (1959), the aesthetic experience may not simply be the pleasure taken in social closure, but the ways in which it is not are difficult to grasp sociologically.

Second, if judgment is not an analytically separable moment intervening between perception and action, then we are (just as Dewey and Köhler argued) free to consider the aesthetic properties of objects—their "qualities" in the sense used here—as properties of these (phenomenological) objects (also see Heider 1958: 26). Kant's principled refusal to endorse such a solution necessarily followed from his attempt at a philosophically rigorous analysis of judgment, his understanding of the universal nature of reason, and his understanding of the nature of the noumena that we face. He demonstrated that we must appeal to the fellow feeling that comes from coexperience when making judgments of quality, and we must treat the world as if it had been made "for us." But, the contemporary social scientist is more likely to imagine that we have been made "for the world" in the sense that our processing faculties, whatever they are, have developed both ontogenetically and phylogenetically to deal with the world that does confront us (Reed 1996: 69). Thus, just as we reverse Kant's "we see that it is beautiful" to form the sociological "who sees this as beautiful, let him join with me," so we reverse Kant's understanding that the world was made for us into the worldliness of our minds.

But this reversal, rather than implying a subjective uniformity, leads us to the opposite. For the worlds we experience are different. This variability is not inconsistent with an investigation of judgment; it merely forces us to accept that we must be prepared to take seriously the processes whereby we sense the qualities of objects even when there is a lack of social consensus regarding what these qualities are. Thus, it might seem possible and necessary to develop a theory of the cognitive components of social action that would be a social aesthetics.

What Is a Social Aesthetics?

It is this need for a theory of social aesthetics that led to Bourdieu's masterwork, *Distinction* ([1979] 1984). It is not necessary to review Bourdieu's terminology as it is so well known, but this renown has not been without frequent misreading. Presumably because of his earlier interest in the relation between cultural background and success in school (see Bourdieu and Passeron 1990), this work has, in the United States at least, been largely treated as a vast data supplement on cultural differences to *Reproduction*, and Bourdieu's own project in *Distinction*, clearly stated at the beginning, has been ignored. Thus, when people find that isolated propositions found in this book do not hold in, say, U.S. data in 1997, "Bourdieu" has been disproved (also see Vandenberghe 1999).

The connection between aesthetics and stratification emphasized in *Distinction* (Bourdieu [1979] 1984) came not because knowledge of art impelled some persons to ruling positions but because of the relationship between taste and class position. In emphasizing this connection, Bourdieu argued that action that might appear to an outsider as strategic in effecting social closure—for example, favoring the "brilliant" style of the glib upper-class student who has not done his work to the "plodding" insistence of the working-class one who has—was in fact an immediate result of tastes that were as far from subjectively strategic as could be imagined. Thus, action could be seen as coordinated not by conscious goals but by a nonconscious (hence Bourdieu called it "bodily") matrix of dispositions and predispositions, the habitus. The habitus thus serves the same role as Kant's analysis of the supersensible, to explain why one person can "know" that garden gnomes *are* in shockingly poor taste. While the habitus is nonarbitrary on the individual level (and its particular distinctions are hence related to basic vertical oppositions between heavy and light, coarse and refined, sweet and dry, etc.), so we may speak of a more "cultivated" taste, it is neither universal nor inherent in the purposiveness of the world. It is not so much that the "purity" of the cultivated taste is not *really* pure but instead sullied by material interests; rather, it is that purity itself can only have a meaning in reference to divisions between persons.

Instead of establishing some large correlation between cultural practices and socioeconomic status to help "explain" the reproduction of class dominance, Bourdieu aimed to present a sociological aesthetic—to do for Kant's third critique what Durkheim ([1912] 1995) had hoped to do for his first. As we have seen in chapter 4, Durkheim's attempt was as flawed as it was influential, but even if it had been free from defect, it would have been a step in the wrong direction, taking "knowledge" as the model of what we should treat sociologically. Bourdieu's line of attack was better. Aesthetics needs to be treated sociologically not because appreciation for art or museum going is an important component of social stratification (which would be absurd), but because aesthetics is the closest model to the cognitive components of action that we have (cf. Pepper 1966: 48, 561f). Via the two reversals discussed above (experience determines we-ness, our minds are made for our variable worlds), Bourdieu put forward a notion of social aesthetics that he seamlessly wedded to a vision of action whereby our we-ness leads to experiences and whereby we transform the worlds according to what is in our minds. Here, we are only interested in the first part—understanding our experience of social objects. What the Gestalt tradition could not answer—how one object could have contrary affordances to different people—Bourdieu could, at least for a restricted set of objects.[21]

Although Bourdieu thus saw the centrality of social aesthetics, his aim was not so much to provide a general explanation of the retrieval of qualities from objects, but to provide a (long overdue) sociological critique of Kant's idea of a pure aesthetic, resolving this into its underlying social oppositions.[22] We have seen, however, that such a general explanation—or at least a way of forming a minimal vocabulary allowing for such explanation—is of the utmost importance for the social sciences. Thus, while Bourdieu might dispense with a close engagement with the nature of aesthetics for his own purposes, if we are to get a sense of how we might be able to retrieve qualities that possess phenomenological validity without requiring universal assent, it will help to consider the nature of aesthetics more closely. If we can rederive a general aesthetics that does not separate perception and judgment when it comes to the attribution of qualities, we may then use this as a model for a social aesthetics.

The greatest stumbling block to the development of a coherent vocabulary of social aesthetics is our common folk theory of perception. As Ong (1969) emphasized, vision has become synechdochic for our understanding of our sensory relation to the world, and our theory of vision is a particularly problematic one. Kant ([1798] 2006: 46, 48) himself argued that of all our senses, sight came nearest to being a pure intuition,

---

[21] Bourdieu's lack of interest in specifying some of these processes easily leads to the argument of Loesberg (1993: 1041) that in his critique of the pure aesthetic, Bourdieu cuts off the legs on which he is standing, namely, the habitus, which is an aesthetic faculty. Bourdieu's project only makes sense if we imagine that there is an aesthetic faculty, perhaps reasonably well described by Kant, but one that is not (by definition) Kant's pure aesthetic. Put another way, Bourdieu's critique of the pure aesthetic relies not only on positing an impurity but also in having this impurity be itself an aesthetic response.

[22] It is important that it be recognized how completely apposite this critique was, as opposed to the more common case of a "criticism" that simply takes the past to task for not being the present. Kant ([1790] 1987: 231) himself understood and emphasized that his approach to taste was grounded on a division between the elite and the mass, and that the recognition of this taste difference was part of the (presumably Greek) solution to the Hobbesian problem of legitimate order. (Here, one may see the discussion of Lloyd 1995.) Interestingly, Dewey (1929: 399) followed Kant almost exactly in his defense of the need for cultivated taste. It need hardly be said that theories of aesthetics that renounced a focus on corporal sensation and instead assimilated aesthetics to the communication of rarified feeling necessarily led to such a social division, although this became more central for those who emphasized the capacity of the (sensitive) receiver in the audience (e.g., Bell 1958: 416–412) than for those who emphasized the (feeling) transmitter (e.g., Tolstoy [1896] 1960).

uncontaminated by "touch."[23] I will suggest that vision is actually a rather poor choice of sense to use as an analogy for social perception, but it will be difficult to consider our retrieval of qualities from social objects if we do not exorcise our current assumptions about sight. We must therefore begin by tracing the historical process whereby we lost a belief in our ability to see qualities in the world and ended with a "vision of vision" that was tied up with the eighteenth-century philosophy of the epistemic hiatus between our minds and the world. We can then go on to develop a consistent, if loose, vocabulary for our interactions with the qualities of social objects. We begin with the notion of quality, and how we gained and then lost the capacity to perceive it.

FOR EYES

> Perhaps this word "quality" strikes you as queer and uncouth and you don't understand it as a general expression; so let me give particular instances.
> —Socrates in Plato's *Theaetetus*, 182b.

Qualities and Quales

Qualities are generally considered to be properties of things; vaguely following Aristotle, most consider quality to be a mode of being that does not require replication (as might quantity); reference to others (as might relation, possession); reference to an outside (as might place, time, and position); or change (doing and undoing) (it also is distinct from substance, although the idea of substance plays little role in contemporary discussions). The difficulty this poses to the modern physical imagination (see Burtt 1927) is that when we subtract all of these we are left with little, usually "form"; we therefore make a concession to phenomenology and slide from qualities to qualia (the basic intuitively accessible but otherwise inexpressible units of phenomenal experience). Thus, we may say that a certain substance has a certain microscopic texture that disproportionately reflects electromagnetic radiation with a wavelength of around

---

[23] At the other extreme was smell, the most "ungrateful" sense—being "taste at a distance, so to speak," it involves us being *forced* to share experiences "whether [we] want to or not. And thus smell is contrary to freedom and less sociable than taste, where among many dishes or bottles a guest can choose one according to his liking, without others being forced to share the pleasure of it" (Ibid., 50). Thus, smell is *hypersocial*, for it crowds in on us, especially where there are concentrations of people, who give off far more unpleasant than pleasant scents. The sociability of taste is, for Kant, not herd sociality.

700 nanometers. Yet, when we say it "is" red, we base our understanding of the quality of this substance on our own quale of "redness." This is, if we take Dewey seriously, an eminently reasonable conflation, for what we *mean* by quality is its experience.

In this sense, we feel free to discuss any reliable mapping between some thing or state with our qualia as a "quality" of this thing or state. Thus, an apple not only is red but also is fragrant; if it has half a worm in it, writhing and leaking innards, we say that the apple has the quality of being nauseating.[24] All this is unremarkable and can be accepted as a reasonable way of discussing qualities. What is perhaps of note for our further use is that (at least in this example) there is a clear duality between the qualitative experience and a disposition on the part of the perceiver. It is this direct linkage between perception and action that makes it key for us to understand the nature of qualitative experience, especially as it pertains to social objects.

But the scientific revolution of the seventeenth century led Europeans to abandon the belief that there was a quality on the other side of every quale. This was related to the general epistemology of arbitrariness that we saw imported into sociology to its detriment. Here, like Dewey, we must return to Greek theories, and trace the process whereby we assumed some sort of falsity to qualitative perception.

From Aesthetics to Perception and Back

Our conventional idea of perception is that visual sense data "come" from the outside in the form of light rays, then enter the eye, and are somehow assembled afterward. As a result, our understandings of this process seem a forced choice between the sorts of errors we saw in the grid-of-perception theory (see chapter 4) and the naïve view according to which what we sense "is just out there" (which we found the Gestalt theorists sometimes tending toward in chapter 5). It is entirely true that light enters our eyes from without. It is also largely true that our understanding of qualities comes from processing the results of such light entry. But it is not *entirely* true, and the part that is missing leads it to be utterly false to imagine that the qualities we perceive in objects come from the postperceptual processing of the effects of neural patterns corresponding to a focused beam projected on the retina. To uncover this, let us frame the question in the terms that are of interest to us: how do we retrieve the qualities of the objects that surround us? We review the history of theories of vision to see how the reaching out of our sense apparatuses has been thought of—until these arms were amputated.

---

[24]Interestingly, I find this also used as an example of quality by Pepper (1937: 92); also see James ([1912] 1943: 153).

We turn to the earliest Greeks, for here begins a coherent tradition investigating vision and beginning with qualitative experience.[25] Specifically, we begin with Empedocles, the first known Greek philosopher to give some empirical attention to organic processes, especially those involving the relation between the organism and its environment. How can we perceive? First, Empedocles proposed that "there are effluences from all things in existence" [*Physics* 73(89) 1981: 229f]—things send out parts of themselves. Second, we take these in on the basis of some sameness: "With earth we perceive earth, with water water, with air divine air, with fire destructive fire, with love love, and strife with baneful strife" [*Physics* 77(109); 1981: 233]. More particularly, he argued that the eye was fashioned so that it contained an internal fire [*Physics* 85(86), 88(84); 1981: 239, 240].

What is key is that Empedocles's understanding was based on an assumption of *consubstantiality*—that it is the fundamental *sameness* of our interior mental world and the external physical that allows for perception (also see Cassirer [1910] 1923: 327; van Hoorn 1972: 43, 51f). With the exception of Sophists such as Protagoras and Gorgias and the atomists

---

[25] We might imagine that, like Kant, we should use "the beautiful" as our example of intuited qualities. It is understandable that to a late eighteenth-century philosopher there were few other options—almost all "qualities" had seemed successfully reduced to attributes of textured matter in motion. But, beauty turns out to be a treacherous example when we attempt to retrace the development of ideas about the perception of qualities precisely because as the theories that guided the development of aesthetics were developed (especially beginning with Plato), beauty (that is, absolute beauty) was *not* generally considered a quality perceived through the senses. Indeed, in *Greater Hippias* 303d (Hamilton and Cairns [1961] 1989: 1558), Socrates convinces his interlocutor that "it is impossible for the pleasant which comes through sight and hearing to be beautiful." This absolute beauty is better seen in the purity of geometric figures or pure sounds than in art or in living creatures (*Philebus* 51c,d; Hamilton and Cairns [1961] 1989: 1132f).

The senses, thought Plato, were simply unable to reach such absolutes, and hence we should rely on the intellect whenever possible, making use of the senses only when necessary (*Phaedo* 66a,d, 76a,e, 83a, 100d; Hamilton and Cairns [1961] 1989: 48f, 59f, 66, 81; also see *Republic* VII 524; Hamilton and Cairns [1961] 1989: 756). Despite this conventional denigration of the senses, Plato did give consideration to how they operated. Here, Plato's thoughts were basically along the same lines as Empedocles (discussed shortly).

This transition from (1) beauty as an absolute only available to the intellect and not to the senses to (2) beauty as paradigmatically sensuous was smoothed by an emphasis on regularity of form. William of Ockham (see chapter 7), with his rejection of any inherent form in the created world, then made form refer merely to the arrangement of parts, as opposed to the Platonic conception, and hence something that could be taken in through the senses (see Eco [1959] 1986: 5, 50, 71, 86ff).

such as Democritus (see fragment 9, Freeman 1971: 93), other Greeks (e.g., Anaxagoras) followed along similar lines. Thus, perception involves some combination of one fluid (*pneuma*) from our soul or our eyes and one from the other bodies, two fluids that share an essence.[26]

This emphasis on consubstantiality means that we can be confident that the qualities that we perceive in objects are indeed qualities of the things themselves (Zeller 1955: 79, 82ff, 93, 98f, 105). Or, more interestingly, we can say that the quality is *attached* to the object in the act of perception. Sight, argued Plato (*Theaetetus* 154a, 156d–e; Hamilton and Cairns [1961] 1989: 858, 861) involves an interaction between the motion of the eye and something from the object, and it is this interaction that gives rise to quality. "As the vision from the eyes and the whiteness from the thing that joins in giving birth to the color pass in the space between, the eye becomes filled with vision and now sees, and becomes, not vision, but a seeing eye, while the other parent of the colors is saturated with whiteness and becomes, on its side, not whiteness, but a white thing" (also see Vernant 1995: 14; compare James [1912] 1943: 57). Thus, the object perceived (the "agent") becomes something laden with qualities (*Theaetetus* 182b; Hamilton and Cairns [1961] 1989: 886).

Qualitative perception, then, is based on the consubstantiality of soul and world (*Letters II* 312e; Hamilton and Cairns [1961] 1989: 1566); such an assumption guided Greek and scholastic philosophy afterward. As Plotinus (third century) writes, "Perception of every kind seems to depend on the fact that our universe is a living whole sympathetic to itself," and vision is the successful apprehending of the external object by the soul. Against the idea that vision is akin to a process whereby (as Aristotle suggested; see note 28) an object pushes its form into wax, Plotinus protested, "If to see is to accept imprints of the objects of our vision, we can never see these objects themselves; we see only vestiges they leave within us, shadows: the things themselves would be very different from our vision of them" (Plotinus 1956: 331f, 337f/IV.5.3, IV.5.8, IV.6.1).[27]

---

[26]Speaking of how the gods created man, Plato argued, "So much of fire as would not burn, but gave a gentle light, they formed into a substance akin to the light of everyday life, and the pure fire which is within us and related thereto they made to flow through the eyes in a stream smooth and dense,. . . . when the light of day surrounds the stream of vision, then like falls upon like, and they coalesce. . . . And the whole stream of vision, being similarly affected in virtue of similarity, diffuses the motions of what it touches or what touches it over the whole body, until they reach the soul, causing that perception which we call sight" (*Timaeus* 45b,d: Hamilton and Cairns [1961] 1989: 1173). One will note that here, in contrast to *Theaetetus*, Plato adds a third factor, namely, daylight, to these emanations (*Timaeus* 61e, 62a, 65e, 67a,b; Hamilton and Cairns [1961] 1989: 1187, 1190).

[27]Plotinus's views on vision are interesting. He denied that objects farther away appear smaller because they subtend a smaller angle, citing as evidence that a

Of course, there was an evolution—later theorists were more likely to propose that the agent's effect was mediated by some sort of change in an ether, or they downplayed the role of emanations from the eye (Couliano 1987: 9; Lindberg 1976: 10; although see Seneca [ca. 62 CE] 2010: 2.9.1, 167 on eye rays; also van Hoorn 1972: 105).[28] Yet, they tended to emphasize the role of attention, and that although the vision might in some sense come from the seen object, it also must come from the perceiver, for it is only the *will* that directs our vision (e.g., Augustine in On the Trinity 2002: 62–66).

But, a second strand of thought was to turn out to be crucial for the development of theories of perception. Euclid had initiated a quiet revolution by joining geometry to the study of the retrieval of qualities.[29] Euclid's own optics dealt with the case of projections of objects of certain sizes and orientations to the eye, and how their relative perceived sizes, locations, and velocities might be affected by their spatial relations to the eye. By drawing rays connecting the eye to the edges of the different objects, geometric relations could be used to determine their sizes and how much of each was seen and so on (e.g., see figure 6.1). To some

---

mountain far away, but still large enough to completely fill our field of vision, still appears smaller than the mountain up close. Rather, it seemed to him that objects farther away were only able to transmit their form, and lost their magnitude along with other qualities. He thought the idea that vision was a result of objects transmitting themselves through the air quite implausible, for if, for example, fire radiated out its own form, there would be an end to all darkness, yet we can see a fire at night surrounded by darkness. We know that the eye has some light within it because when we rub our eyes, we squeeze some out and hence see colored shapes. Finally, although he admitted that an intromission theory could be compatible with the absence of a medium between the object and the light, he argued that the sealing wax metaphor implied that an object would impress its form on the medium near it, which would then impress its form on the portion of the medium near *it*, and so on, until one got to the eye, at which point only a tiny portion of the form could be received (Plotinus 1956: 130f, 329ff, 338, 409/ II.8.1,2, IV.5.2,3, IV.6.1, V.5.7).

[28]Aristotle is the most important example here; not only did he highlight the role of the intellect in uniting perceptions, but he denied that the eye contributed an "inner fire" and compared vision to the simple unidirectional process of stamping an image in wax—if the underside of the wax (corresponding to the medium) maintained the form, it would be like the way the air carries the shape and color of an object to our eyes (*De Anima*, 435a5–8). Thus, what is key is the transformation of a medium as opposed to the transference of substance (van Hoorn 1972: 92, 115; also 77 on likeness and unlikeness in Aristotle's theory). Yet, Aristotle (1961) still seemed to assume that sort of internal *pneuma* leaves with the gaze, else how could he accept the belief that menstruating women who look in a mirror leave drops of blood on its surface? (*De Somniis*, 459; this passage is discreetly omitted by McKeon [Aristotle 1941b]; also see Zeller 1955: 204; Couliano 1987: 8, 29).

[29]Here, I use the translation of Burton (1945).

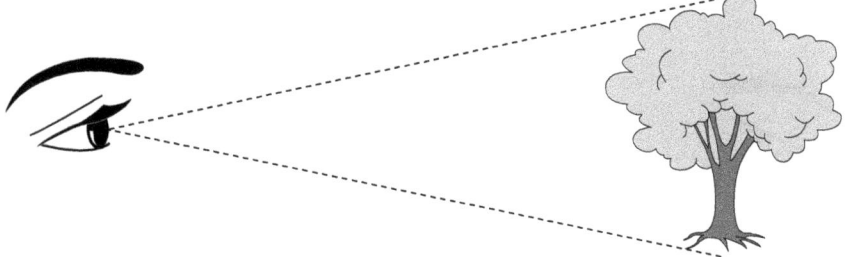

Figure 6.1 Euclid's cone

extent, on examination, his drawings might seem closely related to current optics, but there are some fundamental differences. Most important, Euclid assumed that the rays of vision were emanating *from* the eye and *to* the objects. The sun also emitted rays (and hence similar triangles could be used to measure the height of an object by viewing the sun behind it) (Burton 1945: 360); the sun and the eye thus implicitly contain somewhat similar fires. Second, there was no break with the idea of quality. Thus, the Euclidian breakthrough helped solidify the approach to vision that treated perception as an active retrieval of the actual qualities of the world by an organism. After Euclid, optics involved a combination of a consideration of the geometry of looking and this retrieval of qualities.

This approach was perhaps perfected by Abu Yusuf Yaqub ibn Ishaq al-Sabbah al-Kindī in the ninth century. His approach is worthy of special consideration because it can be understood as a fork in the road; afterward, optics increasingly abandoned the idea that vision involved a grasping of the qualities of the environment. From the perspective of the progressive history of science, al-Kindī's theory is most interesting in its use of the idea of radiation. That is, compared to Euclid, al-Kindī made a dramatic reversal, in which the "cone" of rays crucial for seeing came not from the eye, but from the object seen (figure 6.2). This reversal was necessary for understanding the properties of *lenses* and was later used to explain the inversion of an image under a single lens following a logic that is reproduced in elementary optics today (figure 6.3).

Yet, to al-Kindī, the question of vision was still one of grasping the qualities of objects. From our contemporary perspective, which believes vision to take place because of the effect of light radiation coming from objects and into the eye, we laud al-Kindī for his breakthrough here and scratch our heads disappointedly that he somehow did not see this as forcing a rejection of the old metaphysics of vision. But, al-Kindī's general understanding had a coherence. While accepting the idea that the eye did not project substance but rather effected a transformation of the air around it, he still argued that perception involved the acceptance of the qualities of external objects, objects that actually radiated their nature and acted on others. Indeed, his ability to move beyond Euclid was related

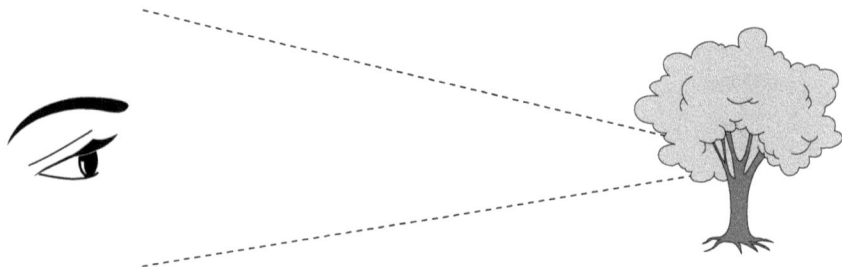

Figure 6.2 Al-Kindī's cone

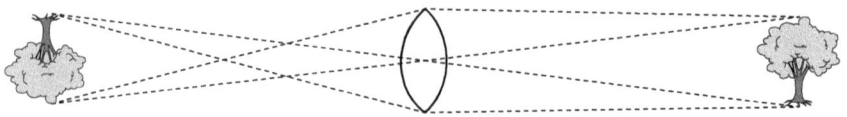

Figure 6.3 Optics of a single lens

to this understanding of the way in which creation announced itself: according to al-Kindī, "Everything that actually exists in the world of elements emits rays in all directions, which in their own way fill the entire rudimentary world." Just as magnets act on metal from afar, and the motion of the stars and planets act on earthy fates, or words expressed by the mind can affect others, so objects reach us through light and air (Lindberg 1976: 19, 31; Couliano 1987: 120).[30]

Although al-Kindī saw the eye as taking in rays from objects, he did not accept a simple intromission theory because the eye was not passive—it clearly moves about and actively selects objects (Lindberg 1976: 22). For example, al-Kindī (¶9; 1912: 11, 49) points out that when someone looks at a book, he "perceives the individual letters not at once, but one after another, and thus only after a passage of time. The reason for this lies in the fact that the power of sight that emanates from the eye in straight lines, and that which the eye seeks, must be aligned. Otherwise, it would grasp it the object immediately," and indeed, we would perceive *all* things at once. Yet, we know that such instantaneous and total perception does not occur. Instead, we see most clearly precisely in the center of where we direct our vision; further from this central point, clarity decreases, and eventually reading becomes impossible.[31]

---

[30]Al-Kindī (1974: 62) did still assume the possibility of a superior intellectual perception in addition to perception through the senses.

[31]Unfortunately, this work has not been translated into English; I base my translations on the somewhat free German translation of 1912 but provide the original Latin. *Ex eis etiam, quae id, quod diximus, verificant, est, quod aspiciens res visui suo expositas, sicut librum fortasse inquirit, eius litteram, quam non comprehendit nisi post tempus. Cuius causa existit, quod rectitude vitutis visus impimentis non cadit super id, quod quaerit. Quia postquam super ipsum ceciderit, statim ipsum comprehendit.*

A Social Aesthetics

Thus, contrary to the intromission theory, by which the forms of objects rush through the air into our eyes, "If we would see any object, so we must turn our eyes to it, otherwise we see nothing of it" (¶10, cf. 12; 1912: 11f).[32]

It is worth pointing out that, first, al-Kindī's comments regarding reading in particular[33] and the role of fixation in general are quite correct. An eye that does not move has little to do with what we mean by eye.[34] Second, we cannot see al-Kindī's views as a hodgepodge of precursors to later science with mystical holdovers, for al-Kindī's idea of radiation, far from sitting awkwardly beside his belief in the qualitative nature of perception, was integrally related to it. It is *because* objects radiate their qualities, and because we reach out to them via attention, that we can see them, and we can trust to the consubstantiality of sense because of our createdness: "All organs of sense are, from their creator, appropriate for their function" (¶10; 1912: 49). This idea of radiation was adopted and freed from its mystical assumptions by al-Hazen in the eleventh century and Roger Bacon in the thirteenth (van Hoorn 1972: 112). While there was still a widespread sense in the Middle Ages that images preserved something of the original nature of the objects (and hence the ability to impress something of themselves into the perceiver's soul), the emphasis on the mediated nature of vision increasingly led to an abandonment of the Greek idea that perception involved direct retrieval of qualities.[35]

Now, the general study of optics involved three interwoven strands: the study of the nature of light, the geometry of vision, and theories of the eye

---

[32]*Quare cum rem aliquam visu nostro recipere volumes, oculos nostros ad ipsam revoluminus. Quod si non, minime eam comprehendimus.*

[33]If the letters four or more spaces to the left and eight or more to the right of the word you are reading right now were changed into gibberish, you would not notice. You believe that the parts you are not looking at are the same, and indeed you "see" them as the same, but this is because your perceptual system fuses judgment and perception. See the experimental work of Underwood and McConkie (1985).

[34]As Plotinus (1956: 338f, 341/IV.6.1–3) said, "In any perception we attain by sight, the object is grasped there where it lies in the direct line of vision; it is there that we attack it; there, then, the perception is formed; the mind looks outward. . . . ." The active nature of the eye was key for Plotinus, for we have a visual power, and characteristic of a power is that it does not passively receive impressions, but within its allotted sphere, it acts. Finally, he saw the use of *memory* in perception as also supporting his view of vision as a *power*. If memory was a vestige of a passive process, the person with the best memory would be the person with the least-active nature. Yet, we know the opposite is true—the person with the greatest memory is the most active and capable.

[35]This is not to deny that there were those who retained an assumption of consubstantiality. For example, the fifteenth-century Platonist Marsilio Ficino (2004: 23) wrote, "Eyes shining with light see objects shining with light by means of a common light; ears of an airy nature hear airy objects by means of a common air." At the same time, Ficino also used Aristotle's metaphor of the wax and the ring, although in a more metaphysical way (27, also see 29).

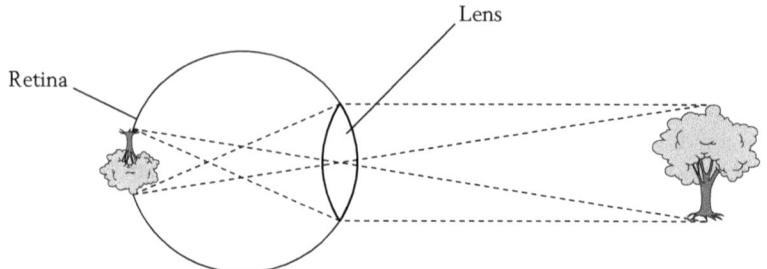

Figure 6.4 Optics of vision

and brain. With breakthroughs in the optics of lenses and a new comparison of the eye to the instruments then being developed, the second of these assumed a critical position in the Renaissance. It both had implications for the nature of light and suggested a way to understand human vision. (Here, I obviously follow Gibson [1979] 1986.) The fact that the eye has a lens allowed figure 6.3 to be combined with figure 6.1, as in figure 6.4. (A similar figure is found in Descartes' 1664 *Treatise on Man* [1985: 105] and in the 1637 *Optics* [2001: 92, see 91 and 96f for the comparison to a camera obscura].) The question of vision was "explained" by the projection of the image onto the retina—but only insofar as, as Gibson pointed out, theorists imagined someone inside the eye, then looking at the cast image.[36] (This is seen in the repeated bemusement that we do not see all things upside-down [cf. Boring 1942: 224; Wade 1998: 33ff for Berkeley and Reid's critique]. Descartes [1664/1985] has the nerves leave the retina and maintain their ordering; there is then an inversion before they reach the seat of consciousness.)

Further, by cementing Europeans into the assumption that one "looked at looking" by drawing diagrams of lines passing through the lens and onto the retina, the focal position of geometry led the Mediterranean world to a theory of vision that dovetailed with assumption of an epistemological hiatus between the phenomenal and noumenal worlds (Lindberg 1976: 73, 9, 104, 116, 176, 181–184, 188, 206; Park 1998: 262, 265; Eco [1959] 1986: 50, 68; van Hoorn 1972: 174; also see Pomian 1998: 217f).[37] When "we" look at the looking, we have a sense of a sort of "meta-looking," a looking from *outside* the eye. This implicit meta-looking can then be used to criticize the partiality of looking. Reflected light of different frequencies

---

[36]Descartes ([1637] 2001: 101) himself noted this error.

[37]Kepler actually made clear the division between the science of optics, which covers the path of light until it hits the retina, and the physics of vision, which takes over from there. Descartes' approach to the latter is usually understood as the most influential, and it emphasized this hiatus (in England, Descartes' approach, although popularized by Jacques Rohault, remained subordinate to that of Newton [Cantor 1983: 115ff]).

may re-create the relative position of parts of the tree on our retina, but the verdure of the tree is not a quality of the tree itself. And this basic epistemology supported the dim view taken of cognition that we explored in chapters 3 and 4.

Despite the great advances made in the neurology of vision between the sixteenth and the nineteenth century, these rejections of al-Kindī's view in favor of a simple intromission theory led to errors.[38] As Gibson ([1979] 1986) emphasized, in the excitement of treating the eye just like the telescope, theorists forgot that they *saw through* a telescope using their eyes, and failed to answer the question of the nature of the seeing eye. They were unable to deal with a number of obvious anomalies for the idea of a simple projection. One of the earliest recognized with dissection of the eye is that we have a blind spot (where the optic nerve is attached) but do not see the lack of vision in our visual field. Second, our vision fades gently away as we move away from the center of the visual field, but we have no sense of a boundary. More generally, we have the sense of "seeing" things in the visual field where we have insufficient retinal input, but we somehow "fill in" (see Pessoa, Thompson, and Noë 1998). These well-known difficulties were pushed to the side, given the indubitable success of the geometric approach.

Further, this approach also increasingly rejected the active nature of the eye, which we also saw was crucial for al-Kindī, and this rejection led to a number of incoherences.[39] Most important, the idea that the retina paints a picture for us of the entire visual field sits poorly with the fact that our eyes constantly dance about (around three times a second), as only the central portion of our fovea has good resolution. There is no reason to imagine that we laboriously construct a stable internal drawing of the field (how could this be done if our heads are mobile anyway?) out of these ever-changing fixations—and there is no need to, for the organization of the visual field is out there, in the world; it would frustrate the

---

[38]The critique of theories of vision made here is not related to the issue of the philosophical definition of vision; one may accept a causal theory of vision (e.g., Vision 1997; although see Merleau-Ponty [1942] 1963: 193, 199) without wanting to accept the particular philosophical connotations that this approach had in the modern West.

[39]Descartes ([1637] 2001: 68, 114), beginning by comparing sight to the sense of touch used by a blind man with a cane, which combines the action of the senser with the action of the sensed, quickly argued that no action came from the eyes except for creatures like cats who can see during the night. "As for the ordinary man, he sees only by the action which comes from the objects." Thus, he confidently asserted, "We can reduce all the things that must concern us here to three principles, namely the objects, the internal organs [i.e., the nerves and brain] which receive the impulses of these objects, and the external organs [i.e., the eyes] which dispose these impulses to be received as they ought."

principle of cognitive economy to make an internal copy. (See the forceful statement of O'Regan 1992; also cf. Ballard et al. 1997.)[40]

Interestingly enough, we have become so bound to this theory of vision that these incoherences often appear to us as necessary facts. Perhaps the clearest example is in the development of linear perspective by the Renaissance artists. Although their artificial conventions of depiction now seem both scientific and natural to Westerners, one cannot "look" at a painting in linear perspective—unless one fixes one's eyes on a particular point and does not move them, distortions result (Edgerton 1991: 9, n16; Goodman 1976: 12, 14, 16, 37).[41]

More troubling, the active nature of the eye was also overlooked by behaviorist psychologists, who developed a theory of perception that fought against the living nature of their subject matter (Gibson [1979] 1986; Churchland, Ramachandran, and Sejnowski 1994; also see Pepper 1966: 188).[42] As Merleau-Ponty ([1942] 1963: 34, 45, 185, 92, 194) insisted, this whole approach treated the light that "hits" any portion of the retina as a "stimulus" that should always produce the same "reaction" in the nervous system.[43] This mechanistic view was unable to recognize that the optical system functioned as a teleological totality. The assumption of passivity led to a unidirectional model whereby light hit the retina and slowly worked its way toward the brain through a succession of steps (preserved in Searle 1983: 266)—ignoring the fact that there seem to be far more neurons proceeding the other way from the visual cortex back to the area that first processes the retinal information coming from the optic tract (the lateral geniculate nucleus) (Churchland 1995: 99). Rejecting the active nature of the eye, the behaviorists literally had to fight against the organism they were supposedly studying—trying to fix the eyes of animals by in some cases bolting their skulls to plywood (later developing more complicated procedures [e.g., Talbot and Kuffler 1952]), they thought that they were truly getting at sight. But, as some retinal cells do

---

[40]As O'Regan (1992: 472) says, "We do not see a hole . . . where the blind spot is, nor do we see . . . color or surface quality as less clear in the regions we are not directly fixating, because our feeling of 'seeing' comes not from what is on the retina, but from the result of using the retina as a tool for probing the environment."

[41]Certain cubist works actually have increased verisimilitude in that they have relations that exist under more than one glance.

[42]Correctly noting that (contrary to the wisdom of the social sciences, in which the same cause always has the same effect) the effect of continuous or repeated stimulation tended to lessen over time, the French philosopher of habit Maine de Biran ([1803] 1929: 61, 91, 94, 96; discussed in more detail in chapter 7) proposed that this was the more true the more passive the sense organ; the motion of the eye was necessary to prevent the extinguishing of sensation. (See Heider [1958: 156] for his appreciation of de Biran.)

[43]Indeed, he argues, the pure "reflex" really occurs only in the particular situation of the controlled laboratory and has no general ecological validity.

not bother firing when there is no movement in the visual field, they were actually decreasing vision, not studying it (Tovée 1996: 143).[44]

This neglect of the active nature of the eye was necessary for the development of that faith in a completely causal account of action that we found threatening to fall apart in chapter 1. Defenders of this faith will grimly insist that, at least in principle, there is a fully causal explanation of any action that remains unshaken by the seeming presence of will. Indeed, they possess a sort of anti-philosopher's stone that can turn this supposed will into external causality! It accomplishes this transubstantiation by tracing out biochemical processes intervening between sensation and intellection, tracing—at least in principle, in the last imaginary analysis—actions to neurochemical processes to sensations to mechanical processes involving some sort of aggressive bombardment of the body from the outside. But the conviction is wrong. Even if we decided to claim on faith that any action (say, I reach out a hand toward an apple) is itself "caused" by neurochemical processes in the brain, in turn caused by neurochemical processes in the optic nerve, the retina, and so forth, until we reach the first cause in light rays bouncing off the apple, we find that this account is no more persuasive than the diametrically opposed but equally monistic argument that all action can be explained by will, by in-order-to.

Because what caused these stimuli in the first place? Unlike the cats, my head was not fixed to plywood, staring at nothing until an apple was placed before me. Instead, I have been turning my head every which way, and I have been doing this because, as a hungry body, I am searching for something to eat. It is my in-order-to that precedes the sensations that supposedly cause my actions (Reed 1996). If my sensations "cause" my will, and my will "causes" my actions, no less do my actions "cause" my sensations. Even if we reject Dewey's formulation of the reflex arc (1896), we cannot avoid admitting that there is no justification for according

---

[44]Even more, there is evidence that attention determines which neurons in the lower levels of the visual cortex fire. As these are cells that are still arranged in geometric correspondence to positions in the retina, this shows the problem with the conventional approach that assumed passive reception (see the papers collected by Braun, Koch, and Davis, especially Corbetta and Shulman 2001: 1, 8; Heeger et al. 2001: 25; Ito, Westheimer, and Gilbert 2001: 89, 91). Even before this point, the retina itself greatly reduces and organizes the information produced by the arrival of photons; precisely as the Gestalt theorists argued, this is in large part through searching for edges and other structural features such as texture; these features, even when illusory, are "seen" at a relatively low level of processing (von der Heydt, Peterhans, and Baumgartner 1984). It may also be that texture and movement are picked up by specialized circuitry that can give an independent action imperative (Something wicked this way comes! Get away!) without going through all the recognition circuitry (Tovée 1996: 27, 65, 74, 82, 160, 169).

priority to the outside and treating the actor as the patient. But through mere dint of repetition we have convinced ourselves that, in the last analysis, any sober materialistic explanation is based in external causality. Thus the flawed theory of vision supported the flawed ontology underlying our approach to human action.

But the gravest problem arising from this new sense of vision was a subtler one: the extinction of the ideas of quality and consubstantiality. Vision became the sense par excellence for the modern philosophy (see Latour 1986; Bourdieu [1997] 2000: 22) and the model for intuitions regarding the relationship between the mind and the world. Objects are passive—they reflect light. Eyes are passive—they absorb light rays. To that extent, there is some consubstantiality between them. But, there is none between our minds and the light itself and none between the light and the objects. The object does not reach out to us through our vision; it merely puts a particular spin on the particles differentially bouncing off its surface, which then crash into our retina, making a pattern that we must identify by going through a file of culturally defined templates. There can be no qualities *in* nature because of this lack of consubstantiality. We get information of some sort across the epistemic divide between minds and things, and yet we would not dare say that some quality such as the "color" of an object is truly a quality of the object "in itself," in that silent, gray world of matter that Hobbes perhaps saw most clearly. Here, we imagine that what a tree looks like "to us" is not what it "really" looks like, if we could somehow climb outside our eyeballs and see it in some other way (cf. Köhler 1938: 15, 112). This makes no sense, but the transformation of optics into applied geometry led to centuries of studying vision as a set of rays *as seen from* the outside. The sense that we are somehow able to "see seeing" through a science of optics gives us the illusion that there is some sort of scientific seeing outside of the human seeing.[45]

This idea of vision as in some ways exemplifying the lack of consubstantiality is hard to shake.[46] But, it is not obviously correct. Vision was perhaps the wrong sense to use as our generic prototype. Consider, instead, taste (understood as the unification of taste and smelling). Here, we have

---

[45]Robert Benchley (1940: 133) puts it this way in a spoof of that form of disillusioning science writing entitled "Did You Know That . . . ?": ". . . . No one has ever *seen* the Brooklyn Bridge? It is merely an action of light waves on the retina of the eye."

[46]Although as Goethe emphasized, there is a serious way in which we must recognize such consubstantiality in vision: "The eye owes its existence to the light. Out of indifferent animal organs the light produces an organ to correspond to itself; and so the eye is formed by the light, for the light so that the inner light may meet the outer. . . . If the eye were not sunlike, how could we perceive the light?" (Goethe [1810] 1970: liii, although I use the translation of Zajonc 1993: 184, 341; also see van Hoorn 1972: 70).

the most undeniably qualitative experience. And, our taste sense involves the most direct relationship between our subjectivity and the world possible: it is a module for identifying the presence of (rare amounts of) particular molecules. It would seem very silly (and it *would be* very silly) to say that the quality of saltiness is not what salt *really* tastes like. Because it is just as obvious that "taste" is about our experience of salt as it is that salt *really* tastes salty because "salty" is our register of the presence of salt. The taste of salt is a particularly successfully stylized experience of salt—any taste of salt must by definition be a salty one. So, too it is nonsensical to ask if things really look like what they look like.

Again, I doubt that any high school physics student has spent much time wondering what electrons taste like. Yet, many certainly have yearned to know what electrons *look* like; although this makes as little sense as the query about taste, it shows how easy it is for us to imagine a sight outside our sight because of the ease of representing sight visually. But, we have no experience of "tasting taste" the way we have a deceptively simple experience of "seeing sight." We take for granted that to understand taste is not to taste it and find that it is wanting according to some illusory standard we set up only for the purpose of such discrediting (which is what we do for sight). We know that if we wanted to study taste, we would do so not by overcoming the limitations of taste but by correlating our experienced tastes with other forms of information we can produce. That is, we would begin by trusting taste and not doubting it, for taste is a stunningly successful way of reporting about the nature of things that surround us. Vision also, despite the geometry, is a particular form of uniquely successful experience.[47]

At the same time, we have recognized that taste (in the sense of an aesthetic sensibility) tends to be cultivated, and this holds for the sense of taste. The person with a cultivated taste of wines does not simply make a cognitive conclusion (of high vs. low quality) that a person without this cultivation would not. She almost certainly has a qualitatively different experience. The experience is in the two cases different, yet in each case, *what* they experience, what they taste, is undoubtedly the wine. As we shall discuss, this also holds for vision.

In sum, the evolution of theories of vision after al-Kindī, coupled with the position of vision as our exemplar of sense, led to a widespread notion of perception that denied its activity and its consubstantiality. I have argued that the first of these was dead wrong, and the second still misleading (in that if our eye is not made of light, it is made *for* light). It is this

---

[47]Further, there is neurological evidence that just as taste is a tasting-what (e.g., saltiness), so vision is organized into a "what" recognition system in addition to the more obvious "where" system that the Durkheimian model begins with. Thus, as said in chapter 5, the evidence is that when we see something, we see it *as* what it is (Tovée 1996: 68f, 112f), although the "where" system can function semi-independently (Pylyshyn 2003: 50f).

view that implied the fundamentally arbitrary nature of perception and the need for grids of perception and led to the views of social knowledge of regular actors that we saw possessed neither sense nor sensitivity. I go on to argue that accepting the active and correlative (if not consubstantial) nature of perception is necessary for our understanding of the cognitive components of action.

The Presence of Others

The Durkheimian approach to social cognition did not deny that there was activity on the part of the cognizer. But, there the active side of cognition was *postperceptual*. In contrast, the notion of vision defended in the preceding section, and the analogous social perception, finds the active nature to be *preperceptual*; the perception itself is nonproblematic in that what is communicated depends solely on the nature of the perceived.[48] This makes a great deal of phenomenological sense (and in fact is argued by Merleau-Ponty [1962: 75, 217f, 242, 278f, 327], who also stressed the activity of the eye and argued that our perceptual field must be analyzed in terms of such consubstantiality).[49] In chapter 4, we found that, contrary to the Durkheimian assumptions, the natural world comes to us rather clumped. But, this preorganization of the world does not mean that the act of perception can be treated as purely passive. To take an example from Pepper (1966: 434; also see Merleau-Ponty [1942] 1963: 88), consider looking for a seat when entering a room. It is not the *word* seat that organizes our perception, in the way that armchair philosophers might discuss the unification of particulars under the abstractions "table" or "chair."[50] We do not look for a chair, but rather a seat, and a seat is defined *by* the nature of the task and the implicit range of appropriatenesses. The upside-down chair is not a seat, although it is a chair; the stranger's lap is not a seat, although one could sit on it; and, most important, neither is *perceived* as a seat. Thus, it is reasonable that we must allow for a

---

[48]Pylyshyn (2003: 69) puts this in terms of the "cognitive penetration" of vision—that is, whether what we *see* can be affected by what we *think*. The lower cells in the temporal cortex seem to respond more to the visual character of what is going on than to its significance.

[49]"My eye for me is a certain power of making contact with things, and not a screen on which they are projected." We can assume this "connatural" relation between eye and world because what we mean by a "world" (*Welt*) is precisely an inhabiting, the creation of coherent experience so that the things we confront are "true objects" (*Gegenstände*), in contrast to the mere "centers of resistance" (*Widerstände*) that surround the dumb animal in its environment (*Umwelt*) (327, also [1942] 1963: 129).

[50]Armchair philosophers sitting at their worktables seem to be very interested in chairs and tables.

preperceptual activity to our investigation of our environments (cf. Cassirer [1923] 1953: 268; James [1890] 1950: II, 562).

The Durkheimian view, we recall, assumes the need for postperceptual processing because it maintains that there cannot be any unique mapping between the structures of the world (if such a thing even can be said to exist) and the structures of our mental apparatus. We have found that this assumption is nothing more than an assumption, and a good deal less reasonable than many others. There is nothing in the nature of our senses to lead us to imagine that they *can* take in unordered data that can then be sorted according to cultural templates. And there *is*, we recall, good reason to expect a form of consubstantiality between our sensory apparatuses and the structure of the world: if the world was not made for us to perceive (as Kant thought), we are made to perceive it.

One of the most interesting things about vision is that it grows. The baby is born with a potential for vision—one that develops with astounding speed—but not the particular vision itself. Cats raised in all-dark environments do not develop a proper optic system; humans born blind but whose sight is surgically restored do not immediately see (Tovée 1996: 89, 93, 98).[51] It takes them a while to learn how, and some never quite master it. Indeed, we might say that one never senses a quality "once"—the child raised apart from offices and their furniture entering a classroom for the first time may actually not see the seats even if she sees the chairs. But, repeated interaction will lead her to see the seats. In James's ([1890] 1950: II, 78; cf. 7) words, "every perception is an acquired perception."

Generalizing this principle, we find that there is nothing troublesome in assuming a high degree of consubstantiality between our perceptual systems and the world; indeed, when it comes to social life, the assumption that our mind is not of the same nature as what we are minding can only result from a lack of serious thought or an embarrassingly adolescent solipsism. For other persons *are* like us, often frighteningly so.[52] Further, the social world around us is one that we have created, if not in our image, then certainly correlative to our image, in the same way that the handle of a hammer is correlative to the shape of our hand (cf. Pepper 1966: 215, 247, who makes these same points in turn; also cf. Sartre 1956: 323). The social world has what Walter J. Ong (1969) calls "presence." *Presence* is a

---

[51]Indeed, kittens raised in environments with only horizontal (or vertical) stripes can later only see stripes with this sort of orientation. They grow to see the particular sort of world that they are in.

[52]Those studying truly different cultures—those becoming rarer in the world by the year—may have a bit more work to do than others in determining the limits of such consubstantiality. But, as we can no longer accept the nineteenth-century view of cultures as spheres (of coherent meaning and isolation) as opposed to glomps of practices undertaken by persons in constant contact with others, this has little in the way of strong implications for our current question.

word to describe the relation of one human to another, and in a real way, that relation is inherent in a humanly constructed world (cf. Dilthey [1883] 1988: 98; Merleau-Ponty 1962: 153; [1942] 1963: 172).[53]

Indeed, we might even say that presence is the apperceptive counterpart to consubstantiality. When we deliberately perceive other persons, we take for granted our mutual equivalence by looking into their lookers, their eyes.[54] The resulting sense of presence is qualitatively different from our interaction with objects and is felt as a form of immediacy. It is this immediacy that, we recall (see chapter 5, note 9), makes children orient to the doll referred to as "Zon" but not the one referred to as "a zon"; in English, the mere act of a grammatical insertion of an article (a, the) is incompatible with the "face-to-face" and "eye-to-eye" encounter of two persons.

Further, and most remarkably, our perception of others includes nonphysical aspects such as their mood and in some cases intentions. This was a key claim of the Gestalt theorists and one echoed by Heider (1958: 30, 155; also see Wieder 1974: 83; Merleau-Ponty [1942] 1963: 173; Kant [1798] 2006: 196): "In social perception . . . the direct impressions we form of another person, even if they are not correct, refer to dispositional characteristics." For example, people who are agitated *look* agitated. People who are friendly *look* friendly.

Of course, the problem is that some friendly looking people are *not* friendly. Rather than sweep this under the rug, the following discussion turns on this issue.[55] But, note that the perception of the quality of friendliness, which we use to illustrate this approach to vision, also exemplifies the nature of judgment. We could prove to person B that person A is over 5 feet 10 inches or weighs no more than 160 pounds. But, we cannot prove that A "is" friendly through evidence and concepts. When we see that A is over 5 feet 10 inches, there is a single attribute we examine, and we might even be able to imagine A unchanged in every way except this (say, we shrink him to 5 feet 9 inches). But, our perception of the

---

[53]"We need no longer project presences into the world, for they are already there" (Ong 1969: 647; cf. de Biran [1803] 1929: 118f).

[54]Of course, in perhaps every culture there are social situations in which such eye contact is inappropriate, although not because the relationship between the locked gaze and equivalence is contested. Rather, precisely to prevent a sense of equivalence, eye contact cannot be made.

[55]We might note that what is crucial here is not the inerrancy of social perception but its this-sided and consubstantial nature. A presenceful encounter is experienced as contact with personhood and orients actors to a set of intersubjective practices (from eye contact to the use of proper nouns) that do not invoke third-person perspectives. If we are able to systematize these, we may move toward a social science that also does no violence to first personhood, although it is not identical to it.

dispositional nature of A as friendly is different: even when this comes from a single visual encounter, it somehow involves a conjunction of many elements, such as body position, relaxation of arms and motion of hands, eye movement, pupil dilation, head position, mouth placement and upper cheek motion, nasal dilation, and so on. But this is simply to say that, as we saw in chapter 5, we are indeed quite able to perceive Gestalts.

Thus, rejecting the problematic assumptions about vision and perception more generally leaves us in a position to use what the Gestalt theorists already developed to understand our perceptions of qualities, including qualities that are uncovered in unitary experiences of collectivities, aggregates, and other social forms.

Gestalts and Qualities

We have seen that the dominant model of perception lacks an understanding of how we grasp qualities; the exception was the Gestalt theory that arose to explain how we were able to have simple and unitary experiences when facing conjunctions. This suggests that if the problematic assumptions of the post-al-Kindī theories of vision—the rejection of the active nature of the eye and of consubstantiality—pose particular problems for an examination of social cognition, the Gestalt approach may be a fruitful basis for generalization. For the things in the social world are themselves conjunctions analogous to those studied in the visual field. This social world, with its transindividual objects and relations, is often assumed to be related to the individuals "below" it through some process of "emergence." Although there is nothing obviously flawed with the idea of emergence in general, there is a common error whereby we imagine that we can assimilate this to the case of "levels" in which the higher ones "include and add to" the lower ones.

Interestingly, this same idea of emergence had also been applied to the nature of our qualitative perception, but as Pepper (1966: 51; 1955: 160–163) pointed out, this is empirically wrong or rather reversed—the quality of, say, a timbre (a tonal quality) does not "emerge" through the "superposition" of simple components, for these supposed components only are created by an analytic procedure. Technically, the timbre may be denoted as a periodic wave that, subjected to Fourier analysis, can be seen as composed of many different sine waves of different wavelengths and amplitudes. But, in actuality, the tone is generally neither created thusly nor heard as such.[56] As Pepper (1955: 164–171) says, it is no contradiction

---

[56]Indeed, it may well be that the destruction of our true understanding of qualitative perception was related to the increased reliance on the visual (Ong 1988; Latour 1986; Edgerton 1991), the sense that, operating in nearly three dimensions, has the least blending (especially compared to smell or taste, which are nearly of dimensionality 0).

to say that a quality is, *at basis*, a "fusion," in that it *can* be analytically decomposed.[57] Because a quality is by nature fused, that which we experience may have "parts" or at least may be partitioned, but the experience cannot be similarly decomposed.

Such qualities cannot be analytically separated from their substrate without fundamentally transforming it (as in imagining person A slightly shorter); thus, we cannot consider the qualities "subtractable" (cf. Cassirer [1910] 1923: 154) in the same way that a rainbow, while phenomenologically an "object," cannot be removed from the sky (Dewey [1930] 1960: 196 made this same point). At the same time, these qualities can, the Gestalt theorists claimed out, be transposed from one substrate to another (in the way that a melody remains the same when we transpose keys) (Köhler 1920: 37). For example, the two drawings in figure 6.5 induce the same phantom rhombus; it does not exist apart from its background, yet it is "the same" across contexts. Neither rhombus consists of "its parts" plus "something more," as in the classic idea of emergence; rather, both are our experience of a particular organization of a set of relations.

Thus, the Gestalt approach forces us to recognize that we can have a qualitative experience of and about the relations of things to one another.[58] But, these relations also include those between ourselves and the things. For our qualitative perceptions are "funded," to use a word of Dewey's,[59] in that they blend aspects—the frighteningness of a sudden noise folds in not only its precise dynamics but the overall situation, indeed, my own history (Köhler [1938: 81] referred to these as "tertiary qualities"). Rather than treat this as an exception or a problem to be

---

[57]Pepper makes the interesting hypothesis that there are no elemental qualities at all, but rather that "qualities are intrinsically fusions of field structures which interpenetrate." Also see Merleau-Ponty ([1942] 1963).

[58]But, as Cassirer ([1910] 1923: 200f, 297, 301, 303, 306, 154; also see 396f) emphasized, the sense of quality that we reach is not a return to that of Aristotle; the qualities that Aristotle introduced were really "only hypostatized sensuous properties." We can accept that, phenomenologically, actors may be able to treat qualities *as if* they were sensuous properties. But because we specify these qualities as attributes of objects that are nodes of relations, we do not mistake the reciprocal position of objects for qualities that would be preserved even were we to consider the objects in isolation. That is, the qualities indicate properties not of any "thing" considered singly, but as qualities of a constellation as a whole. Using the example of work on theories of distances, Cassirer stressed that we can have a "physics of qualities" because there can be invariant relations between qualities—not because the qualities taken individually could be analyzed.

[59]Considering physical Gestalts such as a structure of charge on a conductor, Köhler (1920: 58; also see 1938: 71) also proposed that we need a new word in the place of "distribution" (*Verteilung*) that implies division into "parts" (*Teile*) and suggested *fundieren*, "to substantiate," "to be the fundament of." Also see James ([1912] 1943: 164) equating *gestaltqualität* and *fundirte inhalt* [sic].

A Social Aesthetics

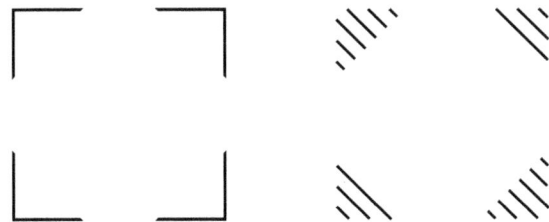

Figure 6.5 Two rhombuses

explained or a form of bias, we must accept it as the normal form of qualitative experience (cf. Metzger 1966: 11; James [1890] 1950: II, 80, 82; Merleau-Ponty [1942] 1963: 15). Phenomenology is not a train which one can have stopped at one's pleasure; so far, the tracks have run straight and forced us to remain with the nature of our qualitative experience, and there is no reason to jump off now. Indeed, it is this seeming paradox—that an acceptance of the veridical nature of our perceptual system implies an acceptance of systematic differences between perceivers—that allows us to imagine that it is noncontradictory to propose a social aesthetics.

We built on the idea of the consubstantiality of perception to understand our interaction with the presence of persons. As Köhler ([1917] 1925: 102; cf. Merleau-Ponty [1942] 1963: 102, 125) emphasized, there was nothing unscientific about describing the nature of, say, the behavior of some chimpanzees as "agitated." This was not, insisted Köhler, an attribution of their mental life, but an observable quality of "the elementary phenomenology of their behavior." So, too, we are able to note the dispositional qualities of persons; it is in fact easier for us to tell whether they are friendly or hostile than it is to assess their weight.

And yet, we may disagree—the person whom you think is coy and winning (to use an example we will focus on below for historical reasons), I may think is aloof and cold. This should hardly be surprising, because the perceived person may like you and dislike me. Our qualitative perceptions of this person are not perceptions of this person as abstracted corporal entity but as a set of relations, relations that naturally include ourselves (cf. James [1912] 1943: 140). Indeed, if qualities are dual to dispositions to act, and our different histories with the objects we confront give us different dispositions, we could not maintain that we should agree in terms of our perceptions and be perceiving correctly. Sticking with the example of judging the personality of another person—how he or she will act—we would be quite mad to insist that the disagreement between two people regarding the dispositional qualities of a third was proof that humans did not have a veridical capacity for such perception. Yet, that is largely what the social sciences have done. We have been unable to fathom how people produce social knowledge because we have rejected the possibility that they directly perceive qualities of the social world.

To summarize, the Gestalt theorists found that we are able to perceive relations in our environment immediately, and this makes sense, as these experiences make reference to things we need to *do*—some things are behind others, to take the case of the rhombi above. Similarly, we may be able to have unitary experiences of sets of *social* relations and have experiences that are reasonably veridical in that they also tell us what we are to do. To generalize this approach to qualitative experience, we begin with the case of social objects.

QUALITY (AND QUANTITY) OF SOCIAL LIFE

Objects and Relations

The secret of the fetishism of the commodity, said Marx, is that in the commodity, we perceive in frozen form the living relationships between persons. Whether we wish to accept Marx's own reasoning here, this provides a wonderful model. The power of the object in this case is simply that it can objectify—that is, freeze relations, make them permanent and available to inspection (cf. Simmel [1907] 1978: 60, 73, 129, who emphasizes the relation to aesthetics; also Pepper 1966: 448). Some complex property of perhaps a large set of relationships (e.g., relationships of investment, employment, and exchange) can be perceived as a single quality of the unitary "object" (e.g., it is "valuable") that is not present in the *thing* (e.g., a particular piece of crockery).[60]

Now, what do we perceive in the social world? Certainly, we do perceive other human beings, but there are other things that have phenomenological validity as quality-bearing units. In chapter 5, we followed the Gestalt theorists in accepting that "a" mountain *is* a mountain (even though its boundaries may not be definable) because of its phenomenological validity. It is worth emphasizing that this validity is not the same thing as consensus. The mountain is not a mountain because we say it is so, but because it can have perceivable qualities. Thus, a mountain may *look* forbidding.

So too here are things in the social world that we perceive as objects that are capable of bearing qualities. Consider, for example, institutions such as the Internal Revenue Service (IRS). This is not a group for it does not include *persons*, but rather a set of *relations*. We consider such sets of social relations to be "social objects" when two (presumably equivalent) conditions are satisfied: first, that they have first-person plausibility as

---

[60]One of the nicest discussions of the nature of qualitative experience in sociology is by Katz (1988: 5). Also see Dewey (1929: 318, 32).

objects (actors agree that there is an IRS), and second, that we experience these objects as capable of bearing qualities.

For another example, we may consider a political party a social object—something that has intersubjective validity as a "thing" in social life whether or not it has a corresponding physical status. Nonmembers may have a confidence in *knowing* this party—sensing its relevant qualities—that seems more like the ways in which one knows a person than the ways in which one knows some complex assemblage (cf. Hayes 2005). The qualities possessed by social objects clearly include those that are most important to us in ordering our action toward them—namely, whether they are good or bad, honest or deceitful, worthy or corrupt. It is, we recall, not only possible but assured that such qualitative perceptions embrace such antitheses, as we have abandoned Kant's assumption that there is only one transcendent ordering allowing for intersubjective agreement about qualitative experience.

This linkage between quality and relationship is not new to us; we previously saw that if the aesthetic experience intrinsically implies that we demand intersubjective agreement, it also then defines a "we," a set of like-minded persons. Put somewhat differently, following Bourdieu for the ideal-typical case of appreciation of high art, we found the retrieval of the quality of the beautiful to establish a set of particular social relations, in this case "sameness"; technically, we might say that the social object (a painting, say) is dual to this set of relations.[61] But there is no reason to limit ourselves to the relation of equivalence—a phenomenal object can objectify other relations, such as "greater than," "opposite to," or "choosing." Thus, we may extend Dewey's conception and propose that social objects are tangles of social relationships (cf. Merleau-Ponty [1942] 1963: 142).

It is for this reason that Bourdieu was able to argue that what tastes "mean" is precisely what social relationships they reference. Mountain climbing "means" teachers as against chief executive officers (CEOs; on the one hand) and shopkeepers (on the other) not because teachers may experience a fellow feeling when encountering each other on a mountain (they may hate running into others), but more because the mountain expresses the social distance between the teachers and these other groups.[62]

---

[61]Here, we may follow the technical exposition of Breiger (1974) regarding this duality. Also compare Boltanski and Thénevot ([1991] 2006: 17).

[62]Bourdieu ([1979] 1984) found sports such as mountain climbing that involve isolation and low capital expenditure to be characteristic of those with low economic capital but high cultural capital: they facilitate the separation characteristic of an elite without the conspicuous consumption characteristic of plutocrats. Mitchell (1983: 185) finds applied mathematicians and such also disproportionately represented among climbers—again, those not only with high technical training but also with an orientation to solo engagement with physical "things."

Such a critique of judgment does not involve *criticizing* judgment—the point is not that "this is what mountain climbing *really* means"—but rather in explicating the ways (and the for whoms) in which things are what they are: the mountain appears to be a mountain to everyone, but only to some does it say, "climb me" (also see Merleau-Ponty 1962: 436, 439).

Thus, Bourdieu's general approach suggests a clarification of the qualitative nature of objects that is aesthetically retrieved by actors. To illustrate, we can take one such quality that was used as an example by Köhler ([1944] 1971: 364; cf. 1938: 77; similarly Dewey 1929: 405) to illustrate his claim that the qualities of things that impel us to action must phenomenologically be understood as located in the things, as opposed to in us. This example, conventional for male German scholars of his day, was men succumbing to the charms of women. Could it be said that the charms are really in the men, as would be implied by a conventional account that considered all values subjective? Obviously not, he concluded; therefore, the charms must be in the women.

Köhler thus made an opposition between (on the one hand) each man singly as perceiving subject and (on the other hand) each woman singly as perceived object. He discounted the possibility that the charms are in the men as organized aggregate or in the entire ensemble of social relations. But, that is more or less what Waller (1937) argued was the basis of the dating logic: that women desired by many men were desirable simply on account of their own desirability. Building on the quite different logic of Levi-Strauss ([1949] 1969), Rubin (1985) emphasized that it made perfect sense that women would serve as units to order relations between males. What is so important about the objectification of women, then, is not simply that an object is not a subject (which is not even necessarily true), it is that an "object"—at least its phenomenological qualities—may best be understood as a crystallization of a set of social relations (also see Emerson [1841] 1940: 141; James [1890] 1950: II, 10; von Wiese 1932: 142; Knorr-Cetina 1997; cf. Merleau-Ponty 1962: xx, 157). In this case, it is not at all that the objectification of women devalues them; it is on the contrary that it *values* them, with values that index the internal relations of members of an exogenous set (men).

Let us return to the example of the social object of the political party: Despite the fact that our nonmember can "know" what "the" Republican party is all about, say, this social object is actually a set of relationships, not only of comembership and coordination but of mobilization, of opposition, and of selective indifference. Yet, our actor is not wrong to treat this knot of relations as a unitary phenomenological object.

The struggle over this separation and purity is then replicated within the field of climbing (see Fuller 2003; also see Simmel [1907] 1978: 87f).

Objectionable Objects

The first chapter began by emphasizing that the problems in sociology came from a distorted idea of explanation, which in turn came from an unnecessary opposition of third-person terms (our "theoretical" constructs) to first-person ones (the lived experience of those we study). This was related to and supported by the assumption (discussed in the third and fourth chapters) that we can only approach general terms by some sort of theoretical construction—but how we (as analysts) define some object of social investigation is similar to how (we generally believe) actors define them. Both are, at base, arbitrary, although either can be defended on pragmatic grounds.

The reasoning pursued in the current chapter now allows us to see this as a fundamental error: the transindividual entities treated by actors have just as much (or just as little) reality as anything else in their perceptual field. We may accordingly desist from peppering our discussion of social action with flags to remind us that this or that, rather than being "objective," is instead socially constructed or rooted in intersubjectivity, because that is what an object *is*. We do not consider objects to be "socially constructed" on the basis of some mysterious social volition but because what we mean by an object is a constellation of relations.

These social objects, we have seen, have properties that integrate to a presence: we face them on the basis of the same consubstantiality that guides our perceptions of other persons.[63] It is for this reason that social explanation need not contravene, sidestep, or delegitimate first-person perspectives. On the contrary, it must systematize them. Yet, although the logic bringing us here has been as good as one would reasonably hope, we are left in a disquieting place: we have been forced to conclude that we perceive social objects such as parties or groups as bearing qualities, and that our perception of such qualities is as veridical as any of our other perceptions, perhaps a good deal more so, despite the lack of social consensus.

It is all very well and good to say that we perceive the dispositions in another person; if it is not always easy to explain, it would be hard to deny. It is also far from shocking to point out that the person who is aloof to one person is encouraging to another, or that to some people the Republicans are "irresponsible" and to others they are "responsible." But, what about when we "see" in his appearance that someone is untrustworthy, although really he has every intention of dutifully fulfilling his promise to us? And, what if when we see that not only he but his entire ethnic group is untrustworthy? We seem to be in the uncomfortable position of either affirming that every racist belief is veridical or rejecting the chain of reasoning until now.

---

[63] As Merleau-Ponty (1962: 327; cf. White 1992) puts it, "I experience the unity of the world as I recognize a style."

The error in this reasoning is to assume that we are talking about racist (say) *beliefs*, as opposed to racist *perceptions* (or intuitions). So far, we have refrained from making any claims regarding propositions-about-experience and have considered only experiences. The white person who perceives hostility and treachery in "blacks" is confronting a social object—a set of relations. These relations are relations of antagonism, of suppression, and of repression. The problem that leads to the production of the perception is not that this person has improperly perceived the qualities of the non-problematic social object. Rather, it is that she has correctly perceived the qualities of the intrinsically distorted social object, a set of relations including her own.[64] The problem is not in the perception, but in the world, and it makes little sense to put people in a distorted world and ask them to see straight.[65]

For example, imagine that we talk to two white persons, the first of whom (A) displays biased perceptions that we would label as racist (say, she generally perceives blacks *to be* untrustworthy), while the second (B) does not. If, as either actors or analysts, we choose to censure the first morally but not the second, it seems reasonable that we do so not on the basis of her perceptions, but on the basis of her social actions, which we can compile into a set of *relations*.[66] We only believe that the perceptions

---

[64]For example, Americans playing a video game in which they are told to shoot the characters holding weapons are more likely to shoot weaponless black characters than weaponless whites (Correll et al. 2002). One might imagine that this stereotype effect is greatest among whites who do not have good relations with blacks and have personal stereotyped beliefs. But, black adults also share this bias; although they are less likely to make false positives for black targets (and shoot the unarmed), they are more likely to make false negatives for whites (and not shoot the armed). Second, it seems to be not personal animus but exposure to representations of cultural stereotypes that predicts bias by whites. Finally, those whites with *more* black friends and black contacts—those more enmeshed in actual relations and those who were *less* racist—had higher bias rates.

[65]It is for this reason that I believe that Joas (2000: 11f) does Dewey an injustice to think that the accomplishment of his theory of values was distorted by an untenable sacralization of democracy. Far from this being an ideological appendage, it is basically implied by a serious consideration of Dewey's approach. Dewey's own passionate belief made him somewhat inarticulate regarding democracy, but our pursuit of this logic implies that all deviations from democracy necessarily lead to problematic perception and an attendant misvaluation.

[66]The conditional phrasing is because once we see things this way, we realize that it may not be the case that we wish to censure one and not the other. For example, if when examining the relations, we find that the B owns the factory at which both A and black persons C, D, and E work, we may decide that the object perceived by A is constituted as much by the relations with B as it is by the relations with A. We are of course still free to censure whomever we want, but the horizon defining those whose conduct we evaluate may be expanded.

A Social Aesthetics

"explain" the relation when we challenge the person with those sorts of Why questions that we have seen to be intrinsically problematic. Similarly, when we demand that others see us as we really are, and not make untrue assumptions, we are not asking for them to *look* at us differently but to change the set of objective relations.

Thus, the very consubstantiality of mind and world means that we can expect our perceptions of the world to be just as twisted as that world itself. The fact that our perceptions of the qualities of social objects are distorted, cruel, oppressive, and antagonistic in no way demonstrates that our capacity for perception is weak; on the contrary, it shows that we are healthily oriented to the real world.

Put another way, our investigation of taste supported Dewey's contention that experience is by nature "funded," in that things are blended, up to and including our own pasts. No one can pursue an aesthetics very far without accepting this: that when two different persons, with differently cultivated tastes, confront the same painting or drink the same wine, they do not have the same experiences; indeed, they do not perceive the same object. This *does* lead to difficulties: we must account for the obduracy of the world and its variability, as we also investigate the differential directions the cultivation of taste may take, as well as the fundament that is being tasted. Without minimizing the difficulties for a systematic aesthetics, we need not let this trouble us unduly—my argument is not that aesthetics *solves* all difficulties, but that a coherent sociological investigation leads us to the *same* difficulties that we find in aesthetics.

Insight Outdoors

When we make our armchair theories, we tend to insert various forms of logical operations between perception and action. The sorts of deductions and subsumptions that may actually only occur in the social context of challenge and justification—"I voted for Schwarzenegger because he is more likely to clear up legislative gridlock"—assume key positions in a logical chain of reasoning. But the considerations here have forced us to seriously entertain the possibility that we directly perceive the dispositional qualities in social objects such as the public persona of a political candidate.[67]

Indeed, our attention to aesthetics may give us the capacity to grasp the curious combination of seeming superficiality and simultaneous depth in actors' ability to extract information from their social environment. In chapter 5, we saw that Köhler was widely ridiculed for introducing "insight" as a crucial term in his description of intelligence (particularly when applied to problem solving by apes); he insisted that such insight

---

[67] And we do, which is one reason why subjects can determine the political party of candidates simply from looking at their faces (see Rule and Ambady 2010).

was as rigorous and appropriate a term as any other but was unable to convince many, perhaps because he had some difficulty defining this insight. But, such a definition *is* possible. Insight, as Dewey (1929: 329) says, means "that sight is employed to form inferences regarding what is not seen." That is, the senses are used to uncover information that is not, strictly speaking, apparent to the senses.[68] As the Gestalt theorists found, these "inferences" are not made in the consciousness through reflective thought; rather, they are "seen" in the way that certain visible configurations suggest what is not seen (also see Fodor and Pylyshyn 1981: 152f).

Bergson (1911: 172f), in his attempt to formulate the nature of intelligence in contrast to instinct, gives the example of *Ammophila hirsuta*, a wasp that preys on a Grey Worm caterpillar.[69] Like many wasps, it stings its prey to paralyze but not kill it to provide its larvae with food. The Grey Worm has nine different nerve ganglia in its body; *Ammophila* unerringly hits each one in turn as if it could see through the skin of the caterpillar and understand its nervous system. It can do neither, which makes this skill the object of wonder, but is it any the less wondrous that we can divide people and programs up into friends and enemies, those to be voted for and those to be voted against, with a similarly cursory overview? The actions of the wasp clearly come from its perceptions of the outside of the larvae, but it has (as Bergson says) a sensorimotor system that has coevolved with the nervous system of the worm. So too, we have an intelligence that has codeveloped with its social environment, allowing for insightful behavior. Just as the wasp can correctly orient to superficial aspects of the worm's morphology and somehow trace these lines below the surface to effectively reach a point she cannot directly see, so we may be able, by seizing on perceivable aspects of social life, to orient ourselves correctly to problems we cannot explain.

It is worth restating that I am not here claiming that this demonstrates that our "knowledge is correct." First, insight need not be "knowledge,"

---

[68] As de Biran ([1803] 1929): 107, 109, 118), emphasized, some of our insight can be seen as the result of habit—having seen one person in the past from many angles, once this person is recognized from afar we may fill in and indeed perceive aspects that technically are beyond our visual capacity. Returning to Dewey's point discussed in chapter 5 regarding actuality of experience, with de Biran we can say that the sailor who sees a speck on the horizon *as* a vessel *sees* a vessel. We make the link to habit in the next chapter, which returns briefly to de Biran.

[69] It might seem a bit out of place to use this example of instinct being offered as a contrast to intelligence when our object is to explain the nature of human intelligence. But as Burke (1952: 151f), following Spinoza's discussion of how we might intuit relationships, comments, "By the time we get to Bergson, for instance, it is hard to distinguish a super-rational 'intuition' from a sub-rational 'instinct.'" Both are ways of bringing the organism into alignment with the requirements of the environment without requiring conscious serial processing (cf. James [1890] 1950: II, 391).

A Social Aesthetics

which we continue to retain for the class of cognitions that are propositions about experience (or about potential experience). I *am* claiming that the *way* that we get our insight (and perhaps some of our knowledge) is that we see it through presenceful encounters (see, e.g., Klein 1998: 16). To the extent that this is the source of our knowledge, our knowledge *is* knowledge *of* the world, and not surprisingly is no better than the world from which it is drawn. This means that such knowledge (say, our knowledge about a political party) comes from insightful perception of a mammoth web of relations. It is not at all obvious *how* we do this. It is also not at all obvious how we take in the fourth quartet of Arnold Schoenberg and understand it on an emotional level, although we may.[70] Similarly, it is not obvious how we infer dispositional qualities (such as friendliness) from superficial perceptuals (not only vision, but also tone of voice, holding of the body). Whether we know that we are making these insights, let alone know how we do, we undoubtedly *are* able to make them.[71]

Directions and Limitations

We may imagine that our capacity for such insight has been disproved by a line of work that shows our serious deficits in making even simple inferences. The most famous such demonstration (see Johnson-Laird and Wason 1977 for a review) presents subjects with four cards, each of which has a letter on one side and a number on the other. The visible faces of the cards display A, D, 4, and 7. The subject is then asked which cards would be necessary to test the following hypothesis: "If a card has a vowel on one side, then it has an even number on the other side." The only cases that could falsify this statement are the A card (if it has an odd number on the other side) and the 7 card (if it has a vowel on the other side). But, few respondents make this selection.

How can one propose that we have the *Ammophilic* capacity to see into a political party from the nature of superficialities if we cannot use logic to determine what is on the back of a playing card? The resolution might be that even if we are not very smart, we are still too smart to answer *very* stupid questions—that is, those that require decontextualized manipulations that serve no purpose for us, only for the career purposes of the demented experimenter who insists on wasting our time by asking us questions the answers to which interest neither him nor us. As Margolis (1987: 149) suggests, outside the lab, were we attempting to determine if (to take

---

[70] I hope not to hear "not very happily" from the reader!
[71] For example, recent experimental evidence suggests that undergraduates do better than chance at determining sexual orientation of men from photographs of faces alone, even though they do not understand that they have this ability (Rule and Ambady 2008; Rule et al. 2008; Rule, Macrae, and Ambady 2009).

a standard example) all swans are white, we would not be impressed by someone who argued for the proposition by noting that worms were green—the exact analogue to the Wason task. (That is, $\sim B \rightarrow \sim A$ implies $A \rightarrow B$.) The failure in the laboratory system is indicative of a mismatch between this particular environment and our cognitive apparatus. (Indeed, there is experimental evidence that shows that the same subjects can complete such tasks when the problem approaches one that they might deal with in real life, such as determining whether someone's identification allows them to purchase alcohol [Griggs and Cox 1982].) What we are good at is not processing pointless information but orienting to situational features and making strong inferences. Further, there is every reason to think that we are quite good at making *social* inferences—that we, like other chimpanzees, have an inherent "triadic awareness" that allows us to directly cognize relations of relations (such as "the friend of my friend") (see, e.g., de Waal 1998).

It might at first seem impossible that we can tell, say, the "compatibility" or "trustworthiness" of a political party, which we never experience perceptually as a unity. But, if social objects are bundles of relations, then by perceiving the relation of one such object to another, we may well be able to perceive other relations. That is, on merely logical grounds, there are relational inferences we can make: if Harry is stronger than Irving, and Irving is stronger than James, I know that Harry is stronger than James. Similarly, we may in many cases be able to infer relations of liking, dislike, greater than, less than, same as, different from, to the right of, to the left of, and so on. Of course, as said, the whole need for the aesthetic approach is that there is little evidence that we actually *make* these inferences, although we somehow come to similar conclusions.

Thus, when it comes to people, we are able to fill in parts of a set of relations that we do not directly perceive (cf. Bradley 1987). It seems that we somehow have a similar capacity to take relations that are inherently relative (e.g., the Republicans are "right") and perceive them as properties of phenomenal objects. Therefore, something brought into conjunction with Republicans (say, "young white men," which also is a set of relative terms seen as stable attributes of an object) may immediately induce the proper relationships.[72]

So (to adapt an example from Köhler [1938: 228]; cf. James [1890] 1950: I, 245), we can immediately see in figure 6.6 not only that the size difference between a and b is greater than that between b and c, but also that it is the same as that between c and d. Somewhat analogously, we

---

[72]It may be that political stereotypes are akin to the corners that occupy critical functional roles in vision—just as we do not seem actually to create a full three-dimensional map of our world, but rather flag the corners that are determinative for our navigation, so too these hyperpersons may encapsulate information that can be used to reproduce the larger set of relations that constitute the world in which we may need to act.

A Social Aesthetics

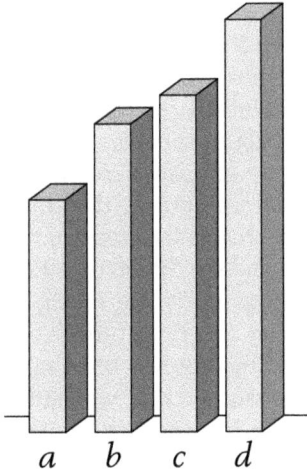

Figure 6.6 Two differences

may have the capacity to perceive relations directly, and relations between relations, as opposed to needing to use various forms of logical inference.

Some work in social psychology has already pursued such themes, but in a different guise; the most relevant work is probably in political psychology, for it is here that social relations are most explicit. We "hear about" social objects (such as political parties) from other objects in our world (a newspaper, a person), and how we understand the nature of the target object depends on our relations to these sources. We see what this party is all about on the basis of the relations we have with other things that we believe to be related to the party and so on.

These are tentative suggestions made on the basis of analogy and extrapolation. Yet, the argument is in no way weakened: although we do not yet know *how* we perceive such relations (as opposed to gathering information and manipulating it in the form of beliefs), it seems that we cannot deny that we *do*. It seems safe to imagine that a clearer understanding requires not only information about various forms of cortical processing, but, even more, closer phenomenological studies of interactions and attributions.

We saw in chapter 4 that Durkheim proposed to base his understanding of our cognitive system on his understanding of language. We saw that this was wrong, as he adopted the early structuralist vision of language as a set of nested boxes—an idealization—as opposed to examining the actual social practices of language. Yet, if we try to figure out what our cognitive strengths might be—those things that could be the basis for complex interactions with the world as called for by aesthetic insight—we would have to admit that language use is near the top of the list. Fortunately, it may indeed serve as a good model for understanding social cognition.

But this is not because it represents a cultural arbitrary, as in the structuralist approach to cognition reviewed in chapter 4. Language is not about mastery of a set of nested definitions, but the establishment of intersubjective validity (see Fauconnier [1985] 1994). In particular, our use of language demonstrates our remarkable ability to correctly parse logically ambiguous statements by reference to previous utterances, to the social relationship between the speakers, and to variations in tone and even bearing that are not consciously perceptible. We can behave in such situations with insight that confounds the sort of artificial intelligence that would master the Wason task because we sense intention as a quality of the concrete situation (also see Silverstein 1976).

Such sensing of intentionality is, we recall, nothing other than what Kant meant by our capacity to orient ourselves to beauty.[73] Thus, if we return to this question of beauty, we see that Kant, starting from the model of artistic creation, assumed that we could only rigorously see ends in objects when those were the ends of a conscious being (or could be treated as such); hence, we could only demand intersubjective agreement with our judgment of beauty if we could treat the world as if it was made for our cognitive system.[74] But we are perhaps more like the wasp *Ammophila* than Kant's abstract subject. We can treat qualities or meanings as inherent in objects not because some creator has kindly decided to use our cognitive conventions as a guide for the expression of his or her inner feelings but because our conventions are developed to make sense of preexisting regularity. The crucial intentionality to which we orient ourselves is not only that of concrete individuals but also includes social objects and the human-created environment.

Recapitulations

We have now rediscovered the Gestalt theorists' key point that our cognitive system is such that we may treat the qualities of objects as phenomenologically valid properties, but for the case when "objects" are bundles of social relations. The fundamental reasoning is the same in both cases:

---

[73]There is currently no small confusion in the social sciences about intentionality, fostered in some part by Luhmann, who draws both on the phenomenological and the action theory traditions, which use the word in diametrically opposed ways. In contrast to the more commonsensical use of the term in the action theoretic tradition, phenomenology follows Brentano's resurrection of intentionality, a term used by medieval scholastics to denote how things in the mind point to something outside it. Interestingly, the Gestalt-inspired psychologist Egon Brunswick, when he had to translate intentionality into English, chose "functionality" because his point was that, in an evolved and fit organism, the correspondence of inner and outer is an appropriate and hence functional mapping (see the discussion in Bischof 1966: 48, who ties this to pragmatism).

[74]It is worth pointing out that similar simplifications are constantly made by those who claim to examine the role of aesthetics in politics, as they create a fictitious superactor who creates various images for various ends.

our cognitive system is correlative and consubstantial to the world of objects. Further, the nature of qualitative experience is such as to give us a head start in our understanding of the relation between subjectivity and action because we may be oriented to qualities that have inherently dispositional quales. We thus need introduce no accessory model of motivation: *nauseating* things, by definition, are those that are sickening and produce "an inclination to vomit" (as the *Oxford English Dictionary* puts it). We need not postulate a model of the actor that includes the axiom, "People are motivated to vomit up nauseating things." That is what the quality of nauseating *means*.

Further, we have seen that our qualitative experience of social objects is one that is funded; those with different biographies and different relations have different experiences. This must be understood as *increasing* our estimation of the veridical nature—the "this-sidedness"—of our qualitative experience. Because, as Mead (1934) argued, what something means is "what we are going to do about it," our aesthetic capacity is the capacity to learn about our *own* intentions from the quality of social objects, that is, their potentiality to evoke our action. And, as we are different, our actions are different.

This is in some sense tautological, which is to say that it is true and unimportant. No one in the social sciences dreams that we see the world the same way. The crucial issue related to the variability of qualitative experience, and the fact that we confront different objects, is a twofold one of *adequacy*. The first is, Is there more to individual variability than compulsion and determination? That is, if due to a childhood trauma I find all healthy food nauseating, we will not admire the adequacy of my perceptual system, but rather infer its weakness. The second part of the adequacy question is, Can we determine ordering in this individual variability, or is the project of a social science lost in confusion?

These are both empirical questions. Here and in previous chapters, we have seen reasons why the social sciences have vastly underrated the this-sidedness of our qualitative perception. In all cases, we must remember that we are interested in how people cognize and deal with the social world; the "propositions about experience" that actors formulate in specific social environments are of some interest, but not very much, for such a task. We have found that there is every reason to think that people are oriented toward the retrieval of the qualities of social objects, which are themselves nexi of relations. This implies that the objects that actors deal with differ systematically by these actors' positions in such nexi. Finally, there is no reason to think that the aesthetic intuition that is used to extract an understanding of qualities, and what we are to do about them, is irremediably jarred by such differences. Our experiences regarding the qualities of social objects may not invariably be "right" in the sense that propositions constructed on their basis can successfully be proven to others through concepts. Yet, these qualitative experiences *are* experiences (as opposed to being inferences, guesses, or cultural tropes), they are experiences *of* the world (as opposed to being experiences of a veil that lies between us and the world), and they are equiprimordial with any other sources of knowledge (as opposed to being postperceptual processes).

Of course, one may still hold out a standard by which our experiences are found wanting. It would be unfortunate if this were used simply to reject our experiences and hope for some new, as-of-yet-inexistent form of perception that a creator filled with second thoughts might bestow. Certainly, it would be a bad beginning for a social science, which must build on whatever cognitive capacities we all have and not simply undermine them.

This brings us to the second question: can the social sciences find principles of regularity in the nature of qualitative experience that can be the basis for rigorous empirical inquiry into social action? The rest of this book argues that it *can*, and that it *must*, in that there is no other reasonable way of producing general statements about human action. I begin with a conveniently pure case that demonstrates the possibility of such a rigorous social aesthetics, and then attempt to move to more general considerations.

Chapter 7

Valence and Habit

THE POSSIBILITIES OF AN EMPIRICAL SOCIAL AESTHETICS

Taking Stock

In chapter 6, we ended with a need for a social aesthetics—a study of the processes whereby actors take in the qualities of the social world around them. It is worth emphasizing that the call for a social aesthetics has absolutely nothing to do with the antithetical ideal that sociology should be done in a more aesthetic fashion—the sort of self-indulgent program that arises every so often. Those who want an aesthetic sociology hope to increase the creative power of the individual sociologist (e.g., Redfield 1948: 188), while the aim here is to constrain the social scientist to occupy the same phenomenological world as others; those who want a more artistic sociology take pride in the abstractions introduced by sociological theory (e.g., Nisbet 1962: 67f), while the aim here is to completely do without them.

Such a project, further, is an empirical one—our purely nonempirical considerations to this point have only allowed us to reject implausible although common assumptions and to develop a minimal vocabulary for the formation of noncontradictory explanatory statements. This vocabulary gives us little, which is quite proper, for a social aesthetics should not be a simple song and dance that can be repeated whenever necessary, but a cumulative research tradition. But, is it possible to approach the qualities of social objects with any rigor?

Let us assume that we recognize the need for a social aesthetics, one that probes further into the ways in which persons orient themselves to the world (as opposed to a critique of their folk theory of this orientation).[1] The contours of such an aesthetics cannot be laid out in

---

[1] It is worth emphasizing that such an aesthetic of qualitative percepts is necessary even for other types of research questions often handled in terms of quantity. For as Kant ([1790] 1987: 107) argued, "Our estimation of the magnitude of the basic measure [used for any analysis] must consist merely in our being able to take it in directly in one intuition and to use it, by means of the imagination, for exhibiting numerical concepts. In other words, all estimation of the magnitude of objects of nature is ultimately aesthetic." That is, every

advance since it pertains to empirical questions. However, Bourdieu clearly thought that the most reasonable approach to such a social aesthetics would involve a field theory. It is worth emphasizing how unusual a decision this was for a late twentieth-century French theorist—to embrace a theoretical vocabulary with scientific overtones and one that was associated with a rather defunct research tradition in Germany and the United States. What is it about field theory that gives it promise for a social aesthetics?

One way of answering this is to return to Cassirer's ([1910] 1923: 248) defense of judgment as opposed to abstraction. Just as there are wholes that must be treated as prior to their parts, Cassirer argued that synthetic judgment did not need to have preexisting categories into which we sort individual cases. This is because, rather than inducing general laws from experience, we tacitly assume the law in each

---

numerical magnitude must be connected by a regress to our understanding of the quality of magnitude of the unit used in counting. So, while we can compare dollar returns per year of education for men and women, we do not have a magnitude in any literal sense without a qualitative idea of how *valuable* a dollar is in itself (not in terms of pennies) and how *long* a year is (not that it is 365 days).

This is no mere word play, but has a direct and experienceable psychological correlate. One particularly interesting optical illusion is the "harvest moon," the dramatically increased apparent size of the moon when it is close to the horizon. This illusion so blatantly flew in the face of the conventional theory of optics that incredibly weak pseudoexplanations based on atmospheric distortion were promulgated (e.g., by Hobbes), although the Gestalt psychologists—and Merleau-Ponty (1962: 31; also Bischof 1966: 44f; James [1890] 1950: II, 92f)—immediately understood it. (Interestingly, Descartes [1637/2001: 11] did as well; see Wade 1998: 379f; Plug and Ross 1989.) The harvest moon occupies no greater relative proportion of the entire visual field than does the moon at its apogee. According to conventional understandings, it is simply impossible that it "look" bigger. But our optical system, which (as Kant would say) must be treated as if it were designed to do something, has the job of giving us important information. When something is close to the horizon yet beyond it, our built-in circuitry understands that it must be extremely far away; no such benchmark exists for something simply in the air. Hence, as the moon gets closer to the horizon, every inch or arc of it in the visual field *looks* (is) bigger. The qualitative understanding of the unit (arc of visual field) has changed. Christopher Smart ([1758–1763] 1954, fragment B2, line 426): "For the phenomenon of the horizontal moon is the truth—she appears bigger in the horizon because she actually is so."

It must be admitted that there is still dispute regarding the neurophysiological basis of the moon illusion and some evidence that processes involved in focusing may actually contribute to the effect by changing the size of the retinal projection (see Roscoe 1989 and Enright 1989 for arguments). However, the balance of the evidence still seems to support the Gibsonian view that the most important thing is the position of the moon in an overall visual ecology.

experience. (As we recall, this was a key idea coming from Stumpf's work.) This can be compared to how we see position. In the world of experience (which is basically a Newtonian one), position is a purely relational artifact. "There" is given to us by other things that are closer or farther away. Thus, the "position" of, say, Radio City Music Hall is not given as some absolute reference to the center of the universe (should there be one) but its relation to other parts of New York City, in turn drawn from a set of relations to other areas of the (ever-moving) earth, such as the poles. But we easily treat the position of any object as an attribute of this unit considered in isolation. This is in effect to do what Köhler's charm-succumbing man did—to read regularities between relations into each individual observation.[2]

That is, to avoid the arbitrariness of the grid of perception, we turned to judgment, and we found this judgment to be nonarbitrary because the objects that it classifies are not self-subsistent atoms, but are nodes in sets of relations—judgment need not *add* anything to the nature of the elements to connect them to other elements, for the elements are defined by their reciprocal positions. To analyze them suchwise is to think in field theoretic terms. In the remainder of this chapter, we see two directions by which social scientists have been led to examine field theory, and I argue that they converge precisely because there is an implicit appositeness to the project of a social aesthetics, and this project is (as argued in the succeeding chapter) satisfied by a rigorous, even mathematized, field theory, should one prove possible. But first, we must handle the plausible reaction that there must be some contradiction between an emphasis on aesthetics and the use of a theoretical vocabulary derived (however loosely) from physics.

From Qualities to Quantities

We have seen that social cognition can be considered a unification of perception and judgment whereby people orient themselves to qualities that are treated as present in the others and the objects with which they interact. In the social sciences, "quality" raises the specter of one side of an old opposition, between "qualitative" and "quantitative" approaches, easily mapped onto "idiographic" and "nomothetic," "humanist" and "scientist," even, at its most base, "warm fuzzy" versus "cold prickly." The great battle between these two pseudoapproaches no longer rages in the epistemic era of good feeling in which all oppositions are unified in the "both/and"

---

[2]Cassirer: "Just as the relational character of position and distance inheres in the individual point, so the character of a universal law inheres in the individual experience," and thus "the advance from the individual to the whole . . . is possible because the reference to the whole is from the first not excluded but retained, and only needs to be brought separately into conceptual prominence."

formulae discussed in chapter 1.³ But, like any corporatist resolution, this harmony only reinforces the categorical opposition since *both* qualitative *and* quantitative approaches (or their designated representatives) are to be socially valorized.

Given this background, it may seem odd to propose that the most promising approach to a social aesthetics is through a field theory, taking as at least a vision, if not a model, a completely mathematized treatment such as that found in classical electromagnetism. But, we cannot deny that qualities can vary in intensity even when we are unable to correlate this variation in intensity with a similar numerical variation in some particular property of the object (Metzinger 2003: 184). Of course, in some cases such a correlation is possible. For example, (given any density) larger objects are heavier, and we may explain the increase in intensity of the quality of heaviness by the increased volume.⁴ But in other cases we cannot transform intensity of quality into some magnitude in the object.⁵ For example, certain wormy apples are more nauseating than others, and while we can describe what about them gives them this increased intensity of quality, we cannot simply explain it as due to, say, the proportion of the insides of the worm that are currently exposed or the number of revolutions made by the expiring animal in its death agonies.

The same may be said for situations. "Security" as a feeling may be held to be a quale; we may also reasonably attribute security as a quality of certain situations. Situations may be more or less secure; we may (as actors) gauge the intensity of this security simply by paying attention to our own subjective experience.⁶ Given any quality that differs in intensity across situations, if there is any relation between intensity of the quality and probability of situational change (which might be the case if, say, people are motivated to put themselves in situations of higher or lower intensity), then a mathematized field theory is, at least in principle if not in practice, entirely applicable for explaining the change in or distribution of persons across situations (cf. Köhler 1938: 368).

---

³Of course, this is presumably only due to the stable division of turf between the two; one can expect a shift in the balance between undergraduate instruction (which disproportionately supports warm fuzzies) and state-sponsored research (which disproportionately supports cold pricklies) to lead to new discoveries that the previous understanding of the importance of *both* kinds of research was overly hasty.

⁴Actually, recent careful research by psychologists in the Gestalt tradition has demonstrated that what we perceive as the quality of "heaviness" of an object is not so much its weight but our difficulty in wielding it, and hence has to do with the distribution of mass and not simply its sum (Turvey, Shockley, and Carello 1999).

⁵We are, of course, free to imagine that it is *possible* to mathematize such qualities; all that matters is that should we find such a project outside our reach, we have available another avenue of exploration.

⁶Our gauging may not be error free, but occur it does.

For example, Stephen Pepper, whose work I cited approvingly in terms of his attempt to reintroduce quality to the understanding of action, when proposing his own theory of art explicitly formulated a field theory if only because our qualitative experience of the aesthetic power of some work is likely to vary. He posited a "consummatory field" in which we are attempting to move to the area of maximum satisfaction vis-à-vis quality, and a relation to objects in which, like a rat following the cheese, we are drawn to a particular position because of an overriding sense of "ought" that is differentially distributed as vectors in a field (1937: 19; 1955: 44, 50–58; 1961: 568; also see Merleau-Ponty 1962: 429).[7]

More generally, field theory is a rigorous approach to a social aesthetics because qualities *do* vary across situations and because people *are* motivated to increase the intensity of some, and decrease the intensity of other, qualia. And, as we recall from chapter 6, in some cases we need no additional theoretical arguments because the dispositional nature of certain qualitative experiences contains their action counterpart—a nauseating apple is that which we are moved to spit out. The most fundamental qualia for a science of action is that of valuation or requiredness—the sense that in some situation, something is called for. We have followed Dewey and Köhler in accepting that such requiredness may be immediately experienced (although it may also be reflected on and mediately experienced).

This simple case highlights why a field approach is a reasonable one for a social aesthetics; indeed, it shows why Bourdieu's own approach did not do itself justice. Bourdieu ([1979] 1984: 488), rejecting Kant's whole approach to judgment, endorsed Hegel's critique of Kant's approach as one that "remains in the register of *Sollen*, ought."[8] But even if Kant himself misrecognized (as Bourdieu might have it) the nature of this "ought," confusing a social opposition with inherent properties of beauty, Kant's

---

[7]Pepper argued that we may be drawn to increase the number, duration, intensity, and vividness of certain experiences of felt qualities. (For example, we may move continuously in geographical space to get the best view.) Thus, we may accurately say that the "ends" are in the objective constitution of the object, for it is effectively the object that directs us—that contains an implicit imperative—and not we who impose an arbitrary predeliction. It is from the "oughtness" of aesthetic experience that Pepper (1937: 11, 226, 239, 241ff; 1955: 93) derives the need for a cultivated taste—just as we would not want poor external conditions (e.g., lighting) to interfere with our aesthetic experience, so we do not want poor *internal* conditions to hamper our ability to attain the peak experience.

[8]It is worth pointing out that Bourdieu's critique here is different from the conventional pseudo-Hegelian critique of Kant as wallowing in "shoulds" as opposed to scientific "isses" made by some self-described Marxists; Bourdieu is not arguing against the use of normative "shoulds" so much as linking them to concrete social divisions. For Hegel's own discussion of Kant, see ([1835] 1975: 57–60); Hegel does imagine that Kant's understanding is "only" subjective, but Hegel's supposed advance requires a return to Platonic downgrading of sensual intuition without abandoning Kant's emphasis on the purity of the aesthetic (36, 39, 111).

terminology is more useful, and his approach more revealing, than Bourdieu perhaps appreciated. For objects *do* have an ought; one may protest that the imperatives of an object are borrowed from the relations in which it is embedded, but as we have been unable to define these objects as anything independent of these relations, it is unclear what such a protest may accomplish. And it is because oughtness gives a vectoral interpretation to experience—that is, we actually feel in the environment a push to do or be something—that a rigorous aesthetics may turn toward a field theory.

We may thus say that a field theory in the mathematized sense is an account that links intensity of something to position, and movement to intensity, where the movement is across these same positions. Interestingly, there has been a convergence toward such a field theoretical conception in the social sciences. The roots of this lie in the Gestalt tradition discussed in chapter 5. Let us return and pick up those threads and see to what extent they point toward a coherent approach.

THE DEVELOPMENT OF FIELD THEORY

Social-Psychological Fields

Previously, we examined the Gestalt theoretic tradition, which derived from a line of comprehensive or wholistic thought that had special importance in Germany. While the wholism of these thinkers was related to more general intellectual trends, it took a specific form in their psychology. Rather than being a vague demand to "see the whole picture," wholism for the Gestalt theorists was an empirical argument about the nature of perception: one bit of perception ("percept") could not be isolated from another that was near it. Thus, Köhler recalled that his goal was to determine "why percepts at a distance have an effect on one another. This is only possible, we assumed (and we followed Faraday in doing so), if the individual percept has a field and if the 'field', which surrounds the percept, does not merely reveal the presence of this percept but also presents its specific properties" (cited in Mey [1965] 1972: 13ff; also see Köhler [1917] 1925: 191; Ash 1998: 171; Reed 1996: 51; for a discussion of the relation of Gestalt theory to field theory, see Mohr, forthcoming).

Now, it is not the case that this was some vague and impressionistic use of natural-scientific metaphors, as is often the case in the human sciences. The Gestalt theorists were well educated in physics, and the physicists of their day considered the Gestaltists' ideas seriously.[9] Thus, when the Gestalt theorists talked of fields, they meant to imply the current state of

[9] For example, Köhler had studied mathematics and physical science, with, among others, Max Planck, who together with Einstein (a friend of Wertheimer's) supported Köhler in a number of instances (see Ash 1998: 112f, 170, 196, 214, 262). Köhler also wrote a controversial book (1920) arguing that Gestalts were present in physical systems.

field theories in the physical sciences. Most of the Gestalt discussions pertained to the fields of force of objects in the field of perception; they had little to do with action. Yet, from the first, there were hints that the Gestalt theory implied that the behavior of an organism could be seen as akin to the motion of an object in a field of force.

Most famously, in his early work with apes, Köhler ([1917] 1925: 14, 89, 180, 182; also 1938: 95) had described their movement in some cases using a metaphor of traversing one of the "lines of force" that Faraday saw emerging from magnets. One example was the inability of an animal near a desired object to move away in order to take a successful indirect path around an intervening obstacle, this inability increasing the closer the animal came to the object, such that an animal beginning on an insightful, indirect path might be drawn helplessly to the object if it came too near it and would end up abandoning the successful initial plan. In such cases, the action of the animal would be better explained by proposing that the object had a gravity-like pull than by attempting to explain the animal responding to differential stimuli from the environment.

Thus, the early field theoretic approaches led to an explanation of behavior that took the perspective of the acting animal and treated objects as having qualities that directly inspired certain forms of action. It is this aspect of field theory that may satisfy our criteria for a social aesthetics; here, we can trace the stages by which the field theory of perception was transformed into a field theory of action.

The first problem for this, as for any field theory, pertained to the nature of the force involved—for forces are, we are told, always only seen by their effects. In this case, however, we might have an advantage, in that we are ourselves able to report the qualitative experience of social forces. (Indeed, recall that this is where Durkheim [1912/1995] imagined that our idea of "force" must originate.) We may have the sense of requiredness in some social environment; it is this experience that allows us to generalize to other cases and use such a notion of force as something that intervenes between an acting animal and its surroundings, an internalization of the objective potentialities present at a particular environmental position. Most important, this notion of "force" could be generalized to cases in which we feel anything but forced. Thus, Tolman and Brunswik (1935), psychologists both of the Gestalt tradition, argued that the perceptual system of an animal had to be understood correlative to an environment that has a particular "causal texture." Rather than the animal being "forced" by some field, the job of the animal as a perceiver was to "get" the principles that would allow for effective action.[10]

---

[10]This suggested to Tolman that animals should have the ability to orient themselves to a complete spatial whole when learning a path as opposed to simply memorizing a set of reinforced actions such as turns, something he demonstrated with rats (Tolman, Ritchie, and Kalish 1946a, 1946b), although his work was ridiculed and ignored by a generation of orthodox behaviorists (see Gould and

This approach to action was brought into American social psychology largely by Kurt Lewin.[11] Lewin argues that the phenomenological lifeworld of the animal (or person) in question is intrinsically *affective*—in contrast to stimuli considered solely as stimuli (light stimulates retinal cells), these phenomena are perceived immediately as desirable or undesirable. These "*Aufforderungscharakters*" (usually translated "valences," although I shall follow Gibson [1979/1986], and White [1992] is using the neologism "affordances")[12] determine how objects and other beings induce a field.

Because this field is a psychological construct, Lewin correctly concluded that in his approach the past cannot directly affect the present. In contrast to what he considered primitive views of causality, Lewin (1936: 10, 30–34) argued that behavior should not be seen as caused by something in the past (let alone the future) but must be grounded in an understanding of the totality of the current situation. (We may then ask how this situation came into being, a historical question quite different from the systematic question posed by field theory.) (Lewin 1936: 33, 35; Cassirer [1910] 1923: 238; cf. Koffka 1935: 429; Merleau-Ponty 1962: 140; Abbott 2005: 247).[13] (This conclusion has implications for the supposedly "causal" explanation of action investigated in chapter 2.)

But Lewin's conception of the field was beset with paradoxes. Most commentators have seized on the incoherence of his attempt to combine a metric notion of field taken from physics with a wholly distanceless understanding from topology (Eng 1978; Rummel 1975: 38, 41, 43; Spiegel 1961: 17; though see Lewin 1936: 53, 55, 85; Mey [1965] 1972: 40 for a defense). Because he simply liked to draw diagrams of whatever

---

Gould 1999: 67). The orthodox behaviorist model, as Brunswik (1952: 40), Rummel (1975: 25), and Köhler (1947: 106, 121) point out, is comparable to the mechanistic interpretation of action at a distance in contrast to a field one: without an explicable chain of elements banging in to one another, the phenomenon had to be wrong.

[11]Lewin was a student of Stumpf and a colleague of Köhler and Wertheimer at the Psychological Institute (see Marrow 1969: 13; Ash 1998: 266) but was perhaps more influenced by Cassirer, from whom he had taken classes.

[12]While "valence" is the standard translation, Allport (1955) and Koffka (1935: 35) used "demand character" and Brown "invitational character" (Marrow 1969: 56f, 61). Rummel (1975: 50, n. 40) argues that the English word *valence* was used by Lewin's translator because of its prescientific meaning of value or worth, although to many readers it seems deliberately "scientistic." "Demand character" is not only literally accurate but also links to the economic idea (stemming from Say's law) that, in Koffka's (1935: 48) words, it is not only that the factory produces the goods, "but also the demand for the goods" that produces them.

[13]Lewin called this the "principle of 'contemporaneity.'" Dewey ([1922] 1930: 200f) made the same argument: action must be explained not in the basis of some future state desired and anticipated, but on the basis on the current state.

argument he wanted to make, he concentrated on such "topological" drawings, and his few forays into formal equations were vacuous (see Lewin 1951).

A more fundamental problem arose because Lewin's conception was both impossibly vague (including "everything relevant") on the one hand and frustratingly limited on the other, as it was a psychological entity. The paradox becomes obvious in his conception of valences. A *valence* is something that pulls one toward or pushes one away; the field itself may be seen as the product of many valences, as a gravitational field may be seen as the product of many objects, each with its own gravitational field.

This seemingly unremarkable definition, however, leads to paradox, because Lewin considered the valence to be "in the head" of any person in question (hence Brunswik [1952: 78] reasonably calls Lewin's field "solipsistic").[14] Accordingly, any need, desire, or drive held by the person or animal *itself* has a valence. It then becomes not the cheese that has the valence, but the hunger of the rat. The field continually collapses to a point; Lewin is in the position of someone holding one end of a string, and forced to argue that the pull he feels comes not from the other end, but his own end.

In some ways, these puzzles return us to the issue of optics discussed in chapter 6—the puzzle over whether to think of the cone of rays as coming from the eye or from the object. Let us say that the desirable object in our case is a banana, and the self is that of a hungry ape. The vector connects the self to the object, and what is of importance for an explanation of the resulting behavior is its "charge" and orientation (e.g., positive, toward banana). Thus, as Köhler (1938: 75; also 73) argued, "it is not very important whether we say that an interest [i.e., affordance] is directed from the self to the object or, perhaps better, that in the form of an interest the self is directed toward the object."[15] What is key is the relation, the reciprocal orientation of the two, expressed as a unity in the form of qualitative perception. Further, the (nonuniversal) intersubjective validity of such perception allows us to begin to move toward generality in our analyses. The same banana draws in other hungry apes, and our focal ape may be attracted to other foodstuffs. Although her state of hunger may sensitize her to the properties of the banana, these properties are not inside the ape. Thus, both the self and the object must be placed in some sort of social, as opposed to psychological, field (cf. Simonis 1974: 368, 372; Heider 1958: 14; Heider 1983: 144) or at least

---

[14]The critique is justified, yet we can sympathetically view Lewin's decision, which was probably derived from his classic (e.g., [1926] 1999) work, which seemed to demonstrate that an unfulfilled intention had the same psychic effects on a person as an external need.

[15]Indeed, Köhler (1938: 78) had a conception reminiscent of Plato's idea of sight, involving the creation of value-properties by the web of relations in the field.

a transpersonal or geographic field as in Koffka (1935: 63, 345, 357, 376, 664, 675).

At the same time, this may appear to involve taking an intramental entity (such as a "need" or a "desire") and putting it outside any particular mind (see the explicit argument of Köhler [1938: 87f] contra Lewin). What kind of existential support could there be for such a concept?

Fields of Organized Striving

Whether or not it could be justified, a parallel concept already existed in the social sciences, namely, "value." Like a shared valence, a value—definitions abounded then as now, and few are exceptionally enlightening—by definition had to be something that *eo ipso* called people to itself, and was shared. Value theory had (again, then as now) as many mushy spots as an overripe banana, tending to remain safely inside the range between the incontestably obvious (we don't eat our children because we think it is bad) to the impossibly tautological (we do good things because we think it is good to be good).

Talk of values now often brings to mind some vaguely Parsonian theory in which all things fit nicely together. But, in the early decades of the twentieth century there was in Germany some serious interest in values not because of a desire to come up with a grand, unified theory of harmonious action, but because of the opposite—the conviction that there is always necessary conflict, indeed, ethical conflict, between spheres of value with their own "inner laws" (as Burger [1976: 8] says, these ideas were "in the air").[16] Like many others, I examine the work of Max Weber as the most important output of this more general concern.

There was a belated sense of urgency to this concern—Nietzsche's work was understood as destabilizing previous philosophies that were

---

[16]Other examples are Friedrich Naumman and Georg Simmel and. later, Karl Mannheim (1940: 159f); see the work of Goldman (1988: 136); Schluchter (1996: 278, n18); and Habermas ([1983] 1996: 409). Husserl ([1900] 1970: 86) proposed "normative disciplines," each "unambiguously characterized by its basic norm, or by the definition of what shall count as 'good' in a discipline." In his mammoth undertaking attempting to describe the different ways in which the human spirit reached out to the world, Cassirer ([1923] 1953: 91, 95, 98) made similar arguments, although he emphasized not variance in the value pursued but variance in the ways of connecting the inner and the outer. This sort of approach has been revived by Boltanski and Thénevot ([1991] 2006: 147ff), who tie this notion of judgment to Aristotle's "phronesis" (and Cicero's later *prudentia*). The difference between taking this path and that of hexis/habitus (as we saw Bourdieu and Dewey choose) may seem small, but it seems to lead one more to *ethics*, perhaps practical reasoning, and a conscious capacity, as opposed to the *judgment* that may be embodied.

based on values, and scholars cast about for ways to reintegrate their thoughts.[17] Perhaps the most influential treatment was that of Heinrich Rickert (1913), previously encountered in this book as formulating one version of the view of concept formation that became the orthodoxy for the social sciences. In this piece, Rickert attempted to respond to Nietzsche with a more flexible sort of value system; he formalized the notion of competing values and logically derived six types. Yet, the mere fact of a formal arrangement defused some of the conflict, for there were some sorts of values that were intrinsically different from others—one would, say, hardly make up for a shortage of "fulfilled particularity" of the contemplative sort (e.g., artistry) by adding a bit more "infinite totality" of the social form (e.g., ethicality).

The dominant criticism of Rickert's approach has been that it was nonempirical and ahistorical, which is somewhat unfair, for this was his deliberate strategy to respond to Nietzsche's challenge to systematizers. At least his ex cathedra pronouncements could be defended by logical argument (of a somewhat scholastic kind). But, what happens when one attempts to make an empirical schema along the same lines? This is what we see in the key theoretical piece by sociologist Max Weber, "Religious Rejections of the World and Their Directions," published a few years after Rickert's (Weber [1915] 1946).[18]

Like Rickert, Weber gave six spheres—the religious, the economic, the political, the aesthetic, the erotic, and the intellectual—and emphasized that each possessed an "inherent lawfulness" (*Eigengesetzlichkeit*). That is, something in the nature of each principle of ordering tends toward a purification or rationalization of purpose and consequent tension between

---

[17]Weber liked to pretend that he saw Hegel as the only rival to his own approach (whatever that was). But, like other neo-Kantians, Weber was chiefly trying to pick up the shattered pieces of system building, and it was Nietzsche whom Weber, as others, accepted as the one who had justly destroyed the Kantian edifice. There have been occasional flurries in the secondary literature when someone wishes to exaggerate Weber's borrowings from Nietzsche; the actual influence of Nietzsche was, as Joas (2000) in particular has emphasized, in setting the problems for Weber's whole circle to solve in terms of the nature of value.

[18]Bruun (2008) has justly criticized an earlier treatment in which I simply declared that Weber had adapted Rickert's scheme, largely because of the closeness between the two treatments and the number of identified spheres. Bruun (2007: 9, 33, 35, 37, 194, 199; cf. 122 on Rickert's scheme) makes clear that Weber's own ideas regarding value conflict go back to at least 1895, and that he saw Rickert's own system as one possible division of values, but not necessarily the only one with empirical validity. Further, because Weber introduced six spheres, as did Rickert, and one can see a close parallel, I was too ready to imagine that this was a simple adaptation. However, the connection between Rickert's philosophy and Weber's treatment is a strong and important one; I will give a more complete treatment of this in a future work.

the spheres, as one could not "serve two gods" (e.g., religion and science) at the same time (cf. Burke 1952: 43). Thus, one who chooses to pursue wealth is driven toward action according to rational cost-benefit calculations in the market and toward treating persons merely as things, while one who is oriented to salvation must utterly reject this orientation. This fundamental idea that the mature individual must choose some "cause" (*Sache*) in order to transcend the pettiness of individual subjective inclinations and act in a truly "objective" (*sachlich*) manner is hardly derivable on the basis of empirical considerations, but it felt deeply right to a generation schooled in neo-Kantian ideas of duty. We do what we do because we must, because it is right, because there *is* a value, some good thing, that we pursue.

At the same time, this line of thought was producing an important reorientation for social theorists. The idea that social life in the Western world increasingly involved some sort of differentiation was hardly new—it was the central ideal of Spencer's sociology and universally accepted. The increasing specialization of the sciences kept this alive for all academics to see, even when they were at their desks. But most (Durkheim, obviously) followed Spencer in assuming that this differentiation was fundamentally a *functional* one. Different areas of social life were to each other as were different organs in a body. By tying this differentiation to values, Weber (and others in his circle) transferred the issue from one of function to one of *motivation*.

But, whence came these goals? What is the nature of the value spheres? Why these and not others? While Rickert was criticized for the ahistoric nature of his scheme, Weber has been criticized for the fact that he took historically specific forms and treated them as if they were eternal. Certainly, to someone like Weber, often as, if not more, concerned with making chilling pronouncements regarding the necessarily tragic position of the modern actor as with explaining some particular ensemble of social actions, it was tempting to overstate the *givenness* of these values.[19] To the extent that these values were fixed by "the nature of the world," then one could demand that the individual *recognize* the nature of constraint in mature action and hence the measure of heteronomy implicit in any true autonomy. But, if the philosophical pretensions are removed, then instead of saying "we all strive for X because it is an instantiation of some value," we simply say "what we call a value is some thing that we happen to be striving for."

Such a rethinking came as a result of the introduction of Gestalt and field theoretic ideas to this neo-Kantian sociology. In this light, value spheres exist not because of the transcendent nature of human action but because of the existence of some social logic to the goals held by actors.

---

[19] I have discussed (in somewhat crude terms) the ethical reasons why Weber required this givenness in Martin (1998) and return to this in a future treatment.

It is this less-sweeping understanding of the nature of shared goals that leads to the idea of a "field" in the sense of a professional field.[20]

In this conception, to take the words of Victor Turner (1974: 135), the field is "an ensemble of relationships between actors antagonistically oriented to the same prizes or values." And, just as we saw Pepper deriving a field theoretic interpretation from aesthetics, so we can derive a field theoretic approach to action as striving for, as Heider (1958: 109) wrote, "'Trying' has a directional aspect and a quantitative aspect." That is, it is a vector, and a set of organized "tryings" is a field.[21]

The first notable effort in this direction was Friedrich Fürstenberg's ([1962] 1969) analysis of the process of upward social mobility or social ascent (*Der Aufstiegsprozess*) using a mixture of field theoretical concepts and closure theory (although also see Brandt 1952: 188). We can understand the progress of someone through a "sector of ascension" in field theoretic terms because the result of any individual's action is due to the interaction between the state of the field and the states of the individual. The social mobility process can thus be seen as a "chain of interrelationships between the ascending individual and the current social environment" (Fürstenberg [1962] 1969: 51f; also 122).

More interestingly, Fürstenberg ([1962] 1969: 36, 37, 42, 49, 54f) argued that the form of the interrelationships was not merely an interaction (such as "*both* the individual *and* the objective factors matter," as in the mantra of the pseudosolutions discussed in chapter 1), but rather a duality, as one's objective structural trajectory must have a "subjective correlate" in an individual striving for success. In particular, Fürstenberg ([1962] 1969: 159) attributes to each person a subjective "aspiration level" (*Anspruchsniveau*)[22] consisting of expectations, in addition to an objective aspiration level corresponding to the demands (*Anforderungen*)[23] of the individual's social environment. While making due allowances for various complications, Fürstenberg ([1962] 1969: 142f) believed that subjectivity will tend to correspond to objective position.

[20]The use of the word *field* for such cases obviously pre-dates the sociological approach; however, I believe that it was first used to mean the open spaces of possible actions and not a set of similarly motivated competitors. Thus, one might speak of a "field of trade" to denote the vast and level realm of openness for merchant actions, to take the example suggested by Karl Mannheim (1940: 295–298), in his introduction of the idea of a "sector field" of parallel strivings.

[21]"Both ought and want belong to the dimension of force or force field. They refer to an actual process, like enjoyment or perception" (Heider 1958: 224).

[22]Fürstenberg ([1962] 1969: 52, n. 2) explicitly noted that he took this term from a student of Lewin's, Ferdinand Hoppe, who did a dissertation investigating the "level of aspiration," a term first coined by Lewin's student Tamara Dembo (Marrow 1969: 44, 56).

[23]This has, I believe, a somewhat harsher sense than Lewin's *Aufforderung*, which is a bit more to the "invitation" side of demand, and thus indicates a "calling out for" as opposed to the "now you must"-ness of roles.

This idea is crucial: while acknowledging the importance of socialization, reference groups, and the other central findings of the sociology of his time, Fürstenberg also argued that one's current motivation must be understood as an effect of current field position. Even if a field does not have organizations in the usual sense, it will possess differentiated action imperatives that Fürstenberg ([1962] 1969: 53, 63, 102, 121f) termed "role demands" (*Rollenanforderungen*). These role expectations are equivalent to the field effect: the situation is experienced by the individual as a chain of objective requirements (*objektiver Anforderungen*)—whether these are formal or informal is of secondary importance.[24]

Thus, the "affordance" that Lewin saw as being—inexplicably—in the head of the actor is seen as part of the organization of some sector. Fürstenberg was, however, somewhat thin on the phenomenology of the perception of objective demands. Pierre Bourdieu's extension of this approach to fields of organized striving comes into its own here. First, while Fürstenberg ([1962] 1969: 51), influenced by Lewin's wholism, considered it impossible to analyze one sector in isolation from the others, Bourdieu (e.g. 1985b: 723) argued that by definition, fields should be treated as analytically distinct (although the degree of autonomy of any field is of course an empirical question). Each field has its own themes and problems and its own rules of proceeding, its own inherent lawfulness (Bourdieu [1966] 1969: 161f; 1990b: 389; 1993: 72).

Most important, each field possesses—indeed, each field *generates*—its own value, that which is at stake (*enjeu*, correlative to the specific subjective libido to pursue this goal).[25] Because of this, the collective goal is the object of struggle (Bourdieu 1985b: 734): what is at stake in a chess, tennis, or sumo tournament is not simply which individual will be the winner, but what *kind* of chess, tennis, or sumo (and hence, what *kinds* of players) will dominate the field in the future. (I return to this issue in the next chapter and defend this statement.)

Bourdieu tended to be oriented to agonistic aspects of field behavior, in which participants are oriented to a goal that is in part positional (that is, not everyone can succeed equally). But if, as Bourdieu says, the field generates its own libido, then more generally and more properly we would note that participants are oriented not so much to a goal as to one another. Indeed, the "goal," like other social objects, has only a virtual existence expressing in simplified form the ensemble of social relationships. Thus, we see the answer to the puzzle of how valences could have intersubjective validity: because they are induced by a field of persons aligned toward one another, they not only *can* have intersubjective validity, they *must*.

---

[24]Giddens (1979: 117) also suggests the possible generalization of the idea of role to that of position in field.

[25]I am grateful to Vanina Leschziner and Loïc Wacquant for discussions regarding the translation of different French terms.

Valence and Habit

To be "in" the field means to participate in the validation of an *enjeu*. There is no "necessary" conflict between "the" value spheres, but since we only recognize a field *as* a field if it is sufficiently differentiated from others, action that facilitates action in one field is unlikely to be as useful in another.[26]

In other words, we have followed the development of a second idea of field (the first being the social-psychological)—a concrete set of individuals oriented by similar motivations. Pursuing this, we find ourselves meeting up with the social-psychological idea of field and, indeed, going far to concretize the project of a social aesthetics. We first derived a field as a set of vectors expressing the intensity and action implications of a quality, especially that of some sort of "oughtness." But, as Heider (1958: 226) wrote, "the ought can be considered a cognized force with objective validity; value can be considered a cognized positive property of something, a relevance with objective validity." Thus, "value" is in some ways our folk theory of the organization of our situational experiences of "oughtnesses"—the objective correlative to our sense of "what it is we are to do." The folk theory relies on the attachment of the oughtness to objects, but objects that are, as we have emphasized, best understood as bundles of relations.

When investigating the field of striving, we found a set of relations that generates some organized perception of "what is to striven for." We thus have a simple case of the direct perception of action implications from sets of social relations. The reason oughtnesses converge on the object-of-value is that the object is defined as that convergence point among a set of vectors. And, when our oughtnesses are parallel, we

---

[26]This issue of differentiation is key and complex in that it is easy for Bourdieu to allow analytically for multiple capitals and multiple fields, but not necessarily for multiple habiti. Here, one may compare the approach of Randall Collins (2004: 108), which is similar, although with the advantage of clarity: rather than speak vaguely of capitals, Collins posits that we have a certain amount of emotional energy—positive participation in group rituals increases a person's stock of emotional energy which then, capital-like, can be used to initiate or dominate other interactions, thus leading to a further increase in energy. This energy—an "anticipation of being able to coordinate with someone else's responses, of smoothly role-taking in the ongoing flow of the interaction" (119)—has great phenomenological validity. One problem (pointed out to me by Elizabeth Williamson and Benjamin Zablocki) is that it cannot be true that we preserve a high state of emotional energy—if this has anything to do with the emotions, such energy must ebb and flow, or it would destroy us. A second problem is that of differentiation—how can we store one sort of emotional energy for work, and another for soccer, say? If the office boy beats the law firm partner on the soccer field, we must imagine some sort of distinction, but it is not clear how this would be retained if we imagine that persons store this energy. Rather, pursuing Collins's logic, the energy would be stored in the *environment*. But, this is, as we will see in the next chapter, precisely the definition of a field effect.

pursue the "value" in itself (cf. Simmel [1905] 1977: 159; also Cooley 1913: 553).[27] Bourdieu's own approach goes farther and allows for (and indeed anticipates) cases with neither universal convergence nor universal parallelism—that is, conflict over what is the legitimate goal. While this does make serious progress in answering the questions with which we began, we have already noted Bourdieu's disinclination to give serious and close attention to the processes whereby qualities are retrieved from social objects. Indeed, closer inspection demonstrates that the problems that result from Bourdieu's incomplete rejection of some of the assumptions explored in chapters 3 and 4 became especially pernicious for the comprehension of the subjective components of action.

The Perils of Socioanalysis

To some extent, Bourdieu's approach reached toward the integration of multiple points of view. In contrast to others who imagined reflexivity to involve merely the sociological hero baring his (invariably noble) value commitments, Bourdieu argued that reflexivity required the analyst to correctly position him- or herself in the field of relations in which both other analysts and other actors were situated. This allowed him to go beyond Mannheim's ([1929] 1936) reasonable, if simplistic, argument that correct knowledge requires the multiplicity of views, by positing that what we need is less the points of view themselves than an overall understanding of the relative placement of these points (Bourdieu [1984] 1988: xvi, 11). As Mead (1938: 606f; also see p. 64) says, "A perspective can be recognized as such only when lying in a field within which it is no longer a perspective."[28] Yet, Bourdieu preserved some of the agonistic epistemology that resolves all scientific questions into a battle of wills.

---

[27]While we are tempted to reverse things and explain the emergence of parallelism on the basis of the intensity of the value that "of course" beckons all of us, such accounts rarely withstand empirical scrutiny. As Weber ([1920–1921] 1976) remarked, strivers after economic success have feeble explanations of why they are doing something that is substantively irrational.

[28]Or, even more precisely, Merleau-Ponty ([1942] 1963: 186, also 212) put it this way: "Perspective does not appear to me [that is, a living person] to be a subjective deformation of things but, on the contrary, to be one of their properties, perhaps their essential property. It is precisely because of it that the perceived possesses in itself a hidden and inexhaustible richness, that it is a 'thing.'" That is, our criticism of "perspectival" knowledge makes the same mistake as previous theories of vision—it assumes the motionless eye. But, we are free to get up and walk around things, and their richness comes from their nonrandom alteration under such walks. It is the set of relations of such nonrandom alteration that allows us to have a "world."

Although Bourdieu drew on the Gestalt/field theoretic tradition, he was unable to completely ignore the Cartesian division of body and mind whereby whatever is not conscious is bodily. One sees this in his idea that we must wed the two sides of objectivism and constructivism, as opposed to the insistence of both Gestalt theorists and pragmatists that there was no such division in the first place. And this Cartesian splitting of course introduces the wild insecurity that there may be no basis to our knowledge. As we saw Dewey point out in chapter 6, we do not wonder how the stomach can "really" digest food because we understand that the stomach and food share a substantial nature, but Cartesianism prevents us from having the same insight regarding how the mind knows the world. Despite his attempts to overcome this division, by starting with it Bourdieu could not avoid implicitly endorsing the Durkheimian assumption of the arbitrary nature of the categories of perception.

Bourdieu never hid his admiration for Durkheim's attempt (discussed in chapter 4) to develop a social ontogenesis of knowledge ("one of the finest texts of the sociological literature" [Bourdieu 1992: 39; also see Bourdieu 1990a: 24f; Wacquant in Bourdieu and Wacquant 1992: 12–15]) and frequently used the idea of Durkheimian categories of perceptions in service of his own points (Bourdieu [1989] 1996: 2; 1984 [1979]: 471). Like Mary Douglas, Bourdieu was only critical of Durkheim for not applying the same reasoning to himself, "and seeking in the social structures of the academic world . . . the sources of the categories of professional understanding" (Bourdieu [1984] 1988: xii; also see 7, 11f, 197, 201ff; 1992: 39f; cf. 1990a: 178; [1989] 1996: 30; 1994: 7, 13; cf. 1990a: 136f).

Now, I believe that many of the alleged inconsistencies in Bourdieu's work come more from his attempts to explain it to a particular audience than from the nature of his ideas. Certainly, Bourdieu often had difficulty in expressing in what way a habitus is "cognitive" and in what way it is "bodily" (for definitions, see Bourdieu 1968: 705f; [1972] 1977: 82f, 97; 1984 [1979]: 170, 466; 1990b: 56, 66, 68f; 1990a: 130f; 1992: 54; 1994: 14; Wacquant's [2004] view of habitus is perhaps more consistent). This was in part because many readers, especially in the United States, seemed to imagine that habitus was an analytic concept he had invented, and insisted on calling it a "black box." (While the precise way in which the spleen filtered blood was not understood for a long time [cf. Weber 1978: 15], it would be silly to try to make progress on this front by demanding that someone *define* it more clearly.) But it was also because, unlike Kant, Bourdieu tended to assume that judgment, although bodily, involves some sort of subsumptive classification (vision and division). His explication of habitus, at least at times, made it seem a bit more like Durkheim's "framework of thought" than is consistent with his own starting point.

And Bourdieu was perhaps least consistent when it came to the relation between this principle of division and political change, in part because he suffered (as do most synoptic social thinkers) from ill-posed accusations that "his system" could not "account for change" (change here being understood in some vaguely voluntarist if not Leninist fashion). Indeed, we see an oscillation between Bourdieu's ([1998] 2001: 39ff; [1997] 2000: 180) emphasizing the futility of attempting to change the world by changing consciousness, and his insistence that not only is such consciousness raising an effective tool of subversion but also, indeed, that demonstrating its efficacy was one of his most important contributions to the discipline (Bourdieu [1980] 1990: 141; 1992: 38ff; 1990a: 16, 116, 180; [1997] 2000: 186). To the extent that Bourdieu actually did reduce his vision to a two-stroke engine of internalization and objectification, either could be used to deny the efficacy of the other alone.

The final step was for Bourdieu to conclude that his own researches had given him sufficient knowledge to be able to determine superior principles of division and, although not to impose them on others, to use these to interpret how others think. It was thus that Bourdieu began to describe his project as one of "socioanalysis," deliberately highlighting the comparison to Freud's theory. At the same time, he began to invoke the importance of denial as opposed to his earlier term "misrecognition" (e.g., Bourdieu and Wacquant 1992: 143; Bourdieu [1989] 1996: 383).[29] Indeed, he even ended up postulating a collective, phylogenic unconscious, perhaps Freud's most outlandish idea (Bourdieu [1998] 2001: 54). Thus, Bourdieu went from merely pointing to the intersubjectively valid nature of action to emphasizing the discrepancy between this working consensus and what the theorist believes.

This point should not be overstated—Bourdieu used this concept of denial in an extremely restricted and substantively reasonable fashion, namely, pertaining to the denial of power differences on the part of the more powerful. Further, Bourdieu's restraint in judging the cognitions of others by their distance from his own remained a notable characteristic of his concrete analyses. Finally, Bourdieu retained a critical understanding of the problems with the epistemology of psychoanalysis.[30] Yet, to the extent that Bourdieu fell back on the Durkheimian way of treating the cognitive components of action as a framework of sorting particularities (and this extent, while not insignificant, is also not overwhelming), there was the potential to resurrect the imposition of arbitrary standards of rightness taken from the authority of the analyst.

---

[29]Here, Bourdieu (e.g., [1997] 2000: 96) himself emphasized that he was thinking of the German term *Verneinung*, sometimes rendered "denegation" in translations of Bourdieu, which in English is simply an archaic form of "denial."

[30]In his posthumous *Self-Analysis*, despite the psychoanalytic title, Bourdieu (2008) mentioned that the appeal of psychoanalysis to French philosophers came from its noble elevation of the freedom of the thinker as opposed to the lowly or common social sciences.

Most critiques of Bourdieu's use of the concept of habitus have been relatively superficial (in that they are general features of any concept, such as simplification and limitation), or they take him to task for his "formulation" of what is taken to be a novel explanatory element. This certainly accords with the nominalism typical of the approach to theory that we explored in chapter 1. But, it leads us to confuse what Bourdieu has said or not said with the nature of habitus—with our general capacity for being that sort of beast that leads us to react in some ways in some situations and not in others.[31] Bourdieu drew on one particular tradition to formulate a more general understanding of aspects of nonrandomness in behavior (we might say personality); there are some defensible reasons (and some not) why he retained a scholastic term as opposed to more simply speaking of "habit" in the contemporary sense, but there is a close relationship between the two, as they grapple with the same real phenomena.[32] And it is not the case that the idea of habit has been shown to be a dead end in our pursuit of these issues; the pragmatists were able to build on first-person understandings of habit in a theoretically

[31] Further, when the habitus is cast as a generic intervening variable in an "explanation" that involves arrows leaving one concept and entering the other, we get the same sorts of vacuous statements that we found in chapter 1, whereby we "explain" someone's communist vote by recourse to the fact that he is a communist. It is important to remember that what is formally empty given one definition of explanation is not necessarily substantively empty. Just as we should not refuse to learn that, in many cases, voting really is merely a matter of preexisting partisan affiliation, so we should not refuse to learn—if it is correct—that much of what seems coherent, serially processed, strategic action is actually a matter of being a certain sort of beast with a set of prereflexive dispositions.

[32] It was largely Mauss ([1934] 1973: 73) who introduced this term into the modern social sciences in the sense of Aristotle's *hexis* as a way of understanding the social shaping of bodily activity. Interestingly, he drew in part from Köhler. This article was drawn to my attention by Lindsay (1996). *Habitus* and "habit" are not the same as one another, but nor is either the same as itself—that is, there are a number of lines of intellectual descent connecting different ideas from Greece to the present, and there is sometimes a bit of slippage in which ones are considered to be identical. Kant ([1798] 2006: 38) argued that in contrast to "facility" (*Leichtigkeit*), which signified possibility, "skill" (*Fertigkeit*), which Kant equated with *habitus*, "signifies subjective-practical necessity, that is, habit (*Gewohnheit*) and so designates a certain degree of will, acquired through the frequently repeated use of one's faculty." Further, using "habit" as opposed to "habitus" did not prevent James ([1890] 1950: 121f) from arguing that habit was the great force for social conservatism by shaping occupational selves, leading parvenus to be unable to buy the right things and speak the right way, keeping social strata from mixing, thus dooming us "to fight out the battle of life upon the lines of our nature or our early choice, and to make the best of a pursuit that disagrees, because there is no other for which we are fitted, and it is too late to begin again."

Habits

The notion of habit has a distinguished career in Western psychology. But, as Camic (1986) has argued, sociology abandoned this idea in part because it became identified with the concerns of behaviorist psychology. This avoidance left a gaping hole in our understanding of personality and its relation to action. Indeed, "habit" now seems one of those terms freighted with an outdated worldview. But, "habit" is no more or less unreasonable a term than "belief," "value," "interest," or any other of the everyday terms borrowed to help explain action. Indeed, it may turn out that habit has a great deal more to offer us than these other terms.

The centrality of habit to a social psychology goes back to Aristotle, who argued that we have to understand virtues not as passions or faculties, but as states of characters, indeed habits.[33] Here, *habit* must be understood as "disposition" or "way of holding oneself" (*hexis*). (This version of habit was related to the explanation of perception as involving consubstantiation discussed in chapter 6, this link being made explicit more by Aquinas than by Aristotle.) It was, however, really William Ockham in the fourteenth century who gave sustained consideration to the idea of habit and shaped how later philosophers would use the term (Fuchs 1952: xii, xv).

Ockham argued that habits are qualities that must be inferred on the basis of the behavior they are supposed to explain. This circularity was to be key for all later serious attempts to understand habits. These habits are both produced by, and productive of, actions; furthermore, the habits are notable for the economy with which they operate, by distilling the fruits of many previous experiences (cf. White 2002: 294). It is such habits that allow us to develop a single, intuitive cognition of the objects in our world of experience (we see "a" ship, for example; compare to de Biran discussed in note 34). Perhaps most interestingly, given the tendency for Western thinkers to consider the will truly free only if it was sheltered from all residues of determinations (which would include past experiences), Ockham also acknowledged the role of habit in the will. Thus, habit refers not only to a *facility* to act but also to an *inclination* to act (Fuchs 1952: 3f, 13, 19f, 47, 67, 69, 77, 79).

In sum, Ockham left us with an idea of habit as a physical nexus in which the residues of past situations and responses to them produced an

---

[33] In the *Nicomachean Ethics* (II 1 or 1103a: 15), Aristotle emphasizes the connection between the word for ethics (*ethike*) and that for habit (*ethos*) and compares (II 5 or 1106a:15) the virtues to other forms of excellence that are acquired through practice and internalized in the body.

agent with a set of predispositions and skills at handling similar situations. While this fundamental understanding of habit was used by the nineteenth-century psychologists such as James (e.g., [1890] 1950: I, 104ff, 561f), it was really Dewey who extended the term in a compelling direction.[34] Dewey's initial use of the language of "reflex" obscured the inherent *intelligence* of habitual action, but he increasingly recognized that one could not approach the cognitive components of action without according habit a central role.[35] We have seen that Bourdieu's exposition of habitus was easily confused with the Durkheimian grid of perception—the theory of arbitrariness tied to an epistemology of clinical authority—thus weakening the leverage that attention to habits

[34]Close in importance is the seminal work of Maine de Biran, which anticipated many of Dewey's arguments. De Biran ([1803] 1929: 47, also 179f) argued that reflective philosophical thought tended to ignore habit because the former "requires a point of support, a resistance: but the most common effect of habit is to take away all resistance, to destroy all friction." His understanding of habit was a coherent part of a global vision of the organism in relation to its environment: de Biran ([1803] 1929: 56f) stressed the active nature of perception (dividing sensation from perception according to whether the organism was relatively passive or active in gathering information, although recognizing that these were poles on a continuum given the close connection between feeling and moving). I mentioned (in note 42, chapter 6) that de Biran emphasized that repeated stimuli tended to evoke lessening response in the organism. De Biran ([1803] 1929: 103ff, 218, 121, 127f) tied this to the increased facility of motion that comes with habit; as we become more skillful, we sense our own motions less. Thus, "habit effaces the line of demarcation between voluntary and involuntary acts, between acquisitions of experience and instinctive operations, between the faculty of feeling [i.e., sensation] and that of perceiving" (104). Indeed, through habit our proprioception becomes confused with exteroception, and indeed we know what our body is doing mediated through our monitoring of objectivity. (De Biran's example is a child learning to play the violin. The child must first concentrate on how he holds his hands as opposed to listening to the sounds he produces; with agility, he *hears* how he moves his body, he no longer *feels* it.) Finally, it is because of our cognitive habits that everything becomes a sign—linked via habit to something else—and objects grow in their meaningfulness and richness over time. Thus, habit is not antithetical to meaning; indeed, even the qualities that we judge as beautiful are built on habits (and hence, contra Kant, conceptions of beauty are historically and socially variable). Durkheim also discussed de Biran's approach to habit ([1883–1884] 2004: 152).

[35]Interestingly, Dewey's ([1922] 1930: 29, 35) example of habit was how one holds one's posture, an idea of bearing (*Haltung* in German) that Bourdieu used as the passive counterpart to the bodily judging *habitus*. (Dewey here explicitly acknowledged the influence of F.M. Alexander, the theorist of bodily posture who pioneered a technique for training movement.) A second example pertained to interpretation of elements in the visual field, where Dewey ([1922] 1930: 32f) proposed that "optical illusions" of the sort examined by Gestalt theorists are due to habit.

can give in prying us loose from the Freudo-Durkheimian approach we found flawed.[36] In contrast to beginning with a Cartesian division between the stuff of the mind and the stuff of the material world and thus emphasizing the arbitrariness of our categories, Dewey (and Merleau-Ponty as well, to a large extent) returned to the Ockhamite idea of habit as a shaping of our apparatus for grappling with the world that points to the nonarbitrariness and indeed fitness of our dispositions. The mountain climber whose actions have become ingrained—who has a set of immediate responses to variations in rock surface that do not require cognitive classifications—is no less skillful for that.

Habit helps us deal with some of the problems we had in thinking through the nature of vision. The Durkheimian approach which emphasizes postperceptual processing led to absurdities, but so did the Gestalt theorists when it was assumed that evolution gave all people a single set of eyes, as it were. But, the optical system develops according to the dynamics laid out by Ockham: we learn to see by seeing, and much of seeing is recognition (James [1890] 1950: II, 103f). Unless eyes are exposed to certain forms of stimuli at a young age, they never recognize them afterward. Western ethnographers report their surprise when finding that their non-Western subjects did not recognize the shapes in a movie as people, did not see faraway objects as cattle, and so on. We generally *see* figure 7.1 as three dimensional. In many cases, no one has ever "taught" us this, yet those raised in very different cultures will not see the third dimension. It is not that they lack a faculty for abstraction; it is that those who grow up in a human environment largely structured with rectangles (of which there are few in nature), as well as a repertoire of two-dimensional representations, develop an internal capacity to recognize the cube as such.[37]

It might be fair to say that, similarly, one never experiences a quality *once*. Just as no one truly tastes wine his or her first time, so more generally, we develop our receptive powers through repeated interactions with the world. The "funded" nature of experience, which seemed radically destabilizing when we first followed Dewey in accepting it, turns out to be quite tame; it is such funding that allows us to develop our sensory capacities to fit the world that we do in fact encounter, and it is repeated encounters that gives us the habitual responses that allow us to know where we are. Indeed, this suggests that some interpersonal differences in the experience of the seeming "same" things, easily ascribed to error, compulsion, or maliciousness, have a simpler basis. In chapter 6, I raised the

---

[36]An extremely incisive and thoughtful critique of Bourdieu's approach by Schatzki (1987, esp. 130) leads to conclusions parallel to those drawn here.

[37]Köhler (1938: 236, 239, 273) proposed that physical neural traces or remnants of past experience guided such perception and future neural activity. He seems to have been basically correct. He also suggested that this could account for mental activity that transcended the concrete phenomenological experience, a more difficult issue.

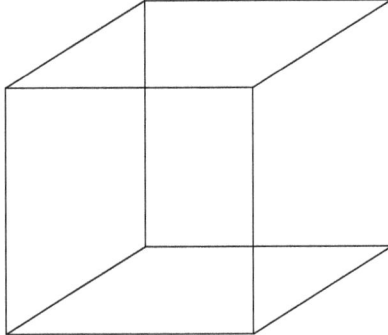

Figure 7.1 Necker cube

example of the person who dislikes a healthy food, perhaps because of some trauma. Such traumatic experiences with particular foods, the more innocuous the better, have been a staple for cheap comedy. More common in real life than "Jell-o-phobia" seems to be the case of someone who has relatively recently come down with food poisoning from one type of food and is unusually sensitive to the presence of toxins. Her conviction that this egg "is" rotten may be a temporarily heightened sensitivity to actually existing sulfur compounds in a nonrotten egg.

Similarly, we should expect social perception to have such variation across persons and times. In every interaction, there are moments of approach and moments of avoidance, trust, and suspicion. Given two persons, one of whom has a greater sensitivity to signals of distrust and avoidance, we expect this one to have fewer trusting relations than the other—that is, this one encounters fewer trustworthy people. Such self-confirming views are not "mistaken," any more than the person who recoils from the egg was wrong—or any more than someone unable to appreciate a century egg or a *balut* (fertilized duck egg) because of a reaction to the similar compounds is mistaken. In all cases, the identified elements *are* present. The necessarily funded nature of qualitative perception inexorably leads us to understand the veridical nature of our engagement of the world as bound up with the formation of habits that both change our worlds and lead to differences in our experiences of it.

This is key, because we might be tempted to believe that we have worked our way back to the Durkheimian view of cognition criticized in chapter 4. That is, we here also reject any simple correspondence of our perception to the physical construction of objects and note the role of the nature of the seeing mind. Perhaps (one might object) the only difference between this approach and that of Durkheim is where we draw the boundary of "the mind": one might say that phenomenologists tend to have a somewhat smaller sense of the mind, as they retreat to within the horizon of consciousness and exclude, for example, the neural processing done close to the optic nerve. If such processing happens according to the grid of perception, then the opposition between the approach taken here and the Durkheimian is an illusion of shifting the terrain of analysis.

This is a serious issue, and by aligning the two approaches most closely, the key differences are brought into starkest relief. The Durkheimian perspective, like the phenomenological, assumes that there is a mental organization of perception, but it also assumes that the percepts in themselves have no necessary organization; the mental organization of culture is an intrinsically arbitrary/culturally willful one.[38] In contrast, the line of reasoning pursued here leads us to insist the active nature of the eye comes not in applying top-down definitions (as if the eye were some dour judge subsuming particular cases into the code Napoléon), but in *recognizing* objects—cultural organization comes not in terms of (arbitrary) mental schemes, but in our actual physical organization of the world that we are to experience. Habit is the recognition of the handle of a tool we are used to using; it is a shaping of our structures of reaching out so that they grasp the objects that are there. And, when we are wrong, as James ([1890] 1950) says, our mistakes are to see things that usually *are* where they are not, and not to see things that are never anywhere.

Thus, habit is a general process of an organism shaping itself to an environment (and in many cases, an environment that it has helped shape) (Dewey [1922] 1930: 14–16, 40–42). Practically speaking, it matters little whether some behavioral pattern is phylogenetically evolved (e.g., binocular vision) or ontogenetically learned (e.g., learning how to interpret vanishing points in the visual field). In either case, the abilities and reactions of the organism are a product of its interaction with the particularities of its surroundings (also see Merleau-Ponty 1962: 139, cf. 79, 144; Pepper 1966: 424).

Habit and Motive

The circular nature of activity—habits from the environment and the environment from habits—that we saw originally pointed to by Ockham might lead us to imagine a perfect seamless equilibrium, indeed a state of unconscious flow, as the natural end point to such a process. On the contrary, argued Dewey ([1922] 1930: 179f), "life is interruptions and recoveries." It is the continual need to readjust, exchange, or revise habits that we call consciousness.

But, it is not that we can oppose conscious willful action to conventional unconscious habitual behavior. The parsing of action into "constraint" and "agency" that, as we saw, bedevils sociological theory leads us, wrote Dewey ([1922] 1930: 24, 30) to "eject the habit from the thought of

[38]It is worth reminding ourselves that Durkheim *himself* did not believe that this was true for modern societies, and he only held for earlier ones that the non-arbitrariness was solely found in the regularities of their social organization of experience.

ourselves and conceive it an evil power which has somehow overcome us." According to this way of thinking, the true person (following Kant [1785] 1938) must be free not only from the determinations of other persons but also from the determinations of nature, up to and including her own nature. That is, our habits are seen as "outside" us, compromising the willfulness of our action. What is left of "us"—and all that can be left, as Hegel ([1821] 1967) noted, when we empty the will of every concrete determination—is a formal abstraction, undetermined, yes, but indeterminate.[39] In opposition, Dewey ([1922] 1930: 38, 43), like Ockham, argued that habits *are* our will; without a preexisting habit we cannot even construct the mental image of our idea. Rather than habit being that which subtracts from or demeans our character, character itself is "the interpenetration of habits"; it is habit that leads to that consistency over time that we consider to distinguish us as individuals.[40]

Habit is then our term for our general capacity to "tool ourselves" to fit the world; it is because we have such a capacity that we are able to establish an ontological complicity between our subjectivity and the world—we are "this sided" in that we are shaped by the "other side." It is for this reason that the faith in our ability to retrieve the qualities of the outside world is not a naïve one. Further, we see that habits may successfully complete tasks that cannot be replicated by conceptual thought, in the same way that we may be able to throw a curve ball but cannot define how a curve ball is different from a straight ball. This, we recall, was precisely the defining characteristic of judgment and the reason to pursue aesthetic theory. Thus, the abstract faculty "judgment" may be resolved into an organized set of habits. Now, when we first followed Kant in deriving the idea of judgment, we seemed to emphasize a relatively passive relation to the world. Of course, even this passivity was less passive than the behaviorist version, as we can follow al-Kindī and de Biran and emphasize the active nature of the eye.

---

[39]Kant ([1797] 1991: 207): "An *aptitude* (*habitus*) is a facility in acting and a subjective perfection of *choice*. But not every such *facility* is a *free* aptitude (*habitus liberates*); for if it is a *habit* (*assuetudo*), that is, a uniformity in action that has become a *necessity* through frequent repetition, it is not one that proceeds from freedom." Thus, Kant ([1798] 2006: 40) explains why another's habits evoke disgust in us—they threaten to reduce us to beast. "As a rule all habits are reprehensible."

[40]For example, our skillful use of a tool is habitual and willful. When the unexpected occurs and we need to readjust, we may be both more conscious and less willful (cf. Merleau-Ponty [1942] 1963: 125). Giddens (1979: 59, 218) discussed the importance of habits in order to explicate the importance of nonintended reproduction (e.g., the way that a language is—according to Giddens—reproduced through speaking). But this was related to his (at least provisional) acceptance of the idea that motivations are paradigmatically *reasons*; I have argued that these two should be treated as analytically distinct.

But we also were forced to accept that, despite the possibility of sound judgment, judgments of taste were *all* "cultivated." This was true for other forms of perception cum action beginning from vision itself. Thus, a consideration of judgment necessarily brings us to consider our engagement with the world via habit. This was basically Bourdieu's approach, and the reason for the close relation between habitus as a matrix of division (compatible with the Durkheimian approach) and the habitus that is inseparable from bearing or hexis. We find these *are* united because habits are a way of being that generates a set of responses to divisions that are not within the body, but without. Habit is the successful response to the qualitative feature of the environment, and not the subsumption of that experience into a class of abstractions.[41]

This is because there is a close connection, indeed a duality, between habit as a set of dispositions and the qualitative nature of our environment. Pepper (1966: 160f) proposed that we may also speak of "passive dispositions"—a mosquito, for example, has a passive disposition to be swatted, in that this becomes activated when the biter is brought into conjunction with those with an active disposition not to be bitten. A nauseating apple has a passive disposition to be vomited—this is what its quality *is*. In other words, the qualities of objects (which, as Dewey said, may be anchored in the response attendant to them) are mirror to our dispositions, and these dispositions are habits that have themselves grown up in a world populated by these objects.[42]

We are now in a better position to specify what of "first-person" experience we are interested in, for we can make a distinction between what we will continue to call motivations (in which we are greatly interested) and answers to Why questions (which are of less interest). By motivations, we will mean "that part of subjectivity which lies behind and alongside the action"—without fooling ourselves that we yet know what this

---

[41]Christian Ehrenfels ([1890] 1988: 106), in the piece that initiated Gestalt theory, argued that we recognize Gestalt qualities precisely when we recognize the "habitus" (here in the sense of bearing or overall nature) of objects as being crucial in organizing them by similarity, even if this "stubbornly resist[s] analysis into relations of identity between individual constituent parts." That is, we see that, say, two passages of music are similar in terms of their overall mood, even though we are unable to find any *parts* that are the same. Finally, it is worth noting that habit satisfies some of the technical requirements of the Gestalt, namely. its existence as a transposable form. Merleau-Ponty ([1942] 1963: 30) points out that our handwriting remains the same when we write on a chalkboard as it does when we write on paper, although the sets of muscles involved are not the same; this habit is a formal organization of reflexes, not an "and-sum" of single reflexes.

[42]"It is thus that the man who is angry sees on the face of his opponent the objective quality of asking for a punch in the nose" (Sartre 1956: 163). Sartre and the angry man are correct—noses *do* afford punching.

means to us. (In the next chapter, we will be able to replace this term.) But, we do at least know the difference between this and those later justifications (or "motives" in Mills's [1940] sense), which are less useful as data (also see Campbell 1996: 68). It is not merely that actors' *abstractions* are of no more inherent value than are analysts'. It is that what we ultimately want to get at is experience and not propositions *about* experience (see Merleau-Ponty [1942] 1963: 183, 185; Collins 2008: 337). This is because the motivation *is* the qualitative experience; motivation is the subjective correlative to the intersubjectively valid qualities of social objects.

Of course, in many cases we are limited to retrospective accounts from actors. But, both by the nature of experience and by the principle of contemporaneity, we are forced to recognize that actors' retrospective accountings-for—their justificatory explanations—may lack environmental validity when it comes to the environment in which we are interested (that of the original act).[43] This does not mean that such reports are useless; on the contrary, they can be most enlightening as long as we can understand them as responses to a particular social task and not as immediate data on experience. Even more important, the same sorts of accountings-for that are of limited utility in understanding past actions have a straightforward meaning for us when they are instead cast forward in time. But, what they capture is the subjective representation of *current* position (and not future action). Thus, we may be better off understanding the nature of motivation by asking about things not (yet) done than things actually accomplished, for the constellation of experienced forces has not yet been dissipated, and the process of forming cognitive justifications not yet begun.

To summarize, the qualitative nature of experience is correlative to imperatives for action—to experience a fright narrows the range of relevant actions. It is such responses to the environment that we here call "motivations." Attention to habit makes us understand that such motivations need not be identified with *accounts* of motivations, that is, "motives" or justifications (here see Scott and Lyman 1968). As we have seen in chapter 2, there is no reason to think that justifications are antithetical to motivations, and that the study of motivations requires the negation of justification. But, it does suggest that to understand motivation we will need more than justifications—in particular, we need a contextualization of experience, which is what has brought us to field theory.

---

[43]This is in no way to align the argument made here with the destructive method of Freudianism and to backpedal on any of the claims made in chapter 3. Far from emphasizing the limited utility of retrospective accounts, psychoanalysis decides to provoke just this sort of response, but lacks any reliable technique for retrieving information from these notoriously unreliable data.

The Role of Habit in Field Theory

We began this chapter with a search for a rigorous approach to a social aesthetics. Elementary considerations suggested that a field theory might satisfy our requirements, at least for certain special cases. We then followed two paths whereby a field theoretic approach has been derived for the social sciences: the first a social-psychological one beginning with the experience of valences and the other a sociological one beginning with the pursuit of values. We found these to converge and to be understood as convergent in the work of Bourdieu on aesthetics. At the same time, we found ourselves brought to the consideration of habits.

This suggests that Bourdieu's emphasis on field and habitus, rather than being some sort of idiosyncratic assemblage (one perhaps requiring some sort of idiopathic genealogy [cf. Bourdieu 1985a]), was a necessary consequence of pursuing the nature of concrete judgments. Indeed, we may say that to some extent the two words (field and habitus) describe the same phenomenon: regularity in experienced valence, one from the collective-spatial perspective and the other from the individual-temporal perspective.

Certainly, it is only the idea of habit that links a field theoretic conception with the general aesthetics of action. The "ontological complicity" of the actor and the world assumed by field theorists (see Bourdieu [1966] 1969: 182; 1985a; 1993: 86), far from being some controversial assumption, follows necessarily from the actor as a bundle of habits. Speaking impressionistically, we may say that just as repeatedly stroking a needle with a magnet turns it into something that will respond to a magnetic field (a phenomenon called "hysteresis" [cf. Lizardo and Strand 2011]), so too it is our capacity to form habits that allows us to develop into the sorts of things that can respond to field effects. Habit, then, is the theory of how we come to have that sort of ontological complicity that allows us to go from the general question of judgment to a field theory—that is, when certain external conditions pertaining to the organization of experiences are such that the processes of habit formation *are* correlative to trajectory through a set of positions.[44]

Habit thus is an indispensible part of any social aesthetics. At the same time, this notion of habit is utterly general; as with the other bits of a vocabulary that we have developed so far, we have solved no problems nor gained deep insight. But this was not our goal, and properly so—all we have looked for is a noncontradictory vocabulary that allows us to frame questions that pertain to the real world. As Moretti (2005: 26) has said, we should beware of the theorist's penchant to ask only the questions for

---

[44]Further, we have seen that this ontological complicity is only a first approximation; any trajectory through the field implies both the potential for recalibration of habits to internalize new affordances, and the at least initially unsatisfactory nature of such recalibration.

which he has an excellent answer. No advance will be made that way. The key is to identify extremely hard problems and then perhaps to attack them in usually clear and simple conditions. The field approach suggests that the difficult problem may be simplest when we have a single qualitative experience that varies in intensity. The next chapter considers the application of existing approaches to such a case, which can be the basis for more general conclusions regarding the explanatory principles of a social aesthetics.

Chapter 8

Fields and Games

In chapter 7, we saw that, merely on logical grounds, a field theory in which quality was linked to position could satisfy our need for a rigorous social aesthetics—a coherent approach to an understanding of the cognitive components of action. The logic was that qualitative experience can be attached to situations that may be structured in such a way that we consider them positions. The resulting conception of field is a narrow one; we only allow for a single qualitative experience varying in intensity. As we move away from this pure case of a single quality, we may lose some of our rigor, but most understandings of a field in the social sciences propose that what is distinctive is not that there is a single underlying experience, but rather that the mutual orientations of persons follow a single principle of organization.

We shall accept this somewhat broader conception of field as we investigate field theory as an avenue to pursue a social aesthetics. While not all social action takes place in fields, that which does is of key interest to us because the mutual alignment characteristic of the field leads social objects to possess a greater "objectivity." That is, because of a field's *eigengesetzlichkeit*—the restricted range of imperatives guiding action—social objects have a greater tendency to be themselves, in the sense of being distinctly that which is distinct to them. We may later be able to extend our approach to the cases in which things are murkier, but there is no shame in beginning with whatever clarity we can find. Here, we can begin by investigating the general promise of a field explanation; in the final chapter, we draw lessons for how the social sciences can reorient themselves to the task of explanation more generally.

WHAT IS A SOCIAL FIELD?

Fields and Spaces

In chapter 7, we saw various thinkers, with more or less conscious recognition of their part in a common enterprise,[1] consistently appeal to the

---

[1] For example, see Lewin ([1949] 1999: 30, 32); Bourdieu and Wacquant (1992: 97), and Swartz (1997: 123).

idea of "field," but we have not seen the emergence of a clearly defined explanatory approach. Most field theorists in the social sciences are inspired by the analogy to a field of force as in classical magnetism.[2] But, they often find it difficult to formulate how and why such a conception can be a reasonable one for social life and, as a result, either bastardize the idea of field to a mere heuristic topology, or confound it with a field of contestation completely reducible to the summation of individual actions. Retrospectively, we can sympathetically understand these temptations; analytically, we can explain their insufficiency.

For the Gestalt theorists interested in the field of perception, it was of course natural that the topological aspect of the field would rise to the fore; the field is phenomenologically experienced as a projection of reality onto a space of particular dimensionality. But when Lewin adopted this basic framework for social-psychological explanation, he turned the field from something that had phenomenological validity for the actor to something that was merely an analytic convention, and generally an idiosyncratic one at that. Unfortunately, it is easy for others to make the same error and imagine that a field is simply an analytic area of simplified dimensionality in which we position persons or institutions, and that a field analysis is simply one of determining the contours of a "social space" (whatever that may be).

Now first, in the technical sense, this is not correct. While a field is, as Bourdieu (1993: 72) says, a structured set of positions, and positions can often be understood in spatial terms (see Brown 1936a: 476), the two are not the same. On the one hand, not all sets of relative positions can be understood as a conventional space, since "distances" may not work according to spatial logic (which implies, for example, that the sum of A's distance to B and C's distance to B cannot be less than A's distance to C) (see Brown 1936b:79f; Heider 1958: 138f). On the other hand, not all spatial models imply a field. The classical mechanics of collision requires positioning objects in a space with a finite number of dimensions but in no way invokes the idea of field.

More important, this trivialization of field theory into some exotic cousin of factor analysis misses the substantive point. Rather than being some conventional act of data reduction that is carried out by the analyst whenever the ratio of empirical complexity to intellectual laziness goes beyond some point, field theory is a substantive assertion. Whether a set of persons or their actions actually forms a field must be an empirical question and cannot be true by definition or methodology. A field theoretic analysis requires that the position of persons in a field must be based

---

[2] Although see Brunswik's (1952: 44) skepticism regarding the connection between Gestalt psychology and electromagnetic field theory; Bourdieu has both compared social fields to the magnetic field (1971: 161) and castigated those who do so ([1984] 1988: 149); see Bourdieu's later work ([1989] 1996: 132) for a comparison to a gravitational field.

on their orientations to each other, either directly through their interpersonal relations (cf. Lundberg 1939: 104, 263) or in a mediated manner via shared goals (which themselves turn out to be coordinations of the relations of the actors).

If there is any reason to take the field theoretic terminology seriously, it is because we believe that such alignment can produce affordances, imperatives for action, and that these imperatives can be attached to position. As we shall see below, sociological theory frequently admits that alignments can produce imperatives for action—for what else are norms but this?—but either ties these imperatives to a concrete set of role partners or immediately generalizes them to abstractions (such as "culture") that require internalization on the parts of actors if they are not to immediately dissipate. Field theory starts from the assumption that these imperatives can be attached to *position*: locally variable, but with a global organization; phenomenologically outside us as individuals, but present in us as organized aggregate. This chapter attempts to explain how field theoretic approaches to alignment satisfy our need for a social aesthetics and how in some cases these explanatory principles may be applied even where we do not have a field, properly speaking.

If we do in fact have a case of a social field in which affordances—felt action imperatives—are attached to position, the intersubjective validity of these affordances allows them to be treated as external (hence the idea that actors are "in" a field). Somewhat more prosaically, we often speak loosely of "social forces" but have a hard time specifying what we mean in terms of acting persons when describing how these forces have their effects. It may be that field theory—field theory in the specific sense of the analysis of a field of forces—is useful in beginning from the position of a person subject to these forces (or pseudoforces, as they may turn out to be). For the phenomenological feeling that "something is required" may provide the starting point for an understanding of qualitative experience that cannot be adequately captured if we restrict ourselves to subsumptive judgments. Further, this starting point, we shall see, necessarily pulls us toward field theoretic issues.[3]

Phenomenologically, certain situations may have the quality of impelling us in a certain direction, in that we feel the rightness of a certain form of action. Immediately commencing a detailed analysis of how these apparent forces are produced may be Herculean, and we may gain great

---

[3] As Köhler (1938: 334; also see 277, 332, 337, 342, 345, 357) said, "I know of only one class of physical facts that represents the properties of a given entity beyond this entity and thus can 'do something' about a second thing with reference to the first. This is the class of 'forces' or 'fields.'" Köhler was admirably consistent in locating this force physically in the neural traces of past experience, for it is here that we can locate, literally and chemically, a gradient (e.g., a proton gradient in the axon of a neuron)—a slope down which thought will roll (see chapter 7, note 38).

analytic insight merely by beginning to map out an overall logic to the dispersion of such forces across positions.[4] Imagine, then, that a phenomenological inquiry identifies "social forces"—that is, what would feel to actors as if they were forces. Rather than explain the social-psychological processes whereby a constellation of actions and ideas generates such felt qualities, we simply attempt to organize reports regarding these felt qualities: which people feel them to what degree in what circumstances. Doing this puts us well on our way to a field theory.

To summarize, in chapter 7 we determined that a set of organized vectors satisfied the requirements of a field, and if the qualities that actors perceive in their environment have action imperatives that we can treat as pseudoforces, we may be able to think of the effect of these pseudoforces in field theoretic terms.[5] Let us then consider the general characteristics of field theories and then what they might look like when applied to the task of social explanation.

General Characteristics of Such Field Theory

To understand field theory, we should start with fluid mechanics, the study of how a continuous substance with some degree of elasticity (or compressibility) behaves in different conditions. In the eighteenth century, physicists developed equations for such fluid mechanics that linked a "flow" to positions in a three-dimensional space. For example, one can predict the increase in the speed of the flow at any point as water proceeding through a straight trough encounters a funnel-like area of constriction. (Since the same amount of water must get through a smaller space, it must go faster, as can be observed in streams.) If we were standing above this trough and looking down, we might imagine dropping a cork repeatedly at different places and measuring its position 2 seconds later. If we drew an arrow from the beginning to ending point, this

---

[4] Again, it should be emphasized that it is empirically possible that there be no overall logic. I propose that some principles discussed for field analysis are still applicable to such a degenerate case, but this is an open question.

[5] Cassirer ([1910] 1923: 163; also see [1928–1940] 1996: 22 on fields and spaces) explicitly drew the connection between such field theories and qualities. "We discover a physical phenomenon . . . at a certain point of space, while we are obliged to locate its 'cause' at a point of space removed from it. In order to establish a continuous connection between these two conditions, we postulate a medium for them by conceiving the space between them continuously filled with certain qualities, which can be expressed by pure numerical values. . . . The more inclusively and consciously physics makes use of the concept of the ether, the more clearly it appears that the object thus signified cannot be understood as an isolated, individual thing of perception, but only as a unification and concentration of objectively valid, measurable relations."

would be a vector indicating the direction and speed of flow in any one place. The whole set of possible vectors represents the dynamics of the fluid in question.[6]

Imagine that we are not really interested in the flow of the water itself but only the movement of the objects that we drop in the water. In that case, the flow can be considered a potential for transmitted force that becomes actualized once we do drop our cork. Now, consider a magnet. We can do something similar by dropping a small piece of iron near it and seeing which way the iron moves; again, we can compose a set of vectors. But in this case, no fluid exists that explains why the iron seems to be carried along in a certain path; the same is true of motion induced by gravity or electricity (Hesse 1970: 181; Rummel 1975: 26; Köhler 1920: 70; also cf. Köhler 1947: 127). Field theories are theories that treat the motion induced in some substances as if there were a fluid present; they link a set of vectors to positions in space.[7]

Perhaps the most important such theory both historically and as an example is classical electromagnetism. If there are distinctive characteristics to field theory, they may have been most apparent in this realm. If we look at classical electromagnetism, we find that the general form of explanation has a number of interesting characteristics (here, see Gillispie 1960: 475; Maxwell [1891] 1954: 68; Koffka 1935: 42, 117; Köhler 1947: 300; Hesse 1970: 196). First, we explain changes in the states of some elements (e.g., a static field induces motion in a charged particle) but need not appeal to changes in states of other elements (i.e., "causes"); instead we make reference to a quality of space or position. Second, the elements have particular attributes that make them susceptible to the field effect (e.g., particles may differ in the degree and direction of charge). Third, changes in state involve an interaction between the field and the existing states of the elements (e.g., a particle of positive charge may move one way and one of negative charge another). Fourth, the field without the elements is only a potential for the creation of force, without any existent force. Finally, the field itself is organized and differential. In other words, at any position in the field we have a vector of potential force, and these vectors are neither identical nor randomly distributed. It is these main points that define field theory as a form of explanation for the social sciences.

---

[6]Such a fluid dynamics-based approach has already been successfully applied to social data for the movement of persons across organizational positions by Stewman (1986, esp. eq. 13; also Stewman 1988; Stewman and Yeh 1991).

[7]Thus, Faraday proposed seeing space as filled with tubes of a fluid flowing in a certain direction (Gillispie 1960: 462f; also see 390). Interestingly, although there were fluid theories of light at the turn of the nineteenth century, these were not the basis for the later field theory as they tended to have a theological orientation and a semivitalist understanding of light and fire (Cantor 1983: 91f).

Field Theories versus General Linear Reality

It is worth pointing out how utterly at odds such a conception is with the conventional understanding of causality in the social sciences that we discussed in chapters 1 and 2. According to this conception, our units of analysis (e.g., individuals) have attributes, with mutually exclusive attributes often considered instances of a "variable." For example, few people are both high school dropouts and hold college degrees, so we may consider "level of education" a variable; similarly, one cannot both have voted for the Republican in the last presidential election and have voted for the Democrat, so "vote choice" can be a variable. Relations between units of analysis are interpreted as by-products of relations between variables, and causality is said to exist when a change in state in one variable produced by external manipulation would *impel* a change in state in another variable (education → Democratic vote). Causality follows a mental image of external impulsion taken from classical mechanics (basically the conception of Hobbes) but recasts this in terms of variables, as opposed to substances (a set of assumptions about the world that Abbott [1988b] called "general linear reality").

Our current methods are almost uniformly based on such epistemological assumptions and consequently form an inventory of ways of linking variation in one attribute of some unit to variation in another of its attributes. Since sociologists tend to be suspicious of things that do not vary—after all, sociology's claim to a domain distinct from those of biology and psychology largely rested on the irreducibility of variation—this methodological imperative has generally been a congenial one. But it is folly to go on to declare that the essence of explanation *is* explaining variation, and that other approaches are nonscientific.

In his classic critique of the conventional methodology of the social sciences, Stanley Lieberson (1985) gave the hypothetical example of a sociologist attempting to understand why things fall. Methodologically acute, our researcher assembles a set of different objects: a cannonball, a feather, a potato, and so on and begins to drop them, measuring their acceleration downward. Linking this acceleration (the "dependent variable") to various attributes of the plummeting objects, such as volume, weight, composition, density (the "independent variables"), our researcher may (if lucky) come up with a rather large R^2 (the measure of explained variance) and conclude that he understands why things fall.

"What is going on here? Something must be wrong if social researchers think that they have a full grasp of falling objects without ever invoking gravity." Lieberson (1985: 103) argues that this researcher has confused variation in the acceleration or accumulated velocity with the fact of acceleration itself—a constant and hence invisible to us. "What we get at is variation in the impact of the force. But we do not get at what the force is."

Here, Lieberson left matters, happy to have used this example to make an important point. But, our researcher may, thus enlightened, now diligently go back to try to "get at" what this force is. Our researcher will not get far. Few of us are Newtons, and even Sir Isaac did not feel that he had "gotten at" this force (Jammer 1957: 137). Are then further efforts necessarily in vain? In between the bumbling foolishness of our researcher's first attempt and the most sophisticated science in human history lies field theory.

It was a protofield theory—including the postulation of an invisible "occult force"—that was able to explain regularities in acceleration due to gravity, both on earth and in the heavens. Field theory posits an enveloping gravitational field that we can neither see nor measure except via its effects and, instead of trying to maximize explained variance, proceeds by assuming in principle a perfectly simple determination. As Ernst Cassirer ([1910] 1923: 254) said, "Galileo did not discover the law of falling bodies by collecting arbitrary observations of sensuously real bodies, but by defining hypothetically the concept of uniform acceleration."[8] Indeed, we see here a transformation of the idea of "gravity" from a variable characteristic of *bodies* ("heaviness") to a uniform characteristic of *space*.

It is one thing to earnestly wish to be the Galileo—or the Maxwell—of the social sciences. It is another to actually find explanatory principles in the field theoretic approach that are relevant, novel, and shed light on what otherwise are confusing aspects of the task of social explanation. If we consider the distinguishing characteristics of field theory with reference to social phenomena, we may see the attraction of field theory as a general social aesthetics.

Explication of These Points with Reference to Social Phenomena

The first distinctive characteristic of field theory was that it explains changes in the states of some elements without appealing to changes in states of other elements ("causes") (see Mey [1965] 1972: 7). Instead, explanation makes reference to a characteristic of the *position* of the element, a characteristic that is usually seen as a vector (Hesse 1970: 192; Köhler [1917] 1925: 35; Speigel 1961), which is to say a combination of an intensity and a direction. If we were able to speak of action as a change

---

[8]Lewin (1949/1999: 32; also see Marrow 1969: 9) cited this passage in his tribute to Cassirer, from whom he took a course in philosophy; it was also used by Brandt (1952: 47) in the first introduction of field theory to the social sciences and by Heider (1958: 4). For other field theoretic discussions of the importance of this example, see Mey ([1965] 1972: 92, 239). The obsession with Galileo (as opposed to, say, Newton) seems somewhat strange both because Galileo never achieved the breakthrough to be able to formally solve the problem of motion induced by gravity and because, unlike Newton, Galileo was more solidly within the mechanist tradition. Indeed, Galileo's own impatience with field theories led

of position, then such a vector would be the simplest way of distilling the relationship between local environment and future position: the vector is a push, an imperative, in one direction. And at no point do we rely on tortuous analogies to mechanical causality (although of course those who compulsively need to see such causality everywhere are in no way hindered from recasting the field effect in those terms at a minor cost of a loss of parsimony).

There is, however, one way in which a field theory used as a social aesthetics may differ from a physical field theory, and this is in the nature of the organization of positions. All field theories in physics employ metric spaces; that is, the position of any object is defined by its placement on each of a set of infinitely divisible dimensions that follow a logic that distances add as real numbers.[9] But, position in a social field is generally understood to be an analytic construct pertaining to complexes of relations.[10] For this reason, it is not *necessarily* the case that position must be defined in terms of continuous dimensions. For example, one's position in an occupational hierarchy may be one of twelve discrete categories, not all of which can be ordered in terms of "greater than."

---

him to castigate Kepler for having "lent his ear and his assent to the moon's dominion over the waters, to occult properties, and to such puerilities," namely, linking the tides to the—obviously impossible—influence of the moon (Galileo [1629] 1967: 445, 420). Kepler, in contrast, had been "profoundly impressed" by Gilbert's work on magnetism (Gillispie 1960: 32, 120), and by treating gravity as akin to magnetic lines of force, Kepler used this phenomenon of the tides to conceive of celestial gravity as a general attractive force (Jammer 1957: 83, 89). (While Galileo [1629] 1967: 399f] was also convinced by "the magnetic philosophy of William Gilbert," he was so enamored of his own [fallacious] explanation of tides as a massive sloshing that he felt no need to appeal to magnetism here.) Galileo's appeal seems to be in part because to early twentieth-century Germans, facing an intolerant conservative militarist government with an obvious affinity for censorship, Galileo represented the struggle against contemporary obscurantism (as in Bertolt Brecht's [1955] *Life of Galileo*; also see Einstein's introduction to *Two World Systems* [Einstein 1967: xviif]).

[9]In most cases, we might find that distances add according to Cartesian principles (e.g., $d_{ij} + d_{jk} = \text{sqrt}\,[d_{ij}^2 + d_{jk}^2 - 2\,d_{ij}d_{jk}\cos(\theta)]$, where θ is the angle between vectors i-j and j-k); things are naturally more complex in the field theory of general relativity. In the field theory of quantum mechanics, time is treated as imaginary. I do not pretend to understand this.

[10]Further, it is also possible to derive the same field theoretic conception directly from relations between relations; doing so, Cassirer ([1910] 1923: 21, 76f; 1910: 100) linked a scientific approach based on relations to a geometry of positions as opposed to one of measure (magnitude). The former, he argues, requires that "we restore intuition [*Anschauung*] to its full scope and independence." But, rather than the intuition of the individual figure (somewhat like that of Faust, meditating on the meaning of one distinct form), this intuition is an investigation of the *relation* of forms, their dependency on one another.

The second point was that elements have particular attributes that lead (or do not lead) them to be susceptible to a field effect. For example, free neutrons are (nearly) unaffected by a magnetic field.[11] Similarly, the failure of some set of persons to be influenced by a social field does not disprove the claims regarding the existence of the field. Of course, if we find no commonality among these persons other than their immunity to predicted effects, we are allowing the field theory to be self-confirming, a pathological result. We must be able to figure out, sooner or later, which persons are and which are not susceptible to an effect, just as we can specify which metals are drawn to a magnet. Indeed, such a specification is as integral a part of the field theory as is the description of the field.

In contrast, in conventional explanation, scope conditions (the range of situations over which some purported generalization holds true) are always considered accessories to the "main" part of the theory. The importance of such accessories is repeatedly emphasized but just as repeatedly forgotten. Because the great theory, we assume, is the general one, accessory statements that then limit the scope of application seem like the small print that tells you that you have not yet, in fact, won the grand prize that you seem to be promised at first.

Yet, such embarrassment at having to specify scope conditions is bizarre since it is really the set of scope conditions that comprises (or should be seen as comprising) any significant theory. The truly abstract statement (e.g., that "people rely on general statuses as a key to task competence") is as empty and useless as a bumper-sticker philosophy. The field theoretic conception may be attractive precisely because it does not relegate the problematization of the actual terrain of applicability of claims to an epistemological ghetto of "scope conditions."

The third point was that we find not only that some elements are immune to the field effect but also that different elements behave differently (Verschuur 1993: 101). This variability has a corollary: we are not continuously close to tautology by saying "the field has certain effects . . . except where it doesn't," for in many cases we can exploit the patterning of reactions to the same position using conventional understandings of individual-level attributes. Thus, those of, say, different birth cohorts or different educational backgrounds may respond differently when placed in the same field position. To some degree, it may well be (as some would like to think) that individual-level differences turn out to be explicable as field effects—as the result of previous trajectory through the field, as Bourdieu has emphasized. But this is irrelevant to the issue of the nature of the production of the field effect; all

---

[11]Because neutrons seem to be composed of other particles, as opposed to being treatable as neutrally charged points, they have a minor magnetic moment. In general, things become complicated in an electromagnetic field, for the measured value of field strength at a point depends on the inertial reference frame used.

that is necessary for a field explanation is that we have *some* external leverage on the dispersion of constitutions.

This variability is not a disappointing "residual variance" that we have not explained, for it comes from a key premise of field theory, namely, that the field effect involves some interaction between the value of the field at any position and the states of the elements within the field. The "force" that impinges on some object in a field is then a function both of the field effect and of some characteristic of the object itself. Köhler (1938: 360f) emphasized that this leads the understanding of the force that acts on persons to be different from the seemingly similar idea of force in, say, Durkheimian sociology. The Durkheimian social force is something that impinges on us from without—it necessarily enters as constraint.[12] Indeed, Durkheim's most extended discussion of the nature of these forces, his derivation of the very idea of force from the moral nature of social experience (Durkheim [1912] 1954: 208–210), emphasizes that we only feel social forces *as* forces because these social imperatives contradict our own egoistic impulses. Thus, in this root conception of force, the object is even *beyond* passivity; far from the force expressing the nature of the object, the force only appears as such because of the willful *resistance* of the object.[13]

In contrast (as we saw in chapter 7), Köhler's understanding of the vector is that it is fundamentally a relation between the self (with its particularities) and the object (ditto), and this relation is one of calling out, not hitting against. Thus, while for the Durkheimian approach, the phenomenological validity of forces—that is, that we may experience social pressure—tends to increase the misplaced concreteness of "society" as an abstract entity, for the field theoretic approach, it leads to an exploration of the configuration of a local situation.

The fourth point was that the field without the elements is only a potential for the creation of force, without any existent force (Brandt

---

[12]See, for example, Durkheim ([1902–1903] 1961: 29; [1897] 1951: 89). I recognize that despite his repeated insistence that social facts are forms of external constraint, Durkheim also argued that, at least in certain fortunate circumstances, social facts occur as a perfect harmony between the inner and outer and hence have "nothing of constraint" in them. This is not Durkheim qualifying his understanding of force as inherently external, it is Durkheim contradicting his sociology when his ethics comes into conflict with it.

[13]Again, Durkheim went on to explore the contrary of this way of seeing things: that we also understand the force as *inside* us, and that rather than nullifying us, it magnifies us. Durkheim's way of reconciling these contraries was a rigorous dualism in his understanding of human beings, going so far as to make each of us a split personality, one part social and one part individual. Although this follows as a sociologization of Kantian ethics, it is difficult to maintain without leading to either paradox or Cartesianism.

1952: 180). Thus, the field explains the otherwise-inexplicable transfer of energy to an element that is not necessarily in contact with any other element. Consider the case of the piece of iron suddenly "dropped" into the magnetic field. While the field was present before, there was no identifiable transfer of energy taking place at that position; yet, when the iron is present, there is an instantaneous transmission of force. However, we are unable to perceive any new effluent coming from the magnet that may be far away in space.

In consequence, field theory is generally applicable for cases in which the alternative form of explanation involves action at a distance, a form of explanation that has generally been treated with suspicious dislike by Western (in contrast to Eastern, especially Chinese) science (Needham 1981: 14; although see Hesse 1970: 187). While the distinction may seem like hair splitting, a field replaces the idea of action at a distance, in which X somehow *directly* affects some Y, which it does not touch, with a purely *local* explanation. The field directly induces a potential energy in Y; the presence of a continuous medium like a fluid is sufficient but not necessary for such local action. X may somehow "cause" or anchor the field, but we do not say that X itself affects Y. The potential for force is in the field, not in the magnet (Maxwell [1891] 1954: ix, 67, 70; Koffka 1935: 41; Schwinger et al. 1998: 2ff; Hesse 1970: 195, 201; cf. Mey [1965] 1972: 8; Verschuur 1993: 98; cf. Marrow 1969: 31).[14]

On the one hand, this implies that our analysis is global in that we do not assume that we can adequately explain what is happening to something of interest only by recourse to what we observe in the immediate neighborhood, but instead must draw on our overall theory of the field (Maxwell [1891] 1954: ix). It is for this reason that field theories are said to be wholistic, or to pursue "the way from above to below" (Metzger [1975b] 1986: 213). But, on the other hand, we do not allow the explanation to make reference to "what is happening" far from our position. In the social sciences, the analogous bifurcation (between localism and action at a distance) is a narrow mechanism or a sweeping functionalism (as discussed in further detail below). According to those insisting on mechanisms in the social sciences, nothing that does not appear in front of us wearing shoes and a hat can be taken into account. Those reaching toward functionalism instead find themselves facing a problem of action at a distance: how is the individual affected by some transcendent whole? The responses are usually recourse either to some vague mysticism or to

---

[14]Indeed, this distinction was key for Faraday's discovery of the electromagnetic field: action at a distance should proceed in straight lines, while purely local effects could take curved forms. On the development of Faraday's understanding of the lines of force and his rejection of the possibility of action at a distance, see Williams (1965: 200, 250, 284, 298, 435).

an oversocialized conception of the personality according to which people fortunately come programmed to reproduce a complex order.[15]

The solution to this problem—how we can explain the local action with reference to the global patterning—is to attach action to position. As Herbert Simon (1955: 113), in his classic piece deriving a model of boundedly rational action, argued (interestingly, using the Gestalt concept of "aspiration level"), we cannot make a plausible model of action that assumes that the actor conducts each choice independent of all others, but it stretches credulity to imagine that the actor is capable of computing payoffs for all different combinations of strategies across many situations. "A possible middle ground is to define for each trial [i.e., choice] a pay-off function with two components. One would be the 'immediate' pay-off (consumption), the other, the 'position' in which the organism is left for future trials."

That is, each position has a characteristic "potential" for the future: in the economic model used by Simon, a good position has a potential for high rewards or—and this is crucial—a potential for attaining a better position. (Of course, this "better" position is also recursively defined in reference to other better positions.) But a set of potentials, we recall, is what we mean by a field. And, as Köhler (1938: 229) points out, a vector is one way of understanding a gradient, and a gradient develops where and when we have a juxtaposition of two different potentials. For Simon's case, it is the felt impulsion to leave one position and move to a better one when the second is proximate to the first.

To recapitulate this discussion, approaching the problem of the relation of the act to the wider environment—the dilemma that leads to the appeals to mechanism or to function—brings us to a sense of positions with potentials. This in turn implies that some of the organization of action resides not in the actors themselves but in the positions. The virtue of this conclusion is largely negative; it prevents us from ascribing unbelievable qualities to actors and from reifying society. The field conception may remain vague here. But it can still be of great analytic value, which brings us to the final point.

This was that the field itself is organized and differential (Köhler 1920: 1). In the words of Brandt (1952: 183), the usefulness of a field concept presupposes that any variation in the vectors of potential force over some space-time is lawful. These variations are frequently seen in topological terms of some sort, since they may be understood as variations in the strength and direction of motion induced in a particle. At any point, then, the field consists of a slope (a gradient) down which an object will "roll" (cf. Gibson [1979] 1986: 151f). If there is a logic to the dispersal of vectors across positions—a logic that we can grasp both as analysts and as

---

[15]As discussed in more detail below, there is one version of functionalism that corresponds closely to the Gestalt/field conception.

actors—then the field representation may add analytic insight even though it remains obscure on the central point of the nature of the field effect. I have proposed that actors have an ability to determine the objective imperative in social objects and supported this with a plausibility argument, although this fell short of a complete psychological treatment. But this does not hamper the ability of the field theoretic approach to shed light on empirical problems. In other words, even if we are unable to "get" the nature of gravity, if we are trying to understand the path water will take—either because we are trying to explain the overall mathematical characteristics of rivers or because we are trying to build a canal—it will be of the utmost importance to accurately map the contours of the hills and valleys that we see.

Field theory, then, has several generic characteristics no matter what the domain of application. As such, it has inherent limitations (some of which have been alluded to here). It is not difficult to discover these limitations, but since field theories were obviously considered acceptable, indeed crucial breakthroughs, in the physical sciences, we know that these limitations are not in themselves fatal. The challenge is not to uncover limitations but to determine the extent to which they will affect the development of field theoretic concepts in the social sciences.

CONTROVERSIES IN FIELD THEORY

Field Theory, Tautology, and Occultism

Perhaps the biggest danger of field theory is a tendency toward tautology. Because fields are only known by their effects, it is tempting to proliferate invisible fields that "explain" whatever is in question. Such an explanation may simply be a restatement of the problem, with the world *field* inserted somewhere. Of course, this is also a temptation for competing theoretical orientations, which make it costless and painless to propose theoretical entities that have no observable correlates other than the observations they supposedly explain. The use of the idea of "preferences" in economics is perhaps the most glaring and well-analyzed example. (Why do people go to work? Because they can generally be assumed to be attempting to maximize utilities, and money from work is useful for doing so. But, why do people give money to a charity? Because they have a "preference" for the subjective state of feeling charitable, and thus charitable giving actually creates the utility associated with this state. But that is simply to replace an observable act with an unobservable preference.)

A similar problem haunts most social functionalism: instead of inventing an invisible preference for an individual, one basically does the same thing but for the group. The particular functionalist tradition that gave rise to the sociological notion of causality discussed in the previous chapters formalized this invention of explanatory terms not as pathological but as the acme of scientific reasoning. Both Spencer and Durkheim affirmed that the cardinal principle of scientific investigation was "one cause, one effect" (cf. Maxwell [1877] ca. 1952: 13)—a central principle of Galileo's. But, this statement, intended to emphasize that (all else remaining the same) the same cause could not have different effects, can fallaciously be reversed to produce the incorrect assumption that "a given effect has always a single corresponding cause." The words are those of Durkheim ([1895] 1938: 128, 95).[16]

Far from being a minor mistake, this idea of Durkheim's gets to the heart of his widely lauded methodology in *Suicide* ([1897] 1951; and it forced him to divide suicides according to invisible characteristics in direct violation of his own [1895/1938] methodological *Rules*). Every social fact—and what counted as a social fact was quite broad indeed—could be assured of having a specific cause in another social fact. There is then not merely a temptation but indeed a methodological requirement to find a "cause" for every effect even if this requires invention of a previously unknown factor. There is little reason to complain that to substitute field terminology in place of Durkheimian causality will *introduce* a tendency toward tautology; on the contrary, because of the commitment of field theory to limit itself to phenomenologically valid explanatory entities, we are less likely to invent degenerate abstractions if we follow the strictures laid out here than if we follow conventional practice in the social sciences.

To summarize, tautology is a problem for field theory, but no more so than for all the other major explanatory approaches in the social sciences. In the physical sciences, the charge of tautology is usually more damning, but successful field theories such as electromagnetism could point to the explanatory consistency and parsimony attained (cf. Hesse 1970: 135, 141, 202; Verschuur 1993: 82f, 99; Gillispie 1960: 452). In the social sciences, however, we are unlikely to attain a formal expression such as an equation that allows us to appeal to parsimony as a reasonable criterion; indeed, here what is often claimed as parsimony is better described as ignorance, strained logic, or fanaticism. The theorist who has an explanation for everything rightfully strikes us as just as suspicious as the apprehended lawbreaker with a ready alibi for every time and place. We must recognize the absolute poverty of a "theory" that simply relabels what is to be explained, as in the wonderful case of Moliere's scholastic philosopher who explains the effects of morphine as being due to "its soporific quality."[17]

---

[16]This is akin to assuming that the inverse of a function is a function. In fairness, we should note that Galileo ([1629] 1967: 445) himself made this same error, as did Hume ([1738] 1911: 170).

[17]Of course, in the seventeenth century it was easier for holier-than-thou mechanistic explanations to repeat this mistake, only putting the tautological explanation in supposed physical qualities of unobservable corpuscles (Shapin

While the physical sciences can appeal to formal elegance and parsimony, the social sciences must appeal to the intuitive accessibility and first-person plausibility of field constructs. This takes the field approach in a direction diametrically opposite to that of the hypothetico-deductivism that forms the generic model for the contemporary social sciences as discussed in chapter 3. In the hypothetico-deductive model (especially as used in the social sciences, which seized on the "operationalism" of Percy Bridgman [see Hempel 1965: 123; Cartwright 1987]), the ultimate defense of theoretic terms is a retreat to heuristic: "We do not say that what we are talking about *really* exists," one is supposed to say when cornered, "just that things are so much *easier* to explain if we *hypothesize* that this is the case." Such shrinking and shirkings—a career of scientific inquiry leading to the obituary, "Here lies someone who successfully evaded making a statement about the world she passed through"—are not particularly compelling in themselves. But, one might be sympathetic to the tactic when it comes to dealing with arcane matters of certain areas of physics.

Yet, as we have seen in chapter 7, field theory itself was, at least in the social sciences, largely derived from a general scientific trend in early twentieth-century Germany that insisted that scientific theory had to "get at" the real world, not simply rearrange observations. This "getting at" the real world implied that the terms of the theory had to be intuitively accessible (*anschaulich*) as referring to a world we could understand and inhabit (for importance of *Anschaulichkeit* in the case of physics, see the classic work by Forman 1984).[18] In this light, it seems preposterous for social scientists to retreat to heuristic instead of staking their claim on the strongest part of our material, namely, the consubstantiality of analyst and

---

1996: 57). The essence of the mistake is not the ontology but, first, the optimistic projection into nature of just what is needed for our explanation and, second, confusing labeling and explanation. This problem did not escape Galileo: in *Two Great Systems*, Galileo's alter ego asks his interlocutor (Simplicio) about why things fall, and Simplicio replies that everyone knows that; the answer is gravity. The former replies, "What you ought to say is that everyone knows that it is *called* 'gravity.' What I am asking you for is not the name of the thing, but its essence" (Galilei [1629] 1967: 234; italics added; see p. 410 for critique of reliance on labeling instead of analysis).

[18]Interestingly, Gilbert, who pioneered the study of magnetism, also emphasized that while his conception was untestable, it offered intuitive accessibility, and Euler's conception of pressure that led to a flexible fluid dynamics compatible with field theory succeeded precisely because, in contrast to Bernoulli's, it was impressionistic and nonoperational. Similarly, Faraday and Maxwell unashamedly relied on analogies to well-understood processes (such as elasticity or fluid dynamics) that they did not mean to defend literally (see Hesse 1970: 100, 191, 208f), not because these "fit" the data but because they allowed for a form of intuitive comprehension. Köhler (1920: 73, 98) cited Maxwell insisting that intuitive "eye-knowledge" could be used to find the choice of the proper method of

analyzed. Thus, we should propose a field not when it has parsimony but when it has intersubjective validity.

It is worth repeating that this means neither that analysts find some field account subjectively satisfying nor that actors must agree with the theoretician's account in every respect. It is that the set of positions and their overall topography as constituted by the field theory have recognizable counterparts in the lived experience (and not the retrospective accounts) of participants. That is, the field approach requires that the key explanatory elements receive the existential assent of actors. They need not agree with our argument (and certainly there is no reason to imagine that any particular actor must agree with us regarding the construction of the overall field, any more than a cartographer would insist that any person in the area mapped have the analyst's bird's-eye view). They may not invariably recall having experienced the vectors we postulate, for there is no field theory that requires a social-psychological model of the actor turning on perfect recall of subjective experience, but we imagine that patterns of forgetting here will parallel patterns of forgetting uncovered in other research.[19]

However, the field theoretic account *does* require that our key elements be discoverable in first-person experience, and pushes us to collect our data whenever possible at such junctures; there is a strong preference for the present and the future as against the past. For actors demonstrate the this-sidedness of field constructs not only when they report the experience but also when they explain how they envision the future. Then, when we get their theories of the world, these are not the justifications provoked by a challenge. Instead, these theories are actors' forecasts of what others are likely to do. Thus, they are strong evidence of the first-person plausibility of the constructs. By this, we mean not that they have a folk theory of others compatible with pluralistic ignorance (as when each individual tells us "everyone here is a racist except for me"), but that

---

solution to a problem and emphasized the importance of Faraday's lines of force of giving *Anschaulichkeit* to the conceptions (also see Maxwell's letter to Faraday reprinted in Williams [1965: 512]). Faraday's own intuitive gift was stressed by contemporaries—"He smells the truth" said the German electrical physicist Kohlrausch (Tyndall 1890: 45). He had a visually oriented intelligence and, in the words of Gillispie (1960: 441), "a sense of the spatial." For his explicit argument regarding the centrality of intuition and judgment, see Williams (1965: 336). For Dewey on the relation between this intuitive accessibility and the nature of qualitative experience, see ([1930] 1960: 184).

[19]Finally, there is no reason to imagine that there are *no* circumstances in which people choose to deny certain experiences even when they recall them. But, there is also no reason to think that these circumstances will prove so common, even given proper research techniques, that simply giving up any attempt to investigate these experiences will be a fatal setback for social science.

they can chart an organization to experience that allows for a correlatively organized plan of action, as well as an experiential link between position and action. The field concept not only gives analysts such intuitive accessibility but is available to actors to organize their own action. It is robust evidence of the appearance of the field terms in first-person experiences that leads us to accept a field theoretic account in the social sciences without being incapacitated by a fear of tautological explanations leading to pathological science.

Mechanical Critiques

The charge of tautology has not been the only one leveled at field theories. Perhaps even more fundamentally, field theories in physics have frequently been opposed because they violate the assumptions of the mechanistic materialism that was the largely dominant metaphysics in the early modern scientific West (see Burtt 1927; Gillispie 1960: 144f on the reaction to Newton). The most important of these assumptions is that all creation or transmission of force must be explicable in terms of contact—in Leibniz's words (as he struggled to propose a fluid-based mechanism for gravitational attraction), that "a body is never moved naturally, except by another body which touches it and pushes it" (Leibniz [1716] 1908: 355).[20] Because field theories dispense with such mechanical contact, many rejected them out of hand even if they were successful in terms of explanation and prediction, attempting instead to introduce a mechanical intermediary that could explain the observed effect.

One way to do this is to propose that the effects are due to an otherwise-unobservable ether (Newton himself, unable to dismiss mechanistic

---

[20]While the West has generally been suspicious of all nonlocal effects, there have been periods in which action at a distance was considered theoretically acceptable (Hesse 1970: 106, 157ff, 187). Gilbert's pioneering work on magnetism in 1600 led to the first such acceptance (Verschuur 1993: 38); Newton's work led to a further acceptance of the "occult" phenomenon of gravity, although he himself was troubled by the lack of mechanism. Newton, in his *Opticks*, query 31, noting that material bodies seem to have "certain Powers, Virtues, or Forces by which they act at a distance . . . ," says, "These principles I consider not as Occult Qualities, supposed to result from the Specific Forms of things, but as General Laws of Nature, by which the things themselves are formed" (Newton [1730] 1952: 401, 388; cf. Westfall 1977: 141). Note that "occult quality" was a technical term of the Aristotelians to denote qualities that were hidden in bodies and were responsible for manifest effects, an explanatory practice Newton abhorred. In contrast, he meant that we know the qualities of the objects (e.g., mass) but not why they lead to falling: "For these are manifest qualities, and their causes only are occult." He reasonably pointed out that those who attempt to explain such forces (e.g., atomic attraction) with convenient mechanical claims such as "hooked atoms" are also inventing occult qualities.

criticisms of his conception of gravity, later added an "explanation" in terms of an ether composed of mutually repelling particles [Westfall 1977: 157; Cantor 1983: 147].[21]) An ether differs from the fluids of fluid dynamics in being a medium that responds as if it were a fluid but apparently has the ability to penetrate any other object (e.g., Huygens's proposed gravitational ether [Jammer 1957: 114f, cf. 139, 141]). Yet, these ethers are clearly just as nebulous as the field and, unless one dogmatically holds that all that exists must be treated as substance, have no scientific virtues. They needlessly complicate without adding to the explanation. Indeed, the social sciences have had their share of such unproductive ethers, from Parsons's (1951) various media of exchange to the ubiquitous "power" of Foucault ([1975] 1979).

The second way to explain away the field effect is to argue that it is actually reducible to mechanical interactions. Of course, because the particles supposedly interacting in this mechanistic way cannot be identified, theorists often must specify a plenum—that is, a space completely filled with particles that interact according to the conventional rules of particle mechanics. Both Descartes and Leibniz took this route,[22] Descartes proposing the existence of myriad spiral particles that, when rotating, would move objects in their wake (Westfall 1977: 143; Hesse 1970: 58f, 106, 157, 160f; cf. Jammer 1957: 105, 188, 197).

Indeed, in some cases it *did* later prove possible to replace a field theory with a more "mechanical" theory; hence, in the physical sciences at any rate, there is perhaps no reason not to consider field theories as provisional attempts to describe in cases in which information about mechanisms is lacking.[23] Thus, before quantum electrodynamics, it was a field

---

[21]It has been suggested by those attentive to Newton's appreciation of alchemical reasoning that this protest may have been more strategic than genuine, and that indeed, it was the magical notions associated with the Hermetic tradition that allowed Newton to go beyond the mechanical philosophy (for a discussion, see Cohen 1994: 175). This point has almost certainly been overstated and seems to come from a determination to force Newton into later contrasts between atomist-materialist as opposed to mystical modes of thought. (Also see Cantor [1983: 25] on Newton's ambiguous relation to particle theories of light.)

[22]Those proposing a plenary explanation usually maintained that magnetism worked via some effluvia from the magnet. It is perhaps interesting to compare to such mechanistic interpretations the spiritual ones that became popular in the eighteenth century. See Darnton (1970: 10f, 115) and Zweig (1932: 44, 52) on the French enthusiasm for mesmerism—a forerunner of the hypnotism on which Charcot was to rely (cf. chapter 3, note 19)—and its relation to electromagnetism and fluid dynamics.

[23]As Maxwell ([1891] 1954: 165f) wrote, "It must be carefully borne in mind that we have made only one step in the theory of the action of the medium. We have supposed it to be in a state of stress, but we have not in any way accounted for this stress, or explained how it is maintained. This step, however, seems to me

theory that made it possible to explain "magnetism" by recourse to the regular properties of the field, even though the mechanistic properties of magnets remained baffling (Verschuur 1993: 99, 111, 121).[24] (On the opposition between mechanistic accounts and field theory, see Köhler 1947: 348; Brunswik 1952: 41; Cassirer [1910] 1923: 404f.) Further, it is significant that Faraday was able to develop his understanding of fields of force by imagining the interactions of contiguous particles. He diverged from the orthodox mechanists in understanding that it was one thing to *imagine* particles and another thing to *hypostatize them* merely to avoid talking about force (for he eventually conceived of the interactions as interactions of forces and not of particles or an ether [Williams 1965: 250, 257, 311, 454]).

Thus, while one may insist that field theories in the physical sciences are destined to be sublated by more mechanical theories,[25] this has never been accomplished by the hopeful invention of mysterious particles possessing just the right familiar properties (e.g., shape) to explain the observed effects. When simple mechanisms have been proposed to explain field effects, the theories were useless because of prematurity, and temptation to a premature mechanism is not the same thing as the epistemological high ground.[26] More important, in the social sciences there is good reason to think that the field theory, rather than the provisional device to allow for the formulation of regularities, is intrinsically preferable than either of the major alternatives, namely, explanation via function and explanation via mechanism.[27]

---

to be an important one. . . . [But] I have not been able to make the next step, namely, to account by mechanical considerations for these stresses in the dielectric. I therefore leave the theory at this point. . . ."

[24]Similarly, Newton emphasized that while he would analyze the results of forces of attraction he was "considering those forces not physically, but mathematically: wherefore the reader is not to imagine that by those words I anywhere take it upon me to define the kind, or the manner of any action, the causes or the physical reason thereof" (Gillispie 1960: 141, 147; also see Whewell [1860] 1971: 199).

[25]Note that I do not propose that this is true, just that it may be conceded without fault. According to my limited understanding of quantum field theory, it appears that the basis is at least as "fieldy" as it is "particley."

[26]In discussing his introduction of an imaginary fluid to explain the magnetic field, Maxwell wrote that he did so "to attain generality and precision, and to avoid the dangers arising from a premature theory professing to explain the cause of phenomena" (Gillispie 1960: 462; also 477, 488f, 492).

[27]Some readers have questioned whether it really is the case that these two alternatives arise as some sort of forced choice; I believe that there is a reason why there are no other distinct contenders, stemming from the basic grammar of the act (as understood by the Why question) referred to in chapter 1. We saw that the clearest understanding, that of Kant, made a distinction between causal explanations rooted in the past and motivational explanations rooted in the future. We see

Mechanisms and Functions

By *mechanism*, sociologists generally mean to refer to some readily understandable causal sequence that explains some theoretically accounted-for pattern (Lundberg 1939: 375). While it has never been demonstrated that such mechanisms *must* be at a lower level of analysis than the theoretical units in question, this seems be the case in practice.[28] It is important not to confuse mechanisms with the theoretical claims themselves. Mechanisms are usually what is invoked when someone accepts a theoretical claim, but insists on asking "how" it comes to be the case.[29] (In classic Lazarsfeldian survey analysis, a search for mechanism implied the use of intervening variables, although now such a search is more likely to lead to an appeal to a simplified accessory model.) While providing mechanisms is not necessary for a theory to be useful or correct, such provision often increases its plausibility.

As an example, consider the theory of evolution, that is, the claim that species change over time, and that a range of species that originally included only very simple organisms developed into a range that went from the very simple to the fabulously complex. "Natural selection" is a mechanism that was offered by Charles Darwin to explain *how* evolution might actually occur. As this example makes clear, a successful mechanism need not be the empirical focus of work guided by a theory: evidence for or against evolution coming from the fossil record or overlaps in DNA rarely bears on natural selection. Indeed, little empirical evidence is brought directly to bear on the issue of whether natural selection "explains" evolution, given that the mechanism is so plausible and alternatives other than theism so few. Finally, the introduction of this extremely reasonable mechanism has not led to any appreciable predictive power (although

---

here that, transferred to the realm of social explanation, these correspond closely to mechanisms and functions. One may also see Kant's ([1790] 1987: 266) explicit discussion of the relation between these two forms of explanation in the *Critique of Judgment*.

[28] Definitions of mechanisms are generally poor; usage confirms my claims here (see, e.g., Gross 2009; Hedström and Swedberg 1998; Hedström 2005: 11; Stinchcombe 1991; the classic use of such mechanisms is by Schelling 1978). Elster (1989: 4, 9) has a clear discussion of the relation between mechanisms and explanation.

[29] There is a new interest in using assembling explanations out of mechanisms without having an overarching theory. With the apparent expiration of any serious functionalism worthy of the name in the United States, this seems to be the most attractive alternative to field theory broadly conceived. Given that this sort of use was employed by Elias ([1939] 1982: 98f), it has been influential in historical sociology. For examples, see Tilly (2000), Mische (2003), and the references therein. In Germany, there is still serious interest in systems theory (which has a functional side); also see the next footnote.

this is of course not always the case). Mechanisms, in sum, turn on making an accepted relation or set of relations plausible. In the case at hand, the intuitive accessibility of the mechanism of natural selection was considered by many sufficiently great to allow them to jettison theological or functionalist explanations of evolution.

Such theological or functionalist explanations, in stark contrast to mechanistic explanations, usually appeal to a *higher* level of analysis to explain a theoretical claim as opposed to a lower. Here, we are totally uninterested in explaining "how" something comes to be; our claim is that it *must* be, and the mechanics are theoretically trivial (see Brunswik 1952: 34 for this same contrast). The problems with functionalist explanations are obvious and largely unanswerable except by wholesale retreat to heuristic: such explanations assume from the start the existence of a doubtful entity. As Tweedledee famously says, "If it was so, it might be; and if it were so, it would be; but as it isn't, it ain't. That's logic."[30] Mechanistic arguments, in contrast, are attractive precisely because they are less grandiose.

That is not to say that all mechanistic arguments are parsimonious and reasonable—many are not. Instead, they involve positing sprawling, Rube-Goldberg-like cascades of elementary interactions that add up to an acceptable explanation only because of a dogmatic refusal to entertain nonmechanistic alternatives (see especially Wertheimer 1922: 50). Such dogmatism is incompatible with a deliberate restriction of explanation to the employment of phenomenologically valid constructs. That is, if we follow this principle, we would not replace a field explanation that makes use of explanatory elements that would be recognized by those whose conduct is being explained with a mechanical explanation if actors could not recognize the validity of the components of this reduction in lived experience. (That is, this is not to say that they *accept* or *believe* the reductive account, but that the elements it appeals to were actually phenomenologically existent for them.) If indeed the imperative attached to a position is a quality that actors directly perceive, then there is no great

---

[30]The other possible recourse for a functionalist approach is a transformation into a systems theory as in Luhmann ([1984] 1995); to the extent that a systems theory emphasizes the self-organization of the system, it may tend to converge with a field theory as expounded by Köhler (1920). Metzger ([1975b] 1986: 219f) discusses the relations between Gestalt theory, field theory and systems theory. He notes that all are fundamentally dynamic and assume interdependence of elements, and suggests that systems need to include open systems that lack single and stable equilibria. It may be (and here I draw on conversations with Jan Fuhse) that Gestalts are the most general case of nonindependence of elements: fields are the case in which the organization is one oriented to the current set of relationships (distilled to a vector at any position), while systems are the case in which the organization is oriented to relationships of elements with members of some *other* set of elements.

advantage in coming up with a more cumbersome explanation that defies their cognitive processing ability.

But, even worse than the case when there is no consensus regarding the validity of some mechanistic reduction may be the case in which there is. Indeed, formulaically we may say that the problem with plausibility arguments is that, by the nature of the beast, they are generally plausible. Such plausibility is not the same thing as a restriction of theoretical terms to those with first-person accessibility. For example, generosity, whatever else it is, is an emotion that can be experienced on occasion at least by many of us. The phenomenological validity of the experience of a generous sentiment cannot be doubted (although its theoretical utility may, of course). However, there have been many and unfortunately still are many (among the ungenerous, one would hazard) who consider altruism some sort of occult phenomenon incompatible with their model of the fundamental unit actor and hence tire us with a predictable decomposition of this sentiment into a cascade of altogether different actions of expanded self-interest.

Now, many people who share the assumption of the ungenerous that all actors are ungenerous will find this mechanistic account plausible, even though it makes reference to entities that do not have first-person recognition. (For example, many persons in the midst of a feeling of generosity have no sensation of making predictions about the results of their actions, although this may be posited by the mechanistic elaboration.[31]) Thus, we may reasonably expect many explanations, mechanistic ones in particular, to have plausibility not because they reflect our first-person experiences (although of course they may), but because they appeal to our folk theories of ourselves. Unfortunately, we probably have a great number of prejudices about our own constitutions that we cannot rid ourselves of because we do not know what all of them are. There might not have been any theory of natural selection if the Galapagos finches were the theoreticians; Galapagos finches may have very different ideas about what it means to be a Galapagos finch.

This does not mean that mechanistic reductions that have independent explanatory power should be rejected just because we believe them—the categorical warning applies only to post facto plausibility arguments that account for already-known facts. Nor should we refrain from serious investigation of the biopsychological processes involved in action (as Lizardo [2009: 58] calls for). But social scientists tend to make a little bit of

---

[31]Interestingly, many such mechanistic accounts incoherently jump to functionalism when their case becomes weak—and the weaker the case, the more ridiculous the functionalism, until we get to evolutionary psychology, which justifies its invention of mystical mechanisms by insisting that their existence is literally a matter of life or death.

psychology go a long way, as we have little reliable third-person knowledge about "how we really work," despite incredible advances in neurology and in cognitive psychology. For the elements of knowledge float like little bits of candied fruit in a vast congealed Jell-O dessert of our prejudices. At any time, there has been "a" body of psychological science on which social scientists can draw. This has swung wildly back and forth, and those who built their house on this unstable foundation found their constructions appearing ridiculously out of plumb a generation later.[32]

Thus, while field theory can satisfy the criteria for a social aesthetics, which means beginning with the adequacy of the phenomenologically valid qualities of social objects, it still forbids us to apply our self-understanding wholesale, let alone to crown these prejudices with the title "mechanism" and congratulate ourselves on a truly *scientific* understanding. Although field theory partakes of *Verfremdung* in Brecht's sense of distantiation,[33] it retains intuitive accessibility. While we cannot see magnetic fields, we can quickly come to accept that they are there and understand how to navigate and manipulate them. Things are even easier, said Köhler (1920: 77, 83), when it comes to the gestalts of human perception, for we are able to grasp the characters of many intuitively accessible structures as wholes, as opposed to needing to painstakingly re-create the equivalent of the "lines of force" of a magnetic field.

At the same time, it is in no way the case that the retention of the idea of fields of force implies a lack of attention to people's conceptions of the importance of themselves as actors. That is, while logically, one might expect that conceiving of action as a result of position in a field of forces implies that people can be treated as wholly passive, indeed, inanimate bodies, sociologically that seems not to be the case. As we saw in chapter 1,

---

[32] In a fascinating piece, Lizardo (2007) has argued that the discovery of mirror neurons—a class of neural cells in certain primates that seem to fire identically when an action is made and when the action is observed—strongly supports the Bourdieuian understanding of the development of habitus. I very much *want* mirror neurons to operate in such a manner as to simplify my treatment of habit and would not be surprised if it this were to pass. But, I am willing to wait 50 years to be pretty sure it is so before I treat it as the foundation for an understanding of how to conduct sociological research.

[33] As Bourdieu (1982; I use the translation of Bourdieu and Wacquant 1992: 96, n. 48; see also Bourdieu 1993: 21) says, "To think in terms of field demands a conversion of the whole ordinary vision of the social world which fastens only on visible things [i.e., the individual and the group]. . . . In fact, just as the Newtonian theory of gravitation could only be constructed against Cartesian realism which wanted to recognize no mode of action other than collision, direct contact, the notion of field presupposes a break with the realist representation which leads us to reduce the effect of the *environment* to the effect of direct action as actualized during an interaction."

work in the psychology of attribution demonstrates that when people think most "self-centeredly," they tend to accentuate the importance of situational pressures. While conventional approaches assume that it is implicitly paradoxical to emphasize both willful motivations and situational pressures, and hence a theory that includes both must involve some special work of "resolving" such contraries, we will see that field theory does not. To make this point, we can consider a somewhat different sense of field also used in the social sciences, namely, the field as a field of contestation.

FIELDS AND GAMES

Fields of Contestation

This idea of fields of contestation initially seems somewhat at odds with the conception of fields of force. Yet, the two have tended to coexist in the heads of the same thinkers: While Bourdieu more than others has stressed this meaning of the word *field*, the more Gestalt-inspired field theorists also relied on this conception (Mey [1965] 1972: xv).[34] In particular, Lewin, who rarely discussed social conflict as such, may still have had the same martial images in the back of his head that one sees in Bourdieu: one of his early articles (Lewin 1917), "Battlefield," was a striking phenomenological analysis of the landscape of conflict.[35]

The idea of a field of contestation may often be attractive to analysts if only because the explanatory concepts evoked tend to be the same as those of the actors. The analogy to the field of physics initially seems arcane and perhaps even mystical, while we all understand a fight. Further, fighting and striving seems to fit well with many of our folk theories

---

[34]For example, Turner (1974: 42) seems to have considered the political field—an ordering of relations of latent or potential conflicts—to be the single best example of a field. Mannheim (1940: 298) combined these senses when he spoke of the field as composed of "warring social atoms."

[35]Rummel (1975: 35), Eng (1978), and Marrow (1969: 11) discuss the importance of this experience for Lewin's intellectual development. This is perhaps because an intuitive understanding of field theory can be gained from the experience of danger. Koffka (1935: 43; Koffka cites Lewin's essay on p. 44) gives the example of someone in an idyllic setting suddenly hearing a cry for help: "Whereas all directions were dynamically equal before, now there is one direction that stands out, one direction into which you are being pulled. This direction is charged with force, the environment seems to contract, it is as though a groove had formed in a plane surface and you were being forced down that groove."

At the same time, the element of interpersonal struggle was not developed in Lewin's theory due to his psychological focus and his understanding of vectors. The rise of Nazism led Lewin, like others, to be more concerned with social psychology

of actions, quite unlike the fields of force, which we may acknowledge experiencing but rarely employ in everyday explanations. This difference may make the two conceptions of field seem quite different, indeed joined only by their common label. Field theory would then be simply a set of overlapping metaphors, loosely and inconsistently applied when convenient. But, closer examination demonstrates that the two conceptions do refer to the same explanatory construct. This is because the terrains of social struggle are not the physical terrain of a landscape, but, to a large extent, an endogenous product of aligned social action. And it is such alignment, and not the mere fact of placement in the same analytic space, that is key for field theory.[36]

I go on to trace analytically the connection of the ideas of games, fields, and rules, making the argument that the field conception that we first derived through the organization of phenomenological vectors is identical to that which we derive from the mutual alignment of actors in a game. Although Bourdieu ([1972] 1977: 10–15, 22–30) has already pointed to the centrality of these connections, I do not think that most readers have appreciated the consistency of these arguments. This is in part because Bourdieu's analytic strategy is here like that of poorly disciplined mercenaries who cease pursuing their objective when the opportunity to loot arises; he repeatedly abandons his central argument to deliver kicks at his opponents instead of sticking to his theme, the place of the "game" in social explanation.

There is, I confess, at first blush something vaguely repellant about the use of a game metaphor as a fundamental part of our explanation of social action (for a balanced evaluation, see Billig 1996: 47; also Nadel 1957: 41f). On the one hand, it smacks of triviality—games are what children or foolish adults play. On the other hand, the idea of "game" may seem to

---

and influence (Mey 1972: 51) than with conflict. While Lewin's (e.g., 1936: 47) basic understanding was oriented to a field of striving (since all locomotion is generally toward something desired or away from something disliked), his general restriction of attention to the individual led him to ignore conflict. In some places, Lewin suggested that conflict arises from opposing but overlapping fields of force, which (as Mey [1972: 43f] pointed out) does not make technical sense: at any point, there is, by definition, one and only one vector in a field (two vectors in opposite directions cancel each other out). Lewin's student Brown (1936a: 55f), following Lewin's topological model, tended to emphasize boundaries when dealing with conflict, thereby completely inverting the nature of the field from that which induces motion to that which impedes it.

[36]Although we might speak of two persons' actions being aligned if they are mutually oriented (formulaically, they are facing each other), I shall emphasize that sort of alignment that arises when two or more are facing in the same direction—most obviously, pursuing the same goal. It is this simple case of alignment that is most elegantly handled with game metaphors (also see Mannheim 1940: 298).

stress competition, and those who tout a game metaphor may be reasonably expected of being of that particularly nasty form of human who is devoid of fundamental feelings of fellowship and will corner us and then begin a tirade about how everyone else is as shallow and obnoxious as he. It is unfortunate that the game metaphor brings with it such baggage.[37] But the game metaphor brings something important pertaining to the relation between overall pattern and individual action, in particular, in the idea of rules.

Rules and Laws

In its most common usage, a *game* is an intersubjectively valid set of restrictions on interaction that leads to vertical social differentiation among persons. Most simply, this differentiation is into winners and losers, although there can be a continuous differentiation as well. But, not all social processes that induce such differentiation are games; for example, total war or unconstrained aggression may be an excellent way of creating winners and losers, but it seems to have nothing of a game about it. A game is a game only if it is played by rules. We generally use the game metaphor to shed light on the nature of rule-governed action (here see Abbott 1997: 176).

Now, it may reasonably be objected that in the game of life, there *are* no rules, nor consensus regarding goals or referees. (There are, however, an awful lot of players.[38]) There is something quite important in this seemingly misguided objection, and this is that if goals could be treated as wholly given—wholly exogenous to the game—then to equate the field with a game would imply the possibility of a successful mechanistic reduction. In such a case, the overall field effect can be, at least in principle if not in practice, satisfactorily explained by devolving to the compound results (even if unanticipated) of strategic actions. But in other cases, it may be that we are unable to treat the goals of action as exogenously fixed; instead, they are better seen as an endogenous outcome of what goes on *in* the game, a field effect.[39] Although it might initially seem paradoxical, the strength of the game metaphor is that it highlights

---

[37]Interestingly, Dewey (1934) noted the inadequacy of utilitarianism in understanding motivation because striving is more like a "game" in that the ends we pursue have an aesthetic captivation for us (what Bourdieu would call "illusio").

[38]I am indebted to Anne R. Martin for this observation. Anne Rawls (2001: 64) has similarly (and equally nicely) put it as follows: we are not "trying to explain the relationship between voluntaristic actors and an external constraint system. The result is something more on the model of a game of chess (only without the rules)."

[39]It is for this reason that we cannot simply embrace game theory as a solution for all problems. Game theory *should* be treated as the most fundamental reductive approach for all social action, and its capacity for generating more complex

a relationship of actors to rules that sheds light on how such endogeneity is possible and thus how there can be a game *without* stably defined goals. This in turn illuminates how fields can be both fields of force that seem to impose directionality on persons and fields of contestation in which persons strive with or against each other.

Because this idea that (as Bourdieu often puts it) the struggle is both with and over the rules may initially seem self-contradictory (and is explicitly denied by, e.g., Rawls 1955: 16, 26), we need to consider the relationship of games to rules.[40] Now, one reason to be interested in the game metaphor in the first place is simply that it provides this idea of rule, and "rule" may turn out to be preferable as a notion of regularity to "law" (discussed briefly in chapter 2 and to which I return in the final chapter). One source of recurring explanatory difficulties in the social sciences has come from the assumptions that their purpose was to uncover laws, that such laws should be determinative of action, and hence that we would find ourselves uncovering some sort of overarching formal framework that in some obscure way *forces* persons to do this or that (see Turner 1994, esp. 115). In games, illegal action is not "unthinkable," but legal action is more than a description of a central tendency that emerges from independent actions (these two extremes of unthinkability vs. central tendency being most conformable to the Durkheimian vision).[41]

But beyond this, it is not entirely clear what the game metaphor brings us, in part because there are different sorts of games, and they

---

explanations has hardly been tapped, especially in sociology (cf. White 2008: 49, n. 23). But, there may be a large class of phenomena that game theory cannot account for, due to the endogeneity of goals. This is in effect to restate Emery and Trist's (1965) point: when the ultimate goal of profit requires that firms focus on the proximate goal of attaining a "position" in the field, then "profit maximization" ceases to be enlightening as an explanatory principle.

[40]One response to the issue of whether it is possible to struggle over the rules would be to attempt to introduce the idea of "legitimacy." In this case, we would claim that some people might play the game but not accord the rules legitimacy; such persons would be willing to change or break rules in certain circumstances. I have not been persuaded that this is anything other than a tautological statement, as legitimacy seems to be a heuristic we use for "it's unlikely to work for me to change the rules." But, a sustained exploration will require a more sophisticated understanding of the difference between felt valuation and justification, as our independent empirical assessments of legitimacy come from the latter but are interpreted as the former.

[41]Köhler (1947: 131) clarified the difference between the conventional idea whereby regularity is a result of such compulsion and his own by contrasting the Aristotelian conception of the motion of the planets with the Newtonian. In the former, the regularity of motion had to come from some external constraint—crystal spheres *forced* the planets to stay in their paths. In the latter, it is the "free

have different flavors of action (DiCicco-Bloom and Gibson 2010). The games that are most often used to explain rules are *strategy* games, in which participants take turns—each one's turn is made solo, in response to the turn of opponents (and in some cases allies). This highlights the nature of the *decision* as a part of action—the choice of what to do, conditional on what others have done. Competitions in which such dialogic decision making is absent tend not to be seen as games. And we do not use such competitions (races, ski jumping, eating contests, and so on) as game metaphors, despite the fact that they too have rules that define acceptable play and who wins. Our usage should, perhaps, orient our understanding of what we find interesting in the rules that games have.

Most discussions of the idea of rule begin with the distinction between two sorts of rules; following Searle (1969: 33f, 36, 52), these are distinguished as regulative and constitutive.[42] A constitutive rule might be that "the game of ice hockey shall be played on a white ice surface known as a 'rink,'" or, "the team scoring the greatest number of goals during the three 20-minute periods shall be declared the winner." In Searle's original conception, a regulative rule corresponded to an "ought," in contrast to the "is" (or "*X* counts as *Y*") of the constitutive rules. So, in hockey one *should* try to score a goal, but to do this, we must have a *goal*, defined as "when

---

play of gravitational vectors" that leads to the orderly arrangements of motion that we see as due to the "law" of gravity.

This understanding that regularity was not incompatible with freedom actually was a fundamental part of the vision underlying field theory and its relation to mechanics. Maxwell was in no way congenitally opposed to the reduction of abstract force to mechanical interactions—this is precisely what he did in creating statistical thermodynamics. But, his underlying vision was different from the Hobbesian model of particles that are in themselves inherently passive. While it goes somewhat beyond the bounds of the current work, it is relevant to the arguments regarding the consistency of the various approaches treated here that in creating this vision of thermodynamics, Maxwell first drew on the work of Quetelet and the other social statisticians—Maxwell treated molecules like Quetelet treated persons (we return to Quetelet in the next chapter). Second, in contrast to those assumed an antithesis between order (or regularity) and liberty, Maxwell (in a letter) stressed that not only were the two compatible, but disorder came from an interference with liberty (see Porter 1986: 195; 1987). Thus, Maxwell avoided the logical mistake of the French school, down to and including Durkheim, of assuming that regularity could only be produced by external constraint, as opposed to internal freedom.

[42]This distinction is generally traced to Rawls's (1955) attempt to separate the justification of an institution from a justification of an act subsumed in that institution; as an analogy (p. 16), he argues that a player *in* a game cannot defend his choice of move by arguing that the game itself should be changed in some way or another. (To Rawls, acting within an institution or practice makes no sense if it can reflexively undermine that practice.) The distinction between "regulative" as opposed to "constitutive" is from Kant, fundamental to his first critique, but also found in his discussion of the opposition between mechanistic and functional explanations cited in note 27.

the puck completely crosses the goal line."[43] But, consider the constitutive rule regarding the definition of *high sticking*: first, note that the game does not cease to be hockey if someone high sticks. Second, is there an associated regulative rule (that one should not high stick)?[44] Certainly, in a way this is true, but not so true that there are no specific penalties to the offending player. That is, if one should *never, ever* high stick, wouldn't we want to throw people out of the game forever (as opposed to giving them, e.g., a minor penalty)? It seems that part of the game of hockey involves determining when it is worth the risk of the penalty to break the rule. If there is no high-sticking regulative rule, then does that not seem to imply that for any game there is only one regulative rule—to try to win?

This might seem to imply that in games there is one type of rule, that which constitutes the nature of the game. But, this too seems to introduce more difficulties. For while there are rules against hooking, butting, spearing, and slashing those on the other team, there is apparently no rule against attacking those on one's own team,[45] even with firearms, or against lighting fires to melt the ice in front of one's goal—indeed, it is never specified by the International Ice Hockey Federation rules that all twenty team members must be human beings, as opposed to bears or robots. This is because a game in which robots shoot bears by a large fire on the ice is not recognizably "hockey" to us. The most important constitutive rules seem not to be explicit.[46]

---

[43] Actually, it is somewhat more elaborate: the full definition of a goal in the International Ice Hockey Federation (2006: 49) is as follows: "1. When the puck has been put between the goal posts below the crossbar and entirely across the goal line by the stick of a player of the attacking team; 2. If the puck has been put into the goal net in any way by a player of the defending team; 3. If the puck has been deflected into the goal net from the shot of an attacking player by striking any part of a team-mate; 4. If a player of the attacking team has been physically interfered with, by the action of any defending player so as to cause him to be in the goal crease when the puck enters the goal net, unless if in the opinion of the Referee, he had sufficient time to get out of the crease; 5. If the puck should become loose in the goal crease and then put into the goal net by the stick of the attacking player; 6. When the puck deflects directly off the skate of an attacking or defending player; or 7. If an attacking player being in the goal crease at the moment the puck crosses the goal line and in no way affects the goalkeeper's ability to make a save, unless the cases described in Rule 471."

[44] Searle's attempt to map the constitutive/regulative distinction to "counts as"/"should do" does not work very well, and most of those who have followed this have, like Pollock (1982), interpreted regulative rules to mean rules for penalties and that sort of thing.

[45] Unlike most other rules on aggressive play, the prohibition on kicking does not specify that one is kicking an opponent, but only "another player." But, in all other cases, it is assumed that the victim is someone on the other team.

[46] Actually, the International Ice Hockey Federation (2006: 85) does have a catchall rule, that any player who "makes a travesty of or interferes with or is

If this is so, it becomes difficult to explain precisely how constitutive rules are rules at all. (We would not want to accept the infinite number of true statements regarding what some game is *not* as its "constitutive rules.") That is, we have not formulated the rule "no firearms to be used" in hockey because presumably until now no one ever dreamed that this was an option. There is no rule that *kept* us from this conception; rather, we simply *call* the fact that we do not waste our time with such a ridiculous idea a rule after the fact.

Further, it is not the case that in a game the regulative rules (in Pollock's [1982] sense) cannot be constitutive in terms of the qualitative nature of the activity in hand.[47] For example, in basketball in the early 1980s the "three-point field goal" was introduced. One might reasonably argue that this reward system for one type of shot (an extra point is gained if a basket is scored from further than 22 feet from the basket) is a good example of a regulative rule. Yet, this rule was put into place precisely to change the nature of the game, indeed, to change it *back* to what it was believed to be before the astounding shift in the height distribution led to basketball becoming a very different game (in which "aim" was progressively deemphasized).

This example shows that changes in the game can take place without changes in the rules. And it is in this way that it is not at all wild to argue that part of the struggle is "what the game is about." As Shore (1996: 105f) has emphasized, games are defined not only by constitutive and regulative rules but also by the strategies used by players—new strategies lead to a new game and can undermine old rules. A new kind of aggressive tennis against which previous styles cannot win turns each game *of* tennis into a game *over* tennis—what kinds of players will dominate the field and what sorts of strategies must be adopted by those who would dislodge them. The influx of Hawaiian, Samoan, and now Mongolian wrestlers into Japanese sumo competitions drastically changed the nature of the game and left many Japanese with the feeling that the existing "rules

---

detrimental to the conducting of the game" gets a penalty. But, clearly this rule returns us to the issue of the intersubjective validity of synthetic but nonsubsumptive judgments.

[47]Pollock (1982: 210–214, 229) made this observation, but argued that the problem is that the constitutive rules include those that are senseless to break because they define the institution (e.g., what constitutes a goal in hockey) and the prescriptive rules regarding what one is supposed to do (you are supposed to try to get a goal). He pointed out that such rules cannot be assimilated to the regulative ones because without a prescriptive rule we have no game at all—so what if we define what a goal is? If there is no prescription attached, people will just sit on the ice. Pollock's approach was to include a sense of conventional obligation. But, it seems to me that this is what should be explained on the basis of the configuration of actors, and not the other way around. Giddens's (1979: 67f) discussion was more congenial to the current approach.

of the game" did not work given the new types of competitors; hence, sumo was now a *different* game *because* the rules were the same. Despite the obvious importance of national pride (foreign entrants have been heckled and indeed the subject of death threats[48]), the situation is similar to that in basketball: formal rules do not by themselves define the character of the game.[49]

This becomes crucial when we begin to apply the lessons from games to more weighty forms of social life, in which the absence of referees leads to a blending of "rules" and "strategies," for what you "should" do depends on what others do (also Fligstein 2001). This leads not only to instabilities but also to intransitivities, seen most clearly in the history of war. Mounted knights using stirrups deliver such a huge blow to one another that they require as much protection as possible. Sustained competition can lead to steady increases in their armoring, making their movements clumsier and their riding slower. The warrior who opts for riding a faster, thinner horse and who wears little armoring may hope to rush in and strike a blow at such heavily armored troops before they can get to him. Such light cavalry, however, can suffer greatly at the hands of massed archers, who would be easily dispersed by heavy cavalry. At the most general, and least useful, level, one may insist that the rules of war are not changing—they are always "win by hurting the enemy." But, what this means specifically, and what soldiers will actually learn as rules of war, incorporate shared understandings of the likely tactics of others.

In sum, when we take seriously the metaphor of the game, we find that what we mean by rules refers not only to the formal prescriptions, whether regulative or constitutive, but also to a larger set of shared understandings and expectations that establish a sense of appropriateness.[50] For example, there is an unspoken understanding regarding how hard a gratuitous

---

[48]See *Japan Today*, Tuesday, July 15, 2003.[a]

[49]Indeed, it is unclear to what extent "X counts as Y" has much to do with "constituting" the nature of the game. In chess, we know what "counts as a checkmate" and what it means for a pawn to capture a piece, including the en passant move. It does seem that without "checkmate," we do not have chess, but without the en passant rule we would still have something very chesslike. Further, while competition chess involves rules regarding time usage, this is not generally believed to be constitutive of the game of chess. Hence, two persons can begin a noncompetition game without a clock and still be considered to be playing "chess." But this means that a key issue—how long one can take in making a move before one has actually conceded—is a matter for local negotiation.

[50]Many readers have asked why, at this point, I do not turn to Wittgenstein's famous discussion of the limits of rules and the voluminous secondary literature. The reason is that I do not think that such a discussion can do us any good, and I suspect that it can do us some harm. I believe that the great value of Dewey's philosophy is to demonstrate to us that we should shun with horror all such unforgivably vague analyses of implausibly precise statements and instead work

"check" in hockey must be before it is penalized; without this understanding, the written rule is of little use. Further, such shared expectations may be challenged by those who will gain by a change in the rules (that is, how the rules are actually interpreted); the sense of how strict to be regarding these body checks has indeed changed. Thus, we can understand how in a conventional game the player might *want* to change the rules as part of the play—and in a world without referees this is precisely what happens.

Fine (1987: 20) points out that in their self-organized baseball games, children continually negotiate over the rules during the game—exactly the sort of behavior that seems internally contradictory to the formalist (Rawlsian) perspective.[51] Yet, such games still seem more like the phenomena in which we are interested than the more rule-regulated contests that involve "parallel play," whereby competitors carry out their actions

---

toward maximally clear analyses of inherently vague phenomena. By choosing an analytic philosophy based in mathematics that at the time was understood as an inherently contradictory enterprise, Wittgenstein could be sure that he could pose questions that others could not answer and, if he could skirt around proposing an answer himself, would have an elegant piece of work. But, things without possible solutions are not problems.

Further, the approach of the Wittgensteinians in the social sciences has largely proceeded according to the following syllogism: (A) Wittgenstein can throw any discussion about rules into confusion; (B) X is a case of "rules"; hence (C) I can derail the current discussion of X. The claim that social life, meaning, habit, or action necessarily is "rule" bound (e.g., Winch 1958: 59, 87) has simply been assumed by such authors, and I think it is not correct in the way that they mean it.

Finally, it is no accident that the adoption of Wittgenstein into the social sciences has come by blending his approach with that of Durkheim—quite deliberately in some cases (e.g., Bloor 1983: 20; in chapter 4, I cite Gellner's acid discussion of the same blurring). There is still demand for a pseudo-Durkheimian philosophy of arbitrariness, and those who recognize the incoherence of Durkheim's strong claims about cognition may find Wittgenstein's paucity of claims a better grounding (Campbell 1996: 55). In a way, there *is* a part of Durkheim's corpus that is relevant to this problem, but it is not the psychology of language: it is his argument regarding the insufficiency of formal contract. Contra Spencer, Durkheim ([1893] 1933) argued—quite successfully, as it appears to me—that every formal agreement does rely and must rely on unstated common (or presumed-to-be-common) assumptions about the intention and extension of the terms used. This not only supports my arguments regarding the interpretation of rules here, but is in accord with legal philosophy, with common sense, and it easily indicates why any overly analyticomathematical approach to rules will be a disaster. This *without* spending too much time with Wittgenstein.

[51] As an only somewhat malicious experiment, I suggest playing a game with a child and systematically winning by breaking unspecified rules to watch how people struggle to formalize the rules that are implicit (e.g., no punching in thumb wrestling; okay, no punching *or* head butting; okay, no punching, head butting, *or* foot stomping; and so on).

independently. (For example, competitive eating rules have been adumbrated by the International Federation of Competitive Eating, but we would not use these rules as the core examples with which to think through social action.) If sandlot baseball is more like social life than is competitive eating, then whatever is essential in the rule-governed nature of games does not seem to be negated by the case of "disputes over the rules" during the game. We began by considering the extremely detailed rules and regulations of the International Ice Hockey Federation and found that even here there were necessary appeals to tacit understandings. But to take the special case of the game with outside authorities as our model for game-like behavior in general is a serious error akin to taking formalized "languages" as our model for linguistic capacity (discussed briefly in the next chapter; also see Wieder 1971: 108f). The virtue of the game metaphor is that it can lead us away from an overly formal/subsumptive understanding of rules to one highlighting the alignment of expectations.[52]

Rules and Patterns

We can either wring our hands in despair that game metaphor breaks down when we accept that we cannot usefully distinguish between constitutive and regulative rules, and that rules can be negotiated during games, or we can see whether perhaps we have misunderstood the most important part of the game metaphor. Let us begin with the more general and open-ended nature of rules and see if we can shed light on the key issues that brought us to the idea of the game in the first place. The resulting understanding of rules is not necessarily innovative, nor is it intended to be. It is, I believe, held by a number of those who attempt to understand the nature of "institutions," which is what first brought Searle and Rawls to the case of games.

No one is quite sure what *isn't* an institution, but everyone seems to be sure that institutions do all sorts of things. The most common definition of an institution is something akin to "a pattern of regularized conduct," which leads to two immediate problems for the development of institutional analysis. The first is that our term is evidently coterminous with the subject matter of our discipline (the social sciences by nature being ill-equipped to study things that only happen once). The second is that institutions obviously cannot "do" the things that they are often said to do (e.g., Douglas 1986) because by definition institutions are themselves the doing.

---

[52]For examples of our key pragmatist sources turning to game analogies to explore the nature of action, see Pepper (1966: 573) and Dewey ([1922] 1930: 145, 220). Perhaps it is significant that when Wittgenstein ([1945–1949] 1958: 39) raises the possibility that we "make up the rules as we go along," he switches to English.

When theorists look at institutions more carefully, however, they often conclude that the most important thing about institutions is not that the observer can see the regularity, but that the participants can (e.g., Parsons and Shils 1954). From this perspective, the thing that is distinctive about an institution is not that it is regular, for there are patterns of conduct whose regularity may be seen by an acute ethological observer but are missed by the participants themselves. Instead, what is distinctive to institutional conduct is that you know, when interacting with some type of person or in some setting, more or less what to do.

This alignment takes place, as Bloor (1997: 31, 34; cf. Searle 1969: 51) has emphasized, when ego cannot make reference to her own ideas without circular reference to alter's—put another way, an institution exists when and to the extent that our first-order beliefs ("in a handshake one should do so-and-so") have collapsed into our second-order beliefs ("other people believe that 'in a handshake one should do so-and-so'").[53] We know what-to-do "when" shaking hands because to know "shaking hands" is just to know this what-to-do. It is, to anticipate, largely for this reason that language is of some use as a template for social action—for as Mead (1934) said, it is the paradigmatic case of the significant symbol, in which our own gesture must (or so we say) evoke in ourselves the same response it evokes in the other, leading to one sort of intersubjective alignment.[54]

Another common example of such an institution is "marriage": this institution is not defined in terms of concrete patterns of conduct between particular persons; rather, we say that it is an institution because if two people do get married the range of arbitrary actions they could take is considerably narrowed (Swidler 2001; Turner 1974: 17). While they need not fulfill any particular expectations, nonfulfillment will have a clear semiotic import, whether or not this is intended. Normative accounts have had difficulty in explaining how persons manage to walk around with the vast catalogues of rules they are supposedly following (also see Taylor 1995: 175, 177). Yet scoffing at the implausibility of such

---

[53] Thus, Bloor (1997: 33) undersells his point in calling an institution a stable pattern of interaction, for there can be stable patterns of interaction—social structures in the sense of Martin (2009) or perhaps systems in the sense of Giddens (1979: 64)—that lack this coterminal relation of first- and second-order beliefs. Searle's (1995: 5, 32, 106, 144) take manages to combine the fuzziness of Bourdieu's with the implausible requirement that all persons have the same subjectivity (hence leading to the postulation of some sort of collective intentionality).

[54] Things only become interesting when we understand that the Meadian criterion is just partially met in practice. What is a stumbling block for definitions that *assume* identical subjectivities across persons and places is completely expected when we begin from Dewey's insistence, discussed in chapter 5, that our understanding of how we get the knowledge we *do* have is not shattered when it turns out that this same process brings in the knowledge we later reject (that is, "misunderstanding").

accounts—and pointing to the fact that the nonfulfillment of norms can be explained neither by randomness nor by orneriness—does not answer the remaining question of how social life *is* as regular as it is.

We have very plausible, if somewhat bland, theoretical explanations—each act reinforces the general understanding that is then drawn on for further acts (e.g., Giddens 1979, 1984; Bourdieu [1979] 1984). But, as Turner (1994) has argued, such accounts—seemingly impervious to assault due to their absolute generality—make an unfounded assumption, and this is that there is "an" institution. Again, we find social scientific theories tending to assimilate things to a subsumptive framework, a formalized one in which a particular action falls under the more general heading ("shaking hands") to which are attached shared meanings. Just as we tend to assume the particular case of a formalized language—one that has a government commission to standardize usage—and not the more common case of a dispersion of dialects, so we assume the case of the International Ice Hockey Federation and not pick-up street hockey games. Both are relatively misleading choices of analogy to social action.

Consider spelling. A movement to systematize English spelling really only got under way in the eighteenth century (Carney 1994: 467; Strang 1970: 107f). In documents, especially handwritten ones, from the seventeenth century and before, it is common to see the same author spell the same word differently in a single sentence. Official state documents from the early sixteenth century are a marvelous profusion of creative answers to the question, "How shall I transfer this word to paper?" Now, it is not that there were *no* rules to spelling; one might write "the Kinges Majestie" or "the kings majesty" or "the Kinges maiestie" but not "dee keeenghs madgesteee" or "xxx xxxxx xxxxxxx."

This sort of unsystemized rule-bound action no longer occurs in our spelling, but it does in our pronunciation and our accents. For example, Searle (1969: 42) points out that if we were to make a word "longer" in the sense of "someone who longs," we would know that it should be pronounced differently from the comparative "longer" (which has a hard "g"), although we would not know why. This case is useful because it is widely accepted across America. Yet, these same sorts of rules often vary *within* languages (often regionally or ethnically), leading to a dispersion of lawfulnesses that the formalist perspective can only see as anarchy.

Generalizing, we may propose that although it is not mistaken to see rules as related to institutions, we cannot claim that every institution exists because it possesses crisp definitions and clearly demarcated jurisdictions. But, not all forms of patternings are institutions—as we have seen, there are forms of patterning for which we do not understand "the rule"—that is, we intuit the pattern and can judge the rightness or wrongness of usage, a "sense of" appropriateness (Bourdieu [1980] 1990), although we cannot formalize this propositionally. If we return to the findings of the Gestalt theorists reviewed in chapter 5, we can understand that such pattern recognition is something that we do on a fundamental level (as opposed to needing to use conscious serial processing). Thus, for most of us, the "glitch" in +1, 0, −1, 0, +1, 0,−1, 0, +1, 0,−1, 0, 0, 0,−1, 0 and so on is immediately recognizable because we visually *pattern* the regularity as a succession of ones and zeros although few re-create the formula guiding the pattern[55] or experience a similar violation in 0 1 1 2 3 5 8 12 21 even though there is also a violation of the principle of regularity of the Fibonacci series.

There is every reason to think that our perceptual system is oriented to perceiving such regularities in space, and some reason to expect the same for temporal regularities. In some cases, our "getting" the pattern is brought to consciousness, and in such cases (if the material is human action) we would speak of an "institution."[56] Thus, we can use the term *institution*, then, to refer not to a *pattern* of regularized conduct, but the intersubjectively valid representation of the *patterning* of that regularized conduct (cf. Kant [1785] 1922: 39, 57, 80; [1785] 1964: 29, 45, 65). It is this subjective version of the regularity that allows for extrapolation and expectation—for surprise and confirmation.

All this is unremarkable, but it implies that we may make a distinction between people's abilities to navigate patterns of regularity (which may or may not be formulated as a conscious principle) and their capacity to give names to these regularities. Institutions are simply one particular subset of a more general, and nonproblematic, process of intuiting patterns. Just as the horse Clever Hans could add numbers by tapping his hoof (as long as he could perceive the abatement of tension in his owner, Wilhelm von Osten, as Hans approached the sum), so we may calibrate ourselves to complex regularities that are partially stored, in subjective form, across many different interactants.

While it is implausible that people carry around rules *as* rules, that is, as formal prescriptions, it in no way strains credulity to imagine that people can develop subjective correlates of the imperatives associated with particular positions. In particular, not only can we bring some patterns to consciousness as institutions, but also we may solidify some aspects of these in the form of "official" rules, and the choice of which aspects are solidified may pertain to historical and practical matters (say, how to ensure reasonable transposability across generation or locale).[57]

But the most important thing about the case of rules in games is the more general action imperatives that come when we recognize what is called for, whether or not we can specify it in propositional form. To each

---

[55] For the ith number this series is $2[\cos(\pi i/2) + 1]$ where i is considered a radian.

[56] A general approach to social life based on the simple idea of patterns inspired the work of Ruth Benedict and Margaret Mead, but they seem to have been unable to transmit their excitement in the idea of pattern to others.

[57] This is exactly the opposite of the argument of Searle (1969: 13) that such rules could *not* be empirical generalizations.

individual, these imperatives are conditional on position, but seen from the point of view of the position, they are conditional on the individual—at least, those attributes that are relevant. We all understand that the rule "people expect the gentleman to let the lady enter the door first" has a different imperative depending on whether we are the gentleman or the lady and whether we wish to be polite or rude. Similarly, the imperative attached to a position (e.g., what a first-year law student "is" to do) may vary by characteristics and trajectory.

Not all social action is made in reference to these common understandings; one can be blissfully unaware of what others think, want, or expect and act efficaciously nonetheless. But the degree of "sociality" of our action may be treated as proportional to the degree to which it only makes sense against a backdrop of others' actions. When action is highly social, we see the unity between the two senses of field, the field of force and the field of contestation: action is oriented to social objects that have phenomenologically valid qualities with subjective counterparts—action imperatives—that may be experienced as if they were "social forces," but this force is only the tension inherent in a set of highly leveraged expectations. And we are free to pull even the most dangerous of these levers.

This sense of rules may seem disappointingly unstructured, but it has important implications for how we think of explanation. In particular, it is compatible with the idea of explaining aggregate action by recourse to myriad interactions by actors, each conditional on the past action of others. This type of explanation is getting a great deal of popularity these days because of dramatic increases in computational power, allowing for simulations of complex outcomes from simple models. Unlike most explanatory fads, this one is important and may be the single most promising path forward (and was suggested before it was practicable by Homans [1967: 82]). It is not the use of simulation or agent-based models that is important, but that we derive our vision of explanation from the reciprocality of interaction and realize that only in simple cases are actors interchangeable or have the convenient distributions on certain parameters that allow for a single equilibrium. The rules in the sense of the emergent patterns are quite different from the laws, which refer to the principles of action on the part of myriad individuals; the Durkheimian approach establishes a one-to-one correspondence between these.

This understanding of rules, then, is compatible with a more general sense of the emergence of social regularity via processes whereby each acts conditional on the acts of others—"bootstrapped induction," as Barry Barnes (1983; also 1995: 60) calls it. The general assumption of the social sciences that staying the same, being average, need not be explained, only deviation from the average or change, leads us to tend to imagine that in the absence of "resistance," institutions are perpetuated. "Habit" is often invoked as part of a noiseless feedback loop of reproduction, as one pole of a continuum, on the other end of which we find "agency." But, as Barnes (2000: 55, 67) has stressed, if individuals were to act according to pure habit they would make a hash of institutions.[58] Keeping the social nonproblematic nonproblematic is a problem for actors and requires their continual readjustment and mutual susceptibility. Thus, in general there is not "an" institution but some dispersion into variants. Any absence of dispersion implies that normal processes have been arrested (e.g., by state power, as in the case of the formation of languages). Just as we saw Durkheim's fundamental epistemology needing to be stabilized by the presence of authority, so too we see that the conventional understanding of rules is one that requires the policing of subjectivity to prevent us from wandering away.

Rules and Alignment

We first approached this issue of rules by thinking about fields in the sense of spaces for contest. But this unfolding has brought us back to the other understanding of fields, namely, fields of forces, and this is because we now realize that the rules are themselves subjectively understood patterns of alignment. And it is such alignments that generate force fields. To return to the root metaphor for field theory (classical magnetism), a normal iron bar has a number of magnetic domains, each with its very small, local, magnetic field. When placed in a magnetic field, however, these domains align themselves so that they have a common orientation, and the iron becomes a magnet. If we somehow freeze the position of the units generating these local fields (often involving cooling an alloy), then the field effect is permanent. The parallel to social life is direct and useful: fields arise from alignment of local vectors.

This idea of alignment is nothing new; many sociological theories begin with some form of alignment (no matter what word is used). For example, when Parsons and Shils (1954) begin from expectations, they are considering the action alignment of an abstract ego and alter. Indeed, we may see an institution as arising when patterns of alignment are persistent enough to survive the replacement of individuals. (That is, rather than some particular ego and alter developing idiosyncratic expectations and each aligning herself to the particularities of the other, we have a situation in which alter can exit and be replaced by a third person without ego needing to change her expectations.)

Thus, it is not the mere fact of alignment, nor the obduracy of alignment, that leads us to speak of a field. Further, the subjective effects of a field of force—the phenomenological experience of requiredness—may

---

[58]Barnes suggests imagining a parade or orchestra in which all individuals operate independently according to habit. He justly emphasizes that this point is missed by the recent theoretical arguments that draw on pragmatist and field conceptions (such as those of Bourdieu and Giddens), who would fain make a smooth transition from the sorts of nonproblematic individual practices of interest to Dewey and the large-scale nonproblematic social practices that we call institutions.

be fundamentally the same whether the alignments are those of particular dyadic ones of a significant other or those of a full-scale field. It is the presence of some sort of large-scale organization to these alignments that leads us to speak of a social field.

Here, we may consider the development of the idea of the organizational field as a guide.[59] No one doubts that organizations themselves are institutions and thus imply significant regularity of expectation and hence alignment of actions. But we only speak of organizations forming a field when the pattern of alignments makes use of the idea of *position*. Here, the key idea was put forward by Emery and Trist (1965: 21, 28), who started from the Gestalt theorists, from Lewin, from Pepper, and from Tolman and Brunswik (1935). Emery and Trist proposed that we can understand an organization, like an organism, as situated in an environment, such that the actions of the organization have to be treated as correlative to the degree of structure of its environment. In some cases, this environment has no overall structure, so the organization—like an organism in an undifferentiated environment—may as well be one place as any other. "There is no distinction between tactics and strategy" (24) since all action is local, and one attempts to do as well as one can without needing to plan a trajectory (link local action to global pattern).

In other cases, there is some rudimentary organization to the environment (such as might be the case in a market in which any organization could only serve one "niche" in a preference space). Far more structure enters when organizations have to be cognizant of the actions of *other* organizations. But what Emery and Trist (1965) called a "turbulent field" only arises when the strategy of any organization is not only cognizant of the actions of others but primarily oriented to these others. Thus, one does not simply pursue one's goal with regular attention to the actions of others (and hence have the alignment characteristic of those running in parallel to the same finish line); as the archetypical strategy now becomes attaining or maintaining some position in the field, alignment is pursued as at least a proximate goal, if not an end in itself.

This sort of alignment is amenable to empirical study. Thus, DiMaggio and Powell (1983) proposed that this sort of structuration is largely a result of the patterning of relations, for it is these sorts of patternings that

---

[59] An alternate approach to the regularities across organizations would be the ecological. In particular, Abbott (2005: 248f) has put forward a general approach to such ecological analysis that is closely related to the field conception. A set of relations forms an ecology when there are partial interdependencies between them; the ecology (like the field conception) parses these into actors and positions, using similar spatial metaphors. Like the field, the ecological space is not an empty one waiting for people to be dropped into it but rather is an endogenous product of the set of relations themselves. One might propose that the more "local" the action—the more the world is like an English muffin as opposed to a pancake—the more the ecological perspective will be preferable to the field conception.

allow positions to emerge from sets of relationships. Drawing on White, Boorman, and Breiger (1976), we may say that they are relations of both direct interaction and structural equivalence in ties (DiMaggio 1986). Two different—even hostile—firms may be drawn closer because they share suppliers and distributors.

Returning to the more general case of social action, we may also say that fields exist when patterns of local alignment—the sorts of things that we often derive when we consider an abstract ego and alter interacting—become globally organized (although not necessarily globally uniform), so that the felt imperative that ego has is attached not to a particular alter, nor to an institution, but to a position in a larger set of positions. Indeed, it may well be that the field effect involves a reduction of these myriad relationships to a manageable position, in the same way that a role simplifies many interactions with different concrete others (cf. Bourdieu and Wacquant 1992: 113f). If so, this would suggest that field theory has an advantage over other approaches in that its form of analytic simplification does not cut across the principles of our subjects but instead dovetails with actors' attempts to simplify social reality into a sense of imperative attached to position.

Finally, we find that the sense of rules *as* alignments that we have come to by considering fields as spaces of contestation is just the material that we need for fields as fields of force, for these are the sorts of local alignments that *can* be globally organized. The field theoretic approach to regularity, unlike the conventional causal one, is consistent in being based in the general process of the formation of rules. Thus, although this view of rules is hardly new, it is key to the coherence of a social aesthetics.

We have seen that both senses of the field—the field as field of force and the field as terrain of contestation—point to the same understanding of the lawfulness or purposiveness of action. This understanding, while not antithetical to those common in sociological theory, yet is somewhat different as it pertains, first and foremost, to our capacity to intuit patterns and respond appropriately, whether or not we bring these patterns to consciousness as part of the process. What is key is that this supports one of the central claims of field theory, on which all else rests, namely, that persons feel the imperatives for action associated with any situation. Having established this as at least plausible, we can see what light it sheds on the key issues of motivations with which the book began.

GOODS AND MOVEMENT

Motivation

There is a tradition of social analysis, inspired by economics, that is able to explain every bit of social action quite satisfactorily, with one exception—what people are trying to do in the first place. Here, analysts can only shrug their shoulders helplessly and say that whatever people are doing allows them to reach some end state that they subjectively desire. Their desires, however, must be treated as fundamentally inexplicable (see Birken 1988). We previously saw theorists associated with the field tradition arguing that such subjective representations of "what is good to strive for" (e.g., Bourdieu's "enjeu" or Emery and Trist's [1965: 28] "values"), instead of being considered external to the system of action, should be understood as a product of it.

This completely general statement—a vague promise that we should be able to discern the origin of values in the set of actions that seem to be explained *by* these values—is hardly as empty as it first appears, for it implies the dissolution of the standard idea of "values." We found ourselves seeking a social aesthetics because social action engages phenomenological objects that we found intrinsically value laden. These objects, we then concluded, must properly be understood not as things but as sets of relations. We then found ourselves led toward field theory because any coherence in sets of relations might be understood as a position in a phenomenologically consistent world (as opposed to a mere set of "surrounding conditions" [*Umwelt*]; see chapter 5). Thus, the reason that values are endogenous to a system of interaction is that there simply are no "exogenous" values at all. Put somewhat differently, values as conventionally understood are not themselves motivations; rather, they are a term for a *folk theory* of motivation, a folk theory that those in the social sciences cling to even though they know it is wrong.

In this folk theory, we have transcendent "conceptions of the desirable," such as "freedom" or "justice," that motivate our behavior. The small print immediately comes in the form of an acknowledgment that these do not inform our behavior in any particular situation. For this, the value must be translated into specific "norms" (see Hitlin and Piliavin 2004: 361). Unfortunately, even these norms do not do quite as much in terms of predicting behavior as seemingly less-relevant social expectations (see Maio et al. 2001). (Thus, in the famous Milgram [1974] experiments, behavior had less to do with fundamental values such as "don't torture the innocent" than with actors' unwillingness to go against others' expectations regarding how a standard action unfolds in a particular institutional context.[60])

In other words, research demonstrates that in different situations we feel pressure—a virtual "social force"—to act in some way as opposed to some other, and that these pressures vary in a nonrandom way across situations (Mey [1965] 1972: 168; Barnes 1995: 59). This is simply to say

---

[60]Of course, it is quite true that many resisted the "force" of these situational expectations, but it is far from clear that this resistance should be attributed to "values" as opposed to "habit" in Aristotle's sense; going against expectations, like other difficult acts, is likely to be facilitated by drill.

Fields and Games

that situations have their own affordances. But, in certain circumstances in everyday life we attempt to *account* for our action by invoking a trans-situational—indeed, occult—factor, namely, values. These values are "measurable" in interview-type situations, though, sadder but wiser realists that we are, we accept that numerous "other factors" also "affect" our action in particular (concrete) situations.

If a value is a folk theory of motivation, then in what way is it different from an institution, which we saw was the consciousness of a patterning that required the coterminal alignment of first- and second-order beliefs? It seems quite plausible that the major difference is that we produce "institutions" (in the sense of bringing them up) when we are queried about *what* we are doing, when we feel that the question comes from an eager learner interested in the substance of our action, but we generate values when we are queried *why* we are doing things, when we feel that the questioner is potentially critical or at least at arm's length and uninterested in the particular situation and substance. (Here, we can compare the discussion of these questions in chapter 1.) There need be no experienced difference between the two until the social situation that calls them forth.[61]

The value, then, seems to be some sense of appropriateness abstracted from any situation.[62] Of course, actors are never nowhere, but some particular situations (e.g., the pub debate or the pencil personality test) are, in their concrete experiential nature, abstracted from something else.[63] Any acceptable explanation must simply consider the interview one type of situation, and the imperative associated with this situation (that is, to

---

[61]For an example, when I first interviewed at the University of Chicago, I teasingly asked at dinner why everyone was dressed up all the time (I did not get the job). One senior faculty member reflected seriously and said, "We do this to show respect for our students." I thought that a fine answer, and when I years later joined the university, I made sure to wear a jacket because I too want to signal respect for my students (even though I am around as comfortable in a sports jacket as I would be in a gorilla costume). But, reflecting on Turner's work made me realize that this might be this one person's *theory* of the institution, one invoking a value ("respect"), and not part of the institution itself.

[62]This in no way implies that all are poseurs and that people do not "live up to" their values. Many do, and we have many reasons to be impressed with this. But this is an empirical question, not a definition of values. The very fact that we are impressed and often surprised by those whose situational conduct does not differ from their values supports the contention that what we mean by values is something that refers to a particular class of abstract situations.

[63]Thus, "being in an auto accident" is a situation different from others, but it is not inherently *abstracted* from others. Answering a hypothetical question about what you would do were you in an auto accident, however, *is* abstracted, in that it is abstracted from the situation of being in an auto accident.

display "values") has no inherently hierarchical relation with the imperatives associated with other situations. The problem with the idea that concrete situations are influenced by values that can be treated as exogenous to the system of social interaction is not that "we don't *really* pursue ultimate values." It is that (as Dewey [1918, 1923] and James [1890/1950: I, 479] also insisted) only the phenomenologically concrete is capable of *bearing* value. Rather than there being two types of values, ultimate and situational (corresponding to Kant's two types of imperative, the categorical and the hypothetical), there is (if the arguments made here are correct) only one. The conception of field is so apposite because it suggests an overall linkage of positions such that, when in any position, we need not make the cumbersome translation of some "ultimate" value (evidence for the existence of which has never been found) into a conditional strategy, but rather find the appropriateness of an action in the qualitative nature of the experience of *being* in that position—that is, having a set of relations.

In chapter 7, I tried to retain the term *motivation* to indicate the subjective states that lie behind action (whatever this might turn out to mean), while distinguishing this from the productions in response to the particular situation of challenge discussed in chapter 1, which I called *motives*. These verbal productions arise in retrospective accountings; hence, they are not causes, but effects, of actions (here see Merleau-Ponty 1962: 435). Given the possibility of confusion, it would be preferable if we were able to be more specific regarding what a motivation might be. For want of a better term, we can provisionally use "impulsion" to denote the lying-behind-action that we generally confuse with motives.[64] (Although impulsion does not do justice to the nature of the field effect as a *pull* and not merely a *punch*; perhaps it can be pronounced as *impullsion*.) The field approach attempts to describe this "impulsion" as a joint feature of experienced environment and individual position.

In hockey, the puck being down the ice gives a phenomenological sense of tension and danger for those on defense. Until the puck is away, there is a sense of what to do—get the puck and send it to a forward.

---

[64] As we have seen, phenomenologically there may be no difference between impulsion and invitation—whether you are pulled by a string from the front or pushed by a rod from behind. It is only our insistence on attaching heavily value-laden and paradoxical interpretations to the phenomenological description that leads us to imagine that using one word is equivalent to determinism and the other equivalent to indeterminism. Or in Köhler's (1938: 357) words: "In a metaphorical fashion the springs of human action have often been called 'forces.' It appears that, if these springs have any counterparts, these counterparts can only *be* forces in the strict sense of the term. On the other hand, if they are actually forces, their behavior within contexts of neural events will resemble human motivation to such an extent that I doubt whether structurally and functionally any difference will be left."

What is notable is that the defense player's objective is *not* to (himself) score a goal, which is the forward's objective (and which might be given as a "rule" of the game in a verbal presentation to a novice). The forward and the defenseman neither share a value just because they play on the same team nor is their "disagreement" regarding what is to be done problematic. Thus, one can conceive of a game in which every position is tied to a conception of "what is to be done" without overall agreement about what is "good."

In other words, if we use the word *values* to mean that which leads us to prefer some states as opposed to others (and not "explanatory productions in particularly abstracted situations"), there is no intrinsic difference between values and impulsions (again, in the specific sense used here). From a phenomenological perspective, both cases involve things that strike the actor (and justifiably so) as qualitative features of the immediate environment (cf. Merleau-Ponty 1962: 49f). In everyday life, however, we generally use *values* to denote the imperatives that we believe to be widely shared, perhaps because they only appear in situations that are abstracted from the pressures that divide us.[65]

Thus, it is not only struggles for obviously positional goods (such as in the game "get to the head of the line"), which require that we reject models of decontextualized motivation (e.g., "maximize utility") in favor of a positional analysis. The simplest null model of action is not an isolated actor carrying out a discrete, individual goal; it is rather the actor whose actions are comprehensible and effective because they are embedded in a nonproblematic field of partial solutions. We would not, in general, take "a road" (one particular road abstracted from all others) because of our "desire" to attain "one place" divorced from other roads and connections.

In sum, the field conception does three things. First, it highlights the importance of the felt motivation of impulsion (as opposed to retrospective accountings) and connects these first-person experiences with felt valuation. Second, it attaches impulsion or, more generally, subjective representations of "what is good to strive for," to positions. Third and consequently, it defines the ethical or imperative nature of such motivations as

---

[65] Actors may christen those of their impulsions that they deem worthy "values," but this is simply to anticipate the universal assent of others that these impulsions indeed are (or better, that they will turn out to be) acceptable motivations as opposed to impulsions that either lack legitimacy or need to be further justified. In other words, the division actors make between values and "other motivations" is the subjective counterpart to that which analysts make, and turns on the degree of consensus, not a phenomenologically valid felt difference between "being moved" and "valuing." If, as in chapter 6, we invert Kant's formulation, we might say that an impulsion paradigmatically becomes a value when we believe that we can appeal to others to recognize its intrinsic rightness without apology. More generally, it may so become value when we realize we can—and anticipate needing to—answer challenges abstracted from substance without lessening our personhood.

akin to a social object, external and (locally) intersubjectively valid, that is, valid conditional on position and history.

Thus, the seemingly different ideas of fields of contestation and fields of force are at worst somewhat loose metaphors that each express one side of a single phenomenon. A field is that which induces conceptions of conduct appropriate to a position—both actors and analysts will agree that there is no conceptual difficulty in seeing action as involving objectivity and choice since one can be counted on to distill a sense of "where to go from here" from one's position. Where the failure to understand the phenomenological validity of such imperatives leads mainstream theoretical traditions to parameterize this situation as some sort of puzzling and unstable mixture of "structure" and "agency"—thereby managing to combine both an uncritical acceptance of actors' self-conceptions and an adherence to nonsensical philosophical abstractions—we can describe a single motion.[66]

Even more important, we are returned to the problem uncovered in chapter 6 pertaining to the translation of the Gestalt model of perception to the case of social objects. It makes perfect sense that we can retrieve qualities of our physical environment in such a way that we know what we are going to do. Phenomenologically, we decided to treat such affordances as qualities of the objects themselves. But it was not at all clear how something similar could be done with the case of social objects, because here the same "object" may have different affordances—and indeed, different qualities—for different persons. We can now return to the question of affordances and consider how they appear in the social field.

To anticipate, we first derived the field approach as the organization of qualitative experiences that could be interpreted as vectors. We returned to this from a somewhat different route, considering the field as a field of contestation with its own "rules." This gave us a sense of how to consider the channeling of actions toward regularity—not an external structure, but the outcome of processes of mutual alignment. This allows us to shed additional light on the central issue of how we might understand actors grasping action imperatives from the environment, and the key role of position in leading to the emergence of a field.

The Nonarbitrariness of Social Perception

We saw in chapter 4 that the social sciences repeatedly rely on an understanding that there are "socially constructed" categories that define objects for interaction. But making this argument has always required emphasizing

---

[66]Thomas Hobbes ([1651] 1909: 162) had a similar idea in trying to circumvent the common inability to deal with human action other than through law as opposed to choice, giving as an example of his conception fluid mechanics: "As in the water, that hath not only *liberty* but a necessity of descending by the Channel;

the nonnatural if not arbitrary nature of these categories, and assuming (for the purposes of derivation) consensus among all those in some culture. (That is, any systematic distinction in how objects are "constructed" undermines the coherence of the explanatory project, so only one or two possible ways of dividing up the world are permitted in any particular case.) Thus, when people speak of the "social construction" of gender, they implicitly discount the possibility of tens of thousands of different theories of gender in the same society. Such a catastrophic situation would strike us not as a case of social construction but as individual idiosyncrasy, and the social scientist responds to the prospect with the same intolerant disapproval with which a Stalinist might view Woodstock.

This (presumed) uniformity of subjectivity is correlative to the (presumed) arbitrariness of the phenomenon: our principles of division are so disconnected from the nature of the world (whatever that might mean) that they can only exist if we *all* agree that it is so.[67] If in the "modern world" we have the (presumed) anomalous case of groups within a single society possessing different subjectivities, then each group must close itself off as a "subuniverse of meaning" (Berger and Luckmann 1967). No group's arbitrary principles of division could withstand scrutiny from an outsider. Not only does the destruction of traditional religion follow as

---

so likewise the actions which men voluntarily doe." Also see the discussion of Barnes (2000: 18) and White (2008: 16).

[67] According to Berger and Luckmann (1967: 103): "The institutional order ... is continually threatened by the presence of realities that are meaningless in *its* terms. ... All societies are constructions in the face of chaos." Similarly, Schutz ([1932] 1967: 9, 42, 69, 84) began by criticizing perhaps the least shaky of Weber's postulates, namely, the existence of intersubjective agreement; for Schutz, in contrast to the Gestalt theorists, phenomenology was not a science of phenomena (as actualities) but a tendentious derivation of the possibility of phenomena (as if such a thing were necessary). Beginning with the armchair theorist's abstract actor, he injected a subjective willfulness in accounting for the meaningful nature of experience, using not the reflection of Dewey, part of a cycle of response to a largely patterned but frequently troublesome environment, but the reflection of the sedentary philosopher. Not surprisingly, this led him to assume that there was a necessary moment of synthetic interpretation of experience before it (experience) could be itself. While generally appealing to the phenomenology of Husserl as his starting point, Schutz ignored the fact that while Husserl ([1900] 1970: 226, 249, 309) saw this phenomenology as an attempt to "lay bare the sources" of general experiences (e.g., logic), he emphasized that the object was given "as" itself to our knowledge, as opposed to synthesized by consciousness out of sensations. Husserl's emphasis ([1900] 1970: 359, 367, 426, 428, 430f) on the phenomenological validity of universal objects (as opposed to the Lockean/Millsian conception, which makes these classes of particulars united by an abstract concept) has important implications for the nature of the abstract as opposed to the concrete (discussed in chapters 1 and 9).

obvious from any such pluralistic confrontation with unbelievers (Berger 1969: esp. 16f, 159ff), but the same may be said of *any* cognitive orientation: only let a child point out that the emperor has no clothes, and all will collapse (cf. Zerubavel 2006).[68]

In contrast, we saw that the Gestalt theorists argued that percepts are fundamentally organized because they come from a world or environment with its own principles of organization.[69] The task of the perceiver is to establish an ontological complicity—to take advantage of the preexisting structural principles or "causal texture" of the social order (Heider 1958: 80).

Yet, at the same time, we recognized that the processes of adequate response to the principles of environmental organization varied by position of the actor; what originally seemed paradoxical given some Gestalt theorists' enthusiastic acceptance of naïve realism turned out to be quite prosaic when we realize that what we find veridical is not persons' *accounts* but their ability to retrieve appropriate imperatives for action. A cliff that one is on top of is not the same thing as the cliff that one is under—the first looks and feels dangerous as one nears the edge because one fears dropping off. The second only feels dangerous to the extent that one may be dropped upon. The qualities of the cliff are an interaction between positions; the dangerousness of the cliff tells us not only about the cliff but also about our current position vis-à-vis it.

Thus, the field terminology captures a crucial aspect of social aesthetics, namely, the inseparability of perception and apperception (perception of one's own person as perceiver). The process whereby the actor takes in information about the world (exterospecific information [Gibson [1979] 1986: 183]) is not merely *relative* to this person's position in the field (as in the early work of Mannheim [1929/1936]); it actually provides the actor information about his or her own position (as in Mannheim 1940: 212f; cf. Köhler 1947: 297), that is, "interospecific" information. Our ability to orient to our surroundings in terms of "position"—Bourdieu (1985b: 728) termed this "a sense of one's place"—implies that rather than it being analytically more complex to move from the perception of individual social objects to a whole, to an organized constellation of objects (a social field), it is easier.

Position, then, is itself or can be a simplification of the infinity of practical imperatives that threaten to swamp the conventional "roles-and-rules"

---

[68] This is related to the assumption that we have seen in a number of forms, namely, that there is "a" grid, "an" institution, "a" rule, "a" language—this sort of uniformity, one that we find in *ruled culture*, probably *does* generally require the thought policing that social constructionism imagines is inherent to social thought.

[69] As Koffka (1935: 67) argued, "The environment is neither a mosaic of sensations nor a 'blooming, buzzing confusion,' nor a blurred and vague total unit; rather does it consist of a definite number of separate objects and events, which, as separate objects and events, are products of organization."

approach. We found that situational sensitivity might allow persons to know what to do when they are in one position (and actually to leave this knowledge behind when they leave). This suggests that position may be key to the idea of cognitive economy that motivated the Gestalt approach.

Terseness and Position

We began with one critical quality of objects that was obviously interactional and relational, namely, their affordances—what they call on us to do. As the distillation of the objective requirements associated with a position, such affordances are notable for their cognitive economy. To know that a fruit is sweet, one need not perform a chemical evaluation; it *looks* sweet—and it is (with unpleasant exceptions that in no way undermine the ecological rationality of acting on the basis of this affordance but, like all forms of evolved mimicry, presuppose it). There is an exact parallel in an actor's ability to know that garden gnomes are tacky (see Bourdieu [1979] 1984). Returning to the issue of this economy highlights some of the open questions that are left by an attempt to use a field theory for a social aesthetics.

The Gestalt theorists argued not only that we see things as wholes because it is as wholes that we interact with them, nor only that they have qualities that call out for us to do certain things with them, but that our position vis-à-vis the objects allows or does not allow us to solve the problems we set for ourselves. Thus, there is not only cognitive economy in our tending to perceive ordered groups or structures of objects (and not many unordered individuals), but also a cognitive economy is our making use of whatever predictability or structure there is in the environment. Just as Köhler ([1917] 1925: 130) found that chimpanzees are much more likely to reach a novel solution to a problem when the elements are physically arranged in such a way that it is possible to literally see much of the answer in the environment, so our intelligence may similarly be dependent on the structure of our surroundings. The cognitive tasks actors carry out are not cultural schemes that independently exist within their psyches, but are generally merely minor completions to what the environment already "affords" (also see Swidler 1992; Hutchins 1995; White 1992; Gibson [1979] 1986: 246).[70]

---

[70] It is worth noting that this view of human cognition as fundamentally deictic—pointing toward meaningful arrangements outside the mind (Clark 1997: 152)—dovetails with the argument about the nature of vision made in chapter 6. As Ballard et al. (1997) persuasively argue, our use of vision in everyday cognition makes use of the external organization of the environment: the eye does not passively intromit a scene, transfer it to memory, and then manipulate it; instead, successive fixations use the spatial organization of objects in the world as a virtual memory.

Because the environment has a causal texture, it actually has information about its own causal relationships and indeed parameters. A sailor can tell which way the wind is coming from by looking at the waves. You do not need to remember what is the acceleration of objects under gravity—all you need is a yardstick and a stopwatch—the earth contains the rest of the information. And we collectively modify our environment to make such computational tasks easier (see esp. Clark 1997: 6, 36, 68, 179, 191, 201, 217). It is this richness of the environment that Simon (1996: 131f) posits makes our decision-making process potentially intelligent. He gives the wonderful analogy of number scrabble, a deceptively simple game in which two players take turns choosing one of nine cards numbered from 1 to 9—the first to get three cards that sum to 15 wins.

What would be trivial without the presence of a second player becomes extremely difficult—there are tens of thousands of possible ways the game can evolve. But, exactly illustrating Simon's (1955) point, this cognitively daunting task could be made manageable if the player could conceive of a *position*. Most people will have a hard time doing this on their own. But, with a simple card with nine numbers properly arranged, the game can be turned into one of tic-tac-toe (also see the work of Hutchins 1995). In a similar way, the coherence of a field—a set of organized positions such that "where one is" contains information on "where to go from here"—allows us to empty our minds of all but specialized skills needed to complete what the environment already affords. We do not need to reproduce an external social structure by internalizing it; on the contrary, we often deliberately make certain adjustments to the environment to allow it to take *more* cognition out of our heads (also see Bourdieu 1992: 89; Dimaggio 1991: 87f).

The aptness of a comparison of the regularities in social life to language is because we are neither dupes who unwittingly re-create what frustrates us the minute we mention it nor saboteurs who can unmake the world with a magic word. It is that in social action, just as in talk-in-interaction, we off-load as much as we possibly can into the social environment. That is, in real talk, we can easily and quickly refer to things near us in space and time—and thus the economy of our expression actually varies by our spatiotemporal position. (Compare "you just dropped that" to "at 5:14 P.M. on December 14, 1997, Alan Murin dropped his grocery list.")

Thus, we see that an organization of positions in a field is not only a nonarbitrary set of vectors but stored information on how to construct meaningful trajectories of appropriate action. Like a treasure hunt, any one place can hold the information about how to get to the next. Recall that Simon proposed that one way of organizing action given bounded rationality was simply to choose the best position for future action. Although Simon emphasized the great economy that comes with replacing a maximization problem with a set of positions, the actor was still required to determine which of a potentially very large set of next positions was the best one. But, if the field is a set of vectors attached to positions, these vectors being both a relationship between positions (that is, a "push" from one to another) and qualitative experience (a quasi-ethical imperative), then our actor need not make even this simple calculation—she need only feel.

Object and Position

The field approach works well when everything that confronts our actor is attachable to position. But more generally in chapter 6 we saw that sets of relationships were distilled into "social objects," which also were experienced qualitatively. We should of course in general be wary of any conceptual apparatus that makes parallel implications for seemingly different forms of organization in the way that I claim that both object (with its accordant value) and position (with its accordant imperative) are sets of relationships that induce an integral qualitative experience.

It will not and should not be possible to resolve all related ambiguities in advance, but closer attention to the nature of the qualities of objects and positions suggests that this parallel is due neither to overeager harmonization nor to vacuous proposition forming. First, we can maintain both that field positions are ways that actors make sense of sets of relationships, and that social objects "are" sets (or tangles) of such relationships without identifying the two. Most obviously, "position" appears to actors as a heuristic; although the imperatives attached to a position have actuality, actors do not feel that that a position "is" in the way that they will argue that a social object is.

Second, although position and object are thus distinguishable, the two coexist in a single phenomenological world. Actors and analysts will argue that objects can "have" positions and be "in" a field (e.g., parties have locations in the political field). Further, we will recognize that that the qualities of objects as experienced by actors in a field depend on the reciprocal relations of object and actor. Formulaically, qualities are intersubjective correlates (conditional on position) that reparameterize the vector of social distance between actors and social objects in a field of mutual alignment. That is, they are distillations of positions in a way that makes distance and direction palpable. A political candidate's honesty and dishonesty are not the same quality to Republicans and Democrats any more than the directions to San Francisco are the same if we are coming from San Diego, California, or Seattle, Washington. But they are clearly not contradictory. Thus, to propose that objects and positions are different ways of saying the same thing is no more odd than pointing out that the "southern" nature of San Diego to San Franciscans is a different way of expressing the geographic positions of both.

Third, it seems likely that there is a strict duality between objects and positions; the two are related to one another as perception is to apperception (as discussed in chapter 5). Let us consider Köhler's proposed phenomenological quality of the "charm" of women. In chapter 5, we saw that

Köhler may have been overhasty in going from the (correct) argument that the charms were attributes of the women as social objects to the (supposition) that the charms therefore could not be in the men, for they could be in the set of relations between the men. The objectification of women in this specific sense was a good template for objectification in general: the transmutation of a set of relationships into a sensible "thing" with attributes that index these relationships.

Seen from the perspective of the men (as did Köhler), this set of relationships may appear incarnated as quality, but seen from the perspective of the women, it may appear as position (in this case, perhaps a position of differential "charmingness" in a specifically sexual field [Martin and George 2006]).[71] Thus, we might hazard that (again following Köhler) social objects induce a local field; what we generally take as "a" field is an overall regularity in such local fields due to a patterning of the reciprocal arrangements of such objects. For example, in the field of high cuisine, chefs not only understand that they occupy positions with particular imperatives for creational styles, but also see this field as shaped by "restaurants," large-scale social objects that, although bundles of relations, are perceived as unitary constructs (Leschziner 2007).

It is worth emphasizing that, phenomenologically, positions are generally occupied places; a field does not consist of a hypercube of continuously divisible spaces, as do the analytic constructs that we make to represent them. Places without objects only appear as places to the extent that they offer possibilities of entry. Positions are dual to objects if only because where nobody is or will be is nowhere. This notion of the duality of position and object is necessarily somewhat impressionistic, but it may serve to indicate the directions whereby a more rigorous field theoretic approach may deal with social objects.[72]

Finally, we must bear in mind that the cognitive economy of the field of positions is not a constant because not all action takes place in fields. The field theoretic approach is in some sense to look where the light is good—to assume the sorts of regularities that make it easy to construct a social science. But there is nothing wrong with this. First, social sciences will always focus on regularities of some form or another. Second, we are

---

[71]In chapter 1, we noted the relevance of parallel findings from attribution theory, namely, that what we attribute to our immediate environment when it is a question of seeing our own action we impute as quality to others.

[72]At the same time, I mean this duality literally and technically, in the sense of Breiger (1974) (also see Duquenne 1995; Mohr and Duquenne 1997); this is one of the ways in which correspondence analysis turns out to have an extremely rigorous interpretation in field theoretic terms (the other has to do with conceiving data as having axes of resistance to transformation, in a structuralist sense), for correspondence analysis determines the position of persons as dual to the constitution of objects. A similar duality can be established in some simplified cases. For one, imagine a set of individuals and a set of relations connecting them (here

heartened to find that there is every reason to think that actors can also focus on these regularities. Third, we find that even outside the clearest cases, actors seem to be using the same basic processes of pattern recognition and the intuition of action imperatives. In the murkier cases for which we lack the structure of the field, it is not, it must be admitted, wholly clear regarding how we could generate explanations of social action, but it is also not clear how well our actors will function.

Indeed, thinking about action outside of fields helps clarify the relationship between field and institution. Generalizing from the work of DiMaggio and Powell (1983), one might propose that a field is an organization of institutions; we might then expect there to be cases in which there are unorganized institutions—institutions but no field. While this is almost certainly true, it would be wrong to imagine that institutions are the "building blocks" of fields. Following the principles laid down by Köhler (1920; also Merleau-Ponty [1942] 1963: 147), we must expect that it is the very patterning that gives institutions their objectivity—the isolated institution may not appear as a true institution, rather as an anachronism, a residue, or an irrationality.

As we move away from the clarity of the field, then, what we have is not a set of unorganized institutions or objects but mutual orientation without the cognitive economy of position. There may of course be other forms of subjective heuristic compatible with such situations; for example, many social scientists have proposed that "identity" in what we may call the subsumptive or set-theoretic sense ("I am a liberal" $\Leftrightarrow a \subseteq S$) is such a way of facilitating action. But evidence that these other heuristics can substitute for the economy of position is not strong. To stick with the example, to the extent that a purely subsumptive logic is used (as opposed to the mutual orientation of reciprocal position taking), we are likely to find serious difficulties confronting an actor. So I am a liberal—now what do I do? Evidence suggests that this heuristic is only helpful in orienting action when combined with a sense of position—as liberals are

---

restricted to be binary and symmetric for simplicity's sake) and define a social object as some subset of these relations. Let us rule out reflexivity (people do not have relations with objects that include them) and make objects nonintersecting (no person is involved in more than one object) and exhaustive (every person belongs to one object). Consider the strength of relations between any two objects to be the number of relations between the persons in each and use this strength to determine the relative position of objects (and hence the positions of the persons involved in them). In this case, we find a partition of the relations into object-constituting relations and position-determining relations. Leaving this simple case (e.g., allowing multiple relations, allowing reflexivity, allowing higher-order relations, allowing continuous relations, allowing interpenetrating objects, and so on) makes things much messier, but the basic logic is unchanged—from a single set of relations, we find both positions and objects dually constituted.

against conservatives, what conservatives are for I must oppose (Sniderman, Brody, and Tetlock 1991).

Thus, we may propose that even when there is not a field, to the extent that action is social it involves not only sets of relationships of mutual orientation but also the distillation of imperatives—felt motivations—from these sets of relationships. Any explanation of action must find the regularity in these experiences, as opposed to looking for some sort of external causation. In the final chapter, I consider the implications of these points for the task of social explanation.

Chapter 9

Explanations Explained

> First of all, an abstraction is made from a fact; then it [the fact] is based upon the abstraction. That is how to proceed if you want to appear German, profound and speculative.
> —Karl Marx and Frederick Engels, *The German Ideology*

MAKING AND BREAKING LAWS

In chapters 7 and 8, we examined one way to approach the explanation of regularities in social action. This way is quite different from that increasingly dominant in the social sciences, namely, the causal understanding discussed in chapter 2. There, we saw many particular problems with the idea of causality as we currently use it, but these were indicative of a more fundamental problem in the way in which the task of explanation was conceived. To refresh ourselves, we previously found three related problems with the dominant idea of explanation. First, there has been an assumption that in order to study the general, we must ignore aspects of the particular, because generality has been identified with subsumption. Second, this act of analytic subsumption was then taken to justify the use of abstractions without phenomenological validity. Finally, the abstractions were linked via relationships of causality that were then said to constrain the acts of the persons in question. This has led to a science in which statements are made about the connection of imaginary elements in an imaginary world, and our justification is the hope that these will explain no case but rather an unknown portion of every case.

We have also seen that the considerations in the previous chapters suggest that these problems stem from unjustified and indeed unjustifiable assumptions. It remains to point out what rejecting these assumptions implies for the task of explanation. I begin by reconsidering the idea that social science comes up with explanations indicating some form of constraint—that there are social "laws." The idea of explanation implicit in the "rules"-type account in the chapter 8 opens up a different way of conceiving the successes—and failures—of explanation. I then discuss the criteria of good explanation that are compatible with this approach before considering a few final possible objections.

Constraining Laws

In the first four chapters, we traced the development of a social science that explains the particular experiences of persons by recourse to relations between general abstractions, these relations being interpreted as ones of causation. Further, while there is no disjunction (which is not to say difference) between causality and motivation on the level of first-person experience, this is not at all how causality is currently understood in the social sciences. Instead, these "causes" can only "explain" the action of individuals to the extent that they appear to *constrain* the action of individuals.

This is largely because the Quetelian-Durkheimian approach to science treated the concrete instantiations as less real than the mathematical construct—like a Platonic form, the "average man," although an otherworldly abstraction, could be held as responsible for the production of those phenomena that people would take as incontestably concrete. It is not surprising that the same denigration of the capacity of individuals to contribute to the process of explaining their own actions that we saw in chapters 3 and 4 went along with a denigration of the importance of individuals as individuals. In a real way, the past 100 years of statistics has built on this attempt to take the individuality out of people and treat them as replicable units without motivation, and then to fix the problems that necessarily arise from this attempt.

But more important than the mathematics themselves has been their interpretation. Quetelet assumed that if the deviations from the average followed a Gaussian curve, the distinctly social average must be understood as *uniform* and *constraining*. This allowed an assimilation of the descriptive results of the social sciences—that is, compiled outcomes of what people have done—to the idea of natural "laws" (itself an ambiguous category of thought) and hence the assertion that the people *had* to do these things. It was precisely this understanding that became the linchpin of Durkheim's ([1895] 1938) method. There are three things for us to note here. The first is that this interpretation is mathematically incorrect—by using a probabilistic form that was the aggregation of individually independent actions (as is the classical error law) and then denying the very independence that gave rise to it, these statisticians—and, to a large degree, Durkheim himself—who took the stability of certain properties of these aggregate statistics to indicate *global* laws, were neither finding the true realm of the distinctly social nor unveiling a new form of determinism worthy of the term *law*. They were making what is undeniably a simple error.[1]

---

[1] This was demonstrated by Lexis in 1879—in a nutshell, only underdispersion or overdispersion indicates the nonindependence that points to something beyond individual propensities (Porter 1986: 249), and even these are compatible with independent but heterogeneous individuals.

The second thing to notice is that this interpretation of social statistics leads to a new idea of law that combines the predictive capacity of a Newtonian law with the causality of a mechanical one. The "equation" that results takes on a form deceptively similar to some of the laws of physics: there is one thing on the left-hand side of an equals sign and one or more things on the right. But, rather than express an ideal invariance irrespective of causality, we formalize a set of partially independent causal relationships. The task of the social sciences, then, would be to accumulate and systematize a set of general propositions that would describe macroscopic constraints on human behavior.

It is not surprising, then, that social science quickly took on the characteristic of the sadder-but-wiser counselor who must point out that we are not in fact as free as we might think. As the founder of sociology, Comte ([1842] 1974: 434f; also see 806–808, 828–832), wrote: "A true resignation ... can proceed only from a deep sense of the connections of all kinds of natural phenomena with natural laws. ... True liberty is nothing else than a rational submission to the preponderance of the laws of nature, in release from all arbitrary personal dictation." Debate within the social sciences thus was narrowly constrained. On one side were the "right wingers," who argued that *no* deliberate change was possible, even on the part of the elite (to borrow William Graham Sumner's[2] famous phrase, "stateways cannot change folkways"). On the other side were the "left wingers," who argued that only enlightened experts could, using their knowledge of causal laws, improve society (compare Breslau 2007: 55). And most were in the confused middle, well charted by Durkheim in his tortured but honest conundrums regarding how to fuse his enlightened liberal republicanism with his monstrously totalitarian understanding of social facts as the uniformly constraining.

Everyone agreed that when it came to everyday actions by the laity, the laws established by the social sciences were, in Kant's terminology, laws of necessity and not of freedom. The most one could do was to accept this heteronomy willingly. As Durkheim ([1902–1903] 1961: 115) said, "Because we understand the laws of everything, we also understand the reasons for everything.... Hence, to the extent that we see that it is everything as it ought to be—that it is as the nature of things implies—we can conform, not simply because we are physically restrained and unable to do otherwise without danger, but because we deem it good and have no better alternative." The social sciences could of course also tell us how "we" could reformulate a more rational society, but the flip side was of course that "we" must recognize to what we must bow (see Billig 1982: 26; Marcuse [1941] 1954: 256, 343f; Porter 1986: 56, 59, 105; Pearson

---

[2]This is if in fact it is his phrase at all. People commonly cite this along with "legislation cannot make mores," which is from *Folkways* (1906: 77), but the term *stateways* does not appear in this work, and I have not seen it attributed to any other piece of Sumner's.

[1921–1933] 1978: 493, 495). As one might imagine, the social scientists themselves seemed to be more often part of the first "we" than the second (cf. Giddens 1979: 72).[3]

The third thing to notice about this philosophical interpretation of social statistics is that it is basically the same conception that is dominant today. We ignore the one place in which we have direct phenomenological evidence of causality—namely, in our motivation—when looking for it, and indeed assume that any effective motivated action (should we be forced to admit it) must be antithetical to a causal account. Like the Humean philosophers who imagined that—as good philosophers—we are only passive observers and can approach causality only through the observation of regularity (cf. Bunge 1959: 68), we too have ignored our fundamentally active nature when thinking about causality. Largely as a methodological residue of the interpretation of the regression equation, we assume that any phenomenon must be the result of myriad causes, the lesser of which are dismissed as bothersome "error" that subtracts from our ability to understand the simpler determinations involved. The paradoxes in reconciling our understanding of liberty with the determinism supposedly revealed by these statistical laws began with Durkheim (see [1897] 1951: 38f) and have continued in largely the same form; instead of rethinking the assumptions producing the paradox, we are content to resign ourselves to seeing social life as a combination of regularity and irregularity and partition these into "explained variance" and "error," the general law and the particular case. What are considered the boldest theoretical innovations are merely minor changes in the emotional connotations of the error term, such as declaring that this or that is a product of both structure *and* agency, and this is a wonderful thing, not merely a vexing thing.

In the second chapter, we saw the limitations inherent in the fact that this approach emphasized a counterfactual understanding of causality—the social sciences have constructed a set of explanatory principles that might, just possibly, work if analysts were walking about a set of cages and injecting every other monkey with some strange solution. But, in our discipline, the monkeys are out of the cages and are busily jabbing each other and themselves with whatever hypodermic needle comes readily to hand. We do not get far by increasing the sophistication of our mathematics for describing *how* the seeming chaos departs from the imposed order of the laboratory. However, we have now seen that the problem is a broader one.

---

[3] "While it's true that no one completely lacks the power of causation, some human beings have more will than others. . . . So not all selves are persons to the same degree" (Durkheim [1883–1884] 2004: 93f). As Gigerenzer et al. (1989: 32) write, "Although the moral scientists greatly admired the successes of Newtonian mechanics and aped its language of natural laws, they constantly harangued their fellow citizens to obey these laws," for humans, unlike inanimate objects, were free to "err."

It has to do with the key idea that there is some sort of explanation for action that exists in a world populated purely by abstractions, and with the idea that this shadow world can then be the true cause of actions. In seizing on a third-person answer to the question, Why? the social sciences produce a class of answers—a whole understanding of what it means to explain—that is contradictory.

Explanation and Aggression

The sense that we have of "explain," far from being the universal scientific one, is peculiar to the contemporary social sciences and laden with paradox. As we saw in chapter 2, it derives more from the substantive implications of our methodological tools than from any understanding of scientific method, and these implications are generally ones that almost no social scientist would be willing to defend.

One explains something in this sense by linking the variation in one attribute of some units to their variation in other attributes. For example, the income of adults is explained as an "effect" of their parents' income, their parents' education, and their years of experience in the workforce. Since our interpretation of the statistics is to consider the links between these attributes to be a causal one, then to take the claims seriously we must conclude that one attribute of persons (say) *causes* another attribute of those persons (who presumably have little to do during this whole process) (see Abbott 1992; Emirbayer 1997; Goldthorpe 2001: 3). Now I am sure that in practice researchers recognize this as an informal shorthand for something quite different (for if they really believed that education caused income, they wouldn't bother showing up for work at all, but would just let their many years of education bring home the bacon). But still, they cannot conceive of any true explanation that is *not* causal in such a sense.[4] Researchers can spend a great deal of time arguing about, say, whether education is or is not a cause of income—without ever connecting their debates with what they know from their first-person experience, and this is that we do not cause our own income. Someone else gives us our income, and usually this other party chooses how much to pay us. It isn't just that we are making unforgivable simplifications when we ask whether individuals' education "causes" their income: we are studying the wrong people. Surprisingly for a science that generally claims to concern itself with social interaction, our core methodologies make it difficult, if not impossible, to employ such analytic elements in our explanations (cf. Gangl 2010: 40).

---

[4]As Bunge (1959: 10, 195) emphasized, "determination" is not the same thing as "causality"—in some causal processes that can be written as an equation, time may be determinative in terms of the outcome without time being a *cause* of the outcome. Because there are noncausal determinations, even in a causal world a causal explanation cannot be a complete one.

Because our methods assume a model of causation that is intervariable but intraperson, we make a mockery of our whole intellectual enterprise. If we want to argue for a rigorous social science, we must accept some definition of explanation that refers to the *real* phenomenon in question (some persons allocating income to others) and not an imaginary one.[5]

But, in the social sciences, "explanation" has more or less meant an aggressive relationship between a researcher and a phenomenon—in most cases, the term *explanation* could be replaced with "disappearance," as the analysts' goal is to make some unaccounted-for phenomenon go away as a thing in itself (cf. Koffka 1935: 178f; Köhler 1938: 92). Once the proportion of variance in this "dependent variable" explained by the "independent variables" (the R^2) approaches 1, "explanation" has occurred because there simply *is* no phenomenon sui generis any more. The basic understanding of what it means to explain is formally parallel to the thinking denounced by Marx and Engels: first variables are made out of people, and then the actions of the people are "explained" on the basis of the variables (cf. James [1907] 1946: 263). This is just no explanation at all.

And yet this follows from the logic we explored in chapter 2, in which every instance is to be decomposed into that which is predicted by something else (this heteronomy being equivalent to our successful explanation) and some error that speaks poorly either of ourselves as inadequate analysts or of the phenomena as unruly. The understanding of action as game-like, however, suggests a very different way of understanding the relation of those who fall into a central tendency and those who do not. This has strong implications for how we determine the adequacy of our explanations. Again, the claims made here are familiar to many. But this familiarity has not led to a reorientation of how we try to learn about the world, and that is the focus here. If anything, it has inoculated us against a serious crisis of faith in our measures by giving us a reasonable ontology, a one-size-fits-all vision of social life that can be appended to any argument, even one attached to the problematic version of explanation current in the social sciences.

Rules versus Laws

In the most straightforward versions of conventional social science, we attempt to use data on how people are distributed to make law-like statements regarding what has caused this distribution—for example, regressing income on various individual-level variables gives us not a descriptive statement, but (we pray) a causal one. And, that means that it is also a

---

[5] Just as with the race of the discriminated seeming to "cause" the discriminatory actions of others, we see here how the conventional approach to explanation is as likely as not to reverse the direction in which effective action proceeds.

recipe for how we can, say, increase our income. In arguing against this common mistake (one that becomes obvious when discussed in such a plain light), Lieberson (1985) argued that analysts were missing the most important social dynamics lying behind these regularities: "Those who write the rules, write rules that enable them to continue to write the rules" (167). That is, if the losers under the current regime threaten to assemble the ingredients previously used for success, the recipe may miraculously turn out to have changed. Of course, rule writers do not always triumph.[6] His more general point is that by confusing patterns of regularity that are constructed via the compounding of persons' actions (on the one hand) with a law that constrains them (on the other), social scientists ignore the most fundamental fact of stratification: it is not the outcome of an impersonal process but an interpersonal struggle.[7]

What is difficult for the conventional approach to understand follows naturally from the discussion in chapter 8. Rather than the regularity of social life being a law that constrains, that is, the *cause* of individual actions, it is the *outcome* of actions undertaken by actors with some sense (presumably imperfect) of the expectations others have and the likely reactions attendant to confirmation or nonconfirmation of various expectations. When patterns of conduct are recognized by actors as forms of regularity, conformity or nonconformity to the pattern, whatever advantages or disadvantages may also follow, has semiotic import (here, see Swidler 1986, 2001, and Barnes 2000: 47; I find that Sewell [2005, ch. 10] has made parallel arguments here. This was also an emphasis of Malinowski's; see Young 2004: 75, 404). As Goffman (1971: x, 45, 173, 177, 185) said, when we try to investigate the rules that supposedly bind us, we find not laws but *meanings*.

In chapter 8, we saw that one source of our confusion regarding the nature of social action and its relation to subjectivity came from the classical assumption that the mental system of human beings—the regularities

---

[6]Lieberson was probably thinking of how college entrance policies were changed so that they could have the same socially exclusive results and hence emphasized the successful attempt.

[7]These arguments were made elegantly by Wieder (1974: 37, 43, 156) in his discussion of the nature of rule following. Investigating a shared set of expectations regarding how convicts and staff at a halfway house would interact, Wieder (1974: 165, 170, 174f, 196ff, 217, 219, 222) noted that these expectations could be used and were used strategically to induce another to take an action or to justify an action one had already taken, and although actors might subjectively experience these expectations *as if* they were predictive, one could not treat them as a high-level set of propositions from which guides to action in the situation could be deduced. These shared expectations were not rules that guided action; they were part of the environment that actors took into account—indeed, these expectations could not explain the pattern of action because these expectations were *part of* this pattern.

in their perception and action—could be understood to correspond to language. Further, this vision of language was an unusually crisp one, taken from the case of French, which since the seventeenth century had a governmental organization to ensure uniformity of usage. Indeed, just as the neo-Kantian approach to concept formation was the equivalent to the code Napoléon, theorists' approach to language took as a generic human faculty the historically unusual case of rationalized, national-level "languages." Such language is the exception, and not the rule, which is the dialect, a set of far-from-perfect regularities not backed up by centralized state power (White 1995). As Bruce Porter (1994: 19) says, "A language is a dialect with an army."

But with our totalitarian understanding of language came an implausible sense of what it meant to obey or break rules. Although there was grammar before there were grammarians, social theorists tended to assume the perspective of the dour instructor faced with recalcitrant pupils who did not understand the *proper* use of (say) "the King's English." Change in such a system would be equivalent to a schoolboy rebellion—willfully breaking *the* rules. An empirical investigation of language and language change (e.g., Strang 1970 on English; see 46, 91, 267, 273), however, finds that changes in grammar are not independent from changes in pronunciation; further, both are affected by speakers' *theories* of the regularities in each—even when these theories are (initially) incorrect, they can become self-fulfilling prophecies. Thus, a comparison to language confirms the conclusion of chapter 8 that when we think about "games," we cannot properly divorce our understanding of "rules" from that of "strategies."

But conventional understandings of language did the opposite, and by ignoring strategies, they turned rules into laws. These laws of language then seemed to be the laws of what could be thought—even those who had a sophisticated view of the nature of the rules of social action (esp. Giddens 1979: 77) might imagine that every statement made within that structure somehow "reinforces" these rules. When, as has been conventional, we begin with the assumptions of some opposition between "structure" and "agency," the simplicity with which actors go about this struggle is first perplexing and troubling, and then the site for tedious wordplay and false breakthroughs. That those standing in some position of opposition (e.g., workers, gay men) make use of the shared expectations that have been misunderstood as "constraints" (e.g., they have "trade union" consciousness, they call themselves "faggots") leads to either supercilious dismissals of their impoverished capacity for alternative visions or tendentious claims to uncover "resistance" (or reclaiming, or subversion, or what have you) in this very lack of resistance. Tired with this, we come to the triumphant discovery that these patterns of regularity *both* constrain *and* enable—that, say, unfortunately, 73% of our following previous patterns reproduce these horrible strictures, but fortunately, 27% resists them! Finally, we reach the deep understanding that there is a deep, deep relationship between resistance and reproduction, between conformity and originality, such that we find there is a very, *very* fine line between structure and agency—or between clever and stupid.

Thus, in their quest to find the pure negation of the rule, analysts entangle themselves in paradox. For the breaking of the rule, like its use or adaptation, has communicative efficacy only because of the expectations of others. Breaking the rule does not *obliterate* the rule in the sense of wiping the traces of memory from others' minds and in fact may make the rule salient. Or, it may not. It is an empirical question, and not an abstract one deducible from the nature of language, what is at issue, what is at stake, and how people orient to common expectations in the use of language. When we see language as one of a more general class of semiotic practices that involve the emergence of and reflexive use of patterns of regularity, we do not find language giving us any strong model for the nature of social action. Indeed, it would be likely that to explicate such use of words (and tones and pauses) we would need to appeal to game metaphors.[8]

For we generally have a poor understanding of the nature of our own speech; as Goffman might have said, we are better speakers than we know. Our folk theory of language turns on the rare cases of unambiguous propositional speech ("this is that"). But, as actual experts in language, we deal gracefully with subtler and harder to formalize types of regularity, some of which are nongrammatical or antigrammatical. It is of course possible to construct a model of language that has as one form of meaning the contravention of the rules supposedly used to express meaning. (Such an understanding of communication through violation of expectation is a well-hallowed part of poetic and musical criticism.[9]) But, this requires that we reject the idea that language has any privileged place in defining the nature of our consciousness. Indeed, it is then not language per se that forms a good analogy with which to understand the task of explanation in the social sciences; it is banter, flirting, or political speech—all of which are akin to games (here see Leifer and Rajah 2000).

We have seen that mastery of language involves above all else the capacity to gather another's intentions. We can now add that we are not beholden to *respect* them—we are free to use our understanding of the intersubjectively valid patternings inherent in language in a number of ways. We may act within them for clarity and speed, break them for

---

[8]The common idea discussed in chapter 8, in which language is some structure and that is an extreme form of what Bourdieu ([1997] 2000) has termed the scholastic fallacy—replacing a lived experience with a theorist's model of that experience.

[9]A classic example is Gerard Manley Hopkins's "curtailed sonnets" that stopped abruptly where the reader, familiar with the sonnet form, expects a continuation. More generally, his idea of "sprung rhythm," a structure based on a fixed number of stresses but other flexibilities, assumed this sort of constantly evolving backdrop of expectations.

emphasis, or even use them against our interlocutors by forcing their words to take on "meanings" that they did not "mean" (see Gibson 2005).[10]

Surprised by Surprise

We saw in chapter 2 that the conventional approach to social laws assumes that failure to obey the laws is some sort of error, random or otherwise. The more theoretically oriented treatments that attempted to explain how we fulfill our lawful parts in the role play of social life (generally involving our introjecting social regularities—norms—as moral commandments) had a difficult time explaining why people might simply decline to follow the rules. If "socialized" persons have preferences, needs, and desires that are "socially formed," why do they so often display distantiation from "their" own values?[11] Following Goffman (1959; also Barnes 1995: 73, 117), we have found that, like a poet breaking meter for emphasis, players may break the rules precisely *because* they are rules.[12] The error of social science

---

[10]This point might seem identical to the now-common idea that the opposition between structure and agency is factitious because we can use the code to undermine the code and so on. But, the argument here is quite different: we do not violate those communicative expectations that are often misinterpreted as "laws" of language because we *hate* them and are trying to revolt against them, but to communicate, or because our own theories of the regularity lead us to change in our quest to be the same (such as when English speakers added "ly" to the adverb/adjective "slow" to make "slowly"; they have been slow to do this with "fast," but in the future I imagine that they will move more fastly in this regard). Only the wrongheaded equation of law, culture, and language has allowed theorists to begin from the presumption that to understand how, say, oppressed people might want to better their conditions we should imagine a situation in which speakers would consciously *want* to destroy their language. Languages do change, all the time, but not because speakers exert their "agency" in *opposing* the constraints of language. Giddens is often cited as providing support for the idea I claim as wrongheaded, although in his earlier treatment (1979: 68, 114, 245) he makes points closely analogous to those made here.

[11]Parsons and Shils (1954) tried to explain this as a result of "faulty internalization," which can produce the "derivative" need dispositions "to refuse to fulfill expectations," an obvious fudge factor.

[12]Interestingly, in his discussion of the constraints of language, Miller (1964: 98) pointed out that since these rules can be and are violated, it makes little sense to call them laws, and instead invoked the idea of "habit," specifically "productive habits" in a sense close to that of Ockham. Meyer's (1956: 18f, 26, 38f, 65f, 83, 119, 137, 200, 255, 270) approach to music theory based on Gestalt theory also turns on the development of expectations and the deviations from such "rules." The cultivation of taste of the listener, the understanding of a style, and the preceding development of the piece all combine with more formal rules of composition to give a sense of what constitutes closure or a reasonable next step. Meyer explicitly drew parallels between his approach to aesthetics (on the one hand) and game theory and information theory (on the other).

was to assume that deviation was error, and the resulting penalty is that we are continually surprised by surprise.

But, if regularity, far from being assumed to be a causal structure of forces that will compel all future persons to act similarly, is a set of assumptions based on past actions, it is always vulnerable to deliberate upset. For an example, I take what I believed to be the first recorded case in history (371 BCE) in which a social "law"—one that was understood by contemporaries to be explained in terms of individual-level mechanisms—was deliberately undone precisely because it was a law. Greek phalanx (or hoplite) warfare involved the confrontation of two lines of soldiers, each armed with a shield on the left arm and a spear or sword in the right hand. These two lines would slowly rotate in a counterclockwise direction, and the "microlevel" mechanisms of this regular pattern are explained by Thucydides (V:71): each soldier's right side was protected only by the shield of the man to his right. As each instinctively moved closer to the right, the line shifted; to keep the lines aligned, the right flanks would move forward.[13] Captains, aware of this "law," tended to put the most valiant fighters on the right side as they would lead the aggression into the enemy's side. But, the most interesting thing about this "law," of course, was that it was not a law at all, although it was repeated for generations. Then, the Thebans, although vastly outnumbered, won a major battle over Sparta at Luectra by concentrating their forces on the left instead of the right and breaking through this side of the Spartan phalanx (Delbrück [1920] 1990: 165ff, 170; Keegan 1994: 258; 1988: 124; Hanson [1989] 2000: 66).

If the strategic importance of such surprise—such standing apart from patterns of regularity and deciding whether to repeat them—comes as no surprise when the topic is a battle, why is it so difficult for us to comprehend when the issue is the place of education in assignment of persons to jobs? If social life is a game, it is not one with unchanging rules (cf. Giddens 1979: 232, 243). Humans may not be quite as smart as we often assumed, but they have clearly moved toward an ecological niche characterized by flexibility in behavioral patterns (James [1890] 1950: II, 368; cf. Reed 1996: 34). Rigid lawfulness is the least-reasonable thing to find in human action.

This suggests a wholly different criterion for successful explanation than the pseudocausality that is standard in the social sciences. Social explanation is less like charting the invariance relations in heavenly bodies and more like commentary on a chess game; this comparison is apposite

---

[13] Krentz (1985: 53) has cast doubt on this traditional understanding, arguing that a hoplite could protect his right side by turning his body. While other of Krentz's emendations to the traditional view are plausible, he seems to forget that spears were probably only used in the initial stages of battle, and after that, every attacking stroke made by a right hander with a sword would necessarily bring this side of the body forward. For other discussions of the precise dynamics involved, see the work of Greenhalgh (1973: 72f) and Anderson (1970: 106f, 142, 222).

not so much because of what it implies about the nature of social action but because of what it implies about the nature of social explanation. Most important, perfection in predictive capacity cannot be considered an indication of a good analyst, only one of poor actors. A commentator on a game between two grand masters must understand the rules that underlie the playing of the game and (one hopes) is able to remember many other chess games, especially those recently played by the opponents. But, we would not insist that his grasp of the situation be mirrored in some generalized predictive power—say, the ability to look at the untouched board and declare, "White always wins." If one player allowed a knight to exchange for a pawn, we seek to explain it as opposed to considering this an error on the order of $3 - 1 = 2$ (the difference in points between the two). We cannot say in advance how far we must go in our quest to determine the context that led to this move, but this indeterminacy is simply the minimal flexibility required to understand complexity.

Why Not What?

Now, adherents of the conventional approach, forced into a corner, may admit the incoherence of their own methods while replying that there is no true alternative—the project of a social aesthetics, they will argue, cannot provide any functional equivalent that can be called "explanation." If indeed we are not to explain one thing as "really" an instance of something else nor to steamroller over first-person experiences, social science cannot be anything other than a recital of observations, a cinema verité perhaps peppered with tiresome analogies to fields. Rather than give explanations, we will only have *descriptions*.

But this assumption that we must divide our statements about the world into the descriptive and the explanatory (e.g., Hedström 2005: 12) is a false dualism coming from the fundamental conviction that things cannot be trusted to be what they are; an explanation is not (we generally assume) a description because the description reveals the superficial and the static, while the important story is deep and dynamic (also see Katz 1999: 178; Merleau-Ponty 1962: viii; and Boltanski and Thévenot [1991] 2006: 118 on the history of this opposition in the social sciences).

To return to the discussion of chapter 1, we might say that (according to our conventional way of thinking about these things), in the descriptive explanation we may know *what* people are doing (e.g., we see a man wave two outstretched fingers back and forth), but we do not know *why* he is doing this (in this case, what is the motivation? What is the cause?). But, on more careful thought, we found this distinction collapsing. There is a way that when we see our man waving his fingers, we do not know What he is doing until we know Why—let us say we realize that he is hailing a cab. We would then *describe* his action *as* a cab hailing (and not, say, a "strike indicating," although an umpire might make the same physical gesture). The difference between Why and What, between explanation and description (if one insists), is not a scientific one, but a social one—a difference between the problematic and the unproblematic.

Of course, there are situations in which these two diverge beyond remediation—when no answer to Why gets collapsed into a What (as in, "Oh, now I see what she was doing"). This is, as we saw in chapter 3, most clear when the analyst judges the actor as incompetent to act or to describe What his act is. We have unnecessarily attributed such incompetence to actors and, as a result, failed to develop our own competence.

For actors *do* intuit patterns and respond to them. Not everything is easy, and not everything appears. But as Dewey (1929) said, the difference actors may be forced to deal with is not between the apparent and the true (or the error-filled particular observations and the theoretically reached abstract law), but simply between the apparent and that which does not appear. The latter calls for insight—extension of patternings in the apparent to make strong implications for action even where we are unable to see. Fortunately, as human beings we are constitutionally fit for such an enterprise (also see Clark 1997: 168). And it is this that can be at the heart of our notion of explanation.

EXPLANATIONS, PROFESSIONAL AND LAY

Explanation Made Plain

We have seen that the social sciences have wound their way into a cul-de-sac in which they cannot imagine any form of explanation that is not to "explain away." Logically, it seems that we must end up, if all goes well, in a world in which there simply are no phenomena any more. In contrast to this idea of explanation as some act of ontological aggression, I have proposed that we must begin with a sense of explanation so obvious and unambiguous that it has become difficult for social scientists to take seriously: explanation is a social relationship between people in which some phenomenon is explained to some persons so that they understand it (cf. Lundberg 1939: 51; Hilton 1990: 65; Bunge 1959: 287, 289, 298–302). That is, it is a triadic relationship. A explains B to C.

The conventional approach, we saw, begins with a potentially hostile triadic relation. A explains B to C and shuts up B at the same time. This is because A's explanation—at least, to the extent that it is impressively "theoretical"—is a third-person one intrinsically at variance with whatever B might say. This third-person theoretical explanation, however, involves connections between abstractions in an imaginary world. We have lost interest in the one place where theories actually *are*, namely, in our actors (cf. Barnes 1995: 224). Actors intuit patterns; they do not always bring these to consciousness, and there is no reason to imagine that they should. To the extent that each does, she provides "my theory of everyone else's action." We are then in a position to compile these, not to produce the right theory, but rather, to provide the correct description. For the actual pattern of relations is the empirical result of the compilation of conditional theories (each person's action conditional on what others do). We can get the basic data for our compilation by watching, and sometimes asking, people.

Let us imagine that we give up on the quest for a third-person vocabulary of explanatory statements able to drown out B's own answer and instead resign ourselves only to giving answers that we are comfortable B hearing and commenting on as well. What would it mean to explain B's action to C so that C would "understand it"? It would not mean making C approve or feel that she would do the same thing or anything like. But, it would mean that we would have transmitted some sort of intuitive accessibility (*Anschaulichkeit*) in which the action "made sense." And it is this that is the single most important criterion of successful explanation: to allow others to inhabit a coherent world, to "get" the principles at work.[14]

---

[14]On this *Anschaulichkeit* one may also see Gadamer ([1980] 1986: 157f) for an important discussion. This emphasis on *Anschaulichkeit* was a key plank of the tradition that led to the field theory discussed in chapters 7 and 8. Thus, Spiegel (1961: 15f; also Heider 1958: 2; cf. Geiger 1949: 45), in one of the earliest field theoretic analyses in the social sciences, argued that more important than the criteria usually given for model construction is that the model make "a part or an aspect of the reality in question materially or ideally intuitively accessible" (*materiell oder ideell veranschaulicht*). He explicitly claimed that his model, although based on a spatialization (*Verräumlichung*), was not an attempt to produce metric or topological statements but merely an intuitively accessible and spatial form of presentation (*eine anschaulich-räumliche Darstellungsweise*) using distance metaphorically.

Mannheim (1940: 169ff) had perhaps the most complete discussion of the importance of *Anschaulichkeit*, as he sought to adjudicate between the American abstract-variable approach that focused on isolated causal sequences and the German "intuitive" approach that he associated with Romanticism in general and the German Gestalt and developmental (comprehensive) traditions in particular. The former, he argued, excluded the important possibility that we can get valid knowledge of an object through "direct physical and psychic contact and perception." Mannheim tried to correct the impression that such an *anschaulich* science simply uses direct inspection (*Schau*) and intuition (*Intuition*, which Mannheim [1940: 232; 1935: 202] used instead of *Anschauung* when he wished to denote the more poetic sense). Far from there being an opposition of the American and Romantic methods of thought, Mannheim argued, in their most developed form they both reach toward the same goal—"to grasp the concrete object in its concrete context" (also see Pepper [1937: 22] for a similar discussion of the complementarity and difference between analysis and intuition).

Mannheim's attempt to bridge the American and German thought styles (interestingly also an obsession of Lewin's; cf. Koffka 1935: 73) was a failure (here see Kettler and Meja 1994). This is unfortunately seen in the difference between the American translation (by Shils) and the German original. (Since Mannheim expanded this edition, he must be held responsible for its final form, even if the

Can we give a crisper definition of what it means to transmit such intuitive accessibility? I do not know, but I am sure that the faculty required to evaluate such accessibility exists since it is not fundamentally different from what we do in our everyday physical and social environments. As actors, we "get" what is going on, whether or not we can explain precisely what this means (and despite the fact that we can be wrong). The rigor and systematicity of our methods as social scientists, not to say the ethical imperative to rein in partisanship, cannot be thought to make us *less* capable of such understanding than our subjects.

We must recognize that explanation in the social sciences is a special case of the more general phenomenon of explanation between persons. For too long, the social sciences have attempted to invent and defend their own criteria for explanatory success. It seems to me that the purpose of a social science is not to invent new criteria with which to judge what it is going to do anyway—a self-justifying, Humpty-Dumptyish definition "what *we* shall call a good explanation"—but rather, to do a better job of meeting existing standards.

While it is easy to criticize such a loose concept of explanation, the social sciences cannot forever prefer the formulaic to the reasonable. This criterion of intuitive accessibility cannot, perhaps, be formalized to allow for the automatic choice of arguments "untouched by human minds," as can some of the criteria coming from the incoherent pseudocausal idea. It is of course pathological to favor the security of a formalizable illusion to a messier reality, but one can understand the attraction, especially if the illusion is one that can be reliably produced, while if we abandon the familiar method and instead try to grapple with reality, we may lack faith in our ability to identify precisely what it is that we are talking about, even if it is real.

At the same time, if there were no criteria for what it means to "get" what is going on other than a subjective feeling of satisfaction, we would find ourselves back in the situation discussed in chapter 3 in which only the authority of the analyst leads to a situation of epistemic stability. But there are other checks on the acceptability of a proposed explanation. Most important, these checks are social—for we are unsatisfied with our answer when it falls short of intersubjective validity. If our fundamental data are first-person experiences and our explanation is a compilation, there is an inherent validity to any pattern that emerges from the ground

---

error was originally that of Shils.) Mannheim argued that although the *anschaulich*-intuitive approach does not attempt to *analyze* in the sense of breaking up the object with an eye to its possible reconstruction, this does not mean that the information retrieved cannot be transmitted and formalized, since this knowledge can be brought to (analytic) consciousness. Mannheim (1935: 120f) was explicit here: "*Das anschauliche Wissen ist keineswegs dazu verurteilt, stumm und unreflexiv zu bleiben*": "intuitive knowledge is in no way accordingly condemned to remain mute and unreflexive." The translation reads, "intuitive knowledge is for this reason condemned to remain mute and unreflexive."

up. Of course, in the best of cases we may hope for a fully mathematized field treatment of quantified degrees of experience, but outside this case we may also find that the arguments here have implications for the most general criteria that explanations should meet.

The Criteria of Successful Explanation

If explanation involves a coordination of first-person experiences to create a sense of the general phenomenologically valid social objects that constitute a terrain of action, there are three general criteria of a successful explanation. The first is that it exists in the same phenomenological world as the actions it intends to explain, such that the actors could, with dialogue, understand the referent of every term in our explanation. The explanation, then, need not contradict people's understandings of their own impulses (as long as we bear in mind that all people understand the difference between retrospective justifications, especially those made defensively to hostile interlocutors, and felt motivations—that is, experiences), but instead uses these reported motivations as data (not as explanation) (also see Giddens 1979: 246, 253, 258). While we in no way are restricted to accept people's self-presentations, we cannot propose explanations that insist that they are "really" doing something other than what they say they are doing, where this "something other" is an unexperienced abstraction. Sequences of chess moves, especially openings, are often given a name, which might be considered an abstraction. Yet, no commentator would argue that while A may have *thought* that he or she was making an X opening, he or she was "really" doing something else. Instead, one might argue that A made a move anticipating a future of Y and Z, while in fact W and V occurred.

In the same way, we should consider it silly to debate whether, say, the American War of Independence was "really" about political liberty or "really" about economic interests. Such "really" explanations entail a degree of almost-willful misunderstanding regarding the nature of political debate—analysts continually confuse conditions, motives, and rhetoric, using one to negate the other seriatim.[15] Instead, a decent explanation consists of situating actors in such a way that the progression of actions

---

[15]Similarly, there are many articles on political sociology coding the "frames" and justifications used by political actors and concluding that pecuniary interests "really" drove this or that social welfare policy simply because one of the most popular rhetorical strategies for convincing others to support some altruistic act is to argue that it actually fits in with their enlightened self-interest. Analysts end up with a completely inverted understanding of the field of action, taking actors' *opponents*' motivations (or actors' *theories* of their opponents' motivations) for those of the actors themselves. If it seems that I am picking on a small issue, I am not: that this is considered acceptable marshalling of evidence at the crucial juncture of motivation and alliance shows how completely ill equipped we are to understand motivation. Again, we see an inversion of the real relationships (just as we saw with causes).

and events becomes coherent. Rather than dismiss one interpretation as ersatz, we put it in ecological perspective. By assembling and organizing these interpretations, we reconstitute social objects that are inherent in the relations between situated interpretations. Mannheim ([1929] 1936) argued something similar; he called for the consideration of multiple viewpoints to flesh out our understanding of a multifaceted social *object*. But, in a very important sense, the social object is itself of no explanatory import; what is significant is the positions of the viewers, not what they view. The social object *is* only that which allows for the reciprocal orientation of actors and need not "exist" at all, in the same way that apes desiring to reconcile will fix their eyes on the same imaginary object to allow them to move closer without embarrassment (de Waal 1989).

Thus, our explanation does not require that we violate first-person terminology by locating causality in some counterintuitive world of variables (see also Berlin [1960] 1997: 41–44, 55f). The task of explanation is, as said above, about "explaining" to another person, but the way in which this task is accomplished involves the systemization of first-person perspectives and the identification of ecological invariants—"objects" in the sense of obdurate relational patterns. Put somewhat differently, the task of explanation is not to subsume the particular as a case of some abstract theoretical concept. Quite the opposite, it is to identify the concrete.

The second criterion is that our explanation involves a coherent compilation of the first-person perspectives associated with situations, so that we are able to get a sense of the whole and, as a result, of the parts. In some cases, we find that these positions form a *field*, in which people can determine what is to be done—what the environment affords—by making reference to their position. We may also compile regularities across similar fields to build up to more general statements. An excellent example here is Andrew Abbott's (1988a) *System of Professions*, a work that certainly has no lack of scope or generality. The same explanatory themes recur throughout. Yet, there is scarcely an abstraction in the work and no abstractions causing other abstractions. (The seeming exception is the word *system*, and yet *system* brings with it no theoretical baggage and does virtually no theoretical work [see Abbott 1988a: 343, n. 8, for a discussion].)[16] Finally, in no place does the work descend to the fray to determine whether professions "really" are about good responsible people doing important jobs or whether they "really" are about bad, selfish people just lining their own pockets.

In other cases, we do not find that a field has formed, making our task somewhat harder. The same general explanatory principles, however, still work for unique events. An example here is John Markoff's (1996) *Abolition*

[16]Abbott does (1988a: 108f) introduce four key systems properties: connectivity, dominance, residuality, and systematization. He even connects these (dominance and residuality tend to go together). Yet, the ratio of generality of the claims to the abstractness of the terms is still far higher than in other works.

of Feudalism. Although this work, concerned with a single historical case, does not attempt to generalize, it tackles a subject traditionally misunderstood in terms of "really" arguments (the French Revolution) without accepting any set of abstractions as an answer. Instead, Markoff alternates between sketching the development of conditions and the actions made by the relevant participants in order to allow us to understand the French Revolution. He does not need to say that any particular actor's conception of the likely unfolding of events was justified or better than others', but neither is it necessary to dismiss actors' understandings and replace them with the mysterious workings of abstractions. We must bear in mind that the key distinction between experiences and propositions about experience (which the Gestalt theorists sometimes blurred) is not a license to re-create the opposition between actors' and analysts' claims: our goal is not to *replicate* in some more extensive, and hence dreadful, form the distortions that generally enter when people recollect and repackage their experiences; it is to find intersubjectively valid compilations and minimally tendentious redactions of such experiences.

Thus, our explanation may allow us to see more of the concrete than do those whom we study—presumably we devote more time to seeing things from different angles than do the laity—but it cannot involve us seeing any less, as is frequently the case when sociologists attempt to foil the understandings of actors. The old approach was, however, right in one way: there is a parallel between the cognition of actors and theory construction. It is not that both necessarily have the same arbitrariness; it is that both can—to the extent that the mind in question is reasonably competent—successfully be impressed by the same external patternings. Contrary to what is implied in the hypothetico-deductive model, a great theory should not involve *construction* but *instruction*: the patterns that we should be talking about come from the world to our heads and not vice-versa.[17] Yes, this is simplistic, but we have somehow saddled our thinking with the opposite simplism, and this has the potential to be disastrous for empirical social research.

This is the third point—that explanation involves the transmission of intuitive accessibility. And for this, the subjective experience of increased understanding is a necessary, but not sufficient, criterion. There are many "false positives," in which an analyst believes that he has an intuitive understanding of some phenomenon, although he does not. But there are different types of false positives, and the mere existence of false positives does not close off the possibility of explanatory progress. To make this clear, let us return to the approach of Sigmund Freud, discussed in chapter 3 as antithetical in spirit and results to that proposed here. Freud

---

[17]One would call this induction, but the term is too widely used in the sense of producing general statements from examination of a number of particulars. Were this usage not dominant, one might use induction in the electrical, not the philosophic, sense: we are not the subject of the verb *to induce* but the indirect object.

frequently had the subjective feeling that he "got" what was going on, and used this feeling to confirm those very conclusions that I have argued were pathological. But Freud put his subjective belief in his comprehension not only above corroboration from those whose actions he was explaining but also against them, making the simplest correction to a false positive all but impossible. More likely in a social aesthetics is the case of a correctable false positive, the sort experienced when comprehension dawns on us, and we believe we have solved a problem, but our solution turns out to be wrong.

How can we learn that we are wrong? There is no single test for the rightness of such a subjective sense of "getting" it, but there are a number of techniques that are of formidable effectiveness in checking an intuition (in the sense used here of *Anschauung*). None of them will appear novel—all have been raised as criteria (often as *the* criterion) for a good explanation. Prediction is one of the most important, although as we have seen, to fetishize it is to lose the ability to understand the most interesting cases of social action (see Kurzman 2004: 138). Regularity is always vulnerable; hence, so are predictions. But, few surprises come as complete surprises—analysts may often correctly identify the range of likely choices even if they cannot determine which of these choices will follow.

Intervention is a second technique for uncovering false positives: someone who successfully understands the game can play; someone who only thinks that she does but does not will generally run into trouble quickly. In many cases, analysts do not want to play or are ethically restrained from doing so. Corroboration from actors in these cases can help confirm or disconfirm the adequacy of insight (see D'Andrade 1995: 158 for a relevant example).

It is worth reemphasizing that the need to confirm the phenomenological existence of theoretical terms in no way prevents analysts from coming to conclusions that the analyzed do not—the claim is not that actors have a line-item veto over social scientists' conclusions, but that a false-positive sense of insight can be uncovered as a result of an interlocution with actors. Because explanations must make use of terms that have a counterpart in first-person experience, analysts cannot (like Freud) take the refusal of actors to admit that we are correct as evidence of our success. When we get it, we must at the very least be able to demonstrate a familiarity and facility with the manipulation of the same phenomenological objects that confront actors. A false positive can therefore be brought to the surface because an interaction with actors does not go as anticipated (Collins 1983: 73). The person who thinks that he has mastered a language and finds others giggling learns that there is some idiomatic usage previously overlooked; the social scientist pontificating on what (say) motivates the defection of American Catholics who also receives sniggers has similar evidence of a false positive.[18]

---

[18] These, and other points made in this chapter, are emphasized by Barth (1981: 6, 9, 28).

Further, this form of checking the validity of an explanatory account has an additional advantage in that it is possible. Some sort of interlocution may be carried out when our subjects are living, and when they are dead we still have other forms of evidence that can be used to confirm the "this-sidedness" of our explanatory terms. This is in contrast to the conventional causal statements, which can only have their mettle proved in the nightmarish world of the philosopher king, who can ride as roughshod over actors in practice as social scientists do in theory.

Finally, we can check the validity of insight by reaching toward transposability and generality. While an explanation should not employ abstractions that require that something really be a case of something else, this does not mean that we do not seek general explanations. If the explanation is correct, it may shed light on other related substantive considerations. Because explanation, like action, is rooted in what was once adumbrated as the faculty of judgment, it may be easier to determine the extent and direction of transposability in practice than it is formulaically. Thus, Köhler's chimpanzees demonstrated insight when they "got" the solution to a problem (e.g., the idea of stacking boxes before climbing them). The correctness of this insight was proved in its (limited) transposability to related situations.

Now, the criterion of transposability to related situations might seem circular and hence useless, especially if we insist that all generality requires subsumption. That is, as the insight only applies to another situation if that second situation is like the first in "calling out for," say, a stacking-and-climbing solution, then a failed transposition (one might object) can always be excused on the grounds that the second situation was not "really" like the first after all. The supposed "circularity" of this definition has nothing in common with a circular tautology (e.g., Freud's definition of resistance or Durkheim's definition of pathology), for in the tautology, *anything* can be successfully absorbed into the definition. Yet, some situations for the chimpanzee *are* solvable by stacking, and others are not. The chimpanzee with a false-positive sense of insight does not get the fruit. It may seem somewhat ignoble to compare good social science to a chimpanzee straining for bananas, but at least the reader will then admit that the criterion is within the realm of possible application: if a chimp can do it, then so can we.[19]

Thus, our criteria for good explanation are (1) a coexistence of explanatory terms with the first-person experiences of actors; (2) a coherent compilation of these perspectives; (3) intuitive accessibility, which may in turn be proved (in the old sense of "tested") by (3a) prediction, (3b) intervention, or (3c) transposability. These strictures are of course not very

---

[19]Further, by requiring that transposability be a criterion of a good insight, we ensure one cannot excuse the failure of a solution to be transposable merely by claiming there simply are no similar situations. Correct or not, then, this insight is an ignorable one.

impressive; their lack of sophistication may be taken by the hostile critic as a reason to dismiss the arguments made here. Unfortunately, we are frequently greatly attracted to a formulaic solution to problems even if there is no good reason to believe that a correct formulaic solution should exist. In particular, there is nothing intrinsic to the nature of social science that would lead us to expect that there should be a definition of "explain" more exact than that which I have given that is both (on the one hand) free from incoherence and (on the other) applicable to the variety of substantive tasks that confront us.

Some will, of course, say that if there is no possibility of either a coherent theoretical terminology of unifying abstractions or a coherent meta-methodological definition of explanation, then the program laid out here is an empty promise. There can be nothing but disconnected and incommensurable analyses and claims. But this is to confess a failure of faith in the social world to possess its *own* character of regularity. The form of arguments (the theoretical syntax) should follow their function (what we are trying to explain in some case) and not vice versa. Put somewhat differently, the social sciences need only formalize and systematize their *methods*; their substantive statements, if on the right track, will tend to systematize themselves because of the patternings of social behavior (although also see Merleau-Ponty [1942] 1963: 49, 51). Further, we do not need to look for an illusory causal realm in contravention of first-person sensibilities to find such patternings. Close empirical attention to such first-personhood will find the source of regularity in the way in which people orient themselves to objectified relationships.

The Retrieval of the Concrete

It is because of this search for the concrete that a social aesthetics is judged by its intuitive accessibility (*Anschaulichkeit*), as opposed to its generation of counterintuitive subsumptions as in the conventional idea of theory that privileges statements of the form "*x* is not *X* but *Y*." But, this differs from a mere transcription if only because the concrete, far from being the obvious and the given, is the focus of bitter controversy and sometimes only emerges after painful elaborative work on the part of the analyst.

Regarding the first point, it will hardly escape notice that there are often fierce disagreements between actors regarding what is concrete. For example, "alienation," "anomie," and "authoritarianism" may seem to a number of people to be obviously concrete but not so to others; indeed, their presence or absence may be the subject of serious intellectual or political argument. Such disagreement does not disprove the possibility of a rigorous social aesthetics; instead, it demonstrates the need for one. The analyst, it will be recalled, must propose only terms that are phenomenologically concrete to the actors in question, but since, as we have seen, social objects can have different affordances, social actors can be oriented to different concrete actualities. Debates over the nature of the concrete are likely to indicate a particular form—whether in degree or in kind—of social relationship, some stark social opposition. Rather than side with one party in a debate, this is an opportunity (as Bourdieu has also said) for objective relational analysis.

Why is it difficult to determine what is, for actors, concrete? It is worth remembering that the phenomenologically concrete is not the same as the "individual." For example, although the Internal Revenue Service, the United States Marine Corps, or the Trilateral Commission are all in some sense (like other large organizations) abstractions, from an ecological standpoint, they are best treated as concrete, in the same way that an island or a mountain is an abstraction yet has ecological validity (Brunswik 1952: 22). The concrete nature comes because there is little disagreement about the fundamental existence of mountains or islands even though it is impossible to delimit either precisely, and acceptance of this existence facilitates both shared and individual action.

In principle, we might imagine simply seeing through actors' eyes and determining what they treat as concrete. But the data with which we begin, first, generally only have an indirect relation to experience (although the better the data, the less indirect the relation), and second, even with direct data on experience we can only determine what is concrete through the compilation of sundry experiences. Yet, even when our data do not deal with the concrete, they may be of considerable use to us in determining the overall phenomenology of action.

Consider, for example, the frequent case in which we do not have direct access to actors' experience of certain social objects (e.g., a political candidate) and hence, the actual impulsions that, as I have argued, are correlative to the phenomenological properties of these objects. Instead, we have degrees of endorsements of certain abstractions such as "liberty," "family," "integrity," and "equality." A complete outsider—one who lacked a feel for the specific political field referenced (in this case)—would probably be driven to utter distraction attempting to understand political choices as a logical derivation of professed adherence to these values. It is not at all that these terms are meaningless; rather, it is that their meaning—their objectivity—is embedded in sets of relations. In such cases, the intersubjectively valid account can only be reached through the systematic concatenation of relations. Yet, we may be able to relate patterns of holding and not holding beliefs, endorsing or not endorsing values, and so on, to the relations between actors.

I have emphasized that just because we refrain from ontological violence against actors' first-person experiences, we need not give actors' accounts of their own actions—their retrospective justifications or folk theories—any more plausibility than we give those of social scientists. But, rather than dismiss them, we can often use them to identify the valid phenomenological objects to which they orient, and actors' abstractions, like smoke from a fire, can be used to lead us to the concrete.[20] That is, to the extent that we are interested in the cognitive components of action, we will examine the practical nature of a cognition that effectively perceives the imperatives for action associated with "objects" that stand in a certain relation to us. Instead of focusing on how people construct elaborate belief systems about the world to orient them to their action (which we know they do not do), we examine how the intersubjectively valid qualities of the world that they inhabit call on them to act. The abstractions of actors may indeed have a certain kind of social validity in that they are integrated and distilled positional perspectives. They can be of use, just as the *etak* islands are of great use to Polynesian navigators, who use their relative position to these well-known landmarks as ways of determining their bearing when out of sight of land. The interesting thing is that etak islands need not actually exist for them to have this value (Hutchins 1992; also see James [1907] 1946: 128); they are abstractions without actuality, but they may have one sort of ecological validity that other abstractions (such as "true north") may not have for these sailors. This is in contrast to islands that have both ecological validity in that treating the island as "real" facilitates action (even though islands may have no clear boundaries) *and* actuality, in that one can set foot on them.

In chapter 6, I used the similar example of the mountain to sketch the intersubjective validity of social objects. But, if islands that do not exist—and, after all, an island is merely a mountain in the middle of water—can have intersubjective validity without existence, how can we construct a science based on such objects? Is this anything other than affirming whatever illusion on which we all agree? I said that a mountain *is* a mountain because we all agree that it is so. One impatient reader responded, if some trickster convinces a horde of gullible people that the mountain moves, must we as analysts also give consent to this foolishness?

The funny thing is, the mountain *does* move. The illusion that it stands still comes about because we adopt a Ptolemeyan reference system for our everyday tasks taking place on the surface of the earth. The stillness of a mountain comes because of our aggregated relations to the mountain and to each other. Thus, the "objective" reality of the stillness of the mountain is not what this focus on objects as clusters of relations *loses*; it is what it *explains*.

In sum, when we explain, we can let things be what they are, and what they are is sets of relations. We do not need to subsume them as instances of some abstraction, the more counterintuitive the linkage the better. Quite the contrary, what we need to do is compile the intuitions that allow

---

[20]It is worth noting that Pepper's (1961) general philosophy unfolded along similar lines—privileging actuality (the phenomenologically valid qualitative experience), he still recognized the utility of conceptual abstraction from this actuality into what he reasonably called "reality." However, the only extensions he accepted as in principle valid were the past, the future, and the set of mathematical/scientific extrapolations.

social phenomena to be themselves. We need not move to the realm of abstraction to uncover regularities because we have faith that regularity is found in the realm of the concrete. To understand the concrete, we need to treat it as phenomenologically valid without imagining that its valences are the same for all persons. Explanation involves reproducing the patternings in first-person experience either by mapping action imperatives to position where this is feasible or by resolving abstractions into the concrete where this is not. All abstractions used are not only provisional but also, to borrow a phrase from Keesing (1974), self-extinguishing.

CODA: ANALYTICAL DISTANCE AND SOCIAL DISTANCE

An End to Criticism?

So far, the discussion has only dealt with explanation—with our capacity to gain insight into regularities in social action. I have argued that the conventional way of explaining in the social sciences, namely, to subsume particularities into abstractions that lack first-person validity, is fundamentally unstable. The reader may accept many of the points made above and yet counter that the approach advocated here robs analysts of any ability to dissent from majority views or to use analytic insight to criticize, let alone to uncover, the perfidy that masks itself as beneficence. While there is some truth to this objection, it is not the case that refusing to consider things to be something other than what they are destroys the critical perspective.[21] (Of course, many of my readers perhaps take this whole idea of a critical social science as an antiquated folly; they may without loss skip this coda.)

It must be admitted that the idea of explanation laid out here is *not* compatible with the use of analysis as "unveiling," in which the analyst shows the connection between several disparate phenomena and allows others to see a greater significance than might be otherwise supposed. For example, let us imagine a talented essayist writing about a number of different empirical phenomena (I choose only three for reasons of space). One might be game shows on television, perhaps focusing on one that seemed inordinately oriented to players undergoing humiliation to have a chance for a large sum of money. A second might be a case of a public school system that (on the one hand) mandates that a certain amount of class time be spent instructing children to avoid certain foodstuffs but (on the other) allows a corporation that produces one of these countermanded items to advertise and sell its wares inside the school in exchange for grants of money. A third might be the spread of retail "chains" as an extension of "branding" from the production to the distribution sector.

---

[21]An elegant and kindred discussion of the conventional use of "scientific" abstractions as criticism is found in the work of Boltanski and Thévenot ([1991] 2006:10f). For a clear exposition of the logic of a transcendent critique, see Marcuse (1964: 225).

All these phenomena are actual; our essayist, however, might give us additional insight by linking them all to the fundamental change in the human motivational system brought about by late capitalism. Our essayist can then synthesize the otherwise-confusing observations while endowing them with an emotional significance. That is, in first-person experience we do not encounter capitalism, nor do we see, hear, feel, touch, or taste its requirements to (say) dispose of its surplus. Yet, with the theoretical terms provided by the work of this essayist, we have a new perspective that not only gives us a sense of insight, but also may be counterposed to our own first-person perspectives (according to which, say, a beckoning product just *is* "neat" and not indicative of a false need). Because (following our imaginary theorist) we are not restricted to our first-person experience but can explain it away, we have both increased analytic power and a critical perspective on limitations in our current society. For example, in seeing capitalism as a "thing," we are able to explain the concrete (e.g., jogging) with reference to the existence of this thing (e.g., capitalism requires or at least produces jogging, which, as we recall, Turner [1984: 199] argued [see chapter 3]).

There may indeed be merit in such an analysis. But there are two reasons why we should not reject the line of thinking laid out in these pages simply because it would push this sort of activity outside the bounds of social science. First, declaring that this is not good social science does not mean that it cannot take place. We generally assume that it is not necessary that sociological research papers be written in meter without thereby wringing our hands over our contribution to the destruction of poetry.

Second, when considering these juxtaposed facts that help us "see" the true nature and noxious pervasiveness of capitalism, we might find ourselves making cognitive simplifications that lead us to ignore some aspects of the concrete for no good reason. That is, we are creating abstractions that build in certain biases, and these very biases might be necessary for the supposedly salutary clarification to take place. If (again, limiting ourselves to three bits of information pulled out of a hat) we also consider that (1) ancient Greeks put a coin beneath the tongue of the dead to pay Charon, or the boatman would refuse to take the expired across the river Styx; (2) the earliest writing discovered is in the form of lists of goods or tax schedules; (3) there are almost no references to regular intersociety or internation contact before modernization that did not revolve around trade,[22] we might suddenly find that what seemed to be such powerful evidence of capitalism as leading to a historically unique configuration of motives is not so powerful at all.

---

[22]The possible exceptions are warfare for religious purposes, which seems to be relatively infrequent, and the famous exchange of women, which when it did occur was usually combined with other forms of exchange. Note that one would not consider the periodic assemblage of the larger units of hunter-gatherers in "fission-fusion" societies as intersocietal interaction.

Of course, these three actualities do not go far in terms of "disproving" the claim or insinuation that capitalism altered the human motivational system. This, however, is not because the first synthesis was right and its undoing wrong, but because posing the question, Does capitalism produce a special constellation of motives? has left the terrain of actuality where the words "right" and "wrong" have even a chance of doing their proper work. A refusal to dispense with first-person experiences would have prevented us from even raising what turned out to be a fruitless debate. The subjective feeling of insight that, far from elucidating and organizing first-person perspectives, requires trampling them underfoot, must be for us a *datum*, never an explanation. Thus, when we consider more carefully the nature of the critical analytic insight via the use of abstractions that is threatened by the approach proposed here, we conclude that this insight ought not be a part of the social sciences in the first place.

Perhaps this does not wholly allay our concern that we lose a capacity for criticizing immoral perceptions. And, it should not, for there *is* a danger in an aesthetics, a systemization of a set of intersubjectively valid judgments that assume a capacity for insightful behavior given superficial sensory contacts—one can (illogically, but "naturally") go from a recognition that value *is* in the world to implicitly valuing the world as it is. Goethe, who more than any other single person exemplified the wholistic approach to knowledge that assumed a connection of the inner and the outer, and who inspired the Gestalt theorists whose work has been central for our rethinking of explanation, closed the treatment of chemical colors in his remarkable *Theory of Colours* with a discussion of the relation between inner and outer in mammals. He insisted that there is some relation between the spots in animal fur or skin and the underlying parts, although this correspondence so far had resisted our decoding (Goethe [1810] 1970: 263, 265).

This conviction, although wrong, is at least charming, and it is related to important aspects of vision (as seen in the discussion of *Ammophila* in chapter 6) that were neglected by others. However, Goethe did not stop here; he saw this process as inherently valuational. Any dappling, he concluded, especially involving loud primary colors, was itself indicative of a lack of perfection; the most perfect creature would have a uniform consistency combining in its wholeness the entire spectrum of colors. The beauty of the body would then indicate the perfection of the soul. And Goethe understood that this supported his aesthetic judgment that the white race was the most beautiful. He could *see* in the objects of racial bodies their fundamental natural inequality.

Of course, we cannot maintain that the contrary approach inherently took social scientists *away* from racism. Rather than use their subjective sense of beauty to support the claim of white superiority, others laboriously filled brain cavities with shot and counted, and weighed, and tested, and validated claims to their own superiority (see Gould 1981). Indeed, the very statistics that underlie the conventional social sciences were formulated largely in response to eugenic concerns, in turn related to (although not identical with) visions of racial hierarchy (MacKenzie 1981). "Counting" can give as much support for poor ideas as can "seeing." It seems that the problem lies less in the type of knowledge produced than in the social relations connecting producers to the subjects of knowledge.

Indeed, Goethe was perhaps in some ways truer than the biometricians who claimed to be producing isolated facts. Goethe *saw* inequality, and inequality there was. Without being unsympathetic, we cannot but note that mainstream social science, with its egalitarian sensibilities, alternates without a blush between asserting equality as the obvious and incontestable fact and accumulating evidence of inequality. Indeed, those most committed to equality often dedicate their careers to the study of inequality. We, of course, understand that this is not evidence of sloppy thinking; we might say perhaps that researchers are committed to egalitarianism in prescriptive terms although they are committed to recognizing inequality in descriptive terms. This makes it seem like equality is only a potential, not an actual, state, so we might want to rephrase it as that we recognize an existent *moral* equality while we deplore the widespread ignoring of this legitimate claim and hence see existent *material* inequality.

Perhaps. It may well be that a skilled intellectual surgeon can deftly separate equality and inequality; I would not like to try because a tremble with the scalpel is likely to lead to a great loss of blood for all concerned. But it might also be that we have an unsurpassable contradiction here, coming again from the wrong way of phrasing our inquiry. The considerations of chapter 5 suggest that it is implausible that there is correct knowledge to be had in situations of oppression; without denying the goodwill behind the effort of finding how inequality and equality coexist, it seems that any ethical impulse should be directed not so much at the particular *view* taken of the subaltern, but at the destruction of the position of those above. Just as no matter how hard one tries, one cannot get a good view of another's face if one insists on standing on his neck, so too a collectivity of social scientists—even an open and meritocratic one, composed of honest and altruistic persons from all backgrounds—can find no guarantee of correct knowledge in such an environment. A decent social aesthetics, should it prove possible, with its restriction to the data of valid experience as opposed to analytic abstractions, could only document and situate the antagonisms, not see around them.

This might seem an admission of lack. But it does not seem that authoritatively employing abstractions that run roughshod over first-person experiences will secure a "seeing around" for us, as we have seen that this leads to evil at least as easily as it does to good. Goethe's error was the temptation that comes from the embrace of experiences to pass directly from the reality of the experience to the truth of the statement about the experience. It is not implicit in a social aesthetics; indeed, a social aesthetics is our best avenue to explore such errors.

Criticism versus Critical Criticism

Further, the perspective put forward here, far from being antithetical to the spirit of criticism, is actually its essence. To explicate this point, we can follow Marx's caustic remarks on the "critical criticism" of Bruno Bauer and the other Young Hegelians (Marx and Engels [1844] 1975, [1845–1846] 1976). What they saw as "criticism," Marx saw as merely a statement of preferences and a feeling of the moral superiority of the analyst. While such criticism is obviously analogous to actions that would be called "critical" in everyday life, this is a paltry excuse for substituting narcissistic gratification for philosophic labor.

Real criticism was, for Marx, integrally tied to the dialectical method. This dialectical method, in turn, involved a progression from the abstract to the concrete.[23] Most famously, Marx ([1867] 1906) begins *Capital* with the abstraction of the commodity, and by analysis (focusing on the commodity as combination of exchange value and use value), attempts to unravel, in greater complexity as he progressively approaches the concrete, the workings of the production and circulation of value in capitalism.

But, did not Marx then use the idea of capitalism that I gave as an example of the sort of abstraction that should be treated with suspicion? Marx himself did not at this time use the word *capitalism* (which would be an anachronism) but instead spoke of "civil society" or "bourgeois society" (*bürgerliche Gesellschaft*), which, though clearly a term with many different philosophical implications depending on the context, was also a nonproblematic term describing European societies in the eighteenth and nineteenth centuries. (This is similar to someone speaking of the "modern" world without necessarily ascribing to a particular "theory" of modernity.) And, far from assuming the uniqueness or integrity of capitalism as a "thing," Marx (while of course emphasizing the fact that political economists falsely universalized the relations of bourgeois production) pointed to the continuity across economic formations, even arguing ([1858] 1973: 105) that there was a way in which capitalism could help us understand earlier economic formations.

Thus, Marx provides us an exemplar of a critical attitude that does not rely on abstractions.[24] Indeed, Marx mercilessly mocked the Young Hegelians for emphasizing these abstract ideas; he and Engels ([1845–1846] 1976) continually counterpose particular historical facts to the broad-sweeping abstractions of their opponents. If Marx did not understand criticism to entail the revealing of a pervasive and blameworthy abstraction behind the particular concrete, what did it entail? More than anything

---

[23]This use of dialectics is best explained by Hegel ([1803] 1949) in his preface to *Phenomenology*. Marx ([1858] 1973: 100f) has the clearest defense of this method.

[24]Or, as he might say—in the spirit of Hegel ([1807] 1977)—*false* abstractions. See, for example, Marx (1968: 437).

else, criticism was a method of *reaching truth by analysis of contradictions (limitations) in abstractions*. What appears to us initially as "concrete" is, in fact, such an abstraction.[25] Criticism involves taking an abstraction that at first blush seems reasonable and resolving it into the true material conditions from which it arises. When Marx did say that others were mistaken about what something "really" was, it was always that what others treated as an abstraction was really rooted in the concrete—not that it was an instance of some other abstraction.[26] Such criticism is wholly in the spirit of the proposals made here.

Put another way, it would indeed be a setback for social science if we were unable to do more than separately document gender differences in interaction (e.g., interrupting and touch initiation), gendering of the division of labor, and violence against women, lost among the thousands and thousands of other social phenomena to be examined. But, a critical approach does not require the fixing of an abstraction (e.g., "patriarchy") with the attendant mystifications (that such and such is done *for* patriarchy or is required *by* patriarchy). Instead, as Dorothy Smith (1987) has argued, it requires careful attention to the concrete relationships of interpersonal life.

CONCLUSION

Theoretical explanation in the social sciences has placed nearly all its bets on the idea of explanation of social constraint in the form of causal laws. The problem with this idea of "explanation of social constraint in the form of causal laws," however, is (as we have seen) that only the words *of, in,* and *the* in this phrase have any possible meaning. It is time to stop arguing about *how* we are to best accomplish an impossible task and determine how we can build on the less-grandiose, but altogether possible, forms of understanding and explanation that we have. Instead of having an explanatory style that refuses to let things be what they are and obliterates them into analytic moments created at the whim of the analyst, we can begin from what we—like other sentient creatures—can know about our environment.

---

[25]For example, the fetishism of commodities is that the concrete web of social relations *appears* as a commodity—abstracted from the actual relations. See Marx (1971: 130, 139, 378, 453, 485; [1858] 1973: 85).

[26]For example, see Marx's (1971: 87; also see 93 on appearance) criticism of Mill: "Here the contradiction between the general law and further developments in the concrete circumstances is to be resolved not by the discovery of the connecting links but by directly subordinating and immediately adapting the concrete to the abstract." Thus, Habermas (1971: 44), in what he imagined to be a blow against Marx: "*Marx conceives of reflection according to the model of production.* Because he tacitly starts with this premise, it is not inconsistent that he does not distinguish between the logical status of the natural sciences and of critique."

When we consider the environment relevant for social analysis, we find that what confront the actor are not human individuals—corporal bodies possibly motored by consciousnesses—or at least not these alone. For our social action involves other assemblages, social objects, that have phenomenological validity. These social objects are, properly speaking, bundles of relations. These relations have qualities that in turn possess positionally variable intersubjective validity. Actors sense these qualities, react to them, and in some cases theorize them. When there is a patterning to these senses and these reactions, we may employ a field theoretic approach. If we really want to take the idea of "theories" seriously, we find that theories are not something that we analysts oppose to the first-person beliefs of actors or to the trivial descriptions of less-gifted social analysts. Rather, theories are what actors make—sometimes—as they confront patterns in social life. Our task is not to steamroller over these theories but to compile them in a descriptive fashion that allows us to understand and to explain—to go, in a sense, from one interiority to another as we go from one position to another.

This does not mean that everything simply falls into our lap. Although things are not something *other* than what they appear to be to actors, not all *does* appear. And it is for this reason that we need insight—not to unveil the nonappearing by denouncing what appears as "merely" apparent, but to infer on the basis of the actuality of the apparent (Dewey 1929: 137f).

Despite grudging acknowledgments of the veracity of many of the critiques made of the conventional idea of explanation, there will be a strong tendency to dismiss the suggestions made here simply because they are too vague and open ended, and we may prefer the surety of our own formulaic approach to explanation over the chaos of one guided only by good faith. We should be quite self-conscious when we are tempted to criticize an argument that sounds reasonable because it does not contain a prefabricated answer to every problem. One way in which a lunatic can be recognized is that he has an answer for everything and is convinced that everything fits into a system. Any order in our analyses must come from actual regularities in the dispersion of things and thoughts across persons, and not because we have scribbled over the glasses with which we see the social world.

References

Abbott, Andrew. 1988a. *The System of Professions*. Chicago: University of Chicago Press.
Abbott, Andrew. 1988b. Transcending General Linear Reality. *Sociological Theory* 6:160–185.
Abbott, Andrew. 1992. What Do Cases Do? Pp. 53–82 in *What Is a Case?* edited by Charles S. Ragin and Howard S. Becker. Cambridge: Cambridge University Press.
Abbott, Andrew. 1997. Of Time and Space: The Contemporary Relevance of the Chicago School. *Social Forces* 75:1149–1182.
Abbott, Andrew. 1998. The Causal Devolution. *Sociological Methods and Research* 27:148–181.
Abbott, Andrew. 2001. *Chaos of Disciplines*. Chicago: University of Chicago Press.
Abbott, Andrew. 2005. Linked Ecologies: States and Universities as Environments for Professions. *Sociological Theory* 23:245–274.
Adorno, T.W., Else Frenkel-Brunswik, Daniel J. Levinson, and R. Nevitt Sanford. 1950. *The Authoritarian Personality*. New York: Harper and Row.
al-Kindī, Abū Yūsuf. 1974. *al-Kindī's Metaphysics*, translated by Afred L. Levy. Albany: State University of New York Press.
al-Kindī, Jacob. 1912. De Causis Diversitatum Aspectus Et Bandis Demonstrationibus Geometricis Super Eas, edited and translated by Seb. Vogl. *Abhandlungen zur Geschichte der Mathematischen Wissenschaften mit Einschlussl Ihrer Anwendungen Begründet von Moritz Cantor* 26:3–72.
Allport, Floyd. 1955. *Theories of Perception and the Concept of Structure*. New York: Wiley.
Amis, Kingsley. 1954. *Lucky Jim*. London: Gollancz.
Anderson, J.K. 1970. *Military Theory and Practice in the Age of Xenophon*. Berkeley: University of California Press.
Anscombe, G. E. M. 1957. Intention. Oxford: Basil Blackwell.
Antaki, Charles. 1994. *Explaining and Arguing*. London: Sage.
Apel, Karl-Otto. 1984. *Understanding and Explanation*, translated by Georgia Warnke. Cambridge, Mass.: MIT Press.
Aristotle. 1941a. Categoriae. Pp. 7–37 in *The Basic Works of Aristotle*, edited by Richard McKeon. New York: Random House.
Aristotle. 1941b. De Anima. Pp. 535–603 in *The Basic Works of Aristotle*, edited by Richard McKeon. New York: Random House.
Aristotle. 1961. *De Anima*, edited with introduction and commentary by Sir David Ross. Oxford: Oxford University Press.
Armstrong, D.M. 1962. *Bodily Sensations*. London: Routledge and Kegan Paul.
Asch, Solomon E. 1952. *Social Psychology*. New York: Prentice-Hall.
Ash, Mitchell G. 1998. *Gestalt Psychology in German Culture 1890–1967*. Cambridge: Cambridge University Press.

Atran, Scott. 1994. Core Domains versus Scientific Theories: Evidence from Systematic and Itza-Maya Folk Biology. Pp. 316–340 in *Mapping the Mind: Domain Specificity*, edited by Lawrence A. Hirschfeld and Susan A. Gelman. Cambridge: Cambridge University Press.

Augustine. 2002. *On the Trinity, Books 8–15*, edited by Gareth B. Matthews and translated by Stephen McKenna. Cambridge: Cambridge University Press.

Ballard, Dana H., Mary M. Hayhoe, Polly K. Pook, and Rajeesh P.N. Rao. 1997. Deictic Codes for the Embodiment of Cognition. *Behavioral and Brain Sciences* 20:723–767.

Barnes, Barry. 1981. On the Conventional Component in Knowledge and Cognition. *Philosophy of the Social Sciences* 11:303–333.

Barnes, Barry. 1983. Social Life as Bootstrapped Induction. *Sociology* 17:524–545.

Barnes, Barry. 1995. *The Elements of Social Theory*. Princeton, N.J.: Princeton University Press.

Barnes, Barry. 2000. *Understanding Agency: Social Theory and Responsible Action*. London: Sage.

Barth, Fredrik. 1981. *Process and Form in Social Life. Selected Essays of Frederik Barth: Volume 1*. London: Routledge and Kegan Paul.

Barth, Fredrik. 1987. *Cosmologies in the Making*. Cambridge: Cambridge University Press.

Becker, Howard S. 1998. *Tricks of the Trade*. Chicago: University of Chicago Press.

Beebee, Helen. 2004. Causing and Nothingness. Pp. 291–308 in *Causation and Counterfactuals*, edited by John Collins, Ned Hall, and L.A. Paul. Cambridge, Mass.: MIT Press.

Bell, Clive. 1958. *Art*. New York: Putnam.

Bell, Daniel, editor. [1955] 1963. *The Radical Right*. Garden City, N.Y.: Doubleday.

Benchley, Robert. 1940. *My Ten Years in a Quandary, and How They Grew*. Garden City, N.Y.: Blue Ribbon Books.

Ben-David, Joseph and Randall Collins. 1966. Social Factors in the Origins of a New Science: The Case of Psychology. *American Sociological Review* 31:451–465.

Benjamin, Jessica. 1981. The Oedipal Riddle: Authority, Authonoy and the New Narcissism. Pp. 195–224 in *The Problem of Authority in America*, edited by John P. Diggins and Mark E. Kann. Philadelphia: Temple University Press.

Berger, Peter L. 1969. *The Sacred Canopy*. New York: Doubleday.

Berger, Peter L. and Thomas Luckmann. 1967. *The Social Construction of Reality*. New York: Doubleday.

Bergesen, Albert J. 2004. Durkheim's Theory of Mental Categories: A Review of the Evidence. *Annual Review of Sociology*, 30:395–408.

Bergson, Henri. 1911. *Creative Evolution*, translated by Arthur Mitchell. New York: Holt.

Berlin, Brent. 1978. Ethnobiological Classification. Pp. 9–26 in *Cognition and Categorization*, edited by Eleanor Rosch and Barbara B. Lloyd. Hillsdale, NJ: Erlbaum.

Berlin, Isaiah. [1960] 1997. The Concept of Scientific History. Pp. 17–58 in *The Proper Study of Mankind*. New York: Farrar, Straus and Giroux.

Bernert, Christopher. 1983. The Career of Causal Analysis in American Sociology. *The British Journal of Sociology* 34:230–254.

Billig, Michael. 1982. *Ideology and Social Psychology*. New York: St. Martin's Press.

Billig, Michael. 1996. *Arguing and Thinking*, second edition. Cambridge: Cambridge University Press.
Birken, Lawrence. 1988. *Consuming Desire: Sexual Science and the Emergence of a Culture of Abundance 1871–1914*. Ithaca, N.Y.: Cornell University Press.
Bischof, Norbert. 1966. Erkenntnistheoretische Grundlagenprobleme der Wahrnehmungpsychologie. Pp. 21–78 in *Handbuch der Psychologie*, Volume 1. Göttingen, Germany: Verlag für Psychologie.
Bloch, Maurice. 1977. The Past and the Present in the Present. *Man, New Series* 12:278–292.
Bloom, Lois and Joanne Bitetti Capatides. 1987. Sources of Meaning in the Acquisition of Complex Syntax: The Sample Case of Causality. *Journal of Experimental Child Psychology* 43:112–128.
Bloor, David. 1983. *Wittgenstein: A Social Theory of Knowledge*. New York: Columbia University Press.
Bloor, David. 1997. *Wittgenstein, Rules and Institutions*. London: Routledge.
Blum, Alan F. and Peter McHugh. 1971. The Social Ascription of Motives. *American Sociological Review* 36:98–109.
Boas, Franz. 1916. The Origin of Totemism. *American Anthropologist* 18:319–326.
Boltanski, Luc and Laurent Thévenot. [1991] 2006. *On Justification: Economies of Worth*, translated by Catherine Porter. Princeton, N.J.: Princeton University Press.
Boltanski, Luc and Laurent Thévenot. 1999. The Sociology of Critical Capacity. *European Journal of Social Theory* 2:359–377.
Boltanski, Luc and Laurent Thévenot. 2000. The Reality of Moral Expectations: A Sociology of Situated Judgment. *Philosophical Explorations* 3:208–231.
Bonduelle, Michel. 1995a. Charcot's Major Neurological Interests. Pp. 99–134 in *Charcot: Constructing Neurology*, by Christopher G. Goetz, Michel Bonduelle, and Toby Gelfand. New York: Oxford University Press.
Bonduelle, Michel. 1995b. Charcot's Private Life. Pp. 268–304 in *Charcot: Constructing Neurology*, by Christopher G. Goetz, Michel Bonduelle, and Toby Gelfand. New York: Oxford University Press.
Bonduelle, Michel. 1995c. The Development of a Career in Neurology. Pp. 62–98 in *Charcot: Constructing Neurology*, by Christopher G. Goetz, Michel Bonduelle, and Toby Gelfand. New York: Oxford University Press.
Borch-Jacobsen, Mikkel. 1996a. Neurotica: Freud and the Seduction Theory. *October* 16:15–43.
Borch-Jacobsen, Mikkel. 1996b. *Remembering Anna O.: A Century of Mystification*, translated by Kirby Olson. New York: Routledge.
Borges, Jorge Luis. [1942] 1965. The Analytical Language of John Wilkins. Pp. 101–105 in *Other Inquisitions*. Austin: University of Texas Press.
Boring, Edwin G. 1942. *Sensation and Perception in the History of Experimental Psychology*. New York: Appleton-Century-Crofts.
Bornstein, Marc H. 1987. Perceptual Categories in Vision and Audition. Pp. 287–300 in *Categorical Perception*, edited by Steven Harnad. Cambridge: Cambridge University Press.
Bourdieu, Pierre. [1966] 1969. Intellectual Field and Creative Project. *Social Science Information* 8:189–119.
Bourdieu, Pierre. 1968. Structuralism and Theory of Sociological Knowledge. *Social Research* 35:680–706.
Bourdieu, Pierre. [1972] 1977. *Outline of a Theory of Practice*, translated by Richard Nice. Cambridge: Cambridge University Press.

Bourdieu, Pierre. [1979] 1984. *Distinction: A Social Critique of the Judgment of Taste*, translated by Richard Nice. Cambridge, Mass.: Harvard University Press.
Bourdieu, Pierre. [1980] 1990. *The Logic of Practice*. Stanford, Calif.: Stanford University Press.
Bourdieu, Pierre. [1984] 1988. *Homo Academicus*, translated by Peter Collier. Stanford, Calif.: Stanford University Press.
Bourdieu, Pierre. 1985a. The Genesis of the Concepts of Habitus and of Field. *Sociocriticism* 2:11–24.
Bourdieu, Pierre. 1985b. The Social Space and the Genesis of Groups. *Theory and Society* 14:723–744.
Bourdieu, Pierre. [1989] 1996. *The State Nobility*, translated by Lauretta C. Clough. Stanford: Stanford University Press.
Bourdieu, Pierre. 1990a. *In Other Words*, translated by Matthew Adamson. Stanford: Stanford University Press.
Bourdieu, Pierre. 1990b. The Scholastic Point of View. *Cultural Anthropology* 5:380–391.
Bourdieu, Pierre. 1992. Thinking about Limits. *Theory, Culture and Society* 9:37–49.
Bourdieu, Pierre. 1993. *Sociology in Question*. London: Sage.
Bourdieu, Pierre. 1994. Rethinking the State: Genesis and Structure of the Bureaucratic Field. *Sociological Theory* 12:1–18.
Bourdieu, Pierre. [1997] 2000. *Pascalian Meditations*, translated by Richard Nice. Stanford, Calif.: Stanford University Press.
Bourdieu, Pierre. [1998] 2001. *Masculine Domination*, translated by Richard Nice. Stanford, Calif.: Stanford University Press.
Bourdieu, Pierre. 2008. *Sketch for a Self Analysis*, translated by Richard Nice. Chicago: University of Chicago Press.
Bourdieu, Pierre and Jean-Claude Passeron. 1990. *Reproduction in Education, Society and Culture*, second edition, translated by Richard Nice. London: Sage.
Bourdieu, Pierre and Lo c J.D. Wacquant. 1992. *An Invitation to Reflexive Sociology*. Chicago: University of Chicago Press.
Bradley, Raymond Trevor. 1987. *Charisma and Social Structure*. New York: Paragon House.
Brainard, Paul. 1930. The Mentality of a Child Compared with That of Apes. *The Journal of Genetic Psychology* 37:268–293.
Brandt, Karl. 1952. *Struktur der Wirtschaftsdynamik*. Frankfurt: Verlag Fritz Knapp.
Brecht, Bertolt. 1955. *Leben des Galilei: Schauspiel*. Frankfurt: Suhrkamp Verlag.
Breiger, Ronald L., 1974. The Duality of Persons and Groups. *Social Forces* 53: 181–190.
Breslau, Daniel. 2000. Sociology after Humanism: A Lesson from Contemporary Science Studies. *Sociological Theory* 18:289–307.
Breslau, Daniel. 2007. The American Spencerians: Theorizing a New Science. Pp. 39–62 in *Sociology in America*, edited by Craig Calhoun. Chicago: University of Chicago Press.
Breuer, Josef and Sigmund Freud. [1897] 1955. *Studies on Hysteria*, translated by James Strachey. New York: Basic Books.
Brown, J.F. 1936a. *Psychology and the Social Order*. New York: McGraw Hill.
Brown, J.F. 1936b. On the Use of Mathematics in Psychological Theory. *Psychometrika* 1(1):79–90, 1(2):1–14.
Brown, Robert. 1984. *The Nature of Social Laws: Machiavelli to Mill*. Cambridge: Cambridge University Press.

Brown, Roger. 1958. *Words and Things*. Glencoe, Ill.: Free Press.
Brunswik, Egon. 1952. *The Conceptual Framework of Psychology, Volume 1, Number 10 of the International Encyclopedia of Unified Science*. Chicago: University of Chicago Press.
Bruun, Hans Henrik. 2007. *Science, Values and Politics in Max Weber's Methodology*. Aldershot, U.K.: Ashgate.
Bruun, Hans Henrik. 2008. Objectivity, Values Spheres, and "Inherent Laws": On Some Suggestive Isomorphism between Weber, Bourdieu, and Luhmann. *Philosophy of the Social Sciences* 38:97–120.
Bulmer, Ralph. 1967. Why Is the Cassowary Not a Bird? A Problem of Zoological Taxonomy Among the Karam of the New Guinea Highlands. *Man, New Series* 2:5–26.
Bunge, Mario. 1959. *Causality: The Place of the Causal Principle in Modern Science*. Cambridge, Mass.: Harvard University Press.
Burawoy, Michael. 1990. Marxism as Science: Historical Challenges and Theoretical Growth. *American Sociological Review* 55:775–793.
Burger, Thomas. 1976. *Max Weber's Theory of Concept Formation*. Durham, N.C.: Duke University Press.
Burke, Kenneth. 1952. *A Grammar of Motives*. New York: Prentice Hall.
Burton, Harry Edwin. 1945. The Optics of Euclid. *Journal of the Optical Society of America* 35:357–372.
Burtt, Edwin Arthur. 1927. *The Metaphysical Foundations of Modern Physical Science*. New York: Harcourt, Brace.
Buss, Andreas. 1999. The Concept of Adequate Causation and Max Weber's Comparative Psychology of Religion. *British Journal of Sociology* 50:317–329.
Camic, Charles. 1986. The Matter of Habit. *American Journal of Sociology* 91:1039–1087.
Campbell, Colin. 1996. *The Myth of Social Action*. Cambridge: Cambridge University Press.
Cannon, Susan Faye. 1978. *Science in Culture: The Early Victorian Period*. New York: Dawson and Science History Publications.
Cantor, G.N. 1983. *Optics after Newton: Theories of Light in Britain and Ireland, 1704–1840*. Manchester, U.K.: Manchester University Press.
Carley, Kathleen. 1986. Knowledge Acquisition as a Social Phenomenon. *Instructional Science* 14:381–438.
Carney, Edward. 1994. *A Survey of English Spelling*. London: Routledge.
Carter, K. Codell. 1980. Germ Theory, Hysteria, and Freud's Early Work in Psychopathology. *Medical History* 24:259–274.
Cartwright, Nancy. 1983. *How the Laws of Physics Lie*. Oxford: Clarendon Press.
Cartwright, Nancy. 1987. Philosophical Problems of Quantum Theory: The Response of American Physicists. Pp. 417–435 in *The Probabilistic Revolution, Volume 2: Ideas in the Sciences*, edited by Lorenz Krüger, Gerd Gigerenzer, and Mary S. Morgan. Cambridge, Mass.: MIT Press.
Cartwright, Nancy. 2004. Causation: One Word, Many Things. *Philosophy of Science* 71:805–819.
Cartwright, Nancy. 2007. *Hunting Causes and Using Them*. Cambridge: Cambridge University Press.
Cassirer, Ernst. 1910. *Substanzbegriff und Funktionsbegriff*. Berlin: Verlag von Bruno Cassirer.

Cassirer, Ernst. [1910] 1923. *Substance and Function, and Einstein's Theory of Relativity*. Chicago: Open Court.
Cassirer, Ernst. [1918] 1981. *Kant's Life and Thought*, translated by James Haden. New Haven, Conn.: Yale University Press.
Cassirer, Ernst. 1922. *Die Begriffsform im Mythischen Denken*. Leipzig, Germany: Teubner.
Cassirer, Ernst. [1923] 1953. *The Philosophy of Symbolic Forms, Volume 1: Language*, translated by Ralph Manheim. New Haven, Conn.: Yale University Press.
Cassirer, Ernst. [1925] 1955. *The Philosophy of Symbolic Forms, Volume 2: Mythical Thinking*, translated by Ralph Manheim. New Haven, Conn.: Yale University Press.
Cassirer, Ernst. [1928–1940] 1996. *The Philosophy of Symbolic Forms, Volume 4*, translated by John Michael Krois. New Haven, Conn.: Yale University Press.
Cerulo, Karen A. 2010. Mining the Intersections of Culture and Cognitive Science. *Poetics* 38:115–132.
Cerulo, Karen A. 2018. Scents and Sensibility: Olfaction, Sense-Making, and Meaning Attribution. *American Sociological* Review 83:2:361–389.
Chang, Patricia Mei Yin. 1989. Beyond the Clan: A Re-Analysis of the Empirical Evidence in Durkheim's *The Elementary Forms of the Religious Life*. *Sociological Theory* 7:64–69.
Charcot, J.M. [1881] 1962. *Lectures on the Diseases of the Nervous System*, translated and edited by George Sigerson. New York: Hafner.
Chase, Ivan D. 1985. The Sequential Analysis of Aggressive Acts During Hierarchy Formation: An Application of the "Jigsaw Puzzle" Approach. *Animal Behaviour* 33:86–100.
Chattopadhyaya, Debiprasad. 1977. *Science and Society in Ancient India*. Calcutta: Research India.
Chattopadhyaya, Debiprasad. 1991. *History of Science and Technology in Ancient India II: Formation of the Theoretical Fundamentals of Natural Science*. Calcutta: Firma KLM Private.
Churchland, Patricia S., V.S. Ramachandran, and Terrence J. Sejnowski. 1994. A Critique of Pure Vision. Pp. 23–60 in *Large-Scale Neuronal Theories of the Brain*, edited by Christof Koch and Joel L. Davis. Cambridge, Mass.: MIT Press.
Churchland, Paul M. 1995. *The Engine of Reason, the Seat of the Soul*. Cambridge, Mass.: MIT Press.
Cioffi, Frank. 1970. Freud and the Idea of a Pseudo-Science. Pp. 471–499 in *Explanation in the Behavioural Sciences*, edited by Robert Borger and Frank Cioffi. Cambridge: Cambridge University Press.
Cioffi, Frank. 1998. Was Freud a Liar? Pp. 34–42 in *Unauthorized Freud: Doubters Confront a Legend*, edited by Frederick C. Crews. New York: Viking.
Clark, Andy. 1997. *Being There: Putting Brain, Body and World Together Again*. Cambridge, Mass.: MIT Press.
Clark, Terry Nichols. 1973. *Prophets and Patrons: The French University and the Emergence of the Social Sciences*. Cambridge, Mass.: Harvard University Press.
Cohen, H. Floras. 1994. *The Scientific Revolution*. Chicago: University of Chicago Press.
Coley, J.D., D.L. Medin, and S. Atran. 1978. Does Rank Have Its Privilege? Inductive Inferences within Folkbiological Taxonomies. *Cognition* 64:73–112.
Collins, H.M. 1983. The Meaning of Lies: Accounts of Action and Participatory Research. Pp. 69–76 in *Accounts and Action*, edited by G. Nigel Gilbert and Peter Abell. Aldershott, U.K.: Gower.

Collins, John, Ned Hall, and L.A. Paul. 2004. *Causation and Counterfactuals*. Cambridge, Mass.: MIT Press.
Collins, Randall. 2004. *Interaction Ritual Chains*. Princeton, N.J.: Princeton University Press.
Collins, Randall. 2008. *Violence: A Micro-sociological Theory*. Princeton, N.J.: Princeton University Press.
Collins, Steven. 1985. Categories, Concepts, or Predicaments? Remarks on Mauss's Use of Philosophical Terminology. Pp. 26–45 in *The Category of the Person*, edited by Michael Carrithers, Steven Collins, and Steven Lukes. Cambridge: Cambridge University Press.
Comte, Auguste. [1842] 1974. *The Positive Philosophy*, freely condensed and edited by Harriet Martineau. New York: AMS Press.
Converse, Philip E. 1964. The Nature of Belief Systems in Mass Publics. Pp. 206–261 in *Ideology and Discontent*, edited by David E. Apter. International Yearbook of Political Research, Volume 5. New York: Free Press.
Cooley, Charles H. 1913. The Institutional Character of Pecuniary Valuation. *American Journal of Sociology* 18:543–555.
Corbetta, Mauizio and Gordon L. Shulman. 2001. Imaging Expectations and Attentional Modulations in the Human Brain. Pp. 1–24 in *Visual Attention and Cortical Circuits*, edited by Jochen Braun, Christof Koch, and Joel L. Davis. Cambridge, Mass.: MIT Press.
Correll, Joshua, Bernadette Park, Charles M. Judd, and Bernd Wittenbrink. 2002. The Police Officer's Dilemma: Using Ethnicity to Disambiguate Potentially Threatening Individuals. *Journal of Personality and Social Psychology* 83: 1314–1329.
Cosman F., M. Baz-Hecht M., M. Cushman, M.D. Vardy, J.D. Cruz, J.W. Nieves, M. Zion, and R. Lindsay. 2005. Short-Term Effects Of Estrogen, Tamoxifen and Raloxifene on Hemostasis: A Randomized-Controlled Study and Review of the Literature. *Thrombosis Research* 116:1–13.
Couliano, Ioan P. 1987. *Eros and Magic in the Renaissance*, translated by Margaret Cook. Chicago: University of Chicago Press.
Craig, Gordon A. 1956. *The Politics of the Prussian Army, 1640–1945*. Oxford: Oxford University Press.
Crews, Frederick C. 1993. The Unknown Freud. *New York Review of Books* November 18, 55–66.
Crews, Frederick C., editor. 1998. *Unauthorized Freud: Doubters Confront a Legend*. New York: Viking.
Crocker, J. Christopher. 1977a. My Brother the Parrot. Pp. 164–192 in *The Social Use of Metaphor*, edited by J. David Sapir and J. Christopher Crocker. Philadelphia: University of Pennsylvania Press.
Crocker, J. Christopher. 1977b. The Social Functions of Rhetorical Forms. Pp. 33–66 in *The Social Use of Metaphor*, edited by J. David Sapir and J. Christopher Crocker. Philadelphia: University of Pennsylvania Press.
D'Andrade, Roy. 1973. Cultural Constructions of Reality. Pp. 115–127 in *Cultural Illness and Health*, edited by Laura Nader and Thomas W. Maretzki. Washington, D.C.: American Anthropological Association.
D'Andrade, Roy. 1995. *The Development of Cognitive Anthropology*. Cambridge: Cambridge University Press.
Darnton, Robert. 1970. *Mesmerism and the End of the Enlightenment in France*. New York: Schocken Books.
Darwin, Charles. [1859] 1912. *On the Origin of Species by the means of Natural Selection*. New York: Appleton.

Dawid, A.P. 2000. Causal Inference without Counterfactuals. *Journal of the American Statistical Association* 95:407–424.

de Biran, Maine. [1803] 1929. *The Influence of Habit on the Faculty of Thinking*, translated by Margaret Donaldson Boehm. Baltimore: Williams and Wilkins.

Delbrück, Hans. [1920] 1990. *Warfare in Antiquity. Vol. 1. History of the Art of War.* Translated from the 3d ed. by Walter J. Renfroe, Jr. Lincoln: University of Nebraska Press.

Demos, John Putnam. 1982. *Entertaining Satan.* Oxford: Oxford University Press.

Descartes, Rene. [1637] 2001. *Discourse on Method, Optics, Geometry, and Meteorology*, revised edition, translated by Paul J. Olscamp. Indianapolis, Ind.: Hackett.

Descartes, Rene. [1664] 1985. *Treatise on Man*, Pp. 99–108 in *The Philosophical Writings of Descartes*, Volume 1, translated by John Cottingham, Robert Stoothoff, and Dugald Murdoch. Cambridge: Cambridge University Press.

Devereux, George. 1937. Institutionalized Homosexuality of the Mohave Indians. *Human Biology* 9:498–527.

de Waal, Frans. 1989. *Peacemaking among Primates.* Cambridge, Mass.: Harvard University Press.

de Waal, Frans. 1998. *Chimpanzee Politics*, revised edition. Baltimore: Johns Hopkins University Press.

Dewey, John. 1896. The Reflex Arc Concept in Psychology. *Psychological Review* 3:357–370.

Dewey, John. [1899] 1965. "Consciousness" and Experience. Pp. 242–270 in *The Influence of Darwin on Philosophy and Other Essays.* Bloomington: Indiana University Press.

Dewey, John. [1904] 1977. Philosophy and American National Life. Pp. 73–78 in *John Dewey: The Middle Works 1899–1924*, Volume 3, edited by Jo Ann Boydston. Carbondale: Southern Illinois University Press.

Dewey, John. 1905. The Postulate of Immediate Empiricism. *The Journal of Philosophy, Psychology and Scientific Methods* 2:393–399.

Dewey, John. [1905] 1977. Immediate Empiricism. Pp. 168–170 in *John Dewey: The Middle Works 1899–1924*, Volume 3, edited by Jo Ann Boydston. Carbondale: Southern Illinois University Press.

Dewey, John. [1906] 1965. Experience and Objective Idealism. Pp. 198–225 in *The Influence of Darwin on Philosophy and Other Essays.* Bloomington: Indiana University Press.

Dewey, John. 1908. Does Reality Possess Practical Character? Pp. 53–80 in *Essays Philosophical and Psychological in Honor of William James*, by his colleagues at Columbia University. New York: Longmans, Green, and Co.

Dewey, John. [1908] 1965. Intelligence and Morals. Pp. 46–76 in *The Influence of Darwin on Philosophy and Other Essays.* Bloomington: Indiana University Press.

Dewey, John. 1911. Brief Studies in Realism. I. *The Journal of Philosophy, Psychology and Scientific Methods* 8:393–400.

Dewey, John. 1917. The Need for a Recovery of Philosophy. Pp. 3–69 in *Creative Intelligence: Essays in the Pragmatic Attitude by John Dewey and Others.* New York: Holt, Rinehart and Winston; reprinted 1970 by Octagon Books.

Dewey, John. 1918. The Objects of Valuation. *The Journal of Philosophy, Psychology and Scientific Methods* 15:253–258.

Dewey, John. [1922] 1930. *Human Nature and Conduct: An Introduction to Social Psychology.* New York: Modern Library.

Dewey, John. [1922] 1970. Pragmatic America. Pp. 542–547 in *Characters and Events*, Volume 2, edited by Joseph Ratner. New York: Octagon Books.

Dewey, John. 1923. Values, Liking and Thought. *The Journal of Philosophy, Psychology and Scientific Methods* 20:617–622.
Dewey, John. 1929. *Experience and Nature*. New York: Norton.
Dewey, John. [1930] 1960. Qualitative Thought. Pp. 176–198 in *On Experience, Nature, and Freedom*, edited by Richard J. Bernstein. Indianapolis, Ind.: Bobbs-Merrill.
Dewey, John. 1934. *Art as Experience*. New York: Minton, Balch and Company.
Dewey, John. [1935] 1960. Peirce's Theory of Quality. Pp. 199–210 in *On Experience, Nature, and Freedom*, edited by Richard J. Bernstein. Indianapolis, Ind.: Bobbs-Merrill.
Diamond, Jared M. 1966. Zoological Classification System of a Primitive People. *Science* 151:1102–1104.
DiCicco-Bloom, Benjamin and David R. Gibson. 2010. More than a Game: Sociological Theory from the Theories of Games. *Sociological Theory* 28:247–271.
DiMaggio, Paul. 1986. Structural Analysis of Organizational Fields: A Blockmodel Approach. *Research in Organizational Behavior* 8:335–370.
DiMaggio, Paul. 1991. The Micro-Macro Dilemma in Organizational Research: Implications of Role-System Theory. Pp. 76–98 in *Macro-Micro Linkages in Sociology*, edited by Joan Huber. Newbury Park, Calif.: Sage.
DiMaggio, Paul. 1997. Culture and Cognition. *Annual Review of Sociology* 23:263–87.
DiMaggio, Paul J. and Walter W. Powell. 1983. The Iron Cage Revisited: Institutional Isomorphism and Collective Rationality in Organizational Fields. *American Sociological Review* 48:147–160.
Dilthey, Wilhelm. [1883] 1988. *Introduction to the Human Sciences*, translated by Ramon J. Betanzos. Detroit: Wayne State University Press.
Donaldson, Margaret. 1978. *Children's Minds*. New York: Norton.
Dore, Florence. 2005. *The Novel and the Obscene: Sexual Subjects in American Modernism*. Stanford, Calif.: Stanford University Press.
Dore, John. 1985. Holophrases revisited: Their "logical" development from dialogue. Pp. 23–58 in *Children's Single-Word Speech*, edited by M. Barrett. London: Wiley.
Douglas, Mary. 1966. *Purity and Danger: An Analysis of Concepts of Pollution and Taboo*. London: Routledge and Kegan Paul.
Douglas, Mary. 1975. *Implicit Meanings: Essays in Anthropology*. London: Routledge and Kegan Paul.
Douglas, Mary. 1986. *How Institutions Think*. Syracuse, N.Y.: Syracuse University Press.
Douglas, Mary. 1992. Rightness of Categories. Pp. 239–271 in *How Classification Works*, edited by Mary Douglas and David Hull. Edinburgh: Edinburgh University Press.
Ducasse, Curt John. [1924] 1969. *Causation and the Types of Necessity*. New York: Dover.
Dupont, Christian Yves. 1997. Reflections of Phenomenology in French Philosophy and Religious Thought, 1889–1939. Unpublished PhD dissertation, University of Notre Dame.
Duquenne, Vincent. 1995. Models of Possessions and Lattice Analysis. *Social Science Information* 34:253–267.
Durkheim, Emile. [1883–1884] 2004. *Durkheim's Philosophy Lectures*, edited and translated by Neil Gross and Robert Alun Jones. Cambridge: Cambridge University Press.
Durkheim, Emile. [1887] 1987. The Positive Science of Ethics in Germany [Originally in *Revue philosophique* 24] *History of Sociology* 6:2–7:2.

Durkheim, Emile. [1893] 1933. *The Division of Labor in Society*, translated by George Simpson. Glencoe, Ill.: Free Press.
Durkheim, Emile. [1895] 1938. *The Rules of Sociological Method*, translated by Sarah A. Solovay and John H. Mueller. Glencoe, Ill.: Free Press.
Durkheim, Emile. [1897] 1951. *Suicide*, translated by John A. Spaulding and George Simpson. New York: Free Press.
Durkheim, Emile. [1897] 1986. Review of A. Labriola: Essais sur la conception matérialiste de l'histoire. Pp. 128–136 in *Durkheim on Politics and the State*, edited by Anthony Giddens. Stanford, Calif.: Stanford University Press.
Durkheim, Emile. [1900] 1973. Sociology in France in the Nineteenth Century, in *Emile Durkheim on Morality and Society*, edited by Robert N. Bellah. Chicago: University of Chicago Press.
Durkheim, Emile. [1902–1903] 1961. *Moral Education*, translated by Everett K. Wilson and Herman Schnurer. New York: Free Press.
Durkheim, Emile. [1913] 1980. Review of Simon Deploige, *Le Conflit de la morale et de la sociologie, L'Année Sociologique* 12:326–328, reprinted in *Emile Durkheim: Contributions to L'Année Sociologique*, edited by Yash Nandan. New York: Free Press.
Durkheim, Emile. [1911] 1953. Value Judgments and Judgments of Reality. Pp. 80–97 in *Sociology and Philosophy*, translated by D.F. Pocock. Glencoe, Ill.: Free Press.
Durkheim, Emile. [1912] 1954. *The Elementary Forms of Religious Life*, translated by Joseph Ward Swain. Glencoe, Ill.: Free Press.
Durkheim, Emile. [1912] 1960. *Les Formes Élémentaires de la View Religieuse*, fourth edition. Paris: Presses Universitaires de France.
Durkheim, Emile. [1912] 1995. *The Elementary Forms of Religious Life*, translated by Karen E. Fields. New York: Free Press.
Durkheim, Emile. [1913–1914] 1983. *Pragmatism and Sociology*, translated by J.C. Whitehouse. Cambridge: Cambridge University Press.
Durkheim, Emile. [1914] 1973. The Dualism of Human Nature and Its Social Conditions. Pp. 149–163 in *Emile Durkheim on Morality and Society*, edited by Robert N. Bellah. Chicago: University of Chicago Press.
Durkheim, Emile. 2013 [1908]. Debate on Explanation in History and Sociology. Pp. 160–173 in *The Rules of Sociological Method and Selected Texts on Sociology and its Method*, edited by Steven Likes. New York: Free Press.
Durkheim, Emile and Marcel Mauss [1903] 1963. *Primitive Classification*, translated by Rodney Needham. Chicago: University of Chicago Press.
Dutton, Donald G. and Arthur P. Aron. 1974. Some Evidence for Heightened Sexual Attraction Under Conditions of High Anxiety. *Journal of Personality and Social Psychology* 30:510–517.
Eco, Umberto. [1959] 1986. *Art and Beauty in the Middle Ages*, translated by Hugh Bredin. New Haven, Conn.: Yale University Press.
Edgerton, Samuel Y., Jr. 1991. *The Heritage of Giotto's Geometry: Art and Science on the Eve of the Scientific Revolution*. Ithaca, N.Y.: Cornell University Press.
Edmunds, Lavinia. 1988. His Master's Choice. *Johns Hopkins Magazine* 40: 40–49.
Eells, Ellery. 1991. *Probabilistic Causality*. Cambridge: Cambridge University Press.
Ehrenfels, Christian von. [1890] 1988. On "Gestalt Qualities," translated by Barry Smith. Pp. 82–117 in *Foundations of Gestalt Theory*, edited by Barry Smith. Munich: Philosophia Verlag.

References

Einstein, Albert. 1967. Foreword to Galileo's *Dialogue Concerning the Two Chief World Systems—Ptolemaic and Copernican*, second edition, translated by Stillman Drake. Berkeley: University of California Press.

Elias, Norbert. [1939] 1982. *Power and Civility: The Civilizing Process, Volume 2*, translated by Edmund Jephcott. New York: Pantheon.

Elias, Norbert. 1978. *What Is Sociology?* Translated by Stephen Mennell and Grace Morrissey. New York: Columbia University Press.

Ellenberger, Henri F. [1965] 1993. Charcot and the Salpetriere School. Pp. 139–54 in *Beyond the Unconscious: Essays of Henri F. Ellenberger in the History of Psychiatry*, edited by Mark S. Micale. Princeton, N.J.: Princeton University Press.

Ellenberger, Henri F. [1972] 1993. The Story of "Anna O.": A Critical Review with New Data. Pp. 254–272 in *Beyond the Unconscious: Essays of Henri F. Ellenberger in the History of Psychiatry*, edited by Mark S. Micale. Princeton, N.J.: Princeton University Press.

Elster, Jon. 1989. *Nuts and Bolts for the Social Sciences*. Cambridge: Cambridge University Press.

Emerson, Ralph Waldo. [1841] 1940. History. Pp. 123–144 in *The Complete Essays and Other Writings of Ralph Waldo Emerson*. New York: Random House.

Emery, F.E. and E.L. Trist. 1965. The Causal Texture of Organization Environments. *Human Relations* 18:21–32.

Emirbayer, Mustafa. 1997. Manifesto for a Relational Sociology. *American Journal of Sociology* 103:281–317.

Empedocles. 1981. *The Extant Fragments*, edited by M.R. Wright. New Haven, Conn.: Yale University Press.

Eng, Erling. 1978. Looking Back on Kurt Lewin: From Field Theory to Action Research. *Journal of the History of the Behavioral Sciences* 14:228–232.

Engstrom, Eric J. 2003. *Clinical Psychiatry in Imperial Germany: A History of Psychiatric Practice*. Ithaca, N.Y.: Cornell University Press.

Enright, J.T. 1989. The Eye, the Brain, and the Size of the Moon: Toward a Unified Oculomotor Hypothesis for the Moon Illusion. Pp. 59–121 in *The Moon Illusion*, edited by Maurice Hershenson. Hillsdale, N.J.: Erlbaum.

Etzioni, Amitai. 1988. *The Moral Dimension: Toward a New Economics*. New York: Free Press.

Evans-Pritchard, E.E. [1937] 1976. *Witchcraft, Oracles and Magic among the Azande*. Oxford, U.K.: Clarendon Press.

Evans-Pritchard, E.E. 1956. *Nuer Religion*. Oxford: Oxford University Press.

Fales, Evan. 1990. *Causation and Universals*. London: Routledge.

Fauconnier, Giles [1985] 1994. *Mental Spaces: Aspects of Meaning Construction in Natural Language*. Cambridge: Cambridge University Press.

Ficino, Marsilio. 2004. *Platonic Theology*, Volume 4, translated by Michael J.B. Allen. Cambridge, Mass.: Harvard University Press.

Fine, Gary Alan. 1987. *With the Boys: Little League Baseball and Preadolescent Culture*. Chicago: University of Chicago Press.

Fisher, Sir Ronald A. 1956. *Statistical Methods and Scientific Inference*. Edinburgh: Oliver and Boyd.

Fligstein, Neil. 2001. Social Skill and the Theory of Fields. *Sociological Theory* 19:105–125.

Fodor, J.A. and Z.W. Pylyshyn. 1981. How Direct Is Visual Perception? Some Reflections on Gibson's "Ecological Approach." *Cognition* 9:139–196.

Forman, Paul. 1984. Kausalität, Anschaulichkeit, and Individualität, or How Cultural Values Prescribed the Character and the Lessons Ascribed to Quantum Mechanics. Pp. 333–347 in *Society and Knowledge*, edited by Nico Stehr and Volker Meja. New Brunswick, NJ: Transaction Books.

Foucault, Michel. [1961] 1988. Madness and Civilization, translated by Richard Howard. New York: Vintage Books.

Foucault, Michel. [1966] 1973. *The Order of Things*. New York: Vintage Books.

Foucault, Michel. [1969] 1972. *The Archaeology of Knowledge*, translated by A.M. Sheridan Smith. New York: Pantheon.

Foucault, Michel. [1975] 1979. *Discipline and Punish*, translated by Alan Sheridan. New York: Vintage Books.

Fourny, Jean-François. 2000. Bourdieu's Uneasy Psychoanalysis. *SubStance* 93:103–111.

Freeman, Kathleen. 1971. *Ancilla to the Pre-Socratic Philosophers: A Complete Translation of the Fragments in Diels, Fragmente der Vorsokratiker*. Cambridge, Mass.: Harvard University Press.

Freese, Jeremy. 2008. Genetics and the Social Science Explanation of Individual Outcomes. *American Journal of Sociology* 114:S1–S35.

Freud, Sigmund. [1887–1904]. 1985. *The Complete Letters of Sigmund Freud to Wilhelm Fliess*, translated and edited by Jeffrey Moussaieff Masson. Cambridge, Mass.: Harvard University Press.

Freud, Sigmund. [1888] 1963. Hypnotism and Suggestion, translated by James Strachey. Pp. 27–39 in *Therapy and Technique*, edited by Philip Rieff. New York: Collier Books.

Freud, Sigmund. [1893] 1962. Charcot. Pp. 9–23 in *The Standard Edition of the Complete Psychological Works of Sigmund Freud*, Volume 3, translated by James Strachey. London: Hogarth Press.

Freud, Sigmund. [1894] 1962. The Neuro-Psychoses of Defense. Pp. 43–61 in *The Standard Edition of the Complete Psychological Works of Sigmund Freud*, Volume 3, translated by James Strachey. London: Hogarth Press.

Freud, Sigmund. [1896a] 1962. The Aetiology of Hysteria. Pp. 191–221 in *The Standard Edition of the Complete Psychological Works of Sigmund Freud*, Volume 3, translated by James Strachey. London: Hogarth Press.

Freud, Sigmund. [1896b] 1962. Further Remarks on the Neuro-Psychoses of Defence. Pp. 162–185 in *The Standard Edition of the Complete Psychological Works of Sigmund Freud*, Volume 3, translated by James Strachey. London: Hogarth Press.

Freud, Sigmund. [1896c] 1962. Heredity and the Aetiology of the Neuroses. Pp. 143–156 in *The Standard Edition of the Complete Psychological Works of Sigmund Freud*, Volume 3, translated by James Strachey. London: Hogarth Press.

Freud, Sigmund. [1898] 1982. Die Sexualität in der Ätiologie der Neurosen. Pp. 11–35 in *Studienausgabe Band V: Sexualleben*. Frankfurt: Fischer Taschenbuch Verlag.

Freud, Sigmund. [1900] 1938. *The Interpretation of Dreams in the Basic Writings of Sigmund Freud*, translated by A.A. Brill. New York: Modern Library.

Freud, Sigmund. [1904] 1963. Freud's Psychoanalytic Method, translated by J. Bernays. Pp. 55–61 in *Therapy and Technique*, edited by Philip Rieff. New York: Collier Books.

Freud, Sigmund. [1905] 1938. *Three Contributions to the Theory of Sex in the Basic Writings of Sigmund Freud*, translated by A.A. Brill. New York: Modern Library.

Freud, Sigmund. [1910] 1963. The Future Prospects of Psychoanalytic Therapy, translated by Joan Riviere. Pp. 77–87 in *Therapy and Technique*, edited by Philip Rieff. New York: Collier Books.

Freud, Sigmund. [1912a] 1963. The Dynamics of the Transference, translated by Joan Riviere. Pp. 105–115 in *Therapy and Technique*, edited by Philip Rieff. New York: Collier Books.

Freud, Sigmund. [1912b] 1963. Recommendations for Physicians on the Psychoanalytic Method of Treatment, translated by Joan Riviere. Pp. 117–126 in *Therapy and Technique*, edited by Philip Rieff. New York: Collier Books.

Freud, Sigmund. [1913] 1938. *Totem and Taboo in The Basic Writings of Sigmund Freud*, translated by A.A. Brill. New York: Modern Library.

Freud, Sigmund. [1914] 1963. Further Recommendations in the Technique of Psychoanalysis: Recollection, Repetition and Working Through, translated by Joan Riviere. Pp. 157–166 in *Therapy and Technique*, edited by Philip Rieff. New York: Collier Books.

Freud, Sigmund. [1920] 1966. *Introductory Lectures on Psychoanalysis*, translated by James Strachey. New York: Norton.

Freud, Sigmund. [1933] 1964. *New Introductory Lectures on Psychoanalysis*, translated by James Strachey. New York: Norton.

Freud, Sigmund. [1937] 1963. Constructions in Analysis, translated by James Strachey. Pp. 273–286 in *Therapy and Technique*, edited by Philip Rieff. New York: Collier Books.

Fuchs, Oswald. 1952. *The Psychology of Habit According to William Ockham*. St. Bonaventure, N.Y.: Franciscan Institute.

Fuller, Sylvia. 2003. Creating and Contesting Boundaries: Exploring the Dynamics of Conflict and Classification. *Sociological Forum* 18:3–30.

Fürstenberg, Friedrich. [1962] 1969. *Das Aufstiegsproblem in der modernen Gesellschaft*. Stuttgart, Germany: Ferdinand Enke Verlag.

Gadamer, Hans-Georg. [1977] 1986. The Relevance of the Beautiful, translated by Nicholas Walker. Pp. 1–53 in *The Relevance of the Beautiful and Other Essays*. Cambridge: Cambridge University Press.

Gadamer, Hans-Georg. [1980] 1986. Intuition and Vividness, translated by Dan Tate. Pp. 155–170 in *The Relevance of the Beautiful and Other Essays*. Cambridge: Cambridge University Press.

Gagnon, John and William Simon. 1976. *Sexual Conduct*. Chicago: Aldine.

Galilei, Galileo. [1629] 1967. *Dialogue Concerning the Two Chief World Systems—Ptolemaic and Copernican*, second edition, translated by Stillman Drake. Berkeley: University of California Press.

Gangl, Markus. 2010. Causal Inference in Sociological Research. *Annual Review of Sociology* 36:21–47.

Garfinkel, Harold. 2002. *Ethnomethodology's Program*. Lanham, Md.: Rowman and Littlefield.

Garfinkel, Harold and D. Lawrence Wieder. 1992. Two Incommensurable, Asymetrically Alternate Technologies of Social Analysis. Pp. 175–217 in *Text in Context Contributions to Ethnomethodology*, edited by G. Watson and R.M. Seiler. Newbury Park, Calif.: Sage.

Gay, Peter. 1970. *Weimar Culture: The Outsider as Insider*. New York: Harper and Row.

Gay, Peter. 1988. *Freud: A Life for Our Time*. New York: Norton.

Gazzaniga, Michael S. 1970. *The Bisected Brain*. New York: Appleton-Century-Crofts.

Gazzaniga, Michael S. 1998. The Split Brain Revisited. *Scientific American* 279:50–55.
Geertz, Clifford. 1973. *The Interpretation of Cultures*. New York: Basic Books.
Geiger, Theodor. 1949. *Die Klassengesellschaft im Schmelztiegel*. Cologne, Germany: Varlag Gustav Kiepenheuer.
Gelfand, Toby. 1992. Sigmund-sur-Seine: Fathers and Brothers in Charcot's Paris. Pp. 29–57 in *Freud and the History of Psychoanalysis*, edited by Toby Gelfand and John Kerr. Hillsdale, N.J.: Analytic Press.
Gelfand, Toby. 1995a. Fame. Pp. 217–267 in *Charcot: Constructing Neurology*, by Christopher G. Goetz, Michel Bonduelle, and Toby Gelfand. New York: Oxford University Press.
Gelfand, Toby. 1995b. Hysteria. Pp. 172–216 in *Charcot: Constructing Neurology*, by Christopher G. Goetz, Michel Bonduelle, and Toby Gelfand. New York: Oxford University Press.
Gelfand, Toby. 1995c. The Struggle for a Career in Paris. Pp. 31–61 in *Charcot: Constructing Neurology*, by Christopher G. Goetz, Michel Bonduelle, and Toby Gelfand. New York: Oxford University Press.
Gellner, Ernest. 1970. Concepts and Society. Pp. 18–49 in *Rationality*, edited by Bryan R. Wilson. Oxford, U.K.: Basil Blackwell.
Gibson, David R. 2005. Opportunistic Interruptions: Interactional Vulnerabilities Deriving from Linearization. *Social Psychological Quarterly* 68:316–337.
Gibson, Eleanor J. and Arlene S. Walker. 1984. Development of Knowledge of Visual-Tactical Affordances of Substance. *Child Development* 55:453–460.
Gibson, James J. [1979] 1986. *The Ecological Approach to Visual Perception*. Hillsdale, N.J.: Erlbaum.
Giddens, Anthony. 1979. *Central Problems in Social Theory*. Berkeley: University of California Press.
Giddens, Anthony. 1984. *The Constitution of Society*. Berkeley: University of California Press.
Gigerenzer, Gerd, Zeno Swijtink, Theodore Porter, Lorraine Daston, John Beatty, and Lorenz Krüger. 1989. *The Empire of Chance*. Cambridge: Cambridge University Press.
Gillispie, Charles Coulston. 1960. *The Edge of Objectivity: An Essay in the History of Scientific Ideas*. Princeton, N.J.: Princeton University Press.
Glover, Edward. 1952. Research Methods in Psycho-Analysis. *International Journal of Psychoanalysis* 33:404–409.
Godlove, Terry F., Jr. 1989. *Religion, Interpretation and Diversity of Belief*. Cambridge: Cambridge University Press.
Goethe, Johann Wolfgang von. [1810] 1970. *Theory of Colours*, translated by Charles Lock Eastlake. Cambridge, Mass.: MIT Press.
Goethe, Johann Wolfgang von. 1988. Selections from Maxims and Reflections. Pp. 303–312 in *Scientific Studies*, translated by Douglas Miller. New York: Suhrkamp.
Goetz, Christopher G. 1995a. Charcot and the Artistry of Neurological Practice. Pp. 135–171 in *Charcot: Constructing Neurology*, by Christopher G. Goetz, Michel Bonduelle, and Toby Gelfand. New York: Oxford University Press.
Goetz, Christopher G. 1995b. Education of a Physician. Pp. 3–30 in *Charcot: Constructing Neurology*, by Christopher G. Goetz, Michel Bonduelle, and Toby Gelfand. New York: Oxford University Press.
Goffman, Erving. 1959. *The Presentation of Self in Everyday Life*. New York: Anchor Books.

Goffman, Erving. 1961. *Asylums: Essays on the Social Situation of Mental Patients and Other Inmates*. Chicago: Aldine.
Goffman, Erving. 1971. *Relations in Public*. New York: Basic Books.
Goldman, Harvey. 1988. *Max Weber and Thomas Mann: Calling and the Shaping of the Self*. Berkeley: University of California Press.
Goldstone, Jack. 1991. *Revolution and Rebellion in the Early Modern World*. Berkeley: University of California Press.
Goldthorpe, John H. 2001. Causation, Statistics, and Sociology. *European Sociological Review* 17:1–20.
Goldthorpe, John H. 2007. *On Sociology*, second edition (two volumes). Stanford, Calif.: Stanford University Press.
Goodman, Nelson. 1976. *Languages of Art*. Indianapolis, Ind.: Hackett.
Goody, Jack. 2004. From Explanation to Interpretation in Social Anthropology. Pp. 197–211 in *Explanations*, edited by John Cornwell. Oxford: Oxford University Press.
Gould, James L. and Carol Grant Gould. 1999. *The Animal Mind*. New York: Scientific American Library.
Gould, Stephen Jay. 1981. *The Mismeasure of Man*. New York: Norton.
Gould, Stephen Jay and Richard C. Lewontin. 1979. The Spandrels of San Marco and the Panglossian Paradigm: A Critique of the Adaptationist Programme. *Proceedings of the Royal Society of London B* 205:581–598.
Greenhalgh, P.A.L. 1973. *Early Greek Warfare: Horsemen and Chariots in the Homeric and Archaic Ages*. Cambridge: Cambridge University Press.
Griggs, Richard A. and James R. Cox. 1982. The Elusive Thematic-Materials Effect in Wason's Selection Task. *British Journal of Psychology* 73:407–420.
Gross, Neil. 1997. Durkheim's Pragmatism Lectures: A Contextual Interpretation. *Sociological Theory* 15:126–149.
Gross, Neil. 2009. A Pragmatist Theory of Social Mechanisms. *American Sociological Review* 74:358–79.
Guttentag, Marcia and Paul F. Secord. 1983. *Too Many Women?: The Sex Ratio Question*. Beverly Hills, Calif.: Sage.
Habermas, Jürgen. 1971. *Knowledge and Human Interests*, translated by Jeremy J. Shapiro. Boston: Beacon Press.
Habermas, Jürgen. [1983] 1996. Georg Simmel on Philosophy and Culture: Postscript to an Collection of Essays. *Critical Inquiry* 22:403–414.
Habermas, Jürgen. 1984. *The Theory of Communicative Action. Volume 1: Reason and the Rationalization of Society*, translated by Thomas McCarthy. Boston: Beacon Press.
Habermas, Jürgen. 1987. *The Theory of Communicative Action. Volume 2: Lifeworld and System: A Critique of Functionalist Reason*, translated by Thomas McCarthy. Boston: Beacon Press.
Hacking, Ian. 1983. *Representing and Intervening*. Cambridge: Cambridge University Press.
Hacking, Ian. 1990. *The Taming of Chance*. Cambridge: Cambridge University Press.
Hall, Ned. 2000. Causation and the Price of Transitivity. *The Journal of Philosophy* 97:198–222.
Hall, Ned. 2004. Two Concepts of Causation. Pp. 225–276 in *Causation and Counterfactuals*, edited by John Collins, Ned Hall and L.A. Paul. Cambridge, Mass.: MIT Press.

Hamilton, Allan McLane. 1910. *The Intimate Life of Alexander Hamilton, Based Chiefly upon Original Family Letters and Other Documents, Many of Which Have Never Been Published*. New York: Charles Scribner's Sons.

Haney, Craig. 1976. The Play's the Thing: Methodological Notes on Social Simulations. Pp. 177–190 in *The Research Experience*, edited by M. Patricia Golden. Itasca, Ill.: F.E. Peacock Publishers.

Hanson, Victor Davis. [1989] 2000. *The Western Way of War: Infantry Battle in Classical Greece*. Berkeley: University of California Press.

Hart, H.L.A. and A.M. Honoré. 1959. *Causation in the Law*. Oxford, U.K.: Clarendon Press.

Harwood, Jonathan. 1993. *Styles of Scientific Thought*. Chicago: University of Chicago Press.

Haugeland, John. 1989 [1985]. *Artificial Intelligence: The Very Idea*. Cambridge, Mass.: The MIT Press.

Hayes, Danny. 2005. Candidate Qualities through a Partisan Lens: A Theory of Trait Ownership. *American Journal of Political Science* 49:908–932.

Heath, Stephen. 2008. Keywords: Representation. *Critical Inquiry* 50:87–99.

Hebb, D.O. 1946. Emotion in Man and Animal: An Analysis of the Intuitive Process of Recognition. *Psychological Review* 53:88–106.

Heckman, James J. 2005. The Scientific Model of Causality. *Sociological Methodology* 35:1–97.

Hedström, Peter. 2005. *Dissecting The Social*. Cambridge: Cambridge University Press.

Hedström, Peter and Richard Swedberg. 1998. Social Mechanisms: An Introductory Essay. Pp.1–31 in *Social Mechanisms*, edited by Peter Hedström and Richard Swedberg. Cambridge: Cambridge University Press.

Heeger, David J., Sunil P. Gandhi, Alexander C. Huk, and Geoffrey M. Boynton. 2001. Neuronal Correlates of Attention in Human Visual Cortex. Pp. 25–47 in *Visual Attention and Cortical Circuits*, edited by Jochen Braun, Christof Koch, and Joel L. Davis. Cambridge, Mass.: MIT Press.

Hegel, Georg W.F. [1803] 1949. *The Phenomenology of Mind*, translated by J.B. Baillie. London: Allen and Unwin.

Hegel, Georg W.F. [ca. 1807] 1977. Who Thinks Abstractly? Pp. 114–118 in *Hegel: Texts and Commentary*, translated and edited by Walter Kaufmann. Notre Dame, Ind.: University of Notre Dame Press.

Hegel, Georg W.F. [1821] 1967. *Philosophy of Right*, translated by T.M. Knox. London: Oxford University Press.

Hegel, Georg W.F. [1835] 1975. *Hegel's Aesthetics: Lectures on Fine Art, Volume 1*, translated by T.M. Knox. London: Oxford University Press.

Heidegger, Martin. [1926] 1962. *Being and Time*, translated by John Macquarrie and Edward Robinson. New York: Harper Collins.

Heidelberger, Michael. 1987. Fechner's Indeterminism: From Freedom to Laws of Chance. Pp. 117–156 in *The Probabilistic Revolution, Volume 1: Ideas in History*, edited by Lorenz Kruger, Lorraine J. Daston, and Michael Heidelberger. Cambridge, Mass.: MIT Press.

Heider, Fritz. 1958. *The Psychology of Interpersonal*. Relations. New York: Wiley.

Heider, Fritz. 1983. *The Life of a Psychologist*. Lawrence, Kan.: University of Kansas Press.

Helliwell, Christine. 2000. "It's Only a Penis": Rape, Feminism and Difference. *Signs* 25:789–816.

Hempel, Carl G. 1965. *Aspects of Scientific Explanation and Other Essays in the Philosophy of Science*. New York: Free Press.

Herdt, Gilbert. 1991. Representations of Homosexuality: An Essay on Cultural Ontology and Historical Comparison, Part I. *Journal of the History of Sexuality* 1:481–504.

Hesse, Mary B. 1970. *Forces and Fields: The Concept of Action at a Distance in the History of Physics*. Westport, Conn.: Greenwood Press.

Hesse, Mary. 1980. *Revolutions and Reconstructions in the Philosophy of Science*. Bloomington: University of Indiana Press.

Hesslow, Germund. 1976. Discussion: Two Notes on the Probabilistic Approach to Causality. *Philosophy of Science* 43:290–292.

Hesslow, Germund. 1988. The Problem of Causal Selection. Pp. 11–32 in *Contemporary Science and Natural Explanation*, edited by Denis J. Hilton. New York: New York University Press.

Hilton, Denis J. 1990. Conversational Processes and Causal Explanation. *Psychological Bulletin* 107:65–81.

Hirschman, Albert O. 1977. *The Passions and the Interests*. Princeton, N.J.: Princeton University Press.

Hitchcock, Christopher. 1996. The Role of Contrast in Causal and Explanatory Claims. *Synthese* 107:395–419.

Hitchcock, Christopher. 2003. Of Humean Bondage. *British Journal of the Philosophy of Science* 54:1–25.

Hitchcock, Christopher. 2004. Do All and Only Causes Raise the Probabilities of Events? Pp. 403–417 in *Causation and Counterfactuals*, edited by John Collins, Ned Hall, and L.A. Paul. Cambridge, Mass.: MIT Press.

Hitlin, Stephen and Jane Allyn Piliavin. 2004. Values: Reviving a Dormant Concept. *Annual Review of Sociology* 30:359–393.

Hobbes, Thomas. [1651] 1909. *Leviathan*. Oxford, U.K.: Clarendon Press.

Hoffman, Frederick J. [1949] 1962. *The Twenties: American Writing in the Postwar Decade*. New York: Free Press.

Holland, Paul W. 1986. Statistics and Causal Inference. *Journal of the American Statistical Association* 81:945–960.

Homans, George C. 1967. *The Nature of Social Science*. New York: Harcourt Brace and World.

Horkheimer, Max. [1947] 1974. *Eclipse of Reason*. New York: Seabury Press.

Huffman, Michael A. and Richard W. Wrangham. 1994. Diversity of Medicinal Plant Use by Chimpanzees in the Wild. Pp. 129–148 in *Chimpanzee Cultures*, edited by Richard W. Wrangham, W.C. McGrew, Frans B.M. de Waal, and Paul G. Heltne. Cambridge, Mass.: Harvard University Press.

Hull, David. 1992. Biological Species: An Inductivist's Nightmare. Pp. 42–68 in *How Classification Works*, edited by Mary Douglas and David Hull. Edinburgh: Edinburgh University Press.

Hume, David. [1738] 1911. *A Treatise of Human Nature, Volume 1: Of the Understanding*. London: Dent.

Hume, David. [1777] 1985. Of the Standard of Taste. Pp. 226–249 in *Essays, Moral, Political and Literary*. Indianapolis, Ind.: Literary Fund.

Hume, David. [1777] 1993. *An Enquiry Concerning Human Understanding*. Indianapolis, Ind.: Hackett.

Humphreys, Paul. 1989. *The Chances of Explanation*. Princeton, N.J.: Princeton University Press.

Husserl, Edmund. [1900] 1970. *Logical Investigations, Volume 1*, translated by J.N. Findlay. New York: Routledge and Kegan Paul.

Husserl, Edmund. [1927] 1997. Phenomenology [draft of article written for *Encyclopaedia Brittanica*], translated by Thomas Sheehan. Pp. 83–198 n *Psychological and Transcendental Phenomenology and the Confrontation with Heidegger (1927–1931)*, edited by Thomas Sheehan and Richard E. Palmer. Dordrecht, The Netherlands: Kluwer Academic.

Hutchins, Edwin. 1995. *Cognition in the Wild*. Cambridge, Mass.: MIT Press.

Hyman, Ira E. and Joel Pentland. 1996. The Role of Mental Imagery in the Creation of false Childhood Memories. *Journal of Memory and Language* 35:101–117.

Ichheiser, Gustav. 1949. Analysis and Typology of Personality Misinterpretations. *American Journal of Sociology* 55:S26–S56.

Ilyenkov, E.V. [1974] 2002. Activity and Knowledge. Unpublished translation of Deyatel'nost' i Znanie, by Peter Moxhay.

Ilyenkov, E.V. 1977a. The Concept of the Ideal. Pp. 71–99 in *Philosophy in the USSR: Problems of Dialectical Materialism*. Moscow: Progress Publishers.

Ilyenkov, E.V. 1977b. *Dialectical Logic: Essays on Its History and Theory*. Moscow: Progress Publishers.

International Ice Hockey Federation. 2006. *IIHF Official Rule Book*. Zurich: IIHF.

Ito, Minami, Gerald Westheimer, and Charles D. Gilbert. 2001. Attentional Modulation of Contextual Influences. Pp. 89–102 in *Visual Attention and Cortical Circuits*, edited by Jochen Braun, Christof Koch, and Joel L. Davis. Cambridge, Mass.: MIT Press.

James, William. [1890] 1950. *The Principles of Psychology*. New York: Dover.

James, William. [1907] 1946. *Pragmatism*. New York: Longmans, Green and Co.

James, William. [1909] 1943. *A Pluralistic Universe*. New York: Longmans, Green and Co.

James, William. [1909] 1975. *The Meaning of Truth*. Cambridge, Mass.: Harvard.

James, William. [1912] 1943. *Essays in Radical Empiricism*. New York: Longmans, Green and Co.

Jammer, Max. 1957. *Concepts of Force: A Study in the Foundations of Dynamics*. Cambridge, Mass.: Harvard University Press.

Jay, Martin. 1973. *The Dialectical Imagination*. London: Heinemann.

Jay, Martin. 1984. *Marxism and Totality*. Berkeley: University of California Press.

Jeffreys, Harold. 1961. *Theory of Probability*, third edition. Oxford, U.K.: Clarendon Press.

Jernsletten, Nils. 1997. Sami Traditional Terminology: Professional Terms Concerning Salmon, Reindeer and Snow. Pp. 86–108 in *Sami Culture in a New Era*, edited by Harald Gaski. Karasjok, Norway: Davvi Girji OS.

Joas, Hans. 1993. *Pragmatism and Social Theory*, translated by Jeremy Gaines, Raymond Meyer, and Steven Minner. Chicago: University of Chicago Press.

Joas, Hans. 2000. *The Genesis of Values*, translated by Gregory Moore. Chicago: University of Chicago Press.

Johnson-Laird, P.N. and P.C. Wason. 1977. A Theoretical Analysis of Insight into a Reasoning Task. Pp. 143–157 in *Thinking: Readings in Cognitive Science*, edited by P.N. Johnson-Laird and P.C. Wason. Cambridge: Cambridge University Press.

Jolly, Alison. 1966. Lemur Social Behavior and Primate Intelligence. *Science* 153:501–506.

Jones, Edward E. and Victor A. Harris. 1967. The Attributions of Attitudes. *Journal of Experimental Social Psychology* 3:1–24.

Jones, Ernest. 1925. Mother-Right and the Sexual Ignorance of Savages. *The International Journal of Psycho-Analysis* 6:109–130.
Jones, Sue Stedman. 1998. The Concept of Belief in The Elementary Forms. Pp. 53–65 in *On Durkheim's Elementary Forms of Religious Life*, edited by N.J. Allen, W.S.F. Pickering, and W. Watts Miller. London: Routledge.
Joravsky, David. 1977. The Mechanical Spirit: The Stalinist Marriage of Pavlov to Marx. *Theory and Society* 4:457–477.
Kahneman, Daniel and Dale T. Miller. 1986. Norm Theory: Comparing Reality to Its Alternatives. *Psychological Review* 93:136–153.
Kahneman, Daniel and Carol A. Varey. 1990. Propensities and Counterfactuals: The Loser that Almost Won. *Journal of Personality and Social Psychology* 59:1101–1110.
Kalish, Charles. 1998. Reasons and Causes: Children's Understanding of the Conformity to Social Rules and Physical Laws. *Child Development* 69:706–720.
Kant, Immanuel. [1783] 1953. *Prolegomena to Any Future Metaphysics that Will Be Able to Present Itself as a Science*, translated by Peter G. Lucas. Manchester, U.K.: Manchester University Press.
Kant, Immanuel. [1784] 2001. Idea for a Universal History from a Cosmopolitan Point of View. Pp. 11–26 in *On History*, edited by Lewis White Beck. Upper Saddle River, N.J.: Prentice Hall.
Kant, Immanuel. [1785] 1922. *Grundlegung Zur Metaphysik Der Sitten. Sämtliche Werke, Fünfter Band.* Leipzig, Germamy: Inselverlag.
Kant, Immanuel. [1785] 1938. *The Fundamental Principles of the Metaphysic of Ethics*, translated by Otto Mathey-Zorn. New York: Appleton-Century.
Kant, Immanuel. [1785] 1964. *Groundwork of the Metaphysic of Morals*, translated by H.J. Paton. New York: Harper and Row.
Kant, Immanuel. [1787] 1950. *Critique of Pure Reason*, translated by Norman Kemp Smith. London: Macmillan.
Kant, Immanuel. [1788] 2002. *Critique of Practical Reason*, translated by Werner S. Pluhar. Indianapolis, Ind.: Hackett.
Kant, Immanuel. [1790] 1987. *Critique of Judgment*, translated by Werner S. Pluhar. Indianapolis, Ind.: Hackett.
Kant, Immanuel. [1797] 1991. *The Metaphysic of Morals*, translated by Mary Gregor. Cambridge: Cambridge University Press.
Kant, Immanuel. [1798] 2006. *Anthropology from a Pragmatic Point of View*, translated by Robert B. Louden. Cambridge: Cambridge University Press.
Katz, Jack. 1988. *Seductions of Crime: Moral and Sensual Attractions in Doing Evil.* New York: Basic Books.
Katz, Jack. 1999. *How Emotions Work.* Chicago: University of Chicago Press.
Keane, A. J. 1886. The Lapps: Their Origin, Ethnical Affinities, Physical and Mental Characteristics, Usages, Present Status, and Future Prospects. *The Journal of the Anthropological Institute of Great Britain and Ireland* 15:213–235.
Keegan, John. 1988. *The Mask of Command.* New York: Penguin.
Keegan, John. 1994. *A History of Warfare.* New York: Vintage.
Keesing, Roger M. 1974. Theories of Culture. *Annual Review of Anthropology* 3:73–97.
Kelley, Harold H. 1973. The Processes of Causal Attribution. *American Psychologist* 28:107–128.
Kettler, David and Volker Meja. 1994. "That Typically German Kind of Sociology which Verges toward Philosophy": The Dispute about *Ideology and Utopia* in the United States. *Sociological Theory* 12:279–303.

Keynes, John Maynard. 1921. *A Treatise on Probability*. London: Macmillan.
Kihlstrom, John F. 1987. The Cognitive Unconscious. *Science* 237:1445–1452.
Kirsh, David and Paul Maglio. 1994. On Distinguishing Epistemic from Pragmatic Action. *Cognitive Science* 18:513–549.
Klein, Gary. 1998. *Sources of Power: How People Make Decisions*. Cambridge, Mass.: MIT Press.
Knappett, Carl. 2005. *Thinking through Material Culture*. Philadelphia: University of Pennsylvania Press.
Knorr-Cetina, Karin. 1997. Sociality with Objects: Social Relations in Postsocial Knowledge Societies. *Theory, Culture & Society* 14:1–30.
Knorr-Cetina, Karin. 1999. *Epistemic Cultures: How the Sciences Make Knowledge*. Cambridge, Mass.: Harvard University Press.
Koffka, K. 1935. *Principles of Gestalt Psychology*. New York: Harcourt, Brace.
Köhler, Wolfgang. [1917] 1925. *The Mentality of Apes*, translated by Ella Winter. London: Routledge and Kegan Paul.
Köhler, Wolfgang. 1920. *Die physichen Gestalten in Ruhe und im stationären Zustand*. Braunschweig, Germany: Friedr. Vieweg und Sohn.
Köhler, Wolfgang. 1938. *The Place of Values in a World of Fact*. New York: Liveright.
Köhler, Wolfgang. [1944] 1971. Value and Fact. Pp. 356–375 in *The Selected Papers of Wolfgang Köhler*, edited by Mary Henle. New York: Liveright.
Köhler, Wolfgang. 1947. *Gestalt Psychology*. New York: Liveright.
Köhler, Wolfgang. [1958] 1971. The Obsessions of Normal People. Pp. 398–412 in *The Selected Papers of Wolfgang Köhler*, edited by Mary Henle. New York: Liveright.
Köhler, Wolfgang. [1967] 1971. Gestalt Psychology. Pp. 108–122 in *The Selected Papers of Wolfgang Köhler*, edited by Mary Henle. New York: Liveright.
Koriat, Asher, Morris Goldsmith and Ainat Pansky. 2000. Toward a Psychology of Memory Accuracy. *Annual Review of Psychology* 51:481–537.
Krentz, Peter. 1985. The Nature of Hoplite Battle. *Classical Antiquity* 4:50–61.
Kuhl, Patricia. K. 1987. Categorization by Animals and Infants. Pp. 355–386 in *Categorical Perception*, edited by Steven Harnad. Cambridge: Cambridge University Press.
Kummer, Hans. 1995. *In Quest of the Sacred Baboon*, translated by M. Ann Bierderman-Thorson. Princeton, N.J.: Princeton University Press.
Kurzman, Charles. 1991. Convincing Sociologists: Values and Interests in the Sociology of Knowledge. Pp. 250–268 in *Ethnography Unbound: Power and Resistance in Modern Metropolis*, edited by Michael Burawoy. Berkeley: University of California Press.
Kurzman, Charles. 1994. Epistemology and the Sociology of Knowledge. *Philosophy of the Social Sciences* 24:267–290.
Kurzman, Charles. 2004. *The Unthinkable Revolution in Iran*. Cambridge, Mass.: Harvard University Press.
Lakatos, Imre. 1970. Falsificiation and the Methodology of Scientific Research Programmes. Pp. 91–196 in *Criticism and the Growth of Knowledge*, edited by Imre Lakatos and Alan Musgrave. Cambridge: Cambridge University Press.
Lakoff, Robin Tolmach and James C. Coyne. 1993. *Father Knows Best: The Use and Abuse of Power in Freud's Case of Dora*. New York: Teachers College Press.
Latour, Bruno. 1986. Visualization and Cognition: Thinking with Eyes and Hands. *Knowledge and Society* 6:1–40
Latour, Bruno. 1987. *Science in Action*. Cambridge, Mass.: Harvard University Press.

Leach, Edmund Ronald. 1964. Anthropological Aspects of Language: Animal Categories and Verbal Abuse. Pp. 23–63 in *New Directions in the Study of Language*, edited by Eric H. Lenneberg. Cambridge, Mass.: MIT Press.

Lee, D.N. 1980. The Optic Flow Field: The Foundation of Vision. *Philosophical Transactions of the Royal Society of London B* 290:169–179.

Leibniz, Gotfried Wilhelm. [1716] 1908. *The Philosophical Works of Leibniz*, second edition, translated by George Martin Duncan. New Haven, Conn.: Tuttle, Morehouse and Taylor.

Leifer, Eric M. and Valli Rajah. 2000. Getting Observations: Strategic Ambiguities in Social Interaction. *Soziale Systeme* 2:251–268.

Lembo, Alessandra. 2020. He Heard, She Heard: Toward a Cultural Sociology of the Senses. *Sociological Forum* 35:443–464.

Lenin, V.I. [1920] 1951. "Left-Wing" Communism: An Infantile Disorder. Pp. 341–447 in *Selected Works*, Volume 2, Part II. Moscow: Foreign Languages Publishing House.

Leontyev, A.N. 1977. Activity and Consciousness. Pp. 180–202 in *Philosophy in the USSR: Problems of Dialectical Materialism*. Moscow: Progress Publishers.

Leschziner, Vanina. 2007. Recipes for Success: Culinary Styles, Professional Careers, and Institutional Patterns in the Field of High Cuisine. PhD. dissertation, Rutgers University, New Brunswick, N.J.

Levi-Strauss, Claude. [1949] 1969. *The Elementary Structures of Kinship*, translated by James Harle Bell, John Richard von Sturmer, and Rodney Needham. Boston: Beacon Press.

Levi-Strauss, Claude. [1962] 1963. *Totemism*, translated by Rodney Needham. Boston: Beacon Press.

Levi-Strauss, Claude. [1962] 1966. *The Savage Mind* London: Weidenfeld and Nicolson.

Lévy-Bruhl, Lucien. [1926] 1985. *How Natives Think*, translated by Lilian A. Clare. Princeton, N.J.: Princeton University Press.

Lewin, Kurt. 1917. Krieglandschaft. *Zeitschrift für angewandte Psychologie* 12:440–447.

Lewin, Kurt. [1926] 1999. Intention, Will and Need. [Originally published *Psychologische Forschung* Vol. 7]. Pp. 83–115 in *The Complete Social Scientist*, edited by Martin Gold. Washington, D.C.: American Psychological Association.

Lewin, Kurt. [1931] 1999. The Conflict between Aristotelian and Galileian Modes of Thought in Contemporary Psychology. [Originally published in Journal of General Psychiatry Vol. 5]. Pp. 37–66 in *The Complete Social Scientist*, edited by Martin Gold. Washington, D.C.: American Psychological Association.

Lewin, Kurt. 1936. *Principles of Topological Psychology*, translated by Fritz Heider and Grace M. Heider. New York: McGraw Hill.

Lewin, Kurt. [1949] 1999. Cassirer's Philosophy of Science and the Social Sciences. Pp. 23–36 in *The Complete Social Scientist*, edited by Martin Gold. Washington, D.C.: American Psychological Association.

Lewin, Kurt. 1951. *Field Theory in Social Science*, edited by Dorwin Cartwright. New York: Harper and Brothers.

Lewis, David. 1973a. Causation. *The Journal of Philosophy* 70:556–567.

Lewis, David. 1973b. *Counterfactuals*. Oxford, U.K.: Blackwell.

Lewis, David. [1973c] 1986. Counterfactuals and Comparative Possibility. Pages 3–31 in *Philosophical Papers*, Volume 2. Oxford: Oxford University Press.

Lewis, David. [1979] 1986. Counterfactual Dependence and Time's Arrow. Pages 32–66 in *Philosophical Papers*, Volume 2. Oxford: Oxford University Press.

Lewis, David. 1986. Postscripts to "Causation." Pp. 172–213 in *Philosophical Papers, Volume 2*. Oxford: Oxford University Press.
Lewis, David. 2000. Causation as Influence. *Journal of Philosophy* 97:182–197.
Lewis, David. 2004. Causation as Influence. Pp. 75–106 in *Causation and Counterfactuals*, edited by John Collins, Ned Hall, and L.A. Paul. Cambridge, Mass.: MIT Press.
Lieberson, Stanley. 1985. *Making It Count*. Berkeley: University of California Press.
Lieberson, Stanley. 1997. Modeling Social Processes: Some Lessons from Sports. *Sociological Forum* 12:11–35.
Lindberg, David C. 1976. *Theories of Vision from Al-Kindī to Kepler*. Chicago: University of Chicago Press.
Lindblom, Charles E. 1977. *Politics and Markets*. New York: Basic Books.
Lindsay, Shawn. 1996. Hand Drumming: An Essay in Practical Knowledge. Pp. 196–212 in *Things as They Are: New Directions in Phenomenological Anthropology*, edited by Michael Jackson. Bloomington: Indiana University Press.
Lizardo, Omar. 2007. "Mirror Neurons," Collective Objects and the Problem of Transmission: Reconsidering Stephen Turner's Critique of Practice Theory. *Journal for the Theory of Social Behaviour* 37:319–350.
Lizardo, Omar. 2009. Formalism, Behavioral Realism and the Interdisciplinary Challenge in Sociological Theory. *Journal for the Theory of Social Behaviour* 39:39–79.
Lizardo, Omar and Michael Strand. 2011. "Beyond 'World Images': Belief as Embodied Action in the World." Paper presented at the Annual Meetings of the American Sociological Association, Las Vegas.
Lloyd, David. 1995. Kant's Examples. Pp. 256–276 in *Unruly Examples: On the Rhetoric of Exemplarity*, edited by Alexander Gelley. Stanford, Calif.: Stanford University Press.
Lloyd, David. Kant's Examples. *Representations* 28 (Fall 1989):34–54.
Loesberg, Jonathan. 1993. Bourdieu and the Sociology of Aesthetics. *ELH* 60:1033–1056.
Loftus, Elizabeth F. and Deborah Davis. 2006. Recovered Memories. *Annual Review of Clinical Psychology* 2:1–30.
Lorenz, Konrad. [1973] 1977. *Behind the Mirror*, translated by Ronald Taylor. New York: Harcourt Brace Jovanovich.
Luhmann, Niklas. [1984] 1995. *Social Systems*, translated by John Bednarz, Jr., with Dirk Baecker. Stanford, Calif.: Stanford University Press.
Lukes, Steven. 1985. *Emile Durkheim: His Life and Work*. Stanford, Calif.: Stanford University Press.
Lundberg, George A. 1939. *Foundations of Sociology*. New York: Macmillan.
MacKenzie, Donald Angus. 1981. *Statistics in Britain, 1865–1930: The Social Construction of Scientific Knowledge*. Edinburgh: Edinburgh University Press.
Macmillan, Malcolm. 1992. The Sources of Freud's Methods for Gathering and Evaluating Clinical Data. Pp. 99–151 in *Freud and the History of Psychoanalysis*, edited by Toby Gelfand and John Kerr. Hillsdale, N.J.: Analytic Press.
Macmillan, Malcolm. 1997. *Freud Evaluated: The Completed Arc*. Cambridge, Mass.: MIT Press.
Macnamara, John. 1982. *Names for Things: A Study of Human Learning*. Cambridge, Mass.: MIT Press.
Mahoney, James. 2004. Revisiting General Theory in Historical Sociology. *Social Forces* 83:459–489.

Mahony, Patrick J. 1996. *Freud's Dora: A Psychoanalytic, Historical and Textual Study*. New Haven, Conn.: Yale University Press.
Maimonides, Moses. 1947. *The Guide for the Perplexed*, translated by M. Friedlander. London: Routledge and Sons.
Maio, G.R., J.M. Olson, L. Allen, and M.M. Bernard. 2001. Addressing Discrepancies between Values and Behavior: The Motivating Effect of Reasons. *Journal of Experimental Social Psychology* 37:104–117.
Malinowski, Bronislaw. 1922. *Argonauts of the Western Pacific*. London: Routledge and Kegan Paul.
Malinowski, Bronislaw. [1927] 1960. *Sex and Repression in Savage Society*. London: Routledge and Kegan Paul.
Malinowski, Bronislaw. 1939. The Group and the Individual in Functional Analysis. *American Journal of Sociology* 44:938–964.
Malinowski, Bronislaw. 1954. *Magic, Science and Religion*. Garden City, N.Y.: Doubleday Anchor.
Malinowski, Bronislaw. 1967. *A Diary in the Strict Sense of the Term*, translated by Norbert Guterman. New York: Harcourt, Brace and World.
Mannheim, Karl. [1929] 1936. *Ideology and Utopia*, translated by Louis Wirth and Edward Shils. New York: Harcourt Brace Jovanovich.
Mannheim, Karl. 1935. *Mensch und Gesellschaft im Zeitalter des Umbau*. Leiden, the Netherlands: Sijthoff's Uitgeversmaatschappij.
Mannheim, Karl. 1940. *Man and Society in an Age of Reconstruction*, translated by Edward Shils. New York: Harcourt, Brace and World.
Marcuse, Herbert. [1941] 1954. *Reason and Revolution*. New York: Humanities Press.
Marcuse, Herbert. 1964. *One-Dimensional Man*. Boston: Beacon Press.
Margolis, Howard. 1987. *Patterns, Thinking, and Cognition: A Theory of Judgment*. Chicago: University of Chicago Press.
Markoff, John. 1996. *The Abolition of Feudalism*. University Park, Pa.: Pennsylvania State Press.
Marrow, Alfred J. 1969. *The Practical Theorist: The Life and Work of Kurt Lewin*. New York: Basic Books.
Martin, John Levi. 2001. *The Authoritarian Personality*, 50 Years Later: What Lessons Are There for Political Psychology? *Political Psychology* 22:1–26.
Martin, John Levi. 2009. *Social Structures*. Princeton, N.J.: Princeton University Press.
Martin, John Levi and Matt George. 2006. Theories of Sexual Stratification: Toward an Analytics of the Sexual Field and a Theory of Sexual Capital. *Sociological Theory* 24:107–132.
Martin, Laura 1986. "Eskimo Words for Snow": A Case Study in the Genesis and Decay of an Anthropological Example. *American Anthropologist* 88:418–423.
Marx, Karl. [1843] 1977. *Critique of Hegel's Philosophy of Right*, edited by Joseph O'Malley. Cambridge: Cambridge University Press.
Marx, Karl. [1858] 1973. *The Grundrisse*, translated by Martin Nicolaus. New York: Vintage.
Marx, Karl. [1867] 1906. *Capital*, Volume 1, edited by Frederick Engels, translated from the third German edition by Samuel Moore and Edward Aveling. Chicago: Kerr.
Marx, Karl. 1968. *Theories of Surplus Value, Part 2*. Translated by S. Ryazankaya. Moscow: Progress Publishers.

Marx, Karl. 1971. *Theories of Surplus Value, Part 3*, translated by Jack Cohen and S. Ryazankaya. Moscow: Progress Publishers.

Marx, Karl and Frederick Engels. [1844] 1975. *The Holy Family*. Pp. 1–211 in *Collected Works*, Volume 4, translated by Richard Dixon and Clemens Dutt. New York: International Publishers.

Marx, Karl and Frederick Engels. [1845–1846] 1976. *The German Ideology*. Pp. 19–539 in *Collected Works*, Volume 5. New York: International Publishers.

Mauss, Marcel [1934] 1973. Techniques of the Body, translated by Ben Brewster. *Economy and Society* 2:70–88.

Mauss, Marcel [1938] 1985. A Category of the Human Mind: The Notion of Persons; The Notion of Self, translated by W.D. Halls. Pp. 1–25 in *The Category of the Person*, edited by Michael Carrithers, Steven Collins, and Steven Lukes. Cambridge: Cambridge University Press.

Maxwell, James Clerk. [1891] 1954. *A Treatise on Electricity and Magnetism*. New York: Dover.

May, Henry F. 1959. *The End of American Innocence: The First Years of Our Own Time 1912–1917*. Oxford: Oxford University Press.

McNemar, Quinn. 1946. Opinion-Attitude Methodology. *Psychological Bulletin* 43:289–374.

Mead, George H. 1926. The Objective Reality of Perspectives. *Proceedings of the Sixth International Congress of Philosophy* 6:75–87.

Mead, George H. 1934. *Mind, Self, and Society: From the Standpoint of a Social Behaviorist*, edited by Charles W. Morris. Chicago: University of Chicago Press.

Mead, George H. 1938. *Philosophy of the Act*. Chicago: University of Chicago Press.

Melden, A.I. 1961. *Free Action*. London: Routledge and Kegan Paul.

Melville, Herman. 1851. *Moby-Dick; or, The Whale*. London: Bentley.

Meltzoff, Andrew N. and M. Keith Moore. 1995. Infants' Understanding of People and Things: From Body Imitation to Folk Psychology. Pp. 43–69 in *The Body and the Self*, edited by José Luis Bermúdez, Anthony Marcel, and Naomi Eilan. Cambridge, Mass.: MIT Press.

Mendel, Werner M. 1964. The Phenomenon of Interpretation. *American Journal of Psychoanalysis* 24:184–189.

Menzel, Charles R. 1997. Primates' Knowledge of Their Natural Habitat: As Indicated in Foraging. Pp. 207–239 in *Machiavellian Intelligence II: Extensions and Evaluations*, edited by Andrew Whiten and Richard W. Byrne. Cambridge: Cambridge University Press.

Merleau-Ponty, Maurice. [1942] 1963. *The Structure of Behavior*, translated by Alden L. Fisher. Boston: Beacon Press.

Merleau-Ponty, Maurice. 1962. *The Phenomenology of Perception*, translated by Colin Smith. London: Routledge and Kegan Paul.

Merleau-Ponty, Maurice. 1964. Eye and Mind, translated by Carleton Dallery. Pp. 159–190 in *The Primacy of Perception and Other Essays*. Evanston, Ill.: Northwestern University Press.

Merton, Robert K. 1968. *Social Theory and Social Structure*, second edition. New York: Free Press.

Metzger, Wolfgang. 1966. Der Ort der Wahrnehmungslehre im Aufbau der Psychologie. Pp. 3–20 in *Handbuch der Psychologie*, Volume 1. Göttingen, Germany: Verlag für Psychologie.

Metzger, Wolfgang. [1967] 1986. Der Geltungsbereich gestalttheoretischer Ansätze. Pp. 134–144 in *Gestalt Psychologie*, edited by Michael Stadler and Heinrich Crabus. Frankfurt: Verlag Waldermar Kramer.
Metzger, Wolfgang. [1975a] 1986. Die Entdeckung der Prägnanztendenz. Pp. 145–181 in *Gestalt Psychologie*, edited by Michael Stadler and Heinrich Crabus. Frankfurt: Verlag Waldermar Kramer.
Metzger, Wolfgang. [1975b] 1986. Gestalttheorie und Gruppendynamik. Pp. 210–226 in *Gestalt Psychologie*, edited by Michael Stadler and Heinrich Crabus. Frankfurt: Verlag Waldermar Kramer.
Metzinger, Thomas. 2003. *Being No One*. Cambridge, Mass.: MIT Press.
Mey, Harald. [1965] 1972. *Field Theory: A Study of Its Applications in the Social Sciences*. New York: St. Martin's Press.
Meyer, Leonard B. 1956. *Emotion and Meaning in Music*. Chicago: University of Chicago Press.
Michotte, A. [1946] 1963. *The Perception of Causality*. New York: Basic Books.
Middleton, John. 1955. The Concept of "Bewitching" in Lugbara. *Africa* 25:252–260.
Milgram, Stanley. 1974. *Obedience to Authority*. New York: Harper and Row.
Mill, John Stuart. 1872. *A System of Logic, Ratiocinative and Inductive*. London: Longman.
Miller, George A. 1964. Language and Psychology. Pp. 89–107 in *New Directions in the Study of Language*, edited by Eric H. Lennenberg. Cambridge, Mass.: MIT Press.
Mills, C. Wright. 1940. Situated Actions and Vocabularies of Motive. *American Sociological Review* 5:904–931.
Mills, C. Wright. 1959. *The Sociological Imagination*. London: Oxford University Press.
Mills, C. Wright. 1964. *Sociology and Pragmatism*. New York: Oxford University Press.
Mische, Ann. 2003. Cross-Talk in Movements: Rethinking the Culture-Network Link. Pp. 258–280 in *Social Movement Analysis: The Network Perspective*, edited by Mario Diani and Douglas McAdam. Oxford: Oxford University Press.
Mitchell, Richard G., Jr. 1983. *Mountain Experience: The Psychology and Sociology of Adventure*. Chicago: University of Chicago Press.
Mohr, John W. forthcoming. Implicit Terrains: Meaning, Measurement, and Spatial Metaphors in Organizational Theory. In *Constructing Industries and Markets*, edited by Marc Ventresca and Joseph Porac. New York: Elsevier.
Mohr, John and Vincent Duquenne. 1997. The Duality of Culture and Practice: Poverty Relief in New York City, 1888–1917. *Theory and Society* 26:305–356.
Morgan, Stephen L. and Christopher Winship. 2007. *Counterfactuals and Causal Inference*. Cambridge: Cambridge University Press.
Morphy, Howard. 1998. Spencer and Gillen in Durkheim: The Theoretical Construction of Ethnography. Pp. 13–28 in *On Durkheim's Elementary Forms of Religious Life*, edited by N.J. Allen, W.S.F. Pickering, and W. Watts Miller. London: Routledge.
Moretti, Franco. 2005. *Graphs, Maps, Trees*. London: Verso.
Nadel, S.F. 1957. *The Theory of Social Structure*. Glencoe, Ill.: Free Press.
Nagel, Thomas. 1979. *Mortal Questions*. Cambridge: Cambridge University Press.
Nagel, Thomas. 1986. *The View from Nowhere*. New York: Oxford University Press.
Nagel, Thomas. 1995. *Other Minds*. New York: Oxford University Press.

Nederman, Cary J. and Jacqui True. 1996. The Third Sex: The Idea of the Hermaphrodite in Twelfth-Century Europe. *Journal of the History of Sexuality* 6:497–517.

Needham, Joseph. 1981. *Science in Traditional China.* Cambridge, Mass.: Harvard University Press.

Némedi, Dénes. 1998. Durkheim on the Causes and Functions of the Categories. Pp. 162–175 in *On Durkheim's Elementary Forms of Religious Life*, edited by N.J. Allen, W.S.F. Pickering, and W. Watts Miller. London: Routledge.

Neisser, Ulric. 2002. *Wolfgang Köhler 1887–1967: A Biographical Memoir.* Biographical Memoirs Series, Volume 81. Washington, D.C.: National Academy Press.

Newton, Issac. [1730] 1952. *Opticks: Or, a Treatise of the Reflections, Refractions, Inflections & Colours of Light*, 4th ed. New York: Dover.

Nisbet, Robert A. 1962. Sociology as an Art Form. *Pacific Sociological Review* 5:67–74.

Nisbett, Richard E. and Timothy DeCamp Wilson. 1977. Telling More Than We Can Know: Verbal Reports on Mental Processes. *Psychological Review* 84:231–259.

Oakes, Guy. 1988. *Weber and Rickert: Concept Formation in the Social Sciences.* Cambridge, Mass.: MIT Press.

Oberschall, Anthony. 1987. The Two Empirical Roots of Social Theory and the Probability Revolution. Pp. 103–131 in *The Probabilistic Revolution, Volume 2: Ideas in Science*, edited by Lorenz Kruger, Gerd Gigerenzer, and Mary S. Morgan. Cambridge, Mass.: MIT Press.

Ong, Walter J. 1969. World as View and World as Event. *American Anthropologist* 71:634–647.

Ong, Walter J. 1988. *Orality and Literacy: The Technologizing of the Word.* New York: Methuen.

O'Regan, J. Kevin. 1992. Solving the "Real" Mysteries of Visual Perception: The World as an Outside Memory. *Canadian Journal of Psychology* 46:461–488.

Orne, Martin T. 1969. Demand Characteristics and the Concept of Quasi-Controls. Pp. 143–179 in *Artifact in Behavioral Research*, edited by Robert Rosenthal and Ralph L. Rosnow. New York: Academic Press.

Owen, A.R.G. 1971. *Hysteria, Hypnosis and Healing: The Work of J.-M. Charcot.* New York: Garrett.

Parascandola, Mark. 1996. Evidence and Association: Epistemic Confusion in Toxic Tort Law. *Philosophy of Science* 63:S168–S176.

Park, Katherine. 1998. Impressed Images: Reproducing Wonders. Pp. 254–271 in *Picturing Science, Producing Art*, edited by Caroline A. Jones and Peter Galison. New York: Routledge.

Parsons, Talcott. 1951. *The Social System.* New York: Free Press.

Parsons, Talcott and Edward A. Shils. 1954. *Toward a General Theory of Action.* Cambridge, Mass.: Harvard University Press.

Pastore, Nicholas. 1971. *Selective History of Theories of Visual Perception: 1650–1950.* New York: Oxford University Press.

Pearl, Judea. 2000. *Causality: Models, Reasoning and Inference.* Cambridge: Cambridge University Press.

Pearson, Karl. [1921–1933] 1978. *The History of Statistics in the 17th and 18th Centuries against the Changing Background of Intellectual, Scientific and Religious Thought*, edited by E.S. Pearson. London: Griffin.

Peirce, C.S. [1875–1910] 1955. The Principles of Phenomenology. Pp. 74–97 in *Philosophical Writings*, edited by Justus Buchler. New York: Dover.
Pepper, Stephen. 1937. *Aesthetic Quality: A Contextualist Theory of Beauty.* New York: Charles Scribner's Sons.
Pepper, Stephen. 1955. *The Work of Art.* Bloomington: Indiana University Press.
Pepper, Stephen. 1966. *Concept and Quality.* LaSalle, Ill.: Open Court Press.
Pepperberg, Irene Maxine. 1999. *The Alex Studies.* Cambridge, Mass.: Harvard University Press.
Pessoa, Luiz, Evan Thompson, and Alva Noë. 1998. Finding Out about Filling-In: A Guide to Perceptual Completion for Visual Science and the Philosophy of Perception. *Behavioral and Brain Sciences* 21:723–802.
Peters, R.S. 1958. *The Concept of Motivation.* London: Routledge and Kegan Paul.
Phelps, Elizabeth A. 2006. Emotion and Cognition: Insights from Studies of the Human Amygdala. *Annual Review of Psychology* 57:27–53.
Piaget, Jean. [1941] 1952. *The Child's Conception of Number.* London: Routledge and Kegan Paul.
Piaget, Jean. 1954. *The Construction of Reality in the Child*, translated by Margaret Cook. New York: Basic Books.
Piaget, Jean. [1965] 1995. *Sociological Studies*, edited by Leslie Smith. London: Routledge.
Piaget, Jean. 1970. *Structuralism*, translated by C. Maschler. New York: Basic Books.
Plato. [1961] 1989. *The Collected Dialogues*, edited by Edith Hamilton and Huntington Cairns. Princeton, N.J.: Princeton University Press.
Plotinus. 1956. *The Enneads*, third edition revised by B.S. Page, translated by Stephen MacKenna. London: Faber and Faber.
Plug, Cornelius and Helen E. Ross. 1989. Historical Review. Pp. 5–27 in *The Moon Illusion*, edited by Maurice Hershenson. Hillsdale, N.J.: Erlbaum.
Pollock, John L. 1982. *Language and Thought.* Princeton, N.J.: Princeton University Press.
Pomian, Krzysztof. 1998. Vision and Cognition. Pp. 211–231 in *Picturing Science, Producing Art*, edited by Caroline A. Jones and Peter Galison. New York: Routledge.
Popper, Karl. 1959. *The Logic of Scientific Discovery.* New York: Basic Books.
Porter, Bruce D. 1994. *War and the Rise of the State: The Military Foundations of Modern Politics.* New York: Free Press.
Porter, Theodore M. 1986. *The Rise of Statistical Thinking, 1820–1900.* Princeton, N.J.: Princeton University Press.
Porter, Theodore M. 1987. Lawless Society: Social Science and the Reinterpretation of Statistics in Germany, 1850–1880. Pp. 351–376 in *The Probabilistic Revolution, Volume 1: Ideas in History*, edited by Lorenz Kruger, Lorraine J. Daston, and Michael Heidelberger. Cambridge, Mass.: MIT Press.
Powell, Russell A. and Douglas P. Boer. 1994. Did Freud Mislead Patients to Confabulate Memories of Abuse? *Psychological Reports* 74:1283–1298.
Przeworksi, Adam and Henry Teune. 1970. *The Logic of Comparative Social Inquiry.* New York: Wiley.
Pullum, Geoffrey K. 1991. *The Great Eskimo Vocabulary Hoax, and Other Irreverent Essays on the Study of Language.* Chicago: University of Chicago Press.
Pylyshyn, Zenon W. 2003. *Seeing and Visualizing.* Cambridge, Mass.: MIT Press.

Radcliffe-Brown, A.R. 1952. *Structure and Function in Primitive Society*. London: Cohen and West.

Rawls, Anne Warfield. 1996. Durkheim's Epistemology: The Neglected Argument. *American Journal of Sociology* 102:430–482.

Rawls, Anne Warfield. 2001. Durkheim's Treatment of Practice: Concrete Practice vs. Representations as the Foundation of Reason. *Journal of Classical Sociology* 1:33–68.

Rawls, John. 1955. Two Concepts of Rules. *The Philosophical+ Review* 64:3–32.

Redfield, Robert. 1948. The Art of Social Science. *American Journal of Sociology* 54:181–190.

Reed, Edward S. 1996. *Encountering the World*. New York: Oxford.

Rickert, Heinrich. 1902. *Die Grenzen der naturwissenschaflichen Begriffsbildung*. Tübingen, Germany: Mohr.

Rickert, Heinrich. 1913. Vom System der Werte. *Logos* 4:295–327.

Rickert, Heinrich. [1929] 1986. *The Limits of Concept Formation in Natural Science*, fifth edition, edited and translated by Guy Oakes. Cambridge: Cambridge University Press.

Ricoeur, Paul. 1974. *The Conflict of Interpretations*, translated by Kathleen McLaughlin. Evanston, Ill.: Northwestern University Press.

Rochat, Philippe. 2001. *The Infant's World*. Cambridge, Mass.: Harvard University Press.

Roediger, Henry L. III, J. Derek Jacoby, and Kathleen B. McDermott. 1996. Misinformation Effects in Recall: Creating False Memories through Repeated Retrieval. *Journal of Memory and Language* 35:300–318.

Rogoff, Barbara. 1990. *Apprenticeship in Thinking*. Oxford: Oxford University Press.

Rosch, Eleanor. 1977. Classification of Real-World Objects: Origins and Representations in Cognition. Pp. 212–222 in *Thinking: Readings in Cognitive Science*, edited by P.N. Johnson-Laird and P.C. Wason. Cambridge: Cambridge University Press.

Rosch, Eleanor. 1978. Principles of Categorization. pp. 27–48 in *Cognition and Categorization*, edited by Eleanor Rosch and Barbara B. Lloyd. Hillsdale, NJ: Erlbaum.

Roscoe, Stanley N. 1989. The Zoom-Lens Hypothesis. Pp. 31–57 in *The Moon Illusion*, edited by Maurice Hershenson. Hillsdale, N.J.: Erlbaum.

Rousseau, Jean-Jacques [1755] 1967. *Discourse on the Origin of Inequality*, edited by Lester G. Crocker. New York: Washington Square Press.

Rubin, Gayle. 1985. The Traffic in Women: Notes on the "Political Economy" of Sex. Pp. 157–210 in *Toward an Anthropology of Women*, edited by Reyna Reiter. New York: Monthly Review Press.

Rule, Nicholas O. and Nalini Ambady. 2008. Brief Exposures: Male Sexual Orientation Is Accurately Perceived at 50 ms. *Journal of Experimental Social Psychology* 44:1100–1105.

Rule, Nicholas O. and Nalini Ambady. 2010. Democrats and Republicans Can Be Differentiated from Their Faces. *PLoS ONE* 5(1): e8733. doi: 10.1371/journal.pone.0008733.

Rule, Nicholas O., Nalini Ambady, Reginald B. Adams, Jr., and C. Neil Macrae. 2008. Accuracy and Awareness in the Perception and Categorization of Male Sexual Orientation. *Journal of Personality and Social Psychology* 95:1019–1028.

Rule, Nicholas O., C. Neil Macrae, and Nalini Ambady. 2009. Ambiguous Group Membership Extracted Automatically from Faces. *Psychological Science* 20: 441–443.
Rummel, Rudolph J. 1975. *Understanding Conflict and War. Volume 1. The Dynamic Psychological Field.* New York: Wiley.
Sahlins, Marshall. 1995. *How Natives Think; About Captain Cook, For Example.* Chicago: University of Chicago Press.
Sand, Rosemarie. 1983. Confirmation in the Dora Case. *International Review of Psycho-Analysis* 10:333–357.
Sanna, Lawrence J., Norbert Schwarz, and Shevaun L. Stocker. 2002. When Debiasing Backfires: Accessible Content and Accessibility Experiences in Debiasing Hindsight. *Journal of Experimental Psychology* 28:497–502.
Sartre, Jean-Paul. 1956. *Being and Nothingness*, translated by Hazel E. Barnes. New York: Philosophical Library.
Schachter, Stanley and Jerome E. Singer. 1962. Cognitive, Social and Physiological Determinants of Emotional State. *Psychological Review* 69:379–399.
Schaffer, Jonathan. 2000. Trumping Preemption. *Journal of Philosophy* 97:165–181
Schatzki, Theodore Richard. 1987. Overdue Analysis of Bourdieu's Theory of Practice. *Inquiry* 30:113–135.
Scheerer, Eckart. 1980. *Gestalt* Psychology in the Soviet Union: I. The Period of Enthusiasm. *Psychological Research* 41:113–132.
Schelling, Thomas C. 1978. *Micromotives and Macrobehavior.* New York: Norton.
Schimek, Jean G. 1987. Fact and Fantasy in the Seduction Theory: A Historical Review. *Journal of the American Psychoanalytic Association* 35:937–965.
Schjelderup-Ebbe, Thorleif. 1922. Beiträge zur Sozialpsychologie des Haushuhns. *Zeitschrift für Psychologie* 88:225–252.
Schluchter, Wolfgang. 1996. *Paradoxes of Modernity: Culture and Conduct in the Theory of Max Weber.* Stanford, Calif.: Stanford University Press.
Schmaus, Warren. 1998. Durkheim on the Causes and Functions of the Categories. Pp. 176–188 in *On Durkheim's Elementary Forms of Religious Life*, edited by N.J. Allen, W.S.F. Pickering, and W. Watts Miller. London: Routledge.
Schmaus, Warren. 2004. *Rethinking Durkheim and His Tradition.* Cambridge: Cambridge University Press.
Schutz, Alfred. [1932] 1967. *The Phenomenology of the Social World*, translated by George Walsh and Frederick Lehnert. Evanston, Ill.: Northwestern University Press.
Schwinger, Julian, Lester L. DeRaad, Jr., Kimball A. Milton, and Wu-Yang Tsai. 1998. *Classical Electrodynamics.* Reading, Mass.: Perseus Books.
Scott, Marvin B. and Stanford M. Lyman. 1968. Accounts. *American Sociological Review* 33:46–62.
Searle, John R. 1969. *Speech Acts: An Essay in the Philosophy of Language.* Cambridge: Cambridge University Press.
Searle, John R. 1983. *Intentionality: An Essay in the Philosophy of Mind.* Cambridge: Cambridge University Press.
Searle, John R. 1995. *The Construction of Social Reality.* New York: Free Press.
Seltzer, Mark. 1992. *Bodies and Machines.* New York: Routledge.
Seneca. [ca. 62 CE] 2010. *Natural Questions*, translated by Harry M. Hines. Chicago: University of Chicago Press.
Sewell, William H., Jr. 2005. *Logics of History.* Chicago: University of Chicago Press.

Shapin, Steven. 1994. *A Social History of Truth*. Chicago: University of Chicago Press.

Shapin, Steven. 1996. *The Scientific Revolution*. Chicago: University of Chicago Press.

Shepard, Paul. [1978] 1998. *Thinking Animals: Animals and the Development of Human Intelligence*. Athens: University of Georgia Press.

Shore, Bradd. 1996. *Culture in Mind*. New York: Oxford University Press.

Sica, Alan. 2004. Why "Unobservables" Cannot Save General Theory: A Reply to Mahoney. *Social Forces* 83:491–501.

Silverstein, Michael. 1976. Shifters, Linguistic Categories, and Cultural Description. Pp. 11–56 in *Meaning in Anthropology*, edited by Keith Basso and Henry Selby. Albuquerque, N.M.: University of New Mexico Press.

Simmel, Georg. [1905] 1977. *The Problems of the Philosophy of History*, second edition, translated by Guy Oakes. New York: Free Press.

Simmel, Georg. [1907] 1978. *The Philosophy of Money*, translated by Tom Bottomore and David Frisby. London: Routledge and Kegan Paul.

Simmel, Georg. [1908] 1950. Soziologie, in *The Sociology of Georg Simmel*, edited and translated by Kurt H. Wolff. Glencoe, Ill.: Free Press.

Simmel, Georg. [1918] 2010. *The View of Life: Four Metaphysical Essays with Journal Aphorisms*, translated by John A.Y. Andrews, Donald N. Levine, and Daniel Silver. Chicago: University of Chicago Press.

Simon, Herbert. 1955. A Behavioral Model of Rational Choice. *The Quarterly Journal of Economics* 69:99–118.

Simon, Herbert. 1996. *The Sciences of the Artificial*. Cambridge, Mass.: MIT Press.

Simonis, Yvan. 1974. Two Ways of Approaching Concrete Reality: "Group Dynamics" and Lévi-Strauss' Structuralism. Pp. 363–388 in *The Unconscious in Culture*, edited by Ino Rossi. New York: Dutton.

Skocpol, Theda. 1984. Emerging Agendas and Recurring Strategies in Historical Sociology. Pp. 356–391 in *Vision and Method in Historical Sociology*, edited by Theda Skocpol. Cambridge: Cambridge University Press.

Sloman, Steven. 2005. *Causal Models: How People Think about the World and Its Alternatives*. Oxford: Oxford University Press.

Smart, Christopher. [1758–1763] 1954. *Jubilate Agno*. Cambridge, Mass.: Harvard University Press.

Smith, Adam. [1759] 1997. *The Theory of Moral Sentiments*. Washington, D.C.: Regnery.

Smith, Barry. 1988. Gestalt Theory: An Essay in Philosophy. Pp. 11–81 in *Foundations of Gestalt Theory*, edited by Barry Smith. Munich: Philosophia Verlag.

Smith, Dorothy E. 1987. *The Everyday World as Problematic*. Boston: Northeastern University Press.

Smith, Herbert. 2003. Some Thoughts on Causation as It Relates to Demography and Population Studies. *Population and Development Review* 29:459–469.

Smith, J. David, Joshua S. Redford, Sarah M. Haas, Mirana V.C. Coutinho, and Justin J. Couchman 2008. The Comparative Psychology of Same-Different Judgments by Humans (*Homo sapiens*) and Monkeys (*Macaca mulatta*). *Journal of Experimental Psychology* 34:361–374.

Sniderman, Paul M, Richard Brody, and Philip Tetlock. 1991. *Reasoning and Choice: Explorations in Political Psychology*. Cambridge: Cambridge University Press.

Sniderman, Paul M. & Carmines, Edward. G. 1997. *Reaching Beyond Race*. Cambridge, Mass.: Harvard University Press.
Soffer, Reba N. 1970. The Revolution in English Social Thought. *American Historical Review* 75:1938–1964.
Spencer, Baldwin and Francis James Gillen. 1904. *The Northern Tribes of Central Australia*. London: Macmillan.
Spiegel, Bernt. 1961. *Die Struktur Der Meinungsverteilung im Sozialen Feld: Das Psychologische Marktmodell*. Bern, Switzerland: Verlag Hans Huber.
Spinoza, Benedict de. [1677] 1930. *Ethic*, translated by W. Hale White and Amelia Hutchinson. London: Oxford University Press.
Spradley, James P. 1979. *The Ethnographic Interview*. New York: Harcourt, Brace, Janovich.
Stark, Werner. 1958. *The Sociology of Knowledge*. London: Routledge and Kegan Paul.
Starr, Paul. 1982. *The Social Transformation of American Medicine*. New York: Basic Books.
Stewman, Shelby. 1986. Demographic Models of Internal Labor Markets. *Administrative Science Quarterly* 31:212–247.
Stewman, Shelby. 1988. Organizational Demography. *Annual Review of Sociology* 14:173–202.
Stewman, Shelby and Kuang S. Yeh. 1991. Structural Pathways and Switching Mechanisms for Individual Careers. *Research in Social Stratification and Mobility* 10:133–168.
Stigler, Stephen M. 1986. *The History of Statistics: The Measurement of Uncertainty before 1900*. Cambridge, Mass.: Harvard University Press.
Stigler, Stephen M. 2010. Darwin, Galton and the Statistical Enlightenment. *Journal of the Royal Statistical Society A*, Part 3:469–482.
Stiles, William B., David A. Shapiro, and Robert Elliott. 1986. Are All Psychotherapies Equivalent? *American Psychologist* 41:165–180.
Stinchcombe, Arthur L. 1991. The Conditions of Fruitfulness of Theorizing about Mechanisms in Social Science. *Philosophy of the Social Sciences*: 21:367–388.
Stocking, George W., Jr. 1984. Radcliffe-Brown and British Social Anthropology. Pp. 131–191 in *Functionalism Historicized: Essays on British Social Anthropology*, edited by George W. Stocking, Jr. Madison: University of Wisconsin Press.
Stocking, George W., Jr. 1986. Anthropology and the Science of the Irrational: Malinowski's Encounter with Freudian Psychoanalysis. Pp. 13–49 in *Malinowski, Rivers, Benedict and Others: Essays on Culture and Personality*, edited by George W. Stocking, Jr. Madison: University of Wisconsin Press.
Stoller, Paul and Cheryl Olkes. 1987. *In Sorcery's Shadow*. Chicago: University of Chicago Press.
Strang, Barbara M.H. 1970. *A History of English*. London: Methuen.
Stumpf, Carl. 1907. *Zur Einteilung der Wissenschaften*. Berlin: Verlag der Königl. Akademie der Wissenschaften.
Sulloway, Frank J. 1991. Reassessing Freud's Case Histories. *Isis* 82:245–275.
Sumner, William Graham. 1906. *Folkways*. Boston: Ginn.
Swales, Peter. 1986. Freud, His Teacher and the Birth of Psychoanalysis. Pp. 3–82 in *Freud: Appraisals and Reappraisals, Vol. 1*, edited by Paul Stepansky. Hillsdale, N.J.: Analytic Press.
Swartz, David. 1997. *Culture and Power*. Chicago: University of Chicago Press.

Sweet, Michael J. 1996. Male Homosexuality and Spiritism in the African Diaspora: The Legacy of a Link. *Journal of the History of Sexuality* 7:184–202.

Sweetser, Eve. 1990. *From Etymology to Pragmatics*. Cambridge: Cambridge University Press.

Swidler, Ann. 1986. Culture in Action: Symbols and Strategies. *American Sociological Review* 51:273–286.

Swidler, Ann. 1992. How Culture Constrains: Looking from the Outside-In. Revised version of paper presented at conference on Ideology: The Turn to Practice, Tulsa, Oklahoma, April 20–21, 1990.

Swidler, Ann. 2001. *Talk of Love*. Chicago: University of Chicago Press.

Swijink, Zeno. 1987. The Objectification of Observation: Measurement and Statistical Methods in the Nineteenth Century. Pp. 261–285 in *The Probabilistic Revolution, Volume I: Ideas in History*, edited by Lorenz Kruger, Lorraine J. Daston, and Michael Heidelberger. Cambridge, Mass.: MIT Press.

Talbot, S.A. and S.W. Kuffler. 1952. A Multibeam Ophthalmoscope for the Study of Retinal Physiology. *Journal of the Optical Society of America* 42:931–936.

Tarde, Gabriel. [1894] 1969. *La Logique Sociale*, reprinted in *Gabriel Tarde on Communication and Social Influence*, edited by Terry Clark. Chicago: University of Chicago Press.

Taylor, Charles. 1995. *Philosophical Arguments*. Cambridge, Mass.: Harvard University Press.

Thomas, Keith. 1971. *Religion and the Decline of Magic*. London: Weidenfeld and Nicolson.

Thucydides. 1972. *History of the Peloponnesian War*, translated by Rex Warner. London: Penguin.

Tilly, Charles. 1999. The Trouble with Stories. Pp. 256–270 in *The Social Worlds of Higher Education: Handbook for Teaching in a New Century*, edited by Bernice A. Pescosolido and Ronald Aminzade. Thousand Oaks, Calif.: Pine Forge Press.

Tilly, Charles. 2000. Processes and Mechanisms of Democratization. *Sociological Theory* 18:1–16.

Tilly, Charles. 2004. Reasons Why. *Sociological Theory* 22:445–454.

Tilly, Charles. 2006. *Why? What Happens When People Give Reasons . . . and Why*. Princeton, N.J.: Princeton University Press.

Tolman, Edward C. and Egon Brunswik. 1935. The Organism and the Causal Texture of the Environment. *Psychological Review* 42:43–77.

Tolman, Edward C., B.F. Ritchie, and D. Kalish. 1946a. Studies in Spatial Learning. I. Orientation and the Short-Cut. *Journal of Experimental Psychology* 36:13–24.

Tolman, Edward C., B.F. Ritchie, and D. Kalish. 1946b. Studies in Spatial Learning. II. Place Learning Versus Response Learning. *Journal of Experimental Psychology* 36:221–229.

Tolstoy, Leo. [1896] 1960. *What Is Art?*, translated by Aylmer Maude. Indianapolis, Ind.: Bobbs-Merrill.

Tovée, Martin J. 1996. *An Introduction to the Visual System*. Cambridge: Cambridge University Press.

Turnbull, William and Ben R. Slugoski. 1988. Conversational and Linguistic Processes in Causal Attribution. Pp. 66–93 in *Contemporary Science and Natural Explanation*, edited by Denis J. Hilton. New York: New York University Press.

Turner, Bryan. 1984. *The Body and Society: Explorations in Social Theory*. Oxford, U.K.: Blackwell.

Turner, Stephen. 1994. *The Social Theory of Practices*. Chicago: University of Chicago Press.
Turner, Victor. 1974. *Dramas, Fields, and Metaphors*. Ithaca, N.Y.: Cornell University Press.
Turvey, M.T., Kevin Shockley, and Claudia Carello. 1999. Affordance, Proper Function, and the Physical Basis of Perceived Heaviness. *Cognition* 73:B17–B26.
Triandis, Harry C. 1964. Cultural Influences upon Cognitive Processes. Pp. 1–48 in *Advances in Experimental Social Psychology*, Volume 1, edited by Leonard Berkowitz. New York: Academic Press.
Trumbach, Randolf. 1991. Sex, Gender, and Sexual Identity in Modern Culture: Male Sodomy and Female Prostitution in Enlightenment London. *Journal of the History of Sexuality* 2:186–203.
Twine, France Winddance. 1998. *Racism in a Racial Democracy: The Maintenance of White Supremacy in Brazil*. New Brunswick, N.J.: Rutgers University Press.
Tyndall, John. 1890. *Faraday as a Discoverer*. New York: Appleton.
Underwood, N.R. and G.W. McConkie. 1985. Perceptual Span for Letter Distinctions during Reading. *Reading Research Quarterly* 20:153–162.
Ushenko, Andrew Paul. 1958. *The Field Theory of Meaning*. Ann Arbor, Mich.: University of Michigan Press.
Vandebroeck, Dieter. 2016. *Distinctions in the Flesh: Social Class and the Embodiment of Inequality*. London: Routledge.
Vandenberghe, Frédéric. 1999. "The Real Is Relational": An Epistemological Analysis of Pierre Bourdieu's Generative Structuralism. *Sociological Theory* 17:32–67.
van Hoorn, Willem. 1972. *As Images Unwind: Ancient and Modern Theories of Visual Perception*. Amsterdam: University Press Amsterdam.
Vauclair, Jacques. 1996. *Animal Cognition*. Cambridge, Mass.: Harvard University Press.
Vernant, Jeane-Pierre. 1995. *The Greeks*, translated by Charles Lambert and Teresa Lavender Fagan. Chicago: University of Chicago Press.
Verschuur, Gerrit L. 1993. *Hidden Attraction: The History and Mystery of Magnetism*. New York: Oxford University Press.
Vision, Gerald. 1997. *Problems of Vision: Rethinking the Causal Theory of Perception*. Oxford: Oxford University Press.
von der Heydt, R., E. Peterhans, and G. Baumgartner. 1984. Illusory Contours and Cortical Neuron Responses. *Science, new series* 224:1260–1262.
von Wiese, Leopold. 1932. *Systematic Sociology on the Basis of the Beziehungslehre and Gebildelehre*, translated and amplified by Howard Becker. New York: Wiley.
Vygotsky, L.S. [1934] 1987. *Thinking and Speech* (translation of *Myschlenie i Rech'*), translated by Norris Minick, in *Collected Works, Volume 1*. New York: Plenum.
Wacquant, Loïc. 2004. *Body and Soul: Ethnographic Notebooks of an Apprentice Boxer*. New York: Oxford.
Wade, Nicholas J. 1998. *A Natural History of Vision*. Cambridge, Mass.: MIT Press.
Wallace, Anthony F.C. 1958. Dreams and the Wishes of the Soul: A Type of Psychoanalytic Theory among the Seventeenth Century Iroquois. *The American Anthropologist* 60:234–248.
Waller, Willard. 1937. The Rating and Dating Complex. *American Sociological Review* 2:727–734.
Wallerstein, Robert S. and Harold Sampson. 1971. Issues in Research in the Psychoanalytic Process. *International Journal of Psycho-Analysis* 52:11–50.
Warren, Roland L. 1967. The Interorganizational Field as a Focus of Investigation. *Administrative Science Quarterly* 12:396–419.

Waquant, Loïc. 2004. *Body and Soul: Notebooks of an Apprentice Boxer.* Oxford: Oxford University Press.
Weber, Max. [1903–1906] 1975. *Roscher and Knies: The Logical Problems of Historical Economics*, translated by Guy Oakes. New York: Free Press.
Weber, Max. [1904] 1949. "Objectivity" in Social Science and Social Policy. Pp. 49–112 in *The Methodology of the Social Sciences*, translated and edited by Edward A. Shils and Henry A. Finch. New York: Free Press.
Weber, Max. [1905] 1949. Critical Studies in the Logic of the Cultural Sciences, in *The Methodology of the Social Sciences*, translated and edited by Edward A. Shils and Henry A. Finch. New York: Free Press.
Weber, Max. [1907] 1977. *Critique of Stammler*, translated by Guy Oakes. New York: Free Press.
Weber, Max. [1915] 1946. Religious Rejections of the World and Their Directions in *From Max Weber: Essays in Sociology*, translated and edited by H.H. Gerth and C. Wright Mills. New York: Oxford University Press.
Weber, Max. [1917] 1949. "Objectivity" in Social Science and Social Policy. Pp. 1–48 in *The Methodology of the Social Sciences*, translated and edited by Edward A. Shils and Henry A. Finch. New York: Free Press.
Weber, Max. [1920–1921] 1972. *Wirtschaft und Gesellschaft*, fifth edition. Tübingen, Germany: Mohr.
Weber, Max. [1920–1921] 1976. *The Protestant Ethic and the Spirit of Capitalism*, translated by Talcott Parsons. New York: Charles Scribner's Sons.
Weber, Max. 1978. *Economy and Society*, edited by Guenther Roth and Claus Wittich (two volumes). Berkeley: University of California Press.
Wertheimer, Max. 1922. Untersuchungen zur Lehre von der Gestalt. I. Prinzipielle Bermerkungen. *Psychologische Forschung* 1:47–58.
Wertsch, James V. 1981. *The Concept of Activity in Soviet Psychology*. Armonk, N.Y.: Sharpe.
Wertsch, James V. 1991. *Voices of the Mind: A Sociocultural Approach to Mediated Action*. Cambridge, Mass.: Harvard University Press.
Westbrook, Robert B. 1991. *John Dewey and American Democracy*. Ithaca, N.Y.: Cornell University Press.
Westfall, Richard S. 1977. *The Construction of Modern Science: Mechanisms and Mechanics*. Cambridge: Cambridge University Press.
Whewell, William. [1860] 1971. *On the Philosophy of Discovery*. New York: Burt Franklin (original publishers). Reprinted from original by Lenox Hill Publishers, New York.
White, Harrison C. 1992. *Identity and Control*. Princeton, N.J.: Princeton University Press.
White, Harrison C. 1995. *Where Do Languages Come from? I. Switching between Networks*. New York: Center for the Social Sciences at Columbia University, Pre-Print Series.
White, Harrison C. 2002. *Markets from Networks*. Princeton, N.J.: Princeton University Press.
White, Harrison C. 2008. *Identity and Control*, second edition. Princeton, N.J.: Princeton University Press.
White, Harrison C., Scott. A. Boorman, and Ronald L. Breiger. 1976. Social Structure from Multiple Networks. I. Blockmodels of Roles and Positions. *American Journal of Sociology* 81:730–779.

References

Whitehead, Alfred North. [1929] 1978. *Process and Reality: An Essay in Cosmology*. New York: Free Press.
Whitehead, Harriet. 1981. The Bow and the Burdern Strap: A New Look at Institutionalized Homosexuality in Native North America. Pp. 80–115 in *Sexual Meanings, the Cultural Construction of Gender and Sexuality*, edited by Sherry B. Ortner and Harriet Whitehead. Cambridge: Cambridge University Press.
Whitehead, Harriet. 1987. *Renunciation and Reformulation: A Study of Conversion in an American Sect*. Ithaca, N.Y.: Cornell University Press.
Whorf, Benjamin. 1940. Science and Linguistics. *Technology Review* 42:229–231, 247–248.
Wieder, D.L. 1971. On Meaning by Rule. Pp. 107–135 in *Understanding Everyday Life*, edited by Jack D. Douglas. London: Routledge and Kegan Paul.
Wieder, D.L. 1974. *Language and Social Reality*. The Hague: Mouton.
Williams, Elizabeth A. 1992. The French Revolution, Anthropological Medicine, and the Creation of Medical Authority. Pp. 79–97 in *Re-Creating Authority in Revolutionary France*, edited by Bryant T. Ragan, Jr. and Elizabeth A. Williams. New Brunswick, N.J.: Rutgers University Press.
Williams, F.E. 1940. *Drama of Orokolo: The Social and Ceremonial Life of the Elema*. Oxford, U.K.: Clarendon Press.
Williams, L. Pearce. 1965. *Michael Faraday*. New York: Basic Books.
Wilson, Timothy D. and Nancy Brekke. 1994. Mental Contamination and Mental Correction: Unwanted Influences on Judgments and Evaluations. *Psychological Bulletin* 116:117–142.
Winch, Peter. 1958. *The Idea of a Social Science*. London: Routledge and Kegan Paul.
Windelband, Wilhelm. [1894] 1905. *Geschichte und Naturwissenschaft: Rede zum Antritt des Rektorats der Kaiser-Wilhelms-Universität Strassburg*, third edition. Strassburg, France: J.H. Ed. Heitz (Heitz & Mündel).
Wittgenstein, Ludwig. [1945–1949] 1958. *Philosophical Investigations*, third edition, translated by G.E.M. Anscombe. New York: Macmillan.
Wolpe, Joseph and Stanley Rachman. 1963. Psychoanalytic Evidence: A Critique Based on Freud's Case of Little Hans. Pp. 198–220 in *Critical Essays on Psychoanalysis*, edited by Stanley Rachman. New York: Macmillan.
Wong, Paul T.P. and Bernard Weiner. 1981. When People Ask "Why" Questions, and the Heuristics of Attributional Search. *Journal of Personality and Social Psychology* 40:650–663.
Worsley, Peter. 1997. *Knowledges*. New York: New Press.
Wright, William K. 1913 The Genesis of the Categories. *The Journal of Philosophy, Psychology and Scientific Methods* 10:645–657.
Yocom, Jim. 2007. Categories, Categorization Effects and Punitive Attitudes towards Criminals. Unpublished sociology PhD dissertation, Madison: University of Wisconsin.
Young, Michael W. 2004. *Malinowski: Odyssey of an Anthropologist 1884–1920*. New Haven, Conn.: Yale University Press.
Zajonc, Arthur. 1993. *Catching the Light: The Entwined History of Light and Mind*. New York: Bantam Books.
Zeller, Eduard. 1955. *Outlines of the History of Greek Philosophy*, thirteenth edition, translated by L.R. Palmer. New York: Meridian.
Zerilli, Linda M.G. 2009. Toward a Feminist Theory of Judgment. *Signs* 34:295–317.

Zerubavel, Eviatar. 2006. *The Elephant in the Room: Silence and Denial in Everyday Life*. New York: Oxford University Press.

Zimmerman, Don H. and Melvin Pollner. 1971. The Everyday World as a Phenomenon. Pp. 80–103 in *Understanding Everyday Life*, edited by Jack D. Douglas. London: Routledge and Kegan Paul.

Zuberi, Tukufu. 2001. *Thicker than Blood: How Racial Statistics Lie*. Minneapolis: University of Minnesota Press.

Zweig, Stefan. 1932. *Mental Healers*. New York: Viking Press.

Zwilling, Leonard and Michael J. Sweet. 1996. "Like a City Ablaze": The Third Sex and the Creation of Sexuality in Jain Religious Literature. *Journal of the History of Sexuality* 6:359–384.

Index

Abbott, Andrew, 24n1, 306n59
aboriginal/indigenous societies, 122, 124, 125, 126, 154, 154n16
abstraction
  causes of, 30–37
  explanation of social action and, 29–30
  sociological theories and, 6, 8, 344–349
action, objective vs. subjective grounds for, 15–16
Adorno, T.W., 94–95
aesthetics
  communion and, 198–203
  Dewey's theories and, 190, 196, 196n11, 198, 201–202, 201n19, 202n20, 205n22
  intentionality and, 236
  Kant's theories and, 190, 197–198, 197n15, 198–201, 200n16, 202–204, 202n20, 205–206, 205n22, 206n23
  presence of others, 220–223, 222nn53–55
  qualities, 206–207, 223–226, 224n58, 224n59, 225, 236–238
  See also social aesthetics
affordances. *See* valences (affordances)
al-Hazen, Abū Alī, 213
alignment, 252, 305–307
al-Kindī, Abū Yūsuf, 211–213, 212n30, 215
American pragmatist school
  experience and knowledge, 181–183, 182n58, 183nn59–60
  German Gestalt school and the, 181, 181n57, 182
  Naïve empiricism, 184–186, 184n61, 185n62

nature of experience, 186–189, 187nn64–66, 188n67, 190n69
animal intelligence, 189n68
Anschaulichkeit. See intuitive accessibility
Aristotle, 113, 206, 210n28, 258, 258n33
aspiration level, 251
attribution theory, 21–22, 31, 172–176
The Authoritarian Personality (Adorno), 94
authority
  Charcot authoritarian approach, 79–80, 79n16, 80nn17–18
  epistemology and, 92–94
  Freud's authoritarian approach, 81–82, 81n19, 82n21, 85–91
averages, 27, 27nn4–5, 29

Bacon, Roger, 213
Ballard, Dana H., 315n70
Barnes, Barry, 136n41, 173n44, 195, 196n10, 305n58
Beebee, Helen, 63n46
Benchley, Robert, 218n45
Ben-David, Joseph, 75
Benedict, Ruth, 303n56
Berger, Peter L., 313n67
Bergson, Henri, 71, 114n4, 141, 232, 232n69
Berkeley, Lord, 184
Berlin, Brent, 137
Billig, Michael, 178
Bischof, Norbert, 197n12
Bloor, David, 301, 301n53
Borges, Jorge Luis, 135, 137
Bororo Indians, 154, 154n16
Bourdieu, Pierre

on Durkheim, 255
field theory and, 74n1, 240,
  252–253, 253n26, 269, 290n33
habit and, 264
on judgment, 227–228, 227n62
on Kant, 243, 243n8
social aesthetics, 203–205,
  205nn21–22
socioanalysis and, 254–258,
  256nn29–30
Brainard, Paul, 151
Brant, Karl, 279
Brekke, Nancy, 174–175
British empiricists, 117
Brunswik, Egon, 245
Bunge, Mario, 325n4
Burke, Kenneth, 178, 178nn48–50,
  232n69
Burr, Aaron, 69–71

Caesar and the Korean War, 41
Campbell, Colin, 13n11
Capital (Marx), 348
Cartesian dualism/rationalism
  Bourdieu and, 255
  Durkheimian sociology and, 9
  French theory and, 147, 182
  phenomenology and, 163
  Russian activity school and, 158
  See also Descartes, René
Cartwright, Nancy, 59n39, 68n50
Cassirer, Ernst, 75, 75n4, 159–161,
  159nn23–24, 160nn25–27
  on fields, 271n5
  on Galileo, 274, 274n8
  medieval thought and Western
    science, 75, 75n4, 159–161,
    159nn23–24, 160nn25–27
  on position, 275, 275n10
  on quality, 224n58
causality
  causes of, 24–29
  chance and, 55–57, 56n36
  common sense and nonsense in,
    69–73, 71nn52–54, 72n55
  determination vs.
  etymology of cause, 30, 30n10
  in jurisprudence, 61–64, 61n41,
    62nn43–43, 63nn44–46
  motives and, 15–18

necessity and, 33–37, 35n18, 39–43
Piaget's analysis of, 150–152
prediction and, 28, 32–33, 32nn12,
  64
preventing factors, 44
probability and, 46–55, 49n28,
  52n30
in social life, 64–69, 65n47, 66n48,
  68nn49–50
sufficient, 34–35, 35n18, 36n19,
  43, 54
transitivity and, 43–44
will of persons and, 16–18, 16n16
chance, 55–57, 56n36
Chang, Patricia Mei Yin, 124n26
Charcot, Jean Martin
  on abstraction, 79n15
  clinical observation vs. etiological definition, 79–80, 79n16,
    80nn17–18
  on false statements of patients,
    80–81
  Freud, Sigmund and, 76, 77, 77n8,
    80
  hypnosis and authoritarian approach, 76–77, 77n10, 78–79,
    79n14, 85n27
chess, 252, 293n38, 298n49, 332
children
  categories and, 130, 130n34
  cognitive development, 148–152,
    149n5, 151n9
  concept formation, 155–158,
    155n19
  game rules and, 299n51
  motivation and, 30n10
Civil War, 33, 72
classification
  practical, 138–140, 139n42, 141n44
  zoological, 135–138, 136n40–41
Collins, Randall, 75
Comte, Auguste, 76n1, 323
counterfactualism
  chance and, 55–57
  interventions and laws, 57–60,
    57n37, 58n38, 59n39
  probability and, 46–55, 49n28,
    52n30
  simple counterfactualism, 37–48,
    42n25, 44nn26–27

Weber, Max, 34
Cousin, Victor, 114, 117n10

Darwin, Charles, 28n5, 287
Dawid, A.P., 28n6
de Biran, Maine, 32, 216n42, 232n68, 259n34
Descartes, René
  on mechanical interactions, 285
  optic theories of, 214, 214nn36–37, 215n39
  on senses, 215n39
  See also Cartesian dualism/ rationalism
Dewey, John
  aesthetics and, 196, 196n11, 198, 201–202, 201n19, 202n20, 205n22
  on experience, 184–186, 189
  on explaining action, 246n13
  on habit, 259, 259n35, 262–263
  inadequacy of utilitarianism, 293n37
  on Kant, 181–182
  on knowledge, 182–183
  pragmatism of, 182n58
  psychoanalytic approach, 183, 183n59
  theory of judgment, 195
  vs. the Greeks, 190
  See also American pragmatist school
DiMaggio, Paul J., 306–307, 319
The Discourse on the Origin of Inequality (Rousseau), 118n16
disposition, *See* position and disposition
Distinction (Bourdieu), 203
The Division of Labor (Durkheim), 118, 118n14, 119n17
Dore, John, 60
Douglas, Mary, 115, 136, 136n40, 255
Ducasse, Curt John, 65n47, 66n48
Durkheim, Emile
  averages, 27, 29
  on de Biran, 259n34
  German *Gestalt* school and, 76, 76n1
  on hypnosis, 143–144
  method of difference, 34n15
  on pragmatism, 140n43
  on scientific investigation, 281
  on social science laws, 323
  on suicide, 28, 29n8
  use of abstraction, 6, 8
  Wittgenstein and, 298n50
Durkheimian sociology
  beginnings of, 26
  categories of thought, 114, 116–121, 117nn11–13, 118n14, 119nn17–18, 120n19, 127n31, 130–131, 130n34
  causality, 127, 127n32
  classes, 121–129, 121n20, 121n21, 122nn22–25, 124n27, 125n28, 126nn29–30, 128n33, 139–140, 140n42, 141–142, 141n45
  habit, 259–260
  knowledge, 114–116, 114nn5–6, 115n7, 143–144, 144n47, 191–193, 220, 235, 255
  Malinowski, Bronislaw on, 47
  perception, 262
  Quetelet and, 322
  social force, 277, 277nn12–13
  social law, 7
  totemism, 126, 140, 191–192
  vision of the social sciences, 8–9

Eells, Ellery, 36n21
Ehrenfells, Christian von, 161, 195, 264n41
The Elementary Forms of Religious Life (Durkheim), 118
Elster, Jon, 5, 33n13, 71n54
Emery, F.E., 294n40, 306
Empedocles, 208–209
empiricism, 184–186, 184n61, 185n62
Engels, Friedrich, 175n47
Eng, Erling, 291n35
Erb, Wilhelm, 80
Eskimos and snow, 134–135, 135n39
Euclid, 210–211
Evans-Pritchard, E.E., 55
events defined, 42, 42n24
explanation of social action
  abstractions and, 29, 341–344
  criteria for a successful, 336–341, 336n15, 337n16, 338n17, 340n19, 349–350
  current status of theoretical explanation, 3–11
  general vs. particular, 28–29

explanation of social action (*Continued*)
  overview, 333–336, 349–350
  social sciences' traditional, 333–336

Faraday, Michael, 278*n*14, 282*n*18
Ficino, Marsilio, 213*n*35
field theory
  Bourdieu and, 240
  explanatory principles, 10
  fields and space, 268–271
  fields of organized striving, 248–254, 248*n*16, 249*nn*17–18
  general characteristics of, 271–272
  vs. general linear reality, 273–274
  German Gestalt school and, 255
  habit in, 266–267, 266*n*44
  motivation, 307–312, 308*n*60, 309*nn*61–63, 310*n*64, 311*n*65, 312*n*66
  object and position, 317–320, 318*n*72
  quality intensity, 241–244, 242*n*4, 243*nn*7–8
  social aesthetics, 240–241
  social perception, 312–315, 313*n*67, 314*nn*68–69
  social phenomena and, 274–280
  social-psychological fields, 244–248
  terseness and position, 315–317, 315*n*70
  use of the word field, 251*n*20
field theory controversies
  mechanical critiques, 281*n*17, 284–286, 284*n*20, 285*nn*21–23, 286*nn*24–27
  mechanisms and functions, 287–291, 287*nn*28–29, 288*n*30, 289*n*31, 290*nn*32–33
  tautology and occultism, 280–284, 281*nn*16–17, 282*n*18, 283*n*19
field theory, fields and games
  fields of contestation, 291–293, 291*nn*34–35, 292*n*36, 293*n*37
  rules and alignment, 305–307, 306*n*59
  rules and laws, 293–300, 293*nn*38–39, 294*nn*40–41, 295*n*42, 296*nn*43–46, 297*n*47, 298*nn*49–50, 299*n*51, 300*n*52
  rules and patterns, 300–305, 301*nn*53–54, 302*nn*55–57, 305*n*58
first-person explanations
  American pragmatist school, 188
  in a successful explanation, 337, 340
  Freudian theory, 74, 87–91, 88*n*30, 89*n*32, 90*n*33, 91*nn*34–35
  German Gestalt school, 177, 180
  Gestalt critique, 170–181, 170*nn*39–40, 171*n*41, 172*nn*42–43
  Malinowski, Bronislaw and, 100, 102*n*50
  Pepper on, 196*n*9
  sociologists and, 92, 93*n*36, 94–96, 95*nn*40–41, 107–111
  vs. third person explanations, 16–23, 17*n*19, 20*nn*21–22, 74, 143
  See also motivation; third-person explanations
Fisher, Sir Ronald A., 49–50, 50*n*29
Foucault, Michel, 77–78, 77*n*9, 94*n*39, 131*n*36, 285
Freese, Jeremy, 47
Freudian theory
  Bourdieu and, 256
  Durkheimianism and, 115, 144
  first person perspectives in, 74
  habit, 259–260
  Malinowski, Bronislaw on, 104
  motivation, 74, 76–77, 87–88
  subjective components of action, 8
  vs. German Gestalt school, 170–171
  See also psychology
Freud, Sigmund
  Charcot, Jean Martin and, 76, 77, 77*n*8, 80
  cocaine and, 77, 77*n*7
  on dreams, 102, 103
  nationality, 76
  practices and clinical approach of, 81–91, 81*n*20, 82*nn*21–22, 83*nn*23–24, 84*n*25, 85*n*28, 88*nn*29–30, 89*nn*31–32, 90*n*33, 91*n*34, 92, 93–94, 93*n*37, 142, 143
functionality/functionalism, 96–97, 100–104
Fürstenberg, Friedrich, 251–252, 251*n*22

Galileo, 274, 274*n*8, 281, 281*n*16, 282*n*17
Galton, Francis, 27*n*5
games/game theory. *See* field theory, fields and games
general laws, particular cases and, 29–30
German Gestalt school
  American pragmatist school and the, 181, 181*n*57, 182
  cognition model, 160–161, 193–194
  correspondence between outer and inner, 76
  errors, 171–174
  experimenters and subjects, 174–179
  on fields, 244
  field theory, 10, 269, 269*n*2, 288*n*30
  German approach to science, 159
  habit, 264*n*41
  nonindependence of percepts, 161–163
  perception, 76, 179–181, 195, 197, 314
  phenomenology of relations, 163–169, 165*nn*33–34, 168*n*36, 169*nn*37–38
  on qualities, 223–226, 236
  vs. Freudianism, 170–171
German laboratory vs. French hospitals/clinics, 78, 78*n*12
Gestalt school. *See* German Gestalt school
Gibson, James J., 164, 175*n*46, 215, 330*n*10
Giddens, Anthony, 9*n*5, 10*n*7, 252*n*24
Gilbert, William, 275*n*8, 282*n*18, 284*n*20
Goethe, Johann Wolfgang von, 75, 161*n*28, 218*n*46, 347
Goffman, Erving, 94, 330
Goldstone, Jack, 4
Goldthorpe, John H., 24*n*1, 26*n*, 179*n*53
gradient, 270*n*3, 279
Graunt, John, 26
gravity, 273–274
Gunaratna, 71*n*52
Guttentag, Marcia, 7

habit
  Bourdieu on, 257–258, 257*n*31
  motive, 262–265, 263*nn*39–40, 264*nn*41–42
  in Western psychology, 258–262, 258*n*33, 259*nn*34–35, 260*nn*36–37
Hall, Ned, 34, 34*n*16
Hamilton, Alexander, 69–71
Haney, Craig, 178*n*51
Hart, H.L.A., 61, 64
Hegel, Georg W.F., Marx on, 4
Heider, Fritz, 67, 172*n*42, 173
Hempel, Carl G., 11
Hobbes, Thomas, 205, 218, 273, 295, 312, 312*n*66
hockey, 43, 295–297, 299, 310–311
Holland, Fran, 60*n*40
Honoré, A.M., 61, 64
hoplites, 331
Horkheimer, Max, 182*n*58
Humean regularities, 33–34
Hume, David, 34, 113, 199
Humphreys, Paul, 42*n*24, 51–52
Husserl, Edmund, 29, 162, 171*n*41, 184*n*61

Ilyenkov, E.V., 153*n*13, 158*n*21
insight
  aesthetics and, 231–233
  intention and, 236, 236*n*73
  Köhler and, 166, 166*n*35, 231–232
  relations, 233–236
  validity of, 340
institutions, 300–305
interventions, 57–61, 339, 340
intuitive accessibility, 334–335, 334*n*14, 338–339, 340, 341, 343

Jainism, 133*n*37
James, William, 61, 75*n*3, 115*n*7, 185*n*62
Janet, Paul, 114, 117*n*10
Jeffreys, Harold, 48
judgment, cognition and, 191–197, 194*nn*4, 6
jurisprudence and causality, 61–64, 61*n*41, 62*nn*43–43, 63*nn*44–46

Kahneman, Daniel, 45*n*27
Kalish, Charles, 30*n*10

Kant, Immanuel, 205n22
  aesthetic approach of, 197–198, 197n15, 198–201, 200n16, 202–204, 202n20, 205–206, 206n23, 208n25, 236, 239n1
  categories of thought, 116, 116n10
  on causality, 113–114
  on class, 117n12
  critiques of, 243–244, 243n8
  Dewey on, 181–182
  grounds for action, 15–16, 17, 21
  on habit, 263
  objects as a property, 168
  on social science laws, 323
  stability of social statistics, 28n7
  theory of cognition, 117n13
Kepler, Johannes, 214n37, 275n8
knowledge
  American pragmatist school on, 181–183, 182n58, 183nn59–60
  Dewey on, 182–183
  Durkheimian sociology, 114–116, 114nn5–6, 115n7, 143–144, 144n47, 191–193, 220
  insight and, 232–233
Koffka, K., 76, 159n22, 163n31, 197n12
  on conflict, 291n35
  on the environment, 314n69
Köhler, Wolfgang
  ape studies, 151, 151n8, 245
  on Faraday, 282n18
  on fields, 270n3
  on Husserl's phenomenology, 171n41
  insight, 166, 166n35, 231–232
  judgment and perception, 195, 244
  on position, 279
  on psychoanalysis/Freudian theory, 170, 170nn39–40, 171
  on qualities, 224n59, 225
  on regularity, 294n41
  on relations in the field, 247, 247n15
  on sensory experience, 165n34
  on social relations, 228
  source of feelings, 176
  Stumpf and, 163n31
Kohlrausch, Friedrich, 283n18
Krentz, Peter, 331n13
Kurzman, Charles, 22

language
  Cassirer on, 194n5
  Durkheim on, 120, 235
  model for social cognition, 112–113
  rules versus laws, 328–330, 330nn10, 12
  snow and Eskimos, 134–135, 135n39
law and causality, 61–64, 61n41, 62nn43–43, 63nn44–46
law and intervention, 57–61
laws, social
  causality and, 7–8, 16
  failure to obey, 330–332
Leibniz, Gotfried Wilhelm, 284, 285
Lenin, V.I., 157n20
Levi-Strauss, Claude, 228
Lewin, Kurt
  affordance, 252
  on behavior, 246, 246–247, 246n13
  on conflict, 291, 291n35
  field theory, 246–247
  influence on, 246n13
Lewis, David, 38, 38n22, 40, 40n23, 54n31, 72n55
Lieberson, Stanley, 273, 327, 327n6
Linnaeus, Carl, 121n20
Lizardo, Omar, 290n32
Luckmann, Thomas, 313n67
Luhmann, Niklas, 10n8
Luria, Alexander, 148, 159n22

Mach, Ernst, 184
Macmillan, Malcolm, 82n21, 83n24
Macnamara, John, 130n31
magic, 55–57
magnetism, 212, 245, 266, 276
Maimonides, 36
Malinowski, Bronislaw
  Durkheimianism and, 100n48
  Freudianism and, 98–100, 98n45, 99n46, 100–104, 100n47
  functionalism, 100–101, 100n48, 101n49
  Meton, Robert K. on, 96
Mannheim, Karl, 108–109, 254, 334n14
Margolis, Howard, 233–234
Marrow, Alfred J., 291n35

Martin, Anne R., 293n38
Marx, Karl, 4, 175n47, 348–349
Mauss, Marcel, 125, 125n28, 126n30, 129, 130, 141, 257n32
Maxwell, James Clerk, 282n18, 285n23
McNemar, Quinn, 178n52
Mead, George H., 237, 254, 301, 301n54
Mead, Margaret, 303n56
Mechanism, 25, 33n13, 71n54, 216, 278, 284–291
Meinong, Alexius, 161
Merleau-Ponty, Maurice, 188n67, 216, 229n63, 254n28
Merton, Robert K., 3, 96–98, 103, 103n53
Metzger, Wolfgang, 197n12
Michotte, A., 32, 32n11
micro-macro problem, 7
Milgram, Stanley, 21, 22
Mill, J.S., 33, 33n14
Mills, C. Wright, 14n13, 34
Mohave culture, 132, 133
Moliere, 281
motivation
   analysts tradition regarding, 307–308
   causes and, 30–32, 55, 62, 66, 72
   defined, 264–265
   differentiation and, 250
   field theory, 251–253, 311–312
   Freudian theory, 74, 76–77, 87–91
   good theory and, 5
   habit and, 262–265, 263nn39–40, 264nn41–42
   impulsion, 310, 310n64, 311n65
   Mills on, 14n13
   reasons and, 263n40
   social aesthetics and, 237, 243
   values and, 308–310, 309nn61–63, 311n65
motives
   acceptable categories of, 14n13
   causes and, 15–18
   children and, 30n10
   functions and, 96–97, 101, 250
   reasons and, 18–21
   vs. functions, 96–97
   Weber on, 14n12

Why questions and, 15, 23
mountains, 67, 166–167, 169, 209n27, 226–228, 260, 314, 343

Nagel, Thomas, 17
natural selection, 287, 289
neo-Kantians, 17
Newton, Sir Isaac, 275, 275n8, 286n24
Nietzsche, Friedrich, 248–249, 249n17
Nisbett, Richard E., 176–177

objects
   insight and, 233–236
   qualities, 206–207, 223–226, 224n58, 224n59, 225, 236–238
   relations and, 226–228, 227n62, 229–231
Ockham, William of, 208n25, 258–259, 263
O'Regan, J. Keven, 216n40

Parascandola, Mark, 52n30
Parsons, Talcott, 285, 305, 330n11
patterns, 182, 188, 300–303
Pearl, Judea, 35n18
Pearson, Karl, 48
Peirce, C.S., 186, 189
Pepper, Stephen
   first-person and third-person accounts, 196n9
   on preperceptual activity, 220
   on quality, 223–224, 224n57, 243, 243n7
perception
   field theory, 312–315, 313n67, 314nn68–69
   German Gestalt school, 76, 179–181, 195, 197, 314
   Köhler, 195, 244
   nonarbitrariness of social, 312–315, 313n67
   vision theory, 201n28, 207–220, 209nn26–27, 213nn33–35, 214n37, 215nn38–39, 216nn40–43, 217n44, 218nn45–46, 219n47, 220n49, 247
   See also Durkheimian sociology
Peters, R.S., 88n30
phenomenological regularities. See regularities in social action

Piaget, Jean, 30n10, 148–152
Plato, 16n16, 25, 208, 209n26
Plotinus, 209n27, 213n34
political parties, 18, 227–228, 231n67, 233–235, 317
Pollock, John L., 297n47
Pop, Iggy, 66
position, 251–252, 268–272, 274–279, 303–304, 306–315
　and disposition, 204, 222–225, 229, 231, 233, 237, 241–244, 258, 264
　and terseness, 315–317
　and objects, 317–320
Powell, Walter W., 306–307, 319
pragmatism, 181, 186
pragmatist school. *See* American pragmatist school
prediction
　causality and, 28, 32–33, 32n12, 64
　field theories and, 284
　successful explanation and, 339, 341
Przeworksi, Adam, 18
psychology
　birth of, 75–76, 75nn3–4
　clinical doctor/patient relationship, 76–81, 78n11
　See also Freudian theory
Pullum, Geoffrey K., 135n39
Pylyshyn, Zenon W., 220n48

Quetelet, Adolphe, 26–28, 26n2, 322

race and racism, 47, 94–95, 229–231, 237, 283, 346–347
Rachman, Stanley, 90n33
Radcliffe-Brown, A.R., 100, 100n48
Rawls, Anne Warfield, 116, 127–128, 293n38
Rawls, John, 295n42
reasons and motives, 18–21
Recherches statistiques (Durkheim), 28
Reed, Edward S., 177
regularities in social action
　deviation from, 330–332
　Humean, 33–34
　Köhler on, 294n41
　as objects, 9–10
Renouvier, Charles, 114, 116n10
Rickert, Heinrich, 193, 193nn2–3, 249, 249n18, 250

Rousseau, Jean-Jacques, 118, 118n16
rules, 293–307, 326–329
Rummel, Rudolph J., 291n35
Russian activity school
　cognitive theories, 157, 157n20, 158–159
　concepts, 155–159
　individual ontogeny of categories, 147–152
　vs. Durkheimian sociology, 152–155
　See also Vygotsky, Lev

Saussure, Ferdinand de, 113
Schmaus, Warren, 112n3, 117n10, 118n14, 127n32
Searle, John R., 295n44, 302
Secord, Paul F., 7
sex and gender, 131–134, 131n36, 133n37, 134n38
Shils, Edward A., 305, 330n11
Simon, Herbert, 279, 316
Skocpol, Theda, 33
Smith, Herbert, 53
snow and Eskimos, 134–135, 135n39
social aesthetics
　empirical questions and, 240
　field theory and, 240–241, 314–315
　motivation and, 237, 243
　need for, 239, 239n1
　See also aesthetics
social laws. *See* laws
social sciences
　criticism in the, 344–349, 344n21
　deviation from regularities in social action, 330–332
　explanation and aggression, 325–326
　rules versus laws in the, 326–330, 326n5, 327nn6–7
　theory in the, 3–5, 322–325, 322n1, 323n2, 324n3
sociology/sociologists
　conflicting statements and, 112
　Durkheimian theory of cognition and, 143
　first-person explanations and sociologists, 92, 93n36, 94–96, 95nn40–41
　social construction, 145–147, 146n2, 147n3

third-person explanations and
  sociologists, 92–93
 types of questions asked by, 11–14
 Weber on, 5, 11–12
Spencer, Herbert, 250, 281
St. Hubbins, David Ivor, 329
Starr, Paul, 77
Stoller, Paul, 56n33
Stumpf, Carl
 Gestalt psychology and, 161, 162, 163, 163n30, 163n31, 167
 on nothing, 185
suicide, 28, 29n8, 281
Suicide (Durkheim), 281

Teune, Henry, 18
The Interpretation of Dreams (Freud), 102
Theses on Feuerbach (Marx), 153
third-person explanations
 necessity and, 35
 Pepper on, 196n9
 sociologists and, 92–93
 vs. first person explanations, 16–23, 17n19, 20nn21–22, 74, 104–107
 See also counterfactualism; first-person explanations
Thomas, Keith, 56
Thucydides, 331
Tilly, Charles, 61, 61n41
Tolman, Edward C., 245, 245n10
Tolstoy, Leo, 197n11
totemism, 126, 140, 154, 154n15, 191–192
transposability, 340
Trist, E.L., 294n40, 306
Turner, Bryan, 108
Turner, Victor, 251, 291n34

unintended consequences, 10n7

valences (affordances)
 American social psychology and, 246
 German Gestalt school on, 167, 179
 Lewin on, 246–247, 246n13
values, 21, 167–168, 190, 193n3, 201, 228, 248–254, 308–312
Varey, Carol A., 45n27

vectors, 243, 247, 251, 253, 271–276, 279
Venn, John, 48
vision theory
 al-Kindī and the Middle Ages, 211–214, 213nn33–35
 early Greeks, 207–220, 209nn26–27, 210n28
 habit, 260
 Kepler on, 214n37
 Renaissances to modern, 114–120, 214n37, 215nn38–39, 216nn40–43, 217n44, 218nn45–46, 219n47, 247
Vygotsky, Lev
 concepts, 155–158
 Gestalt theory and, 159n22
 on Piaget, Jean, 152, 152nn10–11, 153
 Russian activity school and, 148
 vs. Durkheim, 152–155, 152n12
 See also Russian activity school

Weber, Max
 birthday of, 66
 causal explanation, 12nn9–10
 counterfactual theory, 34, 34n15
 explanatory meaning, 12, 13
 first person accusative answers, 22
 Rickert philosophy and, 193, 193nn2–3
 on sociology, 5, 11–12
 value system, 249–250, 249n18, 249nn17–18
 on why questions, 15
Wertheimer, Max, 76, 161, 163, 163n31, 195
Whorf, Benjamin, 137
Why questions
 first person vs. third person answers, 16–23, 17n19, 74
 Freudian theory and, 74
 German Gestalt school, 180
 motivation and, 15, 23
 sociologists and, 92–93
 types asked by the social sciences, 11–14, 15n14, 24
 vs. What questions, 332–333

Wieder, D.L., 327
Wilson, Timothy DeCamp, 174–177
witchcraft, 55, 56, 56nn33–34
Wittgenstein, Ludwig, 32, 298n50
Wolpe, Joseph, 90n33

World War I, 35, 35n17, 40, 41
Wundt, Wilhelm, 75

Yule, G.U., 28

zoological classification, 135–138, 136nn40–41

www.ingramcontent.com/pod-product-compliance
Ingram Content Group UK Ltd.
Pitfield, Milton Keynes, MK11 3LW, UK
UKHW021328180426
11947UKWH00017B/1516